VICTIMS OF THE CULTURAL REVOLUTION

VICTIMS OF THE CULTURAL REVOLUTION

Testimonies of China's Tragedy

WANG YOUQIN

TRANSLATED AND EDITED BY STACY MOSHER

Oneworld Academic

An imprint of Oneworld Publications

First published by Oneworld Academic in 2023

Copyright © Wang Youqin 2023
Translation copyright © Stacy Mosher 2023

The moral right of Wang Youqin to be identified as the Author of this work has been asserted by her in accordance with the Copyright, Designs, and Patents Act 1988

All rights reserved
Copyright under Berne Convention
A CIP record for this title is available from the British Library

ISBN 978-0-86154-223-9
eISBN 978-0-86154-295-6

Typeset by Geethik Technologies
Printed and bound in Great Britain by Clays Ltd, Elcograf S.p.A.

Oneworld Publications
10 Bloomsbury Street
London WC1B 3SR
England

Stay up to date with the latest books,
special offers, and exclusive content from
Oneworld with our newsletter

Sign up on our website
oneworld-publications.com

Contents

Foreword	ix
A Mighty Project to Rescue Memory	xii
The Witness: A Preface to Victims of the Cultural Revolution	xviii
Translator's Note	xxii
Chronology	xxiv
Introduction: The Status of Victims	xxviii

PART ONE: THE CULTURAL REVOLUTION IN THE
UNIVERSITIES 1
   · Attacks on University Administrators, 1966 1
      Why Were So Many University Administrators
         Persecuted to Death? 1
      Top University Administrators Who Died during the
         Cultural Revolution 11
   · Other Early Victims of Violence at the Universities . . 36
      The Four S's 37
      Beijing 74
      Shanghai 104
      Tianjin 111
      Fujian Province 111
      Hebei Province 111
      Henan Province 112
      Hubei Province 112
      Hunan Province 113
      Jiangxi Province 113
      Liaoning Province 114
      Shaanxi Province 116

PART TWO: THE RED GUARDS IN PRIMARY AND SECONDARY
SCHOOLS 118
   · Beijing 118
   · Shanghai 225

- Nanjing — 263
- Fujian Province – Xiamen — 265
- Guangdong Province — 266
- Hebei Province — 267
- Hubei Province – Wuhan — 267
- Hunan Province — 267
- Jiangsu Province — 269
- Shaanxi Province – Xi'an — 269
- Sichuan Province — 278
- Tianjin — 278
- Yunnan Province – Kunming — 279
- Zhejiang Province — 280

PART THREE: OTHER KILLINGS EARLY IN THE CULTURAL REVOLUTION — 281

- Cultural Figures — 281
  - *Literature and Journalism* — 281
  - *Music* — 298
  - *Film and Theatre* — 305
  - *Religious Practitioners* — 307
  - *Others* — 308
- Cadres — 310
  - *The Death of Senior Officials and the Death of Ordinary People* — 310
  - *Central Committee Propaganda Department* — 324
  - *Shanxi Province* — 330
  - *Shanghai* — 330
  - *Sichuan Province* — 334
  - *Chongqing* — 335
  - *Tianjin* — 335
  - *Shaanxi Province* — 335
  - *Fujian Province* — 336
  - *Liaoning Province* — 336
  - *Ningxia Hui Ethnic Minority Autonomous Region* — 337

PART FOUR: VICTIMS OF FACTIONAL STRUGGLE — 338

- Beijing — 338
- Chongqing — 345
- Chengdu — 346
- Gansu — 347
- Anhui Province — 348

- Henan Province · 348
- Jiangxi Province · 349
- Jiangsu Province · 349
- Zhejiang Province · 349

PART FIVE: 1968 CLEANSING OF THE CLASS RANKS · · · 350
- Beijing · 355
- Shanghai · 424
- Other Provinces and Municipalities · · · · · · · · · · · · · · 448
    - *Tianjin* · 448
    - *Jiangxi Province* · 450
    - *Shanxi Province* · 450
    - *Guangdong Province* · 451
    - *Hebei Province* · 451
    - *Chongqing* · 452
    - *Chengdu* · 453
    - *Shandong Province* · 454
    - *Wuhan, Hubei Province* · · · · · · · · · · · · · · · · · · · 454
    - *Jiangsu Province* · 455
    - *Xi'an, Shaanxi Province* · · · · · · · · · · · · · · · · · · · 456
    - *Harbin, Heilongjiang Province* · · · · · · · · · · · · · · · 461
    - *Dalian* · 462
    - *Anhui Province* · 465
    - *Yunnan Province* · 467
    - *Fujian Province* · 467
    - *Henan Province* · 468
    - *Xinjiang Province* · 468
    - *Jilin Province* · 468
- The Medical Profession · 469
    - *Beijing* · 493
    - *Shanghai* · 493
    - *Tianjin* · 494
    - *Chongqing* · 496
    - *Jiangxi Province* · 496
    - *Wuhan, Hubei Province* · · · · · · · · · · · · · · · · · · · 496

PART SIX: THE 1970 ONE STRIKE AND THREE ANTIS CAMPAIGNS · 498
  Gu Wenxuan and the 'Rightists' · · · · · · · · · · · · · · · · 498
    Sentenced to Death during the Cultural Revolution · · · 499
    Death Sentences Without a Basis in Law · · · · · · · · · 502

Death Sentences Passed by the 'Triumvirate' of Public Security, Procuratorial and Judicial Organs	502
Death by Campaign	505
Designated and Imprisoned as a Rightist in 1957	506
Quotas for Attacking Rightists	508
The Outcome for the Peking University Party Secretary	508
Fei Xiaotong's Sympathy and Forgetfulness	509
The Sentencing of Gu Wenxuan	510
Zhou Duo's Tragic Fate	511
Imprisoned during the 1955 Campaign to Eliminate Counter-Revolutionaries: Gu Wenxuan's Autobiography – 'My Experience'	514
The Terror of the Campaign to Eliminate Counter-Revolutionaries	516
Execution by 'Mass Discussion'	518
Conclusion	520
· Purge of the 16 May Conspiratorial Cliques	533
· Zhejiang, Qiaosi Military Reclamation Farm	535
PART SEVEN: LATE CASES	**537**
Alphabetical Index of Victims	541

Foreword

RODERICK MACFARQUHAR

(1930–2019, Leroy B. Williams Professor of History and Political Science, and former Director of the John King Fairbank Centre for East Asian Research)

The Cultural Revolution was the watershed in the history of the PRC. Before 1966, China was an amalgam of Maoist class struggle and a Stalinist command economy. Since 1976, China has become a mixture of capitalist economics and Leninist single party rule. The Chinese Communist Party (CCP) is certainly still capable of class struggle; the events of 4 June 1989, and the suppression of the Falun Gong since 1999 are only the most brutal examples. But the unrelenting campaigns of the 1950s and 1960s and the anarchy and violence of the Cultural Revolution decade thankfully seem to be only memories. The struggle now is to make money or to make ends meet.

But the remembrance of things past is still crucial. As the contrasting examples of Germany and Japan show, it is important for a nation to confront the crimes in its recent history. The Germans underwent denazification under the occupation of the victorious allies of World War II, and subsequently their writers and historians pored over the past, so that eventually every German was forced to understand the guilt of the previous generation. Germany is a healthier democratic nation today as a result.

Many Japanese, however, still do not grasp the guilt of the previous generation because they have not been exposed to it in history texts or novels. Except under intense international pressure, the Japanese have never explored the terrible deeds perpetrated by them in Asia before and during World War II. Consequently, war crimes are still an aggravating issue between Japan and its neighbours.

In the case of the Cultural Revolution, the CCP has grappled with the need for a reckoning in its 1981 Resolution on party history. The Resolution blamed Mao Zedong, 'a leader labouring under a misapprehension', for initiating and leading the Cultural Revolution, but described the actions of the Gang of Four and Lin Biao as 'of an entirely different nature... [they took] advantage of Comrade Mao Zedong's errors, committed many crimes behind his back, bringing disaster to the country and the people'; they incited people to 'overthrow everything and wage full-scale civil war'.

Despite this acknowledgement of the terrible stain on the CCP's record in running China, full-scale research and instruction on the Cultural Revolution is frowned on in academia. One or two excellent accounts of the events of that decade have been written by historians under such official auspices as the National Defence University and the Central Party School, but a professor at Beijing University who undertook a similar study would be risking damage to his career.

There may be two reasons for the uneasiness of the CCP at opening up the Cultural Revolution for research. The Resolution blames the Chairman for Leftist ideological theses, but unfettered research would surely reveal that he played a far more hands-on role, and was complicit in or assented to many of the misdeeds of the Gang of Four. The reputation of Mao Zedong could not be allowed to suffer such denigration; it is still too central to the legitimacy of party rule.

The second reason has more to do with China than the Chinese Communist Party. Because the Chairman wished to steel a new generation of revolutionaries, he incited the youth with the slogan 'to rebel is justified', and urged them to 'bombard the headquarters'. By first removing colleagues who tried to restrain the youth, Mao cleared the way for what became in many places a Hobbesian state of nature, two years of terrible violence on the part of high school and college students, first against teachers, then against Party cadres,[1] and finally against each other. 'Scar literature' in the immediate aftermath of the Cultural Revolution and Red Guard memoirs since then only skimmed the surface of what happened. If realised, the writer Ba Jin's suggestion that there should be a Cultural Revolution Museum would have dug much deeper. But real research could amount to an indictment of a generation – those who participated and those who looked on – that is now on the verge of taking over the leadership of their country.

Such an indictment should only be made by a Chinese. In his most famous novel, *Lord of the Flies*, the Nobel Prize-winning British writer, William Golding, suggested that young people anywhere can behave brutally if freed from parental and societal restraints. At the start of the Cultural Revolution, Chinese youth were not just freed from restraint, they were egged on from the highest levels, and those who did not grow

---

[1] In China, a 'cadre' refers to an individual rather than, as in the West, a group of people.

up under China's communist system with its culture of violence cannot be sure how they might have acted in the heady days of Red Guard rampages.

Wang Youqin is one of a number of Chinese-born scholars in the United States who have been undertaking the Cultural Revolution research that cannot be done in China. In this book, Professor Wang takes a very important step in the direction of making her fellow Chinese confront their recent past. With painstaking efforts, and doubtless much frustration and many impediments, she has lifted the veil on the violence, particularly in two periods which she considers the worst of the Cultural Revolution, the Red Guard summer of 1966, and the 'Cleansing of the Class Ranks' by Revolutionary Committees during the winter of 1968. She does this by recounting, one by one, the fates of many hundreds of victims, thus ensuring that they will not be forgotten. But those victims will have died in vain, if thorough analysis of the violence of Red Guards and subsequently of officials, such as Wang Youqin has pioneered, does not lead the Chinese to appreciate the importance of putting in place systems which can prevent such events ever taking place again, at least on the scale of the Cultural Revolution.

A Mighty Project to Rescue Memory

YU YING-SHIH

(1930–2021, Emeritus Professor of East Asian Studies and History at Princeton University, and Fellow of Academia Sinica, Taiwan)

Dr Wang Youqin's investigative study of victims of the Cultural Revolution is a mighty project. From 1980 onwards, she has methodically collected material, entirely on her own, without assistants or collaborators. Gathering this material has been an unimaginably difficult process. Basically, Youqin has carried out one-on-one interviews with more than 1,000 people who were students or teachers during that time. Most of the interviewees, as well as family members of victims, suffer from lingering fears or are still so traumatised by their memories that they were initially reluctant to relate what happened. This required Youqin to patiently convince them and earn their trust so they would eventually open themselves up to an interview. In order to avoid the loss of these memories, Youqin has also devoted great effort to further investigative work in order to verify information through school records that determine the timing and circumstances of these deaths. She has carried out investigations at more than 200 schools (secondary and primary) in Beijing, Shanghai, Tianjin, Jiangsu, Zhejiang, Guangdong, Jiangxi, Fujian, Shanxi, Shaanxi, Sichuan, Xinjiang and other provinces and municipalities. Apart from face-to-face interviews, she has supplemented her material through letters, telephone calls, the internet and other methods. Following the interview and investigative stage, Youqin then spent years pulling all of the information together in this book, which contains information on 659 victims. Conservative estimates place Cultural Revolution fatalities at more than 1.72 million.[1] In this context, Wang Youqin's compilation of 659 names may seem miniscule and insignificant.

---

[1] See Chen Yongfa, *Seventy Years of Chinese Communist Revolution*, 1st ed., Taipei, Linking Publishing, 2001, Vol. 2, p. 846.

Apart from a tiny number of famous personages and senior officials, however, the vast majority of victims remain anonymous and unknown. Youqin's single-handed effort to rescue 659 names from physical and historical obscurity should be lauded as a kind of resurrection. Although expanded over time to encompass students, workers, farmers, doctors, housekeepers and housewives, Youqin's interviews focus mainly on secondary and primary school teachers, who in fact constitute a particular 'species' among the Cultural Revolution's victims. The large quantity of material about them in this book forms the kind of collective biography found in standard histories (such as the 'Biographies of the Great Proscription' in *History of the Latter Han*) that will greatly facilitate the efforts of future historians; given the extensive range of the Cultural Revolution, effective research requires a categorical classification of its victims. I therefore find this book to have enormous historical value, and believe it will serve as a foundation for future historians carrying out research into the political, educational and social history of this period.

In terms of the nature of the historical material, this book qualifies as the kind of 'oral history' that has become popular in the West. Columbia University has established a large-scale 'oral history project' in the mid-twentieth century, while Academia Sinica's Institute of Modern History in Taiwan launched oral history research in the 1960s and has published many volumes since then. Oral history in these two programmes is basically centred on the individual; in other words, a form of oral autobiography. Conversely, this book covers a much broader scope of more than 600 people. Even so, the interviews and on-the-spot investigations used in this book are actually in line with the historical tradition of ancient China. Confucius says, 'Records and elders are insufficient; if sufficient, I could use them to support my words,'[2] thereby distinguishing between written and oral sources. The stories told by elderly people are a source of history. That's why the Grand Historian Sima Qian always stated his process of investigation and interview, as in the quote below:

> Sima Qian says: I went to the areas of Feng and Pei, interviewing old men well versed in the past age, and visited the houses where Xiao, Cao, Fan Kuai, and Teng Gong once lived, and heard their stories. What I heard was very interesting... I interviewed Fan Kuai's grandson, Guangtong, who described the prosperous period of the meritorious statesmen as I wrote it here.[3]

---

[2] *The Analects*, 'Ba Yi.'
[3] *Historical Records*, Vol. 95, Biography No. 35.

Aren't Youqin's interviews and investigations cut from the same cloth? There are many such examples in the *Histories* that need not be enumerated here. This method of gathering living historical material continued to be used in subsequent eras, especially in local gazetteers from the Song dynasty onwards. For example, the 'User's Guide' to the *Wuyuan County Gazetteer* of the early Republican period even denotes the 'interviewer's report', which shows that much of the factual information came from investigation and interviews. I'm thrilled to see this book continuing this excellent tradition of Chinese history, which provides future generations with so much reliable first-hand material.

A HORRIFYING BLEND OF THE SOVIET COMMUNIST SYSTEM AND CHINESE COMMUNIST CHARACTERISTICS

Of course, Youqin did not devote so much of her life to writing *Victims of the Cultural Revolution* merely to collect material on the Cultural Revolution for the purely objective research of future historians. She has brought a religious fervour to this mighty project driven by conscience, unable to reconcile herself to countless victims of Red Terror disappearing without a trace from the memories of the Chinese people. On 5 August 1966, the vice-principal of the Beijing Normal University Affiliated Girls' Secondary School, Bian Zhongyun, became the first victim of Red August when her students beat her to death. At that time, Youqin was a thirteen-year-old student at that school. This horrific tragedy branded her young soul with indelible pain and terror. This is the actual motivating force that has propelled this book forward from beginning to end. Although I was overseas at that time, I can provide second-hand verification of the results of Youqin's investigations. In October 1978, I led a delegation of American Sinologists on a tour to view archaeological relics in various parts of mainland China. We initially gathered in Beijing, where I had quite a few relatives who still lived in the ancient Bei Bingmasi district. I took the opportunity to return to this district for reunions with family members on two occasions. The first story I heard about the Cultural Revolution was how Red Guards in Beijing's secondary and primary schools had beaten their principals and teachers to death; my relatives related these circumstance as vividly as if they had been there themselves. What I found most unforgettable was how students at one secondary school (I've forgotten which one), used nail-spiked boards and brass-buckled belts to beat their teacher until blood and flesh spattered the walls. My relatives told me that the wife of one of my nephews, a secondary school teacher in Anqing, was beaten to death by her students after the Cultural Revolution erupted. At that time, our travel group included the archaeologist Zhang Guangzhi, now deceased. He had attended primary school in Beijing as a child and was very fond of his school principal. After he heard me retell these stories, he found them difficult to believe. Two days later, he made a special trip to visit his former principal, and when he came back, he told me that the principal's legs had been broken by students, and he could no longer walk. What I heard back then was basically consistent with what is written in this book, and I have no doubt that everything written here is factual.

China is an ancient civilisation in which teachers have always been revered. From the late Ming dynasty onwards, nearly every household paid veneration to 'Heaven, Earth, the sovereign, parents and teachers' (with 'the sovereign' changed to 'the nation' beginning in the Republican era). So why is it that at the outbreak of the Cultural Revolution, the first round of violence was aimed at teachers? It's impossible for me to discuss such a broad issue in detail here, but I can point out two salient facts: the first is that from 1949 onwards, China was completely subjugated by the Soviet Union's Leninist–Stalinist system; and the second is that this system developed even more horrific 'Chinese characteristics' when implemented in China.

There is no need to elaborate on the totalitarian nature of the Leninist–Stalinist system, which is well known to everyone. In the cultural and educational arena, its basic approach was the combating of knowledge and hostility towards educated people. This is because totalitarianism requires a single party to completely and ruthlessly subjugate the entire country and its people. The party therefore needs to use all available means, including deception and brutality, to preserve the power it gained through violence. For such a party, losing power is tantamount to cosmic annihilation. From an individual perspective, every party member must likewise use all possible means to preserve the authority in their grasp, and to ensure that this authority increases and never decreases. Power is everything, and loss of power means losing everything – that is the basic tenet of every party member. This is what Stalin meant when he said, 'Communist Party members are made of special stuff,' and it is why intra-party struggle is likewise unending. The legitimacy of one-party rule is built entirely on an ideology of absolute truth, because the smallest doubt will shake the foundations of one-party rule. That is why one-party rule instinctively opposes knowledge and is hostile to educated people. The Leninist–Stalinist system of the former Soviet Union reflected a thorough anti-intellectualism from the very outset. All subjects, including philosophy, literature and art, sociology, the sciences and history, were tightly controlled by the party, and official ideology maintained absolute unity of thought. The natural sciences were no exception. We all know the jokes about 'Stalin's linguistics' and 'Lysenko's biology', but this tendency was already apparent during Lenin's lifetime. Soviet Communist publications began to attack Einstein and other 'idealist' scientists in 1922.[4] In terms of 'Chinese characteristics', Mao during the Cultural Revolution succinctly described himself as 'a combination of Marx and Qin Shihuang'. Equating himself with Marx was pure narcissism; it would be more accurate to say that he was a combination of Stalin and Qin Shihuang, with Stalin referring to the system rather than the man, and Qin Shihuang symbolising 'Chinese characteristics'. China's First Emperor went down in infamy for 'burning books and burying scholars', and it was precisely this legacy that Mao claimed for himself. In political application, Mao and his party thoroughly resurrected the ruling methods of Chinese despotism, including the Ming-era secret agent system and literary inquisition. Even Mao's *Quotations* and the Red Guards can be said to have originated with the first Ming Emperor. Zhu Yuanzhang wrote three Grand Pronouncements that were essentially his *Quotations*. He not only required all students in the land (from the Imperial College to community schools) to study his Grand Pronouncements, but furthermore issued the edict that every household had to possess a copy and treat it as a great treasure.

Isn't this 'treasure' that every household was required to possess just like Mao's Little Red Book during the Cultural Revolution? The *Ming History Criminal Law Annals* states: 'At that time [1386], more than 190,000 teachers and students throughout the land purchased the Grand Pronouncements and paid their respects at court.'

Isn't this reminiscent of how a million Red Guards stood in Tiananmen Square waving their copies of Mao's *Quotations* and shouting, 'Long life'? China's population at the outset of the Ming dynasty was only around 100 million, so for more than 190,000 to gather in Nanjing is about on the same scale of impressiveness as a million Red Guards. That is why Mao's one-party rule was influenced not only by the imported Leninist–Stalinist system, but also by 'Chinese characteristics'. The combination of 'Stalin and Qin Shihuang' was truly formidable. This is not only true of China; the one-party dictatorship of the former Soviet Union likewise had its 'Russian characteristics' courtesy of the Tsarist system. As early as 1920, the Russian writer Miliukov pointed out that the theory of Bolshevik dictatorship came from the West, but its practice was deeply rooted in the substratum of Russian historical culture.[5] After Lenin came to power, the first thing he

---

[4] See Roger Pethybridge, *One Step Backwards, Two Steps Forward*, Oxford, 1990, p. 213.
[5] Paul Miliukov, *Bolshevism: An International Danger*, New York, Charles Scribner's Sons, 1920, p. 5.

did in the educational sphere was to reduce academic salaries and attack the prestige of teachers. A secondary school teacher earned a little more than half as much as an ordinary worker at the school, and the party arranged for students to humiliate their teachers in the classroom. Eventually one writer wrote a novel in the form of a fifteen-year-old student's diary, describing in hair-raising detail how students brutalised a female science teacher until she finally fled in terror. The only difference from the Cultural Revolution was that the students didn't resort to physical violence.[6] Slavishly imitating the Soviet Union, the CCP autocracy likewise reduced teachers to third-class citizens and goaded students to attack them. In 1952, Chen Yinke wrote a poem in the classical style entitled 'Lü Bushu', which included the stanza:

It has become common to testify against one's father for taking a sheep, while rare to lend one's father a hoe.

People treated their fathers this way, not to mention their teachers.

I have written about this poem in detail elsewhere,[7] but suffice it to say that Mr Chen was extremely sensitive and could see how the situation was developing already in 1952. It was by no means coincidental that students began killing their teachers fourteen years later; and the Cultural Revolution was not launched by Mao all on his own. All of this is inherent in the system of one-party rule, and the Chinese version of the Leninist–Stalinist system developed into a Cultural Revolution that involved the continuous killing of teachers and other types of intellectuals.

The Cultural Revolution was therefore not a stand-alone historical event, but rather the climax of a process through which one-party rule developed its true essence, and of which the 1942 Yan'an Rectification Movement and the 1975 Anti-Rightist Campaign served as harbingers. It was not the culmination of this process, however, as one-party rule continues to take on new qualitative forms in each stage of history. For most Chinese, the scene at Tiananmen in 1989 has largely faded from memory, but some people can never forget it. For a nation afflicted with serious historical amnesia, Dr Wang Youqin's book serves as a timely remedy.

Princeton, 3 December 2004

---

[6] See Richard Pipes, *Russia under the Bolshevik Regime*, New York, 1993, pp. 318–319.
[7] See my *Evidential Interpretations of Chen Yinke's Poems and Essays in His Later Years*, new and expanded edition, Taipei, Dongda tushu, 1998, pp. 54–56.

The Witness:
A Preface to Victims of the Cultural Revolution

SU XIAOKANG

(Journalist, cultural critic and veteran of the 1989 Democracy Movement)

Years ago I referred to Wang Youqin in an article, describing how she went to Beijing every year at her own expense and carried out house-to-house investigations into cases of students killing teachers in 1966, collaring an entire nation with her feeble voice. 'A lot of people probably hate her,' I observed. A friend of Wang Youqin's read these words and asked her, 'Why would he write something like that? It would be better for him to have written nothing than to remind people...' When Wang Youqin reported this to me later, I was surprised and felt the shadow looming darker than ever.

In the late 1980s, when I was in Beijing producing a documentary film about the Cultural Revolution, a university professor refused to allow me to interview his wife, a victim, explaining: 'One of the students who beat her back then now occupies a very high position. How can we dare to speak out? Please don't bother us any more. Let us spend our remaining days in peace, won't you?' At the time, all I could see was his wife from the back, sitting in a wheelchair.

I had tracked down this victim by chance at the Postal and Telecommunications Hospital across from Wang Youqin's former secondary school, the Beijing Normal University Affiliated Girls' Secondary School, where I was reporting on the killing of Bian Zhongyun. At an early stage of the Cultural Revolution, Red Guards from nearby secondary schools had come to this hospital with teachers whom they'd beaten unconscious or to death. Doctors and nurses there mentioned in passing that one-time Red Guards had brought a female teacher there in a pedicab and asked, 'Do corpses sell for 800 *kuai* each?' A doctor discovered that the teacher wasn't yet dead and managed to save her life. I was unable to locate the teacher at that time, but the detail of selling corpses implanted itself in my memory. When I came to the United States and learned that Wang Youqin was researching teachers who had been killed in secondary schools, I told her, 'Your school had a female teacher they tried to sell off, thinking she was dead.' To my surprise, she corrected me: that teacher's name was Han Jiufang, and she wasn't from Wang Youqin's alma mater but rather was vice-principal and chemistry teacher of the nearby No. 8 Boys' Secondary School. She had survived, but Red Guards pounded two large cavities in her back with brass belt buckles, and she was never able to stand again.

Detailed memory of the Cultural Revolution has been largely lost. Wang Youqin has forsaken all else in her effort to discover and preserve these details, and her one-woman struggle against collective amnesia has made her a living storehouse of information on the Cultural Revolution's victims. She has mounted a one-woman resistance against the amnesia of hundreds of millions. I remember during my reporting having someone at the Girls' School point out where Bian Zhongyun had been beaten to death, and I stood in that spot and imagined it as an instance like the Bund Deutscher Mädel, the female branch of Hitler Youth, which was the closest comparison I could come up with. But I lacked the ability to imagine a different scenario: one in which after Bian Zhongyun's death, another girl student would stand up and demand justice on her behalf.

Wang Youqin, a student at that school, was there when it happened. Starting out as an eyewitness, she later became a witness. Years later, Jay Nordlinger, a reporter who interviewed her at the University of Chicago, spoke of her 'calling' in an article for *The Weekly Standard*:

> Even as the Cultural Revolution was in progress, she read *The Diary of Anne Frank*, a book that inspired her to record what was happening around her. It was impermissible to speak of the daily horrors; so she confided what she saw and heard to a diary, addressing it as 'Kitty', as Anne had. But unlike Anne, she destroyed her pages shortly after she had written them. You could be killed for what you said in your diary; many were.[1]

Undoubtedly, Nordlinger was putting Wang Youqin in the context of Western history and experience. Although there should be a universality to bearing witness to violence, in China and in the Chinese language sphere we have seen only Wang Youqin. For that reason, Nordlinger mentioned her again in an article about Solzhenitsyn:

---

[1] Jay Nordlinger, 'What She Saw at the Revolution: Memorialising the victims of the Cultural Revolution', *The Weekly Standard*, 20 August 2001, http://ywang.uchicago.edu/history/docs/2001_08_20.pdf.

> Solzhenitsyn has inspired both ordinary men and extraordinary ones. Let me tell you about an extraordinary one. She is a woman, actually – Youqin Wang, a lecturer in Chinese at Chicago. But that's merely her day job. She has devoted her life to memorialising the victims of the Cultural Revolution... It was at Beijing University that she found Solzhenitsyn... she managed to get a hold of one of the very few copies of *The Gulag Archipelago* in the whole of China. When she read it, she knew what she had to do with her life: commit the lives of the lost to historical memory. I like to think of that woman out in Chicago, with probably the two greatest witnesses of the century at her back: Anne Frank and Solzhenitsyn.[2]

Yet, doesn't the emergence of Wang Youqin stand to reason even more within the scope of Chinese history and experience? Her inner drive might be explained very simply as that of a student reclaiming justice for her teacher. Wang Youqin was an outstanding student, achieving the highest score in the 1979 national college entrance exam; but over and above this, she feels a kinship with the teachers who died in the Cultural Revolution, and awareness of their distress made it impossible for her to live in peace. She herself is the eldest daughter of teachers, and perhaps this has endowed her with the kind of 'inner calling' she describes in her account of the cattle and the chickens: cattle will grieve over the death of another, but chickens will not. In this sense, Wang Youqin not only subverts Mao's Cultural Revolution, but also negates it from the most traditional and classical Chinese standpoint of restoring the dignity of teachers. This is one of the foundations of Chinese civilisation.

Wang Youqin's dialogue with the silent multitudes has put her in the peculiar situation of serving as a substitute for the bystanders who should be witnesses. Our shame is not only the extreme rarity of witnesses, but also the witnesses who cannot bear witness. The dreadful silence Wang Youqin confronts shows her dogged determination. The Cultural Revolution taboo results from systemic information blackout and amnesia, and from subconscious aversion and rejection that has become ingrained in a populace whom the Great Leader forcibly made into his co-conspirators. That's why this great catastrophe has never truly ended, but has become suspended in a collective amnesia that forsakes the victims. Year in and year out, Wang Youqin has dwelled among these suppressed outpourings, the dried blood and tears, the terrified rejection, the helplessness... Her testimony requires not courage so much as tenaciousness. It goes without saying that locating

---

[2] Jay Nordlinger, 'A Long Way from '78', *National Review*, 6 June 2003, http://www.nationalreview.com/article/207148/long-way-78-jay-nordlinger.

more than 600 victims and the details of their fates has been a kind of spiritual purgatory; her exchanges with family members and other sources, the advising, consoling, compelling and rejecting have taken a mental toll on both sides, but have become an important page in the individual spiritual and cultural history of the Chinese people. Her solitary confrontation of systemic lies and defiance of the mainstream discourse that has consistently drowned out the voices of victims and survivors has gradually earned her a following of like-minded 'historical volunteers', contributing to an unvarnished history of those times. It remains to be told how her masterful 'Students Attacks against Teachers: The Revolution of 1966' launched the process of victims bearing witness to history, and how her work was circulated, plagiarised and distorted. Her own testimony could previously only be published on the Internet, reflecting the discrimination against victims; and even that Online Holocaust Memorial has long been blocked by the Chinese authorities.

The first person to advocate a Museum of the Cultural Revolution was Ba Jin in the 1980s. His long-cherished wish symbolised a time when countless people looked forward to a political dawn and few doubted its possibility. Looking back after the 4 June Massacre, people felt the 1980s were truly naïve. Ba Jin's proposal was an implicit call for witness, and he was by no means naïve, having personally experienced that time when 'children became wolves overnight'. We were fortunate to have a Ba Jin, and we are fortunate now to have a Wang Youqin.

Translator's Note

This book should be treated as a companion volume to general histories of the Cultural Revolution. The most important of these volumes available in English include *Mao's Last Revolution*, by Roderick MacFarquhar and Michael Schoenals; *The World Turned Upside Down: A History of the Chinese Cultural Revolution*, by Yang Jisheng; *The Cultural Revolution: A People's History*, by Frank Dikotter; and *Turbulent Decade*, by Yan Jiaqi and Gao Gao. These books typically devote more than 500 pages to charting the origins and course of the Cultural Revolution, and can devote only scant attention to the fate of individual victims. Wang Youqin's purpose is different; her book is a tribute to the victims against the larger backdrop of the Cultural Revolution.

Wang Youqin arranged the original Chinese edition of this book alphabetically, according to the names of the victims, in the style of China's traditional biographical dictionaries. With her help, I have employed a spacio-temporal arrangement for the English edition that brings together people who were victimised at specific stages of the Cultural Revolution and in particular locations or institutions. The aim is to help readers see the connections and trends that unite these individual deaths. This English edition also contains additional information on victims that Wang Youqin continued to collect following the publication of the Chinese edition. In order to aid English-speaking readers, I have added translator's notes in the text to provide further information. These footnotes begin with 'TN' to distinguish them from Wang Youqin's original footnotes.

Wang Youqing's book is more than an objective recounting of fact. She ruminates over the irony of persecutors in one political campaign who become victims in the next; she expresses outrage over the destruction of human talent and its long-term effect on China's development; she relates poignant details, such as the professor forced to shave off the facial hair that had won him a 'best beard' contest in happier times, or the couple who laid out a Bible and sprayed their home with perfume before hanging themselves. In this way, Professor Wang not only highlights the tragedy of individual deaths, but also resurrects them as human beings, worthy of being remembered and mourned.

Stacy Mosher

Chronology

1966

15 May: The CCP circulates a 7 May letter from Mao to Lin Biao stating that 'the phenomenon of bourgeois intellectuals controlling our schools cannot be allowed to continue.'

16 May: The CCP central leadership issues a comprehensive 10,000-word notice, the 16 May Circular, which launches the Cultural Revolution and explicitly calls for a 'thorough criticism of academia, educators, journalists, artists, publishers and other representatives of the bourgeois class, and seizing the leadership of those cultural spheres'.

Students at Peking University put up the first big-character poster, attacking school administrators and calling for 'determined and thorough eradication of all ox demons and snake spirits'.

29 May: Three members of the Politburo Standing Committee, Liu Shaoqi, Zhou Enlai, and Deng Xiaoping, decide to send work groups to the *People's Daily* and Peking University. On 4 June, the new Beijing Municipal Party Committee dispatches work groups to other college campuses.

June: The Beijing Municipal Party Committee is dismissed and replaced by the 'new Beijing Municipal Party Committee'.

1 June: China Central People's Broadcasting Network broadcasts the contents of the Peking University big-character poster.

17 June: The *People's Daily* publishes the CCP Central Committee's decision to eliminate university admission exams and adopt political performance as the criterion for selecting university students.

18 June: At Peking University, students ignore the work groups and carry out struggle sessions against 'reactionary academic authorities'. The university's work group criticises the students, and President Liu Shaoqi endorses the work group's report with a memo stating, 'The Central Committee believes that the Peking University work group was correct in its handling of the phenomenon of unauthorised struggle sessions.'

Late July: Mao accuses Liu Shaoqi and Deng Xiaoping of 'stultifying' the movement and takes over leadership of the Cultural Revolution with the Central Cultural Revolution Group.

Late July: Mao's wife, Jiang Qing, goes to Peking University and declares the 18 June incident to have been a 'revolutionary incident'.

29 July: During a 'Capital City Revolutionary Teachers and Students Congress' held at the Great Hall of the People, the work groups are declared disbanded. Red Guards take control of the schools, along with the 'Cultural Revolution Committees' established by the work groups.

August: Eleventh plenum of the Eighth CCP Central Committee is in session. Liu Shaoqi and Deng Xiaoping are demoted, and the supreme military commander, Lian Biao, becomes the second most powerful man in China.

1 August: Mao writes a letter 'ardently supporting' Red Guard violence at the Affiliated Secondary Schools of Tsinghua and Peking Universities.

5 August: The CCP Central Committee formally rescinds the document Liu Shaoqi issued to curb 'unauthorised struggle' at Peking University. The new directive, No. 395 of 1966, consists of just one sentence: 'The Central Committee's authorised dispatch on 20 June 1966, of the Peking University Cultural Revolution Briefing Report (No. 9) was in error, and the Central Committee hereby rescinds this document.'

9 August: 'The CCP Central Committee's Resolution Regarding the Great Proletarian Cultural Revolution' is broadcast over national radio. The Resolution admonishes, 'struggle but do not resort to violence,' but also endorses student violence by stating, 'A large group of hitherto unknown

revolutionary youth have become daring path-breakers... their revolutionary orientation is ultimately correct.'

18 August: Mao receives one million Red Guards at Tiananmen Square, an event broadcast live over radio and television.

'Red August': The rally at Tiananmen Square promotes the Red Guard movement to a revolutionary organisation present in every educational institution. Campus violence escalates and extends into the wider community in the 'Smashing of the Four Olds', which continues for two months.

September: The Central Cultural Revolution Small Group issues an internal bulletin entitled 'Utterly Routing the Old World', which reports one of the 'accomplishments' of the Red Guards as the killing of 1,772 people from 20 August to early September.

1967

24 January: Mao renames the Shanghai People's Commune as the Shanghai Revolutionary Committee, launching a new power structure of 'Revolutionary Committees' based on a 'three-way alliance of Red Guards, Party cadres and the military'.

27 November: At a workers forum, Jiang Qing first raises the need to 'cleanse the class ranks' (*qingli jieji duiwu*).

1968

July: Mao orders Worker and PLA Mao Zedong Thought Propaganda Teams to take over the schools.

5 September: Revolutionary Committees are established in all provinces, municipalities and autonomous regions of mainland China. They are finally abolished and replaced by people's governments in 1979.

1969–1970

The One Strike and Three Antis Campaign (*yi da san fan*) attacks counter-revolutionaries and opposes corruption, profiteering and waste.

1971

13 September: Lin Biao and others die in Mongolia during an attempt to escape from China.

1976

8 January: Premier Zhou Enlai dies.

9 September: Mao Zedong dies.

6 October: The Gang of Four is arrested. The Cultural Revolution effectively ends.

1977

12 August: Hua Guofeng officially declares the end of the Cultural Revolution.

Introduction: The Status of Victims

WANG YOUQIN

BETWEEN COWS AND CHICKENS

When I began writing the history of the Cultural Revolution many years ago, my first step was to interview hundreds of people who had lived through that period. My emphasis on interviews and investigation rather than on collecting written materials was due to the great discrepancy I found between written records from the period and historical fact. Much of what happened during the Cultural Revolution was not reported or recorded at the time, and first-hand investigation is critical to a faithful portrayal of events.

My heartfelt thanks go to all those who spent their valuable time recalling and retracing past events. These recollections were often very painful and distressing, but morality, courage and desire to support my work enabled these people to overcome deep-seated avoidance and dread. People not only assisted my search for historical facts regarding the personalities and events of the Cultural Revolution, but also shared the lessons of their personal experiences.

One elderly interviewee was a teacher who during the Cultural Revolution had been labelled an 'active counter-revolutionary' and as a result spent many years on a reform-through-labour farm. One of his chores was tending cattle, an area in which, as an engineer, he lacked experience. He was initially intimidated by the herd of massive beasts that could move at will but could neither understand nor speak human language. Over time he realised that the herd was neither hostile nor dangerous, and as the cattle began gradually to obey his commands, he learned to get along with them.

On the farm there was a large willow tree under which the grass was especially lush and succulent, and the teacher often led the herd there to graze. Later, an ox that had grown too old to work was slaughtered beside the big willow tree. The next time the teacher led the herd to graze there, the cattle refused to budge, and lowed mournfully where they stood. He tried twice more, but still the herd refused to graze beneath the willow, bellowing so plaintively that even he felt sad. From then on, he never again took the herd to the willow tree, even though the grass there remained more plentiful than elsewhere. In the ensuing years, he continued to marvel at the memory and steadfastness of those beasts.

Curious, I asked, 'Are beasts really so capable of empathy and memory that these cattle would recall where their companion was slaughtered, and mourn and refuse to return there?'

The teacher said this was true of cattle, but not necessarily of other creatures. Chickens, for example, were different; they would frolic where their companions had been butchered, as if nothing had happened. Sometimes a few chickens would be grabbed from the flock and butchered, plucked and gutted on the spot, and if the intestines were tossed on the ground, the other chickens would fight each other to eat them.

As I listened, the tableaux of the cattle and the chickens scrolled through my brain so realistically that I knew this teacher was describing his actual experience rather than concocting a fable or satire; only personal observation could lend the stories such detail. On further thought, these stories of cattle and chickens reminded me of people: in the post-Cultural Revolution era, we ordinary people often find ourselves placed between cattle and chickens.

Large numbers of people were persecuted to death during the Cultural Revolution, some beaten to death in public, some tortured to death in prison, others committing suicide after being beaten and humiliated, while others died of starvation, illnesses or mental torment. They were teachers, parents, classmates, friends, relatives, colleagues, neighbours and members of the community. What do we recall of their deaths? How did we respond? What did we do? Protest? Sympathise? Help? Keep silent? Turn our backs? Revel in or add to their misfortunes? Were we accomplices or bystanders? Did we forget, embellish, or devote ourselves to the search for truth and justice? In spite of the oppressive atmosphere of the Cultural Revolution era, some leeway existed among these various options. Since the Cultural Revolution, remembrance and the recording of facts have met with multiple obstructions, but the scope of personal choice is much wider; hence the even greater need for individuals to decide where they stand.

The ways cattle and chickens regarded their dead companions, as observed by the teacher on the labour farm, reveal two patterns and provide co-ordinates for measurement and comparison. It could be said that the position of victims in today's historical record, including their presence and how they are depicted, is decided first and foremost by the choice of the majority of survivors, and whether that choice is reminiscent of cattle or of chickens.

The work involved in producing and publishing this book, including the investigation and writing, can likewise be viewed as the struggle of individual conscience between the way of cattle and the way of chickens.

DEATH AND THE CULTURAL REVOLUTION

The Cultural Revolution had its own rationale. Generally speaking, this was to establish a centralised and highly concentrated power structure with no restrictions or balances; an economy with no market, no commodity production and optimally no currency; and media that expressed only one view, all in the same way. The ultimate goal was to transform China's populace into 'the new socialist man', with every individual no more than a cog in the wheel of a great machine, incapable of even fleeting self-interest. Attaining the revolution's goals justified utilising state power and the 'dictatorship of the masses' to beat, detain or even kill those designated 'enemies' by the revolution's leaders.

Violence climaxed during two points in the Cultural Revolution. The first occurred in 1966, during the 'Smashing of the Four Olds' (old thinking, culture, customs and habits) that accompanied the formation of the Red Guards; the second occurred from 1968 to 1969 with the establishment and consolidation of the new power structure of Revolutionary Committees, a process referred to at the time as the Campaign to Cleanse the Class Ranks.

In August 1966, with Mao Zedong's enthusiastic support, the Red Guards rapidly developed from a high school student group into a revolutionary organisation present in every educational institution. Campus violence arose and burgeoned under student Red Guards, who rounded up large numbers of education workers into 'ox demon and snake spirit teams'[1] and subjected them to 'struggle' – the term used for mass denunciation, beating and humiliation. Some of these educators were beaten to death by

---

[1] Translator's note (TN): The term 'ox demons and snake spirits', originally coined by Tang dynasty poet Du Mu to refer to fantastical creatures. In Chinese mythology, *'niugui sheshen'* were shape-shifting evil spirits that could take human form. (For example, the Monkey King battles an Ox Demon in the classic *Journey to the West*.) The term was used to dehumanise the political underclass during the Cultural Revolution.

their own students, in secondary and even in primary schools. It was the first such violence in the 2,000-year history of China's education system.

Guided by the Cultural Revolution's leaders, violence progressed and expanded beyond the campus grounds. Red Guards marched into the streets, beating ordinary citizens and ransacking their homes. They burned books and destroyed cultural artifacts, while killing many designated 'ox demons and snake spirits' and expelling multitudes of city dwellers to rural exile. Some of those driven out were beaten to death en route, while others died of starvation soon after reaching their destinations, or killed themselves when survival proved impossible.

This massacre lasted for about two months. Throughout China, not a single school was spared violent attacks on its teachers and staff. In Beijing alone, some 100,000 residents were driven from their homes, and thousands were killed. Against the red insignia of revolution, blood-soaked bodies were piled into trucks or cargo pedicabs and hauled through the streets to the crematorium. Burning day and night, the furnaces could not keep up with demand, and corpses rotted in piles. The ashes were then discarded like ordinary trash.

The massacre of 1966 had several distinguishing features: the victims underwent no legal process – not even so much as a kangaroo court – before being killed; no written record was made of their deaths; they were not shot or beheaded by professional executioners, but were beaten with clubs or tortured to death; and most of the killings were perpetrated by teenagers who were authorised to torture, plunder and kill.

Two years later, in 1968, guided by of a number of 'memos' written by Mao, or 'Central Committee documents' that he had amended or endorsed, the newly established power structure of multi-level 'Revolutionary Committees' launched the Campaign to Cleanse the Class Ranks. The cleansing was not of rubbish but rather of individual human beings. A large group of people was designated for 'vetting'. Every work unit, from university to village primary school, from government department to factory, established jails where people were incarcerated for months or even years. Because the Cultural Revolution's leaders referred to its targets as 'ox demons and snake spirits', these workplace jails were commonly referred to as 'ox pens'.

All classes and work were suspended, and everyone was engaged morning, noon and night in 'unearthing... deeply hidden class enemies'. Older people became 'pre-liberation counter-revolutionaries' on the basis of their activities decades earlier, while younger people found that careless remarks made them 'active counter-revolutionaries'. Accidentally damaging a picture of Mao or reciting a slogan incorrectly was a 'heinous crime'. People set off for their units in the morning unsure of whether they would return home in the evening or find themselves locked up in an ox pen. Corporal punishment such as floggings and beatings, as well as humiliation and psychological torture, were carried out non-stop, sometimes in public and other times behind closed doors in the 'ox pens'. In Beijing alone, at least 10,000 people were beaten to death or 'committed suicide' under questionable circumstances in the course of these 'investigations'.

Suicide was especially prevalent during the Cleansing of the Class Ranks and its successor campaign, the 'One Strike and Three Antis'.[2] Bodies floated in lakes and ponds, blood dripped through ceilings, brain matter spattered pavements. Leaping from windows, drinking insecticide, slashing wrists, drowning, electrocution, hanging, throwing oneself beneath a train – a variety of horrifying methods were employed. Deaths in the 'ox pens' under 'isolation and investigation' were declared suicides by the same people who were watching and investigating the victims; there were typically no suicide notes, and family members were not allowed to view the bodies. Even after death, targets could be subjected to struggle sessions over their caricatures or even their corpses, where they were vilified for 'committing suicide to escape punishment' and 'unatoned crime'.

Eventually, some of those who survived 'isolation and investigation' spoke of their physical and mental torment, and some of those in charge of the 'ox pens' admitted that many so-called suicides were in fact homicides in which victims were tossed out of windows or hanged from the rafters. Even those who ended their own lives were typically driven to despair by unimaginable humiliation and abuse, and suicides were to all intents and purposes murder by revolution. Such murderous suicide, one of the unique products of the Cultural Revolution, comprised one of the most appalling slaughters in human history.

The Cleansing of the Class Ranks was one of the darkest periods of the Cultural Revolution, its oppression more systematic and protracted than the 'Red August' of 1966. 'Special investigation groups' were established and dispatched throughout the country. Interrogating their targets in the dead of night with threats that coming clean would bring leniency, while refusing to confess would be treated with severity, they coerced numerous 'confessions' and 'self-criticisms'. These texts remained hidden away in work unit 'archive rooms'; in one high school, they filled several sacks.

Many more people died during various other 'campaigns', but the 1966 Red Guard massacres and 1968 'Revolutionary Committee' slaughters represent the two apogees of violence. Most of the deaths recorded in this book occurred during those two periods.

---

[2] 1969–1970, attacking counter-revolutionaries and opposing corruption, waste and opportunism.

People who died around the same time typically showed a striking uniformity in the details of their deaths. For example, the circumstances of those who died during struggle sessions or in 'ox pens' during 'isolation and investigation' were clearly and directly connected to those respective stages of the Cultural Revolution. These deaths were not isolated incidents or mishaps; people were killed after being targeted for attack under the Cultural Revolution's specific arrangements.

Mass persecution was in fact the main scenario and crime of the Cultural Revolution. In terms of the nature, scale and degree of its brutality, the Cultural Revolution is comparable to Hitler's slaughter of the Jews, or Stalin's Gulag Archipelago. The main difference is that much less of what happened during the Cultural Revolution is a matter of record, as a result of which its horrors are more liable to fade from human memory.

RECORDING THE NAME OF EVERY VICTIM

Deaths have been recorded since the dawn of human civilisation. In Chinese tradition, graves were marked with cone-shaped mounds. Since the invention of writing, deaths have been commemorated on stone tablets, in bronze, on bamboo slips and even more prevalently on paper. Deaths are recorded for any number of purposes, and the records have many kinds of significance. Generally speaking, however, a record signifies attaching importance to the death, and commemorating the dead signifies a respect for life.

Ever since the judicial process came into existence, there has been the additional necessity of recording murders. This record is not only for the deceased, but also for the living. If the taking of human life is regarded as too trivial to be put down in writing, killing will run rampant. For the sake of preserving the safety of the living, it is essential to record the death of the victim and the punishment of the assailant. This has been one of the primary motivations behind recording such deaths over the millennia.

The deaths of the Cultural Revolution's victims, however, have gone largely unrecorded. When I began tracing the history of the Cultural Revolution, I was repeatedly shocked, not only by the deaths, but also by the fact that they had not been recorded or reported.

Death during the Cultural Revolution was exceedingly brutal and horrifying, the torment often prolonged, public and involving numerous participants. The reasons for these unconcealed fatalities going unrecorded are worth contemplating.

The refusal to report or record Cultural Revolution fatalities, or to allow the preservation of the remains, was further insult, humiliation and punishment inflicted posthumously. After the Cultural Revolution, the authorities allowed newspapers and books to publish names and biographical details only for the minority of victims who were high-level cadres or prominent members of society. The deaths of ordinary people were cast outside the framework of historical record.

The deficiency of death records has resulted, perhaps intentionally, in a distorted picture of the Cultural Revolution. Eradicating all trace of the great majority of its victims has obviated the need to track the origins of the Cultural Revolution, which would necessarily implicate the highest leadership, as well as the ideology and social system that engendered it; this cannot be allowed in China.

In addition, the slaughter of the Cultural Revolution distorted the way people regarded the lives of their peers. People were forced to accept these deaths, and once this loss of life was no longer regarded as a serious crime, the lack of victims' names in the historical record became a matter of course.

Two thousand years ago, Sima Qian wrote his *Records of the Grand Historian*, with great effort on bamboo slips. His history focused on the Emperor rather than on the population at large, but his 'Annals of the Qin Emperor' recorded the three-year-long incident subsequently referred to as 'the burning of books and burial of scholars', including its causes, methods, process and aftermath. Sima Qian unambiguously noted that in the year 214 BCE, the Qin Emperor 'buried alive more than 460 scholars as punishment and as a warning to the whole empire'. He did not write out the names of those 460 scholars, possibly because he considered it unnecessary, but even more probably because written records of that kind didn't exist at the time, and Sima Qian, writing one hundred years after the event, had no way of finding such information.

In contrast, no record was made of the Cultural Revolution's victims, such as those killed by the Red Guards in 1966 and persecuted by Revolutionary Committees in 1968. The victims vanished without a trace, and the two incidents do not even have a formal name in history.

Fortunately, most people who experienced the Cultural Revolution are still alive, and some recall the deaths of that period. In my investigations, I interviewed hundreds of survivors, and communicated with others by mail or telephone, as well as by email once that became possible. I asked questions and joined them in recalling past events. They helped me discover and verify the names of victims, as well as when and how they died. Where possible, I also consulted published documents and private records, but the voluminous written material extant from that time only rarely offers collateral evidence of deaths.

I began with the schools, recording the names of teachers who had been beaten to death, along with their stories. Educators had been killed or had committed suicide at all of the schools I covered, and the stories I heard were often far more horrific than I had ever imagined. I recorded all the details as thoroughly as possible, even when they might seem incredible to my future readers.

The first story I wrote, in 1986, was of the first education worker to be killed in Beijing during the Cultural Revolution, Bian Zhongyun. I then continued my interviews and investigations and compiled records, adding names and stories to my notebooks and computer files, teachers first and then people of all types and professions, including students, workers, farmers, doctors, nannies and housewives.

Before the Cultural Revolution, these had been ordinary people, doing their work and living their lives. Almost none of them were opponents of the Cultural Revolution, yet it had made them into targets, 'ox demons and snake spirits', 'reactionary gang elements', 'landlords, rich peasants, counter-revolutionaries, bad elements, rightists or capitalists' and 'active counter-revolutionaries'. Silence surrounded their deaths; they offered no resistance to their persecution, nor did any around them protest on their behalf. Their forbearance is nevertheless no reason for us to forget them.

I have emphasised the stories of ordinary people, my attempt to record every victim based on the simple conviction that every life should be valued, and therefore every death should also be valued.

In addition, I believe it is a scholar's responsibility to probe and record historical fact. The victimisation of ordinary people was an important aspect of the history of the Cultural Revolution, and when this fact is obstructed on all fronts, scholars need to apply even more effort. That is why I continued with my investigations in spite of unanticipated difficulties and harassment.

When I began in 1998 to create biographies for each Cultural Revolution victim, I found it shook my existing assumption that 'biographies' were only written for the great and mighty, heroes and tyrants, as has been the normal practice since the time of Sima Qian. On further thought, however, I felt that failing to record the stories of these silent victims would imply that the suffering and death of ordinary people was irrelevant, or that I lacked the will to carry out this time- and energy-consuming task.

THE TRAUMA OF SURVIVORS

Even if the stories of the Cultural Revolution's victims were not written, they would continue to exist in distorted form in the psychic wounds of survivors.

At one point I interviewed a woman who had been a student in Beijing in 1966. She recalled how, during the Red August of 1966, she had watched a cargo pedicab burdened with a dozen corpses emerge from the *hutong* where her family lived. The dead were 'class enemies' who had been beaten to death, their clothes ripped to shreds, and they resembled nothing so much as 'the pale, fresh pig carcasses stacked in the street market'. She then quickly added, 'I can't tell you the name of the *hutong*, because then others will know I told you.' This conversation took place thirty-four years after the fact. Her terror and sudden loss of composure stunned me.

I attempted to put her mind at ease, observing that the *hutong* was very long and well populated, and that many people must have seen the pedicab; no one would be able to identify her as the source of the anecdote. I went on, 'I have my principles, and I will never reveal the source of my information.' I quickly realised, however, that she was not ignorant of this fact, and that it was a terror buried deep in her heart for the past thirty-four years that gushed forth and contorted her face. After regaining her composure, she told me the name and location of the *hutong*. She said that the scene had repeatedly haunted her dreams over the past thirty-four years, and that this was the first time she had had the chance to tell anyone about it.

Another time I interviewed a man who had been a secondary school teacher during the Cultural Revolution. He had once spent three months in an 'ox pen' set up by Red Guards, during which time he had been beaten and humiliated and had carried out the corpses of fellow prisoners who had been beaten to death. He said it had never occurred to him to write of his experiences; since great men such as President Liu Shaoqi had suffered similar persecution, the travails of an ordinary man counted as nothing. He said this with absolute sincerity.

I wanted to impress on him that an ordinary person's life was just as important as that of a senior official. Those in positions of power know the risks they face, but an ordinary school teacher had no reason to expect that a power struggle would become a matter of life and death to him. Yet I also realised that it was not a matter of this former teacher never having heard that 'all human life is of equal value'; rather, having no opportunity to divulge what happened or to obtain justice for all these years, he had to regard himself as a second-class citizen in order to gain some release from the rage and repression he felt over his misfortune.

I know of one family that in recent years experienced tragedy in the form of cancer and a traffic fatality; in their grief they believed they had brought this misfortune on themselves, because back during the Cultural Revolution, a member of their family had been persecuted to death, yet they had neither helped that person nor even claimed the body. Seeking to remedy the lapse by performing funeral rites for the victim, they could not find out what had been done with the corpse. In their terror, the family finally went to the wasteland where the body had been discarded, and they collected some earth in a funerary urn and carried out a ceremony on the spot.

In fact, this family knew that the persons responsible for the death of their loved one had not yet received retribution, and that Heaven's penalty would only come in the next life. But it was clear that after refusing to retrieve the body and 'drawing a clear distinction' from their loved one, and suppressing their anger for three decades, an intense terror had remained in their hearts – not only a terror of the revolution's violence, but also a horror at their own cowardice, and that is what made them feel deserving of retribution. It is my hope that the belated funeral rites finally afforded them some spiritual solace.

Survivors share long-distance bonds resulting from the intense dread, sense of inferiority, and guilt-induced anxiety brought about by Cultural Revolution deaths. These psychological scars, while not as obvious in their pain and symptoms as physical wounds, require healing all the same, and obliterating and suppressing survivors' memories prevents this healing. Recording, narrating and contemplating is not something survivors do for the victims, but rather is a step towards their own recovery.

BANNED MEMORIALS

Despite various pressures, all victims had survivors attempting to remember them. A little more than a year after Bian Zhongyun's death, when the tide of Red Guard ransackings had subsided, her husband and children constructed a spirit shelf for her inside a closet, a tribute kept secret from everyone outside their home. In 1986, the famous writer Ba Jin proposed establishing a Museum of the Cultural Revolution to recall and draw lessons from history. More than twenty years later, no progress has been made in this direction, not even so much as a blueprint or written or oral discussion.

On 16 October 2000, when I uploaded documentation on nearly 1,000 Cultural Revolution victims onto the Internet, I was filled with gratitude for the possibilities afforded by modern technology. At last, when the physical world provided no means of erecting a memorial to these victims, new technology provided a way for ordinary people to do so with relative ease in cyberspace. My new website was called the 'Online Chinese Cultural Revolution Holocaust Memorial'. Readers from all over the globe could access the website at their convenience, read the stories of these victims and provide their feedback by email.

Seventeen months later, in March 2002, my website was blocked in mainland China. If anyone tries to access the website within China's borders, a web page pops up stating, 'Page not available.' In fact, my website has been active and fully functional all along. But of course, it is not the computer that is lying.

While this was hardly surprising, I was still shocked. These victims had been dead for more than three decades without their remains being preserved, much less laid to rest, and it was still not permitted for them to rest in peace in cyberspace. Why? Who made the decision to ban the listing of victims' names on the Internet?

In detective novels, one method for cracking a case is determining who has motivation and who benefits. It is obvious that the names and stories of the Cultural Revolution's victims testify to the evil of the Cultural Revolution, and that concealing and obliterating these names makes this evil less tangible and thereby dilutes the guilt of its leaders. It is because Mao Zedong's corpse and image are still displayed at Tiananmen Square that the names of the Cultural Revolution's victims must be suppressed, even on the Internet.

This is the long and difficult back-story to this book, and why I so treasure its publication. I hope this feeling is evident to my readers.

DATA SOURCES AND ARRANGEMENT

Most of the information from this book is the result of my investigations and interviews. The fact that much relating to the Cultural Revolution has gone unreported obliges us to reach beyond the typical resources of historical research, such as extant written materials or visual records. Investigation of primary sources, while requiring considerable expenditure of time and effort, is essential. I have spoken with around 1,000 people who lived through the Cultural Revolution. Some were in Beijing at the time, others in the outer provinces, in major cities or rural villages. Some of those I interviewed were the family members of victims.

Apart from one-on-one conversations and correspondence, I carried out an online survey in 1994 and 1995. When my Online Chinese Cultural Revolution Holocaust Memorial went live in 2000, I received many letters from readers, some of whom took the initiative to provide me with the names and stories of more victims.

Most of my interviewees were willing to describe what they had seen and heard. In order to avoid errors in their recollection, some interviewees consulted records relating to the individual or work unit in question, or carried out cross-verification. There were minimal opportunities, however, to access official archives, and some people who had participated in the violence refused to speak with me. Surmounting 'selective memory' of the Cultural Revolution was therefore one of my main challenges in compiling this book.

I also read all accounts of the Cultural Revolution published by official sources or distributed by student organisations, including the complete *People's Daily* archives of that period and many tabloids produced by 'mass organisations'. Since the propagandistic media controlled by the Cultural Revolution's leaders intentionally concealed much of the truth, they praised it without the slightest mention of violent persecution and death. Some interviewees said this was because acts of violence were usually regarded as 'the unavoidable extreme behaviour' of 'revolution'. The vast disparity between historical fact and contemporary written accounts reflects to some extent the views and attitudes towards violence and death at that time.

I have also availed myself of materials published after the Cultural Revolution. Where no third-party sources are cited, the material is the result of my own investigations and interviews.

The widely varying length of the biographies is solely dependent upon how many facts I was able to obtain. I hoped to write detailed stories for each victim, but the truth is that complete information was very hard to come by. Even after years of effort, in many cases I have been able to provide only a few sentences.

ACKNOWLEDGEMENT OF UNNAMED BENEFACTORS

A book normally includes a space for acknowledgements, because it is seldom the product of one person's efforts alone, and the author should acknowledge the contributions of others. This is especially the case with this book, which involved the assistance of some 1,000 individuals, some of whom I have met personally and others not. Most of the contributions relate to names and stories, while some people provided technical assistance. For me, this support was not only practical but also psychological. In a typical project, progress brings gratification, but in researching the Cultural Revolution, progress means the discovery of even more death and injustice, and causes sorrow and pain. In research of this kind, psychological support is all the more important and meaningful.

One of those who assisted me referred to himself as a 'volunteer for history'. With that formulation in mind, I here offer my heartfelt thanks to all of the 'volunteers' involved in this book, and I consider myself one of them.

The word 'volunteer' implies one who receives no compensation for performing a good deed. This book should therefore start out with a list of these 'volunteers', not just as convention, but as an expression of genuine indebtedness and detailing many moving stories aglow with human kindness and justice. Yet in the end I have written a simple acknowledgement without names. This is due to the wishes of those who assisted me; I don't wish to cause them trouble, or to provide intelligence to those concealed in darkness who shut down my online memorial.

A very long acknowledgements page does exist, however, and it is my great hope that I might someday publish the names of my 'volunteers' and the stories connected with the production of this book.

I would also like my readers to know that, painful though the content of this book is, I invite everyone to join in my work. Provide any leads or information in your possession, write out all you know about victims of the Cultural Revolution, and then compile the information for publication as a further volume. Writing about and memorialising victims is not the work of one person, but must be the shared effort of those of us fortunate enough to have survived.

PART ONE

The Cultural Revolution in the Universities

ATTACKS ON UNIVERSITY ADMINISTRATORS, 1966

WHY WERE SO MANY UNIVERSITY ADMINISTRATORS PERSECUTED TO DEATH?

Prior to the Cultural Revolution, presidents ran the universities under the leadership of the university Party Committee. The Party secretary was the university's top leader, and in practice a single person was usually both Party secretary and university president. Most appointments to university leadership were based on status within the Communist Party.

The experiences and deaths of these individuals were very similar: in June 1966, the Party organisation designated them 'members of reactionary gangs' or 'representative bourgeoisie'. They were suspended or dismissed from their duties and subjected to 'exposure' and 'criticism' at public rallies. After the Red Guards were established throughout China in August 1966, deposed university administrators suffered violent attacks from Red Guard students, including having their heads shaved and being beaten, marched in the streets, detained and subjected to 'struggle'[1] and

---

[1] TN: In this context, the Chinese word for struggle (*douzheng*) can be a noun, adjective (struggle rally, struggle session) or transitive verb. It refers to verbal and/or physical abuse inflicted on an individual by small or large groups of people seeking to force the person to admit to political offences.

'labour reform'[2] on campus. In the course of this barbaric persecution, many succumbed to their injuries or ended their own lives in 1966, 1967, or 1968 – in some cases people who apparently died from abuse in custody were said to have committed suicide. Among the cases listed below, only one person survived this long-term incarceration and torture long enough to die in 1970.

The uniform distribution of these incidents in universities throughout China was due to the top-down mobilisation of the Cultural Revolution under the direction of Mao and his Cultural Revolution leading group.

Even under the limited scope of my inquiries, I was able to identify twenty cases, which do not include people who were permanently crippled by the abuse they suffered. This death roll indicates the brutality of the treatment university leaders suffered during the Cultural Revolution, and the extent of the violence at China's universities. During the Cultural Revolution, all university leaders were struggled and placed in 'ox demon and snake spirit' teams; all were detained at some time or other, and all suffered physical and psychological abuse and torture. I have been unable to identify a single university that was an exception to this rule.

During the Cultural Revolution, the university, originally a social space characterised by culture and civilisation, became a breeding ground for mass violence and persecution. In terms of social fluctuation, the transformation of China's universities to campuses of mass violence is a prime example of the intense change the Cultural Revolution imposed on social conventions and behavioural standards.

According to my inquiries, it was at the universities that violent 'struggle sessions', 'labour reform teams' and informal prisons (later referred to as 'ox pens') first appeared on a major scale and developed even further. These persecution methods then spread throughout the country, leading to the deaths of untold numbers of people.

It was university leaders who were first 'ferreted out' and subjected to 'struggle' during the Cultural Revolution.

Prior to June 1966, the Cultural Revolution consisted of official criticism of Wu Han's play *Hai Rui Dismissed from Office* and of the pseudonymous newspaper column 'Notes from the Three Family Village' written by propagandists Deng Tuo, Wu Han and Liao Mosha, as well as the dismissal of senior Party cadres Peng Dehuai, Luo Ruiqing, Lu Dingyi and Yang Shangkun at high-level Party conferences. The Cultural Revolution became

---

[2] TN: 'Labour reform' was a process in which an individual was made to perform hard labour, often in the countryside, in order to reform his or her thinking. This labour was sometimes carried out in prison-like labour reform (*laogai*) camps.

a large-scale mass movement after Central People's Radio broadcast the contents of a big-character poster[3] at Peking University on 1 June 1966. The title of this big-character poster was 'What Have Song Shuo, Lu Ping and Peng Peiyun Done in the Cultural Revolution?' Song Shuo was head of the University Department of the Beijing Municipal Party Committee, Lu Ping was president and Party secretary of Peking University, and Peng Peiyun was deputy Party secretary of Peking University. The big-character poster accused them of implementing a 'revisionist line that thoroughly opposed the Party Central Committee and Mao Zedong Thought' and attacked the Peking University authorities as 'members of a reactionary gang', while appealing for the 'steadfast, thorough, total and comprehensive elimination of all ox demons and snake spirits'.

This big-character poster shifted the Cultural Revolution's main focus of attack to educators. On the evening of the broadcast, the Central Committee sent a 'work group' to Peking University, and Lu Ping and Peng Peiyun were dismissed from their posts. All classes were suspended. The broadcast of the big-character poster and the official praise lavished on it ramped up the intensity of the Cultural Revolution and became a turning point in its development.

Lu Ping and Peng Peiyun were the first university leaders to be 'plucked out'. Ten days later, Tsinghua University's work group announced the suspension of university president Jiang Nanxiang, who was also China's Minister of Higher Education. Provincial Party Committees across China plucked out their own university leaders and reported the news in Party newspapers. The criticism and struggle against Nanjing University president Kuang Yaming and Wuhan University president Li Da received national coverage in central-level newspapers as well.

Even after the broadcast of the Peking University big-character poster, many people were reluctant to oppose university leaders. Once the work groups entered the campuses, however, and announced that the original university leaders were 'standing aside' or were 'temporarily relieved of their posts', the climate changed abruptly and dramatically. Literary figures and losers in political power struggles were replaced by university leaders and instructors as the main targets of attack. The attackers no longer consisted of a handful of Leftist writers producing critical essays, but were made up of tens of thousands of university students.

Under the guidance of the work groups, students exposed and criticised the 'anti-Party, anti-socialist, anti-Mao Zedong Thought' crimes of their

---

[3] TN: Big-character posters were handwritten in large Chinese characters and mounted on walls in public places as a means of protest or propaganda. They became especially prevalent during the Cultural Revolution.

erstwhile leaders. The work groups then convened rallies at which people demonstrated their 'revolutionary spirit' through impassioned speeches and violent and demeaning assaults on these former administrators.

Wang Guangmei, the wife of China's then President, Liu Shaoqi, led the Cultural Revolution at Tsinghua University as a work group member. Without a high-profile person such as Wang lending authority to the work group, students would never have dared 'strike down' Jiang Nanxiang. As a representative of the Party's influence within the academic community, Jiang was more than a university president, and wielded a degree of power no student or teacher could think of challenging. Even so, in June 1966, a decision by the top leaders of the CCP Central Committee rendered Jiang a prisoner. It took little time for Jiang's administrative team and subordinates to assess the situation and leap as one to the side of his attackers.

The work groups' method was to strike down the 'reactionary fortress' of the original university leadership, even if those leaders were senior Party cadres who had never voiced the slightest opposition to the policies of higher-level Party Committees. Even so, the work groups did not condone mass violence against the struck-down targets, and insisted that struggle should be carried out only under their leadership. A violent incident at Peking University on 18 June led Liu Shaoqi to order universities to cease all 'unauthorised struggle'.

The Peking University work group clearly reflected its intentions in an essay entitled 'One-Month Situation Report Outline for the Cultural Revolution at Peking University', published in newspapers on 3 July 1966.

The outline stated that Peking University was a 'key stronghold of the revisionist former Beijing Municipal Party Committee'. Lu Ping had 'joined up with Peking University's reactionary social foundation, relying on and making use of a large number of politically impure individuals, forming anti-Party factions and cliques to control the leadership at the university and departmental levels, and implementing a ruthless bourgeois dictatorship'. Peking University had become 'stubbornly anti-Party and anti-socialist' and 'a stubbornly reactionary fortress where landlords, rich peasants, reactionaries, bad elements and Rightists flocked together.' The outline said that the 18 June Incident 'created chaos with the intention of throwing the work groups' war preparations into chaos' and 'led the Cultural Revolution along the wrong road'.[4]

During the time that the work groups were leading the Cultural Revolution at the universities, a large number of academic leaders killed themselves. Five of the people on my list of twenty died during this stage.

---

[4] *Peking University Chronicle, op. cit.*, p. 647.

In late July 1966, Mao accused Liu Shaoqi and Deng Xiaoping of 'stultifying' the Cultural Revolution and ordered the withdrawal of the work groups from all universities. After that, Jiang Qing and her cohorts went to Peking University several times, convening mass rallies and declaring the 18 June Incident a 'revolutionary incident'. At one such rally on the evening of 26 July, in the presence of Jiang Qing and other Party leaders and before the full assembly of students and teachers, Peng Xiaomeng, a student at the Peking University Affiliated Secondary School, whipped work group leader Zhang Chengxian with a brass belt buckle, and Jiang Qing ardently embraced her. This was the first major and formal public occasion at which a student physically attacked a target of the Cultural Revolution, and it received immediate support and encouragement from the revolution's top leaders. On 27 July, Nie Yuanzi, a philosophy professor who had taken control of Peking University after the work group was stripped of its power, announced the establishment of a campus 'labour reform team'. On 28 July, Jiang Qing explained to a secondary school assembly Mao's saying, 'When a good person beats a scoundrel, that's proper; when a scoundrel beats a good person, it's a test; when a good person beats a good person, that's how they get to know each other.' On 1 August, Mao wrote a letter expressing his enthusiastic support for the Red Guards of the Tsinghua University Affiliated Secondary School and for Peng Xiaomeng of the Peking University Affiliated Secondary School.

The withdrawal of the work groups, the rise of the Red Guards movement and the endorsement of violent acts by the leaders of the Cultural Revolution were the three factors that led directly to the upsurge in mass violence on college campuses in August 1966. Under these conditions, the university leaders uprooted by the work groups became the primary targets of attack, suffering severe abuse and humiliation.

On 3 August 1966, Nanjing Normal University dean of studies **Li Jingyi** and her husband, **Wu Tianshi**, died after the university's students struggled them and marched them through the streets for three hours. My information indicates that Li and Wu were the first people to die during a struggle session. The violence and humiliation dragged on, with persecution continuing between the first upsurge of violence in summer 1966 and the second in 1968.

Even university leaders who survived the Cultural Revolution suffered unimaginable torments. In June 1968, Peking University president Lu Ping was locked up in the university's biological sciences building. It was claimed that he hadn't followed all the necessary formalities when he joined the Communist Party in the 1930s, and his interrogators tried to make him admit to being a 'fake Party member' by hanging him from the rafters and beating him. He was interrogated around the clock, and the light in his detention cell was never turned off. Lu's persecutors believed that if deprived of rest, Lu would eventually suffer a mental breakdown and speak the 'truth'.

On the evening of 24 August 1966, Tsinghua University's top leaders were locked up in the science building and then summoned one by one into a small room, where they were beaten bloody. Their detention continued into the next day, and only at noon was each one given a steamed corn bun, after being forced to say 'The son of a bitch is eating a corn bun.'

Jiang Nanxiang, Tsinghua's president and the Minister of Higher Education, had his head shaved and was forced to undergo 'labour reform' in the ministry compound. At night he slept in a corridor of the administration building, where he continued to be harassed and humiliated, and he was dragged off to struggle sessions at the university's Affiliated Secondary School and other work units.

The Cultural Revolution is commonly blamed on the inferior education and ignorance of the Chinese people. This explanation is generally logical, in that as people's level of education rises, they gain a greater capacity for independent thought and reasoning. It nevertheless fails to explain why during the Cultural Revolution the most brutal and fanatical thinking prevailed not in areas with poor educational standards, but rather in China's premier institutions of higher learning and their Affiliated Secondary Schools, and why all kinds of violence occurred at the universities.

The fact is that university leaders were ruthlessly struggled for no other reason than that Mao had designated them as targets of attack in the Cultural Revolution. On 16 May 1966, the CCP Central Committee issued what became known as the 16 May Circular which included the following passage personally drafted by Mao:

> The entire Party must comply with Comrade Mao Zedong's directives, raise high the banner of the Proletarian Cultural Revolution, thoroughly expose the bourgeois reactionary standpoint of those anti-Party, anti-socialist so-called 'academic authorities', thoroughly repudiate bourgeois reactionary thinking in academic, cultural, news, arts and publishing circles, and seize power over these cultural spheres. While doing so, it is necessary to simultaneously repudiate, purge and in some cases transfer the representative bourgeoisie who have infiltrated the Party, the government, the army and the cultural sphere. By no means should these people be entrusted with leading the work of the Cultural Revolution; it is extraordinarily dangerous that many such people have in fact been doing this work in the past and at present.

Educators became one of the five prime targets of the Cultural Revolution, and the leaders of educational institutions became the 'representative bourgeoisie' who were to come under attack.

Among the documents issued at the same time as the 16 May Circular was a letter that Mao wrote to Lin Biao on 7 May 1966, which later became known as the '7 May Directive'. In this letter, Mao wrote, 'The education system must be reduced and education must be revolutionised; the domination of our schools by bourgeois intellectuals cannot continue.'

Who was actually dominating the schools at that time? It was in fact the people who served as the presidents and Party secretaries of China's universities. Although they were not actually 'bourgeois' and many were not even 'intellectuals', they were nevertheless targeted for attack because of this directive by Mao.

After the isolationism of the Qing era, China's modern universities had been established imitating Western universities. Their curricula and management were modelled on the Western principles of pursuit of knowledge, academic freedom and management by professors. When the Cultural Revolution began in 1966, all of these principles were virtually wiped out.

The fact is that the university administrators who were so ruthlessly struggled in the Cultural Revolution had from 1949 onwards been following Mao's itinerary, and the series of campaigns – from the Thought Reform Campaign for Intellectuals on through the Loyalty and Honesty Campaign, 'departmental restructuring', Campaign to Eliminate Counter-Revolutionaries and the Anti-Rightist Campaign – had significantly transformed China's university system in line with Mao's policies.

The pre-1966 university leaders had established Party Committee leadership over their campuses, along with a system of political councillors. They imposed unified administration over what students ate, where they lived and what they did and thought, including the jobs they took after graduation. The greatest change was the unprecedented control schools gained over the individual – groups of students and teachers could be convicted of 'contradictions between the enemy and us' and punished accordingly. By 1957, university leaders enjoyed unprecedented power to label and punish students and professors as Rightists, but Mao still felt reform hadn't gone far enough. The Cultural Revolution was part of his 'sustained revolution'. He ordered attacks on the leaders and teachers of educational institutions, using methods of unprecedented brutality imposed at the hands of students.

It had been Mao's longstanding practice to identify a group of people for persecution and slaughter, and through that process to drive home his ideology and coercively achieve his intentions. The 'rectification of incorrect work styles' in Yan'an in the early 1940s, Land Reform, the Suppression of Counter-Revolutionaries and the Three and Five Antis campaigns could all have been carried out peacefully, but instead were executed with violence. These same methods were imposed on a massive scale in China's schools, not only on teachers but also on the Party's own administrators. In 1966, university leaders joined 'landlords', 'rich peasants', 'bourgeoisie' and 'Rightists' as targets of attack in the class struggle.

The suffering this large-scale persecution brought about was clearly of no concern to top officials. Li Da had been a friend of Mao's for more than forty years, but Mao expressed not the slightest regret or pity when Li was struggled to death. In photographs and documentary footage from the Cultural Revolution era, the faces of Mao, Lin Biao, Zhou Enlai, Jiang Qing and other leaders reveal an unusual complacency and youthful energy, as if they were invigorated by their persecution of others.

This kind of broad-brush persecution proved highly flexible and effective in the Cultural Revolution. The university presidents were not the kind of people to suffer indignity in silence; only strong-willed individuals could have attained the positions they held. Yet they showed no resistance while being insulted, beaten and dragged through the gutter. Even those who survived showed no signs of bearing a grudge. This is one of the lessons of the Cultural Revolution: the more ruthless the regime, the more invincible it is, and the more effectively it can rule without resistance or challenge.

Deng Xiaoping subsequently attributed the Cultural Revolution's large-scale violence and slaughter to Mao's miscalculation of domestic conditions – in other words, presenting the Cultural Revolution as an excessive self-defence mechanism, and an example of cognitive error. This attempt at mitigation does nothing to explain the frenzy of violence inflicted on university leaders.

Several factors combined to produce this phenomenon on university campuses. The first was Mao's ultra-radical plan for social reform, which called for eradicating currency and the commodity economy, and eliminating the traditional educational system. Second was one of Mao's 'pioneering undertakings' in the Cultural Revolution, which was to order the long-term suspension of classes and encourage students to inflict violent abuse on their teachers.

Mao created groups such as university leaders who were to be obliterated through persecution, as well as groups such as student Red Guards who served as tools of persecution.

This role gave student Red Guards an enormous sense of self-worth; decades later, some of them still express pride at having taken part in acts of grotesque cruelty that stun the outside observer with their callousness.

Some people wonder why Mao would persecute this group of university leaders, who would have followed without hesitation whatever orders he passed down. As their performance after the Cultural Revolution demonstrated, these people were loyal to Mao, and given their merciless labelling of young students as Rightists in 1957, there is no reason to doubt that they would have complied with Mao's demands a few years later to shrink the education system, eliminate exams and change class content. Mao's infliction of brutality and humiliation on these steadfast loyalists seems inexplicable.

It is by taking note of the type of people Mao appointed as the new university leaders that we come to understand the third factor leading Mao to forsake those who had previously served him so well.

At the end of July 1968, Mao dispatched a 'Workers' and People's Liberation Army Mao Zedong Thought Propaganda Team' to Tsinghua University, then to all of China's universities and secondary schools to implement what was referred to as 'the working class leading the superstructure'. The actual leaders were soldiers, and among these troops, Unit 8341, known as the 'Central Security Bureau', played a key role. Chi Qun and Xie Jingyi were major figures in this unit. Chi served as Party secretary and chairman of the Revolutionary Committee at Tsinghua University, while Xie served as the university's deputy Party secretary and vice-chair of the Revolutionary Committee. Both also served as members of the Party Committee at Peking University.

Eventually Chi and Xie came into conflict with leading Tsinghua cadres such as Liu Bing. Liu Bing had been one of Tsinghua's leaders before the Cultural Revolution, and after being criticised during the Cultural Revolution, he was 're-integrated' into the new leadership ranks. On 13 August 1975, Liu Bing and others wrote a letter to Mao criticising Chi and Xie's work at Tsinghua.

On 26 October, the CCP Central Committee issued a 'Notice' in which Mao wrote, 'Tsinghua University's Liu Bing and others have written a letter informing on Chi Qun and Xiao Xie. I feel the motivation behind their letter is not intended to unseat Chi Qu and Xiao Xie alone; their spearhead is aimed at me.'[5] 'Xiao Xie' or 'Little Xie' referred to Xie Jingyi, and the tone of Mao's writing revealed he felt protective of these two individuals.

Just who were Chi Qun and Xie Jingyi? According to *Tsinghua University Annals*,[6] Chi Qun was born in 1934, joined the army in 1951, and in 1968 became deputy director of the propaganda section of the political

---

[5] *Manuscripts of Mao Zedong Since the Founding of the People's Republic*, Vol. 13, Beijing, Zhongyang wenxian chubanshe, 1998, p. 486.
[6] *Tsinghua University Annals*, Qinghua daxue chubanshe, 2001.

department of Unit 8341.[7] Xie Jingyi was born in 1936 and joined the army in 1952.[8] Neither Chi nor Xie had received more than a lower secondary school education, and they had no experience working in the educational field. *Tsinghua University Annals* makes no mention of the fact that Xie Jingyi had served as Mao's personal assistant, handling his phone calls and correspondence, and that her relationship with Mao was so close that he referred to her as Little Xie.

Chi also headed the Ministry of Education under the State Council, and Xie was secretary of the Beijing Municipal Party Committee and a member of the Standing Committee of the Fourth National People's Congress. Chi and Xie continued to wield control over Tsinghua University and the Education Ministry right up until Mao's death in 1976, while Mao's memo resulted in Liu Bing and the others being subjected to criticism, and became one of the reasons for Deng Xiaoping being stripped of power a second time during the Cultural Revolution. People such as Chi Qun and Xie Jingyi, whom Mao had personally appointed to take charge of the universities during the Cultural Revolution, were in an entirely different class from the university leaders who came under persecution. Apart from Li Da (a professor of Marxist philosophy), none of these pre-1966 administrators were professors – i.e. they didn't teach classes or undertake scholarly research. Their curricula vitae show, however, that most had received some form of higher education, some even overseas, even if not all were university graduates. They were all relatively experienced Party members, and were among the best educated of the cadres.

Prior to 1949, university presidents were invariably scholars and professors who had not only obtained academic degrees but also had academic status and had made substantial contributions to their fields, in line with Western academic tradition. After 1949, the Communist Party seized control of the universities, dismissing the existing administrators and charging them with crimes. At the outset, the Party appointed Leftist scholars to replace them. For example, while Jiang Longji, a Party member since 1927, was appointed vice-president and Party secretary of Peking University in 1950, the president was economist Ma Yinchu, who had obtained his PhD in the US and had been an intense critic of the Chiang Kai-shek regime in the 1940s. When Ma promoted family planning policies in 1959, he was dismissed and replaced by Lu Ping, who became both university president and Party secretary. Jiang Longji was transferred to Lanzhou University, where he became president and Party secretary. Even before the Cultural Revolution began, the ranks of the university leadership had been quite

---

[7] *Ibid.*, p. 409.
[8] *Ibid.*, p. 497.

thoroughly purged; leaders were no longer scholars but rather 'political cadres', while also possessing a certain degree of culture.

After the Cultural Revolution began, the university leadership was taken over by such people as Chi Qun and Xie Jingyi. Under their leadership, Tsinghua and Peking Universities compiled a set of policies towards intellectuals, which the CCP Central Committee then distributed nationwide to direct a campaign of often fatal persecution. Within the narrow timeframe of the Cleansing of Class Ranks alone, twenty-four people were persecuted to death at Tsinghua and Peking Universities.

After the major changeover in university administrators and the ruthless 'investigation' of educators, on 26 October 1969 the CCP Central Committee issued a 'Notice Regarding the Rustification of Institutions of Higher Learning', which ordered the removal of universities to the countryside 'to carry out genuine struggle, criticism and transformation.' Preposterous as this demand was, no one opposed it; on the pretext of 'battle readiness', urban dormitories were taken over by soldiers and their families, and many universities were disbanded. The process of completing the relocations within two weeks resulted in damaged scientific equipment and the disappearance of prized book collections. By the middle of the Cultural Revolution, Beijing's fifty-five universities had been reduced to just eighteen.

After classes had been suspended for five years, universities began to gradually reopen in the early 1970s. A large poster on the Peking University campus read: 'Go to the university, change the university, use Mao Zedong Thought to remould the university.'

The most important and obvious aspect of 'using Mao Zedong Thought to remould the university' was administration by 'military representatives', which continued for more than ten years. It was only in 1978, after Mao's death and at Deng Xiaoping's direction, that presidents were once again appointed to run the universities.

TOP UNIVERSITY ADMINISTRATORS WHO DIED DURING THE CULTURAL REVOLUTION

Jiang Longji, born in 1905, president and Party secretary of Lanzhou University in Gansu Province, was denounced in June 1966 and committed suicide on 25 June.

A native of Xixiang, Shaanxi Province, Jiang was admitted to Peking University in 1924 and joined the CCP in 1927. In that same year he was admitted to Japan's Meiji University and became an operative of the CCP's Tokyo branch. After being deported from Japan for taking part in a patriotic protest in 1929, he studied economics at the University of Berlin and helped organise the Anti-Imperialist League among Chinese in Germany and other parts of Europe following the Mukden Incident of 18 September 1931.[9] After returning to China in 1936, he wrote extensively on education and held high-level administrative positions in various schools and universities and regional government departments, ultimately becoming the top administrator at Lanzhou University.[10]

Jiang Longji's Experience during the Cultural Revolution

Three sets of documents relating to the Cultural Revolution's development at Lanzhou University indicate that Jiang Longji's experience was typical of university administrators at that time.

In May 1966, following a series of meetings by the CCP Central Committee on how to launch the Cultural Revolution, provincial Party Committees began drawing up lists of major targets. Most of the people on these lists were from the academic and cultural communities. The Gansu Provincial Party Committee included Jiang Longji on its list.

On 10 May 1966, Lanzhou University convened a 'rally to denounce the anti-Party, anti-socialist crimes of Deng Tuo, Wu Han, Tian Han and Liao Mosha'.[11] Jiang Longji delivered a mobilisation speech at the rally, after which big-character posters were put up all over the campus, and many more 'denunciation meetings' were held. The university Party Committee decided to suspend classes on 25 May.

Following the 1 June 1966 nationwide broadcast of the big-character poster attacking the leadership of Peking University, the Gansu Provincial Party Committee on 4 June dispatched 'Cultural Revolution work groups' to lead the Revolution in all of the province's tertiary institutions in the same manner and with the same timing as in Beijing. By the time the work group entered Lanzhou University, more than 25,000 big-character posters had been plastered onto campus walls, mainly targeting the school's 'old Rightists' and 'reactionary bourgeois academic authorities'. Jiang Longji led this first stage of the Cultural Revolution, probably unaware that his own fate was sealed.

Once the work group arrived, Lanzhou University's original administrators were obliged to 'stand aside'. On 6 June, the work group convened a

---

[9] TN: On this date, Japanese troops staged a bombing of their own railway by placing explosives near the railway line at Mukden (now Shenyang), then blamed the incident on Chinese troops to provide a pretext for Japan's invasion of Manchuria.
[10] *Biographical Dictionary of the Chinese Communist Party, 1921–1999*, Zhongguo guoji guangbo chubanshe, 1991.
[11] TN: i.e. the writers of the column 'Notes from the Three Family Village'.

university-wide rally to deliver a 'mobilisation report'. Jiang Longji represented the university Party Committee in examining the 'Right-deviating errors' of the first-stage campaign they had led. The work group then organised students to expose and attack the university's original administrators through meetings, big-character posters and other such methods, and Jiang Longji became one of the targets of struggle.

The essence and escalation of the attacks against Jiang are encapsulated in the titles of big-character posters: 'The Seriously Right-deviating Conservative Thinking of Our University's Leader Must be Immediately Corrected', 'Jiang Longji Openly Vilifies Mao Zedong Thought', 'Strip Off the Mask of Education Expert Jiang Longji', 'Denounce Jiang Longji's Criminal Opposition of the Cultural Revolution'.

On 17 June, students supported by the work group arrived at Jiang Longji's home and dragged him to the sports ground, where they made him climb a stack of tables and chairs with a ten-kilo birdcage on his head. More than seventy people were struggled that day, with some forced to wear dunce caps while others were beaten.

Liu Shaoqi's 18 June order to end 'chaotic struggle' had no effect on the Gansu Provincial Party Committee and the violent persecution it orchestrated. On 22 June, it informed Lanzhou University students that Jiang Longji would be dismissed from his post. The next day, the university convened another rally to struggle Jiang and once again presented him kneeling and wearing a dunce cap, then beat and kicked him and paraded him through the streets while forcing him to admit to 'opposing the Party, socialism and Mao Zedong Thought'.

On the morning of 25 June, the Gansu Provincial Party Committee convened a mass rally at which it announced the 'revocation of all Jiang Longji's postings within and outside of the Party'. Jiang killed himself that afternoon.

After Jiang's death, on 11 July, the provincial Party organ *Gansu Daily* published an editorial that served as the final verdict on Jiang Longji's 'crimes'.

The reason Jiang Longji committed suicide was all too clear: the violence and humiliation inflicted upon him during mass struggle, and the treatment he had received from the Party organisation. From June to August 1966 alone, six others at Lanzhou University also killed themselves after being criticised and struggled, and fourteen more made unsuccessful suicide attempts, with some permanently crippled as a result.

Jiang Longji died before the Red Guard movement began. Although those who humiliated and tormented him at the struggle session were mainly students, the Cultural Revolution was conducted under the tight control and effective management of the Party organisation at all levels.

So-called 'mass struggle' was in fact the result of revolutionary directives and theoretical guidance issuing from the upper levels of the Party and Mao himself. Apart from those in the top leadership in Beijing, those most responsible for Jiang Longji's death were his direct superiors in the Central Committee's Northwest Bureau and the Gansu Provincial Party Committee.

Three months after Jiang's death, in September 1966, Gansu Provincial Party Committee leader Wang Feng and others who had led the struggle against Jiang were similarly 'ferreted out' and subjected to struggle at mass rallies as the Cultural Revolution extended its attacks to those who had initially directed struggles against others.

On 26 January 1978, the Gansu Provincial Party Committee 'rehabilitated'[12] Jiang Longji. This occurred a year and a half after Mao's death, and more than twelve years after Jiang's death, as part of the first round of rehabilitations granted to victims of the Cultural Revolution.

Jiang Longji's Responsibility for the Fate of Another Victim

Jiang Longji was responsible for the death of **Gu Wenxuan**, whose story will be related in detail later. The two serve as a classic example of the common fate suffered by oppressor and victim in the Cultural Revolution.

While serving as vice-president and Party secretary of Peking University after the CCP seized power in 1949, Jiang led the Thought Reform and Loyalty and Honesty campaigns, the university 'departmental restructuring' and the Anti-Rightist Campaign. During a rally at Peking University on 25 May 1957, Gu Wenxuan denounced the injustice and persecution he had witnessed in his native Hangzhou during the Campaign to Eliminate Counter-Revolutionaries.[13] It appears that Jiang Longji censured Gu without verifying his claims, and on the basis of that speech, the university authorities labelled Gu Wenxuan a Rightist and sentenced him to five years of labour reform. Gu was eventually sentenced to death after attempting to flee China, a fate set in motion by Jiang Longji. Gu was one of 716 people (589 of whom were students) labelled Rightists at Peking University. Comprising 5% of its staff and students at that time, they suffered mental and material humiliation, and some were eventually executed like Gu Wenxuan.

---

[12] TN: Rehabilitation was a process of restoring the reputation of people who had been victimised in political campaigns. The rehabilitation often occurred years after the victimisation, and sometimes posthumously.
[13] *Peking University Chronicle (1989–1997)*, Beijing daxue chubanshe, 1998, p. 517.

Although rehabilitated twenty-two years later, they never received any form of apology from the government.

Jiang Longji had directed the purging of 526 Rightists, but his superiors considered his efforts inadequate. On 1 November 1957, the Beijing Municipal Party Committee gave notice that Jiang Longji was being demoted from First Secretary to Second Secretary and that Lu Ping was being sent to replace him as Peking University's Party secretary. Before the transfer, Zhou Enlai called Lu Ping in for a talk, and Lu Ping's harsh 'Anti-Rightist Supplement' increased the number of Rightists by more than a third. In January 1959, Liang Longji was transferred to Lanzhou University, where he served as president and Party secretary until the beginning of the Cultural Revolution.[14]

It was Mao and the other central leaders who formulated the theory behind the Anti-Rightist Campaign and who directed its progress, but the specific implementation was carried out at the hands of people such as Jiang Longji. Jiang spent seventeen years representing the Party as leader of two major universities. During these years, he and others like him persecuted large numbers of people, including young students, and transformed the original university system.

Universities were originally purely educational organs, and the harshest penalty a university could impose was to expel a student or dismiss a teacher. Jiang and his colleagues spearheaded the reforms that empowered university authorities to label students or teachers 'class enemies' on the basis of their thinking or speech, and to carry out long-term systematic persecution on those grounds.

Jiang Longji and his successor, Lu Ping, had both studied at Peking University, later becoming Party members and professional revolutionaries. Was a university system that suppressed and persecuted students one of their objectives when they joined the revolution? If not, why did they not speak out to oppose it? Without answers to these questions, their reputations remain ambiguous at best.

One feels compelled to ask, when Jiang Longji imposed the Rightist label on Gu Wenxuan and more than 500 others, mainly students, in 1957, did he realise that ruthlessly severing this group of young people from the body of society was paving the way for himself to be similarly treated further down the line?

Other questions likewise suggest themselves. When Jiang decided to end his life in the face of the Cultural Revolution's horrors, did he give any thought to Gu Wenxuan and the 525 other 'Rightists' who had suffered

---

[14] *Peking University Chronicle, op. cit.*

by his hand? One hopes that he failed to foresee the brutality of the Anti-Rightist Campaign and the Cultural Revolution, rather than purposely devoting his life to merciless attacks on others. One hopes that he killed himself not merely out of a sense of personal failure and frustration, but out of despair over the cruelty of this revolution.

Zhao Zongfu (aka Zhao Jinzhi), the fifty-one-year-old president of the Taiyuan College of Engineering in Shanxi Province, leaped to his death on 21 June 1966. He joined the CCP in 1933 as a student at Yenching University and at one point worked for the intelligence unit of the Communist International's Far East Red Army.[15]

Gao Yunsheng, the fifty-six-year-old director and Party secretary of the Beijing Steel and Iron Institute (now the University of Science and Technology Beijing), killed himself after being struggled on 6 July 1966.

Chen Chuangang, the fifty-four-year-old vice-president and deputy Party secretary of Shanghai's Fudan University, took an overdose of sleeping pills in June 1966 after his superiors declared him a 'counter-revolutionary revisionist'. Chen graduated from Fudan University in the 1930s with a degree in journalism. His wife, Wang Ruqi, was a graduate of the university's Law Department. The two of them joined the CCP in 1938 and went together to the Communist base in Yan'an in 1940. In 1966, Wang was the director of the Shanghai Foreign Languages Institute.

Another vice-president of Fudan University, **Li Tiemin**, also killed himself during the Cultural Revolution, but the date of his death is unknown.

Zheng Siqun, the fifty-four-year-old president and Party secretary of Chongqing University, was dismissed in June 1966 and slit his own throat on 2 August 1966.

Zheng joined the Communist Youth League in 1926 and became a CCP member the next year. He studied in Japan, but was deported during a crackdown on 'red students' in 1929. Resuming his studies in Japan under an alias in 1931, he returned to China later that year out of indignation after the Mukden Incident. Zheng became deeply involved in CCP activities in Shanghai, then went to Japan a third time in 1936 to study sociology at Nihon University. He returned to China in 1937 when the War of Resistance against Japan broke out, and resumed his involvement with the CCP as political commissar in military educational units. After

---

[15] *Biographical Dictionary of the Chinese Communist Party, 1921–1999*, Zhongguo guoji guangbo chubanshe, 1991.

the founding of the People's Republic, he served in a series of educational postings, culminating in his appointment as president and Party secretary of Chongqing University in October 1952.[16]

The *History of Chongqing University*[17] and a report by leaders of the Chongqing Municipal Party Committee provide the background to Zheng Siqun's death: on 4 May 1966, in accordance with arrangements at the provincial and municipal level, Zheng Siqun delivered a mobilisation report to the entire university criticising the 'Three Family Village' and around the same time organised denunciations of Wu Han, Deng Tuo and others. A university Party Committee Cultural Revolution leading group headed by Zheng Siqun was established in 13 May.

Following publication of Nie Yuanzi's big-character poster at Peking University and the Central Committee's reorganisation of the Beijing Municipal Party Committee, big-character posters targeting university leaders began appearing at Chongqing University. On 4 June, the university Party Committee called an urgent meeting and decided to suspend classes for three days to ramp up the Cultural Revolution. On 8 June, a Municipal Party Committee work group entered the university to 'assist' its Party Committee in leading the movement and to encourage posters exposing 'problems'. Within a few days, the number of big-character posters reached a new high, and more than 170 people were criticised by name, including the university's president and vice-president and leading cadres at all levels. Zheng Siqun called a meeting of university cadres and demanded that order be restored, as a result of which the number of posters exposing problems dropped precipitously.

Someone reported to the work group that President Zheng was holding 'clandestine meetings', and the work group accused Zheng Siqun of 'suppressing the masses and obstructing the development of the movement'. On orders from the Municipal Party Committee, Zheng Siqun and other cadres and administrators underwent self-criticism at university-wide rallies on 16 June. The next day, spontaneous assemblies and big-character posters criticising 'the big reactionary gang led by Zheng Siqun' emerged in the student dormitories. The head of the Municipal Party Committee Propaganda Department, He Zhengqing, announced to the university that the Cultural Revolution movement was now being led by the work group. On 21 June, a new work group sent by the Municipal Party Committee and led by vice-mayor Yu Yueze held a rally for the entire student body, announcing that Zheng Siqun

---

[16] *Who's Who in Chongqing, Today and Yesterday*, Chongqing daxue chubanshe, 1989, pp. 381–382.

[17] *History of Chongqing University*, Chongqing daxue chubanshe, 1994, pp. 125–129.

would be suspended from duty and made to undergo self-criticism and that his 'reactionary gang' would be arrested.

On 22 June, *Chongqing Daily* published that decision and publicly criticised Zheng Siqun by name. Around 90% of Chongqing University's academic cadres were immediately sidelined and became 'targets of the movement'. On 29 July, the work group convened a small-scale symposium attended by special investigation team members to expose and denounce Zheng Siqun to his face. Yu Yueze announced that Zheng Siqun had committed the four major offences of opposing the Party, socialism and Mao Zedong Thought, and maintaining illicit relations with the Soviet revisionists. Specifically, Zheng was accused of saying things such as 'Mao Zedong Thought is not a magic charm', 'An atomic bomb won't explode just because it's red', 'The errors of 1958 can't be repeated'[18] and also of 'harbouring anti-Party, anti-socialist elements and ox demons and snake spirits and putting them in important positions'. That afternoon, the work group told Zheng Siqun to prepare to make a frank confession. Zheng asked for the specific allegations against him and requested that his wife, Wu Gengshu, be allowed to visit him so they could discuss arrangements for their children. The work group said that Zheng would be provided with the material against him as it was compiled, and in the meantime brought Wu Gengshu to spend the night with Zheng at the university. The next day, Wu told the work group that Zheng was in 'good spirits', and later that day Zheng was moved to the Songlipo Guesthouse to be kept 'under observation'. That night, the work group held a university-wide rally to expose and denounce Zheng Siqun. Some teachers, cadres and students questioned the work group's accusations against Zheng, only to be denounced for 'failing to draw a clear distinction'.

On the afternoon of the 31st, Zheng gave a self-criticism at a meeting of the special investigation group, admitting to having the wrong attitude towards the Cultural Revolution, problematic implementation of the Party's education policies and adulating Soviet revisionism and Soviet experts. The work group found that 'his attitude wasn't proper enough; especially on the third problem, he hemmed and hawed and didn't talk about any problems,' and Zheng was denounced. On the afternoon of 1 August, Zheng handed over a half-page self-criticism. At midnight he was reported to have gone to sleep after eating a cake. Early in the morning of 2 August, the guard outside Zheng's room heard a noise and listened at the door. Hearing a

---

[18] TN: Zheng was no doubt referring to the economic policies of the Great Leap Forward, which led to the Great Famine that caused tens of millions of deaths in China in the late 1950s and early 1960s.

loud groan that sounded like weeping, he went to the group leader on duty. They entered the room together and found Zheng lying on his bed in a pool of blood, the artery on the right side of his neck severed with a shaving razor. They immediately contacted the hospital for emergency treatment, but Zheng was dead. The Public Security Bureau inspected the scene and didn't find a suicide note, but told the medical examiner that they had concluded that the death was a suicide. It is believed that Zheng may have brought the shaving razor in his tea container or trouser pocket when he was moved to the guesthouse.[19]

On the morning of 2 August, the work group called urgent meetings in all departments and announced that Zheng Siqun had killed himself at 5:20 that morning. This aroused intense resentment against the work group, and some students sent telegrams to the Southwest Bureau and the Central Committee accusing the work group of persecuting Zheng Siqun to death. On the night of 4 August, the work group convened a university-wide rally, and municipal Party secretary Lu Dadong announced the permanent expulsion of Zheng Siqun from the Party, stirring further controversy. The work group withdrew from the university on 5 August.

A few months later, Yu Yueze and Lu Dadong, who had purged Zheng Siqun, were also struggled at a city-wide mass rally as 'anti-Party elements'.

The series of events surrounding Zheng Siqun in Chongqing was like a chain of interlocking rings in a drama. During each new upsurge of the Cultural Revolution, there were new targets of attack and new victims, and it was altogether possible that people who had started out leading the Cultural Revolution would be crushed in its attack. It is because of this chain of persecution that the people in each link, if they were fortunate enough to survive the Cultural Revolution, had difficulty squarely facing this tragic and shameful history with courage and wisdom.

Li Jingyi, born in 1914, was dean of studies and deputy Party secretary of Nanjing Normal University. Her husband, **Wu Tianshi**, born in 1910, was the director of the Jiangsu Province Education Department. The Provincial Party Committee criticised Wu by name in the newspaper at the outset of the Cultural Revolution. On the night of 3 August 1966, Li and Wu were beaten and paraded through the streets. Li died that day, and Wu fell into a coma and died two days later.

Based on available information, Li Jingyi and Wu Tianshi were the first educators to be killed during a Cultural Revolution 'struggle rally'.

---

[19] 'The CCP Chongqing Municipal Party Committee's Report Regarding the Suicide of Zheng Siqun'.

The Cultural Revolution Would Not Accept Surrender

Nanjing Normal University, formerly Jinling Women's College, was one of China's first modern colleges, with very high academic standards and an elegant and beautiful campus. The school's name was changed after 1949 when its administrators were replaced by Communist Party members. Li Jingyi, a native of Nantong, Jiangsu Province, became dean of studies and deputy Party secretary at Nanjing Normal University after years of working in Suzhou's public schools.

After the CCP Central Committee issued its 16 May Circular calling for educators and other intellectuals to be criticised, Wu Tianshi became one of the key targets first selected in Jiangsu Province.

A native of Nantong, Jiangsu Province, Wu lost his father when he was young and grew up in poverty. After graduating from Wuxi Academy of Sinology in 1932, Wu returned to Nantong to serve as an instructor in Chinese studies at the privately established Chongying Girls' Secondary school, until Nantong's Kuomintang authorities detained him for expressing radical views and expelled him from the province. Wu returned to Nantong after the War of Resistance broke out to teach and take part in the Communist underground. From 1944 onwards he was appointed to a series of positions in which he contributed significantly to cadre education in the liberated areas. After the founding of the People's Republic, he continued to devote his life to education through university and political postings in Suzhou.[20]

Apart from being a leader in one of the sectors from which power had to be 'seized', Wu had co-authored a booklet in 1962 entitled 'Remarks on the Spirit and Methods of Study of China's Ancient Historians', which was designated a 'poisonous weed' during the upsurge in criticism against the play *Hai Rui Dismissed from Office* and the newspaper column 'Notes from the Three Family Village'. Few leaders in the education sector had published books, so writing this pamphlet was considered a crime in itself.

The deaths of Wu Tianshi and Li Jingyi are not recorded in general histories of the Cultural Revolution, but because they were struggled to death, almost everyone in Nanjing knew of it. Some people say that Wu Tianshi was persecuted because he was one of the most educated and cultured people in the Communist Party. Others say there was pressure to carry out purges, so cadres at every level cast aspersions on others to protect themselves.

---

[20] Information provided by Wu's family.

According to an essay published after the Cultural Revolution by Chen Guang,[21] who was Party secretary of Jiangsu Province in 1966, when Wu Tianshi came under criticism, he went to Chen's home and asked if his booklet could be handled in the same way as the works of the prominent writer and scholar Guo Moruo, who had publicly announced his willingness to consign his writings to the flames. Chen replied, 'I understand your feelings, but your status is different from Guo's. Even if the Provincial Party Committee agrees to your idea, it won't do any good!'

Wu was referring to a speech Guo Moruo made to the NPC Standing Committee on 14 April 1966, when he said, 'I'm a man of letters, and many people refer to me as a writer and even a poet and a historian. Over the decades, I've wielded my pen and written things and have also translated some things. In terms of word count, I've probably written millions of characters. But by today's standards, the things I wrote before, strictly speaking, should all be burned. They have not the slightest value.' Guo Moruo's speech was published in the *People's Daily* on 5 May 1966, reportedly under Mao's direction. To date, no one has said what was demanded of Guo Moruo. Clearly, after taking this stand, Guo Moruo 'passed the test'. He was probably the only man of letters who escaped being denounced at rallies during the Cultural Revolution. Although he was criticised in big-character posters and came under pressure, and his college student son was arrested and died in custody, Guo Moruo still put in an appearance at the Gate Tower of Tiananmen Square on every holiday or public occasion, his name continued to appear in the newspapers and he retained his spacious home. That house on West Qianhai Street, with its vast garden and painted beams and pillars, was originally the property of the Tong Ren Tang Chinese pharmaceutical company that had been operating in Beijing for 300 years. After confiscating the property, the government gave it to Guo Moruo.

Wu Tianshi wanted to follow Guo Moruo's example; that is, he didn't resist and was willing to consign his writings to the flames, admit his error, negate himself and submit to the Central Party's directives. Yet he wasn't given permission to do this. Wu Tianshi was dismissed and criticised by name in the Jiangsu Provincial Party Committee's official newspaper, *Xinhua Daily*.

In his elegy, Chen Guang sighs that Wu Tianshi, 'that erudite scholar, naively believed that all he needed was to sincerely acknowledge his "error" (the truth is, he had done nothing wrong) and consign his writings to the flames, and that would allow him to charge through the

---

[21] 'Unforgettable Commemoration', *Xinhua Daily*, 3 August 1986.

barrier and escape this "disaster"'. Chen Guang's lament sounds sincere, but he doesn't tell the reader how a less naïve person should have dealt with the situation.

In fact, most of the people who came under attack during the Cultural Revolution adopted the approach of acknowledging their 'errors' and criticising themselves. Only in very rare instances did anyone publicly express resistance. Members of the 'Pang-Luo-Lu-Yang Clique' criticised themselves right from the outset. Then Liu Shaoqi and Deng Xiaoping criticised themselves. Millions of people being denounced all criticised themselves. But that was not punishment enough. Like Wu Tianshi, they were dragged to denunciation rallies and subjected to violent struggle, and many, like Li Jingyi and Wu Tianshi, died in the process.

In wars, when one side surrenders, the war ends. Soldiers who surrender are taken prisoner but their lives are preserved. During the Cultural Revolution, surrender wasn't allowed, and those who acknowledged their errors were still brutally beaten and humiliated or even killed. The rules of the Cultural Revolution were harsher than war.

This special characteristic of the Cultural Revolution can only be explained by saying that attacking these people was not only an end but also a means. It could be said that relentlessly pursuing and attacking targets at every level and not allowing surrender was how the revolution established its supreme authority. The practice was therefore continued throughout the Cultural Revolution.

Death in Violent Public Denunciation Rallies

After Mao expressed his ardent support for the Red Guards and withdrew the work groups from the universities, people such as Li Jingyi and Wu Tianshi who had already been exposed and criticised by the work groups were quickly subjected to violent struggle.

On the night of 3 August 1966, students from Nanjing Normal University burst into Li and Wu's home and dragged them out. Li and Wu were wearing slippers, and while they were being dragged to a platform on the school's campus, Wu Tianshi's foot was injured and trailed blood along the way. Li, Wu and other cadres and teachers were pulled onto the platform to be struggled. Some had ink poured over their heads, while others were beaten. By the time someone pushed a wire rubbish basket over Li Jingyi's head, the couple were both badly injured.

The struggle targets were then paraded through the streets. When Li Jingyi and Wu Tianshi passed out, they were dragged half a kilometre down the scorching road to the busy downtown area. Li died in the process, her body reduced to mangled flesh.

After being paraded through the streets, Wu Tianshi was taken back to the campus, where someone bound him to a stairway with rope for 'public exposure'. In the process, Wu's arms were fractured and his legs became paralysed. His brain swelled and he fell into a coma. He died two days later, on 5 August, without regaining consciousness.

Li Jingyi and Wu Tianshi's youngest son, a fifteen-year-old secondary school student, had been sent to labour in the countryside, and it was only a week later that he heard two older students describe the deaths of his parents in the city.

On the same day that Wu died, the vice-principal of the Beijing Normal University Attached Girls' School, **Bian Zhongyun**, was beaten to death by student Red Guards. It was also on that day that the Central Committee issued a document formally rescinding Liu Shaoqi's June order to 'cease chaotic struggle'. Violence spread and escalated throughout China's schools in early August 1966; many more educators were killed, with even more driven to suicide. The violence then spread off campus as well.

Beijing and Nanjing were both cultural capitals with long histories, and schools were places to preserve and develop culture. But it was in the schools of Nanjing and Beijing that the violence and slaughter of the Cultural Revolution began, and these places came to symbolise the spread of this kind of struggle rally. The term 'struggle' was itself relatively abstract; in early August 1966, it was universally applied to mass assemblies where targets were subjected to violent and even fatal abuse.

Specifically, the violent methods commonly used were: beating, including with brass belt buckles; parading in the streets, with the targets wearing placards around their necks, beating dustpans and proclaiming their crimes; cutting off all or half their hair, especially for women; wearing dunce caps, which were not only insulting but also constructed to be oppressively heavy; and 'flying the jet', which involved standing bent over at the waist with one's arms raised backward to resemble an aircraft. There were also various impromptu torments. Any of these methods could cause the death of the struggle target.

The terror of these violent struggle rallies was mainly in the fierce and arbitrary nature of the violence. Torture is painful, but at least there's a pattern and even a logic to it. At the struggle rallies, the people inflicting the beatings operated under a mob mentality and bore no legal responsibility for their actions. The emotions of a moment could decide whether the torment was light or heavy. There was no predicting whether the target would live or die: he could only submit and bear it, 'bowing his head and admitting his fault' to avoid provoking his abusers to hit him even harder. At struggle rallies, it was impossible to talk reason.

Another terror of these struggle rallies was that they were carried out in the name of revolution. Their violence was accompanied by resounding slogans such as 'Sweep away all ox demons and snake spirits', 'Carry out the Great Proletarian Cultural Revolution to the end' and 'Long live Chairman Mao'. Any protest against this violence would be treated as a counter-revolutionary act and subjected to even harsher punishment.

In early August 1966, struggle rallies became a common feature of the Cultural Revolution. On 4 August, nearly 200 teachers and cadres were struggled at Shanghai's East China Normal University. On 11 August, a mass struggle rally at Jiangxi Normal University resulted in the deaths of teachers **Li Zhongming** and **Xiong Huaqi** and school doctor **Zhou Tianzhu**, while another teacher, **He Ji**, was driven to suicide. On 19 August, the administrators of the Beijing No. 4, No. 6 and No. 8 Secondary Schools and leaders of the Municipal Education Department were struggled at a mass rally at Zhongshan Park.

The threat of these violent rallies was the main reason why countless people were persecuted without anyone actually coming out and publicly opposing the Cultural Revolution.

Mao and Zhou Enlai Knew of the Deaths of Li Jingyi and Wu Tianshi

In 1996, Jiang Weiqing, who was secretary of the Jiangsu Provincial Party Committee when the Cultural Revolution began, published his memoirs,[22] which mention something related to the deaths of Li and Wu thirty years earlier.

In early August 1966, Jiang Weiqing went to Beijing for the 11th plenum of the Eighth CCP Central Committee. During a discussion about amending the '16 Articles' (the Central Committee's 'Resolution Regarding the Cultural Revolution' passed on 8 August), Mao and Zhou Enlai talked with Jiang and Tan Qilong, the Party secretary of Shandong Province. Jiang Weiqing says that by then he'd learned of Wu Tianshi's death through a telephone call. He told Mao and Zhou that students were putting dunce caps on people's heads and parading them through the streets, beating and humiliating them and sometimes killing them.[23] This shows that the Cultural Revolution's top leaders, Mao and Zhou, were aware of the brutal killings that were going

---

[22] *A 70-year Journey*, Nanjing, Jiangsu renmin chubanshe, 1996.
[23] Ibid., p. 528.

on at the time. After the 16 Articles were issued, the violence escalated, and there was no question of the highest authorities being unaware of it.

The 16 Articles enthusiastically commended 'a large group of previously unknown revolutionary youth' that had become 'courageous pathbreakers'. What path-breaking deeds had these young people carried out? Clearly, it was this kind of violent struggle rally.

Likewise, Song Binbin and other Red Guard leaders immediately reported Bian Zhongyun's death to the Second Secretary of the Beijing Municipal Party Committee, Wu De. Unlike Jiang Weiqing, Wu De never said what he reported to the upper levels and how those officials responded. In any case, no one stepped forward to end the bloodshed, and on 18 August, Song Binbin placed a Red Guard armband on Mao at Tiananmen Square in a highly publicised scene that could only have encouraged more such violence.

Because the Revolution's leaders enthusiastically supported the Red Guards, killings on campus were carried out with great fanfare and were considered meritorious and honourable. The struggle rally on 3 August that resulted in two deaths at Nanjing Normal University was commemorated in the name of the '3 August Rebel Army', one of the most active mass organisations in Nanjing during the Cultural Revolution. The person who had directed the activities on 3 August led that organisation and eventually also the Revolutionary Committee that took control of the school, as well as becoming a leader of the Nanjing Municipal Revolutionary Committee. When the 3 August Rebel Army took power, a huge statue of Mao, measuring 8.3 metres high, was erected on the campus of Nanjing Normal University. All of this served to enhance the violent principles embodied by the 3 August incident.

One interviewee told me that a professor in Nanjing Normal University's Foreign Language Department suddenly died in Suzhou in 1999, and his decaying body wasn't discovered until a week later. Among the school's older staff a rumour circulated that his death was 'payback'; this man had been an enthusiastic participant in the fatal beatings of Wu Tianshi and Li Jingyi.

Li Da, the president of Wuhan University, died of heat exhaustion while being criticised and struggled on 24 August 1966.

Li Da helped establish the Chinese Communist Party in 1921, and along with Mao was one of twelve delegates to the CCP's First Party Congress. Li Da left the Party in 1927 but rejoined it in 1949. He was an expert in Marxist philosophy, and in 1950 proclaimed 'Mao Zedong Philosophical Thought' to be a great contribution. He also criticised 'bourgeois scholars'; for example, his 1955 *Critique of Hu Shih's Reactionary Thought*.[24]

---

[24] TN: Hu Shih (1891–1962) was a philosopher, essayist and diplomat who is widely recognised as a key contributor to Chinese liberalism.

Li Da was seventy-six years old when he was 'ferreted out' and struggled in June 1966. The Hubei Provincial Party Committee dismissed Li from his positions, expelled him from the Party and sent him back to his birthplace for 'labour under surveillance'. During this time, Mao arrived in Wuhan on 16 July 1966, and took his famous swim in the Yangtze River to demonstrate his 'lofty aspiration' in launching and leading the Cultural Revolution. Li Da wrote Mao a letter requesting his help, but was ignored.

When the Red Guard movement sprang up in August 1966, the denunciations against Li Da intensified, and a series of massive struggle rallies was convened. Wuhan is rightly known as one of the three 'ovens of the Yangtze region', with summer temperatures surpassing 104 degrees. To subject an elderly man to repeated denunciation rallies in the scorching heat was bound to have fatal consequences, and Li Da died on 24 August.

In that same month, Mao sent out a memo that prevented another man from being persecuted to death, which provides another perspective on Li Da's situation at the time. After Mao decided to withdraw the work groups from the schools, the head of the Peking University work group, Zhang Chengxian, was subjected to whipping and other torments and humiliations by students from the university's Affiliated Secondary School. On 17 August, Mao handed down the instruction: 'Zhang Chengxian can leave with the work group. Zhang Chengxian has heart disease, and shouldn't be persecuted to death for his error.'[25] As a result, Zhang was not among the thousands of people who were killed during Red August.

For Zhang Chengxian, Mao's directive was a life-saver. In comparison, the deaths of Li Da and others show the much darker message behind Mao's 'leniency': other people *could* be 'persecuted to death' without a similar imperial edict handed down on their behalf.

After Li Da was killed, the *People's Daily* devoted an entire page to criticising him on 5 September 1966, including five essays entitled 'Li Da's Traitorous Countenance', 'A Disgrace to His Race and Veteran Anti-Communist', 'Li Da's Ten Great Crimes of Peasant Exploitation', 'Down with the Local Despot Li Da' and 'Arch Foe of the Poor and Lower-middle Peasants'. An accompanying 'editorial note' stated:

> In the grand and spectacular Great Proletarian Cultural Revolution, the vast revolutionary teachers and students of Wuhan University ferreted out the anti-Party, anti-socialist Rightist Li Da. Li Da was

---

[25] See *Chronicle of Peking University*, p. 651. Zhang Chengxian himself published an article after the Cultural Revolution referring to this incident.

not only president of Wuhan University, but also on the academic board of the Chinese Academy of Sciences and former chairman of the Chinese Philosophy Society, an out-and-out bourgeois reactionary academic 'authority.'

The editorial note went on to say that criticism of such people was mandated by the 'Chinese Communist Party Central Committee Resolution Regarding the Great Proletarian Cultural Revolution'.

In 1966, bearing the official title of 'university president' or 'academic board member' constituted a crime in itself. To a certain extent, university administrators in 1966 were comparable to 'landlords' in 1950, 'capitalists' in 1956 or 'Rightists' in 1957 as groups targeted for 'struggle'. As a university president and professor of philosophy, Li Da became a dual target.

Two years after Mao died, in 1978, Deng Xiaoping rehabilitated a large number of people, including Li Da. At that time, newspaper articles about Li Da included one entitled 'The Friendship between Comrade Mao Zedong and Comrade Li Da'.[26] On 16 November 1980, the *People's Daily* published a report stating that the CCP Central Committee Secretariat had recently approved a resolution by the Hubei Provincial Party Committee to 'thoroughly rehabilitate' Li Da, and that his Party membership had been restored. By then, Li Da had been dead for fourteen years.

An academic symposium commemorating the hundredth anniversary of Li Da's birth was held in his native Lengshuitan City, Hunan Province, in 1990. The symposium eulogised Li Da's achievements in 'promoting Marxism his whole life'. No one mentioned that Li Da was one of a multitude who suffered horrendous deaths during the Cultural Revolution, or how this might be explained by the Marxism he spent his life promoting.

Shao Kai, president and Party secretary of Liaoning University, was dismissed when the Liaoning Provincial Party Committee sent a work group to the university on 23 June 1966. After being repeatedly denounced and struggled, Shao killed himself on 23 January 1967.

Tian Xin, acting Party secretary of the East China Institute of Chemical Engineering, died on 2 August 1967, after being beaten and tortured in the institute's unmarried staff quarters.

Sun Yang, vice-president of Renmin University of China, was subjected to long-term denunciations during the Cultural Revolution. His death in early October 1967 was declared a case of 'committing suicide to escape

---

[26] *Guangming Daily*, 23 December 1978.

punishment'. His wife, Shi Qi, was also beaten, humiliated and locked up, and lost her two front teeth.

Wei Siwen, president and Party secretary of the Beijing Institute of Technology, was dismissed on 5 July 1966. On 30 October 1967, students took him from his home and beat him to death at the institute.

In a 'Selection of Big-Character Posters' mimeographed at that time, I found one entitled 'The Sudden Death of Wei Siwen at the East is Red Headquarters of the Beijing Institute of Technology is a Serious Political Incident'. This poster reports that while a student group, the Red Flags, was searching for firearms and ammunition inside Wei Siwen's home, another group, East is Red, rushed to the scene and took Wei to an unknown location for two hours. They then drove Wei to the East is Red headquarters in the institute's gymnasium, and he died there during the night. The poster raised the question of Wei Siwen's political alliances, accusing him of being a 'henchman' and 'diehard follower' of the 'Peng-Luo-Lu-Yang Anti-Party Clique' and being involved in factional struggle at the institute, resulting in his death. The 'serious political incident' that the big-character poster refers to is not that of an institute administrator being seized from his home and killed – by the time Wei died, such incidents had become common and even routine – but rather the opposition faction's involvement in his death.

The Cleansing of the Class Ranks in 1968 brought a new upsurge in violence, and some university administrators who had survived persecution during the first stage of the Cultural Revolution were less fortunate this time around. (For more on the Cleansing of the Class Ranks, see Part Five of this book.)

Tang Lin, born in 1911, was vice-president of Hunan University. He was struggled, beaten and paraded through the streets when the Cultural Revolution began, and during the Cleansing of the Class Ranks, he was locked up in the school and fell to his death from a third-floor window on the night of 18 February 1968. His death was declared a suicide, but his family suspected he may have been pushed.

Tang Lin joined the Communist Party in 1938, and in the 1950s he served as director of the Propaganda Department of the Hunan Provincial Party Committee. After being designated a 'Right-deviating opportunist' in 1959, he was dismissed from his position and sent to labour in the countryside until he passed a 'screening' in 1962, after which he was appointed vice-president of Hunan University.

In June 1966, the Hunan Provincial Party Committee declared that the leaders of Hunan University, Wei Dongming and Tang Lin, had been 'temporarily relieved of their posts' and the *Hunan Daily* published an article calling for Wei Dongming to be 'thoroughly exposed and criticised' on 27 August.

By then, large-scale violence had broken out at Hunan University and Hunan Normal University. More than a hundred teachers and cadres were paraded through the streets wearing dunce caps and carrying placards while they were made to shout, 'I'm a black devil! I'm guilty!' They were forced to walk barefoot on the steaming hot streets, and some had half their hair shaved off and were viciously beaten, including Tang Lin. By the time he got home, his feet were swollen and covered with blood.

After this 'parade', a middle-aged teacher surnamed Zhou was criticised for 'Leftist ideology' and he and his wife hanged themselves, leaving behind three children, the eldest of which was fifteen. This was the first suicide at Hunan University during the Cultural Revolution, but eventually there were dozens of others who found their torments unbearable and chose to end their lives. Unfortunately I've been unable to learn their names.

Beginning in summer 1966, Tang Lin was put into the 'ox demon and snake spirit team'. When the struggling was less intense, he taught his daughter English with an English edition of *Quotations from Chairman Mao*, one of the few foreign language books that could be published at that time.

One twist during the Cultural Revolution was the mistaken belief that when authorities were 'struck down', the people they had purged would have their verdicts overturned. While Tang Lin was propaganda chief in Hunan in 1957, many editors and reporters at the *New Hunan Daily* were designated Rightists, including a man named Bai Yuan. When provincial leaders were unseated during the Cultural Revolution, those Rightists believed this was their opportunity to reverse their verdicts, and in fact, Tang Lin criticised himself and expressed his regret for persecuting the *New Hunan Daily* staff at a fact-finding meeting at Hunan University in mid-October 1967. Even so, the Rightists did not get their verdicts reversed, and Tang Lin died four months later. In his book *Man-made Disaster*, Bai Yuan expressed sympathy for Tang Lin:

> To tell the truth, my impression of him in the past had not been very good. I'd been designated a Rightist and harshly punished because of him. But his tragic end aroused my sympathy. He was a brilliant, high-level intellectual who became a sacrificial lamb for taking the Left-deviating road. Before he died, he spoke up for the *New Hunan Daily* staff who had been wrongfully designated Rightists and blamed himself and expressed regret, and this was a sincere act. He was a scholar with a conscience. Among all the people who committed wrongdoing during the Anti-Rightist Campaign and the Cultural Revolution, how many were able, like him, to express repentance and publicly apologise for their crimes?

Bai Yuan refers to Tang Lin as a 'high-level intellectual', but in fact he had only a secondary school education. Even so, Tang was very well-read, and among cadres of his generation, he could be considered an educated man.

Tang Lin was locked up and deprived of his personal freedom in February 1968, just as the Cultural Revolution was reaching a new climax and had started a mass campaign of setting up jails in every work unit, the notorious 'ox pens'. Tang was held in a classroom on the third floor and slept on a table.

After Tang Lin had been imprisoned for ten days or so, on the night of 18 February, he fell to his death from the window of the room where he was being held. It is claimed that he jumped out of the window when members of the 'rebel faction' began pounding on the door at 9:00 that night. He was unable to speak as he was taken to the hospital, and died soon afterwards.

The day after Tang Lin died, his sixteen-year-old daughter was forced to attend a rally and declare that she had severed relations with her father. On the third day after his death, Tang Lin's body was sent to the crematorium in his bloodstained clothes.

Tang Lin's family didn't believe he had killed himself. He'd left no suicide note, and he was a strong man who had been bearing up under his persecution since 1959. His family believed he was pushed out of the window, possibly after being beaten to death. After the Cultural Revolution, Tang Lin's children repeatedly petitioned for his case to be investigated, but nothing was ever done.

Peng Kang (also known as Peng Jian and Peng Jiasheng), the sixty-seven-year-old Party secretary and president of Xi'an Jiaotong University, was paraded through the streets all day on 27 March 1968, and dropped dead during a protracted struggle session on the morning of 28 March. He had also been repeatedly struggled in 1966.

Born to a landlord family in Pingxiang, Jiangxi Province, Peng went to Japan to study in 1919. After returning to China in 1927, he took part in Shanghai's renowned progressive literary group, the Creation Society, and was involved in editing and writing for *Cultural Criticism* and other literary publications. He joined the CCP in 1928, and was elected to the Executive Committee of the newly formed Chinese Writers' Association. In 1929, the Party Committee entrusted Peng with translating and publishing major European Marxist texts. Peng was imprisoned for seven years by the KMT for his activities with the Communist Party. After his release in 1937, he served in a series of Party postings relating to culture, propaganda and education. Provincial-level academic and political appointments followed with the establishment of the PRC, and Peng was elected a delegate to the first Shanghai Municipal People's Congress and to the CCP's Eighth National Party Congress. When rehabilitated ten years after his death, Peng was praised as 'a Marxist educator and philosopher, and a good cadre who worked hard for the Party and the people and who devoted his full energies to Communism and to the undertaking of liberating the Chinese people.'[27]

Like Wuhan University president Li Da, Peng Kang was struggled to death. The difference between them was that Peng Kang survived for another year and a half.

Peng Kang was designated a 'bourgeois Rightist' and 'counter-revolutionary revisionist' by the Shaanxi Provincial Party Committee after the 16 May Circular was issued in 1966, and on 2 June of that year, a Party Committee work group took control of Xi'an Jiaotong University and attacked the former administrators. At that time, a big-character poster accused Peng Kang of 'vilifying and slandering Mao Zedong Thought' and of being an 'anti-Party, anti-socialist element'. The main basis for these accusations was that Peng Kang had once said that one person climbed a pole, and another stayed below memorising quotations for half a day without being able to climb the pole. He meant that learning Chairman Mao's quotes was not concrete action. Peng Kang didn't actually oppose learning Mao's quotes, but was merely criticising a trend that he felt was incorrect. Yet his words were used as evidence that he opposed Mao and Mao Zedong Thought.

Peng Kang was designated a 'Three Antis element' and brutally struggled. In the heat of August 1966, he was paraded through the streets with a heavy placard hung from his neck by a fine wire that cut into his flesh, and he passed out at one point, but didn't die.

Nearly two years later, on 27 March 1968, student Red Guards took Peng Kang to Xi'an's east gate and struggled him for the entire day, and at around six o'clock the next morning, they took him out to struggle him some more. A small, thin, elderly man of sixty-seven, Peng Kang was wearing an old black quilted jacket when he was forced to run laps around the sports ground while others ran behind him, shouting and whipping him.

At around nine o'clock, Peng Kang collapsed. Some accused him of 'playing dead', but eventually the Red Guards ordered some of the school's 'reactionary academic authorities' to take Peng Kang to the hospital. He died that same morning.

---

[27] Drawn from the entry on 'Peng Kang' in *Who's Who in Modern Shaanxi*.

Chang Xiping, born in 1917, was president and Party secretary of Shanghai's East China Normal University, and director of the Education and Health Department of the Shanghai Municipal Party Committee. He was 'ferreted out' in 1966 and subjected to brutal 'struggle' and detention at the university for an extended period, enduring frequent beatings and humiliation. On 25 May 1968, he fell to his death from a lecture theatre window.

After Chang Xiping's death, his ashes were discarded, but that wasn't humiliation enough. The university's Revolutionary Committee designated him an 'incorrigible capitalist-roader' who had resisted the Cultural Revolution by committing suicide.

There was a particular reason that Chang Xiping was subjected to brutal struggle. In 1964, he had been a member of a 'work team' that led the Socialist Education Movement at Peking University, and he hadn't supported Nie Yuanzi and others at that time. Once the Cultural Revolution began and Nie Yuanzi became a major figure vigorously supported by Mao Zedong, Nie went to Shanghai to personally launch an attack against Chang Xiping and accuse him of even greater crimes.

Some people at the school believed that Chang may have been murdered; he didn't write a suicide note, and was a person who had endured great hardship in the past.

An ordinary teacher who was designated a Rightist in 1957 said that more than 400 people were declared Rightists at East China Normal University under the leadership of Chang Xiping. It was the continuation and development of this persecution that led to his death. I've collected the names of fourteen people who were persecuted to death at the university from 1966 to 1968, and this is an incomplete list (see Part Five).

Li Qiuye, the fifty-three-year-old director and Party secretary of the Beijing Institute of International Trade, had been under criticism and struggle since the Cultural Revolution began. He leaped to his death on 30 June 1968.

Li Qiuye, like other college administrators, was 'plucked out', subjected to criticism and struggle and deprived of his personal freedom at the outset of the Cultural Revolution. He spent his days undergoing 'labour reform' with a placard around his neck stating that he was a 'capitalist-roader power-holder', and at night he was locked up in one of the institute's buildings.

At that time, the institute was located in Beijing's western suburb, Chedaogou, later the location of the Central Marching Band. The institute had an administrative building and four classroom buildings.

A family member of an institute staffer who was a teenager at the time said that he saw Li Qiuye after he jumped to his death. Li had jumped from the south side of the second storey of Classroom Building No. 1, a grey four-storey structure with a clinic on the ground floor. When my interviewee arrived at the scene with several young companions, Li wasn't yet dead, and his body was still moving in a pool of blood. Li was later taken to the hospital, but reportedly no one was willing to give him a blood transfusion, and he soon died. My interviewee later heard that while undergoing 'labour reform', Li Qiuye had picked up a large nail, and after being taken back to lock-up, he'd driven it into his head with a brick in an attempt to kill himself. This attempt was unsuccessful, but the pain was excruciating, and he'd tried to finish the job by hurling himself against the wall. When that also failed, he leaped from the window. Another version, however, was that Red Guards had been torturing him in the room and slamming his head against the wall; some said that Red Guards had pushed Li out of the window.

My interviewee said he knew the names of four people who leaped to their deaths at the institute, and had personally seen three of them.

The first was **Luo Juemin** from the teaching materials section. After being struggled, Luo leaped from a balcony on the top floor of the administrative building. My interviewee said he saw a heap of clothes without human form on the ground in front of the building, surrounded by blood. The second victim my interviewee saw was Li Qiuye. Not long after that, **Li Guozhong**, from the dean's office, also leaped to his death from the second floor of Building No. 1. My interviewee didn't see his body, but only a chalk outline drawn on the ground where he had fallen. The fourth was **Fu Weiliang** from the General Affairs Department. Fu leaped from the top of a room on the roof of the administrative building, perhaps a water tower or a place from which the flag was hung. It was the highest point in the institute, and there was no doubt that leaping from it would be fatal. At that time, his eldest son was around eleven years old, and the youngest only five. After his body was taken away, someone wrote in white on the ground, 'Fu Weiliang alienated himself from the Party and the people.'

My information comes from two people who were children at the time. No adult witnesses have told me their recollections.

Gao Yangyun, the sixty-three-year-old vice-president and Party secretary of Tianjin Nankai University, drowned himself on 27 July 1968 after being struggled and flogged.

Apart from being attacked as university administrator, Gao Yangyun was accused of having been a traitor to the CCP in the past.

During the time that the Kuomintang government declared the CCP illegal, some Communist Party members were arrested, and some were released on bail after writing 'confessions' or 'statements of repentance'.

During the Cultural Revolution, such people were labelled traitors and became major targets of 'struggle against the enemy'. Incited by the Cultural Revolution's leaders, student Red Guards whipped up a nationwide campaign to 'pluck out traitors'. Nankai University students were the most active in this campaign, combing official archives and organising 'struggle rallies' that played a major role in the nationwide campaign.

Li Guangtian, the sixty-two-year-old president of Yunnan University, died on 2 or 3 November 1968, and was found in a lotus pond on the outskirts of Kunming. His death was classified as a suicide at the time, but his family members believe he was beaten to death and then thrown into the pool.

According to a *Who's Who* directory, Li Guangtian graduated from Peking University in 1935 and in 1941 began using Marxist viewpoints to lecture on literary theory at Southwestern Associated University in Kunming. Li joined the CCP in 1948, and after the Party took power in 1949, he became chairman of the Chinese Department and dean of studies at Tsinghua University. He was transferred to Yunnan University in 1951, serving as vice-president and then president.

A student at Yunnan University at that time told me that when the Cultural Revolution began in 1966, there was still no direct train route from Beijing to Kunming, but secondary school student Red Guards from Beijing managed to reach Kunming during the 'great networking'.[28] By then, large-scale violence was already taking place in Beijing. A group of Beijing secondary school students mounted the stage of the Yunnan University auditorium and brandished *Quotations from Chairman Mao* while shouting slogans, performing 'rebel dances' and yelling, 'Kill, kill, kill!' which deeply shocked this student and taught him what revolution was. As a result, although far from Beijing, Yunnan did not lag far behind other areas in the Cultural Revolution.

Li Guangtian soon became a target of violent struggle, and in 1968 he was locked up at the university. A former student says that two days before Li died, she saw him apparently being taken to a struggle rally. This student had once encountered Li Guangtian on campus before the Cultural Revolution, and he had talked to her about translating English poems. She was just an ordinary student, so this conversation with the university president left a

---

[28] TN: During the first year or so of the Cultural Revolution, young people were encouraged to cut classes and travel all over China to propagate Mao Zedong Thought. They were typically provided with free public transport, as well as food and lodging. This programme was known as the 'great networking' or 'great link-up'. Many of the violent practices of the Cultural Revolution spread to distant parts of China in this way.

deep impression on her. In his youth, Li Guangtian had been a poet who had studied foreign languages at Peking University. This student recalls that before the Revolution, Li often wore pale khaki clothing and always looked 'extremely clean and elegant'. One gains the same impression from essays that Li published in the 1930s.

Li Guangtian was brutally struggled during the Cultural Revolution not only because he was a 'revisionist' university president, but also because he was a published writer who had served as vice-chairman of the Yunnan Writers' Association. Writers were a group particularly targeted during the Cultural Revolution.

In the 1950s, a group of Yunnan writers collected folk tales of the Yi ethnic minority and created the epic poem *Ashima*, a love story set against the backdrop of Yunnan's famous Stone Forest. In the early 1960s, a slight relaxing of government control over works of art allowed for the production of some lighter and more entertaining films. The Shanghai Movie Studio turned *Ashima* into a film, but the original compilers of the poem had been designated Rightists in 1957 and had been expelled from cultural circles. By then, Li Guangtian was president of Yunnan University and a person in authority, and he was listed as a 'literary consultant' for the film version of *Ashima*, even though the original authors weren't credited. At the time, some people felt that Li used his status to take credit for someone else's work, but after seeing him so brutally persecuted and dying so tragically during the Cultural Revolution, all one can feel is the cruelty of politics and the sad fate of China's literary figures.

During the Cultural Revolution, *Ashima* was deemed an 'anti-Party, anti-socialist, anti-Mao Zedong Thought great poisonous weed' and became a key target of criticism in Yunnan Province. The movie was never meant as a political allegory either praising or disparaging the Communist Party or Mao, but after it became a target of criticism, its female star, the young and beautiful actress Yang Likun, was brutally struggled and became mentally unbalanced, and the much older Li Guangtian found himself under even harsher attack. In fact, during the 1960s, Li Guangtian also edited and published a selection of poems by members of various ethnic groups entitled *Gold and Silver Flowers Presented to Chairman Mao*. The title clearly indicates that Li Guangtian was following the personality cult energetically promoted by Lin Biao in the early 1960s; he was certainly not expressing opposition to Mao Zedong Thought.

Li Guangtian was detained and struggled from 1966 to 1968, his persecution reaching a climax during the latter half of 1968. Li's wife and daughter believe his death was a case of murder rather than suicide, in particular because there was a large wound as if from a heavy blow on the back of his head. However, the family wasn't allowed to say anything at the time, and no investigation was carried out. Although Li was rehabilitated in 1978, there was still no follow-up on his death.

Jiang Tiyun, vice-president and a member of the Party Standing Committee at Shanghai's Tongji University, was placed under 'isolation and investigation' in 1968. He died after being savagely beaten on 27 July 1968. He was not yet sixty years old.

Someone from Tongji University told me that Jiang Tiyun had been dean of studies and was very strict about cheating on exams, so some students particularly hated him and took advantage of the Cultural Revolution to savagely struggle him.

This was not the only case in which unruly students seized the opportunity to retaliate against teachers or administrators. They could do so with impunity because the Cultural Revolution had abolished the former exam and grading systems, and even more importantly, because its leaders allowed and encouraged violent attacks onthese particular groups.

During the Cleansing of the Class Ranks in 1968, Tongji University 'unearthed' a 'spy cell' of thirty-three cadres at various levels, including Jiang Tiyun. Beginning in May 1968, Jiang Tiyun was placed in 'isolation and investigation', and his interrogators used torture to force him to confess to being a spy, intending to use him to 'make a breach' in the case. (Other victims at Tongji University are listed in the Shanghai section of Part Five.)

Jiang Tiyun fell from a window on 27 July but didn't die on the spot. While being taken to the hospital on a stretcher, he cried out, 'I don't want to die!' For this reason, some people at the school believe he was pushed from the window rather than committing suicide as the authorities claimed.

Zhang Jingren, president and Party secretary of the Shanghai University of Technology, was subjected to denunciations, beatings, humiliation, incarceration and interrogation under torture for a sustained period. When he became too debilitated, he was carried to rallies on a bench. He died of multiple ailments on 7 June 1970.

OTHER EARLY VICTIMS OF VIOLENCE AT THE UNIVERSITIES

Apart from top university administrators, many professors, lower-level administrators and other university staff also became victims of unrest on the campuses at the outset of the Cultural Revolution. Pan Guangdan's case stands out among them.

Pan Guangdan, born in 1899, was a professor at Minzu University of China (previously known in English as the Central University for Nationalities). He began studying at Tsinghua University in 1913, and while there had a leg amputated as a result of a sports injury. In 1922 he went to the United States to obtain his Master's degree. Labelled a Rightist in 1957, he also became a target of struggle and criticism during the Cultural Revolution as a 'reactionary academic authority'. He began 'labour reform' under Minzu University's 'dictatorship team' in summer 1966 and died on 10 June 1967.

Before his death, Pan Guangdan characterised his life with four English words: surrender, submit, survive and succumb.

THE FOUR S'S

By 1967, the second tumultuous year of the Cultural Revolution, Professor Pan Guangdan was critically ill after suffering constant humiliation and beatings as a target of criticism and struggle since the revolution's launch. Apart from the psychological attacks he endured, the physical effect of being struggled was exacerbated by his handicap and advanced age.

A few days before Pan's death, he received a visit from his old friend Ye Duyi, who like him had obtained an advanced degree overseas as a young man. Pan told his old friend that his philosophy of life could be summarised in three English words beginning with S: surrender, submit and survive. Ye told him, 'Then keep following it – keep surrendering, keep submitting, keep surviving.' Pan Guangdan said, 'I'm gravely ill and about to die. My three-S policy will become four S's. The fourth S is succumb.'

These deathbed words could not be circulated during the Cultural Revolution, because they would be investigated as 'reactionary speech' and a 'venomous attack on socialism and the Great Cultural Revolution'. Even Pan's old friend might be implicated and sentenced to death. It was only after the Cultural Revolution that Ye Duyi dared to reveal Pan's words. I subsequently verified the incident with Pan's family. By then, Pan had been dead for nearly thirty years.

It took a scholar of Pan Guangdan's ilk to come up with this uniquely poignant form of expression. It was because he had studied overseas and was fluent in English that he could summarise his life with four English words. His formulation was not a mere word game, but was the result of deep reflection on his identity and experience. People like him who had been labelled 'bourgeois intellectuals' and 'reactionary academic authorities' suddenly became 'patriotic intellectuals' who 'ardently loved Chairman Mao and socialism' when rehabilitated after the Cultural Revolution ended.

The authorities applied these terms to serve various purposes, but the actual thinking of the intellectuals remains a mystery. Our inability to understand them is not because they had no capacity for expressing their thoughts, but rather because they dared not express what they thought, especially in public. Pan Guangdan's dying words could only be spoken on his behalf by someone else, many years after he died. Even after the Cultural Revolution, the living felt unable to speak directly, and could only borrow the utterance of a dead man to articulate the pain and suffering of their generation.

The poignancy of these words lies in how closely they match historical fact, and how perfectly they encapsulate the experience of Pan Guangdan and his generation. Like many true sayings that are long suppressed and concealed, they resonated all the more once allowed to surface.

Twenty-three years after Pan's death, and fourteen years after the Cultural Revolution ended, the 1990 edition of *China Encyclopedia* included the following entry:

Pan Guangdan: 1899–1967

Born on 13 August 1899, in Luodian Township, Baoshan, Jiangsu Province. From 1913 to 1922 Pan studied in the overseas study prep course at Beijing Tsinghua University. From 1922 to 1926 he studied in the United States, first majoring in biology at Dartmouth College in Hanover, New Hampshire, where he obtained a PhD, and then studying zoology, paleontology and genetics at Columbia University, where he obtained a Master's Degree. He returned to China in 1926 and served as a professor at Shanghai's Great China University, Fudan University and Guanghua University. Beginning in 1934, he served as professor, dean of studies and head of the Sociology Department at Tsinghua University, and professor and head of the Sociology Department at National Southwestern Associated University. From 1952 to 1967 he was employed at Minzu University of China, where he was head of the No. 3 research room. He served as a delegate to the second, third and fourth sessions of the Chinese People's Political Consultative Conference. He died in Beijing on 10 June 1967.

This entry omits two important events. One is that in 1957 Pan was designated a Rightist and treated as an enemy of society. The other is that during the Cultural Revolution he was persecuted and abused, and was forced to participate in the university's 'labour reform team' for an extended period in spite of being handicapped. To the day that he died, he was still being referred to as an 'ox demon and snake spirit'. In addition, the entry does not mention that he left Tsinghua in 1952 because the government had eliminated the sociological research that he had been carrying out there. His departure from Tsinghua was mandatory, and not the routine transfer between schools and research institutes typical of a scholarly career.

What this curriculum vitae suggests to the reader is the peaceful life of a normal, typical scholar, indistinguishable from the lives of scholars in other eras or countries. Nobody reading this mini-biography would ever imagine that Pan would have used those four S's to describe his life and death.

Nothing written in the encyclopedia is false or fabricated, yet it cannot be considered accurate; by concealing and editing so much, it ultimately bears little resemblance to the totality of Pan's life. Neither false nor true, it is a special type of lie.

During the Cultural Revolution era, lies were everywhere. A classic example was that at a time of obvious shortages and hardship, newspapers still boasted of the 'excellent situation' and 'market prosperity'. Another classic example is that many who never dreamed of opposing Mao were labelled 'opponents of the Party, socialism and Mao Zedong Thought'. After the Cultural Revolution, publication of anything relating to its history was rigorously controlled, and the truth could still not be told. Official media was less likely to invent incidents that had never actually occurred, however, and that could be considered a kind of progress. Nevertheless, failure to tell people of the bad things that actually happened served to cover up misdeeds and prevent effective restitution. The obliteration and expunging of historical fact became another form of lying.

We will look back on how Pan Guangdan and his generation of scholars surrendered, submitted and survived from the 1950s until they utterly succumbed during the Cultural Revolution.

Secondary source materials are explicitly cited; unless so indicated, the narrative that follows results from my own inquiries. My investigation included large quantities of written records, and conversations with more than 1,000 survivors of the Cultural Revolution.

The Era of 'Self-Criticism' and 'Confession': Campaigns for Ideological Remoulding, Loyalty and Honesty, and to Eliminate Counter-Revolutionaries

Reviewing a string of incidents at Chinese universities after 1949 will give us greater understanding and sympathy for the four S's.

In the latter half of 1951, a Thought Reform Campaign initiated by Mao and directed by Zhou Enlai spread throughout China's campuses.

Zhou Enlai's 29 September 1951 guideline report on this campaign was entitled 'Regarding the Issue of Reforming Intellectuals'. At the third plenum of the first CPPCC (Chinese People's Political Consultative Conference) session on 23 October 1951, Mao used the phrase 'thought reform for intellectuals'.

It was common in Chinese society to refer to anyone who had attained a high level of education, including university instructors, as an 'intellectual', but in daily life no individual would refer to the social group they belonged to as 'intellectuals'. Labelling a particular social group in this way implied that those outside of this social group lacked knowledge or intellect, and at a time when the majority considered knowledge a good thing, this would come across as rather discourteous. In daily life, therefore, a person would describe themselves as a teacher, engineer, doctor or scholar instead.

The 1952 edition of *Lexicon of Neologisms*[29] explains how the term 'intellectual' was applied at the time. The neologisms introduced in this book arguably illustrated new concepts that arose when a society was established that differed from that before it. The 'Society' section of this lexicon included a category for 'social components', set down as follows:

> Labouring people, physical labourer, mental labourer, worker, industrial worker, peasant, intellectual, old intellectual, worker/peasant intellectual, cadre, office worker, public servant, the masses, leader, social activist, activist, patriotic democrat, model worker, advanced worker, heroic individual, revolutionary soldier, revolutionary, professional revolutionary, revolutionary martyr, family of revolutionary martyr, family of revolutionary soldier, handicraft worker, small handicraftsman, middle peasant, wealthy middle peasant, poor peasant, hired farmhand, common people, lessor of small farming plot, enlightened gentry, independent professional, religious professional, handicraft capitalist, shop owners and vendors, commercial capitalists and merchants, rich peasant, quasi-landlord rich peasant, reactionary rich peasant, landlord, sub-landlord, bankrupt landlord, altered landlord status, usurer, caretaker [of a temple or ancestral hall], reactionary, counter-revolutionary, traitor, degenerate, undercover agent, foreman, scab, labour aristocracy, vagrant, loafer, henchman, local despot.

This is how the new leaders segregated society, and it served as the basis for 'class struggle'. From the outset, 'intellectuals' were considered a social

---

[29] *Lexicon of Neologisms*, Shanghai, Chunming chubanshe, 1952.

component that required 'reform' through 'campaigns'. The reason for designating them as a class was their possession of intellect or knowledge, in the same way that possession of land or a factory qualified someone as a landlord or a capitalist.

Eventually, formulations such as 'places with accumulations of intellectuals' began coming up in speeches by the top leaders, with clearly derogatory connotations. When intellectuals were forced to accept criticism and to carry out self-criticism, it was referred to as 'bathing', with the obvious implication that they were mentally tainted and unclean. An even more unpleasant formulation was that 'intellectuals' needed to 'pull down their trousers and have their tails lopped off'. Even now, some people claim to see nothing humiliating or degrading in this expression, and no books published in China have ever come out and criticised it even from a linguistic standpoint. Such callousness is particularly shocking in a country that boasts of its long literary tradition and emphasis on the written word.

The CCP Central Committee's May 1952 'Directive on the Ongoing Campaign to Criticise Bourgeois Thought in Tertiary Institutions and Preparations to Cleanse the Middle Ranks' stated:

> Based on experience in Beijing and Shanghai, in this campaign it is possible and desirable for 60 to 70% of teachers to be passed after undergoing the necessary self-criticism; another 12 to 25% of teachers can be passed after undergoing appropriate criticism; around 13% of teachers will require repeated criticism and self-criticism before they can be passed, while only around 2% will not be allowed to pass and must be dealt with as appropriate. These proportions are generally suitable.

This document was the first to set quotas for purges. It can be traced back to the 1950 Campaign to Suppress Counter-Revolutionaries, during which Mao stipulated that 0.1% of rural residents and 0.05% of urban residents should be killed (for further details, see the entry for **Gu Wenxuan** in Part Six). The earlier killing quotas made the 'pass' quotas for the Thought Reform Campaign seem lenient in comparison, and the threat of death ensured that no one would dare to resist.

During the Thought Reform Campaign, all of China's intellectuals, especially top intellectuals, had to 'reform' their 'bourgeois thinking' and expose and criticise the 'encroachment of American imperialist culture'. Schools suspended classes for the campaign while teachers performed 'self-criticism' at mass rallies and thoroughly repudiated their past thinking and learning. Some people had to undergo several criticism sessions before they were 'passed', and apart from criticising themselves, they had to 'expose and criticise' others. Some with a higher status or who were key targets had to carry out public self-criticism on varying scales.

Pan Guangdan's self-criticism, 'Why It Is Hard to Hate America', was published in the newspapers. Nearly 10,000 words long, this essay laid out and refuted the education that his parents, teachers and classmates had received in their youth, as well as the scholarly research he was engaged in. Self-criticism had reached the point of laying waste to everything. Pan reportedly underwent self-criticism twelve times before being passed.

During the Thought Reform Campaign, philosophy professor Jin Yuelin was another key target at Tsinghua University. Jin's self-criticism, entitled 'Criticising the Bourgeois Educational Thinking of My Idealism', was also published in the newspapers, and went even further than Pan Guangdan's by criticising the students Jin had taught along with criticism of himself, his parents and his teachers.

It was common for professors to have their self-criticisms published in the *People's Daily*, *Guangming Daily* and provincial newspapers in tandem with carrying out self-criticism at their schools. The content of these 'confessions' was similar, with liberal use of emotive adjectives such as 'corrupt', 'reactionary' and 'ugly'. This is how intellectuals were exposed to the public at large.

Did intellectuals write these things of their own volition? I had access neither to Pan Guangdan himself nor to the archives of Tsinghua University from that time, and the 2001 *Tsinghua University Annals*[30] devotes only one sentence to the Thought Reform Campaign.

By way of contrast, the *Peking University Chronicle*[31] includes accounts of the campaign that help us understand how it came about. Just as Pan Guangdan and Jin Yuelin were key targets at Tsinghua University, Zhu Guangqian and Zhou Binglin were key targets at Peking University. Zhu was a professor of Western languages. After graduating from the University of Hong Kong, he had studied in the United States and Great Britain, and had begun teaching at Peking University in 1933. His writings on aesthetics had enormous influence on young people. According to the *Peking University Chronicle*, Zhu carried out self-criticism before an assembly of teachers and students in his department on 7 March 1952: 'After the self-criticism, those in attendance all expressed dissatisfaction. Five teachers and students

---

[30] Fang Huijian, Zhang Sijing (ed.), *Tsinghua University Annals*, Tsinghua daxue chubanshe, April 2001.
[31] *Peking University Chronicle 1898–1997*, Beijing daxue chubanshe, 1998.

from the Western Languages Department spoke at the assembly, exposing and analytically criticising Zhu's bourgeois thinking.'[32]

On 29 March, Peking University's College of Liberal Arts convened an assembly of all teachers and students 'to carry out analytical criticism of Professor Zhu Guangqian's self-criticism.' On 9 April, Zhu carried out a third self-criticism at a university-wide assembly. On 10 April, 'an assembly of all the university's teachers and students expressed opinions on Professor Zhu Guangqian's self-criticism, with fourteen professors, lecturers, assistant lecturers and students making speeches. Finally, university president Ma Yinchu delivered summary remarks. He said Mr Zhu's self-criticism had made progress, but required further introspection and intensified remoulding, fundamentally changing his reactionary standpoint in line with mass opinion, and taking his position alongside the people.'

Zhou Binglin was a professor of law at Peking University who in July 1920 had been sent with four schoolmates to study in the US at public expense by then university president Cai Yuanpei. After Zhou made repeated self-criticism without being passed, he told university president Ma Yinchu that he refused to make any more and was 'willing to bear all the consequences'. It was no use, however; there was nowhere he could go. Ma and others went to Zhou's home to talk with him, and called in more than twenty people for a meeting to 'help' Zhou Binglin until he finally expressed a willingness to 'expose and criticise his reactionary thought'. Ma Yinchu also convened a meeting of the university's leadership to discuss how to resolve the Zhou Binglin issue,[33] probably never imagining that he would eventually find himself on the other side of the equation.

On 21 April 1952, Mao wrote a letter to Beijing mayor Peng Zhen:

> I've read the documents you sent over regarding ideological self-criticisms in the schools. It appears that apart from exceptionally hostile elements such as Zhang Dongsun,[34] it is appropriate to assist people like Zhou Binglin to pass, and the timing can be relaxed a bit. Peking University's recent handling of Zhou Binglin was very good. I hope it can be extended to other schools; it's the method to use on many reactionary or fence-sitting professors.[35]

Mao's letter shows the extent of his hands-on direction of the campaign. He continued to micromanage 'political campaigns' right up until his last years.

---

[32] *Ibid., op. cit.*, pp. 447–448.
[33] *Ibid.*, p. 449.
[34] TN: Zhang Dongsun's situation will be described later in this book.
[35] *Peking University Chronicle 1898–1997, op. cit.*, p. 449.

Ultimately Zhou Binglin carried out self-criticism before a university-wide assembly on 22 April. 'After Zhou carried out self-criticism, fourteen professors, assistant professors and students made speeches to assist him.'[36] It is clear that Zhou had no choice but to surrender and submit. Zhou Binglin died before the Cultural Revolution, but his wife, **Wei Bi**, was one of its victims.

To those who experienced it, the mass criticism during the Thought Reform Campaign set the scene for the Cultural Revolution, though it claimed to 'assist' the targets rather than 'overthrowing and discrediting' them, and required targets to revile themselves rather than inflicting physical punishment.

On 6 May 1952, Peking University president Ma Yinchu convened a meeting at which he said the Thought Reform Campaign was basically finished, as a result of which 'the meeting decided that classes would resume on 14 May, and from now on campaigns and classes should not affect each other.'[37] This indicates that the practice of suspending classes for campaigns originated back in 1952. During the Cultural Revolution, however, the suspension lasted much longer, five or six years – a record for China.

The constant self-criticism was accompanied by a considerable number of deaths. According to the *Peking University Chronicles*, seven people killed themselves at Peking University between March and May 1952. Suicides among victims were therefore not unique to the Cultural Revolution, although the number was far greater.

The Thought Reform Campaign was followed two weeks later by the Loyalty and Honesty Campaign, which required people to confess in detail all questionable incidents in their personal histories. Those considered to have a 'bad attitude' were 'isolated for soul-searching'.

The Beijing Municipal Economizing Committee's opinions on launching a Loyalty and Honesty Campaign were transmitted during a meeting of the university's top leaders on 24 May:

> The campaign will be divided into a preparatory stage and an unfolding stage. The preparatory stage consists mainly of cadre study sessions and discarding mental blocks. The unfolding stage includes four steps: mobilisation rallies and committee meetings for debriefings [i.e. confessions] on problems (other suitable methods can also be considered), all levels of the leadership investigating the debriefed problems and delivering conclusions to the persons in question, summarising the results, and a call for reports. The organisation

---

[36] *Ibid.*
[37] *Ibid.*, p. 450.

method will be division into a certain number of grassroots units according to different categories of person, with committees set up under the grassroots units, each committee consisting of around twenty people.[38]

The 'Economizing Committee', known formally as the 'Committee for Management of Economizing', existed at the central and municipal level, and its functions extended to convening 'public judgment assemblies' where death sentences could be delivered, as well as planning and leading major political campaigns. Since the launch of the Loyalty and Honesty Campaign was decided by the Beijing Municipal Economizing Committee, Tsinghua University, falling under the jurisdiction of Beijing, would follow basically the same practice.

Beginning on 31 May 1952, all classes were suspended at Peking University for the Loyalty and Honesty Campaign. The secretary of Tsinghua University's Party Committee, Yuan Yongxi, went to Peking University to head up the work group and lead the campaign. On 2 June, Yuan reported that the campaign was proceeding normally, with 2,865 people confessing their errors within the space of thirty-six hours. On 3 June, Yuan convened a model reporting rally,[39] which involved bringing those who had made 'good debriefings' to speak before a mass rally. This not only encouraged others to confess their 'errors', but also put pressure on those whose confessions were 'unsatisfactory'. This method of 'model rallies' evolved during the Cultural Revolution into what were known as 'leniency and severity model rallies', where those who made 'good' confessions were 'handled with leniency' and those whose confessions were unsatisfactory were 'handled with severity'.

On 8 June 1952, Yuan Yongxi reported that 3,387 individuals at the university were taking part in study sessions (some overseas Chinese did not participate), with 89.4% confessing to some form of error, and verdicts delivered on all but 580. The campaign was declared a success.[40]

This was the result of one week's suspension of classes for the campaign. At that time, the errors, personal history, family background, social relations and other information that a person provided in his or her 'debriefing', along with the 'verdict' handed down, were all entered into a personal 'dossier'. Under this newly established system of social control, every individual had a file, but enjoyed no access to its contents.

---

[38] *Ibid.*, p. 451.
[39] *Ibid.*
[40] *Ibid.*, pp. 451–452.

From then on, 'debriefings on errors' were expected as a matter of course, and became a fixture of social life during the Cultural Revolution. 'If XXX doesn't provide an honest debriefing, he must be destroyed'; this became one of the slogans routinely shouted during the Cultural Revolution, in spite of the lack of any legal basis for these campaigns. Chinese who grew up in the Mao era considered these 'debriefings' as intrinsic to their existence as the weather.

At this point we can clearly see that campaign methods included requiring teachers to carry out self-criticism and confessions and to form committees for mutual exposure. This resulted in densely co-ordinated campaigns that no one could escape, while the mutual exposure bred antagonism and resentment between colleagues. A tightly co-ordinated campaign carried out with no regard to cost inevitably produced impressive 'results'. The same methods were employed during the Cultural Revolution, but on an even larger scale and for a more extended period, with even more baneful consequences.

What is described above is merely the partial record left behind by the officials who led the Thought Reform and Loyalty and Honesty campaigns. However preposterous and vicious these records are, they present only one side of the story. Much of what happened then was never recorded or reported, just as one searches in vain for information about the victims in official histories of the Cultural Revolution.

During my investigations, several people I interviewed said that even during the Thought Reform and Loyalty and Honesty campaigns, people had been persecuted to the point of committing suicide. Liu Dajie, a professor of Chinese Literary History at Shanghai's Fudan University, leaped into the Huangpu River after failing to 'pass' repeated self-criticisms. He was pulled from the river alive, only to be forced to continue his self-criticism, which now included his new 'error' of attempting to kill himself. Other cases were even more horrifying. **Li Pingxin**, a professor of history at Shanghai's East China Normal University, attempted to kill himself by severing his own head with an axe in 1952. He, too, was saved, but not long after the Cultural Revolution began, on 15 June 1966, he gassed himself to death in his home.

It should be pointed out that in the 1950s, Liu Dajie and Li Pingxin were both sober middle-aged men who were not the kind to cavalierly end their own lives. Neither had voiced opposition to either campaign. They had surrendered by carrying out self-criticism, but their submission was deemed inadequate to 'pass'. It was under those conditions that they resorted to suicide.

Also worth noting is that the aforementioned work group head, Yuan Yongxi, and his wife, **Chen Lian**, had both been leaders of the university student movement. They had joined the Communist Party in the late 1930s, and became high-level cadres after 1949. The early 1950s was the headiest time for such people. Emboldened to impose submission on others, they wielded their new and formidable power with no regard for the suffering they caused. Yuan Yongxi was only thirty-five years old in 1953, and one can easily imagine the atmosphere on campus as he commandeered the 'debriefing' of more than 3,000 professors and teachers at Peking University. Yet in 1957, he himself was designated a 'Rightist' and was sent to Beijing's rural Changping County for five years of labour reform. After being rehabilitated in May 1962, he was sent to teach literature and English at Nangong Secondary school in Hebei Province. After the Cultural Revolution began, five teachers and cadres at that school were beaten to death or poisoned themselves. Yuan himself was beaten into a coma by Red Guards and tossed into a field; it was only by a twist of fate that he was rescued and survived.

After Yuan was labelled a Rightist, his wife, Chen Lian, 'drew a clear distinction' and divorced him, as a result of which she was able to continue serving as a high-level Party cadre. Even so, during the Cultural Revolution, Chen's 'past errors' led to her being accused of 'treason', and she leaped to her death from a building in Shanghai in November 1967 (see the profile of **Chen Lian** in the Shanghai section of Part Three).

One interviewee said that Yuan Yongxi and Chen Lian met with tragic fates because highly educated people within the Communist Party were easily targeted in political campaigns. This makes them sympathetic figures. Another interviewee, however, said that Yuan's status as an 'intellectual' might have made him even harsher than other cadres in purging his fellow intellectuals. Yuan and Chen played key roles in the persecution that took place on college campuses in the early 1950s, with no indication that their education tempered the persecution they inflicted on others. Workers and peasants, though not well-educated, had common sense and a respect for knowledge, and they were not empowered to purge others. People like Yuan, however, were often aggressive, unscrupulous and callous. It is not my purpose here to explore motivations; I seek only to state the facts, and in this respect Yuan Yongxi's trajectory from purger to purged is noteworthy. People who helped build the machinery of persecution risked being crushed alive by that very machine, no matter how clever or capable they might be.

As soon as the Loyalty and Honesty Campaign concluded, 'departmental adjustment' commenced, and universities were completely reorganised. Private or church-funded colleges were closed down. Tsinghua University eliminated its Arts and Sciences subjects and became an institution devoted purely to the applied sciences. All universities removed sociology, humanities, psychology and political science as independent departments. Pan Guangdan was a professor of sociology, which prior to 1949 was a department in twenty of China's universities, enrolling a total of 975 students.[41] The reason given for eliminating Sociology Departments in 1952 was that Marxism–Leninism provided the true explanation for human society and history, and there was no need for other forms of sociology; Soviet universities had no such academic departments, and China should follow suit. Universities did not reinstate Sociology Departments until after the Cultural Revolution.

From that time onwards, China's professors no longer had a choice in their academic postings. Schools were all repossessed by the government and came under the leadership of the Communist Party, which changed the academic personnel system. Professors could no longer seek their own employment, transfer to other schools, or leave the academic profession; they had to 'submit to state allocation'. The state likewise began assigning jobs to college graduates in 1952.

Under these circumstances, Pan Guangdan could not retain his position and field of expertise at Tsinghua University, and he was assigned to the Minzu University of China instead.

Once the 'departmental adjustment' was added to the Thought Reform Campaign for Intellectuals and the Loyalty and Honesty Campaign, the domestication of China's intellectuals was largely complete. Looking back now, we find that from the government's perspective, the remarkable success of these three movements lay in their seamless planning, close co-ordination and complementarity, with each one closely linked to the next.

Any society has three main channels for controlling the individual: 1) culture and morality; 2) economics and benefit; 3) power and fear. The Thought Reform Campaign's compulsory self-criticism transformed the politically incorrect into intellectual Untouchables. The Loyalty and Honesty Campaign purged people on the basis of past relations with the old regime. The 'departmental adjustment' established a 'Party Committee responsibility system' that choked off market forces in professional choice.

At that time, violence was not yet directly employed against teachers, but other campaigns around the same time used terrorist methods against other defenceless groups. Earlier in 1951, 710,000 people had been executed in the Campaign to Suppress Counter-Revolutionaries, while another 1.27 million people were imprisoned and 230,000 more were put under 'supervision and control'.[42] The sight of mass killings without judicial

---

[41] Han Minghan, *The History of Chinese Sociology*, Tianjin renmin chubanshe, 1987, p. 172.
[42] *China Yesterday and Today*, Jiefangjun chubanshe, 1999.

process and heaps of corpses being trucked through the streets inevitably had a powerful deterrent effect.

This was followed in 1955 by the Campaign to Eliminate Counter-Revolutionaries. Every work unit had a 'group of five' to lead the campaign. During the summer school break, all teachers were held in their school dormitories for more than a month for 'debriefings' on their own actions and 'exposure' of others. One elderly teacher told me he had a habit of talking in his sleep, and when all the teachers were boarding together during the campaign, someone was assigned to stay up at night and note down anything he said that might serve as evidence against him.

For anyone who has not experienced this kind of political campaign, it is hard to imagine this living hell in which an individual was either a pitiful purge victim or a merciless purger who gleaned evidence from nocturnal babblings. The Campaign to Eliminate Counter-Revolutionaries often identified 'unacknowledged or undisposed pre-liberation counter-revolutionaries' who eventually became targets during the Cultural Revolution; for example, Shanghai's East China Normal University professor Li Jigu, who had studied in Japan and England, and Peking University biology professor Zhao Yibing, who obtained his PhD in biology from the University of Chicago and had served as an interpreter for Americans aiding China during the War of Resistance Against Japan.

In November 1955, Peking University joined other universities in establishing a 'grain quota provision review committee' in line with nationwide policy.[43] Apart from countering food shortages, grain rationing gave the state unprecedented control over each and every individual. Before then, it had been possible for someone to support the daily needs of another person, but with the implementation of grain rationing, even someone with extra money could not obtain ration cards for someone else. Ration cards fettered individuals even more irrevocably to their work units and places of residence; freeing oneself from those fetters meant starvation. For the sake of survival, it was essential to cling and submit to that system and that core of political power. Trotsky once said, 'In a country where the sole employer is the State... the old principle: who does not work shall not eat has been replaced by a new one: who does not obey shall not eat.'[44] By the early 1950s, control over the individual had advanced to an unprecedented degree.

---

[43] *Peking University Chronicle 1989–1997, op. cit.*, p. 497.
[44] TN: Leon Trostsky, *The Revolution Betrayed: What Is the Soviet Union and Where Is It Going?* (Max Eastman trans.), Garden City, NY, Doubleday, Doran & Company, 1937, p. 263, quoted in F.A. Hayek, *The Road to Serfdom*, Chapter 9, The University of Chicago Press, 2007, p. 147.

1956 is considered the best year in terms of treatment of intellectuals. In a conference on intellectuals convened by the CCP Central Committee, Zhou Enlai delivered a report that proposed 'improving utilisation of and arrangements for intellectuals', which suggested that there would be improvements to other aspects of their treatment. However, after delivering the opening speech at the May Fourth Science Symposium held at Peking University that year, university president Ma Yinchu distributed two treatises: philosophy professor Feng Youlan's 'Self-Criticism Regarding Past Work in the History of Philosophy' and an essay entitled 'A Critique of Mr Feng Youlan's Past Philosophical Thinking'. The titles of the treatises show there was no change to the old tune of criticism and self-criticism.

From the incidents related above, along with the situation of centralised campaigns and unified standards applied to all schools, we can understand why Pan Guangdan used the first two of his S's, 'submit' and 'surrender', to describe his experience. The third S is 'survive', and there is a genuine relationship between these three S's: when the government takes control of all resources, including economic and occupational resources, and when the government decides what is right and wrong, ordinary people can only survive through submission and surrender – and that was not true for intellectuals alone.

The Time of 'Wearing Caps': The Anti-Rightist Campaign

During the 1957 Anti-Rightist Campaign, Pan Guangdan was forced to wear the 'cap' of a 'Rightist'.

Prior to the Anti-Rightist Campaign, what most intellectuals faced were 'debriefings' and 'self-criticism'. The Anti-Rightist Campaign brought an innovative variation to the social discipline mechanism, which was the imposition of labels on certain groups, known as 'wearing caps', with punishments to match.

According to figures published by the CCP Central Committee after the Cultural Revolution, 550,000 people were designated 'Rightists' in 1957. The scholar Ding Shu[45] places the number at one million. At that time, the Central Committee's policy clearly stipulated that workers and peasants could not be labelled Rightists and that any guilty of 'Rightist speech' should instead be labelled 'anti-socialist elements' (for which the penalty was equally senseless and cruel). This is why people labelled Rightists were

---

[45] Ding Shu, *Open Conspiracy (Yangmou)*, Hong Kong, Jiushi niandai zazhishe, 1991.

predominantly professional and technical personnel and the well-educated, China's so-called 'intellectuals'.

At least half of the Rightists lost their employment, and a considerable portion were sent to 're-education' or 'reform' through labour. In a developing country with a shortage of professional and technical personnel, persecuting a large share of scarce human resources was not only damaging to those individuals and their families but also extremely injurious to the interests of China and its general population. It was nothing less than national sabotage.

On 15 May, Mao circulated among the Party's top cadres his essay 'Things Are Beginning to Change', which proposed labelling some 10% of the population as 'Rightists'. In his speech at a cadre conference in Shanghai on 9 July, Mao once again referred to 10% of professors and assistant professors as being Rightists,[46] and this was ultimately set as the quota for applying that label. Under the government's repressive might, no one dared question the legitimacy of labelling and punishing an arbitrary quota of individuals.

At Peking University, 714 people were labelled Rightists, and another 571 were so labelled at Tsinghua University. Pan Guangdan reportedly said nothing during the Anti-Rightist Campaign, nor did he 'respond to the call' for 'suggestions'. Indeed, some say he was the kind of person who always kept his head down; having experienced the previous round of campaigns, Pan had become very circumspect. Even so, he was labelled a Rightist along with his colleagues Wu Wenzao and Fei Xiaotong, also foreign-educated sociologists who had been sent to Minzu University as a result of the 'departmental adjustment'.

Pan Guangdan was mentioned in an article on Fei Xiaotong's 'reactionary activities':

> On the eve of the rectification of incorrect work styles, the old forces of sociology, brought together by Fei Xiaotong, Pan Guangdan, Wu Jingchao and Wu Wenzao, assembled for a meeting in Beijing. On 9 June, Fei Xiaotong, Wu Jingchao, Wu Wenzao et al. held yet another meeting on the restoration of 'sociology', deciding to restore university Sociology Departments in Beijing, Shanghai, Guangzhou and Chengdu, starting with Beijing and Shanghai. In Beijing, Wu Wenzao would become head of the department at Peking University, and at Renmin University a sociological research institute would be established under Wu Jingchao. In addition, learned societies would

---

[46] *Selected Works of Mao Zedong*, Vol. 5, pp. 424, 441.

be established in Beijing and Shanghai, starting with a registration of scholars in sociology. In this way they parceled out turfs and arranged postings, and awaited 'promulgation' of a distorted anti-socialist scientific programme that would allow them to march onto the stage.[47]

It appears that 'plotting restoration of bourgeois sociology' was Pan's main crime, even though Sociology Departments were not restored in the universities until after the Cultural Revolution ended.

Wu Wenzao's wife was the noted May Fourth Era writer Bing Xin. She had studied at Yenching University and met Wu while travelling by ship to study in the United States. While in the US, Bing Xin wrote her book *To Young Readers* in a sincere, lucid and elegant style that has enchanted countless young people. In 1957, Bing Xin's husband, son and younger brother were all labelled Rightists.

Rightists were divided into six categories receiving different grades of punishment, which ensured that punishments would be carried out smoothly, because acceptance allowed people to avoid imprisonment. In order to protect themselves, some Rightists exposed others, and confessions and mutual recriminations were regularly published in the *People's Daily*. This method effectively dissolved potential alliances and destroyed integrity. Rightists stripped of their jobs and facing reform through labour now also lost their dignity and honour – the last bastions of morality in any society.

This round of self-criticisms and confessions concluded without anyone questioning the legitimacy of designating individuals as Rightists, much less challenging the movement itself. This was yet another instance of 'submission' and 'surrender' by China's intellectuals. Although unprecedented in its scale and degree of persecution, the Anti-Rightist Campaign was not as appalling as the Cultural Revolution that followed. Those accused of 'open conspiracy' in the Anti-Rightist Campaign at least had an opportunity to speak their views; subsequently, even this was lost as the Cultural Revolution took the initiative to attack and purge those who had never criticised it.

After the Anti-Rightist Campaign, the status of intellectuals further deteriorated. Peking University chemistry professor Fu Ying had been considered a model of 'thought reform' in 1952, and had delivered speeches as a 'model of progressiveness' during the university's rallies. In 1957 he was designated a 'moderate Rightist', making him the standard against which those designated Rightists were judged. With the arrival

---

[47] 'A Comprehensive Analysis of Fei Xiaotong's Reactionary Activities', *People's Daily*, 19 August 1957.

of the Cultural Revolution, Fu was struggled, imprisoned and sent to labour reform. Professor Fu Ying's example illustrates how as one group after another was routed in successive political campaigns, those who survived descended further down the slippery slope towards annihilation as 'class enemies'.

The Anti-Rightist Campaign was followed in 1958 by the communisation movement and the Great Leap Forward. The activities of intellectuals who were not labelled Rightists are exemplified by US-educated rocket scientist Qian Xuesen,[48] who in 1958 published an article stating:

> If 30% of the solar power that shines on one *mu*[49] of cropland can be put to use by plants, and the plants can use this portion of solar power to convert the moisture and carbon dioxide in the air into nutrients to feed themselves and develop and grow strong, and if only one-fifth of this becomes edible crops, then the grain yield of one *mu* of rice paddy would not be the mere 1,000 kilos or 1,500 kilos we see at present, but rather twenty times that amount![50]

Qian Xuesen later published similar views as president of the Chinese Society of Theoretical and Applied Mechanics in the magazine *Knowledge is Power*, saying that grain yields of 19,500 kilos per *mu* should be possible, and that ventilation of the densely packed crops could be solved through hydromechanics. In September that year, the *People's Daily* reported a (wildly exaggerated) yield of 65,000 kilos per *mu* in Guangxi's Huanjiang County.

Qian Xuesen's essays seem ludicrous to present-day readers, but set against their historical backdrop, they inspire considerably less levity. Qian's participation in the arms industry accorded him much better treatment than most other intellectuals, but these essays show the surrender of science to power and the submission of common sense to arrant fallacy.

Ma Yinchu (1882–1982) came under attack around this time for advocating a reduction of China's population. Ma obtained a PhD in Economics at Columbia University in 1914, and after returning to China he served as a university president and legislator under the Kuomintang government. After harshly criticising the Chiang Kai-shek regime during a lecture in 1940, Ma was briefly imprisoned and became known as a hero of the anti-Chiang

---

[48] TN: Aka Tsien Hsue-shen, b. 1911, Qian obtained his PhD from the California Institute of Technology.
[49] TN: There are fifteen *mu* in one hectare, or slightly more than six *mu* in one acre.
[50] Qian Xuesen, 'How high will grain yields be?', *Zhongguo Qingnianbao* (*China Youth Daily*), 16 June 1958, p. 4.

opposition. Under the new Communist regime, he was named president of Peking University in 1950.

The *Education Chronicle of the People's Republic of China 1949–1982* states that it was Ma Yinchu who launched the Thought Reform Campaign among Peking University's instructors in September 1951.⁵¹ A campaign initiated by Mao and Zhou Enlai cannot be attributed to Ma Yinchu, but it's true that he was exceedingly co-operative and enthusiastic at the time. I earlier described how in 1952 Ma had put pressure on Zhu Guangqian and Zhou Binglin to carry out repeated self-criticisms. In July 1955, he convened an administrative work conference to discuss 'eliminating the problem of all hidden counter-revolutionaries' at Peking University as part of that year's nationwide Campaign to Eliminate Counter-Revolutionaries. Ma had been an impetus rather than a target of the series of campaigns since 1950. Even so, he soon found himself in the same situation as the people he had victimised.

The Party leadership first organised attacks against Ma in 1958 through articles in Party newspapers attacking his theories, and big-character posters went up all over Peking University, including the walls of Ma's residence at No. 36 Yannan Yuan. Ma's remarks that the Chinese were under-educated, lacked a cultural life and had too many offspring were hauled out as 'vilification of the working people'. On 31 March 1960, Education Minister Yang Xiufeng sent Peking University a resolution from the State Council's 28 March meeting: accept president Ma Yinchu's resignation and appoint the secretary of the university Party Committee, Lu Ping, in his place. Ma's dismissal brought an end to the era in which professors served as the presidents of China's universities.

Ma moved off campus, and the government provided him with a residence in Dongzongbu Hutong in Beijing's Dongcheng District. That *hutong* contained a number of dwellings left over from the old days, and someone who once visited Ma said, 'Ma's house is huge; one room follows another, and going through them is like entering a maze.'⁵² Ma's home was hardly as large as all that, but was undoubtedly vastly superior to the cramped, meager lodgings of other Beijing scholars and ordinary residents at the time.

Ma lived to see the end of the Cultural Revolution and the victory of his population control theories. Prior to his rehabilitation, he delivered none of the vitriolic protests against the authorities that he had made against their

---

⁵¹ *Education Chronicle of the People's Republic of China 1949–1982*, Kexue jiaoyu chubanshe, Beijing, 1983, p. 48.
⁵² Shen Ning, 'Second Uncle also lives in Dongzongbu Hutong', *World Daily* (*Shijie ribao*), 1 August 2001, D15.

predecessors in the 1940s. It is said that he used *qigong* breathing exercises to survive ransackings and beatings by Red Guards during the Cultural Revolution. Ma's decision to adopt forbearance instead of protest probably reflected not so much a change of character but rather his understanding that times had changed since his earlier arrest by the Kuomintang. The reality was that if he had voiced any protest, not a single newspaper would have published it; he might have been arrested and disappeared for decades like Hu Feng,[53] or perhaps even have been beaten to death in public by Red Guards. No one would have come forward to defend him, nor would he have been popularly extolled as a hero or martyr.

Compared to those who shift with the winds and pander to those in power, Ma's forbearance and silence could be considered a form of resistance, but his refusal to voice any further criticism was also a kind of submission. Some have said that Ma opposed the KMT government not because he was all that courageous, but because that government was not as ruthless and cruel; an era without protest is more brutal than one in which protest is rife.

This kind of comment could be seen as a severe criticism of people such as Ma Yinchu, but it could also serve in their defence, because otherwise one might wonder what principles guided Ma's life, or whether he had any at all. In this explanation, it was the unprecedented cruelty of the regime that prevented his protesting a second time, not the inducement of a large and comfortable home that caused him to surrender his right and power to resist.

From the perspective of 'knowledge', grain yields and population growth figures are items that can be calculated with crystal clearness. Maintaining that grain yields can reach 5,000 kilos or that birth control cannot be practised therefore represents not only the surrender and submission of experts, but also the ushering of knowledge onto a path of destruction.

When even numerically calculable hard fact can be flatly rejected, sociology and the humanities are left with even less of a leg to stand on. Pan Guangdan was a prolific and wide-ranging author. In 1922 he had written a book, *Feng Xiaoqing*, that psychoanalysed the narcissism of Chinese women. It was the first work by a Chinese scholar to apply Freudian theory to the Chinese psyche and traditional literature. Although short, this book was highly innovative. Pan subsequently researched eugenics and made an annotated translation of Henry Havelock Ellis's *Psychology of Sex*, only to have his research negated.

---

[53] TN: Hu Feng (1902–1985), a writer and literary theorist, criticised Mao's politicised vision of art and literature. He was arrested as a counter-revolutionary in 1955 and was not released until 1979.

As a Rightist, Pan was no longer allowed to write or publish anything. At that time, it was explicitly stipulated that names to which a Rightist cap had been attached could not appear in any publications, even in the sciences, much less in the social sciences or humanities. After Ma Mingqiang, a professor of mathematics at the Beijing Institute of Construction, was labelled a Rightist, he published books on mathematics under someone else's name. Since Pan Guangdan was unable to publish his own research papers, he began to translate, as he had a high standard of both English and Chinese. He began with Darwin's masterwork *The Descent of Man*, with the help of his son-in-law Hu Shouwen. This monumental task was basically completed by the time the Cultural Revolution began.

After 1958 came the Great Famine. Rightists who had been sent to labour camps found the effects of hard labour compounded by hunger, and many lost their health and even their lives. Pan Guangdan was more fortunate; he had been allowed to remain in academia rather than being sent to labour in the Great Northern Wilderness. His two daughters also had the privilege of working at Peking University.

The famine worsened, and by 1960 even many people at the universities were suffering from oedema due to malnutrition. The universities were obliged to suspend physical education classes, and students were allowed rest periods. Masses of peasants, the producers of China's food, starved to death, and China's steadily increasing population suddenly experienced a deficit. Ultimately, tens of millions of people starved to death.[54] When Ma Yinchu was criticised, he was accused of opposing Marxism in the same way as Thomas Malthus, whose 1798 *Essay on the Principle of Population* stated that human populations invariably exceed the subsistence level, and that only famine and war reduce population. In order to criticise Ma Yinchu's advocacy of population control, Malthus's theories were also criticised as advocating war and famine as means of reducing population. The tragic irony is that following population growth in the 1950s, China did in fact experience a famine that substantially reduced the population, just as Malthus would have predicted.

Food allocation became a major issue. The top leaders set a policy allowing higher-ranking teachers special provisions of soya beans and other foodstuffs. In Guangdong in October 1961, the leader of the Central Committee's South Central Bureau, Tao Zhu, directed that 2,000 instructors at the level of assistant professor and above be provided with half a kilo of subsidised cooking oil and five kilos of grain each month. Two hundred of those 2,000 instructors were selected to receive remuneration

---

[54] TN: See Yang Jisheng, *Tombstone: The Great Chinese Famine 1958–1962* (Stacy Mosher and Guo Jian trans.), Farrar, Straus and Giroux, 2012.

equivalent to that of a departmental grade cadre.[55] At that time, it seemed, 'intellectuals' were shown some respect, and they made no complaint. It could be that hunger discouraged people from thinking too much about why being allowed a little soya or half a kilo of oil should have become a form of grace. Control of the individual through starvation and food supply further stifled the acuity and vitality of academic thought.

Pan Guangdan's Rightist 'cap' was removed in December 1959. The removing of caps had a set procedure: the leadership would first notify the individual concerned, saying that he or she had made progress in acknowledging and correcting error, and that removal of the cap was being considered. That person then had to write a detailed summary of his or her thinking that included self-criticism, admission of error and expression of gratitude towards the magnanimity of the Party and the people. The authorities would then authorise removal of the cap. This was the process required for a temporary reprieve from the gaping maw of the purging mechanism, and Pan Guangdan is certain to have followed it to the letter. What is laudable is that he was always fully conscious of his submission and surrender, and that in the end he had the courage to acknowledge it. He never deceived anyone, including himself.

The Cultural Revolution and the Fourth S: Succumb

When the Cultural Revolution began, one of the categories Mao designated for attack was 'bourgeois reactionary academic authorities', which included scholars such as Pan Guangdan.

Nearly every professor, assistant professor, or engineer or scientist of equivalent rank was 'struggled' during the Cultural Revolution. They were 'ferreted out' in big-character posters, made to wear dunce caps and carry placards around their necks, marched through the streets and made to kneel for extended periods, imprisoned, and sometimes beaten to death. They were forced to 'confess' and 'mitigate', write self-criticisms and 'debriefings'; they had to sing out 'I am an ox demon and snake spirit,' and then express gratitude for the 'magnanimity' and 'salvation' bestowed on them by Mao and the Party. This continued on an unprecedented scale from 1966 to 1970.

One of the Cultural Revolution's popular slogans was 'If the enemy does not surrender, he will be destroyed,' reportedly devised by the Soviet writer Maxim Gorky during Stalin's Great Terror of the

---

[55] Quoted in Lu Jiandong, *Chen Yinke's Last 20 Years*, Beijing sanlian shudian, 1995, p. 342.

1930s.[56] During China's Cultural Revolution, however, even those who surrendered often succumbed to brutal persecution.

Before the Cultural Revolution, intellectuals submitted and surrendered under pressure. During the Cultural Revolution, being *allowed* to submit and surrender became 'special treatment' accorded to a fortunate and tiny minority such as Guo Moruo. Almost all other writers were forced to undergo struggle during the Cultural Revolution on the basis of their earlier writings. No matter how often they declared their willingness to burn every word they'd ever written, they were still subjected to merciless criticism that sometimes lasted for years.

Campus violence became widespread in August 1966. Every school was under the control of student Red Guards, and each school established 'ox demon and snake spirit teams', also known as 'labour reform teams' or 'dictatorship teams'. As a 'de-capped Rightist' and a 'reactionary academic authority', Pan Guangdan inevitably ended up in a labour reform team.

Pan Guangdan's leg amputation required him to use crutches to get around, and by the summer of 1966, he was sixty-seven years old. Student Red Guards in charge of the labour reform teams regularly ordered 'ox demons and snake spirits' to pull weeds around a campus as a form of physical punishment; although ostensibly light work, it proved torturous in the blazing summer heat. It was also a means of putting the educators on public display and giving endless streams of revolutionary youth an opportunity to hurl insults at them. Squatting to pull weeds was impossible for Pan, but the Red Guard supervisors refused him permission to use a stool, and he was thus obliged to sit or lie on the ground as he laboured. Someone who witnessed this scene described to me the torment inflicted on the unfortunate old man.

Another interviewee, fifteen years old back then, told me of being taken to Minzu University to observe a struggle session against history professor Zhou Dafu. Those in charge of the struggle session ordered Zhou to say, 'I bow my head and confess my crimes to the masses.' Zhou followed the instructions, only to be rabidly thrashed as his tormenters accused him of having said he was bowing to the 'stupid pigs' – depending on a person's regional accent, the Chinese term for 'masses', *qunzhong*, could be indistinguishable from 'stupid pigs', *chunzhu*. My informant was never sure whether Zhou's accent caused him to be misunderstood, or if he was purposely venting his resentment of his tomenters. In any case, the horror and cruelty of the scene engraved itself on the

---

[56] Roy Medvedev, *Let History Judge*, p. 599. Published in a revised edition by Columbia University Press (George Shriver, trans.), 1989.

memory of my interviewee. Zhou Dafu, who had studied in India in the 1940s, was arrested as a 'suspected spy' in 1967 and remained imprisoned until 1973. His wife, Yang Qushu, who was on the administrative staff of Peking University's Russian Department, likewise spent six years in prison.

In 1995, I had a conversation with Pan Guangdan's son-in-law, Hu Shouwen, who by then had retired as professor of biology at Peking University. He told me about his personal experience.

Hu said that he was a thirty-year-old lecturer when the Cultural Revolution began. Peking University's first large-scale violent struggle session against 'reactionary gangs' occurred on 18 June 1966. A student tied a rope around Hu's neck, yanked him to the ground and dragged him around, and he only saved himself from strangulation by pulling as hard as he could with both hands and loosening the noose around his neck. In a later instance, students whipped him so hard with their belt buckles that he couldn't remove his shirt because the fabric was embedded in his flesh. His ears were boxed on a regular basis, and he was constantly pulled into multi-hour struggle sessions where the more fortunate targets were made to stand with heads bowed as criticisms were hurled at them, and the less fortunate had to 'fly the jet'. Anyone who lost their balance and fell was mercilessly beaten and kicked.

Some 90% of the Biology Department's older professors were struggled. One day, Zhao Yibing (mentioned above) quietly asked Hu Shouwen if he knew how to keep standing during struggle sessions, as he himself found it impossible. Hu advised Zhao to keep shifting his weight from one foot to the other. Later, when Hu himself was old, it occurred to him that Zhao Yibing would have been capable of thinking of this common-sense method himself. Zhao was over sixty at that time, while Hu was only in his thirties and could not fully appreciate the misery of an older person at these struggle sessions.

Pan Guangdan left no written record of his physical torment, but we can imagine how much worse the situation must have been for someone of his advanced age and physical impairment.

Few of those who survived the torments of the Cultural Revolution have been willing to speak of it afterwards; the pain and humiliation were too unbearable to relive in the telling. Regardless of how much one 'confessed' and 'self-criticised', this physical and mental torment was unavoidable. One interviewee told me that he changed the old saying 'A gentleman prefers death to humiliation' to 'A gentleman prefers humiliation to death', and made it his daily mantra. No matter how he was humiliated, he bore and submitted to it, kneeling or crawling, even cursing himself if so ordered. That is how he endured.

Even with forbearance and submission, many people died of persecution. This is the fourth S Pan Guangdan spoke of – succumbing, to death. It is not metaphor or hyperbole but cold, hard fact. Nothing is as merciless and irreversible as death.

Tragically, Pan Guangdan's treatment was not even the worst suffered in that summer of 1966. As a university instructor, Pan wasn't beaten to death by student Red Guards like his fellow educators in the secondary schools. The 'revolutionary masses' in universities and research institutes didn't dare come out and straightforwardly kill people. Persecution and humiliation nevertheless took their toll in China's higher seats of learning. Pan Guangdan's home was ransacked by Red Guards and sealed off, allowing him only a small room off the kitchen to sleep in. He was forced to attend labour reform every day, with no leniency shown for his infirmity. The exposure of sitting on the ground resulted in a bladder inflammation for which he was allowed no treatment, even when it became serious. Pan died in June 1967, after toiling for ten months on Minzu University's labour reform team.

Pan had three daughters. One was in the United States, and Pan had not seen her for years. One of his sons-in-law, **Cheng Xiance**, employed at Peking University, killed himself on 2 September 1966, after undergoing three months of struggle (see the Peking University section later in this part). Another daughter and her husband were imprisoned for long periods because of 'current counter-revolutionary' activities that consisted entirely of conversations between the two of them.

After Pan died, his home was confiscated. His daughter was given permission to collect his belongings, and in one of the sealed rooms she found the rotting manuscript of his translation of Darwin's *The Descent of Man*. She secretly took it with her, and six years after the Cultural Revolution ended, the manuscript was published. It is one of the finest Chinese translations of a Western classic.

Before his death, Pan Guangdan poured out his heart to his old friend, using the four S's of surrender, submit, survive and succumb to describe the last half of his life. Beginning in 1951, he had repeatedly made use of the first three, constantly submitting and surrendering, until he was ultimately destroyed. For him, the final S brought the first three to an end.

After Pan Guangdan's Death

Pan Guangdan died in the second year of the Cultural Revolution, and the mass persecution continued. The Cleansing of the Class Ranks, which began in 1968, was the longest stage of the Cultural Revolution, as well as being the largest in scale and the cause of the greatest number of deaths.

The establishment of 'ox pens' in every work unit began in 1966, and by 1968, all work units in China had these formal detention facilities for what was known as 'isolation and investigation'. Instructors from Peking University told me that a 'reform supervision compound for ox demons and snake spirits' was set up near the university's western gate in May 1968. More than 200 instructors, cadres and students were held there over the course of ten months, with many instances of violent physical abuse and mental torment, but no protest was raised throughout that time. Under Mao's meticulous direction of the Cleansing of the Class Ranks, the only action open to detainees was to fervently deny the 'past problems' or other 'counter-revolutionary crimes' of which they were accused.

On 18 June 1968, the 'ox demons and snake spirits' held in the 'reform supervision compound' were ordered to file out as people on either side beat them with rods and whips. After this flogging, the prisoners were divided among their various departments for further punishment, and the entire campus descended into a blood-soaked frenzy. This activity was a 'celebration' commemorating the day exactly two years before, when the first large-scale violence on the Peking University campus was extolled by Mao and the Cultural Revolution Group as a 'revolutionary incident'.

Chemistry professor Fu Ying was one of those held in the 'reform supervision compound'. In 1952 he had been proclaimed a 'model of teacher thought reform' and in 1957 he had been designated a 'moderate Rightist'. Once the Cultural Revolution began, however, all professors who shared his background and experience were rounded up for attack; all professors and assistant professors at Peking University, without exception, had cases 'filed for investigation and prosecution'.

The 'reform supervision compound' was overseen by a female university student who carried a cudgel for 'beating miscreants'. After every evening roll call, this student beat Cen Dianhua, deputy director of the Asian Languages Department, to force her to admit to having taken part in the Three People's Principles Youth Corps, a Kuomintang youth organisation, prior to the Revolution. Cen resolutely denied having done so. Observing the situation, Fu Ying remarked that on the scale of pre-liberation counter-revolutionary acts, this constituted merely a 'routine' offence, so Cen's insistent denial was probably true. Fu's logical inference was clear and consistent with his professional training, but when reported to those above, it resulted in him being beaten as well.

The aforementioned Zhu Guangqian, a target of the 1952 Thought Reform Campaign at Peking University, came under even harsher attack fourteen years later. While undergoing labour reform in summer 1966, his head was shaved, and he was forced to pick up melon rinds in front of a small shop near the student dormitories, where he was constantly insulted and beaten by Red Guards who had come to the university to 'network' and gain 'revolutionary experience'. The wife of a Peking University professor recalled once seeing what appeared to be a dead pig lying along a campus wall. Upon drawing closer, she saw it was professor Zhu, beaten into unconsciousness. Two other interviewees remembered seeing him beaten while he was in the 'reform supervision compound' in 1968.

I described earlier how 'model rallies' were used to drive the Loyalty and Honesty Campaign. This method was employed to extreme ends during the Cultural Revolution, with even greater violence and brutality. Peking University Chinese Department professor Zhang Tingqian (1901–1981) was accused of once serving as a member of a local Kuomintang Party Committee. By the prevailing standards, this put him on the threshold of 'pre-liberation counter-revolutionary activity'. Zhang steadfastly denied it, as a result of which he was labelled a 'model' for 'harsh treatment'. Zhu was presented to the entire student body and faculty in a 'leniency and severity rally' on the university's eastern sports field, after which was handcuffed and taken away in a police vehicle.

Zhang Tingqian was a native of Shaoxing, like the writer Lu Xun, who was also his teacher and friend. Zhang graduated from Peking University in 1922, and taking the pen name Chuan Dao, he took part in publishing and editing *Yusi (Word Thread) Magazine*. During the Cultural Revolution, his family shared in his persecution: his wife went mad, and his son, **Zhang Xiaonong**, committed suicide at the age of twenty.

Another professor from the Chinese Department, Lin Tao, told me that a few days before Zhang Tingqian was led away in handcuffs, struggle targets were assembled in one of the university buildings for campaign purposes, but were still allowed to return home at night. One evening while they were walking home together, Zhang said to Lin, 'It's so vexing. They insist that I was a KMT party branch member at Associated [referring to Southwestern Associated University, which was set up in Kunming during the War of Resistance against Japan]. I never was – all I did was attend a dinner, and they call that being a party member. Feng Youlan got it wrong.'

Lin Tao described how the 'leniency and severity rally' against Zhang Tingqian was conducted with maximum dramatic effect and horror. The leader of the rally led the thousands of participants in shouting out a quotation from Mao: 'If you fail to attack every reactionary thing, it won't be beaten, just as if you don't sweep, the dirt won't run away by itself.' After this, the Workers' and People's Liberation Army Mao Zedong Thought Propaganda Team leader mounted the stage and shouted through the loudspeaker: 'Are there any counter-revolutionaries within our ranks?' After a short pause, he shouted, 'There are!' He then announced, 'Drag Zhang Tingqian up here!' and henchmen concealed among the crowd dragged Zhang to the stage. After the Propaganda Team leader read out Zhang's record, Zhang was placed in handcuffs and taken away.

Right up until the Cultural Revolution ended, Lin Tao never knew whether the men who handcuffed Zhang Tingqian were public security officers or had come from some other 'organ of dictatorship', nor did he know whether the vehicle took Zhang to prison, a detention centre or some other place. What is quite clear is that this very uncertainty was what lent such horror to the proceedings. There is comfort in knowing that one has access to a trial with normal legal procedures; mysterious and ambiguous authority is vastly more intimidating. The leaders of the Cultural Revolution acted on this knowledge to create an atmosphere of terror.

Under these conditions, Lin Tao was compelled to confess to participating in a KMT espionage organisation, and to taking part in a plot to blow up the water tower along Wuming Lake. He confessed after being told that his college classmate had already admitted to it, and that if he didn't confess, he would be treated with even greater severity. In fact, there was no truth to the allegation. As a professor of phonology, Lin would hardly know how to blow up the water tower, which remains one of the most scenic spots on the Peking University campus. While this trumped-up conspiracy is now forgotten, it brought a whole group of people to the brink of death. Lin's old classmate confessed to the plot because he was being beaten so severely that this absurd admission seemed the only way to bring his torments to an end, and he intended to explain later that the admission had been extracted under torture. He was never given the opportunity to exonerate himself, however, and his confession resulted in several friends and classmates being terrorised into a similar admission.

Traditional Chinese moral education puts the greatest emphasis on dignity, honesty and friendship. Although ethical standards varied among individuals, all in this generation of intellectuals would have received such an education. When people were constantly forced to 'expose' each other during the Cultural Revolution, the process of mutual implication not only put personal safety at risk, but also forced people to abandon and destroy their lifelong moral precepts. The loss of even a basic assurance of personal preservation led to an ethical capitulation in which injury and distortion of a person's moral character could be overlooked or forgotten altogether.

Looking back on these mutual betrayals stirs feelings of dismay. Even more regrettable, however, would be allowing these inglorious episodes to turn us away from a re-examination of history. The individuals referred to as 'intellectuals' were not 'piles of dog shit' as they were accused of being in the Cultural Revolution, but neither were they the steadfast heroes depicted in post-Cultural Revolution fiction. As a person suffers physically under the thrashings of brass belt buckles, fists, feet and cudgels, his spirit and morality will also be vanquished and twisted by those in power. All people have weaknesses, including so-called intellectuals, and their fragility was if anything highlighted by their persecution and abuse under the state apparatus. It is futile to hope for people to be impervious to gun and knife; the best we can do is glean some kind of truth from history and use it to establish a system under which human flesh is no longer obliged to withstand the cold, hard steel of autocracy.

After nearly a year of 'investigations' that suspended people between life and death, in November 1968 Mao directed that intellectuals be 'given a way out', implying that mercy should be extended to those declared to be on a 'dead end road'. Mao particularly instructed that Peking University philosophy professor Feng Youlan and history professor **Jian Bozan** be 'looked after' for use as 'negative examples'. At that time, Mao's words were referred to as 'directives from the highest authority'. The head of Peking University's propaganda team headquarters immediately went to the 'reform supervision compound' to announce Feng Youlan's release and told him to go home. Jian Bozan was released at the same time, and it was declared that Feng and Jian would be given living allowances of 125 *yuan* and 120 *yuan* per month, respectively (at the time the average monthly wage was around 40 *yuan*). Others, however, remained incarcerated in the 'reform supervision compound'. A month after receiving 'preferential treatment' under Mao's directive, on the evening of 18 December, Jian Bozan and his wife, **Dai Shuwan**, took overdoses of sleeping pills in their home at Peking University's Yannan Yuan. (For more on Jian and Dai, see the Peking University section in Part Five.)

I located the transcript of 'A Speech to Pass Along Experience by Comrade Hu Jianzhong of the Mao Zedong Thought Propaganda Team of the Capital Workers' Liberation Army Stationed at Tsinghua University', delivered on 12 March 1969, and distributed in written form to all work units. The title indicates that this speech was meant for the entire country to follow. One section of the transcript reads as follows:

> Regarding the issue of reactionary academic authorities, this is a policy issue relating to high-level intellectuals. Liang Sicheng[57]

---

[57] TN: 1901–1972, second son of Liang Qichai, and an architect and authority on the history of Chinese architecture.

was a First Class professor at Tsinghua who became famous for developing large roofs. During the Cultural Revolution he was attacked and made to stand aside, and was expelled from his home. Liu Xianzhou was a researcher of mechanics. He wrote a book and was an authority on wood and stone. Qian Weichang was a disgusting person who was designated a Rightist in 1957 but later had his cap removed. Before 1957 he managed seven postings simultaneously, including People's Congress delegate and vice-president and professor at Tsinghua, but eventually he was removed from all of them and was demoted from First Class to Third Class professor. In the past, people referred to the 'three Qians' [i.e. Qian Sanqiang, Qian Xuesen and Qian Weichang] who carried out missile research in the United States. Regarding all these people, the first word is 'criticise', as in 'criticise deeply, criticise thoroughly, criticise until they are toppled and disgraced.' But disgrace is not the only objective; even more important is to teach the masses and to purge the toxic influence.

'Criticise deeply, criticise thoroughly, criticise until they are toppled and disgraced' – this was not only classic Cultural Revolution language, but was also the way the revolution was actually conducted. This criticism was not merely carried out verbally and in writing; the psychological attacks were accompanied by brute force. A Tsinghua University instructor in architecture, Tao Dejian, wrote in her 1990 autobiography about how Liang Sicheng was struggled and criticised:

> Mr Liang suffered from chronic pulmonary emphysema, and it had become so serious that he could no longer rise from his bed, and had to be brought over on a flat-board cargo tricycle. At the struggle session, he lay curled up on the tricycle, and I stood beside him as the secondary target. I could hear his every gasping breath, and his entire body trembled. Hearing his panting growing louder and heavier, I felt my own lungs about to burst. But no one paid any attention, and those who were criticising him just kept on as if nothing were happening, even though only their shouted slogans could cover the sound of Mr Liang's gasps. I shared his discomfort, and time seemed to crawl until the session finally ended and Mr Liang was taken away on the tricycle.[58]

---

[58] Tao's autobiography, *A Storm-filled Life*, was posted on the Wuliu Village website of her husband, Tao Shilong.

Sadder yet is that compared with other scholars, Liang Sicheng's dire situation was by no means the worst, not to mention the fact that his persecution took place in public, where others could see it; the abuse and humiliation inflicted behind closed doors on those who did not survive to tell of it will never be known. It is not hard to imagine the effect of these public spectacles on observers. The most direct result was that no one dared sympathise with the person being struggled, much less openly criticise the persecution.

At the time that the Mao Zedong Thought Propaganda Team presented this report, the Cultural Revolution had been going on for three years, during which classes had been suspended at all universities, and many teachers had been persecuted to death. In October of that year, nearly all of China's universities were moved from their original urban locations to the countryside, where they continued with the 'One Strike and Three Antis' campaign and investigation of the 'May 16 Clique' (see Part Six). Instructors from Tsinghua and Peking Universities were banished to Liyuzhou, Jiangxi Province, where they were required to cultivate marshland and build houses in a region plagued with schistosomiasis (snail fever).

What is very clear is that engineering and science professors such as Liang Sicheng, Liu Xianzhou and Qian Weichang, and humanities and social sciences professors such as Pan Guangdan each had their own experience, strengths and weaknesses, but as a group they represented modern Chinese scholarship. This modern scholarship was closely bound with Western scholarship, and these scholars had studied in Western universities. One of the objectives of the Cultural Revolution was to criticise them until they were 'toppled and disgraced' as a means of striking down modern scholarship imported from the West.

The other professor 'given a way out' by Mao, Feng Youlan, was eventually recruited into the Cultural Revolution leadership's Liang Xiao ('Two Schools') writing group. (*Liang Xiao* referred to Tsinghua and Peking universities.) During the Campaign to Criticise Confucius and Lin Biao beginning in 1973, the Liang Xiao group published many essays attacking Confucius and Confucian scholars and praising their philosophical rivals, the Legalists. It's difficult for modern readers to see the point of essays about the Confucian-Legalist rivalry two thousand years before. When the Liang Xiao group fell out of favour after the Cultural Revolution, these essays were explained away as nothing more than following the Gang of Four's orders to attack Zhou Enlai by innuendo. At that time, however, people understood that the main idea behind these essays was to affirm the Cultural Revolution and its cruelty, and to establish a theory to back its persecution and brutality. It is for this reason that the Liang Xiao group repudiated, at tedious length, the Confucian concept of *ren*, or benevolence, while highlighting that Confucius himself had killed Shao Zheng Mao.[59] They didn't suggest that the killing exposed Confucius as a hypocrite, but rather that it demonstrated that *ren* was fundamentally unattainable, and that this world was inevitably filled with 'struggle' and 'dictatorship'.

Soon after Mao died in 1976, Jiang Qing was arrested along with the other members of the Gang of Four. After the arrests, a rumour circulated in Beijing and elsewhere that Feng Youlan's wife had scolded him with the words 'It's almost daybreak and you've pissed the bed.' The meaning of these words was quite clear: Feng played his ignominious role just as the dark night of the Cultural Revolution was ending. This vivid quote has never risen above the status of rumour, but if Feng's wife never said it, some like-minded individual no doubt came up with the story, which was so entertaining that it spread far and wide. Not everyone laughed at the time, however. Some pointed out that if the Gang of Four had been better at rallying support, they would have had little difficulty enlisting even more scholars of Feng's calibre; quite a few people would have been glad to change places with him.

Mao's death brought an end to the Cultural Revolution. This was followed by the rehabilitation of many people and the rectification of numerous wrongful judgments, and later yet by the emergence and establishment of myths about the Cultural Revolution. Various roles were manufactured, from loyal subordinate to treacherous courtier, from hero to hussy, with a series of ups and downs culminating in a happy ending. Absent from these recollections and narratives, however, were those who had submitted and surrendered. One of the most trenchant ironies is how fictional works inevitably rewrote 'intellectuals' as heroes of resistance, or at the very least as people who remained pure and honest during the Cultural Revolution era. In seeking historical truth, it is not enough to focus on how during the 1980s the horrors of the Cultural Revolution were reduced and simplified to 'the struggle against the two anti-Party cliques of Lin Biao and the Gang of Four.' Equally important is to note how its victims were likewise simplified.

The Cultural Revolution presents three great difficulties: gaining a clear record of fact, obtaining fair legal judgment, and carrying out an in-depth examination of its moral implications.

---

[59] TN: Scholars are largely doubtful that this incident, related solely by Confucian scholar Xun Zi (312–230 BCE) and uncorroborated by other sources, ever occurred. According to Xun Zi, Confucius ordered the killing of Shao Zheng Mao, a government official and scholar, because Shao on three occasions incited Confucius's students to abandon his classes.

Intellectuals submitted and surrendered because they had no choice in the matter. Putting ourselves in their position, would we have been able to do otherwise? Would we have been better people? Answering these questions honestly is very difficult. Few of us could withstand that kind of mental and material deprivation, that kind of humiliation and violence.

Nevertheless, as a generation they are not above reproach. They were nurtured under the May Fourth Movement's spirit of science and democracy, unlike the generation that came of age after 1949, who had no access to the resources of modern thought – a generation that mistook 'liberalism' for what Mao criticised in his essay 'Against Liberalism' as 'saying nothing up front but gossiping behind people's backs'; a generation that used all kinds of ration coupons but never a ballot. Indeed, many in this post-'49 generation didn't even know that elsewhere in the world there were countries in which leaders were freely elected by the general populace. Pan Guangdan's generation knew this, however; they knew there were other choices, other social theories and practices.

Even so, after the Cultural Revolution, when the status of 'intellectuals' had been restored to a considerable degree, hardly any among them engaged in in-depth reflection on their lives. In his Author's Preface to *The Hall of Three Pines*, Feng Youlan quotes a phrase from the *Yi Jing* (*Book of Changes*), 'attention to words and establishing sincerity', and says that during the Cultural Revolution, his participation in criticising Confucius violated the principle of sincerity. This is a rare instance of self-reflection, but his recounting is ambiguous and obfuscates what happened and why. In this respect, the younger generation has been let down by their elders. In comparison, Pan Guangdan takes on the colours of a tragic hero. Towards the end, he had an opportunity to express to his old friend what he thought of his own life. He had no ability to change that life, but he expressed his views with a measure of honesty that embodied his spirit of seeking truth.

Conclusion: Hu Shih's prediction

Looking back on the experience of a generation of scholars and the misfortune they encountered makes for heavy and depressing reading.

In the process of writing this chapter, I recalled reading an essay in English by Hu Shih, the Introduction to Liu Shaw-tong's *Out of Red China*.[60]

---

[60] Liu Shaw-tong, *Out of Red China*, New York, Duell, Sloan and Pearce, 1953.

The author of this book, who left mainland China in 1950, describes his experience during the Clean Break with the Past Campaign in Lin Biao's army. Unable to bear this campaign, which called for a 'clean break' with family, the 'old society' and 'old thinking', Liu Shaw-tong found a way to flee the mainland for Hong Kong. In his book he writes, 'A red net is tightening around us.'

In his Introduction, Hu Shih quotes this expression of a tightening 'red net'. He also quotes Jin Yuelin's self-criticism published in the *People's Daily* during the Thought Reform Campaign: 'Two years of study, especially concentrated study of "On Practice,"[61] led me to recognise dialectical materialism as a scientific philosophy, and as truth... I now recognise that the main task of university Philosophy Departments is to foster propagandists of Marxism–Leninism.'[62]

At the end of his Introduction, Hu Shih expresses his deep concern for Jin's fate, and comments, 'A dark era of oppression has begun.'

Hu Shih died in 1962, before he could experience the Cultural Revolution, before he could see how completely the red net tightened, or how the dark era of oppression he predicted would reach its apogee during that time. Hu Shih's observation and prediction were unfortunately all too accurate.

As a reader from a future time, I was astonished when I first read Hu Shih's words. How did he know?

Hu Shih's prescience might be traced back to his recalling how two thousand years ago, the First Emperor, Qin Shihuang, had 'burned books and buried scholars' and 'made officials into teachers'. What happened after 1949 was very similar. The difference was that the scale of persecution during the Cultural Revolution was much greater than that under the Qin Emperor.

Hu Shih may have known this also because he had seen something similar happen in Russia, where a large percentage of the people that Stalin sent to the Gulag Archipelago were so-called intellectuals.

The main reason Hu Shih knew this, however, was most likely that he understood the fundamental structure of the Chinese system, and the essence of the ideology that supported it. This structure and its underlying ideology made inevitable all that was to come. Mao's blueprint for social reform provided no place for free thought, for learning or for scholars. This disaster did not descend upon China by chance; its roots existed for a long time before being recognised by the majority of people.

---

[61] TN: A 1937 essay by Mao Zedong.
[62] Jin Yuelin, 'Criticising the Bourgeois Educational Thinking of My Idealism', *People's Daily*, 17 April 1952.

Hu Shih's Introduction shows that this kind of darkness and disaster can be predicted, and is not inevitable in all places and all times. That gives us cause for optimism when we look back on this history of terror and shame.

Pan Guangdan was not, of course, the only victim at Minzu University. **Fu Lehuan**, a professor of history, drowned himself in June 1966.

The symbolic beginning of the Cultural Revolution was when Jiang Qing went to Shanghai to organise essays criticising Wu Han's historical drama *Hai Rui Dismissed from Office*. The famous critical essay by Yao Wenyuan was published in November 1965, launching the persecution of historians earlier than in other sectors. Fu Lehuan was an expert in Qing history as well as deputy director of the university's History Department. After being attacked in big-character posters and struggle sessions he drowned himself in Beijing's Taoranting Park around the same time as the suicides of history professors **Wang Jian** at Peking University and **Li Pingxin** at Shanghai East China Normal University.

A historian of the older generation, Gu Jiegang, wrote in his journal on 20 June 1966, 'Went to Baixiang's yesterday and heard that Fu Lehuan, reading the newspaper's publication of Wu Han and Hu Shih's correspondence,[63] recalled that he had exchanged letters with Hu Shih, and fearing that he would be exposed, he killed himself. A meaningless death.'[64] This gives an idea of the psychological climate in Fu's circle at that time. Of course, Gu Jiegang's comment may have been coloured by the knowledge that keeping a journal was unsafe and that he needed to say the right thing in order to avoid being investigated. Gu Jiegang is one of the very few people who persisted in keeping a journal during the Cultural Revolution.

In addition to the sin of being a history professor, Fu Lehuan was also the nephew of Fu Sinian, a student leader at Peking University during the May Fourth Era who later became a historian and followed the Kuomintang government to Taiwan, where he served as president of National Taiwan University. This family relationship became an additional reason for attacking Fu Lehuan.

Zhang Dongsun, born in 1886, was a famous political scientist, philosopher and member of the China Democratic League. He headed the Philosophy Department at Yenching University in 1949, and after Yenching was disbanded, he became a professor of philosophy at Peking University.

---

[63] TN: The campaign against Wu Han included 'iron-clad evidence' of his relationship with the discredited liberal scholar Hu Shih in the form of letters between the two.
[64] *The Journals of Gu Jiegang*, Vol. 10, 1964–1067, p. 480.

Zhang's home was ransacked repeatedly in 1966 and 1967. He was arrested in January 1968 and locked up in Qincheng Prison on the outskirts of Beijing. He died in prison in 1973.

Three generations of Zhang Dongsun's family suffered the horrors of the Cultural Revolution.

Zhang Dongsun was eighty-two at the time of his arrest, and after he was seized, his family had no idea of his whearabouts for five years. It was not until the end of 1972 that they learned he was being held in Qincheng Prison.

Qincheng Prison incarcerated prominent people for non-criminal 'offences' – that is, it was a prison that operated outside the jurisdiction of law. Construction on the prison was completed in 1960, but it came into heavier use during the Cultural Revolution. Especially in 1968, this prison took in a large number of senior Party cadres, including the Public Security Ministry head who had been its supervisor before the Cultural Revolution. It also held a number of 'high-level intellectuals' such as Zhang Dongsun. People could be held there for extended periods without any recourse to legal procedure and without access to the courts. I once heard the former Vice-Minister of Civil Affairs, Liu Jingfan, and writer Chen Ming describe conditions at Qingcheng Prison, where both had been held for extended periods. People incarcerated there were subjected to physical and mental torture that differed from, but was just as vicious as, that inflicted in other jails. Prisons for ordinary people were overcrowded and forced inmates to engage in heavy physical labour. At Qincheng, prisoners were held in solitary confinement, going years without hearing another human voice or being allowed to exchange letters with their families.

At the same time that Zhang Dongsun was being arrested and sent to Qincheng Prison, so was his eldest son, Zhang Zongbing, a professor of biology at Peking University. Neither father nor son knew that the other was being held in the same prison. Zhang Zongbing had obtained his PhD at Cornell University, and after returning to China, he proposed the 'army-worm migration system' that helped China deal with armyworms and other insect pests. Described by his friends as absolutely brilliant, Zhang knew several foreign languages and was a gifted poet and artist and an eloquent speaker. Zhang Zongbing's wife, Liu Zhuoru, was on the staff of the library of the Chinese Academy of Sciences Institute of Zoology. After Zhang Zongbing was arrested, Liu Zhuoru was also denounced and struggled at her work unit and was handed over to the Haidian Public Security Bureau (PSB), where she was detained for nearly a year.

As in the case of his father, Zhang Zongbing's whereabouts were a mystery to his family for five years. By the time they were allowed to visit him in prison, he had become unhinged and was babbling incoherently.

He was finally released on medical parole and admitted to a psychiatric hospital, where he gradually regained his sanity. He was rehabilitated and allowed to return to work, and died of natural causes in 1988.

Zhang Dongsun had two other sons besides Zhang Zongbing. His youngest, **Zhang Zongying**, had started out studying chemistry in college but had switched to sociology. When sociology was abolished as a course of study in the early 1950s, he became an ordinary office worker in the purchasing department of the Tianjin Stationery Company. Zhang Zongying, forty-six years old, and his wife, **Lü Naipu**, poisoned themselves to death after being struggled in the early stages of the Cultural Revolution.

Zhang's second son, **Zhang Zongsui**, was a senior research fellow in the Mathematics Institute of the Chinese Academy of Sciences and had obtained a PhD in theoretical physics at Cambridge University, returning to China in 1953. Zhang Zongsui's educational background and academic status made him a target for attack as a 'reactionary academic authority'. He took an overdose of sleeping pills while locked up for 'investigation' by his work unit during the Cleansing of the Class Ranks in 1969.

A relative of Zhang Zongsui said he was a brilliant student who skipped several grades of secondary school, but also excessively bookish and ill-prepared for dealing with political campaigns. A former research fellow at the Mathematics Institute recalled that when newspapers began criticising Wu Han's *Hai Rui Dismissed from Office*, Zhang Zongsui commented, 'Why dig up dirt on Wu Han? Everyone's got a blot somewhere on their record.' This remark was reported to the Mathematics Institute as 'reactionary speech'. There was nothing wrong with what Zhang Zongsui said, but no one else dared to say it; it reflected a fundamental remove from grim reality. In any case, more experienced people than Zhang Zongsui had a hard time coping with the Cultural Revolution, so he was unlikely to emerge unscathed.

While studying in Europe, Zhang had written a dissertation at the University of Denmark's Institute of Theoretical Physics, headed by the famous physicist Nils Bohr. He had stayed in Bohr's home and become friends with his son. In 1962, the younger Bohr visited Beijing, bringing toys and silk stockings for Zhang's wife and children. Bohr asked if Zhang's family had enough clothes coupons, and Zhang, who took little notice of housekeeping matters, automatically said they had enough. Upon returning home and asking his wife, he found he was wrong, so the next day, he took some embroidered satin cushions to Bohr as a gift, and told him that in fact the family's clothes coupons were insufficient. This conversation was cited as evidence of 'illicit relations with a foreign country'.

Zhang Zongsui was struggled at a rally and locked up in the school for 'investigation'. Zhang tried to sneak out, only to be caught and struggled again. While locked up in the institute's 'ox pen', he was beaten by students until he 'cried out as pitifully as an old ox' according to the housekeeper of mathematician Xiong Qinglai.

Zhang Zongsui took an overdose of sleeping pills one weekend in 1969. His wife, Bao Kunduo, returned home from work and found him unconscious, and rushed him to the Beijing Medical School No. 3 Hospital. The director of the hospital said he couldn't treat Zhang without permission from a leader at the Academy of Sciences. The leader of the Mathematics Institute was unwilling to take responsibility and reported the matter to the workers' propaganda team, which was leading the academy at the time, but no one was available. The situation dragged on until Monday, by which time Zhang had died.

The Cultural Revolution deprived China of a brilliant and able person in the prime of life – it is a collective as well as a personal tragedy.

The persecution also affected the Zhang family's third generation.

Zhang Zongbing's son, Zhang Heci, a student at Beijing Normal College, joined with several classmates to form an association to write poetry and discuss politics in 1963. Their activities came to the attention of the PSB, and they were arrested. After being interrogated and jailed, Zhang Heci was sent to the Chadian Laogai Farm for re-education through labour for three years. By the time he'd completed his sentence, the Cultural Revolution had begun, and he was punished even more harshly as a 'counter-revolutionary'. He spent a total of sixteen years at the *laogai* ('reform through labour') farm.

Zhang Zongying's son, Zhang Youci, was a worker in Tianjin when the Cultural Revolution began. After his parents committed suicide in 1966, he was accused of 'attempting to avenge his parents' and other counter-revolutionary crimes and was sentenced to fifteen years in prison. Zhang Youci was rehabilitated and released in 1978 after more than a decade in prison.

So it was that during the Cultural Revolution, Zhang Dongsun died in prison, two of his sons committed suicide and the third suffered mental illness after imprisonment, while two of his grandsons spent long terms incarcerated.

This sounds like some kind of horror story, but the difference between a horror story and what happened to the Zhang family was not in the degree of the horror, but in the unrecorded factual details. The only inkling we gain of this time of horror is through phrases such as 'being arrested' (without legal process), 'secret imprisonment' (Qincheng Prison), 'being handed over by the masses to the public security organs', 'becoming mentally deranged', 'suicide', 're-education through labour' and 'sentencing for counter-revolutionary crimes'. To a great extent, the undisclosed details are even more effective as intimidation and deterrence to multitudes of other people.

Another difference is that a horror story usually involves a private grudge. While personal grievances might have figured in the deaths of individuals in the Zhang family, only the Cultural Revolution's objectives and methods, and the system from which it arose, could have wreaked such havoc on an entire family. The Cultural Revolution attacked 'bourgeois intellectuals' (according to Mao, intellectuals were bourgeois because their worldview was bourgeois), so Zhang Dongsun and his sons were all attacked. The Cultural Revolution attacked anyone who thought differently, so Zhang Dongsun's grandsons were persecuted. The Cultural Revolution closed off China from the rest of the world, so even victims with overseas connections could not escape but could only accept their punishment without a fight.

The horror the Zhang family experienced wasn't unique. Zhang Zongbing's colleague in the Biology Department at Peking University, **Chen Tongdu**, was also held in extremely high regard. While Zhang was in prison, Chen poisoned himself on 28 August 1968, after being investigated and tortured during the Cleansing of the Class Ranks. Two other professors in the university's Biology Department killed themselves that same year.

Because the total number of people attacked and killed during the Cultural Revolution has never been reported, and there is no public access to official files, ordinary people cannot easily grasp the scope of the suffering. But by understanding the effects on one family, we can gauge the extent of the violence and thereby make a basic assessment of the larger scenario of the Cultural Revolution.

The following were persecuted to death at universities during the early years of the Cultural Revolution.

BEIJING

Peking University

Wang Jian was the first person to commit suicide at Peking University after coming under attack in the Cultural Revolution. A fifty-year-old professor and vice-chairman of the History Department, Wang killed himself by drinking pesticide on 10 June 1966, after being denounced and attacked in big-character posters.

Wang was admitted to Tsinghua University in 1934, and after graduation he began researching his history of the Sui and Tang dynasties with the internationally renowned sinologist Chen Yinke, earning him a mention in the influential book *Chen Yinke's Last Twenty Years*. Wang Jian joined the CCP while at Peking University in 1950 before being promoted to professor, so he was not considered a 'bourgeois professor' before the Cultural Revolution.

In early June 1966, when the CCP Central Committee sent a 'work group' to Peking University to lead the Cultural Revolution in early June 1966, Wang Jian came under attack with other university and departmental administrators.

Students in the History Department put a big-character poster on Wang Jian's door, but the poster fell onto the floor and was torn. It's possible that the wind simply blew it off, but students accused Wang Jian of tearing up the poster and of resisting and sabotaging the Cultural Revolution. Wang Jian denied tearing up the poster, and when the work group ordered Wang to make a copy of the poster and replace it on his door, Wang Jian did what he was told and then killed himself.

Wang Jian lived on the second floor of an apartment block on campus. A professor who lived near him said that on that night, he heard muffled cries and thumping, followed by silence. He later learned that Wang Jian had locked himself in a room and drunk a large amount of dichlorvos (DDVP), a widely used pesticide that was lethal to humans in its undiluted form. Wang Jian pounded his head on the wall and cried out because he couldn't bear the pain caused by the poison. By the time someone was able to force open the door, he was past saving.

A teacher in the History Department said that Wang Jian was a clever and somewhat conceited man, and noted that others in the History Department had endured much more severe humiliation and torture than Wang had. This may seem rather cold-hearted and unsympathetic, but the truth is that at the time that Wang Jian killed himself, the work group in control of Peking University wasn't allowing physical violence. Half a month after Wang died, violent persecution at the university became much more serious, and other instructors in its History Department were harshly persecuted.

Professor **Xiang Da**, designated a Rightist in 1957, was one of the 'problematic' history teachers sent to the countryside to labour on 17 September 1966. The teachers were grouped according to the seriousness of their circumstances. The most problematic, including Xiang Da, were put into Group A. Two weeks later, the people in Group B were allowed a home visit, but not those in Group A. By then, Xiang Da had contracted uremia and and his legs hurt so much that he couldn't walk, but he wasn't allowed to see a doctor. In the latter half of October, when he was completely immobilised, he was sent back to the city, but it was too late to save him. Xiang Da died on 10 November.

Mao Zedong's daughter Li Na graduated from Peking University's History Department one year before the Cultural Revolution began. While at the school, she had been part of a 'work group' sent to Beijing's rural outskirts to lead the Socialist Education Movement. The school deployed special security personnel to attend to her every need. When examining and verifying the 'class status' of villagers, history teacher Hao Bin argued with Li Na over her suggestion of upgrading the statuses of several villagers (upgrading a person's class status to rich peasant or landlord could have calamitous consequences). It wasn't a serious dispute, but after the Cultural Revolution began, Mao's wife, Jiang Qing, gave a speech at a mass rally at Peking University on 26 July 1966, during which she accused Hao Bin of 'persecuting' her daughter. Hao Bin was labelled a 'current counter-revolutionary' and wasn't rehabilitated until 1977, after Mao died. Even relatives as far away as Shenyang and Inner Mongolia were dragged down with him.

Around the same time that Wang Jian died, in late June 1966, a young history professor, Yu Weichao, attempted suicide twice after a 'struggle rally'. The first time, he grabbed a high-voltage electrical wire, but the electrical current threw him off, and he only lost the index fingers of both hands in the process. In the second attempt, he lay down on the railway tracks near the Qinghuayuan train station, but the engineer saw him early enough to put on the breaks. Yu was thrown a considerable distance by the locomotive and seriously injured, but he survived. He continued to teach, and his class on Qin and Han dynasty archeology was very popular in the 1980s, but his students always noticed that he had to use his middle and ring fingers for writing and smoking.

In the early 1990s, Yu Weichao became director of the Chinese History Museum (now the National Museum of China). I once wrote to him asking about the Cultural Revolution, sending my letter to the museum, but he has never replied, nor has my letter been returned. Perhaps Yu doesn't want to cross the authorities by helping record the facts of the Cultural Revolution, or perhaps he doesn't want to revisit this painful time in his life; two suicide attempts suggest immense physical and mental suffering, and then he had to live through the rest of the Cultural Revolution with the evidence of his attempted suicides so obvious for all to see, another drawn-out torture. Whatever reason Yu Weichao had for not answering my letter, I think it deeply regrettable for a historian who has held the highest administrative post in China's supreme historical organisation. His pain and that of millions of Chinese during the Cultural Revolution is a key component of history, because the focal point of history should be people and nothing else. I hope that someday he'll have the courage and strength to write something about this time.

Likewise regrettable is that the History Department of Peking University has never recorded its own history during the Cultural Revolution. What is written here is all that I could learn after inquiring among many people and carrying out my own investigations.

Wu Xinghua, a professor of Western languages, died of abuse at the hands of Red Guards in early August 1966. His artistic talent and academic achievement and his death tell us what kind of people the Cultural Revolution chose to grind under its iron wheel, and how injurious it was to a person's life, and also to civilisation and to the nation.

Wu had been head of Peking University's Western Languages Department before being labelled a Rightist in 1957 and demoted two levels. He continued working in the Western Languages Department, and his Rightist 'cap' was removed in 1962. After the Cultural Revolution began, he was put on the university's 'labour reform team', and Red Guards beat him and ransacked his home. His writings and books, including a nearly completed translation of Dante's *Divine Comedy* and a nearly completed novel about the Tang poet Liu Zongyuan, were burned in an open space in front of his house.

While Wu was engaging in 'labour reform' on campus on 3 August 1966, a Red Guard forced him to drink from a gully carrying drainage from a nearby chemical plant. He lost consciousness and died that night at the age of forty-four. But the university's authorities at the time insisted that he had committed suicide as an act of resistance and to escape punishment for his crimes. Ignoring the objections of Wu's wife, Xie Weiyi, they ordered a hospital to carry out a post-mortem on Wu's corpse. Under the circumstances, what dominated the dialogue was whether he had committed suicide rather than pursuing those who had killed him by forcing him to drink the wastewater.

Wu Xinghua had an immense linguistic gift, and wrote and translated some beautiful poetry; his English teaching materials were also first rate. A Peking University English professor named Zheng Peidi told me that the university subsequently published an English textbook based on Wu Xinghua's work. A former university classmate of his, Guo Rui, published an essay in 1986 entitled 'The Road from Poet to Translator: Portrait of My Deceased Friend, Wu Xinghua'. The essay described Wu Xinghua's family background, his early display of intelligence, the friends of his college years, and his works and translations, in a detailed and lively manner depicting a talented and accomplished scholar. But the essay is vague on how Wu died during the Cultural Revolution and prevents an outsider from understanding what happened. Wu had two daughters who were fourteen and six years old at the time of his death, and Xie Weiyi was left to raise them alone. The elder daughter, Wu Tong, was sent to the northeastern countryside as an 'educated youth' for eight years.

Cheng Xiance, the thirty-eight-year-old Party secretary of the university's Chinese Department, and a son-in-law of Pan Guangdan, poisoned himself in Xiangshan Forest on the outskirts of Beijing on 2 September 1966, after being 'struggled', beaten and humiliated as a 'reactionary'.

When I began investigating what happened in each school during the Cultural Revolution, I asked survivors to recall the people and events of that era. That's how I learned of Cheng Xiance. Several teachers from Peking University offered up fragments of his story, which when set against the background of the Cultural Revolution allowed me to gradually piece together what happened to Cheng and detect the thread of events that pushed him towards death.

In January 1966, as Party secretary, Cheng Xiance led a meeting of the Chinese Department's teachers and students and gave a speech on criticising *Hai Rui Dismissed from Office*. Clearly Cheng didn't oppose the Cultural Revolution, and he joined others in the university's Party Committee as a full and energetic participant from the outset.

After Mao ordered the nationwide broadcast of the big-character poster attacking the leaders of Peking University on 1 June 1966, Cheng Xiance was dismissed along with the rest of the university's leading cadres as members of an 'anti-Party, anti-socialist reactionary gang'. Then the work group arrived to support Nie Yuanzi and take control of the administration while leading attacks against teachers and former administrators. Peking University became a template for carrying out the Cultural Revolution as classes were suspended throughout the country.

The work group quickly 'mobilised the masses' to put up big-character posters and convene struggle rallies to push forward the Cultural Revolution.

Cheng Xiance was one of those targeted during struggle sessions held in the Chinese Department's auditorium in mid-June. Members of the work group and student representatives spoke on stage while Cheng stood below the podium listening to their criticism and replying to their accusations. The work group divided cadres and teachers into four types: good, relatively good, having serious problems, and anti-Party, anti-socialist Rightists. Although all cadres and teachers expressed a willingness to criticise themselves and 'correct their errors', they were still subjected to endless exposure and criticism. Apart from verbal attacks, they also suffered personal attacks like being made to wear dunce caps or having big-character posters hung on them, or they'd be pushed, beaten or have their hair pulled. Some people killed themselves.

On 18 June, without reporting to the work group, some students and workers at the university used violence to 'struggle' several dozen cadres and teachers who had already been 'ferreted out'. Dozens of students went to the Chinese Department shouting 'Ferret out Cheng Xiance!' In a panic, Cheng hid in the women's restroom, alarming an older female staff member who was in there at the time. When the woman recognised Cheng Xiance and learned what had happened, she tried to stop the male students from coming in by claiming to be pulling up her trousers, but the students just ignored her and dragged Cheng Xiance out of the restroom. Other professors in the Chinese Department, including Wang Li, Wu Zuxiang and Wang Yao, were also apprehended. The students punched and beat them and smeared their hair with excrement-covered toilet paper from waste bins. Xiang Jingjie, vice-chairman of the Chinese Department, had bottles of red and black ink poured all over him until he was unrecognisable. When he returned home that night, his wife had to apply ointment to his back, which was covered with wounds. Another man violently attacked on that day was Cheng Xiance's brother-in-law, Hu Shouwen, a biology lecturer and the university's deputy Party secretary, whose experience was mentioned earlier.

This incident drew objections from the university's work group, mainly on the grounds that it ignored their absolute authority rather than from human and legal considerations. The central government leader in charge of the Cultural Revolution, Liu Shaoqi, issued a written order backing the work group's demand for the 'chaotic struggle' to cease. Soon afterwards, however, Mao Zedong criticised Liu for 'pouring cold water' on the Cultural Revolution. He declared the 18 June struggle session at Peking University to be a 'revolutionary' act and ordered the withdrawal of the work groups from the schools.

After the withdrawal of the work group, Nie Yuanzi was in control of Peking University. The contemporary *Chronicle of Major Events at Peking University During the Cultural Revolution* states:

> On 27 July 1966, Nie Yuanzi proposed that the university's revolutionary teachers, students and staff establish a Cultural Revolution Committee Preparatory Committee, which met with the enthusiastic welcome and response of the many revolutionary teachers, students and staff. Furthermore, under the suggestion of Comrade Nie Yuanzi, reactionaries were ferreted out by revolutionary teachers, students and staff, and penal labour under surveillance was implemented.

Cheng Xiance was put in a 'labour reform team' and, with several other 'ox demons' from the Chinese Department, was made to scrub the toilets in the student dormitories. One day, while cleaning toilets, Cheng Xiance was called away by a student, and when he came back, his thick hair had a cross shaved out of it. Another member of the labour team, Xiang Jingjie, was called next, and Cheng whispered to him, 'Just stay calm and don't react in any way.'

Cheng Xiance went home that night to the two-bedroom apartment his family shared with his sister-in-law's family. Although Cheng Xiance and Hu Shouwen were both departmental-grade cadres, their living conditions were wretched, and Hu didn't even own a bicycle. Their poverty was directly related to the economic conditions at that time, which resulted from flawed economic policies as well as production being diverted to class struggle. Cheng Xiance asked Hu Shouwen to tidy up his hair for him. Hu had also had his hair chopped off that day, and he said, 'Why bother? Who cares what we look like? They're the ones who did it.' Even so, Hu did his best to tidy up Cheng Xiance's hair. He was worried by how exhausted Cheng looked every time he came home from the labour team, just taking off his shoes and leaning weakly against the bed without saying a word.

Later, Cheng Xiance, Xiang Jingjie and a female professor of classical Chinese literature, Feng Zhongyun, were ordered to carry placards with their names and crimes written on them, and to pick up melon seed husks and other rubbish around the shops near the student dormitories. At that time, many Red Guards from other places had come to Beijing for 'revolutionary networking'; according to contemporary records, on one day 130,000 Red Guards visited the Peking University campus to 'learn from experience'. Crowds of people passed in front of the shops, constantly ordering the 'ox demons' to stand on overturned garbage baskets and give a 'debriefing of their crime' or of their family backgrounds. The only person who tried to step in was a foreigner passing by on the way to the university's south gate, who told the Red Guards, 'What you're doing is wrong. They've already admitted their error, so stop beating them.' But his words had no effect.

Apart from being tormented in the labour team, Cheng Xiance and other 'cow demons' were struggled at rallies of various sizes. One of the larger rallies was held by the university's Cultural Revolution Committee Preparatory Committee at the Beijing Workers' Stadium on 15 August 1966, to struggle Peking University's top leader, Lu Ping. As a departmental-grade cadre, Cheng Xiance was taken there as a 'secondary target'. The main and secondary targets of struggle had to stand bent at the waist with placards hanging over their chests stating their crimes and labels with their names crossed out with red ink like criminals condemned to death.

In the upsurge of violence that followed Mao's review of the Red Guards at Tiananmen Square on 18 August, Red Guards from Tsinghua University on 24 August invited colleagues in the university's Affiliated Secondary School to bring in truckloads of Red Guards from twelve secondary schools. They tore down all the big-character posters attacking Liu Shaoqi and other national leaders (at that time, Mao's intention to unseat Liu Shaoqi was not widely known), and also began ransacking homes and beating people on the Tsinghua and Peking campuses. Students from the Peking University Biology Department and Chinese medicine pre-med course ransacked the shared home of Cheng Xiance and Hu Shouwen and beat them with brass belt buckles.

In the days that followed, students from the university and nearby secondary schools kept coming to Cheng Xiance and Hu Shouwen's home for random searches and beatings, and attacks on the two teachers intensified. Once, Red Guards rolled Cheng up in a straw mat and then beat him mercilessly.

On 30 August, the Peking University Cultural Revolution Congress was held, with top leaders from the CCP Central Committee in attendance. The meeting established a formal authority called the Peking University Cultural Revolution Standing Committee with Nie Yuanzi as chair. She 'affirmed the combat mission henceforth' as 'thoroughly defeating Lu Ping's capitalist-roader reactionary power-holding faction, thoroughly repudiating the bourgeois reactionary academic authorities and thoroughly demolishing the old educational system'. Cheng Xiance and Hu Shouwen were excluded from that meeting, but they could hear Nie Yuanzi's voice over the loudspeaker from their balcony. Cheng Xiance was, as always, depressed and silent. It was only afterwards that Hu Shouwen learned that Cheng had already sunken into irrevocable despair. The violence and oppression had become increasingly systematised, and there was every indication that it was not random but organised and directed.

A new upsurge in killings followed Mao's second review of the Red Guards at Tiananmen Square on 31 August. On 2 September, Cheng Xiance went to the woodlands of the Fragrant Hills, about five kilometres northwest of the university, with a bottle of liquor and two bottles of concentrated insecticide and killed himself.

There's no way of knowing how much torment Cheng Xiance endured. All I can record is what some of his friends and colleagues told me, and they are unlikely to have known everything. When I previously wrote about other victims, someone asked if I was exaggerating, but if anything, my reports omit much of the torture and humiliation these victims experienced. The dead can no longer speak of their bitter sufferings, the perpetrators have done their best to cover up and minimise what they did, and those who observed from the sidelines only saw fragmentary episodes, while the least sympathetic turned a blind eye and purged the incidents from their memories long ago.

When Cheng Xiance failed to turn up for the labour reform team on the morning of 2 September, Xiang Jingjie and other team members had no idea what had happened and were surprised that he'd dare to be tardy. Later they were called to a struggle rally during which it was announced that Cheng Xiance had 'isolated himself from the people' and 'become more despicable than a pile of dog shit', at which point they realised he was dead.

Red Guards still wrote Cheng's name on white paper and tacked it up at the struggle rally with a 'secondary target' standing on either side. A direct result of Cheng Xiance's death was that Xiang Jingjie was 'promoted' to the status of the Chinese Department's top reactionary and was repeatedly subjected to ruthless struggle. One evening, a group of students went to his home, pulled a hood over his head and dragged him away as his family members pleaded for mercy. They tied Xiang up in a room and then removed his hood.

The scene that followed was like the interrogation scene in a movie. Shining a bright light in Xiang's face, they questioned him all night regarding the accusation that prior to the Cultural Revolution, the university's Chinese Department had suspended Lin Biao's daughter Lin Liheng (better known as Doudou, or 'Beany'). This was described as 'persecuting Lin Doudou' and 'persecuting deputy commander-in-chief Lin Biao'. The truth was that Lin Doudou had been studying engineering at Tsinghua University, but when she lost interest, the Ministry of Education had ordered Peking University's Chinese Department to accept her. Far from being persecuted, Lin Doudou had two teachers assigned to tutor her. Eventually she went on extended sick leave but was not asked to withdraw from the university. It was only after it became clear that she wasn't coming back that the Chinese Department terminated her student status. Once the Cultural Revolution began, Lin Doudou's younger brother, Lin Liguo (at that time a student at Peking University), 'exposed' this matter, and Lin Doudou's withdrawal from the school became a crime for which staff at the Chinese Department were cruelly punished.

On 25 January 1968, the Peking University Cultural Revolution Committee held a special rally to publicly denounce the people who had 'persecuted vice-chairman Lin's daughter'. If Cheng Xiance had still been alive, as a leader of the Chinese Department, he would certainly have been dragged to that rally and subjected to struggle, and would have continued to be persecuted during the Cleansing of the Class Ranks.

I've compiled Cheng Xiance's story from multiple interviews with elderly former staff of Peking University. Cheng's step-by-step trajectory towards death was directly related to the progress of the Cultural Revolution. After experiencing three months of escalating violence, he decided to kill himself. At that time there was no sign that the abuse would end; the violent power mechanism was gradually consolidating, and Cheng's situation was becoming increasing untenable. Events following his death show that if Cheng hadn't killed himself, he would have continued to suffer prolonged persecution.

Many people at Peking University met similar fates. Established during the Modernisation Movement in 1898, the university should have represented China's progress towards science and civilisation, but during the Cultural Revolution, it became a place where the most brutal and violent behaviour occurred. Violent 'struggle rallies', campus 'labour reform teams' and campus jails all originated here, not to mention the prevalence of morally degenerate acts such as framing, lying and toadying. The enormous changes that occurred at Peking University were examples of the transformation the Cultural Revolution wrought on social conventions and behavioural norms, a shocking accomplishment that deserves further reflection.

When I was carrying out my interviews at Peking University, I didn't have an opportunity to talk with Professor Yue Daiyun in the Chinese Department. It was not until 2001 that I read her chapter about Cheng Xiance in her autobiography *To the Storm*.[65] I should point out that there are errors in Professor Yue's account of Cheng Xiance's experience in the Cultural Revolution. For example, she says he killed himself in June 1966 rather than in September. Behind this memory lapse is something unfortunate: they had been close friends when young, but after Yue Daiyun was designated a Rightist in 1957, Cheng Xiance, who was still a leading cadre at the time, had nothing more to do with her, and that's why she didn't know all the details of what happened to him.

Even so, Professor Yue's description of how she and Cheng Xiance first met in 1948, and the contact she had with him in the 1950s, reveals much about what kind of person Cheng was and his thinking before the Cultural Revolution.

Professor Yue writes that she was a new college student in 1948 when Cheng Xiance introduced her to the Communist Party's songs

---

[65] Yue Daiyun, *Juese shuangfeng*, Baihuazhou wenyi chubanshe, 2000. TN: Yu previously published an English autobiography with Carolyn Wakeman, *To the Storm: The Odyssey of a Revolutionary Chinese Woman*, Berkeley, University of California Press, 1985. 'Chapter 3: Cast Out from the People' describes her land reform experience in Jiangxi Province and also mentions Cheng Xiance, referring to him as 'Lao Chen', but does not go into the same amount of detail.

and revolutionary thought. In 1951, some students and teachers from Peking University's Literature, History and Philosophy Departments went to Jiangxi Province and joined with local cadres in forming a 'South-central Region Land Reform Work 12th Regiment', of which Cheng Xiance was deputy commander. Yue Daiyu, nineteen years old at the time, was put in charge of a village that was determined to have eight 'landlords'. Eventually these eight people were executed and their corpses were exposed to the elements for three days. Among them was an elderly man who had spent most of his life in Shanghai as a tailor, and who had saved enough money to buy some land in his home village. This made him a landlord and led to him being shot. Yue Daiyu had a hard time accepting such cruelty. As a regimental leader, Cheng Xiance 'straightened her out' by saying:

> You can't rely on moral standards, especially old moral standards, to deal with people and events. Coming from petty bourgeois families, we need to harshly examine our initial reactions, because they result from years of inculcation with feudal education and bourgeois thinking. Humanism and theories of human nature may have motivated our participation in revolution, but they've become the antithesis to Marxist class doctrine and are the greatest obstruction to our becoming of one mind with the Party. For that reason, the most important task before us is to thoroughly criticise humanism and theories of human nature.

Cheng Xiance wanted Yue to regard this kind of 'punishment' as 'essential' and accept in both theory and in practice the cruel methods imposed on people who were designated 'class enemies'.[66] These extrajudicial killings carried out in the name of revolution required the perpetrators to surrender their capacity for humanity and morality. I have no information on how many villages were handled in this way by the 'South-central Region Land Reform Work 12th Regiment' that Cheng Xiance helped to lead, or how many landlords the regiment killed.

Professor Yue's book doesn't say what Cheng Xiance did after Land Reform. Reading in detail the *Chronical of Peking University* published in 1998, I learned that Cheng Xiance became chairman of the university's student union presidium in 1950, and when the CCP established a Party Committee at the university in 1951, Cheng served as deputy director of its Propaganda Department and then of its United Front Department. He was

---

[66] *Ibid.*

appointed Party general secretary of the Chinese Department in 1959, and in early 1966 led the Cultural Revolution until he himself was 'overthrown'.

As a propaganda and united front operative, Cheng would have been involved in the university's thought reform and loyalty and honesty campaigns, as well as the Anti-Rightist Campaign during which 7,716 of the university's students, teachers and administrators were designated Rightists. Yue Daiyun, who had followed Cheng Xiance in carrying out land reform and struggling landlords, was one of those sent down to the countryside for labour reform as a Rightist. Yue's good friend, Zhu Jiayu, whom she had persuaded not to accompany her father to the US for overseas study, committed suicide after being designated a Rightist.

We have no way of knowing Cheng Xiance's thinking as a full-time 'political and ideological work cadre' during this series of campaigns, but he was clearly at the forefront until he became a target of attack. Yue Daiyun writes of Cheng Xiance's charm, the way he smiled and treated people as warmly as an elder brother, and Cheng's colleagues also speak of his cleverness, dynamism and refinement. Even so, engaging in class struggle and abandoning the spirit of humanism will have a significant effect on a person's behaviour.

Once Cheng was a designated target of revolution, he was 'ferreted out', humiliated and abused in the same way as the landlords of Jiangxi and the Rightists of Peking University. Like the political targets before them, the university's 'reactionaries', 'counter-revolutionary revisionists' and 'reactionary academic authorities' lost all legal protections and access to social justice. Cheng Xiance must have had a profound understanding of this repertoire of methods. People I interviewed didn't mention Cheng ever complaining about the abuse he suffered. He bore it for three months, and harbouring no further illusions, he killed himself.

Cheng Xiance's transformation from revolutionary to target of revolution followed an inherent logic. While one group of people took part in persecuting others, they laid the groundwork for their own persecution by negating the rule of law, procedural justice and the civil rights that a citizen should enjoy. Once a mechanism was established that transcended law and sent tens of thousands of people to their deaths, and once an army of young people was prepared to serve as hatchet men, the people who had established that mechanism and cultivated those hatchet men became swallowed up in what they'd created. Cheng Xiance's death was horrible and tragic, but so was the path his life took.

Yu Dayin, a sixty-year-old English professor who had studied in the UK in the 1930s, poisoned herself to death in the university's staff quarters on 25 August 1966, after being denounced and humiliated by Red Guards on 24 August.

Yu Dayin was forced to kneel on the ground while her home was ransacked. She was alone at home at the time. Her husband, **Zeng Zhaolun**, had obtained a PhD in chemistry from MIT in the US, and after returning to China and becoming a professor, he had joined the China Democratic League in 1944, opposing the KMT government. In May 1949, the CCP Military Control Commission appointed him dean of studies at Peking University, and he was then appointed Vice-Minister of Education. But in 1957 he was designated a Rightist and sent to Wuhan University, so he wasn't living in Beijing when the Cultural Revolution began. Zeng was also persecuted during the Cultural Revolution, and died in Wuhan on 9 December 1967, at the age of sixty-eight.

A relative of Yu Dayin's said that the couple had never had children because they were first cousins and feared that their offspring would have congenital defects. Yu Dayin's elder brother, Yu Dawei, was a senior official in Taiwan. In the 1950s, Yu Dayin had been ordered to carry out 'united front work' on her brother.

Yu Dayin was co-author of the most popular set of English textbooks in China, along with Xu Guozhang and Wu Zhucun. Wu Zhucun had once been Yu Dayin's student, and later became her colleague at Peking University. Wu Zhucun was also savagely attacked during the Cultural Revolution as a 'Rightist who slipped through the net', a 'reactionary authority' and a 'secret agent of the US and Chiang Kai-shek'. He was locked up in the school jail for more than a year and subjected to long-term beatings and humiliation.

Shen Naizhang, a fifty-two-year-old professor of psychology in the university's Philosophy Department, was struggled in summer 1966, also being labelled a 'Rightist who slipped through the net' and a 'reactionary academic authority'; he was forced to carry a placard and sweep floors as a member of the labour reform team. Red Guards from the Philosophy Department ransacked his home and sealed off his books. Shen killed himself with an overdose of sleeping pills on 9 October 1966.

Shen Naizhang had won a contest for his impressive beard while studying in France, but he was forced to shave it off when the Red Guards came to 'smash the Four Olds' in August 1966. A colleague said no one recognised him afterwards, but it was still a minor incident compared with brutal physical and mental torment.

Shen's wife, Hu Ruisi, an English teacher at the Peking University Affiliated Secondary School, was falsely accused of having been a member of a 'reactionary organisation' and was put in one of the school's three labour reform teams. She was further investigated during the Cleansing of the Class Ranks in 1968.

The couple had two children. Their daughter, Shen Enchen, was a first-year student at the Peking University Affiliated Secondary School when the Red Guard movement was launched in August 1966. Ten of the forty-odd students in her class who had 'good family backgrounds' became Red Guards, and they sat in front of the classroom and had students from 'bad family backgrounds' come forward one by one and 'confess their family's problems'. As the daughter of a professor, Shen Enchen was one of those interrogated. The students were asked, 'Do you have any of the Four Olds at home?' 'Does your family have any reactionary materials it hasn't handed over?' During the interrogation, Red Guards whipped the students.

Shen Enchen had a female classmate named Zhao Chongxun who lived in Haidian Town and came from a 'landlord family'. Red Guards destroyed Zhao's home and dragged her mother to a classroom in the school and beat her, ordering Zhao Chongxun to hit her own mother. There was blood all over the floor, and the Red Guards ordered a history teacher surnamed Deng to clean it up while they beat him and accused of having worked for the KMT.

Shen Enchen saw a student named Zhu Tong locked up in a broom closet near the restroom and forced to sit on the wet floor while a Red Guard whipped him. Shen also saw a struggle rally at which the school's teachers and principal were made to crouch on their hands and knees while Red Guards stood on their backs. Only vice-principal Liu Meide didn't have someone standing on her back, because she was noticeably pregnant.

Because she had a 'bad family background', Shen Enchen was not allowed to go on the 'great networking' in September 1966, but was sent to Mentougou District to labour. She saw her father for the last time when she went home in early October to get food ration coupons and clothes. By the time she finished her labour and returned home at the end of the month, Shen Naizhang was dead. The family was soon turned out of their home.

Shen Enchen was sent to Heilongjiang to work in a village production brigade in spring 1969. Her elder brother had already been sent to a mountain village in Shanxi, and was still there in 1972 after better-connected 'educated youth' had found a way to return home. He'd been given an opportunity to work as an electrical repairman in Taigu County, but wasn't allowed to go because Shen Naizhang had disgraced the family by 'alienating himself from the Party and the people'. Seeing no future for himself, the elder brother killed himself in 1972.

After the Cultural Revolution, Shen Enchen was able to go to college. She later studied in the US and became a computer engineer.

Dong Huaiyun, around forty years old, was a lecturer and secretary of the university's Mathematics and Mechanics Department and and chairman of the Public Mathematics Research Institute. He hanged himself on 28 July 1966, after a big-character poster named him in a group of 'problematic individuals'.

Dong Huaiyun's ordeal was emblematic of the political chaos of that era. While at Peking University in 1964, he had come under attack during a political campaign called the Socialist Education Movement (SEM), which was a precursor to the Cultural Revolution. The SEM was quickly reversed, however, and Dong was happy to find his reputation restored. But then once the Cultural Revolution was launched, the reversal of Peking University's SEM was declared an 'extremely serious counter-revolutionary incident' (5 June 1966, a *People's Daily* editorial), and having benefited from that reversal, Dong Huaiyun was declared a 'problematic individual' and placed under 'labour reform'.

After being beaten and forced to kneel and wear a dunce cap and endure other humiliations during the violent struggle rally on 18 June 1966, Dong Huaiyun told someone at his hostel that his health was poor and he had a serious nervous condition, and he feared he wouldn't be able to stand much more. (Dong's family lived inside the city limits, while he kept a bed space in the university's unmarried quarters.)

When the Mathematics Department's Cultural Revolution Committee was established in early July 1966, Dong Huaiyun and other 'problematic individuals' were put into a separate group that worked in the canteen scrubbing glass. Another member of this group was teacher Ding Shisun, who eventually became president of Peking University in the early 1980s. When the 'ox demon and snake spirit' labour reform teams were about to be established after Jiang Qing's visit to Peking University, Dong Huaiyun hanged himself rather than endure further humiliation and injury.

One member of the department's labour reform team was the department head, the famous mathematician Duan Xuefu. Duan was extremely nearsighted, and when forced to scrub bathrooms, he had to practically stick his nose against the wall to see what he was cleaning. Three other lecturers in the Mathematics and Mechanics Department were driven to suicide during the Cleansing of the Class Ranks in 1968, while another became deranged under torture.

Beijing Agricultural University

Lu Jinren, a professor of entomology, was a member of the China Democracy League who had studied in the United States and had been designated a Rightist in 1957. He was struggled at a mass rally and paraded through the streets in August 1966. On 1 September 1966, Lu and his wife, **Lü Jingzhen**, hanged themselves in their home in the university's living quarters.

A teacher who knew the couple at the university recalled in 1990 that Lu Jinren was a 'modest gentleman' and that he and his wife were 'very refined'. Lu Jinren and Lü Jingzhen were among the first of dozens of people who killed themselves at the Agricultural University during the Cultural Revolution.

He Jiefu, born in 1916, was a clerical worker at Beijing Agricultural University, and his wife, Gao Wuji, was an accountant there. In summer 1966, the couple and their two children were 'repatriated' to the countryside. He was beaten to death on 14 November 1967.

He Jiefu was a native of Guangxi. After graduating from college, he worked with Zhang Xueliang's Northeast Army;[67] one of Zhang's high-ranking officers, He Zhuguo, was He Jiefu's relative. He Jiefu's wife, Gao Wuji, was a native of Beijing with a degree in economics from Nankai University. Gao was designated a Rightist in 1957 and was punished with demotion and a 25% cut in pay to around 60 *yuan* per month.

In August 1966, He Jiefu was attacked as a 'historical counter-revolutionary' and Gao Wuji as a Rightist, and they were put on the list for 'repatriation' to the countryside (this process, initiated by the Xicheng Pickets, is described in the section on Beijing No. 4 Secondary School in Part Two). In the meantime, Red Guard students ransacked He and Gao's home and took away their belongings, including charting tools that Gao had used as a student, which were designated 'Four Olds' because they were made in Germany. When the Cultural Revolution was repudiated and people were compensated for seized belongings in 1980, Gao Wuji was paid 50 *yuan*.

Wu Aizhu, the housekeeper of He Jiefu's neighbour, **Wu Weijun**, hanged herself on 25 August, after being accused of being the 'mistress of a landlord' and ordered to return to her home village. Shortly thereafter, Beijing Agricultural University gave He Jiafu and Gao Wuji two months' pay, totalling around 200 *yuan*, and then turned them out of their home along with their thirteen-year-old son, He Ping, and seventeen-year-old daughter, He Wei.

According to the historical records of Beijing Agricultural University, sixty-nine people affiliated with the university were forcibly repatriated to the countryside in summer 1966. Their names were not given, which means

---

[67] TN: Zhang Xueliang or Chang Hsueh-liang, known as the Young Marshal, effectively ruled northeast China after the assassination of his father, Zhang Zuolin, by the Japanese on 4 June 1928. He instigated the 1936 Xi'an Incident, in which KMT leader Chiang Kai-shek was abducted and forced to accept a truce with the CCP in order to form a united front against the Japanese occupation.

that the fates of others apart from He Jiefu and Gao Wuji are unknown; we don't know if they reached the countryside alive, let alone survived the Cultural Revolution. Red Guards taking part in the 'big link-up' struggled He Jiefu's family on the train to Guangxi; they were lucky not to have been beaten to death en route like some others.

The family were sent to Yangmei Commune in Guangxi's Rong County, but the commune production team refused to accept them, because it would mean distributing a share of their land and grain ration to a 'black element' household. At that time, the people's communes controlled all resources in the countryside; rejection meant He's family had no means to sustain themselves. Finally, He Jiefu paid over a sum of money in order to 'join the team'. The whole family toiled relentlessly while other villagers threw stones and clots of earth at them, and He Jiefu gave villagers haircuts in exchange for rice or eggs. Even so, the four of them never had enough to eat.

When He Jiefu's family first arrived, Guangxi was experiencing less violence than Beijing, being behind the capital in the 'progress' of the Cultural Revolution. The struggle sessions became more frequent, however, and He Jiefu was 'seized and struggled' several times before the rally where he was finally beaten to death.

On 14 November 1967, the commune where the family lived convened a denunciation meeting during which twenty-odd people were brought up on a stage and struggled. He Jiefu's wife and children watched from below the stage as the 'rebel faction' beat the victims with wooden rods. After He was beaten to death, his children were told to fetch his body. The two teenagers weren't strong enough to lift their father's corpse, so two others were called over to help drag the body away.

One of those who helped move He's body was a man named **He Houye**, who was a member of He Jiefu's clan from the same generation and a 'landlord element'. Seeing the people who had been struggled lying on the floor, most of them already dead and the rest breathing their last, He Houye considered his own prospects, bound his own hands, and drowned himself in the river.

I learned from the *Chronology of the Cultural Revolution in Guangxi*[68] that the Rong County militia killed sixty-nine 'class enemies' (rich peasant and landlord elements) and others in November 1967.

Furthermore, the *Rong County Gazetteer*[69] records that in mid-November 1967, the Shizhai District People's Armed Forces Department convened a meeting in the county to announce Guzhao Village's supposed unearthing

---

[68] Chronology of the Cultural Revolution in Guangxi Editorial Group (ed.), *Chronology of the Cultural Revolution in Guangxi*, Guangxi renmin chubanshe, 1990.
[69] *Rong County Gazetteer*, Guangxi renmin chubanshe, 1993.

of an 'Anti-Communist National Salvation Army' and to implement the dictatorship of the masses, as a result of which random killings began and 738 innocents were slaughtered throughout the county.

There's a huge difference between these two figures, and none of the victims are named, nor is there any description of how they died. Without a name list, we can't tell if He Jiefu was included in either of these figures. But it should be said that Guangxi's local gazetteers contain more records on the Cultural Revolution than most places.

At the end of 1978 – two years after Mao's death, when Deng Xiaoping and Hu Yaobang rehabilitated many of the victims – Gao Wuji returned to Beijing. Her daughter, He Wei, returned in 1979, followed by her son, He Ping, in 1981. The university compensated them for lost wages. Gao's anger over what had happened continued to plague her until she died in 1996. She could hardly be blamed for this. After experiencing such brutality and suffering and not being given an opportunity to tell anyone of their misfortunes, many victims suffered psychological trauma that never fully healed.

Shen Baoxing, a fifty-two-year-old cook at Beijing Agricultural University, was accused in summer 1966 of being a 'concealed counter-revolutionary'. He hanged himself on 8 September after the university authorities ordered him to be 'repatriated' to his home village in Huairou County.

Shen had served in the army under the Kuomintang. When Beijing was 'peacefully liberated' in 1949, his army unit switched allegiance and joined the People's Liberation Army. His unit was sent to fight in the Korean War in 1950. Following his demobilisation, Shen became a cook.

Shen Baoxing's wife, Yao Rongyi, was a peasant who lived in the village of Shangxinzhuang in Beijing's Xiaotangshan Township. They had five children, and Yao Rongyi's mother also lived with the family. Thanks to the residential permit (*hukou*) system at that time, it was very difficult for the holder of a rural residential permit to obtain an urban permit or to find work in the cities. Shen was therefore obliged to live alone at the university, and returned to the village on his days off.

When the Cultural Revolution began, Shen Baoxing was 'ferreted out' as a 'class enemy in hiding for seventeen years'. This meant that he hadn't committed any recent crimes, but that he was being punished for his time in the Kuomintang Army. On the grounds that he might poison people as a cook, he was relegated to feeding the canteen's pigs instead.

When the Red Guards began ransacking homes and beating people in August and September 1966 and issued General Order No. 4 expelling large numbers of Beijing residents, Shen Baoxin was notified that as a 'class enemy', he was being dismissed from his position, having his urban *hukou* nullified, and being sent back to the village to live with his family.

According to *The History of Beijing Agricultural University*,[70] the university's Cultural Revolution Committee organised the first university-wide parade and began violent struggle against 'class enemies' on 8 August 1966. On 20 and 21 August, it established two Red Guard organisations, which immediately began ransacking homes and beating people, 'smashing the Four Olds' and driving out 'black elements' while also 'seizing and struggling' teachers and cadres. The university descended into a reign of terror; sixty-nine of its people were forcibly 'repatriated' to the countryside and several committed suicide.

The book doesn't provide the names of the people who were expelled, so it can't be confirmed whether Shen Baoxing was included in that number, given that he killed himself before he could be repatriated. In any case, this is the only university history I've found that includes the number of people repatriated. In comparison, the official history of Peking University only provides the names of full professors and high-level administrators who died during the Cultural Revolution. The Beijing Agricultural University historians deserve credit for their effort, and it is only regrettable that other university histories overlook their Cultural Revolution victims to varying degrees.

Before killing himself, Shen Baoxing went back to Xiaotangshan and told his wife about his situation. He was not only losing his position and his monthly income of 50 *yuan*, but after returning to the village he would continue to be subjected to 'dictatorship' as a class enemy. By that time, at the Shangxin production brigade where Shen's family lived, struggle rallies were already being held against landlords and rich peasants, and students of the local primary school had beaten their teachers' heads with cudgels. Some Beijing residents who had already been repatriated to the village had had their hair shaved off and were forced to wear cloth badges stating their names and crimes. They'd been tortured to the point where they were barely recognisable. Shen Baoxing knew that he faced the same fate and that his children might also be dragged into it; he'd heard of nearby villages where 'black elements' had been buried alive with their children. Shen returned to the university, and the next day he hanged himself near the pigs' feeding troughs.

According to the aforementioned *History of Beijing Agricultural University*, on that same day, someone put up a big-character poster calling for students to 'bombard the Party Committee'. This was followed by a great debate about university president and Party secretary Wang Guanlan and the university Party Committee, resulting in the organisation

---

[70] Wang Buzheng (ed.), Beijing nongye daxue chubanshe, 1995.

of different factions. At that time, the CCP Central Committee had already dismissed the administrators of universities such as Tsinghua and Peking as 'reactionaries'. The situation was slightly better at Beijing Agricultural University because of Wang Guanlan's special relationship with Mao. On 18 June, the Vice-Premier in charge of agriculture and forestry, Tan Zhenlin, gave a speech at the university saying that Wang Guanlan and a deputy Party secretary were 'revolutionary Leftists and Red' and that they should be 'preserved'. That's why the big-character poster about 'bombarding the Party Committee' wasn't put up until 8 September. The university's Party Committee was eventually disbanded like those of other schools in October, but at least there had been some debate about it. However, there had been no debate about the firing, expelling and suicide of the old cook Shen Baoxing. No one had expressed a dissenting view about it or even any sympathy for Shen's widow and bereft children. The school's Red Guards and rebel factions could disagree for a time over whether or not to bombard the university Party Committee, but no one seemed to object to a class enemy being abused and stripped of their rights. The unanimity on this point indicates the nature of the revolution taking place at this time.

What real problem could there have been with Shen Baoxing? He was just a kitchen worker and had nothing to do with the 'feudalist, capitalist and revisionist education line' being attacked at the university. The truth is that the Cultural Revolution's leaders could designate whole batches of people as 'class enemies' and 'targets of dictatorship' with no legal basis; the persecution of helpless and powerless ordinary people like Shen Baoxing was conducive to creating an atmosphere of terror.

After Shen Baoxing died, the university authorities sent his body and belongings in a truck to his wife, and the village arranged for his burial. As a class enemy who had committed suicide, Shen wasn't given a coffin, and the grave-diggers didn't go to the trouble of burying him deep enough. As a result, one of Shen's legs protruded from the hole and had to be broken with a shovel so he could be properly interred. Watching her husband's corpse so brutally handled only intensified his wife's anguish, but she was allowed no protest. Shen's unmarked grave eventually became indistinguishable from its surroundings.

The belongings sent back with Shen Baoxing included a small bottle with a little liquor left in it, but a cadre broke the bottle, saying the alcohol might be poisoned.

Shen Baoxing and Yao Rongyi had three daughters and two sons, the oldest of whom was thirteen at the time Shen died. The work points Yao Rongyi earned through her labour at the commune weren't enough to feed her children and her elderly mother, and the family was in dire straits.

On top of that, they suffered all kinds of bias and attacks as a 'counter-revolutionary family'. The children were forced to 'draw a clear distinction' from their father, so Yao Rongyi had them take her surname. There were many instances of similar name changes in that era, and the worst of it was that it brought no improvement to their circumstances; they continued to be treated as the children of a counter-revolutionary.

Shen Baoxing's eldest daughter had fallen in love with a village youth who wanted to join the army, a rare opportunity for advancement. The village leader told him that he couldn't join the army if he continued his attachment to Shen Baoxing's daughter, so the two young people agreed to break up. After the young man returned from the army, the two resumed their relationship and finally married when they were twenty-eight.

Two years after the Cultural Revolution ended, Shen Baoxing's children began appealing to Beijing Agricultural University to have their father rehabilitated. The university Party Committee finally agreed to do so, and provided one of the daughters with a job as compensation.

When Shen Baoxing died, his children were still young, and didn't really know him, as they had spent little time living together. When they went to the university to request rehabilitation for their father, they took the opportunity to ask some of his colleagues in the kitchen what kind of man he had been. The kitchen staff said Shen Baoxin had been honest, loyal and kind. As an uneducated man, he spoke little and concentrated on his work. They were sorry about what had happened to him.

When I spoke to one of Shen's daughters, she said, 'My dad didn't have any real schooling or sense of perspective, so he couldn't see a way out and killed himself.' She said she'd seen others expelled from the city to the village who had suffered greatly, but because they had some education, they were able to bear up and endure.

I told her that Shen Baoxing had been the sixth person at Beijing Agricultural University to kill himself, and dozens more did so after him, most of them highly educated. Every suicide involved individual factors to some extent, but they were secondary; the real cause was that they were persecuted too brutally.

I told her that if her father hadn't died in summer 1966, he might well have been beaten to death like He Jiefu in November 1967. Facing protracted torment and the terror of never knowing when one might be killed, death seemed less horrifying for many people.

Shen's daughter said she hadn't known that so many others at the university had died; she'd thought it was only her father.

I was shaken by her views of her father's suicide. Victims are too forbearing; when persecuted to death, they look for their own faults, or the weaknesses of their loved ones. When I've interviewed family members, I've often heard them say that the victims were too uneducated or had bad tempers or didn't know how to answer the Red Guards' questions, or they blame themselves for not being clever enough to protect their loved ones or help them escape. Conversely, the persecutors are so shameless, refusing to apologise or even to talk about what happened, and forbidding others to do so. When will this ever change?

Beijing Normal University

Liu Pansui, a seventy-year-old professor of paleography in the university's Chinese Department, was beaten to death in his home along with his wife, **Liang Qiuse**, by Red Guards on 28 August 1966. Liu Pansui was the only one of eight professors in Beijing Normal University's Chinese Literature Department who hadn't been designated a Rightist in 1957.

A graduate of the National Studies Institute of Tsinghua University, Liu Pansui spent his life researching ancient documents and was the author of several works on the subject. He was a very learned man, and colleagues and students regularly consulted him on literary quotations, referring to him as a 'living dictionary'. Yet it took me years to find out the details and date of Liu's death.

I spoke with Liu's former students and colleagues and wrote many letters to the relevant people at Beijing Normal University. Some of my letters were completely ignored, while people who did answer had no access to the school's files. Some younger people wanted to help but knew nothing about these past events, while old people who wanted to help worried that they'd be accused of 'criticising the Communist Party'. Finally, in April 2009, with the help of at least eight people, I established when Liu Pansui died.

This may sound absurd. Scholars are able to examine and research matters from a thousand years ago, but no one is allowed to look into Red Guards beating a professor to death in 1966. This is a result of the authorities' long-standing ban on reporting what happened during the Cultural Revolution. I hope the narrative that follows will help readers understand not only Liu Pansui's murder and its background, but also why it is was so difficult to investigate.

When in 1996 I interviewed Xia Weiyun, the widow of the late Wang Li, a professor of Chinese at Peking University, she said that Liu Pansui had been her husband's schoolmate many years ago. She'd heard that Red Guards had beaten Liu to death, but she didn't know further details. At that time, all professors were being denounced and struggled; Wang Li's home on the Peking University campus was also ransacked, and he was sent to a *laogai* camp. The old friends were unable to help each other.

Liu Pansui died at the height of the violence and ransackings that followed Mao's review of the Red Guards at Tiananmen Square on 18 August. The home where he died was in Beijing's Xicheng District, where the largest number of Red Guard killings occurred.

Liu's home was in a *hutong* located diagonally across from Xidan Market. He had taught for many years to save enough money to buy a small quadrangle compound named 'Peaceful Home' on a wooden sign above the door. A colleague who visited Liu many times couldn't remember the exact address, but he remembered the name, which contracted so starkly with the brutal deaths of the compound's inhabitants.

On that day in late August, the Red Guards of Beijing Normal University ordered all members of the 'democratic parties' to gather at the school. Liu was summoned as a member of the China Democratic League, and one of his League colleagues called the public telephone nearest his home to notify him, only to be told that Liu's home had been ransacked and he couldn't come to the telephone. This colleague didn't dare ask any more questions or go to Liu's home.

The Lius had a son who was married but still lived with them, and a daughter who had married but was staying with her parents at the time because she was pregnant. The Lius' compound wasn't large; the couple lived in the principal rooms, while the son and his wife lived in a wing room, and there were two outbuildings used to store books. Liu Pansui had many books, and shelves lined his walls to the ceiling.

After the Red Guards searching Liu's home found a bankbook under the daughter's mattress, they accused the family of hiding gold and began beating Liu and his wife, demanding that they tell them where the gold was hidden. Liu had been a teacher all his life and had spent all his money on his home and his books, but because he was unable to hand over any gold, he and his wife were beaten. They were tied up in the courtyard and weren't allowed to go inside or eat, and they were only given a little tap water to drink.

Red Guards began digging up the ground around the Lius' home, but found nothing. Others continued to beat members of the household, and after several days of this torture, Liu Pansui's wife died.

Liu Pansui's wife was a homemaker and not very well-educated. When colleagues or students visited, she seldom took part in their conversations. They addressed her respectfully but never knew her name. It took a great deal of searching for me to finally learn that it was Liang Qiuse.

Distraught at his wife's death, Liu Pansui pushed his head into a water vat to kill himself, but as it contained little water, he was still alive when the Red Guards discovered him and pulled him out. They then continued to beat him, and he died soon afterwards.

Liu's home was only a kilometre from Tiananmen Square, so Red Guards locked up other neighbourhood 'class enemies' in the Liu family compound. Some were beaten to death, but I've been unable to learn their names.

Liu Pansui's daughter was also beaten so brutally that she suffered a miscarriage. She managed to survive by fleeing to the school where she worked at the dean's office. In subsequent years she gave birth to a son and a daughter.

Liu Pansui's son was tied to a tree in the courtyard and beaten and interrogated. He later managed to slip out the door and ran to Beijing Normal University, where he begged the school to send someone to his home and explain that Liu Pansui wasn't a 'black element' so the Red Guards would release the old couple. By then, the former leaders of the university had been unseated, and a new power structure had been established, so no one from the university went to Liu's home. Liu's son and daughter were incensed that the school allowed their parents to be killed, but with the Red Guards so clearly favoured by China's top officials, few people would have been willing to challenge their actions at that time.

In another respect, however, the university's administrators are blameworthy, because they could have helped at least a little. For example, another professor of Chinese who lived in the same neighbourhood, Yang Minru, also had her home ransacked by Red Guards from the foreign language section of the Trade Institute. The Red Guards destroyed Yang's records, piano, seals, books, paintings and dishes and took away the family's jewelry. Yang Minru's husband was a senior engineer in the Electronics Industry Ministry, and had obtained his PhD at the prestigious California Institute of Technology. He was attacked with big-character posters at his work unit, but the ministry sent someone to tell the Red Guards that he didn't constitute a 'contradiction between the enemy and us'. As a result, although Yang Minru's home was turned upside down and many possessions were destroyed or taken, she and her husband weren't beaten to death like Liu Pansui and his wife. They never recovered their stolen items, even after the Cultural Revolution was officially negated, but they were grateful simply to have survived. Similarly, the chairman of Beijing Normal University's Chinese Department, Xiao Zhang, who also lived downtown, was bound and beaten when a Red Guard patrol discovered he had secretly tossed away some silver items. Xiao begged the Red Guards to telephone the university and verify his class status; the university authorities reportedly put in a word for him, and he wasn't beaten to death.

Someone sympathetic to Liu Pansui and his wife nevertheless felt compelled to say that the Lius were undone by not knowing what to say to the

Red Guards. In particular, before the Cultural Revolution, Liu Pansui had on several occasions visited the home of Lin Biao and his wife, Ye Qun, to teach them about ancient Chinese writings, and Liu might have been able to use his relationship with Lin Biao, by then Mao's second-in-command, to save himself. This suggestion may be too naïve, however. Mao and Lin Biao visibly and vocally encouraged the Red Guard violence in Beijing, so why should Lin Biao show any special favour to Liu Pansui? Zhou Enlai drafted a list of 'cadres who should be protected', which was subsequently used as evidence that he had tried to help people, but that list contained only thirteen of the highest-ranking 'democratic personages' and Liu Pansui could never have hoped for such protection, even as a famous professor at a ranking university.

Some of Liu Pansui's books were destroyed, while others were taken away. After the Cultural Revolution, some were recovered and donated to the university's library, but his valuable Ming dynasty editions were lost forever. Reportedly, someone in the Cultural Revolution's leadership circles took possession of the books, but given that no action was taken on the murders, theft received even less notice.

In the same neighbourhood as Liu Pansui's home was a multi-unit residential compound for the university's teachers and staff, including Ye Cangcen, a professor of pedagogics. After Red Guards ransacked Ye's home and beat his wife to death, the university put Ye in 'isolation', fearing he would engage in 'class retaliation'. I was unable to learn the name of Ye's wife.

Sun Meisheng, professor and head of the university's Mathematics Department, threw himself in front of a train after being denounced and struggled in the summer of 1966.

Sun killed himself on the Feng-Sha Railway line that ran outside the university sports ground. Someone saw him sitting beside the rails reading a newspaper, and when the train approached, he ran straight in front of it and was crushed.

One of Sun Meisheng's colleagues described him as modest and amiable, with a good sense of humour and excellent teaching skills. Shocked and saddened to learn of his death, this colleague went to the railway track hoping to bid him farewell. All she found was the lower half of Sun Meisheng's body with one leg attached.

Lu Zhiheng, a political counsellor in the university's Chinese Department, questioned some of the tactics used in the Cultural Revolution while posted at the university's Linfen branch in Shanxi Province in autumn 1966. After being struggled multiple times, he drowned himself in a river.

Lu Zhiheng had the nickname Badou or 'eighty bushels', from an expression denoting great talent. The university's Linfen branch had been established in 1964; new students would spend their first year studying there for the purposes of 'revolutionising' and 'battle readiness'. Lu Zhiheng left a suicide note criticising the Cultural Revolution.

Ma Te, a professor of psychology in the university's Education Department accused of being a spy, leaped to his death along with his wife from the university's main building.

The main building of Beijing Normal University, built in the 1950s and eight storeys high, was the tallest building in the area at that time, and therefore became a favourite place for committing suicide during the height of Cultural Revolution violence from 1966 to 1968. The building was subsequently razed after being damaged in the 1976 earthquake.

In spite of interviewing many former students and teachers, I haven't been able to determine exactly when Ma Te died, or the name of his wife. Ma Te was not an ordinary university instructor; he was a noted professor in the educational field, yet the circumstances of his death remain a mystery.

Zhang Ruidi, a student admitted to the Chinese Department in 1964, leaped to his death from the university's main building in December 1966.

Earlier that month, two of the university's students wrote a big-character poster criticising Lin Biao under the pen name Xiang Dongbiao. At that time, Lin Biao was the second most powerful man in China, and was referred to as 'Chairman Mao's close comrade-in-arms'. The students who wrote this poster were accused of being counter-revolutionaries and subjected to struggle in a mass rally that eyewitness described as horrifying. After attending the struggle rally, Zhang Ruidi threw himself from the seventh floor of the university's main building, down through the internal stairwell.

Inquiries at the time did not find that Zhang or his family had any political problems, and the PSB concluded that Zhang had simply been scared to death after seeing how the other students had been treated.

Tsinghua University

Zhang Huaiyi, born in 1945, was admitted to the Mathematics and Mechanics Department of Tsinghua University in 1963, and was a member of a sports delegation. After expressing objections to the Cultural Revolution in his journal and in conversation with teammates in 1967, he was accused of 'counter-revolutionary speech' and criticised in a small group. The sports team's leading Party group had decided that Zhang Huaiyi would be denounced at a rally of more than 100 team delegates on the afternoon of 25 March, but Zhang leaped to his death from the roof of a dormitory at noon that day.

In June 1978, the Tsinghua University Party Committee rehabilitated Zhang Huaiyi and paid his parents a bereavement pension of 150 *yuan*, with an additional 150 *yuan* as a 'one-time family hardship subsidy'.

Renmin University of China

Xiang Chong, a professor of international economics, tried to escape to his brother's home in Shanghai when persecuted during the Cultural Revolution. His brother's situation was also bad, however, and Xiang couldn't stay there. After returning to the university, he killed himself by drinking insecticide. He was around sixty years old.

Xu Hui'er, another teacher at the university, had been designated a Rightist in 1957. Red Guards from his school seized him and beat him to death in summer 1967.

Beijing Drama School

Jiang Feng, head of the Beijing Drama School, was struggled by the school's Red Guards in August 1966. After being beaten and humiliated, she hanged herself, leaving behind an adopted son and daughter.

Jiang Feng and her husband, Wu Zimu, were both Communist Party members. Wu Zimu was head of the Universities Department of the Beijing Municipal Party Committee, and came under long-term struggle and criticism when the Party Committee was labelled 'reactionary' and completely reorganised. Wu died of lung cancer in October 1970. A person close to Wu said he was deeply distressed because when his wife came home after being tormented and humiliated by students at her school, their fourteen-year-old adopted daughter also beat Jiang Feng to demonstrate her revolutionary spirit. Even as he neared death, Wu asked, 'How can such a thing happen?'

Beijing Institute of Geology (now China University of Geosciences)

Guang Kaimin, an associate professor, threw himself in front of a train at Wudaokou, near the school, soon after the Cultural Revolution began.

Xie Jiarong, a research fellow at the Geology Institute of the Chinese Academy of Sciences, killed himself with an overdose of sleeping pills in his home after being struggled as a 'reactionary academic authority' in August 1966. He left a suicide note, which his family read when they discovered his body; they immediately destroyed it and reported that Xie had died of a heart attack. Even so, a post-mortem was carried out, and the doctor issued a certificate saying there was no evidence of suicide, thus sparing Xie a posthumous denunciation.

Wang Hong and his wife, **Xue Tinghua**, both graduated from the institute in 1955 and stayed on at the school as teaching assistants. Xue Tinghua was the youngest of three daughters of a secondary school teacher in Fuzhou. Her two elder sisters emigrated to the US in 1949. Both Wang and Xue were designated Rightists in 1957, and during the Cultural Revolution they were persecuted as members of a 'Rightist anti-Party clique'. The couple killed themselves, leaving behind a son, Wang Lei, who was raised by relatives.

Beijing Institute of Technology

Cai Liting was employed at the institute's library. In August 1966, library staff ransacked her home along with the homes of other families living in the same quadrangle. Cai Liting's home was stripped clean. With nothing to her name, she went to someone in the library who owed her money, hoping repayment would tide her over, but that person gave her nothing. Some other staff gave her a little money, and she used it to buy some pickled vegetables, then went home and hanged herself. When the library reorganised its rooms in 2003, several crates of Cai's personal belongings were discovered. Some younger staff who asked the library's elderly director about them learned who Cai Liting was.

Chinese Academy of Sciences

Chen Mengjia, a poet and archaeologist and a research fellow at the Chinese Academy of Sciences Institute of Archaeology, was designated a Rightist in 1957. Denounced and tormented when the Cultural Revolution began, he killed himself on 3 September 1966, at the age of fifty-five.

In the late 1980s, China's young people rediscovered the poetry of Xu Zhimo, and collections of his poems became bestsellers. Xu Zhimo's graceful and exquisitely emotional poetry held particular allure after the brutality, violence and cruelty of the Cultural Revolution. Like Xu Zhimo, Chen Mengjia had been one of the 'New Moon' poets who gained fame in the 1920s and 1930s through publishing their work in the literary magazine

New Moon. In 1931, Chen edited a volume entitled *New Moon Poetry Collection*, which included one of his own poems:

> Water unstirred by wind,
> My mast lit by stars,
> I push toward the Milky Way,
> The new moon my sail.

At that time, Chen Mengjia was just twenty years old. After graduating from college, he joined the research institute to study ancient script and in that way became an archaeologist. He was an accomplished scholar, publishing many books on ancient culture and artifacts.

In the 1940s, Chen and his wife, Zhao Luorui, both studied at the University of Chicago, where Zhao obtained a PhD in Literature in 1948 for her research on the novels of Henry James. After they returned to China, Zhao Luorui became a professor of English at Yenching University, while Chen Mengjia became a professor of Chinese at Tsinghua University.

When the CCP reorganised China's universities, church-funded institutions such as Yenching University were closed down, and Tsinghua University's Humanities Department was eliminated. Chen Mengjia came under harsh criticism and was 'assigned' to the Institute of Archaeology in 1952.

A friend of the couple, Professor Wu Ningkun, had also studied at the University of Chicago, and when he returned to Beijing he stayed with Chen and Zhao for a time. In an essay entitled 'Yenching's Last Days', published in the 1990s, Wu writes that one day an announcement was broadcast over the Yenching campus requiring all teachers and students to take part in exercises during breaks. When Chen Mengjia heard this, he said, '1984 has arrived. So quickly.' However, Chen never openly criticised the Communist Party or the system it imposed.

While at the Institute of Archaeology, Chen Mengjia was designated a Rightist. His main crime was 'opposing reform of the writing system'. In fact, all he had said was that reform should be carried out prudently. Although archaeology was far removed from political struggle, other archaeologists criticised Chen harshly. Zhao Luorui suffered a mental breakdown.

Many of the intellectuals who were designated Rightists had studied in the US or Europe. As one of them, Wu Ningkun was sent to the Great Northern Wilderness for 'labour reform'. Chen Mengjia remained at the Institute of Archaeology with a demotion and reduced salary, but at one point was 'sent down' to labour in rural Henan just as China experienced the Great Famine that killed tens of millions of people.

In 1960, at a time of severe food shortages, a friend of Chen Mengjia found a way for a relative who had been working for the government overseas to bring him some butter from abroad. This friend invited Chen to his home to eat roasted cakes with butter smeared on them, an extraordinary indulgence at that time. While eating the cakes, Chen Mengjia wept. He still had a poet's sensitive heart, but like the rest of China's intellectuals, he endured the three years of hunger with fortitude.

After the Cultural Revolution began, the Institute of Archaeology subjected Chen Mengjia to criticism and struggle. He was forced to kneel for long periods in the institute's courtyard, enduring the blazing heat while people spat on his head. His home was ransacked and taken over by someone else, while he and his wife were relagated to a shed that had once served as a garage. His wife become ill twice but wasn't allowed hospital treatment.

After being struggled once again on the night of 24 August 1966, Chen Mengjia left the Institute of Archaeology and went to the home of a friend who lived nearby. He told that friend, 'I'm not going to be toyed with like a monkey any more.' At that moment, some people from the institute who had tracked him to his friend's house forced him to kneel while they harangued him, and then held him at the institute all night.

This was at the height of the Red Guard violence, and on 24 August, at least six residents were beaten to death by Red Guards in Dongcheng Hutong next to the Institute of Archaeology, flogged mercilessly from noon until deep into the night. 'It sounded like they were butchering pigs,' a neighbour recalled. The wailing of tortured people rang through the night air, and nearby residents could only cover their ears with their pillows.

Chen Mengjia must have heard all of this while locked up inside the Institute of Archaeology. That night, he wrote a suicide note and took an overdose of sleeping pills, but the dosage wasn't enough to kill him. The night of 24 August had a full moon, and I wonder if Chen saw this moon and thought of the poem he'd written all those years ago.

Ten days later, on 3 September 1966, Chen Mengjia attempted suicide again, successfully this time, in his home in Qianliang Hutong.

In the ten days between Chen's suicide attempts, Red Guards killed thousands of Beijing residents, while tens of thousands were expelled from the city. Many others were humiliated and tortured in the 'labour reform teams' established in their work units, and many committed suicide after being subjected to struggle. The brutality and terror of the Cultural Revolution far exceeded what Orwell imagined.

Chen Mengjia was a sensitive poet and a mild-mannered scholar. In the early 1950s he came under ideological attack and lost the freedom to choose his profession. In 1957 he was designated a Rightist, making him an enemy of the people. In the Cultural Revolution, he experienced not only intense mental torment, but also cruel physical torture. After his two earlier calamities, the third was the worst and it destroyed him. It was the destruction of one man, but also of a group of people like him – a small but very important part of Chinese civilisation.

Qi Shiqian was a research fellow in the Modern History Research Institute in the Department of Philosophy and Social Sciences of the Chinese Academy of Sciences. After the Cultural Revolution began, Qi was accused of being a member of the institute's 'Three Family Village Anti-Party Clique' and was criticised and struggled. He killed himself by drinking pesticide on the night of 4 August 1966.

SHANGHAI

East China Normal University

Li Pingxin, a fifty-nine-year-old history professor, gassed himself to death in his home in Huaihai Road after the Shanghai Municipal Party Committee proclaimed him an 'anti-Party, anti-socialist element' on 15 June 1966. Li Pingxin was one of the first people 'struck down' in Shanghai during the Cultural Revolution.

After the CCP Central Committee issued its 16 May Circular, the provinces and cities responded by 'ferreting out' batches of people according to the standards set in the notice.

On 10 June 1966, the Shanghai Municipal Party Committee convened a Cultural Revolution mobilisation meeting attended by some 10,000 people. In his mobilisation report, Shanghai mayor Cao Didi accused eight artists, writers, editors and professors of being anti-Party, anti-socialist elements. On 11 June, the Party Committee's official newspaper, *Liberation Daily*, published an editorial on the subject entitled 'Thoroughly expose, criticise and strike down'. Li Pingxin gassed himself a few days later in the apartment he rented above a shop selling women's products. The others who were attacked along with him were subsequently also tortured, and some died as a result.

Li Pingxin had been a Communist Party member, but he left the Party after 1927. He nevertheless remained a Marxist historian and was the author of many works in which he used Marxism to explain Chinese history, and he retained many contacts among Communist Party members. After coming under criticism during the 1952 Thought Reform Campaign and Loyalty and Sincerity Campaign, he tried to kill himself with a blow to the head with a hatchet, but was taken to hospital and saved. The Shanghai

Municipal Party Committee subsequently arranged for him to teach at East China Normal University.

Li Pingxin's only son, Li Qianwei, was a foreign-affairs cadre in Beijing at the time, and upon learning of his father's death, he reported it to the political and ideological work department above him. They told him he could go back to Shanghai, but he'd be responsible for the consequences. For that reason, Li's son didn't return to Shanghai and 'drew a clear distinction' from his father. Even so, Li Qianwei was subsequently forced out of his position and assigned a job as a handyman at the Beijing 157 Secondary School.

Half a year later, Shanghai mayor Cao Didi was also struck down. A placard was hung around his neck, and he was put in a truck and paraded through the streets.

Ding Xiaoyun, a librarian at the university, killed himself on 4 August 1966, after being paraded through the streets and struggled.

That night, students pulled more than 190 teachers from their homes, made them put on the dunce caps and placards inscribed with the words 'reactionary gang element' and 'reactionary academic authority' and then forced them to parade around the campus while being beaten. After the parade, all of the 'ox demons' were forced to crowd together kneeling in front of the school's sports ground, where a struggle rally was held.

After the rally, the victims were forced to labour in 'ox demon and snake spirit teams' at the school. Most had their homes ransacked. Soon after this, the Shanghai Municipal Party Committee Writing Group that played a key role in the Cultural Revolution in Shanghai at that time came to the university to observe what was happening, and the next day it went to other schools to encourage students to 'begin taking action'.

Other university staff targeted at the 4 August struggle rally also killed themselves later:

Wu Disheng was originally a professor of Russian, but after being designated a Rightist in 1957 was no longer allowed to teach and went to work at the university library.

After the violent struggle rally at the university on 4 August, Wu and his wife, a bank employee, discussed how to deal with their affairs. They sent their adopted daughter to her maternal grandmother and withdrew all their money and put it in a drawer. One day in September, they ate a final meal, wrote suicide notes, changed into clean clothes, and then hanged themselves, each from a separate window casement in their home.

Hu Ming, a professor of Russian around fifty years old, had been labelled a Rightist in 1957 and removed from his position as department head. After being struggled and criticised, Hu leaped to his death from the university's main building on 5 September 1966.

Yao Qijun, a physics professor, leaped to his death from the physics building on 28 September 1966.

Shen Xin'er, a student at the university, was accused of being a 'reactionary student' in 1966. He leaped to his death, landing on a coal heap at the foot of the building.

Fei Mingjun's case spans a longer timeframe. After studying at Japan's Waseda University, Fei became an associate professor at Shanghai's East China Normal University in the 1950s. Labelled a member of the 'Hu Feng Counter-revolutionary Clique'[71] in 1955, he was sent to Qinghai for 'labour reform' under the additional allegation of being a 'Japanese spy'. Fei Mingjun died in Qinghai in 1972.

Fei's family suffered long-term persecution because of him. After he was arrested in 1955, his seven-member family was expelled from their living quarters at East China Normal University, and with nowhere to go, they were forced to take refuge in a cement culvert. The eldest child was only eight or nine years old at the time. Later the Public Security Bureau escorted the family to Gansu Province. On the train there, the family were handcuffed, even though the cuffs kept falling off the youngest child. Once they reached Gansu, the labour reform farm refused to take them. They begged in the streets and made their way back to Shanghai, where they again lived in the culvert and scavenged in garbage piles for food until 1961. Around that time, many people starved to death in Anhui Province due to the Great Famine. Fei Mingjun's family were sent to Yanqiao Commune in Dingyuan County, Anhui Province.

A teacher at East China Normal University once visited Fei Mingjun's family in their village. He said more than half of the people in that village had starved to death, and half of the fields were lying fallow. The farmer's home where the teacher stayed had no door, and a pile of mud served as a table. Many houses in the village had no door, because people who starved to death after being refused food at the communal kitchen were carried away on door planks.

Fei Mingjun's daughter was unable to find a husband for a long time. She finally married a man from a 'class enemy' family, but he was abusive and she passed her days in misery.

When Fei Mingjun died in Qinghai in 1972, the Qinghai Labour Reform Farm notified Yanqiao Commune, which then held a 'struggle rally' to denounce Fei's wife. When Fei's third son asked the commune's militia commander why his mother was being treated this way, he was hung from

---

[71] TN: Hu Feng, a Leftist writer, was imprisoned on accusation of being the leader of a counter-revolutionary clique in 1955. He survived the Cultural Revolution and was rehabilitated in 1980.

a rafter all night long. He later ran off to Shandong to learn carpentry and boxing, and didn't return to the village until two years later.

After the Cultural Revolution ended, Fei Mingjun's third son went to Shanghai and asked East China Normal University to rehabilitate him. The university referred the case to the court, which replied that Fei was not a Hu Feng Clique element but a traitor. The son then went to Beijing and found a classmate of Fei's from Waseda University who was now director of the Counsellors' Office of the State Council. One week later the son was received by the central government leader Zhao Ziyang.

By the time Fei Mingjun's third son returned to Shanghai, East China Normal University had already been notified by Beijing, and he was given a job in the general-service section of the university. When the son took an exam to become a carpenter, he could barely write his name because he'd never been to school. Later he ran a sawmill. His eldest brother was allowed to run a restaurant near the main entrance to the university.

Fudan University

Liu Dezhong, a foreign language teacher in his forties, hanged himself along with his wife on 8 October 1966. I have been unable to learn the name of his wife.

Before 1966, the Foreign Languages Department of Fudan University only offered a major in English, but some teachers also taught required foreign-language courses such as English and Russian to non-English majors. Liu taught courses for English majors, but he was also fluent in German and Russian. One of his students said that Liu gave lively lectures that were a joy to attend; his wit and easy-going style made him one of the most popular teachers.

Liu Dezhong's father was a Chinese diplomat, and his mother was German,[72] so he'd grown up overseas. When the Cultural Revolution began and Mao targeted 'bourgeois intellectuals', Liu's outstanding teaching and family background made him a natural target.

We don't know exactly what torments he suffered, but we can draw some conclusions based on what happened to others at Fudan University. For example, on 8 August 1966, chemistry professor **Zhao Danruo** was struggled by students and made to kneel while wearing a dunce cap and having ink poured on his head. He was then paraded through the streets and beaten. His denunciation rally lasted nearly an hour and a half, and he died soon afterwards. Mathematics professor Su Buqing and others were

---

[72] TN: Liu's given name combines the characters for Germany and China.

made to crawl around the campus on all fours like dogs while they were beaten. An eyewitness says the victims crawled until their trousers were worn through at the knees. In the Foreign Languages Department, teachers were called to the student dormitories and beaten.

Before the Cultural Revolution, Liu Dezhong's wife had been sent to a labour reform farm. It appears she was allowed to return to Shanghai every few months to visit her family. In summer 1966, when the Red Guards began their large-scale violence, Liu's wife had half her hair shaved off at the *laogai* farm. When she returned home in early October, she was beaten and humiliated by people in her neighbourhood.

Liu Dezhong and his wife hanged themselves in their home. Neighbours noticed that no one was taking in the milk deliveries and notified the police, who broke down their door and found they had died some time ago.

A Red Guard leader from Fudan University's Foreign Languages Department who went to Liu's home told schoolmates that Liu and his wife had used newly purchased rope. They died facing each other and wearing their best clothes. On their table was an open Bible with some English words written on a piece of paper on top of it. That Red Guard leader had been an English major for three years, so he remembered what was written on the paper and told his schoolmates. One of them still remembered the sentence more than thirty years later: 'When earthly refuge fails me, can I find a shelter in the love of Christ?'

The Red Guard who went to Liu's home said he smelled a fragrance there, and believed that the couple had sprayed perfume in their home before they died. They wondered if this was part of a rite Christians carried out when committing suicide.

In fact, Christian teachings forbid suicide, so there are no such rites. Christians believe that life is the gift of God, and that only God can take it away. Liu Dezhong and his wife were driven to this ultimate sin because they couldn't face living under the protracted terror of the Cultural Revolution. That's probably why they changed into clean clothes, sprayed perfume, and died in the most dignified way they could manage.

Liu Dezhong was not the only teacher in Fudan's Foreign Languages Department who killed himself. Professor **Yu Nanqiu** gassed himself to death with his wife in summer 1966 after Red Guards ransacked their home and struggled them. Yu Nanqiu was an elderly man, and one of his 'crimes' was that he had been a delegate to the National Assembly under the KMT government. Teacher **Zhang Ruxiu** hanged herself after being struggled in 1966, and the department's deputy Party secretary and political counsellor, **Wu Jingcheng**, also leaped to his death that year. Others were victimised during the Cleansing of the Class Ranks (as described in Part Five).

There were also victims in the university's other departments.

Fu Manyun, a homemaker in her fifties, was married to one of the professors who were made to crawl on the ground like dogs. Fu's husband, Tan Jiazhen, was a prominent biology expert who had obtained his PhD in the US in the 1930s and specialised in genetics. Fu herself had once been a primary school teacher but was no longer working outside the home. During a 'struggle rally' for family members at Fudan University, she was beaten and humiliated, and later Red Guards from the university's Affiliated Secondary School forced her to kneel on a scrubbing board. She hanged herself at home after that.

Mao Qingxian, a teacher of atomic physics around fifty years old and somewhat lame, was very popular with his students, who recalled his humour and intelligence. In 1966, Mao was designated a bourgeois intellectual and accused of making reactionary remarks. Students struggled him on the university's sports field and poured ink on him. Unable to bear the humiliation, Mao jumped to his death from one of the school's buildings.

Wang Zaoshi, born in 1903, was a professor of history who had obtained his PhD after studying in the US and the UK. Labelled a Rightist in 1957, he was arrested on 26 November 1966, on allegations of 'establishing a reactionary organisation'. Wang died in prison in Shanghai on 5 August 1971.

Ye Shaoji, a mid-level cadre in his fifties, killed himself after being struggled in 1966.

Qi Xiangyun, deputy Party secretary of the Chemistry Department, leaped to his death while under 'isolation and investigation' in 1967.

Wu Bixi, vice-chairman of the Journalism Department, leaped to his death from the fourth floor of a university dormitory building in 1967. His body was left on the cement next to the building for nearly a day before anyone took it away.

Wu Weiguo, Party secretary of the History Department, killed himself during the Cultural Revolution.

Qian Xingsu, a physical education teacher, is remembered by a friend as a lively woman and dedicated teacher who excelled at the hurdles and high jump. Qian came under persecution after her husband, formerly the principal of the East Asia Athletic School, was unjustly sentenced, and she hanged herself in a restroom.

East China Institute of Chemical Engineering

Peng Peng, a teacher of politics, killed himself while being struggled during the early stages of the Cultural Revolution.

Zhang Zhendan, a professor of chemical engineering, killed himself after being struggled in 1966.

Shanghai Conservatory of Music

Lu Xiutang, a fifty-five-year-old professor of folk music who played the traditional two-stringed instrument known as the *erhu*, drowned himself in summer 1966.

Yang Jiaren, born in 1912, was professor and chairman of the Conducting Department. Yang had obtained his Master's degree in music in the United States, and had been teaching at the Conservatory since returning to China in 1940. He was brutally struggled in 1966, and on 6 September he and his wife, **Cheng Zhuoru**, killed themselves by taking an overdose of sleeping pills and turning on the gas.

Li Cuizhen, a fifty-six-year-old professor and head of the Piano Department, was a graduate of the school and had studied in England before returning to her alma mater to teach. After being humiliated and paraded through the streets, she gassed herself to death in her home on 9 September 1966.

Zhao Zhihua, forty-five years old, had studied in Japan and the US before becoming an assistant professor in the conservatory's Strings Department. Thrashed and struggled as a 'major Rightist, traitor and spy' on 25 December 1966, Zhao gassed himself to death along with his wife the next day.

Fan Jisen, a fifty-year-old professor and former head of the Piano Department, was already suffering from liver cancer when he was forced to undergo labour reform and was subjected to struggle and various torments. He died in 1967.

Others at the Shanghai Conservatory of Music died during the Cleansing of the Class Ranks and the purge of the 16 May Conspiratorial Clique and are included under those sections.

Other Victims in Shanghai

Wang Renli, a teacher of mechanics at the Shanghai Work-Study Polytechnic University (now the Shanghai No. 2 Polytechnic University), was a beautiful woman. Accused of 'lifestyle problems' during the Cultural Revolution, she had half her hair cut off and was forced to scrub toilets. One day, Wang killed herself by drinking the diluted hydrochloric acid used for cleaning the toilets.

Ma Qishuang, in his sixties, was dean of studies and a professor and head of the Radio Department at the Shanghai University of Science and Technology. After being struggled, beaten and humiliated in 1966, he stayed in the school dormitory, wrapped wire around his wrists and electrocuted himself. The day after he died, the campus was plastered with banners declaring that Ma had 'isolated himself from the people' and his name was crossed out with a large red X.

Yang Dairong, an English teacher at Shanghai Normal College and vice-chairman and Party secretary of the Foreign Languages Department, was born to a 'capitalist family'. Accused of being a 'proxy of the bourgeoisie' during the Cultural Revolution, she hanged herself in one of the school buildings.

Wang Gengcai, principal of the Shanghai Gauge Casting Factory Work-Study Technical School, was in his fifties when, sometime in 1967 or 1968, he was beaten to death by students from the school's 1965 intake.

TIANJIN

Nankai University

Wu Shuqiu, a forty-one-year-old professor of foreign languages who had graduated from Yenching University and studied at the University of Moscow from 1955 to 1957, poisoned himself to death on 9 July 1966.

Xu Zhengyang, the same age as Wu Shuqiu and like him a graduate of Yenching University, taught classical literature in the Chinese Department. Accused of being a member of an 'anti-Party clique', he was struggled, had his home ransacked and was forced to engage in 'labour reform' by pulling weeds in the hot sun. He drowned himself on 4 September 1966. Xu's ashes weren't retained, so when his 'remains were laid to rest' after the Cultural Revolution, a copy of the *Ancient and Modern Novels* that he had annotated was placed in his urn.

FUJIAN PROVINCE

Wang Sijie, a professor of history at Xiamen University, was brutally struggled in summer 1966. He and his wife, son and daughter committed suicide together.

HEBEI PROVINCE

Hebei Normal University, Shijiazhuang

Zhai Yuming, a lecturer in chemistry, slit his wrists in 1966 after being paraded through the streets, beaten and humiliated.

Yang Suhua, a teacher of Chinese, was off campus with her students when the Cultural Revolution began. She was brought back to the school, had her hair shaved off and was locked up. On her third night of captivity, she killed herself with scissors.

Zhu Xianji, a biology lecturer, was struggled by students during the Cultural Revolution and died after returning home that night. The people who struggled him claimed he killed himself, but his family said he died of his injuries. Another teacher in the Biology Department, Wang Yiduo, had his face branded with an iron, leaving a permanent triangular scar.

HENAN PROVINCE

Zhengzhou Normal College

Two historians at the college,[73] both graduates of Peking University who had been put under labour reform in the college library after being labelled Rightists in 1957, leaped to their deaths in summer 1966 after big-character posters called for them to be 'repatriated' to their places of origin. **Tong Junting**, a native of Yanshi, Henan Province, who specialised in Chinese history, had been an instructor before being labelled a Rightist. **Wang Jimin**, a native of Xun County, Henan Province, who specialised in world history, had been head of the History Department.

HUBEI PROVINCE

Liu Yongji, a professor of classical literature in the Chinese Department of Wuhan University, fell ill after being struggled in summer 1966 and died in his home at the end of the year. His wife, a full-time homemaker, had been known as 'Granny Liu' by children in the staff residential quarters, but she was struggled as a 'landlord woman' during the Cultural Revolution. After Liu Yongji died, his wife hanged herself.

Another professor of Chinese at Wuhan University, **Xi Lusi**, went on hunger strike after being struggled as a 'reactionary academic authority' and died as a result in September 1966.

Zhou Wenzhen, a fifty-five-year-old teacher at the night school for staff of the Yangtze River Shipping Management Bureau in Wuhan, was beaten to death by Red Guards in late August 1966.

---

[73] Now Zhengzhou University.

As well as being a teacher, Zhou Wenzhen came from a family that was wealthy before 1949, and these two factors were the main reason why she was beaten to death in Red August. Zhou's daughter, Huang Jingyi, an intelligent and lively student in the Chinese Department of Wuhan University, never recovered from her mother's death. She eventually taught at Huangshi City Normal School in Hubei Province, but poor health forced her to retire early.

HUNAN PROVINCE

Central South University of Mining and Technology, Changsha

A lecturer hanged himself in the university's residential quarters in 1966, and a professor living in the same block jumped to his death in 1968. I was unable to learn either of their names.

The teacher who hanged himself taught foreign languages and had served as a translator for 'Soviet specialists'. He left behind a three-year-old son and a wife who had graduated from a technical school and had to support herself, the child and an elderly parent on a little more than 30 *yuan* per month.

The professor who leaped to his death had studied in the US and served as director of a mine. It was said that he was locked up in an 'ox pen' because gold had been found in his house.

Two-thirds of the adults in the eighteen households living in that residential block were 'struggled' during the Cultural Revolution, most by having half their hair shaved off.

JIANGXI PROVINCE

Jiangxi Normal College, Nanchang

Xiong Huaqi, associate professor and chairman of the Chinese Department, was beaten to death during a large-scale struggle rally at the college on 11 August 1966. He was in his early fifties.

More than 140 people were paraded and struggled at the college that day, beginning around 10:00 a.m. and ending at the 'Red Square' in the middle of the campus around three hours later. There the targets were ordered to kneel on the cement and were struggled for more than half an hour. The weather was stifling at more than 100 degrees, and the scorching concrete mangled the flesh on the legs of the kneeling people. Some older people fainted before even reaching the square, and many more lost consciousness before their torments ended. Chinese teacher **Li Zhongming**, nearly sixty years old, and the school clinic's head physician, **Zhou Tianzhu**, around fifty years old, both fainted during the parading and struggling and died soon afterwards.

Around 2:00 p.m., a student who was chairman of the Cultural Revolution Committee Preparatory Committee that controlled the school at that time came out and announced that each unit should take its 'reactionaries' back to be denounced. This brought the parading and struggling to a temporarily halt, but Xiong Huaqi had already fallen into a coma. He was carried to the doorway of the No. 2 classroom building and lay on the ground foaming at the mouth. A female student shouted, 'Xiong Huaqi is putting on an act!' and kicked him. Xiong never regained consciousness.

He Ji, a history professor around fifty years old, killed himself that night, bringing the death toll to four.

LIAONING PROVINCE

Dalian Engineering Institute

Huang Bixin, a forty-one-year-old teacher of radio at the Dalian Engineering Institute, was designated a Rightist in 1957. He hanged himself in his home soon after the Cultural Revolution began, on 14 June 1966. The youngest of Huang's three children disappeared on 26 October that year and his wife, **Yu Qiyun**, killed herself on 15 June 1968.

Among Huang Bixin's family of eight brothers and sisters, six were designated Rightists in 1957; of the two sisters who escaped this fate, one had a college student son who was designated a Rightist.

'Rightist' Huang Bixin was no longer allowed to teach; his pay dropped by half and he was 'sent down' for labour reform. After his Rightist cap was 'lifted' in 1960, he was allowed to resume teaching. Some of his students were 'cadre college students' who had 'good political qualifications' but lacked a solid secondary school education, and when they repeatedly failed their exams, Huang Bixin was accused of engaging in 'class retaliation' and sent back to the countryside. When the Cultural Revolution began, he returned to school only to immediately be identified as a key target by the university Party branch. He became the subject of big-character posters and struggle rallies and finally killed himself.

Less than a month after his death, the Cultural Revolution further expanded its targets to include members of the institute's Party Committee, and even more teachers were sent to the campus 'labour reform teams', where they were humiliated and subjected to worse physical torment than during the previous phase. Eighteen people were persecuted to death at the Dalian Engineering Institute during the Cultural Revolution. In 1969, people from all nine of Dalian's tertiary institutions were sent down to the countryside, and the Engineering Institute was relocated to Zhuanghe County.

Another of the tragedies in Huang Bixin's family was the disappearance of his fourteen-year-old daughter, who attended a mass public criticism of the municipal Party secretary on 26 October 1966. The girl became separated from her classmates and never returned home. Some people concluded that Huang's daughter had been murdered because of her 'class enemy background', while the school claimed that the girl's mother had sent her overseas to serve as a spy.

Huang Bixin's wife, **Yu Qiyun**, a teacher of physics at the institute, was put under 'isolation and investigation' on 10 June 1968, during the Cleansing of the Class Ranks. Four days later, on the second anniversary of her husband's suicide, Yu Qiyun killed herself in her cell.

Huang and Yu's two remaining children were secondary school students, and four months after the death of their mother, they were sent to labour in the countryside. Families with this kind of background were known at the time as 'carrying a black wok', or being scapegoated, and their hardships were greater than that of most 'sent-down educated youth'. But while in the countryside, the youngsters heard villagers say that the worst times were during Land Reform in 1950 and the Great Famine of the early 1960s, when even children were killed or starved to death. To survivors of these horrors, the torments of the Cultural Revolution seemed less severe.

Huang Bixin and Yu Qiyun were ordinary teachers, but Huang's father, Huang Yanpei (1878–1965), was a famous early advocate of vocational education, as well as being a founder of the China Democratic League. Huang Yanpei had visited Yan'an in 1945 and asked Mao whether the CCP would become despotic and corrupt after taking over like previous dynasties. Mao replied that the CCP would take a new road of democracy instead. After returning to Chongqing, Huang Yanpei wrote his book *Return from Yan'an*, which served as positive publicity for the CCP, and he started a movement to boycott the Nationalist government's censors, which led the Kuomintang Central Committee to rescind inspection of news and publications.

After the CCP took power in October 1949, Huang Yanpei was appointed vice-premier of the State Administrative Council and Minister of Light Industry, and he served as vice-chairman of the CPPCC from 1954 until his death in December 1965. Huang died before the launch of the Cultural Revolution, but he lived long enough to see the CCP go back on Mao's promises for a democratic China, with six of his children and one grandson designated Rightists. One son, Huang Wanli, was a professor of civil engineering at Tsinghua University and wrote an essay that criticised problems with the construction of the Western Highway. After the president of Tsinghua University sent the essay to Mao, Huang Wanli and more than 5% of Tsinghua University's professors were designated Rightists. Years after the tragic deaths of Huang Bixin and Yu Qiyun, their names were not allowed to appear on their own in publications, and even Huang Yanpei's books and essays could not be mentioned.

SHAANXI PROVINCE

Xi'an Jiaotong University

Thirty-six people were persecuted to death at Jiaotong University during the Cultural Revolution (see also Part Five).

Wang Yongting, a twenty-three-year-old student who signed a big-character poster opposing the 'work groups' in June 1966, was surrounded, attacked and made to write thirty-two copies of a self-criticism totalling 162 pages. Wang leaped to her death on 9 July 1966.

Gong Qiwu, a fifty-four-year-old employee of the university library, was beaten and stabbed because of his landlord class status. He leaped to his death on 21 August 1966.

Lu Jiaxun, a forty-one-year-old teacher in the dynamics teaching and research section, had been designated a Rightist in 1957, and was struggled for 'historical problems' during the Cultural Revolution. Lu leaped to his death on 27 August 1966.

Luo Fengjiao, a fifty-year-old associate professor of dynamics at Shaanxi Province Polytechnic (which later merged with Xi'an Jiaotong University), leaped to his death on 13 December 1966, after students put up big-character posters denouncing him.

Hu Junru, born in 1919, joined the Party in 1939 and was head of the organisation department of the university's Party Committee. During the Cultural Revolution he was investigated and struggled for having once been taken prisoner and for losing an important name list. Hu hanged himself on 11 May 1967, in Xingqing Park, across from the university.

Shaanxi Normal University

Huang Guozhang, professor and head of the Geography Department, and his wife, **Fan Xueyin**, a lecturer in the foreign language teaching and research section, hanged themselves in their home after it was ransacked and they were struggled by Red Guards in August 1966.

Huang Guozhang had studied overseas and had laid the foundation for modern geography in China. During the Cultural Revolution, he was labelled a 'reactionary academic authority' and also came under attack for having worked under the Kuomintang government.

Zhu Huang, a lecturer in history, killed himself after being struggled in 1966.

Gao Bin, a native of Hubei Province, had studied in England in the 1940s and was a professor of Russian Literature at the Beijing Foreign Studies University before being transferred to Shaanxi Normal University. During the Anti-Rightist Campaign, he was designated a Rightist and sent to the countryside for 'labour reform'. He was rehabilitated and allowed to resume teaching, but at a lower grade and salary. He killed himself after being publicly criticised in 1966.

Seven staff of Shaanxi Normal University were persecuted to death in 1966, either through beatings or suicide. Seven more staff were killed or driven to suicide in 1968. Ten of the fourteen victims were teachers.

PART TWO

The Red Guards in Primary and Secondary Schools

BEIJING

BEIJING NORMAL UNIVERSITY AFFILIATED GIRLS' SECONDARY SCHOOL

Bian Zhongyun, the school's fifty-year-old vice-principal, was 'exposed' and struggled in early June 1966, and then beaten to death by student Red Guards on 5 August 1966.

She was the first person killed by Red Guards in Beijing during the Cultural Revolution.

The Killing

On 5 August 1966, Red Guards at the Beijing Normal University Affiliated Girls' Secondary School (hereafter BNU Girls' School) struggled the school's five administrators: vice-principals Bian Zhongyun, Hu Zhitao and Liu Zhiping, dean Mei Shumin and vice-dean Wang Yubing.

The Red Guards had declared themselves established at the BNU Girls' School on 31 July, soon after Mao Zedong ordered the withdrawal of the work groups that had been leading the Cultural Revolution in the schools. The Red Guards took control under the leadership of the Cultural Revolution Committee that the school's work group had established; most of the Committee's members were students.

On the morning of 5 August, 'ox demons and snake spirits' who had been 'ferreted out' were ordered to attend a struggle rally at around two o'clock that afternoon. Vice-principal Hu Zhitao, who had been assigned to clean toilets for 'reform through labour', reminded the students that following the departure of the work group, struggle rallies required permission from the Chinese Communist Party's new Beijing Municipal Party Committee (which had unseated the old Party Committee two months earlier). The Red Guards simply drenched Hu with a bottle of ink and dragged the school administrators onto the sports field wearing papier mâché dunce caps and placards bearing the words 'Counter-revolutionary Reactionary' and 'Three-Anti Element'.[1] The administrators were forced to kneel on a concrete platform while Red Guards 'exposed' and denounced them. Some students grabbed broken chair and table legs from the workshop, while others fetched buckets of scalding water from the boiler room. The Red Guards forced the struggle targets to march through the streets beating dustpans and chanting, 'I am an ox demon and snake spirit,' then escorted them to a smaller sports field to engage in 'labour reform' by moving a pile of dirt using baskets on shoulder poles. When Bian Zhongyun had difficulty lifting her over-loaded basket, she was struck on the face so hard that she collapsed on the ground. The five targets were battered with baseball bats, crosspieces from hurdle bars, and chair and table legs spiked with nails that gouged out chunks of flesh.

After the 'labour reform' had gone on for a while, the Red Guards dragged the 'reactionaries' to a dormitory toilet and dumped human waste on them. Blood stained the dormitory's whitewashed hallway.

The school had no principal at that time, and as the most senior of the three vice-principals, Bian Zhongyun was beaten the hardest. After two or three hours of torment, Bian fell unconscious in the dormitory's stairwell. Even then, Red Guards continued to kick and stomp and throw filth on her, reviling her for 'playing dead'.

A little after five o'clock, a school handyman was summoned to load Bian Zhongyun's body onto a wheelbarrow used for moving rubbish. Meanwhile, the struggle session continued against the other four administrators. Vice-principal Liu Zhiping was forced to kneel beside the wheelbarrow. Vice-principal Hu Zhitao saw that Bian Zhongyun's arms were red and swollen and covered with wounds; her eyes were half-open and unresponsive, but she was still breathing. Hu told the Red Guards that Bian was in critical condition and should be taken to the hospital. The Red Guards yelled, 'Reactionary! If you don't reform, you'll end up the same way!' and then locked her in an office.

---

[1] TN: A Three-Anti Element (*sanfan fenzi*) in this context was someone alleged to be anti-Party, anti-socialism and anti-Mao.

Eventually the handyman pushed the wheelbarrow over to the school's north entrance, which was just across the street from the Postal and Telecommunications Hospital. Fearing that taking Bian across the street in broad daylight would 'look bad', one of the Red Guards ordered the wheelbarrow kept on the school grounds, while Bian Zhongyun's body was covered with big-character posters weighted down with a broom. About two hours later, a little after seven o'clock, someone from the school's Cultural Revolution Preparatory Committee telephoned the Beijing Municipal Party Committee to request instructions. By the time Bian Zhongyun was taken to the hospital, she had been dead long enough for rigor mortis to set in.

The four other administrators attacked that day were also seriously injured. Vice-principal Hu Zhitao was beaten to unconsciousness and then pulled upright and beaten again until her spine fractured, confining her to a back brace for the rest of her life. Dean Mei Shumin was beaten across his back with a nail-spiked pole until fabric from his shirt became embedded in his flesh. The physical and mental anguish he suffered resulted in chronic arrhythmia. Liu Zhiping died in the early 1990s at what would not be considered an advanced age. The four administrators suffered sustained physical and psychological damage not only from their own physical abuse, but also from watching their long-time colleague beaten to death before their eyes.

Bian Zhongyun's husband, Wang Jingyao, was notified to come to the Postal and Telecommunications Hospital, where he found his wife's battered corpse. The BNU Girls' School's leaders met with Wang at that time, and he asked them to write down their names on a piece of paper, which he retained. Six of the seven were student Red Guards, including Song Binbin, a third-year student and Red Guard leader.

Although cameras were luxury items at the time, Wang Jingyao went to the Xidan Department Store the next day and bought one, and in the hospital mortuary he took a last photo of his wife. He still has that photo, which shows Bian's wounds distinctly even in black-and-white.

In order to arrange for the disposal of Bian's body, Wang and his eldest daughter met with one of the leaders of the school's Red Guards, Deng Rong, the daughter of Deng Xiaoping. Deng was dressed in the standard Red Guard attire of a military uniform with sleeves and trouser legs rolled up, her waist cinched with a belt and an armband on her upper arm. Deng wanted the hospital's doctor to carry out an autopsy and certify that Bian had died of a heart attack rather than from being beaten. (Later, as the violence escalated, Red Guards were proud to take credit for killings, and corpses were loaded into trucks and transported openly through Beijing's streets.) Wang Jingyao opposed further violation of his wife's body when the cause of death was so obvious. Deng Rong angrily asked Bian Zhongyun's eldest daughter, 'What's your opinion?' The daughter said, 'It's not up to me to decide.' Deng left without saying anything more, and ultimately no autopsy was performed. In line with the Red Guard leaders' demands, however, the hospital released the body with a death certificate stating the cause of death as 'unknown'.

Thirty-four years later, Deng Rong published her book *My Father, Deng Xiaoping: The Cultural Revolution Years*,[2] which made no mention of Bian Zhongyu's death and Deng Rong's own part in it.

The Road to Death: Designation as 'Category 4'

Bian Zhongyun was born in 1916 in Wuwei, Anhui Province. Her father had worked his way up from struggling banking apprentice to wealthy and prominent founder of a private bank. After Bian Zhongyun graduated from secondary school in 1937, her plans to enter college were interrupted by China's war with Japan, and she joined the resistance effort in Changsha. She was finally able to attend college in 1941, and became a member of the Chinese Communist Party that same year. After graduating in 1945, she joined her husband, Wang Jingyao (her college classmate), in one of China's Communist-controlled areas. After the CCP took power in 1949, Bian became a teacher at the BNU Girls' School and gradually rose through the ranks to become vice-principal. By the time of her death, Bian had been working at the Girls' School for seventeen years. She was the mother of four children, and her husband was a historian in the faculty of philosophy and sociology at the Chinese Academy of Sciences.

The BNU Girls' School, established in 1917, was one of Beijing's oldest secondary schools. When the CCP came to power in 1949, all of the school's administrators were replaced with Party members. Noted for excellence, and located only a kilometre from the centre of government power at Zhongnanhai, the BNU Girls' School inevitably counted the daughters of China's top leaders among its students. Mao's two daughters graduated from it prior to the Cultural Revolution, and Liu Shaoqi and Deng Xiaoping both had daughters there when the Revolution began. Entry to all secondary schools required passing a city-wide examination, but this was not the sole criterion; in autumn 1965, half of the students at the BNU Girls' School were family members of senior government

---

[2] Deng Rong, *My Father, Deng Xiaoping: The Cultural Revolution Years*, Beijing, Zhongyang wenxian chubanshe, June 2000.

officials. This became an important factor leading to Bian Zhongyun's death.

Before the Cultural Revolution, when Li Na, the daughter of Mao and his last wife, Jiang Qing, was about to graduate from the BNU Girls' School, Jiang arranged to see Bian Zhongyun. Jiang told Bian that Li Na wanted to study science, but Mao wanted her to study history. Jiang wanted the school's teachers to persuade Li Na to take the university entrance exam for the humanities rather than science. Eventually Li Na majored in history at Peking University. Bian Zhongyun's work diary records her appointment with Jiang Qing. I've mentioned this point to show the kind of relationship Mao and Jiang had with this school: in terms of work relationship, Bian was a school principal under the leadership of the Communist Party, engaged in the work the Party assigned to her; on a personal level, Bian was the teacher of their daughter.

The sequence of events that set the course for Bian Zhongyun's death began on 1 June 1966, with the nationwide broadcast of the first big-character poster at Peking University. At noon the next day, three students put up the first poster at BNU Girls' School, calling for students to 'pledge your lives to the Party Central Committee and Chairman Mao' and attacking the school administration. Among the students who signed it was Song Binbin, an upper-classman and the daughter of Song Renqiong, the general secretary of the CCP's Northeast Bureau. Song Binbin's family background lent a tone of authority and influence to this big-character poster.

In fact, this student protest was responding to more than the broadcast of the Peking University poster. Two weeks earlier, the Party had issued its Circular launching the Cultural Revolution with an explicit call for a 'thorough criticism' of the intellectual class and 'seizing leadership of the cultural spheres', along with the 7 May letter from Mao to Lin Biao stating that 'the phenomenon of bourgeois intellectuals controlling our schools cannot be allowed to continue.' These documents, which shifted the Cultural Revolution's attacks from movies and plays to a group of individuals, in particular educators, were disseminated only to upper-level cadres, and ordinary people were unaware of them. The children of these senior cadres had nevertheless learned of the preparations for the Cultural Revolution through their 'internal channels' and regarded the 1 June broadcast as a comprehensive call to action. They began attacking administrators and teachers the very next day, not only at the BNU Girls' School, but also at the Affiliated Secondary Schools of Tsinghua and Peking Universities.

On 3 June, a work group dispatched by the Communist Youth League Central Committee arrived at the BNU Girls' School and declared its whole-hearted support for Song Binbin and the others at a rally. Work group leader Zhang Shidong expressed elation at the 'exposure and criticism' of school administrators, eliciting wild applause and thunderous chanting of slogans from the students.

After the work group took over management of the school from the original administrators, it established a 'congress of revolutionary students and teachers' (6 June) and a 'Cultural Revolution Committee' (13 July) chaired by the work group head, with the vice-chair positions held by Song Binbin and others who had signed the big-character poster. The Committee included representatives from every grade level, all but one of them the daughters of senior officials, including Liu Shaoqi and Deng Xiaoping. The same process was carried out at Beijing's other secondary schools.

Under Bian Zhongyun's administration, the BNU Girls' School gave preferential treatment to the daughters of senior cadres, and many class monitors and student council leaders were daughters of top officials. Student leaders also included girls from ordinary backgrounds, however, and class monitors, who could exert considerable influence, were elected by the students themselves. Thus, while not all students enjoyed equal status, school administrators clearly did not believe that the daughters of top officials should monopolise leadership positions within the student body. This policy embodied one of the traditional principles that educators brought with them; during imperial times, the exam system was largely independent of the power structure. The full-scale launch of the Cultural Revolution provided the children of top leaders with their first opportunity for a power grab within the schools. Their initial attack on school leaders, subsequently romanticised as a rebellion, was on closer examination a direct extension of totalitarian power.

Before the work group entered the school and supported Song Binbin, some teachers had warned students not to put up big-character posters attacking the school authorities, because people who had criticised grassroots Party organisations in 1957 had been accused of 'opposing the Party' and labelled 'Rightists'. Unlike the children of cadres, these teachers were unaware of the Party Central Committee's arrangements for the Cultural Revolution. Within days of the work group's arrival, the entire school underwent radical change. Classes were suspended and students spent all their time waging revolution. The work group drafted a two-phase plan of 'general exposure' and 'focused exposure' that targeted the school's teachers and administrators. Students no longer showed any respect to their teachers; they called them by their names and reviled and berated them. The school was full of big-character posters attacking its former administrators, and nearly every teacher came under attack.

Historian Gu Jiegang's daughter was a student there at that time, and on 7 June 1966 Gu wrote in his journal, 'Yuan came home at eleven, and we talked until twelve ... she fetched the notebooks in which she had recorded what she'd heard at school over the last few years so she could write up big-character posters reporting statements by the principal or dean that were unsuited to Mao Zedong Thought. She's often at the school until midnight, and her exhaustion can be imagined.'[3]

There were big-character posters put up that accused Bian Zhongyun of a number of 'crimes'. First among them was participation in a 'counter-revolutionary coup d'état by the previous Beijing Municipal Party Committee'. Even allowing that any such plot existed, the principal of a girls' secondary school could not possibly have known about it. However, no one voiced any doubts about the accusation, nor was Bian given a chance to deny it.

Another of Bian's alleged crimes was 'opposing the Party's class road'. The main supporting evidence cited was that one of President Liu Shaoqi's daughters had been denied admission to the BNU Girls' School in 1962 because her exam score fell short by two points. In fact, the city's key schools gave preference to the children of top leaders, but Liu's daughter had still failed to make the grade. The school had consulted the Beijing Municipal Party Committee and the Education Ministry, and on their advice had not admitted Liu's daughter.

Bian was also accused of 'opposing Chairman Mao'. The students cited as supporting evidence an incident in March 1966, just after an earthquake struck the outskirts of Beijing. As a precaution, administrators told students that in case of an earthquake, they should quickly vacate the classrooms. When a student asked whether the portraits of Chairman Mao that hung above the blackboards in each classroom should be taken along, Bian Zhongyun did not answer directly, but told the students to move as quickly as possible into the open areas outside.

None of these accusations would have held up under discussion, but the work group vigorously supported them and added fuel to the flames. This resulted in even more big-character posters, which were categorised and collated, stencilled and mimeographed, then bound into book form.

The volume devoted to Bian Zhongyun listed the nature of her 'offences' as follows:

Opposes Mao Zedong Thought, slanders the Party's guiding policies, opposes the Party, socialism and the Three Red Banners, opposes the

---

[3] Gu Jiegang, *The Journals of Gu Jiegang*, Vol. 10, 1964–1967, Linking Publishing (Taipei), 2007, p. 472.

Party's policies, sabotages the Great Cultural Revolution, prioritises intellectual development, pursues higher rates of university admission, opposes uniting with workers and peasants, assiduously cultivates the sprouts of revisionism, nurtures a coterie of bourgeois teachers, opposes revolutionary insurrection and joins with reactionaries, has vulgar tastes.

Similar summaries of criminal offences were used against many other 'ox demons and snake spirits' during the Cultural Revolution and reveal its essence. Going beyond attacking an individual's 'crimes', the summary condemns the concepts of 'intellectual development' and 'rates of university admission' while emphasising the paramount authority of Mao Zedong Thought, the Party, socialism and the Three Red Banners.[4]

Apart from attacks in political terms, the big-character posters contained large quantities of invective and insults, for example crossing out Bian Zhongyun's name with a red X and replacing it with 'Bandit Bian'. The following is the content of a poster hung on the door of Bian's home in late June 1966:

> You Rightist who slipped through the net, you black element conspiring with the former Municipal Party Committee, vanguard of opposition to the Party, you bastard implementing bourgeois dictatorship over revolutionary students and teachers, you damned petty despot, come clean or face the merciless consequences!

Another poster was affixed to her bedroom door:

> Despotic dog, poisonous snake Bian, you'd damned well better listen: If you dare to continue running roughshod over the working people, we'll whip your dog's hide, rip out your dog's heart and lop off your dog's head. You'd damned well better not place any hopes in a comeback! We'll cut you off without descendants and smash you to smithereens!

This was the language used by female high school students at the beginning of the Cultural Revolution: crude, irrational, uncivilised, obscene and violent. The term *'tama de'* (a term with a harsher and more vulgar connotation than the English term 'damned' with which it is typically translated) was

---

[4] The Three Red Banners were the General Line of Socialist Construction, the Great Leap Forward and the People's Commune, which were regarded as fundamental to building a socialist state.

commonly used on campuses at that time to lend a 'revolutionary' tone. It eventually became a characteristic of Red Guard language.

The mimeographed copies of big-character posters devoted to Bian Zhongyun totalled more than 50,000 words. The authorities provided large amounts of paper, ink and paste for posters, each of which cost about as much to produce as the 30 cents charged for a day's meals at the school canteen. Mere encouragement would have been inadequate to galvanise the 'movement', which could only have been launched by a government in full control of all intellectual and material resources.

On 17 June, the *People's Daily* published the CCP Central Committee's decision to eliminate university admission exams and make political performance the criterion for selection. Competing with displays of 'revolutionary' character, students became increasingly virulent, obscene and detached from fact and logic in their 'exposure' of their teachers.

On 23 June 1966, the school's work group convened a compulsory 'exposure and criticism rally' against Bian Zhongyun. Several students dragged her onto the stage of the assembly hall and escorted the school's four other administrators to the front of the stage to face the assembly. The targets were forced to bend over at right angles to signify 'bowing under their guilt'. The students responsible for exposing and criticising the offenders mounted the stage and furiously screamed accusations at them, beating and kicking them at the same time. Some dashed onto the stage to strike at Bian with iron-clad wooden training rifles. Each time Bian fell to the floor, someone would douse her with cold water and pull her upright by the hair. Rather than intervene, the work group ordered Bian to stand up for more 'exposure and criticism'.

After the struggle session, Bian wrote a letter to Party officials criticising her own 'errors', including some she had never committed, and expressing her support for the Cultural Revolution. She then requested that no violence be used against her:

> During the public criticism, I was shackled and tormented for more than four hours: I had to wear a dunce cap and bow while I was struck and kicked. My hands were tied behind me, and two militia training rifles were jabbed into my back. Dirt was stuffed into my mouth and smeared on my face, and people spit all over my face and body.

Given the risk of being accused of 'slandering the mass movement', Bian would have described the situation accurately and without exaggeration in her letter. She hoped those higher up would help her, but in fact she never received a reply. The quotation above comes from her rough draft, which her husband hid in a space behind a wall until after the Cultural Revolution, fearing that it would be found by Red Guards.

Bian's account is verified in Gu Jiegang's journal, quoted earlier: 'Yuan returned, said the most problematic person at the Girls' School, Party secretary Bian, was struggled in a dunce cap, and that students carrying guns ordered her to "bend over, bend further!" When her hat fell off, she had to hold it on, and she had to stay bent over for more than three hours.'[5]

Meanwhile, the working group divided the school's administrators into four types according to the severity of their 'problems': the first classification being 'relatively good', the second 'in error', the third 'in serious error' and the fourth 'bourgeois Rightist'. According to a report to the next level by the Xicheng District work group, the results of the categorisation were as follows for the district's sixty-one schools: Category 1: 3.3%; Category 2: 33.3%; Category 3: 58.4%; Category 4: 5%. For the 476 leading cadres of the secondary schools: Category 1: 4%; Category 2: 42%; Category 3: 40%; Category 4: 14%. The BNU Girls' School was classified as a Category 4 school, and Bian Zhongyun and another vice-principal, Hu Zhitao, were classified as 'Category 4' cadres.

In its 3 July 1966, 'Preliminary Opinions on Classification of the Leadership Core of the Beijing Normal University Affiliated Girls' School', the work group repeated the accusations against Bian Zhongyun, elaborating, under the charge of 'vulgar tastes', that 'she has a particular admiration for the dissipated and shameless lifestyles of such as Wu Zetian, Yang Guifei and the Empress Dowager Cixi,[6] and her discourse is often extremely vulgar and philistine.' Bian Zhongyun was not even capable of 'promoting a revisionist road in education' or 'nurturing bourgeois intellectuals' among the staff, given that textbooks, syllabuses and teacher appointments were all arranged through a centralised system in which school administrators such as Bian had no input. As for 'vulgar tastes', Bian had worked at the school for seventeen years and inevitably would have chatted with colleagues about mundane topics such as food and clothing; her comments on how the colour green particularly suited her were 'exposed' and included on the work group's list of crimes. All of the allegations were one-sided, with no opportunity given for rebuttal or self-defence.

The officials leading the Cultural Revolution in June 1966 were the PRC's President, Liu Shaoqi, and the General Secretary of the CCP Central Committee, Deng Xiaoping. Liu Shaoqi had at one point personally heard a report from the work group of the Beijing Normal University Affiliated

---

[5] Gu Jiegang, *op. cit.*, June 25, Vol. 10, p. 482.
[6] TN: Wu Zetian (624–705) was a usurping empress who consolidated Tang rule. Yang Guifei (d. 756) was the favourite concubine of Emperor Minghuang. The Empress Dowager Cixi (1835–1908) was the power behind the throne of the Qing dynasty from 1861 until her death.

No. 1 Secondary School, and had written out a detailed directive on how to 'criticise and struggle' the school's principal, Liu Chao, and others. The text stated that big-character posters had attacked the BNU Girls' School for not admitting one of Liu Shaoqi's daughters. This daughter was subsequently admitted to the No. 1 Secondary School, where she became one of the first students to write posters attacking the school's leadership.

On 5 July 1966, the leader of the work group at the BNU Girls' School, along with Song Binbin and other students, joined Hu Qili, a secretary of the Communist Youth League Central Committee and leader of the Xicheng District work group, in reporting directly to Deng Xiaoping on the Cultural Revolution in that school. During the conversation, Deng Xiaoping referred to Bian Zhongyun's plea for help and told the work group to handle it appropriately. Deng asked whether Bian had been beaten during the struggle sessions, and when the work group reported that she had, Deng emphasised that beating was not allowed. He also recommended reclassifying some of Xicheng District's schools and school administrators from Category 3 to Category 2, but raised no objection to the Category 4 classification for the BNU Girls' School and its vice-principals Bian Zhongyun and Hu Zhitao.

During the new phase of the Cultural Revolution that followed Bian Zhongyun's death, Liu Shaoqi and Deng Xiaoping were criticised, and the leaders of the work groups in each school were subjected to even worse violence than they had earlier inflicted on Bian. The leaders of the Youth League Central Committee who had led the Beijing secondary school work groups were also struggled in a mass assembly. One such leader, Hu Keshi, in the 1980s apologised to Bian Zhongyun's husband for classifying Bian as Category 4 and thereby leading to her fatal beating after the work group withdrew. His personal experience as a target of attack and struggle enabled Hu Keshi to express his regret after the Cultural Revolution. This kind of moral rectitude was rare, however, with most people preferring to shift responsibility or to conceal or deny historical fact.

In mid-July, the Beijing work groups sent the majority of the city's secondary school students to military bases for training, while those regarded as 'problematic' were sent to labour in the countryside. Students who qualified as 'Leftists' remained at the schools to deal with the teachers and administrators, whom they rounded up and divided into separate groups for 'debriefing' (i.e. confession) or 'self-criticism'. Teachers from the BNU Girls' School were sent to Mashenmiao Primary School, where the work group required each teacher to write a self-criticism before being processed individually.

All over China, even in the border regions, educators were handled in this same way. In the prefectures under each province, high school teachers were ordered to leave their homes and live in centralised quarters for self-criticism, debriefing and mutual recrimination. Those whom the upper levels designated as 'problematic' were subjected to struggle. Some teachers collapsed under pressure at this stage and committed suicide. All this was clearly a result of the CCP Central Committee's unified leadership arrangements for the whole country.

The plan at that time was to deal with educators according to their 'categories'. After those in Category 4 were struggled to the nth degree, they were to be dismissed and expelled from Beijing for 'reform through labour' in the countryside. This callous decision was made by people who had been Bian Zhongyun's superiors for years. As a high school principal, she had virtually no ability to contravene the directives of her superiors, nor had she ever defied their orders; the children and grandchildren of the Party's top leaders attended the school she administered. Yet, once the revolution needed targets to attack, these senior cadres were able to turn their backs on their loyal subordinates, transforming them into scapegoats in service to the goals of revolution. This callousness was a hallmark of the Cultural Revolution, which virulently attacked not only its opponents, but even those who had never voiced the slightest opposition.

Victim of Red Guard Violence

If things had continued along the lines laid down by the work groups (later referred to as 'Liu-Deng work groups'), Bian would probably not have ended up dead. But when Mao in late July accused Liu and Deng of 'stultifying the movement' and took over leadership of the Cultural Revolution with the help of the Central Cultural Revolution Small Group, the work groups that had been restraining student violence were withdrawn, and schools were taken over by Red Guards and the Cultural Revolution Committees that the work groups had set up.

The Red Guards established themselves at the BNU Girls' School on 31 July 1966. Their organisational principle consisted of a couplet: 'Heroes breed good fellows; reactionaries breed scoundrels,' which designated a young person's status according to his or her family background. Consequently, students whose parents served in the highest reaches of government naturally became leaders of the Red Guards and of the new Cultural Revolution Preparatory Committee. They enjoyed three major privileges: 1) they were allowed to conduct struggle sessions against students designated as 'scoundrels' based on their 'bad family backgrounds'; 2) they could conduct struggle rallies against teachers and administrators without obtaining prior permission; 3) they were allowed to employ violence in their attacks on students and teachers.

On 4 August 1966, the day before Bian Zhongyun was beaten to death, the BNU Girls' School Red Guards carried out struggle sessions against students with 'bad family backgrounds'. The walls were covered with posters proclaiming 'Down with the sons of bitches!' Students with 'good' family backgrounds sat in chairs while those with 'bad' backgrounds were made to stand at the front of the classroom, bound together with ropes around their necks, and students whose backgrounds were 'neither bad nor good' sat on the floor. The bound students were then forced to undergo 'debriefings' on their 'reactionary thoughts' and the 'crimes' of their parents, after which they were forced to repeat three times, 'I am a son of a bitch, I am a scoundrel, I deserve to die.' Similar sessions took place in other classes.

That afternoon, a group of Red Guards chanting 'No reactionary gangs allowed' burst into a classroom where school administrators were being held and beat them with wooden training rifles and leather belts until they were black and blue. That night at home, Bian Zhongyun told her husband, 'Killing someone in my position is like killing a dog.' She knew she was in mortal danger, but could think of no way out. She and her husband discussed whether to send another letter to the leadership pleading for help or simply to flee for their lives. Ultimately they did neither. The next morning, Bian's elderly housekeeper pleaded with her, 'Don't go to school,' but Bian Zhongyun, resigned to her fate, set off punctually as usual.

The reality in Beijing at that time was that there was no place to hide or seek refuge, much less any opportunity to resist. Knowing that the school had reached a crisis point, another vice-principal, Hu Zhitao, rose at dawn on 5 August and went to the Beijing Municipal Party Committee to see the official responsible for education and culture. Hoping for sympathy and support, she told the official that people at the school were at risk of their lives. The reply she received was, 'Go back to school.' Hu returned to the BNU Girls' School in despair, and that same afternoon witnessed the murder of her colleague of many years, beaten to death before her eyes, while she herself was seriously injured.

Grasping a death certificate on which a doctor had written 'cause of death unknown' under the threatening gaze of the Red Guards, Wang Jingyao delivered his wife's corpse to a crematorium in the eastern suburbs. He had covered Bian's head with a cloth to spare their children the sight of their mother's battered face. Their youngest daughter was only ten years old at the time.

While passing Tiananmen Square, the family heard the broadcast of 'The CCP Central Committee's Resolution Regarding the Great Proletarian Cultural Revolution'. Hearing the phrase 'struggle but do not resort to violence', they believed that at least others would be spared Bian Zhongyu's fate. But another portion of the 'Resolution' stated: 'A large group of hitherto unknown revolutionary youth have become daring path-breakers... their revolutionary orientation is ultimately correct.' This powerful endorsement of the violence in Beijing's secondary schools was issued on 9 August, four days after Bian was murdered.

The Fate of One Becomes the Fate of Many

On the evening of 5 August 1966, after Bian Zhongyun was killed, Song Binbin and other leaders of the BNU Girls' School's Cultural Revolution Preparatory Committee and Red Guards arrived at the Beijing Hotel, where they promptly spotted Wu De, the second general secretary of the new Beijing Municipal Party Committee. They told him of Bian's death, and Wu reportedly told them that nothing could be done about it, but from now on they should follow policy.

This was the first case of Red Guards killing someone in Beijing, so Wu De is likely to have immediately reported it to the top leaders of the central government, including Mao, Jiang Qing and Zhou Enlai. To this day, nothing has come to light regarding what Wu De reported or how the government responded. However, soon afterwards, the general office of the Beijing Municipal Party Committee and Premier Zhou Enlai's office both sent cadres to the school to 'gain an understanding of the situation'. They spoke with Bian's husband, Wang Jingyao, and told him it was necessary to 'properly handle the mass movement', which meant that Wang should not protest or express his dissatisfaction or inquire into how the matter had come about. Bian's death did not alert the Cultural Revolution's leaders to the need to curb violence and persecution. Rather, by word and deed they vigorously supported the launch of the Red Guard movement, gradually pushing campus violence to new heights.

Thirteen days after Bian's death, on 18 August 1966, Mao received one million Red Guards at Tiananmen Square (seven more such reviews were to follow). The rally was broadcast live to the entire nation over radio and television, while a documentary was filmed and shown throughout the country. A million Red Guards marched across Tiananmen Square holding aloft copies of the red-covered *Quotations from Chairman Mao* and shouting, 'Long live Chairman Mao!' Some Red Guard leaders ascended the Tiananmen Gate Tower to shake hands and chat with Mao, Lin Biao and Zhou Enlai. Peng Xiaomeng, leader of the Red Guards at the Peking University Affiliated Secondary School, gave a speech on the Gate Tower, while Song Binbin, leader of the Red Guards at the BNU Girls' School, removed her red armband and tied it around Mao's upper arm.

A photo of Song tying her armband on Mao's arm was circulated throughout the country, and newspapers published the conversation in which Mao asked Song her name. When she said 'Binbin', which means 'gentle and refined', Mao said, 'It should be Yaowu' – militant.

After the 18 August rally, in an article entitled 'I Gave Chairman Mao a Red Armband' published in the *Guangming Daily* and *People's Daily*, Song's name was changed to 'Song Yaowu' and the Red Guards changed the name of the BNU Girls' School to 'Red Militant Secondary School'. At the 18 August rally, changes in the highest circles of power were made public for the first time. Lin Biao replaced Liu Shaoqi as China's second most powerful leader, and Song Binbin's father, Song Renqiong, was promoted to alternate member of the Central Committee Politburo.

The two Red Guards who attracted the most attention on the Tiananmen Gate Tower on 18 August were Peng Xiaomeng and Song Binbin, one of whom came from the school that first used violence against teachers and students, and the other from the school where the first educator was beaten to death. For Mao to praise 'militancy' against this background clearly had implications and influence far beyond a comment on a name.

After the 18 August rally, Red Guard violence escalated, and Bian Zhongyun's personal tragedy became the fate of an increasing number of educators and ordinary citizens. In a survey I carried out at 115 schools throughout China, I found that all, without exception, experienced incidents in which Red Guards violently persecuted educators. Every school in China became a torture chamber, prison or even execution ground, and many teachers were persecuted to death. Claims that secondary school teachers came under the greatest persecution during the Cultural Revolution are consistent with the facts; an extraordinarily high percentage of these teachers suffered humiliation, beating and torture, and their persecutors were their own students. The oldest of these students were eighteen years old, and teachers were also beaten to death at primary schools, where the oldest students were only thirteen years old.

Violence quickly spread as Red Guards burned and smashed literary and cultural items, ransacked homes and attacked 'ox demons and snake spirits' in the surrounding neighbourhood. At the Yuhuatai restaurant near the BNU Girls' School, an unmarried eighteen-year-old waitress was abducted and brought back to the school's chemistry lab on accusations that she was a 'hooligan', presumably indicating some kind of illicit romantic attachment. Acting as her judges and executioners, Red Guards bound her to a pillar and lashed her with brass belt buckles. Her screams of agony filled the hallways, and carried through the nearby school gates into the streets, but no one came to her aid. Only after she fell silent and the school's doctor pronounced her dead was her body unbound. As with

Bian Zhongyun, the death of this unnamed waitress was never investigated by the judicial departments, nor was anyone ever punished for it.

The Red Guards of the BNU Girls' School killed seven other people during the summer of 1966, and their behaviour was far from exceptional. According to one 'internal report', in Beijing's Xicheng District (where the Girls' School was located), 333 people were killed by Red Guards, most of them secondary school students, in the last half of August. Since Xicheng District had sixty-one secondary schools, each school averaged at least five killings.

A Central Committee Central Work Conference in October 1966 reported as one of the 'accomplishments' of the Red Guards the killing of 1,772 people from 20 August to the end of September. The actual number of fatalities was probably greater, and in any case did not include Bian Zhongyun and others who died earlier in August.

Pursuing Justice

At dinner on the evening of the day that Bian Zhongyun was beaten to death, all that was heard in the student canteen was gleeful discussion and derisive laughter at the miserable plight of the struggle targets. There was no evident horror or unease on campus over the unwarranted killing, but rather a pervasive exuberance. Bands of Red Guard students in uniforms with cinched belts and rolled-up pant legs marched around the campus with heads high and chests jutting, their voices strident with jubilation and pride over their ability to end a life with their violent dominance.

Blood fuelled the flames and propelled the Cultural Revolution forward, crushing in its path not only ordinary citizens, but even some of its early leaders. Only half a year later, both Liu Shaoqi and Deng Xiaoping were struck down, and Liu's daughter was forced to leave home and board at her school. One day in the dormitory someone asked her, 'Liu Tingting, I hear that you killed three people during Red August – is that true?' She replied, 'That was just boasting. At that time it was an honour to beat someone to death, so I said I killed three.'

'Red August' is how the Red Guards proudly referred to August 1966, when a fourteen-year-old felt compelled to take credit for three murders. The thinking and principles established during the August slaughter permeated the Cultural Revolution as insidiously as the blood that was shed.

In such an environment, Bian's family could not even mourn her death, much less protest it. Bian's young daughter found her father's sleeping mat gnawed to shreds from his effort to suppress his anguish.

A year later, after the spate of Red Guard ransackings had passed, Bian's family set up a 'spirit shelf' inside a cupboard, attaching a photo of her to one wall and placing flowers before it. The cupboard door could be shut at a moment's notice, and no one outside the family was allowed to see the tribute. Because Bian had been beaten to death, venerating or memorialising her would be considered 'hostility toward the Cultural Revolution' or 'seeking to overturn a Cultural Revolution verdict', both of which were considered serious crimes. Some people were even brainwashed into regarding their loved ones as criminals who brought disgrace upon their families.

Bian Zhongyun's death was not the only blow her husband Wang Jingyao suffered at that time. The day before Bian died, on 4 August, a mutual friend from their youth, **Qi Shiqian**, committed suicide by swallowing pesticide after being struggled as one of a group of 'reactionary writers' at the Chinese Academy of Sciences Modern History Research Institute. The day after Bian's death, on 6 August, a university classmate of the couple, **Liu Kelin**, killed himself by leaping from the fifth-floor window of his office in the Central Propaganda Department.

Throughout the ten years of the Cultural Revolution, no one was criticised or called to account for Bian Zhongyun's violent death, nor was it reported or recorded in any of the 'chronicles of events' left behind from that time. The only contemporary record of Bian's death is a letter written by one of the teachers at the BNU Girls' School after witnessing the tragedy. Language teacher Zhang Jingfen wrote to Bian's family describing the incident and expressing sympathy and outrage, but dared not sign her name and even altered her handwriting for fear of sharing Bian's fate. This lonely voice of morality and justice shows that people knew this violence was wrong, and that the Cultural Revolution was not universally embraced. Even so, the unbridled Red Terror deprived dissenters of a hearing, and the majority suppressed their conscience and submitted to the barbarism and cruelty of a minority.

Following the 1971 death of Lin Biao, Mao's 'close comrade-in-arms' and chosen successor, the leaders of the Cultural Revolution began to ease up on purging cadres. In 1973, Bian Zhongyun was given a verdict of 'no problems' and her death was treated as 'work-related'. The school's Revolutionary Committee was ordered to pay her family 400 *yuan*.

After Mao's death in 1976 and the arrest of Jiang Qing and the other Cultural Revolution leaders in the Gang of Four, a cautious and gradual negation of the Revolution began. In 1978, the CCP's Xicheng District Party Committee staged a memorial service in which Bian Zhongyun was 'exonerated'. At another rehabilitation meeting for education workers, the Party head of Xicheng District acknowledged that 276 of the district's middle and primary school teachers had been persecuted to death.

Wang Jingyao repeatedly asked to use the 400 *yuan* payment to erect a monument or plant a row of trees to commemorate Bian at the school where she had been killed, but to no avail. Wang then began considering legal measures to obtain justice for his wife. In April 1979, he submitted a complaint to the Beijing Municipal Public Security Bureau, Municipal People's Procuratorate and Municipal People's Court. Apart from demanding investigation and punishment of those directly responsible for Bian's death – the three or four students whose vicious blows ended her life – he leveled an accusation against an employee of another school, Yuan Shu'e, who had been an enthusiastic participant in the 23 June struggle session. Out of personal spite, Yuan had 'exposed and criticised' Bian and borne false witness by cropping a group photo to suggest that Bian had a 'relationship problem' with a male teacher. Retribution for personal grudges was a major unofficial factor in the Cultural Revolution's rapid development.

On 14 March 1981, the Beijing Xicheng District People's Procuratorate declared that the accused, Yuan Shu'e, had taken advantage of the Great Cultural Revolution to concoct a slanderous allegation, and that the case was serious and constituted libel, but that the incident fell outside of the statute of limitations, and a prosecution would therefore not be filed.

Apart from accusations of murder, the statute of limitations effectively prevented attempts to obtain justice, given that twenty-five years passed between the launch of the Cultural Revolution and its official negation. Anyone daring to criticise the Revolution before then risked accusations of 'verdict reversal', which constituted 'current counter-revolutionary activity'. Some people were actually persecuted to death for their naïve pursuit of justice. That is why, even though Wang Jingyao took the step of buying a camera and photographing Bian's wounds as evidence, he was unable to pursue the case until the political situation changed.

Even at that, by the time the Xicheng District Procuratorate reached its 1981 decision on Bian's case, the official policy was not to prosecute Red Guards responsible for the deaths at the Beijing No. 6 Secondary School and No. 3 Girls' Secondary School. No one was ever punished for the thousands of beating deaths in Beijing in the summer of 1966.

The person who decided how to handle these 1966 cases of Red Guard violence was then-Party General Secretary Hu Yaobang. Hu was a key force behind negating the Cultural Revolution and overturning cases of injustice, but he emphasised that 'a stone dropped in the water cannot be recovered,' and focused on rehabilitating the victims rather than punishing their persecutors. This effectively protected the early-stage Red Guards, most of whom were the children of high-level cadres, and also prevented Mao from being held accountable in spite of his encouragement of their violence.

Wang Jingyao continued to appeal the case using his connections within the upper circles of power, but made no progress. Eight years later, on 25

December 1989, the Supreme People's Procuratorate upheld the decision not to prosecute, stating:

> Upon re-examination, the incident at the BNU Affiliated Girls' Secondary School on 5 August 1966, in which Bian died after being denounced and humiliated with four other school administrators, was a case of the school's students imitating those at the Peking University Affiliated Secondary School, and was not related to Yuan Shu'e. For that reason, Yuan Shu'e cannot be considered to have inflicted intentional injury in this case.
>
> Comrade Wang Jingyao has related that in one instance during 21 or 22 June 1966, Yuan Shu'e tugged Bian's hair. Examination has found no evidence to verify Comrade Wang Jingyao's version of events. Even if this incident could be verified, it was extreme behaviour in the course of a campaign and does not constitute intentional harm as stipulated in the Criminal Law.

This decision stated who was not responsible for Bian Zhongyun's death, but not who was. The procuratorate had the responsibility to pursue the cause of death; there is no statute of limitations in murder cases. This handling of Bian's murder at the very least constituted negligence on the part of the procuratorate.

Furthermore, since the Supreme People's Procuratorate correctly asserted that the violent persecution started at the Peking University Affiliated Secondary School (hereafter PU Secondary), it should have carried out further inquiries there. In fact, the Red Guards at PU Secondary not only viciously assaulted teachers and students, but also fatally beat several individuals outside the school. Even so, the procuratorate took no action against these Red Guards, none of whom ever expressed apology or regret for their acts of violence.

The reason for the Supreme People's Procuratorate acting as it did is all too clear. If it had investigated PU Secondary, one of the points of origin of the Red Guards, it would have exposed the enthusiastic support these Red Guards received from Jiang Qing and Mao Zedong. Although Jiang had been arrested and handed a suspended death sentence by then, it would have been difficult to claim that she bore sole responsibility for the Red Guard violence in 1966, and it was inconceivable that Mao's own responsibility might be investigated. Hence the matter was pursued no further.

Twenty-seven years after Bian Zhongyun's death, her husband ran into a stone wall; the Supreme People's Procuratorate's decision terminated the pursuit of any further redress. Even so, Wang Jingyao's untiring efforts to obtain some form of justice on behalf of his wife deserves the greatest respect.

The Motive for Murder

After the Cultural Revolution, in the late 1970s and early 1980s, newspapers and magazines published a series of articles about the movement's victims – but only those who were high-level officials and famous writers. Very little was said about how they died; the main purpose of the articles was to 'restore the reputations' of the victims rather than to reveal historical truth. Reference to 'fatal assault' and 'suicide' was the new taboo, and a new phrase that became common at this time was 'persecuted to death', which those who had experienced the Cultural Revolution would understand referred to struggle sessions, clubbings, thrashings with brass buckles, and 'isolation and investigation'. The status of the victim was clearly the deciding factor in publishing these articles; lowly school teachers did not meet the requisite criteria, however much they had suffered. Their powerlessness did not exclude them from the persecution that fuelled the fervour of the Cultural Revolution, yet it was this same powerlessness that led to their suffering and death being largely overlooked afterwards. It was not just the official news media who were guilty of this oversight; among three histories of the Cultural Revolution and two books about the Red Guards published in China up to the end of the twentieth century, none named a single educator who had been killed during that period.[7]

This was more than a matter of snobbery: reporting the large number of ordinary victims would change the complexion of the Cultural Revolution and give rise to more in-depth analysis of who was responsible. It is for this reason that a strict line was drawn, not only in the courts but also in books, to exclude the stories of Bian Zhongyun and the many other persecuted educators.

---

[7] TN: After Wang Youqin wrote her book, mainland Chinese author Yang Jisheng published *The World Turned Upside Down: A History of the Chinese Cultural Revolution* (Farrar, Straus and Giroux, 2021, Chinese edition published in Hong Kong in 2016), which specifically mentions Bian Zhongyun and other individual victims of the Cultural Revolution. Yang has been unable to publish his book in mainland China. Another book by mainland author Tan Hecheng, *The Killing Wind: A Chinese County's Descent into Madness During the Cultural Revolution* (Oxford University Press 2017, Chinese edition published in Hong Kong in 2010), narrates Cultural Revolution violence at length, including the deaths of some educators; the violence in this case was factionally based and did not involve Red Guards. Tan's book circulated online for a period of time in mainland China, but was never formally published there. Neither Yang nor Tan are official historians, but compiled their information covertly and published their books as private citizens.

Because of this omission, the Red Guards were not compelled to express apology or regret. One example is Liu Shaoqi's daughter Liu Tingting, a student at the BNU Girls' School who took part in the violence that resulted in Bian Zhongyun's death, and who herself suffered persecution when her father was unseated. Following Liu Shaoqi's posthumous rehabilitation in 1980, his children published an essay that contained this statement on their participation in the Red Guard movement in August 1966: 'More than ten years later, we feel the greatest guilt about this incident.'[8] Yet in 2003, when Liu Tingting was interviewed in Carma Hinton's documentary film *Rising Sun*, she only mentioned her father's persecution and said nothing of her own part in persecuting others. Red Guards from five different secondary schools appeared in this film, including Song Binbin, yet not one of them expressed any apology or regret for the violence of August 1966, even though by that time my Online Chinese Holocaust Memorial included the names of nine victims who had been killed at those five schools over that summer. This cannot be attributed solely to personal factors; the long-term prohibition of any mention of Bian Zhongyun and her colleagues had banished them from collective memory.

Bian Zhongyun's story raises certain questions: Why was she killed? Why kill, humiliate, beat and torture a large number of educators just like her?

As a member of the teaching profession, Bian faced a much higher risk of death. Right from the outset, Mao had designated educators as targets of attack, most explicitly in the 16 May Circular and 7 May Directive – and Bian was a 'Category 4 Cadre' in a 'Category 4 School'. The children of top-level cadres, forming the vanguard of the Red Guard movement at the BNU Girls' School, served as the localised element that converged with the larger trend to make Bian Zhongyun the first of the Red Guards' victims in Beijing.

If Bian had survived the Red Guard tide of 1966, she would have faced another round of persecution during the 1968 Cleansing of the Class Ranks, during which ten of the school's 116 teaching and administrative staff were persecuted to death (as detailed in Part Five). All of them were rehabilitated after the Cultural Revolution, but the authorities didn't allow their persecution to be acknowledged; instead, a more veiled reference was made to 'unnatural death'. The facts, however, were irrefutable: Bian Zhongyun's murder was just the beginning of a large-scale mass persecution.

One of the school's victims was its old handyman **Wang Yonghai**, who had loaded Bian Zhongyun's lifeless body onto the wheelbarrow on 5 August

---

[8] Liu Tingting et al., 'Presenting You with the Victory Garland', *Workers Daily*, 5–8 December, 1980.

1966. Born physically handicapped and mentally slow, Wang had worked at the school for decades. Several months after Bian's death, he sought out her widower to describe what had happened that day and express concern for Bian's youngest daughter, nicknamed 'Precious'. It puts all the others to shame that the only person from the Girls' School who went to Bian's home to express condolences was this humble working man. When Wang Yonghai himself later came up for struggle, he fled and was never seen again. No one knows what became of him or how he died.

If Bian Zhongyun had survived the Cleansing of the Class Ranks, she probably would have shared the fate of school administrators from the Tsinghua University and Peking University Affiliated Secondary Schools who survived the initial campus violence. After being convicted of 'faithfully executing a revisionist education line and committing serious political errors', these administrators were sent to 'May 7 Cadre Schools' for manual labour. During a new round of urban purges carried out in the name of 'war preparedness' in autumn 1969, they were 'sent down' to the countryside for unspecified tenures in the production brigades. It was not until 1973, long after Lin Biao's death, that these educators were finally allowed to return to their schools, and only after the Cultural Revolution ended were they allowed to resume their teaching duties.

On 5 August 1966, while Bian Zhongyun was being beaten to death, the eleventh plenum of the Eighth CCP Central Committee was in session. At that meeting, Liu Shaoqi and Deng Xiaoping were demoted, and the supreme military commander, Lin Biao, became the second most powerful man in China. Mao, Lin Biao and other Cultural Revolution leaders regularly attended mass rallies in 1966, accepting tribute amidst roaring slogans and thunderous applause. All of them, not only Mao, regularly gave speeches at these rallies. Their remarks were recorded and reproduced in print, totalling more than a million words, but in all of this verbiage not a sentence was devoted to any of the thousands of Beijing residents who were beaten to death. These ordinary people seemed beneath contempt, no more than ants to be crushed beneath their thumbs. Bian Zhongyun had been a teacher of Mao and Jiang Qing's daughter, but neither Mao nor Jiang expressed the slightest compassion towards her or any of the other educators or ordinary citizens. By slighting the victims of this tumultuous mass persecution and slaughter, they achieved the ultimate power of life and death over every Chinese citizen, from those just one rung lower in the circles of power, such as Liu Shaoqi and Lin Biao, right down to the lowliest school teacher.

On 5 August 1966, a fault line divided history and formed a new era in which people could be killed in the name of revolution, at the hands of the 'revolutionary masses'. The campus slaughter shook the foundations of Chinese culture, and the death of the educator Bian Zhongyun signified the beginning of a new reign of terror. Let us remember this name and this date, so that we may never forget the reversals and misfortunes that can occur in the course of civilisation.

The school where Bian Zhongyun taught has since changed its name to the Beijing Normal University Affiliated Experimental Secondary School. In 1993, I visited it and took a photograph of the dormitory where Bian had been beaten to death. Four upper-classmen who lived in that dormitory asked me, 'Is it true that someone was beaten to death here more than twenty years ago? No one ever told us.'

TSINGHUA UNIVERSITY AFFILIATED SECONDARY SCHOOL

The general trend of beating and killing in the Cultural Revolution emerged in tandem with the development of the Red Guard movement. This is a plain and simple fact known to everyone who was there, but it is not acknowledged in books and articles published in China, where the authorities maintain tight control over the interpretation, writing and publishing of history. Nevertheless, understanding what happened to the victims requires understanding the Red Guards, and the Tsinghua University Affiliated Secondary School (Tsinghua Secondary) was one of the points of origin of the Red Guard movement.

The term 'Red Guards' was initially the name given to a group of students at Tsinghua Secondary, who began using it on big-character posters put up at the school on 2 June 1966. Their first poster, 'Pledging Our Lives to Defending the Dictatorship of the Proletariat and Mao Zedong Thought!' proclaimed, 'Whoever goes against Mao Zedong Thought, no matter who it is or what banner they carry or how high their status, will be smashed to pieces.' A similar group calling themselves the Red Flag Combat Group had been established at the Peking University Affiliated Secondary School (PU Secondary), located near Tsinghua Secondary, when Nie Yuanzi's big-character poster at Peking University was broadcast on 1 June. The Red Guards subsequently claimed 29 May as their date of establishment, and there is still some dispute on this point. In any event, what is clear is that either on 29 May or two days later, some groups made up of the children of senior cadres emerged in certain Beijing secondary schools under revolutionary-sounding names such as Red Guards, Red Flag, East Wind and so on, in response to internal documents that the CCP Central Committee had issued regarding the Cultural Revolution, namely the 16 May Circular and Mao's 7 May Directive to Lin Biao.

While these directives to 'seize power' circulated in the upper levels, there was news of the purge of the central government cadres 'Peng, Lu, Luo and Yang'. One former secondary school principal I interviewed said that in early May 1966, she was surprised to overhear some children of senior cadres discussing 'problems' that Beijing Party secretary Peng Zhen allegedly had. When she asked her superiors about it, she was told, 'It's none of your business.' The big-character poster by Nie Yuanzi and others went up at Peking University on 25 May, and its broadcast nationwide on 1 June was considered the signal for an all-out offensive. The next day, the Red Guards of Tsinghua Secondary and the Red Flag Combat Group of PU Secondary began putting up their own big-character posters virulently attacking the schools' authorities along the same lines as Nie Yuanzi's poster.

'Red Guards' eventually became the general name for these new organisations, apparently because it seemed best suited to limitless development into a large organisation and could also be applied to members of these organisations. The name also best embodied the climate of personality cult and attacks on 'class enemies'. The CCP's youth organisation, the Communist Youth League, indicated the ideology and age of its members but didn't directly suggest protecting the leaders, the Party and the regime by attacking 'enemies'.

The work groups sent to Beijing's secondary schools in early June 1966 to replace the school administrators were led by the Communist Youth League Central Committee. They announced the suspension of classes and supported students who had put up big-character posters attacking the original school administrators. At Tsinghua Secondary, the work group arrived on 9 June, and on 10 June the school's administrators were seized and struggled as reactionaries. Later these reactionaries and some teachers and staff were locked up in the western compound. The work group supported the Red Guards as a 'revolutionary Leftist faction', the highest commendation at that time, and established a Cultural Revolution Committee that included founding members of the Red Guards.

When Mao ordered the work groups to withdraw from the schools at the end of July, he criticised them for 'stifling the students', but the truth was that the work groups resolutely supported the students in opposing school leaders and organised them to 'expose' and 'struggle' administrators and teachers. Without the guidance of the work groups, few students or staff would have attacked school leaders, with memories still fresh of the Anti-Rightist Movement in 1957, when people who had criticised grass-roots leaders were severely punished. It was the work groups that caused the upsurge in opposition against school leaders, and Mao only accused them of 'stifling the students' because he wanted to guide the Cultural Revolution in a more intense direction.

The difference between the work groups under Liu Shaoqi and Deng Xiaoping on the one hand, and the Red Guards and Mao on the other, was mainly that the former didn't allow large-scale beatings. When some people at Peking University used violent methods to struggle some 'ox demons and snake spirits' on 18 June 1966, Liu Shaoqi issued a document calling a halt to this kind of 'chaotic struggle'. Likewise, at Tsinghua Secondary, the work group stopped a student from dumping a bucket of water on the head of Wan Bangru. People were being beaten, but the work groups generally didn't allow too much of it.

It is unlikely that Liu and Deng and the work groups intentionally opposed Mao's violent itinerary, given their immediate self-criticism when Mao complained about them. It is more likely that Liu and Deng had not anticipated that the Cultural Revolution would involve this degree of violence, and eventually divisions developed between them and Mao as a result.

History is full of examples of rulers killing ordinary citizens, but the killing is usually carried out by professional executioners, police officers or soldiers. Every era has had bandits and robbers who have harmed people, but always within limited parameters. It is only during the Cultural Revolution in summer 1966 that a leader mobilised secondary school students to inflict torture and humiliation on school administrators and teachers, and then enlarged the scope of attack to the wider community.

On 1 August, Mao wrote a letter expressing his 'ardent support' for the Red Guards at Tsinghua Secondary and the Red Flag Combat Group at Peking University Secondary. It became a formal document printed and distributed at a Central Committee plenum. The situation underwent a dramatic change, with Red Guard organisations being set up at every school and taking control, and large-scale beatings becoming ubiquitous. By early August, Beijing's secondary schools were inundated with abusive practices such as parading people around with dunce caps and placards and half-shaven heads and beating them with brass belt buckles. The schools where Red Guard organisations were first established, such as the Tsinghua and Peking University Affiliated Schools, were among the first to engage in this violent persecution. Tsinghua Secondary's Red Guards even changed the name of the school to Red Guard War School. When Mao reviewed a million Red Guards at Tiananmen Square on 18 August 1966, Tsinghua Secondary, as the school where the Red Guards originated, had the supreme honour of sending a representative to the Gate Tower to shake hands with Mao.

By the time of Mao's review of the Red Guards, violence at Tsinghua Secondary was already well underway. One day in early August, students forced vice-principal Han Jia'ao into the assembly room for second-year students, where he had served as deputy head teacher before the Cultural

Revolution. They made Han kneel and then beat him until he collapsed on the floor. All students except those 'disqualified' due to 'bad family backgrounds' were forced to take part in beating Han Jiao'ao with sticks, whips and belt buckles. When one student showed reluctance, a Red Guard egged him on, saying, 'Don't you remember when Han Jia'ao persecuted you? Hit him!' The so-called persecution was when Han had arranged for that student, a bed-wetter, to share a dormitory room with another bed-wetter. This might normally have been considered a sensible arrangement, but under the circumstances, it was turned in to a rationale for hatred and violence.

At one time, Han Jia'ao had set up a 'foreign language book corner' for language students. He had also bought an English dictionary for a student in financial difficulties. Now these acts constituted crimes. After beating him for more than an hour, students began burning books and English dictionaries in a wire basket, and thrust Han's head into the basket so his hair caught fire.

After beating Han, the Red Guards took him back to the western courtyard, where they were holding 'reactionaries' for struggle and labour reform. They stripped off his clothes, exposing the wounds all over his back, and said to the other reactionaries, 'Look here, if you don't behave, you'll be treated like Han Jia'ao!' Han had wounds all over his body, and since the hospital wouldn't treat 'ox demons and snake spirits', all he could do was ask his family to buy traditional Chinese ointment and medicine, and drink strong white liquor every day to deaden the pain. Han Jia'ao was thirty-three years old at the time and had never been a drinker, but he acquired the habit from then on, and he continued to suffer back pain for decades afterwards.

The violence was less severe at Tsinghua University itself; the Red Guards at Tsinghua Secondary criticised their university colleagues as soft and useless and insisted on giving them some lessons. One day in mid-August, Red Guards from Tsinghua Secondary paraded through the university campus, grabbing one of its former leaders, Ai Zhisheng, and forcing him to march along with them. The parade ended at the university's western canteen, where the secondary school Red Guards held a struggle rally and gave Ai Zhisheng a thrashing.

On 24 August, Red Guards from Tsinghua Secondary called in Red Guards from twelve other secondary schools (including the Beijing Normal University Affiliated Girls' Secondary School) to stage a 'rebellion' at Tsinghua University. In essence, the secondary student Red Guards were importing mass ransackings and beatings to the university. Arriving in trucks at the Tsinghua campus for a co-ordinated action with the university's Red Guards, they ordered the destruction of a symbolic structure erected when Tsinghua was first established, a white marble archway with the words *Tsinghua Yuan* engraved on it. (This archway was restored in 1990.) After a crane pulled it down, the Red Guards ordered members of the 'labour reform team' to carry the stones away. As the 'ox demons and snake spirits' moved the rocks, Red Guards from the secondary school and university followed behind, beating and berating them. Blood stained the campus hallways. After professors and cadres from the Radio Department were beaten, someone used their blood to draw a big circle and the words 'dog's blood'. After Red Guards 'rebelled' at Tsinghua University, they went to the nearby Peking University staff quarters and ransacked the home of history professor Jian Bozan, destroying his paintings and sealing off his library.

On the night of 24 August, Red Guards from Tsinghua Secondary dragged vice-principal Han Jia'ao from his home to the Tsinghua University science building, beating him all the way. School principal Wan Bangru was also grabbed. A Red Guard from the school shoved Han Jia'ao's head to the ground and put his foot on it, saying he wanted him 'never to rise again' (quoting Mao). Red Guards also ordered Han Jia'ao to hit Wan Bangru, saying, 'If you don't hit him, I'll hit you.'

That night, Wan Bangru and Han Jia'ao were locked up in the campus science building along with university administrators Liu Bing, Ai Zhisheng and others. They were called into a small room one by one and beaten. After a night of torture, each was given a steamed corn bun to eat the next day at noon. As they took the buns, they had to say, 'The bastard [their own name] is eating a corn bun,' otherwise they'd be beaten again. The university Red Guards took it in turns to torment the administrators the next day.

Wan Bangru and Han Jia'ao were then taken to Tsinghua Secondary by the school's Red Guards. Han's family still didn't know where he was, and when they went out looking for him and saw pools of blood on the ground, they thought he'd been killed and went home weeping.

The secondary school's geography teacher, Zhang Baolin, having watched her colleagues being beaten and committing suicide and not knowing when it would be her turn, knelt on the floor of her home and told her son to hit her as if they were at a struggle rally so she could get used to Red Guards beating her.

When a rain storm caused Tsinghua Secondary's drainage ditches to clog and form stagnant pools, teachers from the school's 'labour reform team' were ordered to clear the gutters, after which the Red Guards ordered them to splash the gutter water at each other and beat each other. Male teachers were ordered to hit female teachers.

An interviewee who was a student at that time said one day at the height of the beatings he saw another of the school's vice-principals, Wu

Yuliang, walking along the road. A Red Guard went up to Wu, slapped him in the face, then punched him until he fell to the ground. After the Red Guard swaggered off, Wu Yuliang crawled back onto his feet and walked away.

Students were also abused along with teachers at Tsinghua Secondary. Red Guards had come up with the concepts of 'children of the five red categories' and 'children of the five black categories' and energetically promoted the couplet 'Heroes breed good fellows; reactionaries breed scoundrels.' Students from 'black category' families (landlords, rich peasants, counter-revolutionaries, bad elements and Rightists) became the targets of attack.

The Red Guards not only wrote out countless copies of the notorious couplet, but also forced 'black category' students to insult themselves by copying it. A third-year student named Dai Jianzhong and three other students were each forced to write 100 copies of the couplet. It was one of the most common items pasted up in Beijing secondary schools in summer 1966.

In the dormitories, insulting big-character posters were pasted over the beds of black category students. A second-year student named Zhang Lifan had his mosquito net and sheets ripped up by Red Guard schoolmates because his father was a famous Rightist, Zhang Naiqi.

An older student named Yang Ailun, whose father had worked for the Customs Department before 1949, was labelled as having a 'bad family background'. She was a good student who had won awards in mathematics, as well as being a long-distance runner in the school sports team and a soloist in the school chorus, all of which also counted against her; Red Guards began struggling her in late July 1966. One of the school's Red Guard leaders came to her class and explained in detail how to punish her. She was locked up in a small room, and her bedding in the dormitory was thrown away. She was forced to write self-criticisms and confessions. On 8 August 1966, Yang Ailun threw herself in front of a train near the Tsinghua train station. Pushed off the track by the locomotive's 'cow-catcher', she survived but was permanently disabled.

Less than two weeks later, on 20 August 1966, another student from a 'bad family', **Guo Lanhui**, killed herself with poison. Her father had worked for the pre-1949 government, which made her a 'son of a bitch'. 20 August was a Saturday, and the Red Guards notified Guo that they would begin 'helping', i.e. struggling, her on the following Monday. Guo Lanhui drank disinfectant on the way home. When she got there, her mother saw her looking ill and immediately took her to the hospital, and she was still alive when they arrived. But according to two students who knew Guo Lanhui, when the hospital telephoned the school to ask about her, the Red Guards said she was a 'Rightist student' and as a result, the doctors didn't treat her and she died on the hospital floor. The Red Guards felt no pity for Guo, even crowing to other students about what had happened, seeing it as a demonstration of their power over life and death. Guo Lanhui was nineteen years old when she died.

At noon on 26 August, 'black category' students Zheng Guangzhao, Dai Jianzhong, Zhao Boyan and Liu Xihong were brutally beaten with belt buckles and rods by Red Guard classmates who berated them as 'sons of bitches'. That afternoon, the students were forced to kneel on the school lawn and pull weeds while Red Guards stood behind them with belts. That night, Zheng Guangzhao and the other students were locked in a room and not allowed to return home. Zheng began passing blood in his urine, had a seizure and fell into a coma, nearly dying. Afterwards he remained in custody in the dormitory.

The daughter of Tsinghua University's president and Party secretary, Jiang Nanxiang, was a student at Tsinghua Secondary. Because the work group that the Central Committee sent to the university in June 1996 had 'plucked' Jiang Nanxiang out as a 'reactionary', his daughter immediately became a 'son of a bitch', and one day, 'red category' students dragged her out and slapped her repeatedly before a crowd of other students.

It was especially popular at Tsinghua Secondary to give girls yin-yang haircuts. The school was unusual in this way, because most Beijing secondary schools reserved this treatment for female teachers. This method of abusing female students is a classic example of taking advantage of the Cultural Revolution to give vent to sadistic tendencies.

The famous writer Shi Tiesheng was a student at the school in 1966. When I asked him if any students had been beaten at the school, he said yes, but not severely. I asked what he considered severe. Shi Tiesheng said two female students, Wang Shuying and Sun Shuqi, had been forced to kneel in the classroom while Red Guards beat them with belts and fists, and half their hair had been cut off. I couldn't help asking, 'That's not considered severe?'

Shi Tiesheng is a writer who has mastered the appropriate use of words, so he would know whether or not to use the term 'severe' in describing the beating of two fifteen-year-old students. He said what he did because much worse things happened to people in the climate of that time. Whatever fell short of beating someone to death or driving someone to suicide could be considered 'not severe'.

Television journalist Xiao Yan was a fourteen-year-old first-year student at Tsinghua Secondary in 1966. His father was the writer Xiao Jun (for more on Xiao Jun, see the entry for **Lao She** in the first section of Part Three). When I interviewed him in 1997, Xiao Yan said, 'My class didn't struggle me too fiercely, but they imposed corporal punishment on me several times and had me stand and talk about my father's problems. Once they spent an entire class period telling me to confess. Several students made up a case saying I'd stolen from them; they took my shoes to check the shoeprints, and they whipped my face with a metal chain.'

When he said he hadn't been struggled too fiercely, it left as deep an impression as when Shi Tiesheng said his classmates hadn't been beaten too badly. It could only make me imagine what constituted harsh treatment at Tsinghua Secondary.

Also beaten was an elderly watchman in the school's reception office. There was no way a doorman could be considered to be 'carrying out a revisionist educational line', nor could he 'attack and persecute the children of revolutionary cadres', but still he was beaten, because the Red Guards could always find a reason. In his case, they said he was a 'landlord'.

On the night of 26 August 1966, the school's Red Guards held a struggle rally in the large classroom of Building No. 5, led by Red Guard leader Bu Dahua. The rally began at seven o'clock with shouting and beatings and didn't end until around midnight. By this time, Red Guards were smashing the Four Olds, and beatings and ransacking went on all day and often all night as well.

The big classroom where the struggle rally was held on the west side of Building No. 5 measured 156 square metres and was the school's largest meeting place. It had two doors, on the east and west, but usually only the east door was open. When the struggle rally began, most of the teachers and staff lined up to enter through the east door and were then made to sit down facing west. The 'reactionaries' who had already been 'ferreted out' as 'class enemies' entered through the west door. They included principal Wan Bangru, vice-principal Han Jia'ao, Youth League secretary Gu Hanfen, office deputy-director Zhang Xiuzhen and teachers who had been designated Rightists in 1957. After the reactionaries entered the room, they stood in a line, waiting to be struggled.

Liu Shuhua, a twenty-six-year-old physics teacher, had not been categorised as a reactionary before then, but when he entered through the east door to sit with the majority of the teachers and staff, Red Guards stopped him and ordered him to stand with the 'reactionaries'. During the struggle rally that night, all of the 'reactionaries' were brutally beaten with belt buckles and whips fashioned out of plastic jump ropes. It was the height of summer then, and the whips shredded the thin clothing people were wearing and left bloody welts on their skin.

The people being struggled initially stood but later were made to kneel, and if they knelt too low or not low enough, Red Guards would curse and beat them. Students 'exposed' and denounced the targets for incidents that had never occurred and labelled innocent acts as counter-revolutionary crimes, while shouting slogans against the 'reactionary gang' and pledging their lives to defend the Party Central Committee and Chairman Mao.

The school's principal, Wan Bangru, and vice-principal, Han Jia'ao, were referred to as the heads of the school's 'reactionary gang'. The Red Guards shaved their heads and ordered them to sew a black strip of cloth to the front of their clothes, on which their crimes were written. All through that summer, they were obliged to wear these labels wherever they went while being beaten and cursed. Eventually Wan Bangru's kidney became seriously injured from the beatings, and he passed blood in his stool. He later suffered from chronic kidney disease and gastric illness. A large wound in his head didn't heal completely for a very long time.

The school's Youth League secretary, Gu Hanfen, fell unconscious in the bicycle shed after being harshly beaten at the struggle rally. Her husband, Liu Songcheng, who worked in Tsinghua University's Department of Electrical Engineering, carried her home from the school. Gu Hanfen went nearly blind in one eye and she was so physically devastated that she subsequently suffered two miscarriages before eventually bringing a third baby to term.

The harshest beatings were inflicted on Liu Shuhua and Xing Jiali. Xing was deputy director of the Tsinghua University dean's office, and was responsible for Tsinghua Secondary, so he was considered the 'ringleader' of the reactionary gang. Students had abducted him and brought him to the school that day. Liu Shuhua wasn't a school administrator or a prominent teacher, so he couldn't be labelled a reactionary academic authority, and he was also too young to have committed any 'historical problems' before 1949. The 'reason' given for struggling him was that he was a 'hooligan'.

At that time, Liu Shuhua had been married just three months. Before falling in love with his wife, Liu had pursued another young woman, who had not welcomed his advances and had complained that Liu was pestering her. Because of this, the school's leaders had spoken to Liu.

Liu Shuhua's romantic faux pas was 'exposed' at the outset of the Cultural Revolution, when the work group was put in charge of Tsinghua Secondary, and once the Red Guards took charge, they included him in their expanded list of 'reactionaries'. On one of the doors to the school's education building, Red Guards pasted a huge caricature of Liu with the words 'Big Hooligan' written on it.

The leaders of the school's Red Guards were from the highest two grades, eighteen or nineteen years old, and they were all male. It is hardly surprising for boys of that age to take a prurient interest in a teacher's romantic activities. Every society has people who maliciously pry into other people's personal lives. Under normal conditions, this abnormal mentality and malice is reined in by social mores and by law, and a normal person engages in introspection and corrects his or her viler inclinations. But in the Red August of 1966, Mao granted the Red Guards unprecedented licence to kill with impunity, and to arbitrarily beat and humiliate their teachers and classmates. Latent perversions and malice burgeoned in the name of revolution, giving rise to obscene fantasies and vicious behaviour. On the night of 26 August, Red Guards beat Liu Shuhua more harshly than any of the other teachers.

The struggle rally continued until the middle of the night. When it ended, the Red Guard leaders declared that all head teachers and course teachers had to go to their classrooms to 'engage in the movement'. All of the teachers understood that this meant they'd all be beaten again the next day.

Before this, the teachers had been assembled to 'engage in the movement' among themselves, so apart from some 'ox demons and snake spirits', most teachers hadn't been exposed and denounced by their students. Now the Red Guards had arranged for all of the teachers to be exposed and denounced by their students, and some classes had already struggled their head teacher[9] that day. One head teacher, Tong Changzhen, had been forced to kneel at the front of the class while her students denounced her, and a parent also came and hit her on the head with a stick. The fact was that Tong Changzhen had given extra attention to the child of that parent, so they felt obliged to engage in an especially intense performance to 'draw a clear distinction' between themselves and Tong. Red Guards from that class also ransacked Tong Changzhen's home. The beating at the struggle rally that day, and the violence and terror already occurring in the rest of Beijing, made the teachers aware that they would be encountering even harsher abuse and humiliation.

Although Liu Shuhua was married, his wife was from Shanxi, and as it was almost impossible for an ordinary teacher to have his wife transferred to Beijing, the two were still living apart. Due to a housing shortage in Beijing, Liu shared a room with other male teachers. After the struggle rally, he returned there, put his bed in order and then quietly left. His roommate, Zhang Yiming, was in the room at the time, but had no idea of Liu's intentions.

Whether Liu went anywhere else after leaving his room, no one knows, but finally he climbed to the top of the smoke stack of the boiler room at

---

[9] TN: In the Chinese school system at that time, each year of students had a head teacher, in addition to higher-level administrators such as deans.

Tsinghua University's southwest gate and leaped to his death. He jumped straight down into the smoke stack, which was very long and narrow, and hit the ground with immense impact; someone who saw his corpse said his legs had been jammed straight up into his body. Liu Shuhua's blood and soot-covered body was found the next day when the chimney was cleaned. The Red Guards accused him of 'committing suicide to escape punishment'.

At the time that Liu Shuhua died, his wife was pregnant, and he supported a blind, elderly father back in his home village. After learning of Liu's death, his wife and father went to the school, but were given no help while the movement was still ongoing. We can only imagine how that pregnant young woman and blind old man must have felt, travelling all the way from Shanxi and learning how their husband and son had died.

The violence continued after the brutal 26 August struggle rally. Students from Tsinghua Secondary ransacked the homes of their teachers and of other families near the school. In the homes of Tsinghua University professors, they destroyed books and works of art and took gold and foreign currency, as well as beating the occupants. One day in late August, Red Guards stacked up the seized items, mostly books, on the school sports field and set them on fire. Smoke and ashes danced in the air and produced an asphyxiating odour while Red Guards stood cheering and clapping around the enormous bonfire. The other students looked on from afar.

The school's Red Guards also went to the train station and beat 'black elements' who were being 'repatriated' to the countryside. Sometimes they scalded them with boiling water. In November that year, some people who had been expelled and found they couldn't survive in the villages made their way back to Beijing. Students from Tsinghua Secondary went to the train station and beat those people in a way one eyewitness described as horrific.

Red Guards from the school also helped launch a campaign against 'petty hooligans' and joined Red Guards from other secondary schools in a mass rally at the Beijing Workers' Stadium where these 'hooligans' were beaten before a crowd of onlookers. Some victims of the campaign died of their beatings.

In late August, the Red Guards began their 'revolutionary great networking' to 'fan the flames' of revolution, and Red Guards from Tsinghua Secondary spread their violent persecution methods wherever they went. One interviewee said that when students from the school arrived in Guiyang, they thrashed the 'ox demons and snake spirits' in the provincial Cultural Bureau, as well as members of the Peking Opera troupe and the principal of the Cultural Bureau Nursery School, a middle-aged mother of four.

Mao's extravagantly publicised reviews of the Red Guards at Tiananmen Square on 18 August and subsequently sent an unmistakable message to young people throughout China, and the term Red Guard, once enclosed in quotation marks, became a neologism in widespread use. On the day Liu Shuhua died, 26 August, the number of people beaten to death by Red Guards in Beijing each day jumped from double to treble digits. The numbers continued to climb with almost no interruption until fatalities reached a new height on 1 September.

On 5 September 1966, ten days after Liu Shuhua killed himself, the Central Cultural Revolution Small Group issued an internal bulletin, 'Utterly Rout the Old World'. This detailed the 'countless battle results' of the Red Guards in half a month, which included 1,762 fatalities in Beijing from late August to early September. Haidian District, where Tsinghua Secondary was located, recorded the third highest number of beating deaths of all the capital's districts, even though its population density was much lower than the downtown areas.

Apart from reviewing the Red Guards at Tiananmen Square and ensuring that the media energetically promoted them, China's top leaders arranged for the police to assist in ransackings and in the disposal of dead bodies, a monumental task that was all the more pressing in the heat of summer. Without the guidance and assistance of the authorities, the Red Guards could not possibly have created so much carnage.

From the perspective of the initiators and leaders of the Cultural Revolution, supporting and encouraging secondary school students in launching the Red Guard movement was a very advantageous, powerful and successful measure. Primary school students were generally too mentally and physically immature to kill (although some did beat their teachers to death), while the well-educated university students were generally more likely to think than to kill impulsively. None of Beijing's universities experienced killings on the scale of the secondary schools, even after Red Guards from Tsinghua Secondary spread their practices to Tsinghua University.

According to an interviewee from the CCP Central Committee Senior Cadre School, although before 18 August the cadre school had big-character posters and people who were 'ferreted out' and had to work with the school's gardening team, people weren't paraded through the streets or made to wear dunce caps or kneel for punishment. It was only after Mao reviewed the Red Guards at Tiananmen Square that large-scale violence began. A leader of the Cadre School, Lin Feng, was one of the people reviewing the Red Guards from the Tiananmen Gate Tower, but that night the school's 'revolutionary masses' ferreted him out and paraded him in a dunce cap along with the other 'ox demons and snake spirits' in direct imitation of what the Red Guards were doing in the secondary schools.

Of course, the Tsinghua Secondary students were not necessarily the inventors of all these practices; for example, labour reform teams were first formally established at Peking University, the couplet on class origins originated at PU Secondary, and the first educator was beaten to death at Beijing Normal University Affiliated Girls' Secondary School. Nevertheless, Tsinghua Secondary was one of the first schools to adopt this set of new practices, which were then replicated throughout the country. In other words, what Tsinghua Secondary contributed to the Cultural Revolution was not only the Red Guard name, but also the pattern of violent persecution. The school served as a model for persecuting teachers, students and residents in the wider community. However, I have described how the Red Guards were propped up, guided and developed every step of the way by the Cultural Revolution's leaders. It would therefore be more accurate to say that Mao took this name, this organisation and this pattern of violent persecution and spread it across the whole country through the Red Guard movement and these schools.

The Theoretical Props of Violent Persecution: 'Revolution in Education', 'Class Line' and 'Rebel Spirit'

I wrote earlier how maliciousness played into the brutal beating of Liu Shuhua, the torture of other teachers and cadres at Tsinghua Secondary, and the cutting of female students' hair. Brandishing whips and clubs at others, watching victims moan at one's feet, and holding power over life and death seemingly became addictive for some. During the Cultural Revolution, the innate evil of humanity was able to express itself through the political concepts and operational objectives of the Red Guards.

The Red Guards at Tsinghua Secondary declared that their group had been established for the purpose of 'revolution in education' and 'implementing the class line'. In carrying out their 'revolution in education', they relentlessly attacked the schools' leaders and brutally beat teachers such as Liu Shuhua, even though these people had never, as the Red Guards claimed, 'persecuted the children of cadres', but rather had given them many privileges. The behaviour of the Red Guards had its basis in ideology and revolutionary theory; they designated their principal and teachers as representative figures of the 'revisionist education line', and that's why they could be beaten, humiliated and even killed. This understanding clearly originated from Mao's 7 May Directive, which stated that 'the phenomenon of bourgeois intellectuals dominating our schools cannot continue.' Like the targets of previous political campaigns, school principals and teachers were a social group that the highest authorities had designated a target of revolution, and there was nothing they could do to change this overall situation.

The second objective of the Red Guards was to 'implement the class line.' I described above how the Red Guards of Tsinghua Secondary invented the concept and terminology of 'five red category offspring' and 'five black category offspring'. The 'classes' they spoke of weren't the ones Marx had referred to, who possessed or formerly possessed the means of production, but rather the offspring of people who had once belonged to a certain class. This clearly suited the needs of Mao's theory of class struggle, which required identifying new targets once the old classes had been defeated and eliminated. The Red Guards expanded the targets of attack under Mao's theory of class struggle to include not only 'black elements' – i.e. landlords, rich peasants, counter-revolutionaries, bad elements and Rightists – but also 'bourgeois intellectuals' such as educators and people in the cultural field, as well as the offspring of 'black elements'.

It was on the basis of this theory that the Red Guards of Tsinghua Secondary felt they had the right to humiliate and beat students with 'bad family backgrounds'. Thirty years after Liu Shuhua died, when his former colleagues talked to me, they made a point of mentioning that he didn't have a 'bad family background' and was at most a 'small proprietor'. They also noted that principal Wan Bangru was subjected to long-term abuse not only for being a reactionary and a representative of the 'revisionist education line', but also because he came from a 'landlord family'. These recollections are indicative of the extreme emphasis placed on 'family background' at the school.

The Red Guards at Tsinghua Secondary explicitly limited their membership to students from the 'five red categories': revolutionary martyrs, revolutionary soldiers, revolutionary cadres, workers, and poor and lower-middle peasants. In a major city such as Beijing, the majority of the population consisted of commercial employees, official functionaries, teachers, medical workers, engineers, service personnel and professionals. Children from such families were not allowed to join the Red Guards, and of course the treatment the adults were subjected to is clear enough. Such people make up the main part of any modern city, and attacking them is tantamount to attacking the foundation of modern urban life, including commerce, technology and science.

The Red Guards were the only organisation with a written requirement stating family background as a condition for joining. Although the Communist Youth League also emphasised this aspect in actual practice, it wasn't stated in the League's bylaws. The Red Guard membership rules required rigorously vetting the parentage of members; any attempt to conceal the truth was punished. One of the female students beaten and humiliated at Tsinghua Secondary, Wang Shuying, had been accused of 'concealing her family background'. Students from different family backgrounds were forbidden to deal with each other on an equal basis, or even to speak to each other.

It was not only the Red Guards of Tsinghua Secondary who put such an unusual emphasis on family background; organisations that later became antagonistic to them, such as the Jinggang Mountain Corps at Tsinghua University, also did so. Documents issued by the Jinggang Mountain Corps' leader, Kuai Dafu, particularly designated his family background as 'revolutionary cadre'. ('Resolution No. 3 of the Jinggang Mountain Red Guards' of 28 September 1966 was signed by three people, all of whom noted their family backgrounds.) People routinely stated their positions along with their signatures, but noting family background was something new.

The method the Red Guards of Tsinghua Secondary used to 'implement the class line' was violent and unconventional. They referred to it as the 'revolutionary rebel spirit' and regarded it as an important characteristic of the Red Guards. Three essays they wrote on the subject were published in the *People's Daily* shortly before the 26 August struggle rally. The word 'rebel' (*zaofan* in Chinese) traditionally describes a movement that opposes the Emperor or those in power, but as they declared themselves Mao Zedong's Red Guards, they weren't actually rebelling at all.

If the Tsinghua Secondary Red Guards can be said to have 'rebelled' in any way, it was against the conventions of civilised society. In a civilised society, crime is punished through judicial processes. That is to say, even if Liu Shuhua, Wan Banru, Han Jia'ao and others had actually committed any crimes, their students had no right to punish them. But in the name of 'rebellion', the Red Guards inflicted every kind of bodily harm on their victims.

In a civilised society, there are regulations stipulating the extent of the penalty to be imposed for a given crime. The extent of punishment is limited: imprisonment by the length of time, and the death penalty by the method of execution. The punishment the Tsinghua Secondary Red Guards inflicted on educators had no limits. By the time of the 26 August struggle rally, the school's vice-principal and other 'ox demons and snake spirits' had already been beaten and tortured for nearly a month, and afterwards they remained in 'dictatorship teams' under the Red Guards. They had no way of knowing when this dictatorship would end or whether they'd end up being beaten to death. This kind of unrestrained punishment creates an immense terror.

Even after the Cultural Revolution ended, the violence of the Red Guards did not become part of the official record. For many years, this period was described as a grand festival for idealistic youth, and the people killed or driven to suicide by the Red Guards were covered up.

In 1990 (Vol. 2), the magazine *Biographical Literature* published a 20,000-word essay entitled 'The Flag of the Red Guards', in which former Tsinghua Secondary Red Guard leader Bu Dahua described how they came into being at the school. This lengthy and beautifully written memoir devotes not a single word to the struggle rally that Bu presided over on 26 August, or to how the school's teachers and cadres were tortured or how Liu Shuhua killed himself that same night. Bu makes no mention of how the Red Guards persecuted and humiliated teachers and classmates with 'bad family backgrounds'. He neither acknowledges nor apologises for the monstrous crimes they perpetrated. What the Tsinghua Secondary Red Guards did to their teachers and classmates was a crime – this has to be stated clearly. But Bu Dahua's narrative doesn't even acknowledge it as an error.

The 'progress' this former Red Guard leader made between 1966 and 1990 was in no longer bragging about the violence as one of the 'achievements' of the Red Guards, as was done at the time. In grand rallies at Tiananmen Square in summer 1966, Lin Biao and Zhou Enlai gave speeches lavishly praising the actions of the Red Guards. By 1990, however, the Cultural Revolution had been negated by Deng Xiaoping, and circumstances no longer allowed for boasting.

In Bu Dahua's 1990 article, the incident he describes with the most relish was when on 24 June 1966 the Red Guards put up the big-character poster entitled 'Long Live the Revolutionary Rebel Spirit of the Proletariat!' which included Mao's quote, 'Rebellion is justified.' At the time, the work group at Tsinghua Secondary was unhappy with this poster, but didn't dare oppose Mao's instructions, and since they'd never heard this quote before, they asked the Red Guards where it came from. Bu Dahua intentionally refused to answer, so the work group sent someone to the Beijing Library to look for the quote in the Party history archives; they failed to find it. Even so, the work group was helpless to control the Red Guards.

After Liu Shuhua's Death

At the end of 1966, the Tsinghua Secondary Red Guards lost their pampered status with the Cultural Revolution leadership as its targets expanded far beyond the original remit of the 16 May Circular. The Cultural Revolution leaders who had so energetically supported the Red Guards shifted their support to other organisations that began fiercely attacking all leaders below the level of the CCP Central Committee. The once-powerful parents of the Tsinghua Secondary Red Guards came under attack, and many Red Guards suddenly found themselves 'children of reactionaries' and victims of the same persecution they had initiated and practised against others. Some Red Guard leaders such as Bu Dahua were arrested by the Ministry of Public Security and held for three months until Mao ordered them released. From then on they were known as the 'Old Red Guards' to distinguish them from the new student organisations that the top leaders were now supporting.

The dramatic shifts of power from the work groups to the Red Guards and then to the rebel faction, which in turn was also abandoned by the Cultural Revolution's leaders, show that what looked like reversals were just powerful people being sacrificed as the Cultural Revolution reached a new level. What on the surface seemed like changes in the course of events actually represented the progress of the Cultural Revolution. From the standpoint of its leaders, this was a very successful tactic.

These turns of events resulted in certain people being transformed from oppressors to victims. Yet, after the Cultural Revolution, these people only talked about how they were attacked and never expressed any regret or repentance over how they'd hurt others. The aforementioned article by Bu Dahua is an example of this, describing how Bu was victimised but glossing over his persecution of others. This moral double standard has greatly distorted the history of the Cultural Revolution and has also allowed its ideology of violent persecution to be further promoted through these narratives.

Withdrawal of support for the Red Guards at Tsinghua Secondary didn't mean loss of support for the violent persecution they espoused. The school's new organisation, Jinggang Mountain, occupied a different school building from the Red Guards. Members of the two groups stood on their respective roofs and berated each other. The Red Guards accused Jinggang Mountain of being 'conservative', so Jinggang Mountain proved its revolutionary character by blindfolding the 'ox demons and snake spirits' currently imprisoned in the school – principal Wan Bangru, vice-principal Han Jia'ao, language teacher Gao Tianhui, and clerical staff Zhang Xiuzhen and Yang Disheng – and escorting them to the doorway of the education building, and then ordering them to climb up to the roof, where students in the Jinggang Mountain group beat them with leather shoe soles.

Principal Wan Bangru and vice-principal Han Jia'ao, who were struggled along with Liu Shuhua on the night of 26 August 1966, remained under 'dictatorship' in the school's 'labour reform team, for the rest of 1966 and 1967, and were locked up during the Cleansing of the Class Ranks in 1968.

They finally received a 'Cultural Revolution verdict' of 'faithfully executing the revisionist education line and committing serious political errors', and were sent to a May 7 Cadre School near Beijing for manual labour. After Lin Biao issued his 'Directive No. 1' in 1969 and launched a new round of purges in the cities in the name of 'battle readiness', Wan and Han were sent down to a village in one of Beijing's outer suburbs for an unspecified term in a production brigade.

In 1973, well after Lin Biao's death, they were allowed to return to Beijing and were assigned work. Wan Bangru was reinstated as principal of Tsinghua Secondary after the Cultural Revolution ended, in 1978.

In the late 1980s, Wan Bangru told other secondary school principals that the emergence of the Red Guards and the violence they engaged in was related to the special privileges he gave cadre offspring before the Cultural Revolution, which fostered a sense of group consciousness among them and directly contributed to the subsequent emergence of the Red Guard organisation with these same students at its core. Unfortunately, Wan Bangru never published his soul-searching regarding his pre-Cultural Revolution practices, and he died in 1992. It's a great pity that this generation of educators who had such intensely painful experiences didn't leave behind their notes and analysis for posterity. Many Tsinghua Secondary teachers and students never forgot the struggle rally at which Liu Shuhua was driven to suicide, and they clearly remember the names of the Red Guards who beat him most brutally. They also felt for Liu's wife and child and his elderly father. But because of the restrictions the Chinese authorities have imposed on articles and books published on the Cultural Revolution, these people have been unable to express themselves, and everything published so far has glossed over the violence.

The son Liu Shuhua never met grew up under the cloud of the Cultural Revolution without his father's love or financial support. He experienced all kinds of trouble and bias because of the way his father died at a time that emphasised politics and family background. Liu Shuhua's wife, losing her husband soon after marriage and forced to raise her child alone, certainly experienced hardships that are hard for an outsider to appreciate.

If we remember the Cultural Revolution as a social calamity on a scale not seen since the Qin Emperor's burning of books and burying of scholars, we should also remember Liu Shuhua and make sure his name is not expunged from the history of this era.

It is notable that of all the deaths I was able to confirm in Beijing's secondary schools in Red August 1966, only three are known to have occurred before Mao reviewed the Red Guards at Tiananmen Square on 18 August; all of the other killings and suicides appear to have occurred during the subsequent surge in violence, even in cases when I was unable to determine the exact date.

BEIJING TONG COUNTY NO. 1 SECONDARY SCHOOL

The other early August death was that of **Cheng Min**, the vice-principal and mathematics teacher at the Beijing Tong County No. 1 Secondary School, who died on 7 August 1966, after being subjected to struggle and torture. A 1947 graduate of Tsinghua University, he was fifty-four years old when he died.

The school suspended classes in June 1966, and Cheng Ming, the school's principal and others were accused of being 'reactionaries'. Red Guards established a 'labour reform team' in the school on 6 August, and beat Cheng and the other 'reactionaries' while forcing them to move large rocks and carry earth in large baskets under the scorching sun without water or rest. Cheng Min reached the point where he could no longer stand. His two sons took him by bicycle to the hospital, where he was given a sick leave certificate. At 4:00 a.m. on 7 August, Red Guards arrived at Cheng's home and forced him to return to 'labour reform', tearing up his sick leave certificate. Cheng Min collapsed upon reaching the worksite. When his wife and sons implored the school's Cultural Revolution Committee head to help him, they were rebuked and then beaten by Red Guards.

After Cheng Min died, Red Guards covered his corpse with a tattered mat and used soil to weigh down a sign stating 'Alien-class element Cheng Min'.

Many of Cheng Min's colleagues and students saw him beaten and tortured to death. That night, the heads of the Cultural Revolution Committee and Red Guards held a school-wide rally during which they quoted Mao by declaring, 'A revolution is not a dinner party, or painting a picture or doing embroidery; it cannot be so leisurely and gentle, restrained and magnanimous. Cheng Min killed himself to escape punishment for his crime, and now that he's dead he's nothing more than a stinking lump of soil.'

After Mao reviewed a million Red Guards at Tiananmen Square on 18 August, Red Guards from Cheng Min's school ransacked his home on 20 August and chopped off the hair of his mother, wife and crippled daughter. Like tens of thousands of others at that time, the entire family was expelled to the countryside, where the handicapped daughter died soon afterwards.

According to the *History of Beijing Tong County No. 1 Secondary School* (1986), fifty-three of the school's seventy-six cadres, teachers and staff (70%) were put into 'reactionary teams', where they were flogged with clubs and steel wire and forced to labour for fourteen to fifteen hours a day, after which they had to write self-criticisms at night. Four female teachers had their heads shaved, and twelve cadres and teachers were forced to carry placards around all day. Principal Fang Tiangu was reportedly beaten until his ribs were fractured, and a language teacher, **Xu Zhong**, was driven to suicide. Two teachers and their families were expelled to the countryside, and twenty-one teachers had their homes ransacked. Eight died after being beaten into a coma, and many were permanently crippled.

In September 1966, the Red Guards of the Tong County No. 1 Secondary School and another school 'staged a rebellion' in Xitianyang Village, during which many people were killed or injured. During the Cleansing of the Class Ranks, the school's accountant, **Meng Xiangyun**, was sent to labour reform while ill and died as a result.

During the Cultural Revolution, the school library's 50,000 volumes were looted, and almost all its furnishings were taken away for personal use or destroyed.

A memorial ceremony was held for Cheng Min at the school on 19 July 1978. The school, which had been founded by American missionaries in 1867, reverted to its original name, Luhe Secondary School, in 1987.

BEIJING 101 SECONDARY SCHOOL

The other Beijing educator I identified who was killed before 18 August was **Chen Baokun**, an art instructor at the Beijing 101 Secondary School, who was beaten to death by student Red Guards on 17 August 1966.

The Beijing 101 Secondary School was built on the old site of the Summer Palace, close to Peking University. Prior to the Cultural Revolution, the campus had a fountain with water shooting from the head of a sculpture of a white stork and falling into a round pool. Chen Baokun was beaten to death next to that fountain.

More than a dozen other teachers, as well as the school's vice-principal and head teacher, were beaten along with Chen Baokun on 17 August after being put into 'dictatorship teams' as 'ox demons and snake spirits'. The Red Guards forced them to crawl around the campus pathways, which were covered with coal cinders that cut into their hands and knees. As they crawled, student Red Guards walked behind them and beat their heads and backs with brass belt buckles.

A student at that school said that during this process, she saw a Red Guard wearing heavy army boots stomp on the hands of a female teacher and then grind his boot into her hand.

Upon reaching the fountain, the group of 'ox demons and snake spirits' was harshly beaten. The stork sculpture had already been destroyed during the 'Smashing of the Four Olds', and water no longer flowed in the fountain. As the students surrounded and beat the teachers, one student grabbed a match and set Chen Baokun's hair on fire.

After Chen was beaten into unconsciousness, the Red Guards threw him face-down into the pool, where he died. The water in the pool was very shallow, so it is possible that Chen was already dead when he was pushed in.

Later the Red Guards pulled Chen's body out of the pool and tossed it into a shed behind the principal's office. They told the other teachers in the dictatorship team, 'That's what happens to class enemies.' They ordered the other 'ox demons and snake spirits' to strike Chen Baokun's corpse on the face or else be accused of 'refusing to draw a clear distinction from a counter-revolutionary'.

The day after Chen Baokun was killed, on 18 August, Mao Zedong held his grand rally at Tiananmen Square to receive and review the Red Guards. Red Guards from the No. 101 Secondary School rushed to the city to take part, leaving Chen Baokun's corpse, which was eventually removed by a crematorium wagon.

Following the rally, campus violence continued to escalate. More than sixty of the school's teachers and administrators were put into the 'dictatorship team', and by autumn the leader of the Beijing Municipal Education Department, Zhang Wensong, and others were detained at the school for 'labour reform'.

The 101 Secondary School had been established in the 1950s as a boarding school for the children of Party cadres. By the time of the Cultural Revolution it had become just an ordinary secondary school, but its student body still consisted of a higher than average proportion of cadre offspring, who in summer 1966 became the leading force behind the Red Guard movement and its acts of violence. The ferocity and destructiveness of the No. 101 Secondary School's Red Guards were famous throughout Beijing.

Apart from beating and torturing teachers and school administrators, the school's Red Guards also attacked family members in the school's staff quarters. Two elderly people attempted suicide after being beaten, one of them dying as a result, and the other being crippled for life.

Red Guards ransacked the homes of teachers and administrators, burning their books and destroying works of art and cultural objects regarded as the Four Olds, while also demanding money and ration coupons even from staff who weren't pulled into the dictatorship teams. Teachers who couldn't bear the harassment rose early in the morning and hid in the sorghum and corn fields near the school, not coming home until late at night.

The Red Guards at the 101 Secondary School divided the school's main entrance into two entryways, the smaller of which was labelled the 'dog entrance' through which teachers and students with bad family backgrounds were obliged to pass. They also beat and struggled such people for no other reason than their 'class origins'.

In October 1979, not long after the Cultural Revolution ended, I rode my bicycle to the 101 Secondary School to view the fountain where the 1966 violence had occurred. There was not a drop of water left, or any white stork; all that could be seen was the grimy concrete railing and blackened pool with the cinder pathway alongside it. When I returned to make inquiries in summer 1995, I noticed that the kitchens of teachers' homes had been refurbished with white ceramic tiles and looked clean and pretty. I also noticed that the fountain had been repaired, and that the pool now had a statue of a group of white storks, their wings spread as if to fly. The history of the fountain at the 101 Secondary School is closely bound to the history of the Cultural Revolution and its aftermath.

After my Chinese Holocaust Memorial website went live on the Internet, a historian who had been a student at the 101 Secondary School during the Cultural Revolution made the comment, 'Chen Baokun was a problematic person. Why doesn't the website make any mention of that?'

My response was that when the Red Guards beat Chen Baokun to death, his 'problems' were not at issue. That is why even though I had information about Chen's 'problems', I made no mention of them on the website. However, this case involves questions of what a 'victim' is, as well as assessments of the large-scale persecution and killings during the Cultural Revolution, so it requires a fuller discussion.

When the Cultural Revolution began in 1966, Chen Baokun was working in a Beijing factory because he had been sentenced to three years to be served out of prison. The reason for his sentence was that he'd engaged in inappropriate behaviour with a male student. Chen and his family still lived in the staff quarters of the 101 Secondary School.

What is clear is that first of all, Chen Baokun's 'problem' was his three-year non-prison sentence. When he was sentenced before the Cultural Revolution, students were not mobilised to attack him. Even if he had committed a crime, the court had already punished him, and beating him would therefore be illegal.

Secondly, his fatal beating by student Red Guards was a case of homicide, which like most killings during the Cultural Revolution was never investigated or even reported.

Thirdly, the violent acts that student Red Guards committed at the 101 Secondary School targeted not only Chen Baokun, but a whole group of educators. The beating of Chen Baokun and other school staff was part of the Cultural Revolution that Mao launched and led and was not an isolated incident. The Cultural Revolution is the key factor in this killing.

In any case, it must be clearly stated that Chen Baokun's so-called 'problem' cannot serve as the basis for rationalising persecution and killing during the Cultural Revolution, and the Red Guard violence of August 1966 cannot be explained as 'attacking evildoers' or 'attacks on evildoers that got out of hand'.

BEIJING NO. 26 SECONDARY SCHOOL

Another death that occurred in Beijing before Mao's review of the Red Guards on 18 August was carried out by Red Guards, but did not involve an educator.

Wang Zhaojun, a retired customs official residing in Chenggen Street in Beijing's Dongcheng District, was beaten to death when Red Guards from the Beijing No. 26 Secondary School ransacked his home on 16 August 1966. Beaten to death with him were his wife, **Xu Lanfang**, and their second daughter, **Wang Peiyuan**, who was visiting them.

Wang Zhaojun was nearly eighty years old when the Cultural Revolution began, and his wife, Xu Lanfang, was two years older and had bound feet. Wang had been a customs agent for most of his life, but had retired years earlier. They lived in one of Beijing's oldest neighbourhoods, near the former Imperial City and very close to the Beijing OBGYN Hospital and the National Art Museum of China.

Wang Zhaojun and Xu Lanfang weren't wealthy people, but they could be considered upper-middle class. They owned their home, and they had eight daughters, most of them doctors with good incomes who provided them with financial support for their daily living. When the Cultural Revolution began, the couple's two youngest daughters were working but not yet married and lived with them. The family had always got along well with their neighbours, and donated clothing and shoes to the poorer among them.

When Red Guards began leaving their schools and invading the surrounding neighbourhoods to 'smash the Four Olds', their main targets included property owners. They ransacked homes and beat their residents

– sometimes to death – expelled some of them to the countryside, and forced people to hand over their land deeds to the government. It is under these circumstances that Wang Zhaojun and Xu Lanfang lost their lives.

At that time, the Red Guards were distributing leaflets in Beijing ordering every family to hang Mao's portrait and quotes on their walls. The Wang family immediately bought a portrait of Mao, which they placed in a frame, covering a photo of Wang Zhaojun's father.

A neighbour informed on Wang's family, telling the Red Guards that the frame with Mao's portrait 'had something else in it'. Red Guards ransacking the home opened the frame and found the photo of Wang's father, who was wearing old-style garments. The Red Guards said it was a photo of Chiang Kai-shek and that the family was hoping for a change of regime. Nothing the Wangs said could convince the Red Guards otherwise, and they began beating the couple for being property-owners and for the old photo.

The couple's second daughter, fifty-three-year-old Wang Peiyuan, was visiting from Tianjin at the time. She was a doctor, but had withdrawn from the workforce after marrying an accountant at a Tianjin hospital, and she was visiting her parents because her father was ill. When she saw the situation deteriorating, she tried to escape, but when she reached the gate, a neighbour saw her and told the Red Guards, 'That's their daughter.' Wang Peiyuan was captured and attacked along with her parents, as was the fifth daughter, who was also at home at the time.

The fifth daughter rolled on the floor with her arms covering her head, and although seriously injured, she wasn't killed. Wang Peiyuan was beaten to death, after which the Red Guards kept beating her parents until they lost consciousness. Later a truck arrived, and the Red Guards dumped the three bodies into it. Wang Peiyuan and Xu Lanfang were dead when they were dumped into the truck, but the fifth sister heard Wang Zhaojun groaning and knew he wasn't dead. He was taken to the crematorium with the others and never came home.

Wang Zhaojun's fourth daughter also lived in Tianjin; she and her husband were both doctors who had graduated from the Xiehe Medical School. Their home was likewise ransacked, and they were beaten to the point where the daughter lost consciousness.

Wang Zhaojun's eldest daughter was also a doctor in Tianjin, and her husband was a famous neurosurgeon. He had polyps requiring regular examination, but after being attacked as a 'reactionary academic authority' during the Cultural Revolution, he was unable to maintain his medical examinations and died of rectal cancer. His widow survived, reaching her 100th birthday in 2003 in good health. The Wang family had a history of longevity under normal circumstances.

The neighbours living north of Wang Zhaojun's home were an old couple surnamed Pan who had a son in the US. They too were beaten to death by the Red Guards. Other people in that street were also killed at that time, but I've been unable to learn their names.

When I spoke to a member of Wang Zhaojun's family, she said several friends and relatives had advised her not to speak to me or she might get in trouble. But after thinking about it, she decided to talk with me anyway. I thanked her for her co-operation and frankness, but I was disturbed by this lingering hold the Cultural Revolution imposes on people: even accepting an interview appears risky, much less exercising one's right to resist evil, to demand punishment for the perpetrators, to seek justice, or to devote oneself to changing society so that such disasters can never happen again.

Red Guards at the No. 26 Secondary School also repeatedly beat and tormented their principal, forty-two-year-old **Gao Wanchun**, who killed himself after a struggle rally on 25 August. Gao had been exposed and criticised after the school had been classified as 'Category 4' by its work group.

When the Red Guards took over at the end of July 1966, they organised forty-six teachers and administrators into a 'labour reform team', forcing them to write 'debriefings', clean toilets and move garbage, and parading them in the streets carrying placards. At the end of their daily ordeal, the team members were given a steamed corn bun and a bowl of cold water.

Before the struggle rally on 25 August, the school's Red Guards (who were also members of the 'Capital Red Guard Dongcheng District Pickets') had already spent an hour beating 'ox demons and snake spirits' in a classroom. After that, they stood on either side of the school building's entrance and beat members of the 'labour reform team' as they passed through the door. One of the victim's glasses were smashed, and the blood pouring into his eyes prevented him from seeing his way. Another bled profusely after having his flesh torn by a nail embedded in a club. Upon reaching the rally venue, the forty-six targets were force to kneel. Gao Wanchun was escorted to the rally bound hand and foot and was ordered to kneel on a bench covered with sharp stones. He was repeatedly beaten until he fell off and was then pulled back up again. After the rally, Gao jumped to his death from a window.

Someone who was a student at the time says that before Gao Wanchun died, the Red Guards had brought a man onto the campus and beaten him to death. This man, reportedly surnamed Su, was said to have been a writer who had been a major in the Kuomintang Army, and who lived near the school. When a third-year student objected to the beating, other Red Guards accused him of 'lacking class sentiment' and beat him as well. After Su was beaten to death, the Red Guards had Gao Wanchun come over and touch the corpse and told him, 'You're next.'

During this time, a teacher at the school also attempted suicide by jumping out of a window while the students were eating lunch. He didn't die, however, only breaking his leg.

The leader of the school's work group was a woman named Li Shuzheng. After Mao ordered the work groups to withdraw, Li and other members of the team were also attacked by the Red Guards. Li Shuzheng was called back to the school to make self-criticisms and admit her crimes. Treated brutally, she attempted suicide by drinking pesticide, but her family rushed her to the hospital in time to save her life.

BEIJING FOREIGN LANGUAGE INSTITUTE AFFILIATED FOREIGN LANGUAGE SCHOOL

Zhang Furen, a language teacher in his forties, and **Zhang Fuzhen**, employed in the school's General Affairs Department, were beaten to death by student Red Guards on the night of 19 August 1966.

The school, located near Hepingmen, was originally called the Affiliated Secondary School, but because it added a primary school section, it was renamed the Affiliated Foreign Language School. It was under the direct leadership of the State Council's Foreign Ministry, as opposed to the Beijing Foreign Languages School near Baiduizi (see next section), which was under the direct jurisdiction of the Beijing municipal government. At the outset of the Cultural Revolution, the Affiliated Foreign Language School had more than 1,000 students, including around 600 in the secondary school section.

During summer 1966, both of Beijing's foreign language secondary schools experienced comparatively high levels of violence. There wouldn't seem to be any connection between studying foreign languages and violence, but at this time ordinary people had no access to international exchanges, and the students at foreign language schools were mainly being trained as diplomats or intelligence agents. These were elevated positions in society at that time, with good remuneration and benefits and requiring the best 'political qualifications', so the children of middle- and high-ranking cadres made up a much higher proportion of the student body than on average. These were the kind of students who played a key role in the Red Guard movement in 1966.

The day after Mao reviewed the Red Guards at Tiananmen Square on 18 August, Red Guards ramped up the scale and degree of violence at the school, and Zhang Furen and Zhang Fuzhen were killed that night.

Zhang Furen was a language teacher for the school's upper-classmen and head teacher for the upper-level Russian class (the other class was for

English and French). A former student at the school said that its upperclassmen had begun studying languages when Sino-Soviet relations were still good and there was much to be gained from learning Russian, so the upper-level Russian class was large and included a substantial number of children of powerful officials. This, coupled with the age of the students, gave the class a leadership role in the school. One student in the class, the son of a senior military official, was the commander of the school's Red Guards and chairman of its Revolutionary Committee.

As a teacher, Zhang Furen was naturally a target of attack, but in addition to that, he was a strict teacher who was likely to have attracted the hostility and resentment of students who happened to be a leading force among the Red Guards. In this, he was a classic example of how the most mundane factors can bring disaster on a person in a society that becomes violent and lawless.

Zhang Fuzhen, for his part, had originally been a history teacher, and from 1960 to 1963 he had been the head teacher of a class, but he had been removed from his teaching position during the Socialist Education Movement in 1964 because he had joined the Three People's Principles Youth League, a Kuomintang organisation, before 1949. Once the Cultural Revolution began, he was punished even more harshly, not only as a bourgeois intellectual, but also because of his 'historical problems'.

The fatal beating of Zhang Furen and Zhang Fuzhen on the night of 19 August came about while Red Guards in the lower-level Spanish class were flogging 'reactionary students' Ye Nianlun and Li Zhongliang. Ye Nianlun was the son of a famous translator, Ye Junjian, and among the children of senior cadres who made up much of the student body, he was considered to have a 'bad family background'. Li Zhongliang's crime was 'bourgeois thinking'. While these two students were being flogged, the school's Red Guard leader came in and said, 'Don't beat them – let's get back at the teachers.' This leader, as previously mentioned, was in the high-level Russian class, and as a result, Zhang Furen and Zhang Fuzhen were dragged out and beaten to death in front of the student dormitory.

At first they were beaten with fists and belts, but when some students felt this wasn't enough, they went to the school's martial arts room to grab the wooden guns used for military drills. The room was locked, so they broke in through a window to take out the equipment they used to beat the two men to death.

The Red Guards weren't sure that Zhang Furen and Zhang Fuzhen were actually deceased. Someone had seen in a movie that an unconscious person could be revived with cold water, so they fetched some and threw it on the bodies. When there was no response, they tried boiling water. In this way, the Red Guards confirmed that both men were dead.

The beating death of Zhang Furen and Zhang Fuzhen was brutal enough, but the further detail of dashing cold and boiling water on their bodies afterwards was also circulated around the school. The corpses were put inside a classroom, and many students went to look at them the next morning after word got around; some students just stood in the doorway, however, repelled rather than amused by the violence. At noon, the Red Guards held a rally for all of the school's teachers and students, where the Red Guard leader of the upper-level Russian class said, 'The saying goes, kill one to warn 100; we've now killed two to warn 200.' (The school had around 200 staff at that time.) While this speech was going on, the teachers stood with their heads bowed, afraid to look up.

Which students actually killed Zhang Furen and Zhang Fuzhen? Some said it was the lower-level Spanish class students who had been beating two of their classmates shortly before. Others said it was students from the upper-level Russian class who beat them hardest. No one took the trouble to inquire into the specifics.

Zhang Fuzhen had a daughter in the upper-level Russian class at that time, and the other students kept an eye on her. On the afternoon of 20 August, she was seen walking calmly to the school exit and dropping a letter into a nearby postbox. The Red Guards discussed among themselves whether she might have written a letter reporting what had happened. Someone said she wouldn't dare, since reporting the Red Guards would be a counter-revolutionary act. I was unable to locate Zhang Fuzhen's daughter, so I don't know if she reported what happened, if she got any response, or what subsequently happened to her family. But what other students said about her being under surveillance, and about her mailing the letter, gives an idea of the atmosphere at the school.

Two days later, the Red Guard leader told others that the 'Centre' knew what had happened and wasn't saying anything about it. The 'Centre' was the CCP Central Committee, the ultimate head of the Cultural Revolution. At that time, its leaders were in close contact with student Red Guards and were well aware of the increasingly violent acts they were committing. The Central Committee didn't question or punish the killings, but rather endorsed and praised them, which is why after the murder of the two teachers on 19 August, violence spread at the Affiliated Foreign Language School, and even more educators were beaten and persecuted.

One female teacher surnamed Cui who worked in the dean's office made an unsuccessful suicide attempt by taking an overdose of sleeping pills after being beaten and humiliated. Students were also attacked if they came from 'problematic family backgrounds'. For example, the chairman of the Chinese Musicians' Association, Lü Ji, was a veteran Party member, but after the Cultural Revolution began, he came under attack just like other leading cadres in the educational sector, and his children were no longer recognised as 'children of revolutionary cadres'. Lü Ji's daughter, a first-year student at the Affiliated Foreign Language School, was derided as a 'bitch's offspring'. In the dormitory, classmates soaked her bedding with water so she had to sleep on a wet bed.

The students Ye Nianlun and Li Zhongliang, who were beaten before Zhang Furen and Zhang Fuzhen, were other examples of this violent persecution. In the dormitory, Red Guards demanded that whenever Ye Nianlun's name was called, he had to stand at attention and say, 'Present,' and then, 'My name isn't Ye Nianlun, it's Dogshit.' Li Zhongliang was beaten so often that while sleeping he would cry out, 'Don't beat me! Don't beat me!'

At one point, Red Guards seized 'class enemies' in the surrounding neighbourhood and imprisoned them in a root cellar used to store cabbages and turnips. No one knew what happened in the cellar, but teachers heard that more than one or two people were beaten to death there.

The school's Red Guards also killed people while ransacking the homes of 'black elements' outside the school. One victim was an elderly woman who lived nearby in a home that had been passed down through several generations of her family. She supported herself by renting out the better parts of the house while living in the more run-down portion. A group of Red Guards went to her house and beat the old woman to death. After the Cultural Revolution, someone investigated the matter, but all of the former Red Guards insisted, 'I just hit her a little.' No one was punished.

In fact, the Affiliated Foreign Language School was exceptional only in that two teachers were killed there in one night. In the schools I have information about in Beijing, apart from the Foreign Language School at Hepingmen, only the Beijing Normal University No. 2 Affiliated Secondary School and the Kuan Street Primary School killed more than one teacher in one day. (If educators who were driven to suicide are added in, the number of such schools increases substantially.)

After the Cultural Revolution, the Affiliated Foreign Language School was abolished, but its former students continued to arrange gatherings, and in 1990 they established an alumni association. A former teacher at the school said that former Red Guard leaders attended and even hosted these gatherings, and when she noticed that these people were as arrogant as ever and showed no shame for what they'd done, she refused to stay for dinner.

When I asked this teacher if she could provide me with detailed information about what happened at the school during the Cultural Revolution, she hesitated and then with a trembling voice said she could not, because she wanted to 'spend her later years in peace'. The logical inference of what she said shocked me: more than thirty years after the fact, talking about the tragic deaths of Zhang Fuzhen and Zhang Furen could still threaten the peace of one's later years. This terror came from two aspects: the government forbidding people to talk about the Cultural Revolution, and the continued refusal of the perpetrators to admit their wrongdoing. As long as no one pursues accountability for the deaths of people such as Zhang Fuzhen and Zhang Furen, and their killers feel no need to repent, the poison of Cultural Revolution terror will continue to pollute the atmosphere of our lives today.

BEIJING FOREIGN LANGUAGES SCHOOL

Liu Guilan, around twenty-five years old, a cook and laundress at the nursery school of the Beijing Foreign Languages School, was beaten to death by Red Guards on August 1966 because she came from a 'landlord' family.

The Beijing Foreign Languages School was located in Baiduizi in Xicheng District. Prior to the Cultural Revolution it was under the management of the Beijing municipal government, and after the Cultural Revolution it was merged and became part of the Foreign Languages Institute of Capital Normal University (formerly known as Beijing Normal College).

Liu Guilan had given birth shortly before summer 1966. She came from a village in Shandong Province, and her family was classified as landlords. After Beijing's Red Guards issued their 'general order' to expel all 'landlords, rich peasants, counter-revolutionaries, bad elements, Rightists and capitalists' from the city, Liu Guilan was ordered to return to her native village, but she was first taken to the Foreign Languages School auditorium to be struggled. She knelt on a washboard while Red Guards beat her with clubs, pipes and belt buckles. Afterwards, Liu was unable to stand. She crawled out of the auditorium but died before she could reach the reception office at the main entrance, just 200 metres away.

After Liu Guilan died, her body was put in a small room next to the reception office. The next day, the Red Guards ordered four 'ox demons and snake spirits' to carry her body on a wooden plank to the crematorium. One of the four was the school's vice-principal, and others were 'rehabilitated Rightist' teachers. They carried Liu's body all sixteen kilometres to the Babaoshan Crematorium. Later someone asked one of the bearers if carrying the body so far had been exhausting. The teacher said, 'With the Red Guards riding bicycles behind us, who would dare to be tired?'

One of the teachers forced to carry Liu Guilan's body was **Yao Shuxi**, a head teacher in her forties. Yao hanged herself in the school's restroom on 20 August 1966, after being ruthlessly struggled.

When the beatings began in early August, Peng Xiaomeng and other Red Guards from PU Secondary came to the Foreign Languages School to launch struggle, and a group of cadres and teachers were put under 'labour reform'. The school had three school-level cadres – Party secretary Cheng Bi, principal Mo Ping, and Yao Shuxi. When the canteen served meals, these three cadres and some teachers had to stand in line at the entrance, bowed at the waist, while Red Guards whipped them and ordered them to sing the 'Ox Demon and Snake Spirit Song' over and over again. Cheng Bi and Yao Shuxi had their hair chopped off so they looked like hedgehogs.

One night, a struggle rally was held in the dormitory for Yao Shuxi and language teacher He Huisheng. He Huisheng was also head of the English teaching and research group, which made him a 'reactionary academic authority', while Yao Shuxi was a 'reactionary academic authority in an important position'. The Red Guards forced them to kneel on a desk with their heads between the legs of small stools.

Yao Shuxi was in her forties, unmarried, and lived at the school, as did all of the schools' students, so it was easy for them to continue beating and tormenting her. Sometime around 20 August, You Shuxi tied a rope around a sewer pipe in a girls' restroom in the school's office building and hanged herself, leaving a note saying she couldn't take it any more.

A school cook named **Luo Guitian** also hanged himself, and a school administrator, **Mo Ping**, committed suicide two years later during the Cleansing of the Class Ranks.

BEIJING NO. 3 GIRLS' SECONDARY SCHOOL

Sha Ping, the school's principal, was beaten to death by student Red Guards on 20 August 1966.

Some people say that of all the educators beaten to death in Beijing, Sha Ping suffered the most. On 19 August, Red Guards beat her with leather whips and nail-spiked cudgels deep into the night. Barely breathing, Sha Ping was then brought to a struggle rally at the school on the morning of 20 August and beaten to death on the spot. By the time she died, almost all of her hair had been pulled out, and even some of her scalp had been torn away.

The fact is that teachers at other schools were brutalised just as badly, but with the victims unable to talk, and the perpetrators maintaining their silence, the details were seldom known.

Sha Ping was one of ten teachers and four administrators held in the labour reform teams established by the school's Cultural Revolution Committee in August. An additional thirty-four teachers and staff had their homes ransacked and were beaten and locked up. Members of the labour reform teams were detained at the school and had to begin working at six o'clock in the morning. They had to keep their heads down when walking, and they had to run while carrying heavy loads. For punishment, they were ordered to stand bent at the waist at a ninety-degree angle for six or seven hours at a time; anyone who fell over was whipped with brass belt buckles. When punished by being made to kneel, they had to lower their heads near the ground, but could not touch it, and sometimes their legs were weighed down with large bricks. People had to kneel holding a wooden placard in their mouths, or on washboards until their knees swelled and bled. Anyone who dozed off was dashed with cold water or beaten with the wooden guns used for military drills.

The day after Mao reviewed the Red Guards at Tiananmen Square, Red Guards at the No. 3 Girls' School interrogated members of the labour reform teams in one of the school's three 'proletarian dictatorship rooms':

'Do you hate Chairman Mao?'

'I don't hate Chairman Mao.'

'You damned reactionary, how can you not hate Chairman Mao? Tell the truth or you'll be beaten to death.'

If the people being interrogated said they didn't hate Chairman Mao, they'd be beaten for lying, but if they said they hated Mao, they would certainly be beaten to death. The Red Guards first whipped their victims with thin leather belts, then with brass belt buckles. They made female 'ox demons and snake spirits' jump up stairs in the courtyard and then ordered them to hit each other; anyone who didn't hit someone else would be beaten with belt buckles. They slapped people with plastic shoe soles until their faces swelled and their noses bled and their features became unrecognisable. The sound of beating and screaming rang through the streets, causing many passers-by to stop and stare. This continued until 3:00 a.m., when the 'ox demons and snake spirits' were again made to kneel on the floor and write 'exposure reports'. Anyone who didn't write a report or who wrote too slowly was punched, kicked or whipped. At 5:00 a.m., the victims were taken out to continue their hard labour.

On the morning of 20 August 1966, the Red Guards held a struggle rally in front of the school auditorium. The 'ox demons and snake spirits' had already been tortured all night and had not been fed. They were bound with rope, and placards labelling each as a 'reactionary', 'Rightist' or some other such term hung from their mouths as they were led to the rally. Another group of 'secondary targets' was forced to stand bent over on each side of the venue. Struggle victims were beaten on a platform while being forced to stand in the 'jet' formation, and if they lowered their arms even a little, they were beaten with wooden drill guns.

When two of the targets fell to the ground and couldn't get up again, the leaders of the rally shouted, 'Don't let them make trouble in the assembly!

Take them down and beat them!' Several assailants then dragged them off to a torture room, where they were beaten with wooden guns and belt buckles and then dragged back to the rally and made to kneel on pebbles while the struggling continued.

At the struggle rally, Red Guards kept yanking's Sha Ping's head around by her hair, which was ripped out and scattered on the floor. When she fell over, Red Guards brought in a hedgehog and had it bite her in the throat to test if she was actually dead. After the rally ended, a pile of hair remained scattered on the floor along with a pool of blood left by vice-principal Xiong Yihua, who had been kneeling next to Sha Ping with three or four bricks weighing her head down until her forehead was fractured.

After the struggle rally, some Red Guards shouted and beat the 'ox demons and snake spirits' while making them crawl around the courtyard. The victims were then herded into the 'proletarian dictatorship room', where the torture continued. In the afternoon they faced several more hours of struggle and 'labour reform'.

In the evening, the victims were locked up in a third torture room and forced to kneel with their hands on the ground while they stared at the ceiling. Anyone who dozed off would have a leather belt tied around his or her neck and would be dashed with cold water or whipped or have menthol ointment rubbed into their eyes.

The No. 3 Girls' Secondary School had only female students, so boys from a nearby school were called over to help beat the 'ox demons and snake spirits'.

Around this same time, mathematics teacher **Zhang Meiyan** hanged herself after being beaten and having her home ransacked.

Red Guards also held the wife of Mao Baoshan, who lived near the school. They said this mother of seven was a 'female hooligan', and after beating her to death, they put her corpse in a run-down shed and forced all of the teachers on the labour reform team to go in and 'touch the dead woman'. The Red Guards laughed in scorn as they told people of one teacher who was so terrified that she was 'shaking from head to toe and didn't dare go in'. The Red Guards then had members of the labour reform team drag the body onto a crematorium truck. When the truck reached a busy shopping area, the Red Guards ordered the teachers out of the truck and paraded them in the streets.

Another elderly man, referred to as an 'old landlord', was also beaten to death at the school. The Red Guards told four members of the labour reform team to drag the body from the school grounds. They never learned his name.

After Sha Ping was killed, the other teachers and staff in the labour reform teams remained locked up in the school and continued to be tortured and humiliated. The school's second-highest administrator, vice-principal Dong Guangtai, had given birth less than a month before. She was dragged to the school, denounced and tortured. Her father, Dong Zhentang, had been a soldier in the Kuomintang Army who had gone over to the Communists and had become a commander of the Red First Front Army's Red Fifth Regiment. An important military figure, he had died in the Battle of Gaotai in Gansu Province. Dong Zhentang had been designated a revolutionary martyr, and his widow had been given preferential treatment ever since. When she heard that her daughter was locked up in the school where Sha Ping had been beaten to death, she wrote to Mao describing Dong Guangtai's situation and begging for his help, passing the letter via someone she knew in the PLA's General Political Department. As a result, Mao sent down a memo, which was brought to the school by someone from the PLA and passed along to the Red Guards and Dong Guangtai. She remembers that it said, 'If this person has committed no great crime, she can be released.' Because of this memo, Dong Guangtai was freed from the labour reform team and survived the Cultural Revolution. But when she talked to me thirty years later, she still felt uncomfortable about Mao's phrase, 'If this person has committed no great crime...'

Dong Guangtai's colleagues from this and numerous other Beijing schools remained in the labour reform teams. What 'great crime' had any of them committed? This should have been a matter for the courts to decide, rather than student Red Guards. But unlike Dong Guangtai, they had no one to appeal to Mao on their behalf.

On 13 September 1966, the school's Cultural Revolution Committee split the labour reform team in two. The staff in Labour Reform Team No. 2 were tormented for more than four months, but those in Labour Reform Team No. 1 were tortured even longer and more brutally.

The fact that Mao authorised Dong Guangtai's release from the labour reform team shows that the Cultural Revolution's top leaders were aware of the brutality being carried out, and that they were able to control the extent and the scope of it; there is no way of claiming that they were 'unaware' or that the 'mass movement spun out of control'. At that time, a variety of intelligence departments were submitting daily reports on the number of people Red Guards had killed in Beijing, and the fact that the Cultural Revolution's leaders repeatedly expressed their ardent support for the Red Guard movement shows that they approved of these brutal methods.

It should be noted that while Red Guards were inflicting mass ransackings and killings on the residents of Beijing in August 1966, the Cultural Revolution's top leaders offered protection to some people. According to currently available documents, Dong Guangtai was the only Beijing educator who was protected and released from a labour reform team. Premier

Zhou Enlai produced a list of people he wanted protected on 30 August. The list, published in 1984,[10] included Song Qingling, the widow of Sun Yat-sen and vice-president of the People's Republic of China, as well as Guo Moruo, Zhang Shizhao, Cheng Qian, He Xiangning, Fu Zuoyi, Zhang Zhizhong, Shao Lizi, Jiang Guangnai, Cai Tingkai, Sha Qianli, Zhang Xiruo, members of the National People's Congress Standing Committee, ministers and vice-ministers, other top officials and leaders of the democratic parties. All were targets of the Party leadership's united front or other VIPs. The contrast between the small number of people on Zhou Enlai's list and the enormous number of Beijing residents who had their homes ransacked and were beaten and even killed implies that the Red Guards were allowed to treat anyone not on the list any way they pleased. Two more teachers at the No. 3 Girls' Secondary School, **Feng Tingzhi** and **Sun Lisheng**, killed themselves during the Cleansing of the Class Ranks.

After the Cultural Revolution, in 1979, the Beijing Municipal Education Bureau investigated Sha Ping's death, but because of the policy of dealing with Cultural Revolution rehabilitations on the basis of 'the big picture rather than details', the investigation was suspended mid-way. Friends of the main culprit claimed it would be unjust for her to be punished when no one else was. This person had been working in Xi'an's Military Hospital University, but was transferred back to Beijing in 1979. Teachers investigating the case went to the Beijing military compound, but were stopped at the compound gate.

BEIJING NO. 8 SECONDARY SCHOOL

Hua Jin, the school's fifty-two-year-old Party secretary, was found hanged on the morning of 22 August after being repeatedly beaten and locked up in the school.

Death during the Red Guard Killing Spree after 18 August

Hua Jin died during the upsurge in Red Guard violence that occurred after Mao reviewed a million Red Guards at Tiananmen Square on 18 August. The day after this event, Red Guards at the Beijing No. 4, No. 6 and No. 8 Secondary Schools held a rally at the Zhongshan Park Concert Hall during which they struggled the leaders of those three schools and of the Beijing

---

[10] *Collected Works of Zhou Enlai*, 1984, p. 450.

Municipal Education Bureau. All three of these schools were located in Beijing's Xicheng District, which was where the largest number of people were killed in August 1966.

Zhongshan Park was near the western side of Tiananmen's Gate Tower, two or three kilometres from the No. 8 Secondary School. Former students recall seeing a Red Guard on a bicycle pulling the school's vice-principal, Wen Hanjiang, to the park by a rope around his neck while other students whipped Wen from behind. On the stage of the concert hall before an audience of at least 1,000, the targets of struggle knelt in a row while having criticism and slogans yelled at them and being punched, kicked and whipped with brass belt buckles. Wen Hanjiang fell unconscious on the stage, covered with blood. The director of the Beijing Education Bureau, Sun Guoliang, was beaten until three of his ribs were broken. Others victims were beaten so harshly that one eyewitness said they 'no longer looked human'.

After the rally, Hua Jin and the others were locked up at the No. 8 Secondary School and beaten some more. On 22 August, the Red Guards announced that Hua Jin had hanged herself from the window latch in the room where she was being held. The latch was very low, but the Red Guards claimed that she had lain prone on the floor in order to hang herself.

At that time, suicide was referred to as 'committing suicide to escape punishment' and 'alienating oneself from the Party and the people', and was a major crime of 'resisting revolution'.

Suicide or Homicide?

Hua Jin's family members and some teachers at the No. 8 Secondary School insisted that she was beaten to death. They couldn't provide eyewitness evidence, because Hua was locked up alone, and it was Red Guards who had last seen her, but they held their views for the following reasons:

1) On the night of 21 August, a school employee who lived nearby heard Hua Jin being beaten in the passageway very late at night and for an extended period of time until the noise finally stopped. He didn't see anything, but only heard the sounds.

2) Based on the beatings experienced by others at the No. 8 Secondary School, the Red Guard violence there was very severe. Han Jiufang, a vice-principle and chemistry teacher at the school, lapsed into a coma from being beaten at the time that Hua Jin died. Han Jiufang's husband, Zhou Xin, a chemistry teacher at Tsinghua University, rushed Han to the hospital, where she was found to have two great

holes gouged into the flesh of her back from being beaten by the brass-buckled army belts. The doctor said she was suffering from septicemia and could not be saved. Zhou Xin donated 400ml of his own blood to save his wife, and had a sample of her blood sent to the No. 3 Hospital under the Beijing Medical School for a bacterial culture, which determined that the antibiotic erythromycin might be effective, so the doctor gave Han Jiufang an extra-large dose. Zhou Xin heard the nurse ask the doctor, 'Is this a reasonable way to cure her?' The doctor said, 'This is called, "healing a dead horse as if it were alive".' After a few weeks, Han's fever receded and her life was saved, but from then on she suffered from epileptic seizures and other after-effects. She was never able to look after herself again, and was confined to a wheelchair for the rest of her life. She was forty-three at the time that she was reduced to this condition, nine years younger than Hua Jin.

3) During this time, the school's Red Guards killed eight 'ox demons and snake spirits' in the surrounding neighbourhood.

4) Hua Jin had never shown any inclination towards suicide. As a senior cadre, she had experienced many political campaigns. When she was being beaten, she never expressed despair and in fact encouraged other teachers to persevere and not give up hope. The No. 8 Secondary School had a language teacher named **Shen Xianzhe** who killed himself after being beaten and humiliated. But Shen was never locked up alone, and before killing himself he'd told his family of his feelings of despair.

5) Deaths falsely reported as suicides occurred elsewhere, as in the case of **Xu Peitian**, a worker beaten to death at the Beijing No. 6 Secondary School, which will be described later in this part.

Although those holding that Hua Jin had been beaten to death provided all of the above reasons, they were unable to state their conclusion at the time because even the beating death of Bian Zhongyun, which had involved so many participants and eyewitnesses, had gone unpunished.

How Did She 'Sacrifice Her Life'?

By the time victims of the Cultural Revolution were rehabilitated, Hua Jin had been dead for twenty-two years. At that time, the question was raised of whether she committed suicide or was beaten to death, but no conclusion was reached.

On 3 June 1978, the Beijing Xicheng District Party Committee issued its 'Decision Regarding Hu Jin's Notice of Exoneration', which read:

> After the Proletarian Great Cultural Revolution began, Comrade Hua Jin enthusiastically took part in the movement and closely observed Party discipline, maintaining truth, principle and a work style of seeking truth from facts, and courageously defended Chairman Mao's revolutionary line, but she was brutally persecuted by the counter-revolutionary revisionist line of Lin Biao and the Gang of Four, cruelly beaten and regrettably died a martyr's death in the early hours of 22 August 1966.
>
> For thirty years, under the leadership of the Party Central Committee and Chairman Mao, Comrade Hua Jin offered all her energies and was an outstanding member of our Party and a good cadre. Comrade Hua Jin's sacrifice is a loss to our Party's educational undertaking.

This was the formulaic language used in all rehabilitation documents at that time, even though it was Mao Zedong who reviewed the Red Guards from the Gate Tower of Tiananmen Square on 18 August 1966, and Lin Biao merely stood behind him waving a Little Red Book. There is nothing to suggest that Mao was in conflict with Lin Biao or the Gang of Four regarding Red August. Their conflict arose later, and had nothing to do with the question of whether to treat ordinary people more humanely.

In Hua Jin's 'exoneration', she is described as having been 'martyred' rather than killed or 'persecuted to death' (the usual phrase used to describe people who killed themselves while being tormented). The writers of the 'decision' probably had no choice but to use these words, but they were inappropriate.

The word 'martyr' in its modern sense, according to the *Dictionary of Modern Chinese*, means 'to sacrifice one's life for a just cause'. Hua Jin could not possibly have wished to be 'plucked out' as a 'reactionary' in June 1966, and being beaten, locked up and losing her life was even less the result of any choice on her part. Hua and her colleagues were stripped of their lives by the Cultural Revolution's leaders for the sake of their own objectives, rather than offering up their lives for any cause. Hua does not meet any of the criteria for a martyr's death.

In its ancient sense, the Chinese phrase for martyr, *xisheng*, referred to 'a domestic animal offered up as a sacrifice in ancient times'. Referring to Hua Jin and other victims as *xisheng* in the ancient sense of sacrificial beasts could explain the reasoning and objectives of the Cultural Revolution's leaders in persecuting them to death. But this expression is inaccurate in one respect: in ancient times, people sacrificed beasts, not living human beings. Furthermore, when the ancients slaughtered these beasts, they killed them quickly, at the hands of a professional butcher; the complicated sacrificial ceremonies of ancient times were used to worship the gods rather than torture the beasts. Hua Jin, tortured on the stage of the Zhongshan Park Concert Hall and in a closed room in August 1966, was treated much worse than any sacrificial beast in ancient times.

It was the Cultural Revolution that caused Hua Jin to die in such a horrific manner. The use of the word 'martyr' to sanitise the brutal death she suffered is just another one of its legacies.

BEIJING NORMAL UNIVERSITY AFFILIATED NO. 2 SECONDARY SCHOOL

Jiang Peiliang, the school's Party secretary, was beaten to death by Red Guards on 25 August 1966.

The Affiliated Secondary School (hereafter BNU No. 2 Secondary) was located directly across from Beijing Normal University in Xicheng District. On 25 August, Red Guards killed three people at the school.

An eyewitness said that apart from Jiang Peiliang, school principal Gao Yun and other teachers identified as 'ox demons and snake spirits' were being struggled on the stage of the school auditorium at the time. Most of the beatings were carried out by lower secondary students. The Red Guard leaders didn't take part in any of the physical attacks, but they had organised the rally. Nail-embedded wooden sticks that ripped into the flesh were used. During the rally, someone yelled, 'Get some salt and pour it on their wounds!'

Jiang Peiliang had a son who was a lower secondary student at the school. The Red Guards called him onto the stage and ordered him to beat his father; the son picked up a stick and hit him. After Jiang Peiliang was beaten to death at the rally, his son became mentally unstable. An interviewee who saw him in 1992 said he still hadn't returned to normal.

Red Guards ransacked Jiang's home after his death to 'destroy the roots and branches'. His youngest child was only two years old at the time and was being looked after by a nanny. The nanny was quick-witted and helped Jiang's family get away while she distracted the Red Guards with her banter.

Believed dead, principal Gao Yun was sent to the crematorium. While lying among the pile of corpses waiting to be incinerated, he regained consciousness and went home. Gao Yun was not the only one to have this bizarre and horrific experience. The head of the Beijing No. 33 Secondary School, a middle-aged woman named Du Guangtian, was also beaten so savagely that she was taken for dead and sent to the crematorium. Its foreman found that she was still breathing, so she was sent home instead of into the furnace.

The other two people killed at BNU No. 2 Secondary that day were **Jin Zhengyu**, a language teacher, and **Fan Ximan**, the mother of a student.

Jin Zhengyu, in his thirties, had studied at Beijing Normal University after serving in the navy. He was single and lived in a small residence at BNU No. 2 Secondary. His colleagues said he didn't get upset over trifles and liked to write doggerel. One time a petty thief stole some items from his home, and he wrote a poem about it entitled 'To the Cat Burglar': 'If you're hungry, there are cold steamed buns; if you're thirsty, there's some water, and there are a few books you can read.' This was also a depiction of his life. It was because of some poems he'd written that Jin was pulled onto the stage with Jiang Peiliang and the other 'reactionaries' on 25 August. He was beaten until his liver ruptured; he was unable to eat, vomited blood, and died soon afterwards.

Fan Ximan, a cadre at the Railway Ministry Party School, was the mother of Cao Binhai, a student at BNU No. 2 Secondary. Fan's husband had been designated a member of a 'reactionary gang' at the outset of the Cultural Revolution, and Fan wrote to her son telling him about the family's problems. Some schoolmates saw the letter and referred to it as a 'reactionary letter'.

On 25 August 1966, Red Guards ransacked Cao Binhai's home. Prior to that, Cao's parents had both been 'revolutionary cadres', so he found it difficult to tolerate this treatment. During the ransacking, Cao began fighting with his Red Guard schoolmates. The Red Guards claimed that Cao Binhai grabbed a knife from the kitchen and wounded one of them.

Cao Binhai was taken to the Public Security Bureau and locked up, while his mother, Fan Ximan, was taken to the school to be struggled by the Red Guards. That afternoon, Fan was beaten to death on a table tennis table.

In the regulated confines of a prison, Cao Binhai wasn't beaten to death like his mother, but he became deranged. A person who saw him in the mid-1990s said he had still not recovered.

After killing three people at their school, the Red Guards at BNU No. 2 Secondary were still not satisfied. They decided to take all of the school's 'reactionaries' to a mass denunciation rally at Beijing's largest meeting venue, the Workers' Stadium. In particular, they wanted to take Cao Binhai, the student whose mother they'd killed, and beat him to death in front of everyone. After Zhou Enlai found out about this, he sent a municipal Party secretary over to express support for their revolutionary actions, but also to say that the rally should not be held and the Red Guards should just go into the community. Zhou Enlai invited two of the school's Red Guard leaders in for a talk, but during the lengthy wait the students fell asleep and were finally taken back to the school without having seen the Premier.

The Red Guards did as they were told and didn't hold the rally, but they went around ransacking nearby homes and killed more people. **Li Congzhen**, a resident of East Di'anmen Avenue who was a worker at a semiconductor research institute, was beaten to death by students from the school on 28 August.

Li Congzhen had earlier worked as a doorman at the home of Dr Zhu Guangxiang, who had studied medicine in France and was the director of Beijing's Ping'an Hospital before his retirement. Li Congzhen continued to live in a room in Zhu's home, and the children of the Zhu family called him Uncle Li.

On 28 August 1966, students from BNU No. 2 Secondary came to ransack Dr Zhu's home, assaulting him and smashing his possessions. Li Congzhen stepped forward to dissuade them, saying, 'Dr Zhu is a good man; don't beat him.' The Red Guards were infuriated and tied Li to a pillar and whipped him with their belts. The Zhu family was forced to stand in the courtyard and watch Li being beaten.

When the brass belts first struck him, Li Congzhen screamed in pain, but after a while he lost consciousness. Some Red Guards said he was dead, while others said he was faking. One of them chopped at Li's shoulder with a cleaver, slicing off a large piece of flesh. When Li didn't react, they decided he was really dead and untied him from the pillar, tossed him on the ground and called the crematorium to take him away.

After Li Congzhen was killed, the Zhu family was forced from their home, bound with ropes and taken to BNU No. 2 Secondary, including the children. They were held for a month, during which time Red Guards burned the feet of the Zhu family adults with red-hot coal hooks and interrogated the children. They asked Dr Zhu's two-year-old grandchild, 'Who is better, Chiang Kai-shek or Chairman Mao?' When the uncomprehending child gave a nonsensical answer, the Red Guards beat the adults for teaching the child to be 'reactionary'. The Zhu family also saw teachers being attacked, including a mathematics teacher named Li Wenying who was beaten half to death. After more than a month, Zhu Guangxiang and his family were released. By then, their home was occupied by others and their furnishings had been sold off. Their dozen family members were given the two worst and smallest rooms to live in.

In the meantime, Mao reviewed the Red Guards a second time at Tiananmen Square on 31 August. The *People's Daily* reported:

After Chairman Mao and other Central Committee leading comrades circled the square in their motor vehicles, they went into the Gate Tower of Tiananmen Square, accompanied by the strains of 'The East is Red.' More than 300 revolutionary young militants from all over the country and the capital who had been invited to the Gate Tower ardently hailed Chairman Mao and wished him long life. They put a red scarf and Red Guard armband on Chairman Mao.

Among those 300 'revolutionary young militants' were representatives of the Red Guards of BNU No. 2 Secondary. This happened less than a week after they killed three people at their school and the neighbourhood resident Li Congzhen.

BEIJING NO. 15 GIRLS' SECONDARY SCHOOL

Li Wenbo, a fifty-two-year-old resident of Beijing's Chongwen District, was beaten to death in his home by Red Guards from the Beijing No. 15 Girls' Secondary School on 25 August 1966.

The Only Victim Named from the August Slaughter

Thousands of Beijing residents were beaten to death by Red Guards in the latter half of August 1966, and even more were driven to suicide, but the names of these victims were never reported in the media, disappearing into the black hole of history.

Among these thousands of victims, Li Wenbo was an exception. His name appears in printed materials from that period because Premier Zhou Enlai mentioned him and his wife in two speeches at that time. The first was Zhou Enlai's 10 September 1966 speech at the Capital University and College Red Guard Revolutionary Rebel Headquarters Networking Pledge Rally, and the other was a speech he gave on 25 September 1966, while receiving the leaders of the Capital University and College Red Guard Revolutionary Rebel Headquarters. In his speech, Zhou said that 'capitalist Li Wenbo' had 'assaulted' Red Guards, but didn't mention that Li had been beaten to death. Zhou's two speeches and those of other leading cadres were published in book form as guiding materials for the Red Guard movement, and they can be read even now. In his speech, Zhou also mentioned the incident involving Cao Binhai at the Beijing Normal University Affiliated Secondary School, but didn't include Cao's name. None of Zhou Enlai's other public speeches mentions the names of any victims, or the fact that anyone had been beaten to death by Red Guards.

The Truth Behind Li Wenbo's Death

Li Wenbo's name became public because he was treated as a case of 'resisting' the Red Guards who ransacked his home, and provided a pretext for violence on an even greater scale in Beijing.

The Red Guards claimed that Li Wenbo attacked them with a kitchen knife and then leaped to his death to 'escape punishment'. After Li died, the Red Guards immediately spread reports of 'reactionary capitalists killing Red Guards' and of 'class enemies engaging in counter-revolutionary retribution'. In subsequent beatings and ransackings, 'blood debts repaid with blood' became the new slogan. One year later, the Red Guard newspaper of the Peking University Affiliated Secondary School, *Xiang River Review*, and *Song of the Red Guards*, a newspaper published by Red Guards from sixty-three Beijing secondary schools, jointly produced a Special Issue celebrating the first anniversary of their movement. One article was about the Li Wenbo incident, and it said that after the Red Guards arrived at Li's home they rummaged through his cupboards and beat Li and his wife, and then went up to the roof to continue their search. Li later asked to go to the bathroom, and when he came back, he slashed at Red Guards with a knife. The article said that Li then jumped from the upper story of his house, after which 'the masses, filled with righteous indignation, grabbed him and rained blows on that old dog and ended his wicked life.' The article went on to say that on 25 August 1966, 'the young militant Red Guards used blood to begin writing history, and on this day, the rising sun of the Red Guards shone with an intense flame.'

In 1998, thirty-two years later, an article under the pen name 'Hong Ming' was published.[11] The writer said that he was one of the Red Guards involved in the Li Wenbo incident. He wrote:

> In fact, that small proprietor and his wife were very honest and timid. I was just a lower secondary school student and didn't know what I was doing. On a hot day we locked the couple upstairs and didn't let them eat, drink or go to the bathroom all day. The old lady couldn't stand it and insisted on coming downstairs, but we pushed her down and kicked her. The old man became upset and came down to reason with us, and

---

[11] *Democratic China*, No. 3, 1998.

we beat him with a stick and made him bleed. He became agitated and grabbed a knife to scare us off. No one actually stabbed anyone. We said he was retaliating, but we didn't know anything, and later it was changed to say he killed someone and he was executed. When I joined the Party while in the Northeast Production Corps, I told the political commissar what had really happened, and he advised me to say nothing, otherwise others would say I had an 'unstable standpoint'.

This rare expression of regret by a Red Guard provides a description of the Li Wenbo incident that differs substantially from previous versions. If Li Wenbo and his wife were alive to tell their story, they might well provide yet another version. What is certain, however, is that Li Wenbo was beaten to death by Red Guards on the spot, and Li's wife was taken away in a police vehicle. After Li was killed, the Red Guards planned to hold a mass rally to denounce him, and to beat his wife to death. Zhou Enlai mentioned the Li Wenbo incident twice in his speeches because he was talking of the need to protect the Red Guards. He also expressed his disagreement with the Red Guards' plan to kill Li's wife at the rally. Instead, two days after Zhou Enlai mentioned Li Wenbo in his 10 September speech, the court sentenced her to death.

Since Cultural Revolution archives are closed to the public, I'm unable to record the contents of the judgment against Li's wife. But several people I interviewed said they'd read it. One legal researcher said that the judgment not only sentenced Li's wife to death, but also Li Wenbo. He added that this was tantamount to sentencing a dead man to death, which was very unusual in legal procedure, and that's why it left such a deep impression on him. He further explained that the authorities may have done this in order to demonstrate the state machinery's full support for the Red Guards.

In Zhou Enlai's speech and the Red Guard's article, Li's wife is never referred to by name. Through further investigation I determined that her name was **Liu Wenxiu**. Liu Wenxiu was sentenced to death on 12 September 1966.[12] The execution was carried out the next day.

Although Liu Wenxiu was sentenced to death by the state apparatus rather than being killed by Red Guards, she was not given the right to defend herself or to appeal, in violation of standard legal procedure. Furthermore, the Red Guards only said that Li Wenbo 'stabbed someone' and never accused Liu Wenxiu of assaulting anyone. Finally, all of the versions and explanations unanimously affirm that no Red Guards were killed or seriously injured in this incident. Yet Liu Wenxiu was sentenced to death.

---

[12] Judgment No. 345 (1966).

The Red Guards who came to Li Wenbo's home that day were from the Beijing No. 15 Girls' Secondary School (since renamed the Guangqumen Secondary School). The ransacking had begun the night before, and they hadn't let the family sleep all night. They searched Li's home and roof and beat Li and his wife, demanding that they hand over gold and guns, but they had no such items. Basically, the Red Guards invaded Li's home and searched it without a warrant; according to the pre-Cultural Revolution law, they were acting illegally, and Li would have been within his constitutional rights to defend himself, his home and his family. But Li and his wife clearly didn't try to prevent the Red Guards from entering their home, and in fact on 24 August, the day before he was killed, Li had signed over his property to the city's housing administration. The couple had Mao's portrait hanging in their home and owned a copy of Mao's *Quotations*. Like the more than 100,000 other households in Beijing where homes were ransacked and people were beaten, Li Wenbo's family submitted entirely to the Red Guards' actions and endured them.

Was the Li Wenbo incident exaggerated by the Red Guards, or was there actual resistance? Based on inquiries from multiple sides, it can at least be determined that Li offered no strong resistance when the Red Guards ransacked his home and beat him and his wife. What probably happened that day was that Li took some obstructive action to protect himself or his wife. Li was not particularly old, and people were dressed lightly in the heat of summer. Household knives back then were made of iron and would have caused serious injury if Li had used one to deliberately attack the female student Red Guards. For that reason, on 26 March 1981, Case No. 222 (1981) found Liu Wenxiu not guilty and declared the charges dropped against Li Wenbo.

Li Wenbo's home at No. 121 Guangqumennei Avenue was built by the government in the 1950s. Because the land had belonged to Li Wenbo before 1949, he was allowed to live in part of the building when it was completed. Li was no longer formally employed, but before the Cultural Revolution he had engaged in secretarial work, and he repaired bicycles to make money.

Li Wenbo and his wife had three children. The youngest, Li Yuhai, was in lower secondary school. When the incident occurred at his home, he was taken from school to the Chongwen District Public Security Bureau and held there. When he was escorted to a new location the next day, he saw the PSB's courtyard filled with hundreds of dead bodies, male and female, young and old, with just a narrow space left to pass between them. They were local residents who had been beaten to death, like his father. Li Yuhai was held for a month and a half. His elder brother was detained for more than a year.

I tried to interview one of Li Wenbo's sons, who was clearly still suffering from post-traumatic stress syndrome from the Cultural Revolution. He said his wife was ill and his child very young, and he begged me not to continue asking about what his family had been through. I understood and sympathised with his situation and hung up the phone, even though it had taken a lot of effort for me to find out his telephone number.

A Pretext for Escalating Violence

The Li Wenbo incident immediately provided a pretext for an upsurge in Red Guard violence in Beijing.

The first to suffer from it were teachers and administrators at the Beijing No. 15 Girls' Secondary School, who had already been subjected to all kinds of inhuman torture and humiliation since being locked up in mid-August. On the evening of 25 August, the day Li Wenbo was killed, Red Guards murdered the school's Party secretary, fifty-four-year-old **Liang Guangqi**.

Wang Kaishun, a language teacher at the school, subsequently self-published a book entitled *Shattered Dreams*, which describes how the Red Guards ordered Liang Guangqi and principal Gao Jiefei to kneel on the ground and drink each other's urine or be beaten. After Liang was struck five times, she didn't get up again.

Wang Kaishun herself was also beaten several times. One time, two Red Guards strode into the 'ox pen' and dragged her out by the hair. They then gripped her by the arms and legs and swung her back and forth like a jump rope. It was a new torture method the girls had learned from outside. They then dropped her on the ground and kicked and punched her. One time a big wooden placard weighing five kilos was hung around Wang's neck with an iron chain that dug into her flesh while two club-wielding Red Guards escorted her to the stage of a struggle rally and made her kneel down. Wang's back became permanently misaligned after Red Guards beat her with clubs while she was scrubbing toilets. The school's chemistry teacher, Wang Xiu, had a huge wound beaten into his back and couldn't stop the bleeding.

Later, the school's Red Guards claimed that it was Red Guards from a different school who came in and beat Liang Guangqi to death. In any case, her killing was never investigated.

Liang Guangqi was a native of Rongcheng, Shandong Province, and she had grown up in a landlord family in decline. She'd had her feet bound when young but unbound them several years later. She attended Weihai Normal School and Jinan Normal School before going to Yan'an in 1938 and joining the Communist Party in 1942. In the 1950s, she was head of the women's section of the Chinese Federation of Trade Unions. When a group of central organ cadres was dispatched to 'assist the localities' in 1958, she was sent to a series of secondary schools, and ended up as the Party secretary at the No. 15 Girls' Secondary School.

Because both Liang and her husband were considered 'revolutionary cadres', her second son became a Red Guard at the Beijing No. 4 Secondary School and took part in ransackings and beatings in August 1966. Yet Liang herself was soon struggled and locked up at the No. 15 Girls' Secondary School. The school notified her son to bring things for her. He and a classmate went to the school's Cultural Revolution Committee, where they were treated rudely but allowed to go to where Liang and others were being held. There they found Liang with half her hair cut off, exposing her scalp. Always a neat and tidy person, she was all but unrecognisable. Her son and his classmate spoke a few words with her and then left, never guessing that she'd be beaten to death a few days later. Liang's son was the last person in her family to see her alive.

Liang Guangqi's body was quickly cremated. Her husband rushed around various upper-level organs trying to get an explanation for what happened to her, but without result. Finally he, too, was locked up.

The father of the classmate who accompanied Liang Guangqi's son to see her, the director of a Finance Ministry mint in Sichuan, was also subsequently beaten to death. The experience of these two boys was quite representative among the Red Guards. When the Cultural Revolution began, they were the children of 'revolutionary cadres' and therefore belonged to the 'five red categories' who harmed others, only to become victims themselves later on. After the Cultural Revolution, many such people talked only about how they had been harmed but not about how they had harmed others. Liang Guangqi's son was one of the few courageous enough to face up to what he had done. His father subsequently married a woman whose first husband had committed suicide during the Cultural Revolution.

Liang Guangqi's son said that Liang got along well with people, and young teachers always came to their home for the holidays; she wasn't the kind of person who attracted hostility. But personal conduct had no bearing on the deaths of most of the people killed during the Cultural Revolution. Liang Guangqi and other school administrators were targets by virtue of their status, and killing them was a group activity for Red Guards.

Liang Guangqi's son said that for a time he hated the neighbourhood resident Li Wenbo, because if not for Li Wenbo, his mother wouldn't have died. Eventually he understood that Li was just a 'little person' and not responsible for the violence leading to his mother's death. I was able to convince him of this by showing that the upsurge in Red Guard violence was already well underway by the time Li Wenbo was killed.

It is a fact that the day after Li Wenbo died, 26 August, Red Guards held a mobilisation rally at the Tsinghua University Affiliated Secondary School and shouted, 'The class enemy has begun retaliating! We can't let them off easily!' and 'The landlord and capitalist classes have raised their butcher's knives against Chairman Mao's Red Guards!' They beat several students with 'bad family backgrounds' as well as administrators and teachers, one of whom, **Liu Shuhua**, killed himself later that night. In the days that followed, Red Guards from other schools beat and tortured their classmates, teachers, school administrators and neighbourhood residents, resulting in numerous killings and suicides. The famous Pingju opera performer Xin Fengxia wrote after the Cultural Revolution that from 26 to 28 August, Beijing was 'rattling the rafters', a theatrical expression used to describe the ransackings and beatings going on at the time; on 26 August she heard Red Guards declare, 'Today Beijing will blossom and rattle its rafters, and no one will get away.'[13] Xin Fengxia was repeatedly beaten by Red Guards at the China Pingju Theatre and became so disabled that she was never able to perform on stage again. Her colleague, the famous Pingju performer **Xiaobaiyu Shuang**, committed suicide after being beaten and humiliated.

In Chongwen District, where Li Wenbo was killed, eyewitnesses say that busloads of Red Guards converged on the area and attacked local 'ox demons and snake spirits' for several days, killing many. In particular, Red Guards confiscated kitchen knives from local homes.

According to the statistics in one internal document, in summer 1966, the four Beijing districts where Red Guards killed the most people were Xicheng, Chongwen, Haidian and Dongcheng. The number of killings in Xicheng District, where the CCP Central Committee and State Council offices were located, was almost as large as the total of the other three combined. Xicheng, Haidian and Dongcheng were districts where the Red Guards were first established and became active, but Chongwen was not. Furthermore, Chongwen is Beijing's smallest district, yet the number of people killed there was higher than in Haidian and Dongcheng, second only to Xicheng. This has much to do with the Li Wenbo incident. However, Red Guard violence was already on a steep upward trend before then.

In summer 1966, intelligence organs filed daily internal reports on the number of people killed; they didn't include the victims' names, but at least there was a record of the numbers. I've compiled this data into a graph using the date as the horizontal axis and the number of deaths as the vertical axis:

---

[13] Xin Fengxia, *The Last Hurrah*, Jiangsu wenyi chubanshe, 1995, pp. 152, 155.

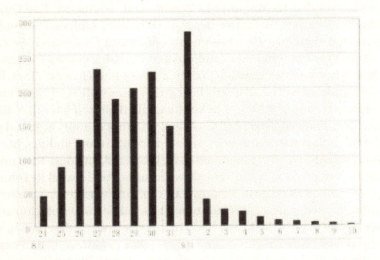

On the day after Li died, 26 August, the number of fatalities jumped from two digits to three digits. The number increased by 50% from 25 to 26 August, and doubled from 26 to 27 August. The number of deaths reached a peak on 1 September. On the day before this, 31 August, there was a dip in the number of deaths. That was the day that Mao reviewed the Red Guards a second time, drawing them to Tiananmen Square and leaving fewer out beating people.

The graph also shows that the number of fatalities doubled from 24 August to 25 August, the day that Li Wenbo was killed. The number of deaths had been climbing steadily in the last half of August, and the trend was already firmly established by then. Mao's nationally broadcast review of the Red Guards at Tiananmen Square on 18 August, and the honouring of the Red Guard leaders at the forefront of the violence, was the real watershed for the upsurge in violence.

One cadre from the CCP Central Committee Senior Cadre School said that on the evening after the 18 August rally at Tiananmen Square, the first large-scale attack against 'ox demons and snake spirits' occurred there, at the Party's highest seat of learning. All of the educators working at the school were highly qualified and experienced, and its students weren't ordinary young people, but fairly high-level cadres. Even so, someone applied the same methods as the secondary school Red Guards to inflict violence and humiliation on school director Lin Feng and others, making them wear dunce caps and parade through the streets while beating dustpans and proclaiming their crimes. Clearly, the actions of the secondary student Red Guards had set an example for Cultural Revolution activities throughout the country. The day after the 18 August rally, violence reached a new high with sometimes fatal beatings in many Beijing schools. All this happened a week before the Li Wenbo incident.

Just before Li Wenbo's death, Red Guard beatings and killings had already spread into the wider community, with famous authors Xiao Jun, Lao She and others from the Beijing Municipal Cultural Bureau and Federation of Cultural Circles beaten and humiliated at the Temple of Confucius on 23 August, and six residents of Dongcheng Hutong beaten to death the same day.

Li Wenbo died in the course of an upsurge of violence that followed the first review at Tiananmen Square; among the thousands of people who were beaten to death at that time, only Li and Cao Binhai were accused of resistance, and both incidents occurred on the same day. The conflicts between Li Wenbo and Cao Binhai and the Red Guards were the result rather than the cause of the massive increase in Red Guard violence. It can be said with certainty that even without these incidents, the sharp increase in killings in August would have occurred just the same.

Why Did No One Resist?

On 5 September 1966, ten days after Li Wenbo died, the Central Cultural Revolution Small Group issued its internal bulletin 'Utterly Rout the Old World: The Countless Accomplishments of the Red Guards in the Last Half Month', stating that more than 1,700 people had been killed in Beijing. These deaths weren't from shootings or knifings, but rather from brutal and sustained torture such as being beaten with belt buckles and clubs or being scalded to death with hot water for days at a time, and were carried out mainly by secondary school students.

Looking back on this period, one feels compelled to ask why Li Wenbo and Cao Binghai were the only two recorded instances of resistance to this brutality. Apparently everyone else – not only the 1,772 murder victims, but also thousands of others who were tortured and humiliated – submitted passively to this torment. Why didn't more people defend themselves in some way? How can this be explained?

I relate elsewhere my interview with the author Xiao Jun, who was beaten along with a large group of other writers. Xiao Jun told me he considered resisting, and having learned martial arts in the armed forces, he was in a position to defend himself. However, he assessed the odds and decided that given the number of assailants and their frenzied state of mind, he would ultimately be killed and might cause his fellow victims to be killed as well, and perhaps even his family. He therefore suppressed the impulse to resist and bore his abuse in silence for three hours. Although we have no way of knowing what Li Wenbo was thinking when he decided to resist, Xiao Jun's story gives us a clear indication of why so many others submitted to their oppression. The violence of summer 1996 was not a case of mob politics running amok; it was backed and encouraged by state power, and that made resistance untenable.

The Death of Li Wenbo and the Legacy of the Red Guard Spirit

On 1 October 1966, a National Day celebration was held at Tiananmen Square, and two representatives of the Red Guards from the No. 15 Girls' Secondary School were invited to the Gate Tower to stand with Mao, Lin Biao and Zhou Enlai to review the big parade. The honouring of those involved in the deaths of Li Wenbo and his wife was an obvious affirmation and promotion of the Red Guard spirit. Apart from the article of praise in a Red Guard newspaper the following year, I also found printed material from March 1968 written by one of the Red Guards who ransacked Li Wenbo's home, and who had the official title of 'Delegate to the Capital Secondary School Red Guard Congress First Assembly for Activists on Chairman Mao's Writings'. The title of the article was, 'What Fear of Bloody Self-sacrifice: Red Hearts Ever Toward Chairman Mao'.[14] The article began:

> August 1966 was a Red August, a militant August, a victorious August, in which Red Guards armed themselves with Mao Zedong Thought and raised high the banner of revolutionary rebellion, breaking down all obstacles in an assault on the old world and declaring war on the old world.
> Red Guard young militant [name redacted], using the invincible weapon of Mao Zedong Thought, in an intense battle to the death, harbouring a red heart pledged to protecting Chairman Mao and the Great Proletarian Cultural Revolution in fearless and valiant battling against the class enemy, has displayed the power and prestige of the Red Guard young militants.
> Chairman Mao patiently admonishes us: **'Never forget class struggle.'** We need to engage in class struggle every day, every month and every year; engage in it in the past, present, for eternity and decisively! We must ceaselessly and without pause attack Liu, Deng, Tao, Peng, Luo, Lu, Yang, Tan and the remaining smidgen of incorrigible capitalist roaders, traitors, spies and black element class enemies. Attack!

---

[14] *Red Guard Daily*, official newspaper of the Capital Secondary School Red Guard Congress, No. 8/9, 27 March 1968.

Attack! Attack! In the fierce battle on the eve of total victory, '**Let the remaining heroes pursue the hard-pressed foe**,' rebelling to the end to display the new power and prestige of the Red Guards!

This was two years after the death of Li Wenbo and Liu Wenxiu. The essay was not only published in the newspaper; a student who was in secondary school at the time said it was reported to her entire school.

BEIJING NO. 11 SECONDARY SCHOOL

Like the Beijing No. 15 Girls' Secondary School, the Beijing No. 11 Secondary School was located in Congwen District, and its teachers were brutalised as soon as the Red Guard movement began. The school's principal had his hair cut off and was made to kneel on a stage while being struggled and beaten. The day after Mao's 18 August event, Red Guards moved the school library's 'feudalist, capitalist and revisionist' books onto the sports field and had all of the school's 'ox demons and snake spirits' kneel in a circle around the pile of books, which was then set alight. As the books burned, sparks flew out in all directions. Red Guards stood behind the teachers and forced them to lift their arms towards the bonfire. Because it was summer, people were dressed in short sleeves, and the heat of the fire blistered their arms.

Other teachers saw what was happening but didn't dare make a move, knowing that the Red Guards could arbitrarily order them to join their colleagues around the bonfire.

Shen Shimin, a librarian in her forties, was one of the twenty-odd teachers who were humiliated, beaten and burned in this way. She had worked at the school for many years, but was said to have a 'bad family background'. After she went home, she found the pain unbearable, and fearing more abuse the next day, she hanged herself. She had one son.

After Shen Shimin died, a language teacher surnamed Wang also leaped to his death because he couldn't bear the abuse of the Red Guards. An elderly worker in the school's reception office was killed by Red Guards that summer, but his name has been forgotten. A total of eight people died at the school during the Cultural Revolution.

NO. 47 SECONDARY SCHOOL

Bai Jingwu, an art teacher, was designated a Rightist in 1957. After being forced to undergo 'labour reform' and being brutally beaten by Red Guards, Bei drowned himself in a river in August 1966.

Students at No. 47 Secondary were among the Red Guards who held a mass rally to struggle 'little hooligans' at the Beijing Workers' Stadium on 13 August 1966. One of the targets, Nan Heling, was sentenced to fifteen years in prison, but his father, grandfather and elder brother met with an even more tragic fate.

The younger son of **Nan Baoshan**, a barber residing in Taipingqiao Street in Beijing's Xicheng District, Nan Heling was working on a farm on the outskirts of the city when the Cultural Revolution began. Nan Baoshan had previously operated a small barber shop in front of his home, which made him a 'small proprietor'. By 1966 he was basically retired. His sons weren't good students, having been held back more than once and sometimes getting into fights. His elder son, **Nan Helong**, didn't advance to fifth grade until he was eighteen, and then ran a portable barber's stall, cutting people's hair on the street to earn a little money.

When the Red Guard movement surged in August 1966, one of Nan Heling's good friends, who was a secondary school student, was beaten by Red Guards, and when Nan Heling heard of it, he went to take revenge.

The Red Guards were all at an age when boys most enjoy fighting. Normally teachers or police officers step in before the situation gets out of hand, but in the summer of 1966 the Red Guards used their privileged positions to turn these antics into 'revolutionary' activity and launched attacks on peers like Nan Heling in the name of 'beating little hooligans'.

In fact, 'beating little hooligans' constituted an important part of the Red Guard violence carried out in August 1966. But because the 'little hooligans' who were beaten and killed at that time lacked social status, little mention was made of their persecution, even after the Cultural Revolution, and some people might even have wrongfully believed there was nothing wrong with assaulting such people. The beating of 'little hooligans' began around the same time as the attacks on educators. At the time that vice-principal Bian Zhongyun was beaten to death by Red Guards on 5 August, some secondary schools also carried out beatings of 'little hooligans'.

On 13 August 1966, the Cultural Revolution's leaders and secondary school Red Guards held a mass rally to 'struggle little hooligans' at Beijing's largest gathering place, the Workers' Stadium. Nan Heling was one of the 'little hooligans' struggled that day.

Ma Bo, a student at the No. 47 Secondary School at the time, wrote, 'In August 1966, our school's Red Red Red group was one of the conveners of the mass rally to struggle little hooligans at the Beijing Workers' Stadium, because someone in their group had been stabbed by a little hooligan. At the rally they beat the little hooligans very harshly, but central government leaders who were present, including Premier Zhou, did nothing to stop it.'[15] At that rally, Nan Heling was sentenced to fifteen years in prison.

After Red Guard violence surged, and a large number of educators and ordinary Beijing residents were beaten to death, Mao said at a Central Committee work conference on 23 August:

> I don't feel Beijing is too chaotic. The students held a mass rally and grabbed some criminals, and there was panic. Beijing is too civilised, and there were letters of appeal. Hooligans are a minority and we don't need to intervene. The Youth League Central Committee is reorganising; they were originally going to hold a meeting to reorganise, but now it's not so clear. We'll see in a few months. Rushing to a decision can be very disadvantageous. Rushing to send out the work groups, rushing to struggle Rightists, rushing to hold a mass rally, rushing to issue letters of appeal, rushing to say that opposing the new Municipal Party Committee is opposing the Party Central Committee – why can't it be opposed? I put up a big-character poster to bombard the headquarters. Some questions have to be decided quickly, like workers, peasants and soldiers not interfering in the students' Cultural Revolution. What does it matter if they take to the streets or write up big-character posters? Let the foreigners take pictures. They're just taking pictures of our backwardness, and why should we care if the imperialists say bad things about us?!

Mao clearly knew about the beating of 'little hooligans' and intended to take the already violent Cultural Revolution a step further. Nan Heling was sentenced to fifteen years in prison instead of being killed, but his father and elder brother were beaten to death in their home during the large-scale violence in the wider community.

When the Red Guard ransackings reached a climax at the end of August 1966, Nan Baoshan was hauled over to the neighbourhood services centre to be struggled, and he was beaten to death with clubs. His father, Nan Heling's grandfather, hanged himself at home.

While ransacking Nan Baoshan's home, the Red Guards beat the elder brother, Nan Helong, then locked him in the house and gave him nothing to eat or drink but a bottle of chili pepper water. A retired primary school teacher who lived next door secretly passed him some water but didn't dare give him any food for fear that the Red Guards would beat him as well.

---

[15] Lao Gui (pen name of Ma Bo), *Blood and Iron*, Beijing, Zhongguo shehui kexue chubanshe, 1998.

After being locked up in his home for nearly a week, Nan Helong died of hunger and his injuries. He was twenty-six years old.

The Nan family disappeared from their Taipingqiao Street home after August 1966. A neighbour said the Nan brothers were rough boys who swore and fought, and they'd never had proper jobs, but was that any reason for the Red Guards to beat them?

Nan Heling's prison sentence ended in 1981, but it appears that he didn't return to Beijing until 1996. In 1998, a neighbour heard that Nan Heling had been seen peddling goods at an open-air market near Beijing's Yuetan Park, but before the neighbour had a chance to see for himself, the market was closed down, and he never heard anything more about what happened to Nan Heling.

PEKING UNIVERSITY AFFILIATED SECONDARY SCHOOL

Chen Yanrong, a thirty-seven-year-old worker at the gas works of the Chinese Academy of Sciences, died on 27 August 1966, after student Red Guards from the **Peking University Affiliated Secondary School** (PU Secondary) ransacked his home and then took Chen and his wife back to the school and beat them.

Chen Yanrong lived in Beijing's Haidian District in the immediate vicinity of the Affiliated Secondary Schools of both Tsinghua University and Peking University, where the Red Guards originated.

PU Secondary was the first place in Beijing where teachers and students were beaten after the work groups were withdrawn at the end of July. The Red Flag Combat Group supported by Mao and Jiang Qing took control of the school, and started out by beating vice-principal Liu Meide, chopping off her hair and stuffing her mouth with filth. Liu was pregnant at the time. Once, when the *Beijing Daily* came to report on events at the school, the Red Guards had the reporter set up his camera, then forced Liu Meide to kneel on a table while a Red Guard stood with a foot against her back to enact Mao's command to 'thoroughly overthrow the enemy and then stomp on them.' Liu's baby died shortly after birth.

A Peking University student who went to PU Secondary during the 'revolutionary networking' said the atmosphere there raised the hair on the back of his neck. The whole school looked like a 'big torture chamber', with classrooms full of people being beaten and the constant sound of people screaming in pain. One blood-spattered Red Guard shouted that his belt was 'carnivorous and not vegetarian'.

PU Secondary was the place where the notorious couplet 'Heroes breed good fellows, reactionaries breed scoundrels' was penned. An upper-classman at PU Secondary named Zhu Tong was the son of a man who had been designated a Rightist in 1957, and as a result Zhu Tong was locked up in a damp cupboard and put on public display like an animal in a cage. He was beaten so badly that he had to crawl home afterwards.

On the evening of 27 August, a Saturday, Chen Yanrong's wife, Liu Wancai, was making dumplings and waiting for her family to come home for dinner. Chen and Liu had seven children, the oldest of whom had just begun working, and tight finances meant that Saturday was the only day they had money to spare for meat to make dumplings. Even then, the filling still mainly consisted of vegetables, but the family considered them a great treat.

The Chen family was crammed into two small cottages, so when Chen's eldest son, Chen Shuxiang, became a teacher at Tsinghua Secondary, he'd moved into the school's unmarried staff quarters. That afternoon, Chen Shuxiang had gone to the Tsinghua campus clinic for stomach pain, which was diagnosed as chronic appendicitis. He then walked from the clinic to his parents' home, but as he arrived around six o'clock, he found it surrounded by twenty or thirty Red Guards dressed in green military uniforms and red armbands. The family's elderly neighbour, Zhang Junying, was standing in her doorway, and when she saw Chen Shuxiang approach, she motioned for him to quickly leave. Chen immediately walked away, and after turning the corner he began running, giving no further thought to his stomach-ache. Reaching the home of a cadre relative nearby, he told him about the ransacking and asked what he should do. The relative didn't know what to tell him, so Chen Shuxiang ran back to his school, but no one there knew how to help him, either. Chen was unsure what was happening, but was filled with terror and a sense of impending doom.

This was the day after Red Guards at Tsinghua Secondary had held a mass rally to 'struggle' the school's principal and teachers, including physics teacher **Liu Shuhua**, who leaped to his death later that night. Liu had begun teaching at the school two years earlier than Chen Shuxiang and lived in the same dormitory. His death cast a deep shadow over Chen, but he never expected his father to meet an even more horrible end.

At nightfall, Chen Shuxiang went back his parents' home and found the Red Guards gone and his parents missing. The eldest of his younger brothers, twelve years old, had been beaten, and his twin sisters, three years old, had been left without food. The house had been turned upside down, and the dumplings his mother hadn't had a chance to cook had been tossed all over floor.

The children had no idea where their parents had been taken or what the Red Guards planned to do with them, but the violence they'd witnessed was enough for them to spend the rest of the night in terror.

The next day, their mother, Liu Wancai, was released and sent home, beaten black and blue. The first thing she said upon entering the house was that the Red Guards were demanding a 28 *yuan* cremation fee. Their father, Chen Yanrong, had been beaten to death.

When Red Guards from PU Secondary's Red Flag Combat Group had arrived at the Chens' home, Chen Yanrong had not yet come back from work, so they beat Liu Wancai and ordered her to hand over the family's gold bars, guns and 'restoration records' (property deeds and other such documents supposedly hidden while awaiting the next regime change), which in fact did not exist. When Chen Yanrong finally neared home, the kind-hearted neighbour signalled for him to run away, as she had for his son, but Chen ignored the warning and went home to see what was going on. As soon as he entered the door, Red Guards tried to tie him up. Chen ran out of the house, but the Red Guards caught him in a neighbouring courtyard. He was first beaten in his own home, and then the Red Flag Combat Group called for a truck and took Chen Yanrong and Liu Wancai to Qinghuayuan Secondary School. The couple were tied to a heating pipe and beaten with leather belts and iron bars. By then, the school's principal, Xiang Kai, had been held there for days and was half-dead.

After being beaten for a while, Chen Yanrong and his wife were taken to PU Secondary, where they were bound and assaulted with fists, feet, clubs and belts. While beating them, the Red Guards of the Red Flag Combat Group asked, 'Are you a landlord? Are you a rich peasant? Are you guilty? Do you deserve to die?'

Chen and Liu were beaten from around nine o'clock until the middle of the night. Around 1:00 a.m., Chen Yanrong died. As he breathed his last, he told his wife, 'I want water.' Liu Wancai asked a Red Guard for water but was refused. Chen then died as his wife watched. He was thirty-seven years old.

A woman somewhat older than the couple was beaten along with them. They never learned her name, but she also died that night.

When Liu Wancai was released, a member of the Red Flag Combat Group told her, 'Go home and bring us 28 *yuan*,' meant for the cremation fee. In summer 1966, there was a saying in Beijing's secondary schools: 'Isn't killing someone just a matter of 28 *kuai*?' The students thought this question amusing, as it showed their limitless power to kill as well as their scorn towards their victims.

In those days, 28 *yuan* was a considerable sum of money, especially for a poorly paid worker with a big family. Chen Yanrong's family couldn't come up with the money, and even people who sympathised with them hesitated to lend them money, given the circumstances of Chen's death.

Chen Shuxiang finally managed to round up the required sum, but before he could collect his father's body from PU Secondary to take to the crematorium, he had to obtain a certificate from his work unit's leaders. That meant going to the Red Guards, who were in control of Tsinghua Secondary by then.

The certificate read:

> Chen Shuxiang from our school is coming to your school to make arrangements for his father (now dead). Please allow him to collect the body and make the appropriate arrangements in accordance with policy.
> Respectfully,
> Tsinghua University Affiliated Secondary School Red Guards,
> 29 August 1966

Under the signature was the large red official stamp of the school's Red Guards.

Chen Shuxiang took this certificate to PU Secondary, but when he reached the school entrance, the horrifying atmosphere made him hesitate. Red Guards at the school were beating not only 'ox demons and snake spirits' but also their children as 'sons of bitches', and Chen Shuxiang was afraid he'd be treated like Zhu Tong. After wavering for a while, he heard someone at the school's entrance say that two bodies had been taken to the crematorium that day, and he guessed that one was his father's. Under the circumstances, he changed his mind and silently left the school, and he gave the money he'd borrowed to his mother. Later, Red Guards from the school came to the family's home and collected the 28 *yuan*.

A teacher at PU Secondary said she at one point saw a body discarded in an empty space in the school, and a Red Guard driving a motorcycle (confiscated from someone's home) back and forth over the corpse. It might have been Chen Yanrong's.

After Chen's body was sent to the crematorium, his ashes were discarded. All that remained of him was the certificate his son had obtained to fetch his corpse, and Chen Shuxiang put it safely away. The Red Guards didn't have special stationery, but they had an impressive seal as wide as the rim of a teacup, the kind of official seal that Party and government organs used to denote their power. It was common at that time to refer to a person in authority as 'holding the official seal'.

This unused certificate was in a sense an indicator of the events and social climate of that time: the degree of violence and persecution in the birthplace of the Red Guard movement, and its control of administrative power. The Red Guards could kill someone without going through any legal process or trial and without obtaining permission from higher-level authorities. Afterwards, they felt no alarm, shock or guilt, and in dealing with the corpses of their victims, the Red Guards of PU Secondary didn't neglect to demand a cremation fee. The corpse-handling 'certificate' provided by the Tsinghua Secondary Red Guards was dated and stamped with an official seal as if it were routine business, the clerical tone showing that someone being beaten to death was a matter of no importance, even if the victim was the father of one of their teachers, beaten to death by Red Guards at another school.

With Chen Yanrong dead, his family lost its main source of income. His eldest son's teaching salary was 37 *yuan* per month, barely enough to feed the family, and there were few other ways to earn money then. Chen Yanrong's children thought of everything they could do to earn enough to survive. They cut weeds on empty plots of land, dried them in the sun and sold them to dairies. They raised rabbits and sold them to the government purchasing station which handled the supply of food when everyone had to use ration tickets. They selected big-character posters that could be taken down and sold to recycling stations. At that time, the government provided limitless amounts of paper, ink and paste for posters that were put up all around work units and in the streets. Old posters could be treated as waste paper and sold to recycling stations for three *fen* per kilo, but tearing one down was a crime of 'current counter-revolution' and subject to arrest. Back then, poor children waited around places that were plastered with posters, and when someone came to paste up a new poster, they'd run over and tear down the old one first. Bands of such children emerged in Beijing in the winter of 1966. Dirty and underdressed, they ran through the streets carrying large baskets, their cheeks and hands chapped red with the cold. Among them were Chen Yanrong's children.

After Chen Yanrong's death, his family petitioned the Beijing Municipal Party Committee that governed the city, protesting the unlawful killing, but they never received a reply. Six years later, Chen's second son was old enough to be assigned work. At that time, a young person's job was mainly determined by his family background, so Chen Yanrong's children had to obtain a 'verdict' regarding their father's death, even though they couldn't demand that the killers be brought to justice.

The investigation was carried out by the neighbourhood committee of Zhongguan Village, which had jurisdiction over the place where the Chens lived. Chen Yanrong had worked in Beijing since his youth, first as a handyman at Tsinghua University and the Beijing Steel and Iron Institute (now the University of Science and Technology Beijing), and then in 1965 becoming a worker at the Chinese Academy of Sciences. The Red Guards from PU Secondary came to Chen Yanrong's home and beat him because he was the offspring of a 'rich peasant' by virtue of a piece of land that Chen's father, although also a long-time handyman at Tsinghua University, had managed to buy in his home village. Chen Yanrong's mother lived there, which led to her classification as a 'rich peasant', although she wasn't made to 'wear the hat'. In 1973, seven years after Chen was beaten to death, the Zhongguan Village neighbourhood committee reached a verdict on his death, but they didn't give a copy to the family, who only learned from a subsequent verdict in 1979 that the earlier one had designated Chen's death 'wrongful'. Back then, a family was grateful to obtain any kind of verdict at all.

In 1973, the leaders of the Cultural Revolution launched a campaign to 'oppose retrogression and restoration', attacking anyone who expressed criticism or discontent. Because Chen Yanrong's eldest son, Chen Shuxiang, had once said that his father had been 'unjustly killed', he was criticised by name during a meeting at Tsinghua Secondary and was accused of 'vainly attempting to negate the Great Cultural Revolution' and 'taking revenge on the Great Cultural Revolution for his father'. At that time, negating the Revolution was one of the most serious crimes anyone could be accused of. The logic of the Cultural Revolution was that a son was committing a crime by feeling aggrieved by his father's death, even if the father's killing was wrongful under the regulations of the Cultural Revolution era. Right after that, the campaign to 'criticise Lin Biao and Confucius' began, and the Confucian concept of '*ren*' or 'benevolence' came under severe attack, creating a theoretical basis for the brutal acts that had resulted in the deaths of Chen Yanrong and countless other innocents.

Mao Zedong died in 1976, and after the CCP Central Committee declared the end of the Cultural Revolution and then negated it, the Zhongguan Village neighbourhood committee reached its second verdict on Chen Yanrong's death in 1979. This verdict was sent to his family members and their work units:

> To the sons and daughters of Chen Yanrong, a resident of District 6 of the Zhongguan Village residential district. Chen Yanrong… was persecuted to death by the reactionary line of Lin Biao and the Gang of Four in 1966 during the elimination of the four olds at the early stage of the Cultural Revolution.
>
> Following study by the Neighbourhood Committee Party Committee, Comrade Chen Yanrong is hereby rehabilitated, and the first verdict on his case is revoked.
>
> We are sending this verdict to you. Please destroy the original verdict and related materials.
>
> Zhongguan Village Neighbourhood Committee Office
Political Section
26 February 1979

A month later, the Party branch of PU Secondary issued its decision:

> Regarding the Pension for the Bereaved and Hardship Allowance for Comrade Chen Yanrong
>
> On 28 August 1966, Red Guards from the Peking University Affiliated Secondary School dragged Comrade Chen Yanrong to the school, where he was persecuted to death by the reactionary line of Lin Biao and the Gang of Four.
>
> The Zhongguan Village Neighbourhood Committee Party Committee Policy Implementation Office has written up a political verdict regarding Comrade Chen Yanrong being persecuted to death.
>
> On 29 December 1978, the Affiliated Secondary School's Party branch wrote a report and was authorised to provide 240 *yuan* in funeral expenses for Comrade Chen Yanrong, along with a bereavement pension of 180 *yuan* and a hardship allowance of 1,000 *yuan*, for a total of 1,420 *yuan*.
>
> Following Comrade Chen Yanrong's unfortunate passing, his wife was in frail health and only one of her seven children was working. Now four of them are working, another is awaiting employment and two are in lower secondary school. In view of these practical hardships, following discussion by the Party branch committee and with the permission of the Peking University Party branch policy implementation office, the family of Comrade Chen Yanrong is granted an additional hardship allowance of 1,080 *yuan*, for a grand total of 2,500 to be paid in full in two instalments.
>
>   Peking University Affiliated Secondary School Party Committee
>   29 March 1979
>   [signed with the seal of the Party branch]

The first paragraph of this document does not accurately state the facts, but that is how it was written. 'Persecuted to death by the reactionary line of Lin Biao and the Gang of Four' was the official boilerplate for rehabilitation documents at that time. Chen Yanrong was beaten to death by Red Guards from PU Secondary who had been supported by Mao in writing, but the authorities were only allowed to place blame for the Cultural Revolution on Lin Biao and the Gang of Four.

Chen Yanrong's wife, Liu Wancai, had been seriously injured and permanently scarred by her beating in 1966. When she received the 2,500 *yuan* in 1979, she said, 'I've never seen so much money in all my life.' Then she broke down in tears and said, 'What good is this money to me? I want my husband!'

The money came from the Party branch committee of PU Secondary, even though at the time that Chen Yanrong was beaten to death, members of this committee had been removed from power as a 'reactionary gang' that 'opposed the Party, socialism and Mao Zedong Thought' and some had been badly beaten by members of the school's Red Flag Combat Group.

Chen Yanrong's death was not an isolated incident. According to internally circulated statistics, on the day he died, 27 August 1966, 228 people were beaten to death in Beijing, and even more were beaten the next day. The hundreds of people killed daily, and the many others driven to suicide, caused a severe backlog at the city crematorium, and the practical hardship of dealing with so many bodies, coupled with scorn for the dead, Red Guard prohibitions against saving ashes for family members, and families' fears of retrieving the remains, resulted in loads of unidentified bodies in ragged clothes being brought to the crematorium by truck or cargo pedicab and stacked on its grounds, with ice piled around them against the August heat, producing a horrific olfactory and visual spectacle.

On 29 August 1966, the day after Chen Yanrong was killed, the *People's Daily* published a headline editorial entitled 'A Tribute to Our Red Guards':

> In the short time since the Red Guards have gone into battle, they have truly shaken society and have shaken the old world. They are invincible before all against whom they direct their spearhead of battle. They have swept away the old customs and habits of the exploiting class like so much rubbish. No parasite lurking in any dark corner has been able to escape the penetrating eyes of the Red Guards. These parasites, the enemies of the people, have been ferreted out one by one. The treasures and valuables they've been hiding away have been taken out and displayed by the Red Guards. All of the restoration records they've been hiding, and all their lethal weapons, have been taken out and publicly exposed by the Red Guards. Such are the great exploits of our Red Guards.

The editorial went on, 'The Red Guard movement is truly excellent!' and 'Long live the heroic Red Guards!' This fanatical encouragement, along with emotive and vague labelling of targets of attack as 'parasites' and 'vampires', led to even more senseless deaths.

Thirteen years later, when the Gang of Four was put on trial, the deceased Xie Fuzhi, who had previously conspired with them, was denounced by name in the *Beijing Daily*. Xie Fuzhi had once been chairman of the Beijing Municipal Revolutionary Committee. The article of nearly 10,000 words referred to 1,772 people being killed in Beijing in summer 1966, but it didn't state who these people were, what any of their names were or who had killed them. Presumably Chen Yanrong was included among those 1,772 dead. During that period, newspapers and magazines published a batch of articles regarding the people who were persecuted to death during the Cultural Revolution and then rehabilitated. But the people written about in these articles were all senior cadres and other prominent members of society, and even at that, the articles focused on their various virtues and provided few details about their deaths. The people killed at the height of the Red Guard movement in summer 1966 were ordinary educators and citizens. They had no opportunity to express the slightest protest. After the Cultural Revolution, their families received some money, typically 240 *yuan*; Chen Yanrong's family received more because of the number of under-aged children. But none of these people, as individuals or as a group, were ever mentioned in the media. Their family members had no way of expressing their sense of grievance to society. They were silent victims from beginning to end.

The Red Guards referred to August 1966 as 'Red August' and wrote it into their anthems. In the decades that have passed since then, not a single Red Guard from PU Secondary has ever apologised to the Chen family. Did they simply forget what they had done, or have they purposely concealed it? Or do they think they didn't do anything wrong? After the Cultural Revolution, one of the leaders of the PU Secondary Red Guards, Peng Xiaomeng, published an article in a newspaper saying that she herself was persecuted during the Cultural Revolution. During the Revolution's first year, she had been personally praised by Mao and Jiang Qing and had delivered a speech from the Gate Tower at Tiananmen Square, but later, as the ruthless 'revolution' expanded the range of its attack, Peng's own parents, high-ranking cadres, came under attack. While all this is true, Peng never made any mention of the killings committed by the Red Flag Combat Group under her command or expressed any regret regarding the teachers and schoolmates they beat and tortured.

Decades after the death of their father, two of Chen Yanrong's sons still blamed themselves for not thinking of some way to save him at the time. They believed they could have found a way to escape from the house while the Red Guards were there and warn their father not to come home, and then he wouldn't have been beaten to death. They felt they should have known that their father, an uneducated and temperamental man, would not fare well at the hands of the Red Guards; that they let their father down by not being smart or quick-witted enough to protect him, even though no one would have expected such an ordinary citizen to be taken away and beaten to death by the Red Guards. Their self-reproach is understandable and human, and they will harbour their guilt as long as they live.

The nameless elderly woman who was taken away and beaten along with Chen Yanrong and Liu Wancai, and who died of her injuries, had no one who went to the 'Party policy implementation office' (the term used at the time to emphasise that the Communist Party was helping the victims, rather than that victims were filing complaints with the courts) on her behalf. As a result, the post-Cultural Revolution leaders of PU Secondary didn't know who she was. Perhaps she had no living relatives, or perhaps the survivors felt it was not worth their while to 'implement policy' on someone who had died so many years ago. On that day, 27 August 1966, she was murdered along with Chen Yanrong and then sent to the crematorium along with him, and the ashes of both were discarded. From that day onwards, both her name and her physical presence disappeared forever. Even more than Chen Yanrong, she was a victim who died in obscurity.

RENMIN UNIVERSITY AFFILIATED SECONDARY SCHOOL

A former Red Guard from that school says that its Red Guards killed more than ten people inside the school and in the surrounding neighbourhood.

One day in late August 1966, they seized a woman from outside, saying she was a 'hooligan', and locked her in a small closet under the stairway of a school building. The Red Guards later beat the woman to death, and teachers saw her being dragged out in a burlap sack the next day. Her name remains unknown.

On 29 August, Red Guards from the school went to the staff quarters of Peking University and killed an elderly man named **Kong Haikun**, who was the grandfather of a female student, Kong Xiang'ai. When Red Guard classmates learned that Kong Haikun had 'historical problems' they ransacked the family's home and beat Kong Haikun, piercing his cheek. They then used an iron chain to hang him from a tree, where he died.

BEIJING NORMAL COLLEGE AFFILIATED SECONDARY SCHOOL[16]

Yu Ruifen, a biology teacher in her fifties, was beaten and scalded to death at the height of the Red Guard violence in late August 1966.

---

[16] TN: Note that this is a different institution from the Beijing Normal University Affiliated Girls' Secondary School.

Yu Ruifen graduated from the Biology Department of China University in Beijing. In 1957, she and the other two biology teachers at the Beijing Normal College Affiliated Secondary School (hereafter BNC Secondary) were all labelled Rightists, and Yu was sent down to the countryside for labour reform. After returning to the school, she wasn't allowed to teach any more, but took care of its living and preserved biological specimens.

On the morning of Yu's death, Red Guards seized her in her home and brought her to the school, where they cut off her hair and put her in the 'dictatorship team', made up of more than fifty teachers and staff who were beaten and humiliated one by one.

When it was Yu's turn, Red Guards burst into the office of the biology teaching and research group, where Yu Ruifen cowered in a corner. They grabbed her and beat her, and when she fell to the floor they dragged her by her legs out of the office and down the corridor to the entrance of the building. An eyewitness said that Yu Ruifen's head slammed against the concrete steps at the entrance to the building as the Red Guards dragged her along, and she lost consciousness. A Red Guard fetched a bucket of boiling water from the school's water room and poured it over Yu. After about two hours of this torture, Yu Ruifen died.

The school's personnel cadre told a teacher from the dean's office who was in the 'dictatorship team' to look up the address of Yu's family and notify them that she had been beaten to death. Yu Ruifen's husband came to the school, but they didn't let him take her body. Instead, Red Guards took Yu's corpse to the school's rear sports field and covered it with a straw mat, as it was beginning to draw flies in the hot weather. Red Guards called the 'dictatorship team' over and pointed at Yu Ruifen's body, saying, 'That's what's going to happen to you.' Then the Red Guards made the teachers strike at the corpse with leather whips, shredding her scalded flesh.

The teacher who was told to look up Yu Ruifen's address later went to Yu's home and found it had been ransacked; the door was wide open, and no one was there. This teacher never learned what happened to Yu's husband and daughter.

The school's principal, Ai Youlan, was also beaten beyond recognition, his head grotesquely swollen and covered with open wounds. One night, the Red Guards called together the 'dictatorship team' and took them to see where Ai was being held under lock and key, and his horrifying appearance shocked the others.

The school's head teacher was given a yin-yang haircut, and Red Guards ordered her to crawl to the school from her home across the street on the BNC campus. The head teacher eventually became mentally ill and began crawling around randomly.

BNC Secondary's school doctor was a single woman in her fifties. One day, Red Guards tied her and the head teacher together in the dormitory and beat them nearly to death. Their screams of pain echoed through the room. Red Guards from the school also went to nearby villages to attack people. One group of Red Guards inflicted fatal beatings on several 'landlords' and 'rich peasants' in one night and then went back to the school and bragged about their cruelty. A former student who wasn't a Red Guard said that after the Cultural Revolution, he ran into one of the former Red Guards and was horrified to hear him say with a laugh, 'Back then I beat a landlord woman, and she yelled Ow! Ow! I beat her for half a day and she didn't die.'

The school's Red Guards also ransacked the homes of their teachers and seized their belongings while tormenting their family members. Administrator Li Gengyin was beaten because she came from a 'bad family background'. The Red Guards confiscated a box of calligraphy and paintings that her father had left her, and her mother was expelled to a Henan village as a 'landlord', dying soon afterwards. Li's father, in his seventies, was tied to his bed and beaten. He became a deaf-mute after trying to poison himself. In 1974, Li Gengyin's younger brother in America telephoned and asked after their parents. Afraid to tell her brother what had happened, Li just said that their mother had gone to the countryside because she wanted to be buried in the earth rather than cremated, as was done in the cities.

The school's Red Guards also fatally beat **Tian Yue**, the younger brother of the school's mathematics teacher, Tian Qin, for 'passing himself off' as a leader of the school's Red Guards.

Tian Yue was a student at the Beijing No. 106 Secondary School, which no longer exists, but which at that time was located between the Drum Tower and Deshengmen. It was stipulated that only young people from 'red five category' families could become Red Guards, but Tian Yue came from an 'office worker' family, which made him a member of the 'grey five categories', and he had once given a speech criticising the Red Guard family background policy. On 19 August, the day after Mao's Tiananmen Square event, Red Guards from BNC Secondary accused Tian Yue of passing himself off as the leader of the school's Red Guard unit and brought him back to the school, where they beat him to death.

Tian Qin wasn't told that his school's Red Guards had killed his brother. A cadre from the Beijing Municipal Party Committee notified Tian Yue's father to come to the hospital to deal with the body. There was no autopsy, and Tian Yue's family wasn't allowed to keep his ashes.

BNC Secondary had two Red Guard organisations. The first to be established was simply called the Red Guards, and the second was called the Maoist Red Guards. Both were very violent; one group killed Tian Yue and the other killed biology teacher Yu Ruifen.

Tian Yue was the third of four children, and the rest of the family didn't tell his mother that he'd been beaten to death, only saying that he'd disappeared. His father never got over Tian Yue's murder and died when he was in his sixties.

A former student of the school told me that he discussed Tian Yue's death with Tian Qin in January 1967, and Tian Qin was still very upset, but he had no way of seeking justice for his brother. This interviewee also noted with satisfaction that one of the Red Guards who beat people most harshly died with his mistress from carbon monoxide poisoning in the 1990s. I thought it strange to have what was clearly an accidental death somehow connected to a killing nearly thirty years earlier, but it shows a wish in the popular consciousness for the evil of the Cultural Revolution to be avenged in some way.

JINGSHAN SCHOOL

Li Jinpo, around sixty years old and a worker in the reception office, was beaten to death by student Red Guards in the latter half of August 1966.

The Jingshan School was located in the heart of Beijing. (Jingshan, a hill near the Forbidden City, is said to have been formed from a pile of coal cinders discarded by the Imperial Palace.) It was unusual in covering all twelve grades from primary school through secondary school, and received special attention from the Ministry of Education and the CCP Central Committee's Propaganda Department. An unusually large number of its students were the dependents of senior cadres.

Li Jingpo worked mainly as a doorman in the school's reception office, so all the students knew him and addressed him respectfully as Uncle Li. When I was investigating deaths at schools during the Cultural Revolution and asked a former Jingshan School student whether anyone had been beaten there, he told me, 'Yes, Uncle Li in the reception office was beaten to death.' My interviewee said Li Jingpo was believed to have served as an army major under the Kuomintang and he was killed as a 'historical counter-revolutionary'. Whether or not this was true is unclear, because during the Cultural Revolution victims' histories and relations with the Kuomintang were routinely exaggerated in order to provide a 'proper reason' for persecuting them.

Another former student said Li was killed soon after Mao's first Red Guard rally at Tiananmen Square, and that teachers and cadres were also beaten. A teacher named Wu Shouxin was forced to kneel on a bench studded with nails. Wu was a very talented individual, but he was not worldly-wise, and combined with his 'bad family background', this led to him being harshly beaten by the Red Guards. My informant said there was a downpour just as Wu was being beaten. Weather reports from that time show that Beijing had a downpour on 22 August 1966. Li Jingpo therefore probably died that day or the day after. There are several other instances in which interviewees could not recall the exact date that someone died, but remembered heavy rainfalls, which helps narrow down the timeframe. Presumably the school recorded the date of Li's death for the purpose of terminating his *hukou* registration and food rations, but until such records can be accessed, we'll have to settle for this approximate date.

Another former student of the Jingshan School said that Red Guards beat teachers to death in the school's basement, but she didn't recall if Li Jingpo was among the victims. The student said the Red Guards then expanded their attacks to the wider community. One day, she was passing by the Gong'an Hospital near the school when she saw a truck pull away stacked with forty or fifty bodies, many of them elderly people. She said students from the secondary schools on both sides were sure to have been involved in the killings. The other school involved was the Beijing No. 65 Secondary School.

I once interviewed a woman who had been a Red Guard at the Jingshan School in 1966. She said her school's Red Guards were considered insufficiently 'revolutionary' and 'too mild' so a visit to the No. 6 Secondary School was organised for several of them to observe the 'revolutionary experience'. This woman recalled seeing the floor covered with blood, as well as bloodstains on the walls. In summer 1966, the Red Guards of the No. 6 Secondary School beat three people to death on campus, so the single death at the Jingshan School was considered 'mild' by comparison.

BEIJING NO. 4 SECONDARY SCHOOL

The No. 4 Secondary School, located in Xicheng District, was a boys' school and one of Beijing's best schools. Many of its students were the children of senior Party cadres, partly due to its proximity to Zhongnanhai, and partly because its administrators had been replaced with Party cadres even before the Cultural Revolution began.

On 18 June 1966, the *People's Daily* published a letter that the 'revolutionary students' of the No. 4 Secondary School had sent to Mao, agreeing to the abolition of the old school promotion system. The examination system for entering college was scrapped from then on and wasn't revived until 1977.

At the end of July 1966, this school's Red Guards proposed 'kicking aside the nursemaid and making revolution themselves'. The 'nursemaid' they referred to was the work group that was leading the Cultural Revolution at the school. After Mao ordered the withdrawal of the work groups, student Red Guards took control.

On 4 August, the No. 4 Secondary School experienced its first large-scale violent attacks against teachers and staff, who were struggled and then paraded around the sports field. Principal Yang Bin had ink poured all over her, and vice-principal Liu Tieling's shirt was torn to ribbons, while some head teachers were punched.

News of the attacks at the No. 4 Secondary School spread rapidly, and Red Guards at other schools began to imitate them. The next day, 5 August, vice-principal Bian Zhongyun was beaten to death at the Beijing Normal University Affiliated Girls' School.

The Red Guards at the No. 4 Secondary School composed the 'Ox Demon and Snake Spirit Song' and forced teachers and staff to sing it. This song eventually spread throughout China and became one of the methods used to humiliate people. The song went like this:

> I'm an ox demon and snake spirit, I'm an ox demon and snake spirit,
> I'm guilty, I'm guilty,
> I've offended the people, the people impose dictatorship on me
> I bow my head and admit my guilt
> I must be honest and not speak or act carelessly.
> If I speak or act carelessly, smash me to bits, to bits,
> Smash me to bits, to bits.

This hideous song was the pride and joy of the Red Guards of the No. 4 Secondary School.

Principal Yang Bin was locked up in the sports equipment room and given a yin-yang haircut. She and other members of the 'ox demon and snake spirit dictatorship team' were put to work weeding the sports ground while students dumped weeds and soil on their heads.

Vice-principal Liu Tieling had a resonant voice (after the Cultural Revolution, he became active in a teacher's chorus in Beijing), so he was made to lead the singing of the 'Ox Demon and Snake Spirit Song'. A former student I interviewed said he considered Liu slavish and spineless at the time, but now that he was around the same age as Liu was then, he could imagine what he might have done under the circumstances; if even bystanders didn't dare to intervene, the victims must have found it even more impossible to resist.

On 19 August 1966, Red Guards from the No. 4, No. 6 and No. 8 Secondary Schools held a mass struggle rally at the concert hall of Zhongshan Park near Tiananmen Square. On the stage of the auditorium, before an audience of over 1,000, more than twenty 'reactionaries' from the three schools and the Beijing Municipal Education Bureau were made to line up, after which Red Guards punched and kicked them and beat them with belt buckles. The Education Bureau's director, Sun Guodong, had three ribs broken.

A former student of the No. 4 Secondary School said the school's Red Guards killed two men who lived near the school. Word went around that the men, who were killed on separate days, died not only from their beatings but also because they were given cold water to drink afterwards. Apparently the school's Red Guard headquarters investigated the killings, because after the death of the second man, word circulated among Red Guard groups that beaten victims should not be given water to drink, and that if they requested water, it should only be splashed on their bodies.

Another former student said that the school's Red Guards killed one more local resident as well, in the staff dining hall.

Besides the struggling teachers and staff, the school's Red Guards also brought in 'ox demons and snake spirits' from outside and locked them up in the school. The music room was one room were people were held and beaten. The school's Red Guards also beat and humiliated schoolmates who came from 'black five category' families.

Apart from composing the 'Ox Demon and Snake Spirit Song', the Red Guards of the No. 4 Secondary School were notable for establishing and leading the notorious Capital Red Guards Xicheng District Pickets. The power and prestige of the Xicheng Pickets was such that Dongcheng, Haidian and other districts established similar groups.

The Xicheng Pickets played a key role in the Red Guard violence of late August 1966, not only because members of the group were particularly fierce but, more importantly, because they made violence more systematic and standardised. The group issued ten 'general orders' that commanded the mass expulsion of 'black elements' from Beijing, among other abuses. It was this directive that resulted in nearly 100,000 Beijing urban residents (2% of the population) having their homes ransacked and then being expelled to the countryside for 'supervision and remoulding' in the summer of 1966. The media at the time provided no reporting or record of this mass persecution of peaceful citizens, but the Capital Red Guard Pickets Xicheng District Unit's 'General Order No. 4' reveals how it occurred.

The subtitle of 'General Order No. 4' is 'Suggestions Regarding Search and Seizure Carried Out in the Homes of Landlords, Rich Peasants,

Counter-Revolutionaries, Bad Elements, Rightists and Capitalist Roaders'. Its seventh section, entitled 'Providing a Way Out', proposed that the 'black elements' listed in the order's title should be 'provided with a way out in terms of politics and livelihood' by 'returning to their native village for manual labour and remoulding under the supervision of the masses, thereby giving them on opportunity to turn over a new leaf'. Such people were to leave Beijing by 10 September, with some flexiblility allowed under special circumstances.

'General Order No. 4' was issued on 29 August 1966. Two days later, on 31 August 1966, Mao reviewed the Red Guards a second time at Tiananmen Square. Photos of Lin Biao and Zhou Enlai wearing the red armbands of the Xicheng Pickets published in the *People's Daily* the next day reflected the strong support of the highest authorities for the Xicheng Pickets. Although the Red Guards were only students, their general orders were as authoritative as government decrees.

The frenzied and violent ransackings taking place at that time provided the conditions for carrying out this kind of mass expulsion as people had all of their earthly possessions confiscated, and were forced from their homes and out of Beijing under threat of death. A special entrance manned by Red Guards was established for these people at Beijing's railway stations, where many people were beaten and even killed. Most people left through the Guang'anmen train station. They arrived carrying clothing and cooking utensils, only to have everything taken from them except the clothes on their backs and one bowl per person and one wok per family. Some were beaten to death en route, while others died of abuse or starvation in the countryside. Some of those who survived returned to Beijing when the beatings eased up at the end of 1966, and submitted petitions to the Central Cultural Revolution Small Group requesting permission to live there on the basis that current 'policy' did not classify them among the categories of people to be repatriated. With no place to live and no money, they could only spend the night at the train stations.

On 18 March 1967, the Beijing Municipal Public Security Bureau Military Control Commission issued a notice that repatriated persons 'must immediately leave Beijing, and violators will be forcibly repatriated by revolutionary mass organisations and public security organs. Those who willfully stir up trouble and engage in sabotage will be handled in accordance with law depending on the circumstances.'

This notice listed ten types of repatriated persons. Apart from the categories in General Order No. 4, these included people who had served in public office under the Kuomintang, ranking or full-time members of secret societies, 'reactionary' capitalists and property owners, former prisoners whose behaviour was unsatisfactory, family members of counter-revolutionaries, and 'inveterate hooligans, thieves or other criminals'.

There was much ambiguity in these categories, and complicating the matter further was the fact that the current occupants of their vacated premises had no desire for them to return.

Some of the returnees continued to petition, because they really had no 'way out' in the countryside, but in subsequent campaigns in 1968 and 1973, their behaviour was deemed 'reversing Cultural Revolution cases', a crime of 'current counter-revolution', and they came under renewed attack.

In 1978, two years after Mao died, some of the expellees who were still in the countryside returned to Beijing and requested 'implementation of policy' (i.e. rectification of their unjust treatment). Having nowhere to live, they slept in shacks on vacant land. Beijing residents showed no concern for them. A journalist from Japan's *Asahi Shimbun* who went there was mistaken for 'someone sent by the Central Committee' and people surrounded him and implored him to allow them to return to Beijing to live. They didn't know he was a foreign journalist who could do nothing to change their fates, which were in the hands of the all-powerful Chinese authorities. Deng Xiaoping and Hu Yaobang finally changed the policies and allowed them to return home, but they were not permitted to inquire into who was responsible for their misfortune.

Wang Hanying, an employee in the Beijing No. 4 Secondary School library, was beaten by Red Guards who also ransacked her home, after which she committed suicide with her husband, **Su Tingwu**.

I first learned about Wang Hanying and Su Tingwu from a teacher at the Beijing No. 1 Girls' Secondary School. Su Tingwu was a mathematics teacher at the No. 4 Secondary School, but he was 'on loan' to the No. 1 Girls' School, which is how this teacher knew him. However, this teacher was also under 'dictatorship' at that time and had no personal freedom, so didn't know the details of what happened to Su. In the years since, I interviewed a dozen former students from the No. 4 Secondary School and found that they had almost no impression of Wang Hanying's suicide. One of them had even forgotten his name until my mentioning of it brought to mind a big-character poster with Wang's name on it. Another student recalled seeing Wang in the library before the Cultural Revolution, and described her as a plump, bespectacled and very affable middle-aged woman. The former students heard that Wang Hanying had originally been an excellent geography teacher, and that under the Kuomintang government she had been elected a delegate to the National Assembly of the Republic of China. This brought her under attack.

Understanding what was going on at the No. 4 Secondary School makes it easier to understand why former students don't recall the suicide of

Wang Hanying and her husband; their deaths didn't stand out against the backdrop of so much other violence.

In 1997, I interviewed a retired teacher who had taught at the school and asked him when Wang Hanying and her husband had died. He couldn't remember the date, but an old colleague of his was now an administrator at the school, so he thought he could find it out for me. When I telephoned him a week later, however, his tone of voice and attitude had changed. I learned that the school's administrators had refused his request to check the files, and it appeared that he'd also been warned not to involve himself further in the matter.

As a result, I still don't know exactly when Wang Hanying and Su Tingwu died.

BEIJING NO. 6 SECONDARY SCHOOL

The Beijing No. 6 Secondary School was located in Xicheng District, just a few hundred metres from Tiananmen Square and one block from the Central Committee headquarters at Zhongnanhai. Many of the students were from cadre families, and No. 6 Secondary was one of the first schools to organise Red Guards, who promptly set up a prison where they fulfilled all the judicial functions of police, prosecutors, court, jailers and executioners. They decided of their own accord whom to detain, whom to beat and whom to sentence to death. This prison existed for more than 100 days, during which dozens of people were viciously thrashed, three fatally.

Students from many other schools, including my informant from the Jingshan School, visited No. 6 to 'learn from' its relatively comprehensive jailing arrangements. There they saw walls on which the words 'Long Live the Red Terror' were scrawled in human blood. One teacher held in the jail recalled, 'Red Guards from other schools came in to beat us as if it were some kind of sport.'

After No. 6 Secondary's Red Guards took over control of the school following the withdrawal of the work group in August 1966, some teaching and administrative staff who had been 'suspended for soul-searching' were organised into 'labour reform teams'. By mid-August they were being detained in the school's jail, along with more than twenty students. Nine people remained incarcerated for the entire time the jail was in operation.

The jail was established in what had been the school's music classroom complex, which was set apart from other classrooms because of the sound generated during music lessons. (Beijing No. 4 Secondary School likewise used its music rooms to detain and beat people.) The No. 6 Secondary School Red Guards hung a sign at the entrance to their jail stating 'Ox demon and snake spirit labour reform centre'. They constructed a watchtower in the back equipped with a high-voltage electric light that shone around the clock. After setting up the prison, Red Guards painted the words 'Long Live the Red Terror!' in large red script on the walls.

When Mao stood for the first time at the Tiananmen Gate Tower to review a million Red Guards, he was joined by a Red Guard leader from the No. 6 Secondary School. One of the leaders of the notorious Xicheng Pickets was the student in charge of the No. 6 Secondary jail.

Wang Guanghua, a nineteen-year-old student, was beaten to death by Red Guards at the 'labour reform centre' on 27 September 1966.

Wang's father was dead, leaving Wang's mother to raise him and a younger sister. Teachers who knew Wang described him as a 'polite, well-behaved and diligent' student. His father had been a 'small proprietor' before 1956, and this disqualified Wang from becoming a Red Guard. When the No. 6 Secondary School's Red Guards began preaching 'Heroes breed good fellows; reactionaries breed scoundrels,' Wang expressed disagreement, but the Red Guards immediately suppressed any divergent views and made this slogan the school's paramount principle.

Wang's fatal incarceration came about as a result of the 'revolutionary networking'. The No. 6 Secondary School Red Guards stipulated that only Red Guards could take part in the networking, but reluctant to miss out on the opportunity for government-sponsored travel, Wang Guanghua and four other classmates who lacked 'red backgrounds' left Beijing for Shanghai on September 7. Separated during the train journey, they eventually returned individually to Beijing. On 26 September, one was detained on campus and beaten into a coma. Three others were arrested on the morning of 27 September and taken to the school jail, where they were forced to kowtow to the Red Guards and were then punished with 100 strokes of the rod. All of them lost teeth, and the blood they shed was used to smear the words 'Long Live the Red Terror!' on a nearby wall.

Wang Guanghua returned to Beijing on the evening of 27 September and was immediately arrested and thrown into the school jail, where a dozen Red Guards surrounded him and beat him with rods and belts. When he had been beaten into unconsciousness, the school's former principal, Wang Yijing, who was also being detained, was ordered to give him artificial respiration. After Wang Guanghua revived, the Red Guards beat Wang Yijing until her arm was fractured.

Wang Yijing had been principal of the No. 6 Secondary School in 1964, when the children of cadre families launched attacks on school administrators as part of the 'Socialist Education Movement', also known as the 'Four Clean-ups'. The Party's senior leadership dispatched a work group to the school and relieved its administrators of their duties, sending two of them to the countryside for reform through labour. The main accusation was that these administrators were 'attacking the children of cadre families' and 'not fully implementing the class line'. Wang Yijing had also been beaten back then, but only lightly in comparison with the brutality of the Cultural Revolution. Once the Revolution began, it was felt that these administrators had enjoyed 'protection', and Wang Yijing and the other dismissed administrators were arrested and brought back to the school's 'labour reform centre'.

On that night, Wang Guanghua and the other students who had joined him 'networking' were locked up in that same jail. In the middle of the night, Wang's breathing became laboured, and it was clear that his life was in danger. Even so, the next morning he was beaten again, and that afternoon he died.

The Red Guards didn't notify Wang's mother, but simply called for a truck from the crematorium. The four teachers held in the jail carried Wang's corpse out into the school's front courtyard; by then they had been incarcerated for more than two months. At first, watching the Red Guards take sport in beating people and even killing some of their fellow prisoners, each wondered anxiously if he or she would be next; eventually they became numbed to the proceedings. By the time they carried Wang's body outside, they no longer knew fear; it was as if they had lost all capacity for feeling.

One of the crematorium staff who came for Wang's body observed, 'This young fellow was in good shape.' Wang's body was then taken to a crematorium in Beijing's eastern suburbs.

At the time Wang died, he was carrying 7 *yuan*, and the money and the belongings in his book bag were split among several Red Guards. They then went to Wang's home and took away his bicycle without informing his family of his death. Several days later, Red Guards from the school demanded 28 *yuan* from Wang's mother, saying it was the cost of his cremation.

Twelve years after Wang Guanghua's death, in 1978, the teachers who had carried his body into the school courtyard held a memorial service for Wang at the No. 6 Secondary School. The government provided his family with a payment of 400 *yuan*.

After Wang died, the other students who had joined him 'networking' continued to be held and tortured in the school prison until their release on 2 October. Two months after Wang Guanghua was killed, the Cultural Revolution underwent a shift. University student organisations had begun attacking senior cadres (many of whom were the parents of secondary school Red Guards), and had gained the support of the top leaders who had so enthusiastically supported the secondary school Red Guards as China's 'little suns'. Conflict ensued between the two groups of students, and the Red Guards at the No. 6 Secondary School ordered their prisoners to manufacture weapons for them to use in attacking the university student organisations.

On 19 November 1966, eighty-two days after Wang Guanghua's death, a Central Committee Politburo member and chairman of the Cultural Revolution Group, Chen Boda, arrived with others at the No. 6 Secondary School and disbanded its jails. School staff still in custody were taken to the Public Security Bureau, where they were held for more than two weeks before being allowed to return home. One of them, the school's vice-dean, died a month after being released.

In 1998, Chen Boda's last writings were published posthumously by his son, Chen Xiaonong, in Hong Kong. In a chapter entitled 'Some Circumstances Surrounding the Curbing of Violence', Chen Boda writes, 'I arranged for Beijing municipal leaders to accompany me to various places in Beijing, where we found kangaroo courts and privately run detention centres. We immediately disbanded them and released all detainees. I also went to a number of schools and other organs to deal with this.'[17] The book's explanatory notes take pains to point out that Chen went to Beijing No. 6 Secondary School and disbanded the labour reform centre there.

What goes unmentioned is that Chen Boda also went to No. 6 Secondary School on 6 September 1966, on which occasion he expressed his ardent support for its Red Guards. At that time, the school's jails had been operating for nearly a month. Wang Guanghua was killed just three weeks after Chen Boda's visit. Thirty years later, Chen Boda's book attempted to cover up Wang Guanghua's death and distort the overall picture of the Cultural Revolution by glossing over the inhumanity of its leadership.

In 1996, a scholar researching the Cultural Revolution told me that a former student of the No. 6 Secondary School said that Wang Guanghua had 'committed a crime' and that during his networking excursion to Shanghai in 1966, he had raped the daughter of a Shanghai businessman.

I asked teacher Shan Chengzuo about this allegation. Shan, who graduated from Beijing Normal University in 1951, was vice-dean of the No. 6 Secondary School in 1966 and was held in its jail for more than 100 days. After the Cultural Revolution, he became the school's principal and remained there until his retirement in 1996. He was a very calm and collected person, and even though he suffered great personal harm during the Cultural Revolution, he was able to speak temperately and objectively of that time. Perhaps it was his profession and experience that gave him

---

[17] Chen Xiaonong (ed.), *Chen Boda's Posthumous Manuscript*, Hong Kong, Cosmos Books, 1998.

such self-restraint and diffidence. When I raised this allegation about Wang Guanghua, however, his eyes flashed with shock and indignation. He said, 'That is utter nonsense. When Wang Guanghua was beaten to death, he was never accused of such a crime. Who would invent such lies thirty years later?' There is no arguing with Shan's logic.

Xu Peitian, in his seventies, a retired handyman at No. 6 Secondary, was beaten to death by student Red Guards on 3 October 1966.

Of the first three general histories written in China about the Cultural Revolution, only Gao Gao and Yan Jiaqi's *Turbulent Decade* mentions two ordinary people beaten to death by Red Guards: Xu Peitian and **Wang Guanghua**.[18] Both were killed at the No. 6 Secondary School. (An elderly nearby resident, **He Hancheng**, who was also killed there, wasn't mentioned in *Turbulent Decade*, presumably because he was a property owner and therefore a 'capitalist'.) Because of objections by former Red Guards, *Turbulent Decade* was not made available for sale to the general public in China. Subsequently published general histories of the Cultural Revolution did not name any individual ordinary people who were killed until the twenty-first century, when unofficial historians such as Yang Jisheng and Tan Hecheng detailed the suffering of individuals.

Xu Peitian had begun working at the school in 1940, and by the time the Cultural Revolution began, he had retired but continued to live at the school and rang the school bell. He lived alone, and had no children.

In September 1966, several students put up a big-character poster saying Xu Peitian was an 'old vampire', after which Red Guards seized and beat him. A former student who witnessed what happened said Xu was seized in broad daylight, with hundreds of students watching. One younger Red Guard went into Xu's room with a stick and forced him out and then made him crawl on the ground. The Red Guard drew a line on the ground with his stick and made Xu crawl along it all the way to the toilet while hitting and kicking him. Upon reaching the toilet, the old man was forced to drink from the urinal, after which he was dosed with cold and then boiling water. After torturing Xu Peitian for a long time, the Red Guards left, telling him to go off and die.

The next night, Red Guards went back for Xu Peitian and said, 'Why didn't you die like we told you to yesterday?' Xu knelt on the ground and pleaded for mercy, but they continued to torment him. Finally they tied a rope around his neck and strangled him.

After killing the old man, they dragged him into the school jail and tried to make it look as if Xu had hanged himself from a beam. However,

---

[18] Yan Jiaqi, Gao Gao (D.W.Y. Kwok, trans.), *Turbulent Decade: A History of the Cultural Revolution*, Honolulu, University of Hawai'i Press, 1996, p. 82.

the rope wasn't tied securely enough; the corpse fell to the floor and had to be strung up again, after which an overturned stool was placed beneath his feet. As the stool was more than a foot lower than the old man's feet, it was obvious he could not possibly have kicked it over. The rope marks on his neck also made it clear that Xu had been murdered rather than committing suicide.

After Xu Peitian's body was cut down, some student Red Guards came to look, and one of them struck his head with a pickaxe. At dawn, they called over the Public Security Bureau, the police recorded the case, and the corpse was taken to the crematorium for incineration. The police officers were experienced and could see right away that Xu hadn't killed himself, but under the circumstances they didn't dare say anything. In fact, in the month prior to Xu's death, Red Guards had killed at least 333 people in Xicheng District, but senior police officers ordered their men to support and protect the Red Guards. While the police officers couldn't say anything at the time, they later served as witnesses in judicial proceedings.

At the end of 1966, Xu Peitian's murder was revealed. The main reason for this was that the early group of Red Guards who had killed him had fallen from power, and when they were exposed and criticised, the story of what happened to Xu Peitian was revealed and printed up in a pamphlet. That is how he came to be included in *Turbulent Decade*, unlike the many other victims of the Cultural Revolution.

After the Cultural Revolution, the No. 6 Secondary School held a memorial ceremony for Xu Peitian and Wang Guanghua. The school investigated who had written the big-character poster calling Xu Peitian an 'old vampire' and the writer said he'd heard a political science teacher say it. The teacher denied ever saying such a thing.

In 1979, four Red Guards from the school who had taken part in the killings were arrested by the Xicheng District PSB; they had been upperclassmen and leaders of the Xicheng Pickets. However, the younger student who played a key role in the death of Xu Peitian by forcing him out of his room and making him crawl to the toilet was not arrested, because he was only fourteen years old at the time. His father was a senior cadre whose name was mentioned in the *Selected Works of Mao Zedong*.

After the PSB arrested those four former Red Guards, the district procuratorate asked the head of the No. 6 Secondary School to come and read the formal indictment. However, they were ultimately not prosecuted and were released after half a year. The victims' family members and the school authorities disagreed with their release, and the school administrators went to speak with the leaders of the district Party Committee, but the latter said this was done according to the instructions of central government leader

Hu Yaobang. Hu had sent a letter to the district procuratorate basically stating that the 'Red Guard young militants had been young and made mistakes.' Finally the school demanded that the four write confessions and pay compensation to the families of the dead victims and to a teacher who had been badly injured.

The four former Red Guards wrote confessions and were then released. An administrator of the No. 6 Secondary School said that subsequently, during the investigations of the 'three categories of people'[19] when these former Red Guards were asked about the violent actions of others, they were very unco-operative. But the adminstrator added that at least these four former Red Guards were arrested again, while others who had beaten people weren't punished in any way. One reason for this was that Red Guards from the school had offended the Central Cultural Revolution Small Group at the end of 1966 and had been seized and taken to the PSB. Mao quickly decided to have them released, but by then they'd already been interrogated and had confessed the details of Xu Peitian's killing, thinking it a matter of no importance.

Xu Peitian is not the only school handyman included in this book. What do the deaths of these handymen tell us?

After reading an article I wrote in 1996 that described the death of Xu Peitian, an American professor researching the Cultural Revolution asked me why an ordinary worker like Xu had been killed. I understood his puzzlement. What he meant was that other victims, such as school principals, teachers, 'capitalists', property-owners and others connected to the 'bourgeoisie' were known targets of the Cultural Revolution, but school handymen didn't fall into any of these categories. They had a low social status and no physical or intellectual assets, so why would Red Guards want to kill them? This question is connected to understanding the Cultural Revolution. Over the years, a common misconception overseas has been that the Cultural Revolution was carried out in order to strike down people with money and status, along the lines of 'killing the rich and helping the poor'; the people who opposed it were those who originally had money and status, while the poor benefited from, and therefore supported, it.

But did the Cultural Revolution actually help poor people? The fact that school handymen were killed shows that this was a myth. The number of

---

[19] TN: That is, people made to bear major responsibility for the Cultural Revolution, defined as people who had risen in the ranks as followers of the Lin Biao and Jiang Qing cliques, people with seriously factional thinking, and beating, smashing and looting elements.

school handymen who were killed or who committed suicide after being struggled is far from insignificant, and their suffering was intense.

At the Tsinghua University Affiliated Secondary School where the Red Guard movement began, they brutally beat an elderly watchman at the reception office, saying he was a landlord. Someone from the school said the man was horrendously injured, but wasn't killed.

At the Beijing Normal University Affiliated Girls' Secondary School where Red Guards killed principal Bian Zhongyun, starting the trend in Beijing of killing educators, the Red Guards also brutally beat Xu Zhankui, a watchman at the student dormitory. He was seventy years old, but still ruddy-faced, straight-backed and with a booming voice. He kept a close eye on the door and barred admittance to students who didn't board at the school, and some students objected to his strictness and occasional tongue-lashings. When the beatings began in August 1966, some Red Guards accused Xu of 'impersonating a police officer' and beat him so badly that he was confined to a bed for two weeks. Another school handyman, Wang Yonghai, was born handicapped, being shrunken and hunchbacked and unable to speak clearly. A rumour went around that he was a descendant of Manchu royalty and owed his condition to venereal disease contracted through depraved living. Wang Yonghai was brutally beaten and then disappeared; it's likely that he died during that time.

One of the reasons that school handymen came under attack is that the targets of the Cultural Revolution – 'class enemies', 'ox demons and snake spirits' and 'Kuomintang dregs of society' – were very broad concepts. Many school handymen were of advanced age and had lived under KMT rule. Although the Cultural Revolution began seventeen years after the KMT lost control of China, people were still punished for anything from that era that could be construed as a crime. They were shown no sympathy or mercy merely because they were labourers on the lower rungs of society.

School handymen were persecuted because under the brutal social, political and economic environment of the Cultural Revolution, student Red Guards held power over life and death and could do what they pleased, and they could give vent to their own vicious tendencies to attack even those who weren't explicit targets. Those who were weak and easy to violate like the elderly Xu Peitian were especially likely to be killed. If they had their own living quarters away from the school, the Red Guards usually took no notice of them. If they had family members around them, someone might come forward and save them by pointing out that they weren't class enemies. But Xu Peitian lived alone, and in a time of violence, this kind of person lost even the most basic legal protections, easily falling victim even if not a specific target of the movement.

Although the Cultural Revolution did in fact attack people with relatively better social status and financial resources, there was never any claim of helping people on the lower rungs of society to improve their living standards. An inspection of the directives the CCP Central Committee issued regarding the Cultural Revolution finds no plans for improving the lives of the poor; indeed, its propaganda and theory didn't even acknowledge the existence of poor people in Chinese society, so there was naturally no need for a plan to help such people in any way. The printed matter of that period depicts poor people as existing only during the KMT era and in foreign capitalist countries. There was not even an empty promise that school handymen would enjoy any improvement to their lot due to principals and teachers being 'struck down'.

The only possible 'benefit' for school handymen during that time was a possible feeling of *Schadenfreude* at the persecution of teachers and cadres who had enjoyed a higher status. This feeling can be quite seductive, and sometimes motivated people to enthusiastically throw themselves into the Cultural Revolution, but it didn't constitute an actual gain.

Regrettably, much less is understood about the deaths of these school handymen than is known about the deaths of teachers and cadres.

He Hancheng, a man in his seventies who lived in a private residence in Rongxian Hutong, near No. 6 Secondary, was seized and locked up in the school's 'ox demon and snake spirit labour reform centre' and beaten to death in the latter half of August 1966.

Three or four members of He's family were also beaten to death at the time due to ownership of the Rongxian Hutong property. After He Hancheng was taken to No. 6 Secondary's 'labour reform centre', the Red Guards demanded that he hand over guns and gold bars, and when he said he didn't have any, Red Guards beat him with their belt buckles for several hours and then locked him in the makeshift jail. When the teachers who were locked in the cell woke up the next morning, they found that He Hancheng was dead.

BEIJING NO. 8 GIRLS' SECONDARY SCHOOL

In late August 1966, Red Guards from the school beat to death an elderly woman, the **wife of Ge Panyu**, who had formerly run a coal shop at No. 99 Shifuma Avenue in Beijing's Xicheng District.

During the Cultural Revolution, Shifuma Avenue changed to its present name of Sinwenhua (New Culture) Street. The No. 8 Girls' School was located on this street.

Neighbours say that Mrs Ge was an elderly woman with bound feet. The family had handed their coal shop over to the state in 1956, but in August

1966, the Red Guards ransacked their home and beat up the elderly couple. Neighbours could hear the woman's horrific cries, which gradually became fainter until she finally died. Her husband was subsequently expelled to the countryside. The neighbours didn't recall the woman's name, but knew her husband's younger brother was a 'major Rightist', Ge Peiqi.

Ge Peiqi was a lecturer at Renmin University who was sentenced to a long prison term as a Rightist in 1957; his name was reported in the *People's Daily* during the Anti-Rightist Campaign. After the Cultural Revolution, Ge Peiqi was rehabilitated, and he published a memoir in 1994. In his book he mentioned his second elder brother, Ge Panyu, and his brother's wife, whom he referred to only as 'Sister-in-law'. This is the entire passage: 'My brother's home was ransacked by Red Guards, my sister-in-law was beaten to death, and my brother was repatriated to a village in Shandong. Due to the hard living conditions and lack of medical treatment, he died of illness.'[20]

Ge Peiqi was harshly penalised by being sent to prison as a Rightist, but at least he was properly tried, his conviction was reported in the newspaper, and there was some kind of legal process involved, however superficial. None of this was required for his sister-in-law to be beaten to death by Red Guards during the Cultural Revolution.

On 27 August, students from the Beijing No. 8 Girls' Secondary School and the No. 31 Secondary School beat to death a retired accountant named **Sun Qikun** in Xijiaomin Lane. Two days later, on 29 August, Red Guards killed Sun Qikun's elder sister, **Sun Yukun**, fifty-eight, a resident of Xiwachang near Beijing's Western Legation Quarters.

NO. 13 SECONDARY SCHOOL

The No. 13 Secondary School was originally known as the Furen University Affiliated Boys' Secondary School, but changed its name when the university was abolished. After the Red Guard movement began in August 1966, it became 'Resistance University Affiliated Secondary School'. 'War of Resistance University' was a school during the Yan'an period, with Lin Biao serving as president. Before the Cultural Revolution, an appeal went up for secondary school students to emulate the 'Resistance University manner'. Red Guards used the school's fourth floor chemistry lab for a place to beat people and called it the Red Terror Torture Chamber. Methods used included beating people with wooden guns used for militia

---

[20] *The Memoirs of Ge Peiqi*, Zhongguo renmin daxue chubanshe, 1994, p. 155.

training, tying a person's thigh to a bench and then stuffing bricks under the calf until the knee curved backward; and whipping with leather belts and brass belt buckles.

Among the people that Red Guards locked up in the school were administrators Cao Lishan, Cheng Shuge and a dozen or so teachers, as well as students Wu Supeng and Ren Chunlin.

Wu Supeng, a student with a 'bad family background', was beaten to death by Red Guards in August 1966. Ren Chunlin, who witnessed this, said Wu was an excellent boxer, and in fact, the Red Guards who beat him had boxed with him and been on good terms with him in the past. When Red Guards locked Wu up in the school's 'Red Terror Torture Chamber' and berated him, he answered back, so they stuffed him in a burlap sack and beat him with wooden guns. When they opened the sack and let him out, Wu Supeng asked for water, and a Red Guard sprayed him with a hose. He died soon after that and was dragged away.

Someone said to be a 'capitalist' was also taken to the school's sports ground and punched and kicked by Red Guards until he died.

Like Wu Supeng, Ren Chunlin was a third-year student with a 'bad family background'. He liked calligraphy and often used old magazines for his practice paper, and Red Guards found an old *Red Flag* magazine in which Ren had written the character for 'tomb' over Mao's name. For this, Ren was accused of being a counter-revolutionary who opposed the Great Leader.

On 12 August, Red Guards seized Ren Chunlin in his home, fastened a heavy chain around his neck and forced him to crawl to the school, which was two bus stops away. Ren was struggled three times before the entire student body, along with the principal and a head teacher who was considered too strict.

In the latter half of September, Ren Chunlin's entire family was expelled from Beijing to a village in Shanxi Province. Unlike most of those expelled, Ren considered it a fortunate escape after seeing Wu Supeng beaten to death. About two weeks after they arrived in the village, his eighty-four-year-old grandmother, **Qi Qinghua**, died; she had been beaten by Red Guards on 17 September, before the family was expelled.

Qi Qinghua lived with her two daughters and a son-in-law in a house she owned in Zhao Dengyu Road in Xicheng District. The road was named after a general who died in the War of Resistance Against Japan, but since Zhao had served under the Kuomintang, the Red Guards changed the name of the street and began ransacking homes there on 19 August 1966. At first they destroyed objects classified as Four Olds, but they soon began beating people as well. Qi Qinghua's family had compliantly turned over their property deed to the state and renounced their ownership rights, hoping to avoid being treated as 'landlords' or 'bourgeoisie', but on the afternoon of 24 August, Qi Qinghua's grandson, who was in fourth grade, went to the neighbourhood committee office and overheard the chairman mention his family when telling the Red Guards which homes to ransack. The boy was in the same grade as the chairman's daughter, and the two had been playmates for years. But by then they had fallen out, and the girl's name had been changed from one with a traditional meaning of good fortune to the more revolutionary 'Yonghong', meaning 'forever red'.

That night after dinner, Red Guards from the Beijing No. 3 Secondary School, also located in Zhao Dengyu Road, came to Qi Qinghua's home and ransacked it all night long, followed by students from the Beijing No. 10 Girls' Secondary School.

Qi Qinghua was half-paralysed, and when she heard the Red Guards come in the door, all she could do was lie in bed and chant Buddhist prayers. The girl Red Guards pulled her out of bed and threw her on the ground in the courtyard, then beat her. The Red Guards also shaved the heads of Qi's daughters and son-in-law and beat them.

The Red Guards took some of the family's belongings to a nearby Catholic church, which they had also ransacked and turned into a warehouse for goods confiscated from neighbourhood homes. Other belongings, including the family's quilts, bowls and chopsticks, were sealed in the northern wing of the home. The Red Guards took the Qi family's bankbooks and withdrew money to buy food, then rode off on their bicycles.

After Red Guards from the No. 3 and No. 10 Girls' Secondary Schools ransacked the house, Red Guards from the No. 13 Secondary School arrived. Since one of Qi Qinghua's grandchildren, Ren Chunlin, was a student there and was on bad terms with some cadre children in his class, they made a point of coming to Qi's home for the dual purposes of revolution and revenge.

On 17 September 1966, Qi Qinghua, her daughters Pan Shoukang and Pan Fukang, her son-in-law Ren Jiecheng, and her twelve- and sixteen-year-old grandsons were taken to Beijing's Xizhimen train station and sent to the Dongguan production brigade of Jianxi Commune in Shanxi Province. This was the birthplace of Qi's son-in-law, Ren Jiecheng, who was deemed a 'historical counter-revolutionary' for having operated a law office and a private construction firm.

The crippled Qi Qinghua had to be carried to the village in a wheelbarrow, and she died nineteen days later. Her two daughters eventually also died of illness and deprivation, one in 1974 and the other in 1976. None of them ever saw a doctor.

After the Cultural Revolution ended and the college entrance exams were restored, Qi Qinghua's younger grandson was admitted to university.

He at one point went to see the neighbourhood committee chairman, who apologised to him repeatedly. In 1982, the government restored Qi Qinghua's property to her grandsons. Her son-in-law was also rehabilitated, and his work unit held a belated memorial ceremony for him. Ren Chunlin, the grandson who had been made to crawl to school with a wire around his neck, eventually became a construction engineer. In 1995 he was diagnosed as manic-depressive. His illness manifested itself every spring, when he became paranoiac and believed he was being watched; in summer he became impulsive and fearless. He finally realised that this was an illness, and he believed it resulted from the trauma he'd suffered at the age of sixteen. He admitted himself to a psychiatric hospital for six months.

Qi Qinghua's younger grandson went to the United States after the Cultural Revolution and obtained a PhD. He says that he tries to help people whenever he can because of his experience when he was helpless.

After the Cultural Revolution, Ren Chunlin went to see Wu Supeng's elder sister and suggested that she should seek justice for her brother, offering to serve as a witness in court. But Wu Supeng's sister was too afraid, and Ren understood. To this day, extreme discomfort causes him to take a wide detour around Tiananmen Square and the No. 13 Secondary School.

HUAJIA TEMPLE SECONDARY SCHOOL

Another resident of Zhao Dengyu Road, **Kong Mumin**, a retired doctor in his sixties, was beaten to death when Red Guards from the Huajia Temple Secondary School ransacked his home on 23 August 1966 during the 'Smashing of the Four Olds'.

Kong Mumin had been director of Beijing's Nanyuan Hospital, and he continued to practise medicine at home after retiring, charging 30 cents for a consultation or 1 *yuan* for a house call. The Kong family was famous for producing four generations of doctors. The quadrangle compound where they lived was their private property.

Kong Mumin's youngest daughter was a first-year student at the school, and when her Red Guard schoolmates came to ransack her home, she led the way. Her elder brother never forgave her for it. She was subsequently sent to a farm in the northeast as an 'educated youth' and wasn't allowed to return to Beijing. After Mao died, the 'educated youth' policy changed, and a neighbour of the Kong family said that in spite of all that had happened, the girl's elder brother helped her transfer her residential permit back to Beijing in 1978.

BEIJING XUANWU DISTRICT BAIZHIFANG SECONDARY SCHOOL[21]

Zhang Bingjie, administrator and Party secretary of the school, was beaten to death by Red Guards in August 1966.

Zhang suffered from oedema while being locked up, interrogated and beaten by student Red Guards. She told them, 'I've executed the revisionist educational line, I'm guilty, I'll carry out self-criticism. Please don't beat me!' But the Red Guards continued to whip her with rope soaked in brine until she finally died around midnight.

Zhang Bingjie's husband was a demobilised soldier who worked in the State Council apparatus. When Zhang was locked up and beaten, her husband reported it to the State Council and asked for help. The upper levels told him that they couldn't control what happened during the Cultural Revolution.

BEIJING NO. 52 SECONDARY SCHOOL

Yi Guangzhen, vice-principal, killed himself on 30 June 1966, after coming under attack soon after the Cultural Revolution was launched.

Zheng Zhaonan, a thirty-six-year-old teacher, died on 6 September 1966, after being tortured by student Red Guards.

In August 1966, Zheng Zhaonan was locked up in a dark, fetid room in the school. Red Guards forced her to hang a garbage pail around her neck and wear a dunce cap while being paraded through the streets and shouting, 'I am a Rightist, I am an ox demon and snake spirit,' with a Red Guard following and whipping her like a beast of burden. Sometimes she had to crawl on the ground, and sometimes she had to hit herself while yelling, 'I'm getting what I deserve.' On the hottest days, the Red Guards built three bonfires and put her in the middle. They also forced her to eat apricot pits and grape skins that had been tossed on the ground, and to drink foul liquid from a spittoon.

Zheng's home was ransacked and her belongings destroyed. On 26 August, the Red Guards beat a 'landlord woman' to death in front of her and said, 'If you don't behave, it'll happen to you.'

Zheng Zhaonan finally died after weeks of torment. Her husband, Tang Xiyang, was a reporter for the *Beijing Evening News* who had been designated a Rightist in 1957. The couple had two daughters.

---

[21] Later Beijing No. 138 Secondary School.

BEIJING NO. 10 GIRLS' SECONDARY SCHOOL

Sun Di, a thirty-six-year-old teacher, was beaten to death by student Red Guards in late August 1966.

In my inquiries regarding Beijing's seven girls' secondary schools, I found that in summer 1966, Red Guards killed two teachers and three principals at these schools, and that at least three teachers and one worker committed suicide after being brutally beaten. Red Guards from some of these schools also killed nearby residents.

The No. 10 Girl's Secondary School was located in Beijing's Xicheng District. Prior to the Cultural Revolution, it had been a Christian-run school, but after 1949, its church affiliation was nullified and it was renamed. Later in the Cultural Revolution, the school became co-ed and was renamed the Beijing 157 Secondary School.

Like other secondary schools in Beijing, the No. 2 Girls' School established Red Guards in August 1966 and began inflicting violent struggle on its administrators and teachers. The principal, Tao Hao, was viciously beaten at a struggle rally. She was given a yin-yang haircut, and several of her fingers were broken, permanently crippling one hand.

The school's Red Guards also beat ordinary teachers such as Sun Di. An eyewitness said that on the school sports field, Red Guards encircled Sun Di and beat him with clubs and belt buckles, ripping his shirt to ribbons. The eyewitness saw welts rise on Sun's almost naked torso as he was beaten. The witness was horrified, but she said the Red Guards seemed excited as they beat their teacher.

The half-dead Sun Di was then locked up in one of the outbuildings that Red Guards used for holding the 'ox demons and snake spirits' they were torturing. A student at the school who was not a Red Guard said that when passing the outbuildings, one could smell a horrific stench of blood.

It is not known whether Sun Di continued to be beaten after that, but the eyewitness says that the next morning, she saw his corpse being loaded into a wheelbarrow, carried out of the school, and loaded onto a crematorium truck. Former students said they'd heard that Sun Di had a wife and child, but they didn't know what became of them. My interviewees didn't remember the exact day that Sun Di was beaten to death. I wrote to the No. 157 Secondary School and asked the principal to look in the files to find the date; the school was sure to have a record, since it would have cancelled Sun's household registration and halted his pay, and teachers at other schools had helped me look up records of other victims. But in Sun Di's case, I never received a reply.

My interviewees said that Sun Di was killed at the height of the Red Guard ransackings and beatings that occurred after Mao reviewed the

Red Guards at Tiananmen Square on 18 August. From this I infer that he died in the latter half of August 1966. A former student said that although she never had Sun Di as a teacher, she had seen him before the Cultural Revolution, and her impression was of a pale, round-faced scholar of average build.

As a teacher, Sun Di had been doomed when Mao declared educators 'bourgeois intellectuals'. Moreover, he came from a 'landlord' family, and was therefore despised by the Red Guards as a 'son of a bitch'. Former students of the school said that Sun was further referred to as a 'hooligan' though no one could come up with any specific 'hooligan behaviour' he'd been accused of. Before the Cultural Revolution, schools imposed strict controls on male-female relationships, and if Sun Di had erred in this way, he would have already been dismissed from his job. In the horror of August 1966, accusations were often as arbitrary as the violence, and it wouldn't be out of the question for Red Guards to use the pretext of 'hooliganism' to beat someone to death in the heat of the moment.

The No. 10 Girls' Secondary School had a Red Guard unit called the 13 Reds that was famous for its brutality. All of the members were daughters of veteran Party cadres and took names that contained the word Hong, or 'red'. They also stood out by cutting their hair very short and wearing brass-buckled military belts. After Song Binbin tied a Red Guard armband around Mao's arm at Tiananmen Square and changed her name to Song Yaowu at his suggestion, Red Guards began changing their names to make them more 'revolutionary'. The girls in this group not only changed their names, but also energetically engaged in violence. They were among the Red Guards who encircled and beat Sun Di.

At that time, there were a number of infamously ultra-violent Red Guard groups like the 13 Reds. At the Beijing No. 4 Girls' Secondary School, a group of Red Guards who shaved their heads and were called the Bald Gang became famous for brutally beating people. At the Beijing No. 27 Secondary School, four girl Red Guards who were 'revolutionary cadre offspring' were known as the 'Four Yamas' (regents of Hell) because of how they beat people. It's worth mentioning that at that time, calling someone Yama wasn't an insult; brutality was seen as a praiseworthy expression of 'revolutionary character'.

Although the Beijing No. 10 Girls' School was located in Xicheng District, it did not have an inordinately high number of 'revolutionary cadre offspring' – they made up perhaps 15% of the student body. Before the Cultural Revolution, cadre offspring enjoyed some privileges at the school, but the same scholastic standards were applied to them as to other students, and in theory, at least, the teachers treated all students equally. After the Cultural Revolution began, these 'revolutionary cadre offspring' openly criticised the school's leaders for not giving them enough privileges, and they were the main force behind the violence in August 1966.

A former student who was the offspring of revolutionary cadres said the violent behaviour was influenced not only by the Cultural Revolution, but also by their upbringing. Revolutionary cadres never paid attention to personal feelings but emphasised revolution and struggle, and as a result their children often lacked a basic capacity for empathy and could become extremely cruel. Because the truth about Red Guard violence was covered up or ignored for so long, there has been no significant exploration of why secondary school students would become gleeful participants in violent persecution.

The No. 10 Girls' School was one of the founding groups for the powerful Xicheng Pickets, and four of its Red Guards were members. One of them told her classmates that she beat people until she couldn't raise her arm any more. After the Cultural Revolution, someone asked this Xicheng Pickets member how she could beat people so viciously. She gave three reasons. First, she was initially afraid, but later she realised this was revolution, which required revolutionary courage, so she put in a real effort. Second, other members of the Xicheng Pickets beat people savagely, and she had to keep up if she wanted to stay in the group. Third, she became addicted to violence.

Sun Di was beaten in broad daylight on the school sports field in front of many people. In this time and place we know that this savage cruelty was considered a 'revolutionary action' that could be carried out openly. It was only later that these acts of violence were covered up.

The fact that teenage girls beat a thirty-six-year-old male teacher to death with sticks and belt buckles makes it even more horrifying. In Chinese culture, females are typically reared to be milder; the fact that these girls could beat their teacher to death highlights just how far the savagery of the Cultural Revolution deviated from the norm.

Sun Di's murder wasn't an isolated incident at the time, nor was it an accident or an exception; it doesn't even qualify as an act of extremism. It was just one of many acts of Red Guard violence in 1966. At that time, it was common to see trucks carrying corpses through the streets of Beijing. One former student said that on the first night after mass ransackings began in Xicheng District, while in the doorway of the school she saw a truck drive by packed with fifty or sixty corpses. Later she saw two more such trucks loaded with the corpses of Beijing residents that Red Guards had beaten to death while 'smashing the Four Olds'. Standing there in the school doorway, she saw a total of around 150 corpses. Not long afterwards, that student's own mother, a doctor, was struggled and locked up, and she eventually leaped to her death. When the student was notified of her mother's death, she was so full of grief and rage that all of her hair fell out, and in the decades since it has never grown back.

The Cleansing of the Class Ranks that began in 1968 brought Cultural Revolution violence to a new high. At the No. 10 Girls' School, one teacher killed himself. He was a language teacher surnamed Xia, but former students couldn't remember the rest of this name. They remembered that he was tall and an experienced teacher whose classes were very popular.

In the first three years of the Cultural Revolution, two out of fewer than 100 teachers at the No. 10 Girls' School died. We don't know how many others were injured or suffered serious psychological damage.

NO. 27 SECONDARY SCHOOL

A female student at the school was beaten to death by Red Guards in late August 1966 after sitting on a copy of *Quotations from Chairman Mao*.

The No. 27 Secondary School was located in Dongchen District in the heart of Beijing. Before 1949 it was the affiliated secondary school of the Institut Franco-Chinois, and was named the Kongde (Comte) Secondary School after the nineteenth-centry French mathematician and philosopher Auguste Comte. Among the earliest of the new-style schools founded during the May Fourth Era, it was located in what had once been the Confucius Temple attached to the Forbidden City, so its classrooms looked like an old-style temple. Due to its location near two housing compounds for senior cadres and the offices of the Central Committee's Propaganda Department, many of its students were the children of senior officials or military personnel. When the 'Smashing of the Four Olds' campaign began in August 1966, the school changed its name to the People's Liberation Army Secondary School.

I found three interviewees who knew that this student had been beaten to death, and one even knew the name of the Red Guard who killed her, but no one knew the girl's name or exactly when she was killed. They only knew that it was soon after Mao reviewed the Red Guards at Tiananmen Square on 18 August, and that she was the first person to be killed at the school. Its Red Guards beat not only teachers and students, but also people who lived nearby. Because these killings became so routine, no one knew exactly how many people were killed at the No. 27 Secondary School.

My interviewees recalled the victim as a very well-behaved fifteen-year-old who didn't seek the limelight. She had been killed because during a meeting, when the students had to sit on the floor, she placed a copy of Mao's *Quotations* under her bottom. She was first beaten inside the school and then pulled into the courtyard and ordered to sweep the ground while Red Guards continued to beat her until she fell unconscious. The Red Guards accused her of 'playing dead' and rubbed glass shards into her eyes to see if she would respond. Her eyes began bleeding, and she revived. Red Guards fetched a basin of water and poured it on her, and blood ran over the ground.

Many people took part in beating that student, but she was beaten hardest and longest by the four female Red Guards known as the Four Yamas. They were all the daughters of 'revolutionary cadres', and were all first-year students, just fourteen years old. Everyone at the school knew they were responsible for several deaths. They beat the girl with their brass belt buckles, and when one buckle broke, one of the Red Guards yelled that the girl's family would have to compensate the cost of the belt. The girl died that night, and her body was rolled into a grass mat and taken away to be cremated.

The next morning, my eyewitness returned to the school and found the courtyard a mess, with the water basin still there along with glass shards and some torn paper covered with blood.

One interviewee said he saw one of the Four Yamas in 2000 at a dinner for children of former Propaganda Department officials at the Songhe Pavilion Restaurant. They had all grown up together in the department's residential quarters around the time of the Cultural Revolution. My interviewee wanted to ask this woman the name of the girl she'd beaten to death thirty-four years earlier, but felt it would be inappropriate at such a gathering.

One interviewee recalled that a female teacher was also harshly beaten and locked up in the school, and slit her artery with an eyeglass lens.

I wrote to the school asking its administrators to look in their files for the names of this student and teacher, but never received a response.

BEIJING NO. 4 GIRLS' SECONDARY SCHOOL[22]

Qi Huiqin, a biology teacher around fifty years old, was beaten to death by student Red Guards in August 1966.

Qi Huiqin had taught at the school for many years and got along so well with others that everyone called her Aunty. A few days before she was killed, she gave a student two chicks from the biology teaching and research group, saying, 'Take them home and look after them.' Qi was afraid the chicks would starve to death in the threatening atmosphere that prevailed in the school by then.

---

[22] Now Chen Jinglun Secondary School.

Qi Huiqin's family had property that they rented out, making her a dual target. When the Red Guards learned that Qi owned property, they ransacked her home and took her back to the school to be struggled. After she was beaten, she asked for some water to drink, but the Red Guards told her to drink ink. Qi Huiqin finally died in the school's basement.

A primary school student living nearby at the time saw a group of the school's Red Guards, with shaved heads, khaki uniforms and brass-buckled belts, pushing a fifty-ish woman onto the school grounds, where they held a struggle rally. The woman had a yin-yang haircut, and her remaining hair was gripped by a Red Guard who kept shaking her head up and down. After a while, the Red Guards began beating the woman on the stage, and their belt buckles struck her on the head until blood poured out. This excited the Red Guards even more, and they kept beating her. This witness ran from the sports field in terror, not knowing who the woman was. It might have been Qi Huiqin, or it might have been some other victim; the school's principal, Pan Ji, was nearly beaten to death in summer 1966.

The perpetrators were probably the group known as the 'Bald Gang', who became notorious in Beijing during Red August.

Another teacher at the school, **He Shenyan**, hanged herself at the school in autumn 1968 after being attacked for 'current counter-revolutionary behaviour'. Her crime was leaving out two words from a Mao quote so that instead of 'By no means forget class struggle', it read 'By no means want class struggle'.

BEIJING NO. 1 GIRLS' SECONDARY SCHOOL[23]

Ma Tieshan, a worker at the school, killed himself after being beaten and struggled in summer 1966.

I interviewed several former students of the school, and only one remembered a worker killing himself in late August or early September 1966. He had been beaten by Red Guards because he was categorised as a 'rich peasant' and was therefore a class enemy.

I later interviewed a woman who was vice-principal of the school at the time, and she remembered that the worker's name was Ma Tieshan. The vice-principal had been put in a labour reform team and was locked up with other female 'ox demons and snake spirits'. The school's top administrator, Zhang Naiyi, had been beaten and then covered with filth and nearly died of septicemia. Given the horror of her own experience, this vice-principal

---

[23] Now Beijing No. 161 Secondary School.

didn't know exactly what happened to Ma Tieshan, but she said that he was not a rich peasant himself, and at most had merely come from a 'rich peasant' family.

During the Cultural Revolution, many people were victimised on the basis of standards that had no legal basis and were completely wrong. Other people were victimised for crimes that were fabricated and had no basis in fact. But the leadership turned a blind eye to these injustices because random violence was conducive to establishing an atmosphere of terror and the authority of the Cultural Revolution.

Back in 1950, people who had been 'landlords' and 'rich peasants' before the revolution were beaten and even killed, and residents of Beijing had already been purged before the Cultural Revolution. It was inconceivable that a 'rich peasant' was working in the city at that time, especially at the No. 1 Girls' Secondary School, which was separated by no more than a wall from the central government headquarters in Zhongnanhai. Political vetting of workers was very rigorous even before the Cultural Revolution. If Ma Tieshan had really been a rich peasant, he would have been expelled long ago. In other words, he was not a person who should have been persecuted even under the class designations of that time.

BEIJING NO. 2 GIRLS' SECONDARY SCHOOL

Dong Yaocheng, a language teacher around thirty years old, leaped to her death after being struggled and humiliated in August 1966. Her widowed mother killed herself that same day.

Dong Yaocheng taught language to third-year lower secondary students (around fourteen or fifteen years old), and it was her students who struggled her. Her father had been executed in the 1950s, but family background was emphasised less heavily at the time she took the college entrance exam, so she managed to graduate from Beijing Normal University. Dong was unmarried and living with her mother at the time of her death.

After Dong Yaocheng killed herself, the authorities sent someone to her home and found her mother dead. No one knows which of them died first. They had written the word *yuan* (injustice) in large script on the table.

Cao Tianxiang, a physical education instructor, leaped to his death after being struggled and brutally beaten in August 1966.

Cao Tianxiang was one of only four 'special-class' physical education teachers in Beijing's secondary schools. A former student of the school said he heard Cao had named his sons Jianzhong, Jianhua, Jianmin and Jianguo, which were all patriotic names but could be combined to form the phrase 'Establish the Republic of China.' This was used as evidence that Cao opposed the CCP, socialism and the People's Republic of China and longed for the return of Chiang Kai-shek's Kuomintang regime. Combined with his status as a special-class instructor, this resulted in him being brutally struggled by Red Guards.

Cao Tianxiang leaped to his death from the fifth floor of the school building. Someone saw him jump and said that he curled into a ball mid-air, as if diving into the water.

The Beijing No. 2 Girls' Secondary School was located near the Soviet Embassy. In the latter half of August 1966, the school's Red Guards changed the names of the road on which the Soviet Embassy was located to 'Revisionist Road'[24] and organised a protest of hundreds of thousands of people in front of the embassy. Their actions were commended and supported by the top leaders of the Cultural Revolution.

After Cao Tianxiang leaped to his death, a leaflet disseminated by Red Guards in Beijing said that a class enemy at the No. 2 Girl's Secondary School had died while attempting to leap into the embassy grounds, and that there must be some secret plot behind it. In fact, it was impossible to jump onto the embassy grounds from the school, and Cao had made no such attempt. Even so, this mysterious and vicious rumour fuelled the flames of escalating violence at that time.

BEIJING NO. 25 SECONDARY SCHOOL

Chen Yuanzhi, a forty-two-year-old language teacher, was beaten to death by student Red Guards on 8 September 1966.

Chen Yuanzhi had been teaching at the school for eight years by the time she was killed. The No. 25 Secondary School was located in Dongcheng District, close to the bustling Wangfujing Street. The school was originally called 'Yuying' – 'breeding heroism' – and while it changed its name in the 1950s, it was still a boys' school during the Cultural Revolution. It was one of the first schools to establish a Red Guard organisation and remained a key force in Beijing's student Red Guard movement.

After graduating from Beijing Normal University, Chen Yuanzhi had married Shu Wu, a prominent target of Mao's attack on the 'Hu Feng Counter-revolutionary Clique' in 1956. Shu Wu had been in frequent contact with Hu Feng and others, and under pressure he handed over letters they had

---

[24] TN: A Sino-Soviet split occurred in the late 1950s and early 1960s over interpretations of Marxism. In particular, Nikita Khrushchev's 1956 denunciation of Stalinism horrified Mao and other Chinese leaders, and the PRC were formally denouncing 'Soviet revisionism' by 1961.

written to each other. These letters became crucial evidence for Mao to designate Hu Feng and the others as a 'counter-revolutionary clique'. Shu wasn't arrested and imprisoned in 1956 like others who were close to Hu Feng, but in 1957 he was designated a Rightist, and he and his wife suffered accordingly and were humiliated.

Chen Yuanzhi recorded some of the things that happened to them in her journal. When Red Guards from her school ransacked her home at the height of the violence in late August, they read her journal and discovered 'reactionary language' that they said qualified Chen as an 'active counter-revolutionary'.

Like other secondary schools, No. 25 Secondary had its own jail on campus for 'ox demons and snake spirits'. The words 'Education Room' were written above the door, but in fact the makeshift jail was used for beating and torturing the people they detained.

Chen Yuanzhi was held there, and a former student said that during one struggle session a Red Guard leader stacked one table on top of another and had Chen Yuanzhi stand on top of them, after which the tables were pushed over, toppling her to the ground. Held at the school for two weeks, Chen Yuanzhi was beaten to death on 8 September 1966.

After Chen was killed, her husband was summoned to the school, where he saw her body lying on the floor, her hair dishevelled and her face covered with blood. A Red Guard admonished him: 'Chen Yuanzhi was an active counter-revolutionary. She died after going on hunger strike.' At that point, Red Guards brought in a person wearing a dunce cap and ordered him to write a self-criticism next to Chen's body, threatening, 'If you don't behave, that's how you'll end up.'

A truck from the crematorium came in through the school's back gate to take the body away. The Red Guards told two other detained teachers to help Chen Yuanzhi's husband carry her body to the truck. One of the people in the crematorium's truck demanded a cremation fee from Chen's husband and said, 'The ashes of black elements can't be taken home.'

Chen Yuanzhi was rehabilitated twelve years later. The Beijing No. 25 Secondary School Communist Party branch and the Beijing Municipal Education Bureau Party Policy Implementation Leading Group wrote in their jointly issued 'Concluding Opinion' that 'Comrade Chen Yuanzhi died in September 1966 under persecution by the counter-revolutionary revisionist line of Lin Biao and the Gang of Four.'

A former student of that school said that one day in summer 1966, he saw a mat rolled up under the eaves of the school. He and his classmates were curious, so they went over and poked at the mat with a stick, and found it contained a female corpse, swollen and covered with bruises and emitting a horrific stench. This was probably not Chen Yuanzhi but some other 'class enemy' who had been beaten to death at the school. Students brought people from outside to beat on campus, and also beat some people to death in the neighbouring community.

Among the school's staff, a male worker was also beaten to death in summer 1966. I interviewed several former students who recalled this man being killed, but none of them could remember his name.

BEIJING NO. 65 SECONDARY SCHOOL

Jin Huan, a chemistry teacher around forty years old, leaped to his death from a school window in August or September after being struggled and sent to the school's 'labour reform team'.

The No. 65 Secondary School was located at the centre of Beijing, close to the major commercial area of Wangfujing Street. After Red Guards were established in the school, a group of teachers and administrators were sent to the 'labour reform team' to carry out sanitation work at the school while also being beaten and humiliated. Jin Huan was reportedly targeted for 'historical problems'.

I interviewed three people who were students at the school at the time, two of whom actually saw Jin Huan's body. Jin jumped from a fifth-floor window, and his body made a large crater in the ground. The school handyman moved his body to a small courtyard at the back of the school where garbage was kept. Jin's arm was broken at an unnatural angle, and his forehead had a huge, swollen bruise. Although the handyman covered Jin's body with a piece of cloth, his elbow and feet protruded from under it.

A troupe of Red Guards went to the small courtyard and stood in front of Jin Huan's corpse, then took out their book of Chairman Mao's *Quotations* and read out a paragraph from page 149:

> Everyone has to die, but the significance of their deaths varies. Ancient China had a man of letters named Sima Qian who once said, 'A man dies once, and it can be more significant than Mount Tai or more inconsequential than swan's down.' To die for the benefit of the people is more significant than Mount Tai; to devote one's effort to fascism, to die in order to exploit and oppress the people, is more inconsequential than swan's down.

The students then said that Jin Huan had 'committed suicide to escape punishment' and had 'used death to resist the Great Proletarian Cultural Revolution launched by Chairman Mao'; that his 'crime deserved a thousand deaths' and would 'not be expiated even through death'. They then shouted the slogans 'Down with Jin Huan!' and 'Long live the victory of the Great Proletarian Cultural Revolution!'

ANDE ROAD SECONDARY SCHOOL

A fairly young teacher surnamed Ma who had served as a substitute language teacher in 1964 but had left the school in 1965, was dragged back there in late August 1966 and beaten to death by Red Guards, who then stuffed his body in the school's restroom.

One former teacher said it was possible that Ma was a rather strict teacher, so the students resented him. The Red Guard movement gave students an opportunity to wreak violent revenge on the pretext that a hated teacher was a 'bourgeois intellectual' and because teachers were being beaten all over Beijing. The school's Red Guards were part of the Xicheng Pickets.

The Ande Road Secondary School covered only lower-secondary education, so the students who killed Ma were all only fourteen to sixteen years old. The school wasn't famous in any way, and as Ma was only a former substitute teacher, no one mentioned his death afterwards, and no one was punished for it.

BEIJING NO. 38 SECONDARY SCHOOL

Red Guards from the school beat to death **Huang Ruiwu**, around thirty years old and a technician at the Beijing Glass, Ceramics and Cement Institute of Design, while ransacking his home in Dahong Luochang South Lane in Xicheng District on 28 August 1966. Beaten to death alongside him were Huang's grandmother, **Li Xiurong**, his mother, **Chen Yurun**, his elder sister, **Huang Weiban**, and an elderly servant, name unknown. Only Huang's eighteen-month-old child and nanny managed to escape. The reason for the fatal beatings was that while ransacking Huang's home, the Red Guards discovered a bullet casing that he had kept after taking part in a 'labour and defence system' training course.

The shocking news spread through the Institute of Design, but no one dared step forward to protest this tragedy or to criticise the mass ransackings and beatings that the Red Guards were carrying out. This incident made clear that people not only had to worry about having Red Guards seize their gold and silver, foreign currency, paintings and old books, but also had to take note of anything that could arouse suspicion, like empty bullet casings. It also showed that even a respectable family such as Huang

Ruiwu's, which included a hospital Party secretary, could encounter this kind of disaster. This knowledge radiated from the city centre to remote villages, creating an atmosphere of terror.

The day that Huang Ruiwu and his family were killed, 28 August 1966, marked the height of the Red Guard campaign to 'smash the Four Olds'. Eradicating the 'Four Olds' was specified in the CCP Central Committee's series of documents that launched the Cultural Revolution in May 1966. They consisted of 'old thinking, old culture, old customs and old habits'. On 20 August, the *People's Daily* published on its front page the Beijing No. 2 Secondary School Red Guards' specific proposals for 'smashing the Four Olds'. These included changing the names of streets and shops, burning old books, prohibiting 'bourgeois' clothing and hairstyles, destroying temples and churches, smashing statues and murals and so on. These activities developed into a full-scale invasion of the homes of ordinary people, during which Red Guards not only confiscated cultural items, but also seized gold, silver and foreign currency.

One of the main targets of the mass ransackings were homes owned by private individuals in Beijing. In fact, as soon as the ransackings began, under orders from the Red Guards and under threat of being beaten and whipped, people who owned their homes started turning over their property deeds to the government's housing management bureau; they had to line up to sign over their property, so great was the demand. But giving up their rights of private ownership was not enough to spare householders like Huang Ruiwu from joining the thousands of people beaten to death in Beijing at that time, or the even greater number driven to suicide.

The authorities' confiscation of private property, gold, silver and foreign currency during the 'Smashing of the Four Olds' in summer 1966, can be seen as a new economic policy and social reform. Whatever the merits and demerits of the plan, it should be pointed out that the CCP, firmly entrenched in power for seventeen years, could have achieved this aim through peaceful means. Why did it have to involve the violent persecution and death of so many ordinary people? The requirements of the social reform plan are inadequate to explain the fatalities; slaughter was not merely a means, but also an end in itself. The killing of Huang Ruiwu's household and others like them can only be explained by the need for the Cultural Revolution's top leaders to establish a persecuting society in which they directly controlled the lives and deaths of the population. Diametrically opposite to a democratic society, in which the people vote to decide who will be their leaders, the Cultural Revolution established a new 'revolutionary order' in which the leaders could arbitrarily kill ordinary people.

Huang Ruiwu's home was near Xicheng District's Western Quadrant intersection. The compound, containing more than ten rooms, was the family's private property, as all Beijing homes were prior to 1949. Huang's father had been a professor and translator before 1949, but he had died by the time the Cultural Revolution began. The courtyard at No. 20 Dahong Luochang South Lane housed Huang and his wife and young child, as well as his grandmother, mother and an unmarried servant. Huang's grandmother, Li Xiurong, was a devout Buddhist and vegetarian in her eighties. His mother, Chen Yurun, was a retired primary school teacher, and his sister, Huang Weiban, was the Party secretary of the hospital where she worked. Huang Ruiwu had graduated from Tsinghua University's Electrical Engineering Department in 1961, and had been assigned a job at the Glass, Ceramics and Cement Institute, which is now known as the China Building Materials Academy.

When Red Guards from the Beijing No. 38 Secondary School found the bullet casing while ransacking Huang's home, Huang explained that he had kept it after training at the firing range. They insisted he was hiding a gun somewhere and when Huang was unable to hand it over, the Red Guards tied up his entire family, forcing them to kneel while beating them with clubs and belts.

Huang Ruiwu's elder sister, Huang Weiban, was an OBGYN at Beijing's Ping'an Hospital. She had been living elsewhere since her marriage, but on that day the Red Guards summoned her to her mother's home. When she saw them beating her grandmother, mother and younger brother, as well as the family servant, she tried to stop them, but only managed to turn the attack on herself. Within three hours, Huang Ruiwu, Huang Weiban and the servant were dead, and grandmother Li Xiurong and mother Chen Yurun were breathing their last.

Huang Ruiwu's wife, Wang Kekuan, escaped because at the time of the ransacking, she was at her work unit, the Oriental Song and Dance Troupe. Their eighteen-month-old son was being cared for by a nanny, who told the Red Guards that she was a poor peasant and then fled with the baby, saving both of their lives.

After killing five members of Huang Ruiwu's household, the Red Guards summoned a cart from the crematorium to take the bodies away. The ashes of the dead were discarded. Huang's wife was ordered to move out, and the family compound was confiscated.

The slaughter of Huang Ruiwu and his family was hardly exceptional at that time. A Beijing resident who lived near Xicheng District's Western Quadrant told me that one day in late August 1966, a flat-bed cargo pedicab emerged from Lingjing Hutong carrying at least ten people that the Red Guards had beaten to death in that *hutong*. 'There were so many corpses on the flat-bed, like the pale, fresh pig carcasses stacked in the street market.' Back then, Beijing shops often used flat-bed cargo pedicabs to transport slaughtered pigs to their retailers. Telling me about this thirty years later, the interviewee was still horrified, and also fearful that relating this eyewitness account might bring trouble.

BEIJING YUETAN SECONDARY SCHOOL

Xiao Jing, the school's principal, jumped from a chimney after being beaten by Red Guards in August 1966.

SHEHUI ROAD SECONDARY SCHOOL[25]

Li Peiying, the school's vice-principal, hanged herself in her office on 27 August after being harshly beaten by Red Guards.

Li Peiying was formerly head teacher at the No. 3 Girls' Secondary School, but was transferred to the newly established Shehui Road Secondary School in 1964. A younger teacher at the school said that its administrators and older teachers were struggled with placards hung around their necks stating their names crossed out with red X's as well as their alleged offences, such as secret agent, counter-revolutionary, reactionary academic authority, etc. This younger teacher, although only in his twenties, was also struggled as a 'reactionary sprout of the counter-revolutionary revisionist educational line', and was locked up in the school for more than fifty days. He was made to wear a tasseled dunce cap and had to sing the 'Song of the Ox Demons and Snake Spirits' every day. Sometimes he was kept awake all night and pricked with a dagger.

In August 1966, this teacher saw Li Peiying's corpse, and he also saw Red Guards drag a woman from outside the school onto the sports ground and beat her to death. That woman was reportedly twenty-two years old.

On 16 September 1966, all of the school's teachers went to Lugou Bridge for manual labour, while Red Guards watched over them with wooden guns.

Later, everything inside the school was destroyed and emptied out. Its books were burned, and even its windows were smashed.

BEIJING NO. 3 SECONDARY SCHOOL[26]

Shi Zhicong, a language teacher, drowned herself in Longtan Lake after being struggled in summer 1966.

---

[25] Later 154 Secondary School.
[26] TN: This is a different institution from the No. 3 Girls' School.

Li Jianping, in her forties, a resident of nearby Wu Wanghou Hutong, was beaten to death by students from the school on 27 August 1966.

A former student says that on that day, the school's Revolutionary Committee and Red Guards organised a school-wide struggle rally for neighbourhood 'ox demons and snake spirits', including Li Jianping, who was accused of being a 'bandit woman'. A Red Guard struck her from behind with a baseball bat, and she fell to the ground while the other students cheered. Li Jianping jumped to her feet, only to be struck down again. Someone accused her of playing dead and kicked her, while another dashed water on her face, but Li was in fact dead.

WAIGUAN SECONDARY SCHOOL

He Dinghua, a sixty-six-year-old retired primary school teacher, lived in the hostel of the Chinese Academy of Agricultural Mechanization near Beijing's Anding Gate. She was beaten to death by Red Guard students from the nearby Waiguan Secondary School on 27 August 1966. Her husband, **Yao Jianming**, hanged himself less than two years later.

He Dinghua and Yao Jianming were both retired and lived in the residential quarters of their son, Yao Jianfu. Yao Jianming considered himself a revolutionary who would not have any problems. He had been a member of the Nationalist Army's 110 Division that had revolted under the leadership of underground CCP member Liao Yunzhou in 1948. (Years after Yao died, on 9 December 1985, his children obtained a document from the PLA's Wuhan Military Region stating, 'Comrade Yao Jianming, formerly a KMT soldier, is hereby certified to have taken part in the revolt in the Battle of Huaihai in November 1948.')

The Waiguan Secondary School Red Guards ransacked He Dinghua's home and beat her to death. When a truck came to haul her corpse to the crematorium, He's daughter stood on the driver's cabin and saw her mother's clothing torn, her hair chopped off, her body covered with bruises and a long knife wound in her neck, indicating that apart from being beaten, she had been stabbed to death.

Yao Jianming was beaten at the same time; the blood from deep wounds in his back glued his clothes to his skin. While his wife was being taken to the crematorium, Yao Jianming was driven out of Beijing. He spent two years living in his native village in Anhui's Shusong County, and then the Cleansing of the Class Ranks began. In July 1968, two people from his son Yao Jianfu's work unit (the Chinese Academy of Agricultural Mechanization) were transferred to the village, and they told Yao that his son was a 'current counter-revolutionary' who had attacked Jiang Qing and the Cultural Revolution with 'reactionary speech'. The Commune convened a rally to struggle Yao Jianming, but before it could be held, Yao hanged himself.

BEIJING NO. 30 SECONDARY SCHOOL

Wang Shengguan, the school's principal, died of a cerebral haemorrhage in 1966 after student Red Guards beat him and pushed him down the stairs. Around the same time, the school's Party secretary, Sun Shurong, was blinded in one eye from being beaten.

BEIJING INSTITUTE OF INDUSTRY AFFILIATED SECONDARY SCHOOL

Pang Hongxuan, the school's principal, had been taking part in the 'Four Cleans' (Socialist Education) Movement when the Cultural Revolution began. After being sent back to her school, she was beaten and locked up in a small room, and she killed herself in the makeshift jail.

KUAN STREET PRIMARY SCHOOL

Guo Wenyu, the school's principal, was beaten to death by her students along with the school's head teacher, **Lü Zhenxian**, on 27 August 1966. Guo's husband, **Meng Zhaojiang**, was also harshly beaten and died two days later.

An older friend of mine told me about this case, and although by then I'd already collected material on a large number of violent incidents at more than eighty schools, I was still extremely shocked that primary school pupils could have killed two educators in one day. I later located a former student of the Kuan Street Primary School who knew about this incident. She was nine years old at the time, but she wasn't at school that day, and she didn't know the names of the principal and head teacher. With great difficulty I found the telephone numbers of two former teachers and contacted them to verify the details and the names of the two victims.

It wasn't that I didn't trust the information from my friend, who has always been a very reliable person, nor did I doubt the memory of the woman who had been nine years old at that time, but I subconsciously hoped it wasn't true and that someone had made a mistake. But the message came clearly over the telephone line: principal Guo Wenyu and head teacher Lü Zhenxian had been beaten to death in 1966 by Red Guards among the school's students. The oldest pupils at the school were only thirteen years old.

The Kuan Street Primary School was located in Dongcheng District at the heart of Beijing, close to the National Art Museum. Before Guo Wenyu and Lü Zhengxian were beaten to death, the school's teachers and staff had 'assembled for training' near the Beijing Train Station, criticising themselves and others. They were then told to return to the school, where Red Guards beat them.

Beijing experienced heavy rains in the latter half of August 1966. After Guo Wenyu was beaten unconscious, she was dragged to the sports ground and placed face-down in the jumping pit, which was full of water. That's where she died. Guo's husband, Meng Zhaojiang, who had been designated a Rightist in 1957, was also dragged to the school and beaten until he lost consciousness, dying two days later.

Lü Zhenxian was in her fifties and had grown up with bound feet. People at the school knew she'd long been in conflict with Guo Wenyu, but they were both treated as representatives of the 'revisionist education line', and neither could escape being beaten to death.

In addition to the beating deaths of Guo Wenyu and Lü Zhengxian, language teacher and sixth grade head teacher **Li Yinfu** killed himself.

In an interview with the American journalist Edgar Snow on 18 December 1970, Mao Zedong made the following comment about the Cultural Revolution: 'We don't have university professors or secondary or primary school teachers; they're all Kuomintang members, and they rule here. The Cultural Revolution is targeting them.'[27]

When the Cultural Revolution began, not a single school principal was a member of the Kuomintang.

By the time Mao was interviewed by Snow in 1970, Guo Wenyu and Lü Zhengxian had already been dead for four years, and while this was never made public, Mao and Zhao Enlai had been informed of the beating to death of principals and teachers by Red Guards (see the entry on **Li Jingyi** in Part One). So when Mao used the term 'target', it wasn't metaphorical but literal. The targeting of educators in universities, secondary schools and primary schools was part of Mao's explicit plan.

---

[27] The full conversation between Mao and Edgar Snow is recorded in 'Minutes of talks with Snow' in *Manuscripts of Mao Zedong Since the Founding of the Country*, Vol. 3, Beijing, Zhongyang wenxian chubanshe, 1998, pp. 163–187.

BEIJING XUANWU DISTRICT LIANGJIAYUAN PRIMARY SCHOOL

Wang Qingping, the school's forty-year-old principal and Party secretary, fell to her death in the early hours of 20 August 1966, after being beaten and struggled by Red Guards the day before. It was claimed that she had jumped, but her colleagues and family believe she was pushed.

In 1978, two years after Mao died, Wang Qingping was rehabilitated like many other victims of the Cultural Revolution. Her school issued an official letter to the work unit of her husband, Hu Fusheng, stating:

> The conclusion regarding Comrade Wang Qingping written in a memo in September 1978 by the Party Committee of the Xuanwu District Education Bureau is as follows: 'Comrade Wang Qingping, formerly Party secretary and principal of the Liangjiayuan Primary School, met an unfortunate death on 20 August 1966, due to persecution under the counter-revolutionary revisionist line of Lin Biao and the Gang of Four.'
>
> It would be appreciated if you would return any material inconsistent with this conclusion to this school or destroy it.

A verdict had been reached regarding Wang Qingping prior to this, in 1972, with the 'concluding opinion' that:

> Comrade Wang Qingping had routine political historical problems. In the early stage of the Cultural Revolution, due to a misunderstanding of the mass movement, Wang leaped from a building and died. She is still to be treated as a revolutionary cadre.
> Party Committee of the Beijing No. 147 Secondary School
> 16 November 1972

> We concur with the school's opinion that Wang Qingping's historical problems should be summarised as routine political historical problems. In the early stage of the Cultural Revolution, due to a misunderstanding of the mass movement, Wang leaped from a building and died, and is still to be treated as a revolutionary cadre.
> Party Committee of the Beijing Xuanwu District Education Bureau
> 18 November 1972

The Liangjiayuan Primary School had been abolished by then, and the No. 147 Secondary School now operated at that address, so the conclusion was written by the Party Committee of that school.

This 'conclusion' still affirmed that Wang Qingping had killed herself, but by 1972 suicide was no longer interpreted as 'resisting the Cultural Revolution' or as a reason for being expelled from the Party. For a period of time after Lin Biao died in 1971, the Cultural Revolution authorities criticised the 'ultra-Leftisim' he had represented and relaxed their handling of previous victims of persecution. It was this trend that produced the conclusion that Wang Qingping's death was due to a 'misunderstanding of the mass movement' and that she should 'still be treated as a revolutionary cadre'.

By 1972, Wang Qingping had been dead for six years, so how was she to be 'treated'? The main significance was obviously in the treatment of her children. During the Cultural Revolution, the persecution of people purely for their connections to others reached unprecedented levels, and the problems of a father or mother could have multiple negative ramifications for their offspring.

As for earlier 'conclusions on handling' for such individuals during the Cultural Revolution, the authorities kept these documents in their confidential personnel files and did not let the individual or their family members have a copy. When victims of the Cultural Revolution were 'rehabilitated' from 1978 onwards, the upper levels ordered all work units to destroy any related material. The destruction was carried out in public, but without allowing people to view the contents of the documents being burned. Eyewitnesses say that small work units such as primary or secondary schools would destroy two travel trunks full of documents. The process was claimed to represent 'thorough rehabilitation', but in fact it also prevented the pursuit of legal responsibility and the recording of historical truth. That is why the conclusion reached on Wang Qingping before 1972 can't be recorded here.

Wang Qingping was a victim of the immediate upsurge in violence following Mao's first Tiananmen Square Red Guard rally. Wang had already been struggled multiple times by then; she'd been beaten and had to request permission to return home. One night when she was allowed to go home, her children were already sleeping, but her mother and husband saw that half of her hair and been cut off, her body was covered with wounds, her face smeared with ink and her clothes were too filthy to wash clean. The day after the 18 August rally, Wang was struggled with other school leaders at the Zhongshan Park Concert Hall near Tiananmen Square, and was then escorted back to the school.

The Liangjiayuan Primary School was four storeys high. That night, Wang Qingping was locked up in a room, and she fell to her death in the early hours of the next morning. When the school notified her family several hours later, her husband and mother left the children with a neighbour and rushed to the school, where they found her body. Wang's husband and mother didn't tell the children of Wang's death for many years; the first they heard of it was from other children in their compound.

Wang Qingping had three children aged eleven, nine and eight at the time of her death. As they grew older, they gradually learned about their mother's 'suicide' back in 1966. They always had their doubts; if Wang had really killed herself, why hadn't she left a note for them? They couldn't believe that she wouldn't say goodbye.

The vice-principal of the Liangjiayuan Primary School, Ji Lihua, who was beaten and humiliated along with Wang Qingping, said, 'Under those circumstances, anyone would want to die, but she wouldn't have taken that step.'

One reason for suspicion is that during the night shortly before Wang Qingping fell to her death, three of the school's teachers went to the room where she was being held. Two of the three were undergoing the year of probation required before joining the CCP. One of them had had his probation extended and believed that Wang, as the school's Party secretary, was responsible.

Furthermore, when Wang Qingping fell to her death, her body struck the window casement on the floor below. If she had jumped, she would have missed the casement. That's why her children and colleagues believe that she was beaten to death and then pushed out of the window, or that she was pushed out during a struggle.

After Wang was rehabilitated in 1978, her eldest son, Hu Dajun, wrote a report to the Xunwu District Education Bureau laying out his suspicions. The bureau told him, 'The facts are inadequate' and rejected his report.

Red Guards killed thousands of ordinary residents and educators in summer 1966, but while rehabilitation of the victims began in 1978, families weren't allowed to seek the perpetrators. For all the names recorded in this book, I am aware of only one person who was punished for a killing. This was a Red Guard from the Beijing's No. 3 Girls' Secondary School, whose principal Sha Ping was beaten to death on 22 August 1966. This was key to the policies Deng Xiaoping and Hu Yaobang put in place when the rehabilitations began in 1978: new verdicts could be written for victims, and their families could be financially compensated, but criminal liability was not to be pursued against the perpetrators; furthermore, Lin Biao and the Gang of Four were to be blamed for the persecutions rather than Mao and Zhou Enlai.

From the 'Application Report Regarding Paying Wang Qingping's Funeral Expenses and Comfort for the Bereaved' written by the Party

Committee of the No. 147 Secondary School on 15 August 1978, we know that Wang's family was given 2,190 *yuan*. The two largest portions were 240 *yuan* for funeral expenses and a living allowance of 1,800 *yuan* for the children. The compensation was calculated at 15 *yuan* per month for the eldest child, who was eleven, until he could join the workforce ten years later.

Wang Qingping's experience was typical of primary and secondary school principals on the eve of the Cultural Revolution. She had been born to a 'landlord' family, but while in secondary school in Beijing, she had encountered Communist activists and joined the Party in 1949. She had served for many years as a school principal, and her husband was a relatively high-ranking military cadre. She was not, as she was accused of being during the Cultural Revolution, an 'anti-Party, anti-socialist, anti-Mao Zedong Thought' individual. She was struggled to death because all school principals were struggled, because Mao designated them as 'representative bourgeois personages' in education circles.

BEIJING BEIMENCANG PRIMARY SCHOOL

Zhang Baihua, a teacher in her forties, threw herself onto a railway track after being beaten and humiliated by student Red Guards in August 1966.

The Beimencang Primary School was located in Dongcheng District, near the intersection of North Chaoyangmen Lane and the newly built Ping'an Avenue. During the Imperial era, this stretch consisted of several warehouses, hence the name, which meant 'warehouse at the northern gate'.

The Red Guards of the Beimencang Primary School, although young, were extremely vicious in beating and tormenting their teachers, using all the methods employed by older students at secondary schools. One time, the Red Guards killed a cat and buried it, then forced a dozen or so teachers to kneel in front of the cat's grave and weep for it. The lively imaginations of primary school students often made the Cultural Revolution even more unbearable.

This school had another teacher who also committed suicide, but the person who told me about Zhang Baihua couldn't remember their name.

BEIJING YUPENG PRIMARY SCHOOL

Sun Liangqi, a mathematics teacher in his thirties, leaped to his death after coming under attack in summer 1966.

The Yupeng Primary School was located at Ganshuiqiao outside of Andingmen. In 1966 it catered to the dependents of Air Force personnel, but it later became an ordinary local school.

Sun Liangqi was a mathematics teacher at the school and also head teacher for one of the fifth-grade classes. His students quickly joined in the Red Guard movement in summer 1966. They first attacked a female Young Pioneers troop leader, Lu Fen, who made an unsuccessful suicide attempt after being struggled on a stage. The school's principal, surnamed Xue, a military man who had attained the rank of colonel, was also struggled. He died of liver cancer during the Cultural Revolution.

When the students in Sun Liangqi's class learned that he had once been a soldier in the Kuomintang Army, they put up a big-character poster to 'pluck him out'. Sun was usually quite strict with his students and had once thrown a piece of chalk at some who were talking during class. Troublemaking students especially enjoyed tormenting their teachers when they had the chance. Language teacher Wang Dahai was struggled alongside Sun Liangqi.

Former students I talked to weren't sure exactly what kind of treatment Sun was subjected to – just that he leaped to his death soon afterwards.

Sun Liangqi's wife came from a village in northern Anhui and was not employed at the time. They had a son who was still in nursery school. After Sun died, his wife and child were driven from the school.

BEIJING SINO-CUBAN FRIENDSHIP PRIMARY SCHOOL

Zhao Qianguang, a head teacher in his thirties, leaped to his death from the school's chimney after being beaten and humiliated by student Red Guards in summer 1966.

The Sino-Cuban Friendship Primary School was located in Beijing's Xicheng District, where Red Guard violence was at its worst.

The principal of the school, a woman named Bai Zhi, was also beaten and humiliated that summer. On one occasion, Red Guards pushed thumbtacks into her head.

BEIJING SHIJIA HUTONG PRIMARY SCHOOL

Zhao Xiangheng, the school's principal, leaped to her death in August 1966.

Located near Beijing's busy Wangfujing Street, the Shijia Hutong Primary School was one of the most highly regarded primary schools in

Beijing. A friend from the older generation told me of Zhao Xiangheng's death, which was verified by a Beijing professor who had been a student there in 1966 and still had active ties to the school. The information I received was that Zhao committed suicide along with her husband, a cadre in the Beijing Cultural Bureau. I have been unable to learn his name.

BEIJING JIXIANG HUTONG PRIMARY SCHOOL

Qiu Qingyu, the school's vice-principal, was beaten to death by her students on 1 October 1966.

RED GUARD KILLINGS OF NEIGHBOURHOOD PEOPLE

A female resident of No. 11 Yongning Hutong surnamed Guo, aged around fifty, was a native of the northeast who graduated from Yenching University, and was known by neighbourhood children as **Aunty Guo**. During the 'Smashing of the Four Olds' in late August 1966, Red Guards ordered all households to destroy their old paintings, books and ornaments and to hang portraits of Mao in their homes. Aunty Guo's home had a painting of Zhong Kui, the exorciser of demons, hanging in the central room. She didn't want to destroy it, so covered it with a portrait of Mao. When the Red Guards discovered it, they accused her of wanting Zhong Kui to defeat Mao. After her home was ransacked and she was struggled, Aunty Guo killed herself by drinking pesticide.

Kou Huiling, a resident of No. 2 Dongdamochang in Xicheng District, was beaten to death in her home by Red Guards in August 1966. Kou worked at the Jiujiang Laundering and Dyeing Shop and had once owned shares in it. She also owned the home she lived in. In compliance with orders from the Red Guards, she handed over her property to the state in August, and the housing administration gave her a receipt, but the Red Guards still came to her home and beat her to death and closed off her house. Her daughter, Sun Wenjing, only twelve years old, was taught to regard her mother as a 'class enemy' and prohibited from mourning her. When the authorities eventually told her that her mother qualified as a 'contradiction among the people', she was finally able to vent her sorrow.

Wang Huilan, a homemaker residing in Douban Hutong, killed herself after being persecuted by Red Guards in late August 1966. Wang's husband, Zhao Changze, was an accountant for the Beijing Motorcycle Factory, and at the outset of the Cultural Revolution was accused of being a 'historical counter-revolutionary' and demoted to furnaceman. Red Guards ransacked their home in late August 1966 and forced Wang Huilan to stitch a black patch to the front of her clothing stating that she was a 'counter-revolutionary family member'. Wang killed herself with an overdose of sleeping pills. Wang's sister's eldest son, Yu Luoke, became famous for his essay 'On Family Background' and was executed as a counter-revolutionary in 1970.

The parents of Bian Yongzhen, a seventeen-year-old student at the Beijing No. 65 Secondary School, killed themselves after their home in Heyan Avenue was ransacked in August 1966.

Bian Yongzhen's parents had once run a small general store, as a result of which they were classified as 'small proprietors' in the 1950s. When the Red Guards began their mass campaign to ransack homes and expel 'black elements', many 'small proprietors' were upgraded to 'capitalists'. After Bian Yongzhen's home was turned upside down, her parents decided to kill themselves. The next evening, when Bian came home from school, her parents gave her some money and told her to go to the store to buy some groceries. When she returned, it was to find her parents hanging from the beam of their home. Now an orphan, Bian Yongzhen was humiliated and browbeaten by Red Guards at her school. She later took refuge with her elder sister in Ningxia.

Aunty Zuo and **Aunty Ma** lived at No. 6 Dongcheng Hutong in Dongcheng District. Their neighbours always referred to them in this way and never knew their full names. On the afternoon of 24 August, Red Guards ransacked their home and brutally beat Aunty Zuo, whose husband, Zuo Qingming, was away at the time. Aunty Ma was beaten to death after she warned Zuo Qingming not to come home.

This *hutong*, named after the Ming dynasty secret police organisation, was located near a busy shopping district and was home to the Modern History Institute of the Chinese Academy of Sciences, with the Instiue of Archeology also located nearby.

Aunty Zuo's husband, Zuo Qingming, had once run a shop selling firewood, which made him a 'small proprietor'. They also had some property that they rented out, as well as the house they lived in. The shop had been handed over to the state years earlier, and the rental units were also being 'managed' by the Housing Administration. The couple, in their seventies, were devout Buddhists, and Zuo Qingming had once served on the government-run Buddhist Council.

Aunty Ma and her husband were renting from the Zuos, so the two families lived in the same compound. Aunty Ma's husband was a factory worker, and she herself earned some money by doing housework for other families.

The Red Guards came to ransack the Zuos' home at 3:00 in the afternoon. Like many traditional Beijing quadrangle compounds, it had a grape arbour in the courtyard that provided shade and fruit in the summer. The Red Guards tied Aunty Zuo to it and beat her with their brass-buckled belts. Aunty Ma wasn't able to help Aunty Zuo, but she knew that Zuo Qingming would be home soon and would be beaten even more harshly, so she waited at the entrance to the *hutong* and warned him off when she saw him approach. This probably saved Zuo Qingming's life, but the Red Guards saw what happened and tied up Aunty Ma and began beating her as well. They also poured boiling water over the heads of both women.

One neighbour said the women's cries were so horrifying, she couldn't bear to stay at home, and went and sat along the road outside the *hutong* until it was dark. Even then, the beatings continued and she heard screaming until late into the night. Another witness said the cries were 'like pigs being butchered'. Finally, around 3:00 a.m., there was silence. Around 5:00 a.m. a truck drove up, and someone called out in the dark, 'Where's Number 6?' The neighbours heard the thumping of the bodies being loaded onto the truck.

Aunty Zuo was old enough to be a grandmother, typically the most harmless kind of person, yet she became a target of attack. Aunty Ma was a house cleaner and a relatively poor person who should not have been a target of the Cultural Revolution, and indeed might have enjoyed a feeling of triumph at the beating of someone with more wealth and status. Instead, she was an exception among the many victims of the Cultural Revolution: she died while trying to help another. In a time of horror, she took the path of benevolence and righteousness. She was a hero, but we do not know her name.

A resident of No. 2 Dongcheng Hutong, **Sun Zuoliang**, was beaten to death along with his wife on the same day as Aunty Ma and Aunty Zuo. Sun Zuoliang was famous as one of Beijing's best optometrists. Apart from once operating an optometry shop, he owned his own home, which is why Red Guards beat him and his wife to death.

A mother and daughter living on the western end of the *hutong* were also beaten to death that day, but I wasn't able to find out their names. Someone recalled the mother dressing well and wearing a gold ring.

In total, six residents of Dongcheng Hutong were beaten to death on 24 August.

A retired man in his forties living at No. 1 Baotouzhang Hutong in the southern portion of Xuanwu District was beaten to death in late August 1966. Red Guards ransacked the man's home, claiming he was hiding a gun and demanding that he hand it over. When he said he didn't have a gun, the

Red Guards beat him. Finally he claimed that he'd buried the gun, and then that he'd hidden it in the ceiling of the shed, but when no gun materialised, the Red Guards finally beat the man to death.

Inside the *hutong* was an even smaller dead-end *hutong*, where a plump matron in her sixties lived. She was a housewife who had apparently once had some money, so the Red Guards called her a parasite and beat her. That night, she drowned herself in the lake near the Taoran Pavilion.

Other people also died in Baotouzhang Hutong at that time.

Xiao Shikai, a retired secondary school teacher in his sixties residing in Guang'anmennei Avenue on the south side of Xuanwu Park, died along with his wife after being driven out of Beijing by Red Guards in early September 1966.

Xiao Shikai came from a family of educators; his father had once run the Tongzhou Women's Normal School, and his younger sister was a primary school teacher. Xiao himself had taught physical education and languages at the Beijing No. 1 Secondary School, but by the time the Cultural Revolution began, he was retired and provided tutoring and childcare in his home along with his wife. The couple's own children had died young.

In late August 1966, Xiao Shikai was accused of being a 'rich peasant who slipped through the net'. Red Guards ransacked his home, shaved his head, and sent Xiao and his wife off to Zhuo County, Hebei Province. With no place to live and nothing to eat, they took shelter in a shed by a melon patch. By then it was early September; their urban food rations had been cut off, and it was not yet time for distributing foodstuffs in the villages, not to mention that the couple were 'class enemies' who had been driven out of Beijing. Xiao's younger sister managed to send them some wheat flour, but it didn't last long. Both Xiao and his wife died a month after being expelled.

OUTSKIRTS OF BEIJING

Changping County

Wang Zhanbao, a member of the Heishanzhai production brigade in Beijing's Changping County who had been designated a 'landlord' before 1949, was killed along with his son and grandson in August 1966.

According to *Snowstorm at the Ding Mausoleum: The Mystery of the Underground Xuangong Cave*,[28] in August 1966, Red Guards in the Heishanzhai production brigade near the Ding Mausoleum ferreted out

---

[28] Yang Shi, Yue Nan, *Snowstorm at the Ding Mausoleum: The Mystery of the Underground Xuangong Cave*, Beijing, Xinshijie chubanshe, 1997, p. 338.

'landlord element' Wang Zhanbao and his family for public denunciation. Wang and his son were beaten to death, and in order to 'destroy the roots and branches', the leader of the rebel faction captured Wang's nine-year-old grandson in the wilderness and tore him in half.

The Ding Mausoleum is the only one of thirteen tombs of Ming dynasty emperors in Changping County that has been partially excavated, making it a major Beijing tourist attraction. Several interviewees mentioned having heard of a massacre of 'black elements' and their family members in Changping County in August 1966, around the same time as the massacre in Daxing County.

Around the same time, nineteen 'landlords' and 'rich peasants' and their family members were killed in Huangtunandian Village under the Sino-Vietnamese Friendship People's Commune. The village, at that time called a production brigade, consisted of two production teams totalling around 2,000 people. The village was in the part of the county closest to Beijing, separated by only one street from the urban Haidian District, and only ten or so kilometres from Desheng Gate. The village is now under the jurisdiction of Huilongguan Town, where large numbers of highrises sprang up in the 1990s because of the area's proximity to Beijing.

On that particular day, the villagers were notified to bring clubs to a 'struggle rally' to kill the village's 'landlords', 'rich peasants' and their family members. At first no one made a move, but once a demobilised soldier began beating someone with his club, others in the crowd joined in. All of the victims were buried outside the village – some when they were not yet dead. The victims included people who had been designated 'landlords' and 'rich peasants' during the Land Reform Movement, but they'd given up their land before 1949, a full seventeen years before the Cultural Revolution began. Others killed were small children and distant relatives of the 'black elements'. Secondary school students dispatched to Huangtunandian in 1974 as 'sent-down educated youths' learned of this incident from people in the village.

Daxing County

Daxing County experienced a massacre of 325 'black elements' from 27 August to 1 September 1966. Among the victims were **Han Zongxin**, his wife, their teenage daughter and two sons; **Tan Runfang**, a man in his thirties, and his daughter; and **Fang Junjie**, a man in his thirties. All lived in Dong'an Village, which at that time was part of the Daxinzhuang People's Commune. More than 100 people were killed at that commune on 31 August 1966.

Han Zongxin came from a landlord family. He joined the Nationalist Army but then went over to the Communists, and he returned to his village in 1955. He had a 'certificate of revolt' signed by PLA Marshal Luo Ronghuan hanging in his home in the futile hope that it would bring him a measure of protection. When the Cultural Revolution began, Han's village was still engaged in the Socialist Education Movement. Someone reported that Han Zongxin was concealing a gun. After being detained for several weeks, he was finally released, only to be killed along with his family soon after he returned home.

Han and his wife had one more daughter, but due to their poverty, had given the girl to another family in the commune's Beihe brigade when she was four years old. Although that family was also in the landlord class, Beihe Village was more humane, and they were spared. After the Cultural Revolution, the Zhongxin brigade paid 1,800 *yuan* in compensation to Han Zongxin's surviving daughter.

The 'Daxing Massacre' is mentioned in *Turbulent Decade: A History of the Cultural Revolution*.[29] It was first reported in *Beijing Daily*, so I went to the newspaper's office to make further inquiries. The newspaper said it couldn't find the original materials on which their report was based, but it did provide me with an essay from its *Propaganda Handbook*:[30]

> In the latter half of 1966, under the incitement of Lin Biao and the Gang of Four... Beijing was struck by an unhealthy trend of ransacking, beating and killing. This unhealthy trend rapidly spread to the rural suburbs. Serious incidents of mass killings of black elements and their families occurred in some counties.
>
> On 26 August 1966, the Daxing County Public Security Bureau called a meeting during which it transmitted comments by [Minister of Public Security] Xie Fuzhi at an enlarged meeting of the Municipal Public Security Bureau. Xie Fuzhi said, 'Things that were stipulated against in the past, whether by the state or by the public security organs, are not to be restrained... I don't agree with the masses killing people, but the masses deeply loathe evildoers, and we can't dissuade them, so we shouldn't force them... The People's Police have to stand with the Red Guards, make contact with them, establish friendly relations with them and explain the situation of the black elements to them.' After Xie Fuzhi's order was transmitted, some People's Police officers explained the circumstances of the black elements to the Red Guards, and in that atmosphere, some people started

---

[29] Yan Jiaqi, Gao Gao, *op. cit.*
[30] Beijing Daily Propaganda Handbook Editorial Department, *Propaganda Handbook*, February 1985.

a rumour, saying, 'The communes know about this [killings], the county knows about it, the city knows about it and even Premier Zhou supports it.' From then on, the beatings and random killings became increasingly serious. At first only 'misbehaving' black elements were beaten, but then it was extended to black elements generally. At first a production brigade would exterminate one, two or three 'outstanding examples', but then one brigade would kill a dozen or several dozen at one time. At first only black elements themselves were killed, but then there was indiscriminate killing of their family members and other people with minor issues, and this finally developed into the eradication of entire families. From 27 August to 1 September, in that county's thirteen communes and forty-eight production brigades, 325 Black Elements and family members were killed. The oldest was eighty and the youngest was only thirty-eight days old, and twenty-two households were completely wiped out. This state of affairs did not end until Municipal Party Committee secretary Comrade Ma Li personally went to the county to prevent further killing. This was a deplorable incident with serious consequences and extremely bad influence. The relevant departments investigated the individual participants, and all were disciplined and punished in accordance with Party policy and their varying circumstances.

There are at least two problems with this narrative. The first is that the Daxing Massacre did not result from the instigation of Lin Biao and the Gang of Four, but from Mao's encourgement and promotion of the Red Guards. Secondly, the *Propaganda Handbook* only mentions the Daxing Massacre without mentioning the thousands of killings that the Red Guards perpetrated within the Beijing city limits during this same period. The article doesn't mention the names of any of the victims. One important reason is that these were all ordinary people, not senior officials or prominent members of society. I'm grateful to Yu Luowen, who personally went to Daxing County to carry out an investigation and found out three of the names of these 325 victims.

Nankou

Zhou Fuli, a worker at the Nankou second branch farm, was beaten to death by Red Guards in 1966.

During the Socialist Education Movement at the end of 1965, Zhou Fuli was designated a 'bad element' because he had been a soldier while the KMT was in power. 'Bad elements' were among the 'black elements' who were the main 'targets of dictatorship' at the time.

In August 1966, the Nankou second branch farm established the Soaring Eagle Red Guards. Soon after Mao's fateful rally on 18 August, the Soaring Eagle Red Guards rounded up all of the branch farm's 'black elements' in the open area in front of the canteen and meeting hall, made them wear placards stating their 'crimes' and then beat them with clubs, shovels and pickaxes.

Zhou Fuli was beaten half to death with a club and then tossed into a pit, after which 'revolutionary workers' caught 200 or 300 venomous caterpillars and dumped them on his naked body. Zhou died that night.

Another man in his fifties was beaten to death along with Zhou Fuli. He was a Rightist sent down from the Beijing municipal Grain Bureau, but I haven't been able to find out his name. He was still breathing when he was hauled to the orchard and buried.

Several 'reactionary students' who were struggled that day had their skulls fractured, and the placards around their necks were covered with blood. At that time, Nankou Farm had a labour camp known outside as the 'College Brigade', which held educators and students in two separate divisions. The educators' division held nearly 100 people, mainly Rightists and other 'problematic people' from Beijing colleges. The students' division held 'reactionary students' from Beijing's colleges purged over the past three years, and was under the control of the Beijing Municipal Party Committee Universities Department.

University authorities sent 'reactionary students' to Nankou Farm for labour reform for nothing more than expressing divergent views. When the Universities Department and the leaders of all the universities were struggled as 'reactionaries' in August 1966, the students they had purged were persecuted even more harshly, and they weren't rehabilitated until 1980.

SHANGHAI[31]

EAST CHINA NORMAL UNIVERSITY NO. 1 AFFILIATED SECONDARY SCHOOL

Qin Song, an English teacher, killed himself during the Cultural Revolution.

---

[31] TN: Due to less detailed information, victims in this section are listed according to the alphabetical order of the schools where they were killed.

FUDAN UNIVERSITY AFFILIATED SECONDARY SCHOOL

Yang Hanqing, a language teacher at the Shanghai Fudan University Affiliated Secondary School, killed herself in 1966 after being beaten multiple times by Red Guards from that school and from Beijing.

FUXING SECONDARY SCHOOL

Jin Zhixiong, manager of the school's library, hanged herself after being struggled in summer 1966.

Jin was originally a history teacher, but she'd been working in the library since being designated a Rightist in 1957. Red Guards repeatedly beat and humiliated her and gave her a yin-yang haircut with blunt scissors. Soon after she returned home, her attackers came pounding on her door. Unable to bear the thought of more abuse, Jin hanged herself.

Around the same time, Red Guards from the school killed a student who came from outside of Shanghai, whom they accused of 'passing himself off as the son of a senior cadre' and 'passing himself off as a Red Guard'. After killing that student, the Red Guards ordered the school's music teacher, Peng Zhiwu (who was locked up in the school as an 'ox demon and snake spirit'), to go out in the early hours of the morning to the shop across the street and buy soya milk to wash the blood off their clothes.

Red Guards from the school also killed an unidentified elderly man in his home in Shanyin Road in Hongkou District.

GAOQIAO SECONDARY SCHOOL

Zhang Aizhen was an unemployed woman in her thirties who lived in Gaoqiao Town in Shanghai's Pudong District. In summer 1967, Red Guards from the Gaoqiao Secondary School accused her of 'lifestyle problems', abducted her, and beat her to death in the school building.

GEZHI SECONDARY SCHOOL

Shen Jie, head teacher of third-year students, killed herself after being denounced. Shen had at one point been a soldier in the Communist-led New Fourth Army, but during the Cultural Revolution she was accused of being a 'traitor'.

HONGQI SECONDARY SCHOOL

Qiu Fengxian, around thirty years old and in charge of the chemistry laboratory, fell to her death while imprisoned at the school in summer 1966.

Qiu was abducted from her home one night and taken to the school to be struggled because she came from a 'landlord' family. After being locked up in a six-metre-square storeroom next to the third-floor boys' toilet, she fell to her death while climbing out of a window.

The school's biology teacher, a man in his fifties named Wu Baihe, had his home ransacked twice and was beaten by Red Guards until his head streamed with blood and his leg was broken because he was a 'rehabilitated Rightist'. When another student asked why Wu was being beaten, the assailants wrestled him into a duffle bag and pushed him onto the cement floor. After the Cultural Revolution, the Red Guards who had carried out these beatings were expelled from the Party but didn't have to bear any legal responsibility for their acts.

Another teacher, **Sun Jingxiang**, leaped to her death from the school's education building in winter 1968. (See Part Five.)

Later, other teachers locked up with Sun told her daughter Zhang Xin that conditions were so bad in the 'study class' that death was preferable, and everyone there wanted to kill themselves. 'Only your mama was lucky enough to find a way to die.'

JINGXI SECONDARY SCHOOL

The Jingxi Secondary School was located in Shanghai's Jing'an District. Before 1949 it was called Guoqiang (strong nation) Secondary School, and its name changed again in the 1980s.

Many of the school's teachers were beaten in summer 1966 during the 'Smashing of the Four Olds' campaign. Red Guards ordered them to hand over the 'Four Olds' in their homes, mainly books, which were piled on the exercise ground and burned while teachers were forced to crawl around the bonfire like dogs until some were actually burned.

Yang Shunji, a physics teacher around forty years old, was beaten to death at the school in late August or September 1966. Yang was a quiet person, unmarried, who lived in an apartment on Huaihai Road. He appears to have had 'overseas relations'.

When Red Guards started beating people, Yang Shunji sought refuge with a cousin for a time, but the cousin, fearing that the Red Guards would pursue Yang there, didn't let him stay long. The cousin was extremely distressed for years after that, even though he really had no choice in the matter; if he'd let Yang stay with him, his family would have been victimised as well.

JINGYE SECONDARY SCHOOL

Su Yuxi, the school's principal, was repeatedly struggled after being accused of being a 'traitor'. He hanged himself from a bamboo pole in the school canteen.

Sheng Zhangqi, a personnel cadre in his forties, leaped to his death from a school building sometime in 1966 or 1967. Accused of being a 'bandit', he took his own life after being told to attend a struggle rally.

NO. 4 GIRLS' SECONDARY SCHOOL

The No. 4 Girls' Secondary School, located in Xuhui District, was established by the Catholic Church in 1855. It was one of the first girls' schools in modern China, and one of Shanghai's first new-style schools. After several name changes, it was renamed the No. 4 Secondary School in 1968 and became co-ed.

The school's all-female Red Guards were extremely brutal and cruel, as was the case with many other girls' schools that came up in my research. The principal of Shanghai's No. 3 Girls' Secondary School, Xue Zheng, was forced to eat excrement, and Red Guards attached a big-character poster to her back with thumbtacks driven into her flesh.

Wang Yunqian, a Suzhou native and a mathematics teacher at the school, leaped to her death after being denounced in autumn 1966. An eyewitness said the scene of Wang's death was 'too horrible to look at'.

NO. 56 SECONDARY SCHOOL

Qian Songqi, a school accountant in his fifties, allegedly killed himself while locked up in the school in 1966.

Qian had worked at a bank before being transferred to the school. Soon after he was locked up, his wife, the principal of a primary school in Shanghai's Hongkou District, was notified that Qian had killed himself. When she came to fetch his body, she found pieces of a steamed bun in his mouth. She was suspicious about how Qian had died, but was never able to have it investigated.

Wu Xinyou, in his forties, the exemplary manager of the school's chemistry lab, was found to have some old share certificates from the Nationalist era in his home, as a result of which he was accused of being a capitalist. Struggled and tormented on an almost daily basis, he finally drowned himself in the Huangpu River.

NO. 58 SECONDARY SCHOOL (AKA CHENGZHONG SECONDARY SCHOOL)

Dong Silin, the school's principal, disappeared in 1966 after being subjected to brutal public denunciation.

QIBAO SECONDARY SCHOOL

Zhou Ruipan, a young physics teacher, drowned himself in September 1966 after being denounced.

One night early that month, the school's Red Guards denounced another teacher, Wu Mingji, as an 'agent of American imperialism'. Wu had graduated from the Department of Electrical Engineering of Southwestern Associated University and had been a classmate of Nobel laureate Yang Zhenning, who was living in the US at that time. After struggling Wu Mingji, the Red Guards went next door to Zhou Ruipan's living quarters to make trouble. When they found one of Wu's books on Zhou's desk, they used 'collusion with a secret agent' as a pretext for torturing Zhou for several hours, ordering him to write a confession to hand over the next day. Instead, Zhou Ruipan drowned himself in the school's well.

Yang Jiugao, a middle-aged English teacher, hanged himself in August or September 1966 after poor and lower-middle peasants from his home village came to Shanghai and struggled him as a 'landlord who escaped through the net'.

Zhang Guanghua, a middle-aged language teacher, suffered heatstroke after being sent down to the countryside for labour reform at the outset of the Cultural Revolution. Because he came from a 'capitalist' family, the Red Guards wouldn't allow him to seek medical treatment, and he died as a result.

SHANGHAI CONSERVATORY OF MUSIC AFFILIATED SECONDARY SCHOOL

Li Shaobai, a young teacher in his twenties, threw himself in front of a train after being subjected to struggle for his 'bourgeois' attire during the 'Smashing of the Four Olds' in August 1966.

Cheng Zhuoru, born in 1918, was vice-principal and teacher of basic musical theory. She killed herself with an overdose of sleeping pills along with her husband, **Yang Jiaren**, on 6 September 1966, after coming under attack by Red Guard students in the summer. Yang Jiaren was a professor and head of the Conducting Department at the Shanghai Conservatory of Music. The couple had a son and a daughter who were both college students at the time.

When Cheng Zhuoru was struggled, she was not only beaten by Red Guard students but was also forced to hit other teachers. The Red Guards ordered 'ox demons and snake spirits' to stand in two lines and slap the face of the person standing across from them, and if they didn't co-operate, they would be beaten.

The Shanghai Conservatory shared its instructors with its Affiliated Secondary School. Out of a total of 300 instructors and students at the college level, there were seventeen unnatural deaths at the Shanghai Conservatory during the Cultural Revolution.

SHANGHAI DATONG SECONDARY SCHOOL

Originally the Affiliated Secondary School of Datong University (which was disbanded after 1949), Datong Secondary had a lengthy history and was a keynote secondary school. Once the Cultural Revolution began, in June 1966, its principal, Wang Jixian, was 'ferreted out' as 'ringleader' of the school's 'Three Family Village'.

Li Xueying, a head teacher and language teacher around thirty-six years old, hanged himself in summer 1966 after being repeatedly beaten and humiliated by his students.

According to a big-character poster, Li Xueying had been an editor at a film company at the age of eighteen. He became a language teacher at Datong Secondary School after 1949. Language was a key subject in secondary school, and Li Xueying, who had considerable literary talent, taught it at several levels before the Cultural Revolution.

Attacked as a 'reactionary scholar', Li was savagely struggled by his students in July and August. On the last occasion, they dragged him into the sports field jumping pit, poured sand and ink over him and shaved off half his hair. Li killed himself at home that night. Li's wife was in the graduating class of the Shanghai Medical School at the time. They had no children.

SHANGHAI FOREIGN LANGUAGES INSTITUTE AFFILIATED SECONDARY SCHOOL

The Shanghai Foreign Languages Institute Affiliated Secondary School opened in 1963 and moved into a new school building the following year.

Because it was specially geared towards training future diplomats and intelligence agents, many of the students were the children of senior Party cadres. During the Cultural Revolution, Red Guards at this school were extremely violent. On one occasion, after beating a teacher, they forced him to lick his own blood off the floor.

Wang Yimin, a student, leaped to his death after being beaten and humiliated by Red Guard classmates in 1966. A former teacher said that Wang came from an intellectual family and was a mild-mannered boy who played the piano, and was victimised because he didn't come from a Red family. This teacher saw Wang being pushed back and forth and beaten by other students in a dormitory room. Unable to bear the abuse, Wang fled to his home; Red Guards followed, ransacked the house and brought him back to the school. Wang became deranged and attempted suicide several times. He finally succeeded by leaping from a window.

SHANGHAI PUDONG SECONDARY SCHOOL

Ye Wencui, a teacher, committed suicide after being struggled in 1966.

SHANGHAI TONGJI SECONDARY SCHOOL

Lin Xiuquan, a language teacher around forty-five years old, was beaten to death by Red Guards in late August 1966.

Red Guards from the school were mainly the children of cadres from the nearby No. 2 Military University of Medical Sciences.

A former student of Tongji Secondary School recalls that Lin Xiuquan was well-educated and took his teaching seriously. He had beautiful handwriting, and many students tried to imitate his calligraphy while in class. When the Cultural Revolution began, Lin was 'ferreted out' as the son of a senior KMT official, possibly Lin Sen (Lin Sen, 1868–1943, was chairman of the Nationalist government in Nanjing in 1928). Whether this was true or not, it served as the basis for denunciation.

In late August 1966, Red Guards from Beijing travelling through the country on the 'great networking' joined the school's Red Guards in savagely beating Lin Xiuquan. Soon after that, they took him to the sports field, tied him to a horizontal bar and beat him with their brass belt buckles until he died. Lin had a frail physique, being only around 5'4" and weighing less than 100 pounds, and his screams of pain reached the classroom building, but no one dared step forward to save him.

TONGJI UNIVERSITY AFFILIATED SECONDARY SCHOOL

Ye Maoying, the school's principal, hanged himself after being beaten by students. After the Cultural Revolution began, the schools' teachers and administrators were forced to kneel in a line and were beaten so harshly that some Vietnamese overseas students protested.

WEIYU SECONDARY SCHOOL (NO. 51 SECONDARY SCHOOL)

Sun Chifu, a teacher in his thirties, drowned himself in 1967. Sun had been designated a Rightist in 1957 and as a result had never married. His Rightist label meant that he was persecuted even more harshly than other teachers when the Cultural Revolution began. His mother came from their home village to visit him in 1967, and while accompanying her on the boat back to their village, he jumped into the water and drowned himself. His body was never recovered.

Huang Mengzhang, a teacher, killed himself after being struggled during the Cultural Revolution.

WUSONG NO. 2 SECONDARY SCHOOL

At the outset of the Cultural Revolution, around twenty of this school's 100-odd teachers were put into the school's 'labour reform team' and 'ox pen'.

Zeng Ruiquan, a language teacher in his forties, drowned himself in summer 1966 after a fellow teacher was 'seized and struggled'. Zheng had been a journalist before 1949 and had 'historical problems'; he drowned himself in the Huangpu River before he could be 'ferreted out'.

Zhang Fengming, a foreign language teacher in his thirties, came from a 'capitalist' family. One day, a fellow teacher looked through the window of a classroom and saw Red Guards beating Zhang Fengming with clubs. Zhang leaped to his death the next morning.

XINHU SECONDARY SCHOOL

Zhang Youbai, a mathematics teacher in his thirties, was designated a Rightist in 1957 and 'seized and struggled' in 1966. He electrocuted himself in the school's unmarried residential quarters.

YUEYANG ROAD PRIMARY SCHOOL

Li Wen, a language teacher around thirty-five years old, was struggled brutally at the school (which was merged into Jianxiang Primary School in 1972) when the Cultural Revolution began, and was also humiliated by neighbourhood cadres near her home. She hanged herself in the school's 'ox pen' sometime in 1966 or 1967.

OUTSKIRTS OF SHANGHAI

On the afternoon of 27 August 1966, three Red Guards from Beijing's No. 28 Secondary School who had arrived in Shanghai for the 'great networking' went along with Red Guards from a Shanghai secondary school to 'struggle landlords' in the Zhuhang production brigade of Meilong Commune in the suburbs. They tied up six 'landlords' and some 'landlord offspring' and forced them to kneel on bricks with their heads bowed. The Beijing Red Guards beat them with belts, saying, 'In Beijing, it's no crime to kill black elements.' The Shanghai Red Guards then joined in. Ultimately a woman in her seventies was killed, and the others were badly injured.

NANJING

NANJING FOREIGN LANGUAGE SCHOOL

A former student said that Red Guards from the school, most of them the offspring of senior cadres, beat many teachers in summer 1966. One female teacher was given a yin-yang haircut and was harshly beaten merely because she was religious.

Wang Jin, an ordinary worker, was beaten to death on a bus by Red Guards from the school who said that he had a 'bad family background'. After Wang's colleagues came forward and said he was from the working class, many workers surrounded the Foreign Language School to protest the killing. In order to pacify them, the Nanjing Municipal Party Committee and Public Security Bureau arrested three Red Guard leaders, one of whom was the son of the deputy commander of the Logistics Department of the Nanjing Military Region. Other students were sent to the countryside for a few days and then went on the 'great networking'. The former student who talked to me said that after arriving in Beijing, he attended Mao's second review of the Red Guards at Tiananmen Square on 31 August. He observed that Red Guards from the Beijing Foreign Languages School were even more violent than those in Nanjing.

NO. 2 SECONDARY SCHOOL

A former student of the school recalled that the beatings there began soon after Red Guards returned from being reviewed by Mao at Tiananmen Square. A rally was held in the school auditorium, during which Red Guards marched up to the stage, shoulders squared, behind a flag-bearer.

One teacher whose face was said to resemble a secret agent in the movies was accused of being an actual spy and was brutally beaten. Students from 'bad family backgrounds' were also beaten and humiliated; one student was penalised by being forced to clean the school for several months.

The former student told me that a teacher was beaten to death there in August or September 1966, but he didn't remember a name, only that he was older and taught history. I later met a Nanjing resident who had been a classmate of this teacher's son and had visited their home, and although he too didn't know the teacher's given name (Chinese children would never ask the names of their friends' parents back then), he eventually helped me identify the victim as **Zhu Qingyi**, who was in his fifties.

This man also told me that Zhu Qingyi's son, **Zhu Shiguang**, had gone to work in Hunan after graduating from the East China Institute of Political Science and Law. During the Cultural Revolution, Zhu Shiguang was accused of being a 'current counter-revolutionary' and was executed, leaving behind a son, who was then raised by Zhu Qingyi's widow, a primary school teacher.

During the Cultural Revolution, Zhu Qingyi's former students and Zhu Shiguang's old classmates didn't dare go to the Zhu home and visit Zhu Qingyi's wife and her grandson, but afterwards they wanted to do something for the family, so they went to court on their behalf. But the court said it could only 'restore the good name' of the victims, and wouldn't provide financial assistance to the survivors.

NO. 13 SECONDARY SCHOOL

School librarian **Han Kang** was beaten to death by Red Guard students on 5 September 1966. Han lived near the school, and because he had joined the KMT before 1949, Red Guards ransacked his home and destroyed his belongings. One morning, Red Guards dragged Han Kang to the school's sports ground to be struggled along with **Xia Zhongmou**, the school's physical education instructor, who had a similar 'historical problem' of having belonged to the KMT's Three People's Principles Youth Corps. The Red Guards kicked and punched the two teachers, whipped them with their belts and threw bricks at them, beating Han Kang more harshly because his attitude was 'bad'. Han passed out three or four times, but the students always revived him by throwing cold water on him. He died as night fell.

Xia Zhongmou kept his head down while the students berated him, so he didn't die right then, and was escorted to one of the school's laboratories to pass the night under guard. Having seen Han Kang beaten to death and knowing that his own torture would resume the next day, Xia tore his clothing to make into a rope with which he hanged himself that night.

Two people who were students at the school at that time told me of this incident.

FUJIAN PROVINCE – XIAMEN

The Xiamen No. 8 Secondary School, founded in 1919, was one of the city's best schools. It was originally called the Double Ten Secondary School to commemorate the 1911 Xinhai Revolution, but since 10 October was proclaimed National Day by the government of Taiwan, the school's name was changed during the Socialist Education Movement. It reverted to its original name after the Cultural Revolution.

The school was located close to the Xiamen municipal government offices, and many children of senior cadres were actively involved in its Red Guards. Teachers who had already been 'ferreted out' bore the brunt of Red Guard beatings, after which students with 'bad family backgrounds' were also locked up and beaten.

Sa Zhaochen, a language teacher at the school, was the first educator to be killed by Red Guards in Fujian Province. He, his wife – who worked in the school office – and their four children lived across the road from the school.

One day, Red Guards beat and tortured Sa Zhaochen for an entire day, parading him around the school building from the fourth floor to the first floor and beating him under the broiling sun on the sports field. He died that same day.

Physics teacher **Huang Zubin** fell to his death early one morning in August 1966 after being brutally beaten by the school's Red Guards.

One eyewitness said that all of the school's students were living in the classrooms to engage in revolution. Early one morning, they were awakened by a concussive sound, like a sack of rice dropping. When they looked out of the window, they saw someone lying on the ground in front of the building. The students ran out and found Huang Zubin still alive and writhing.

My interviewee recalls that Sa and Huang both died before 29 August, which is when the Red Guards of the Xiamen No. 8 Secondary School launched a massive campaign in which hundreds of people marched to the provincial capital, Fuzhou, demanding the 'ferreting out' of the provincial education department director, who had been seconded to the school and who was the wife of the provincial Party secretary at the time. This was the beginning of the Red Guard attack on provincial leadership organs. Reports on the '8–29' incident make no mention of Sa Zhaochen, Huang Zubin or other victims, who were apparently not considered important enough to be included in the official record.

My interviewee said that his trigonometry teacher was also beaten and made an unsuccessful attempt to hang himself. A rally was held for all of the school's students to denounce that teacher, who still had a red mark around his neck.

In order to learn more about Sa Zhaochen and Huang Zubin, including the dates of their deaths, I wrote a letter to the famous Xiamen poet, Shu Ting, asking for help. She made inquiries among former students and others, and learned from one source that Huang and Sa had been beaten to death rather than committing suicide. She also learned that another teacher surnamed Lü did commit suicide later, during the Cleansing of the Class Ranks.

I've written many letters requesting help with my inquiries, but I've received few replies. There are any number of reasons for this, of course, but I would like to take the opportunity here to express my heartfelt gratitude to Shu Ting, whom I've never met.

I later identified the third teacher as **Lü Jianyuan**, a mathematics teacher and Xiamen native, who was held in an 'ox pen' during the Cleansing of the Class ranks and hanged himself in the school in early 1971. I also learned that many of this school's teachers and leading cadres were brutally tortured and humiliated. Red Guards made a teacher named Zheng Xiuyue eat insects captured in the school toilet, and Huang Zubin was forced to eat excrement.

GUANGDONG PROVINCE

He Peihua, a language teacher at the Guangzhou No. 17 Secondary School, was subjected to criticism and struggle. Early on the morning of 8 August

1966, he killed himself by lying down on the railway track at the Dengfeng Road crossing near the school.

HEBEI PROVINCE

Xu Jiqing, principal of the Nangong Secondary School in Nangong County, Hebei Province, stabbed himself in the heart with a knife after being paraded and struggled by Red Guard students in August 1966. Around the same time, **Yan Jufeng**, the school's vice-principal, hanged himself, and a mathematics teacher, **Xing Zhizheng**, drowned himself in a well after being struggled. Nangong Secondary School was once a provincial keypoint secondary school.

HUBEI PROVINCE – WUHAN

Yao Xuezhi, a teacher of politics at the Wuchang Experimental Secondary School, had been designated a Rightist in 1957. In August 1966, student Red Guards, who were primarily the children of cadres and military men, seized and struggled Yao, paraded her through the streets and forced her to drink fluid from a spittoon. Eventually they tormented her to death.

Li Dehui, an English teacher at the Wuhan No. 1 Secondary School, committed suicide in summer 1966.

Chen Bangjian, an outstanding mathematics teacher at the Wuhan No. 14 Secondary School and its highest-ranking teacher at that time, was struggled and kept under the supervision of Red Guard students in August and September. While under his mosquito net one night, Chen cut his throat with scissors. His death was long-drawn-out and agonising; he had not yet breathed his last when he was discovered at dawn.

HUNAN PROVINCE

Tang Zheng, a language teacher at the No. 1 Secondary School in Liuyang, Hunan Province, died after being trussed up and struggled in the school's auditorium in August 1966. She was forty-seven years old and left behind three children, including two daughters of twelve and eight years old.

Tang's family members were not allowed to mourn her, and she was hastily buried that same day.

Tang Zheng's husband, Gong Yuren, was also a teacher at the school. When I interviewed him in 2001, he was eighty-four years old, and tears streamed down his face when he spoke of his wife.

Tang Zheng graduated from the Beijing Normal School for Women in 1942 and in 1951 followed her husband to Liuyang to teach. Tang was always a target of every major and minor campaign that came up before the Cultural Revolution, not because she had personally done anything, but because she came from an 'industrial and commercial capitalist family' and had joined the Three People's Principles Youth Corps while a student. In addition, her sister's husband, Gao Binghuang, had been an undersecretary of finance in the Nanjing government – yes, even a brother-in-law's doings could be construed as a reason to purge someone.

After the Cultural Revolution began, Tang Zheng was 'seized and struggled' and apart from being beaten and kicked she was forced to engage in hard labour. A big-character poster was pasted at the entrance to her house, and another poster was hung from the lintel so that people had to stoop in order to pass through the doorway. Spear-bearing student Red Guards were posted outside her home to monitor the family's activities.

One day, Tang's daughter saw her crawling on the ground, too feeble to stand. The Red Guards standing beside her accused her of malingering and hit her in the legs and lower back with their spears. She was unable to say a word. Her daughter ran away in tears.

Tang was tortured until she was reduced to skin and bone and passed blood in her stool. She asked for leave to see a doctor, but was refused. On the night before she died, she developed a high fever. The next morning, her daughter was horrified to see blood in her urine, but didn't know what to do.

Later that day, Tang Zheng was tied up and taken to the school auditorium, where her husband, Gong Yuren, and some other teachers with bad family backgrounds were made to stand next to her as 'secondary targets'. Gong watched helplessly as his wife was beaten until she could no longer stand and fell onto the stage. The Red Guards kept beating her and berated her for 'playing dead'. When Gong cried out in protest, Red Guards beat him to the ground. After the struggle rally finished, Gong Yuren carried his wife home, where she died.

Someone from the school came to dispose of the corpse. Tang Zheng's eldest son was bound and hung in the doorway of the house, and Gong Yuren was hogtied. A few pieces of wood were nailed together to make a box, and Tang's body was tossed into it. Some students spat on the corpse and tossed pieces of tile onto it. At that time, the school's principal hadn't yet been 'struck down' and he stood off to the side. Gong Yuren kowtowed to him and begged him to make the students stop, but the principal replied these were revolutionary actions.

It was not only in Beijing that city dwellers were expelled to the countryside. **Wen Duansu**, a seventy-six-year-old woman, died after being expelled to her native Bashitou Village in Tangquan Township, Ningxiang County, Hunan Province, from Hankou, Hubei Province, in August 1966 due to her 'landlord' status.

Wen Duansu was born to a wealthy and influential family and married a civil engineer. When her husband died of natural causes, Wen went to live with her son in Hankou. When the Red Guards expelled 'class enemies' from the cities in August 1966, Wen had to take a train, a bus and then walk more than forty kilometres to reach her native village. All of her children were working elsewhere and were also persecuted during the Cultural Revolution; her youngest son was jailed as a 'counter-revolutionary'. Wen's daughter came to visit her once and saw she was not only enduring great hardship living alone, but was also suffering constant physical abuse at the hands of the village's 'rebel faction'.

When the rebel faction in Bashitou Village began beating up 'landlords' in June 1968, they ordered another villager to string up Wen Duansu, and when he refused, they told the villager's son to do it. The son tied Wen Duansu's hands and hanged her from the eaves of her house. She died after she was taken down.

JIANGSU PROVINCE

Yang Zhenxing, a mathematics teacher at the Qingyang Centre Primary School in Qingyang Town in Jiangsu's Jiangyin County, leaped to his death after being struggled in 1966. He was in his forties.

Zhang Yun, vice-principal of the primary school at Yangzhou Wantou Commune in Jiangsu Province, drowned herself after beaten and imprisoned in a classroom in February 1967. Before she died, her seven-year-old son heard students talking about the experience of beating people with brass belt buckles.

SHAANXI PROVINCE – XI'AN

Shi Qingyun, principal of the Shaanxi Normal University Affiliated No. 1 Secondary School, killed himself after being beaten in August 1966.

Red Guards struggled Shi along with the vice-principal and head teacher, beating them with belts, iron rods and wooden sticks studded with nails detached from old chairs and tables, and then forcing them to crawl in circles around the school sports ground. The Red Guards stipulated that the person crawling slowest would be beaten, and Shi, being heavier than the other two, was beaten so harshly his entire body was bruised and the fabric of his shirt was embedded in the skin of his back. After this, Shi killed himself. He was the first principal in Xi'an to commit suicide after being beaten by Red Guards. The vice-principal and head teacher were also badly injured.

Bai Sulian, a language teacher at the Xi'an Bao'en Temple Street Primary School, was beaten to death by student Red Guards at her school in summer 1966.

Han Zhiying, principal of the No. 5 Secondary School and a member of the China Democratic League, was killed in August 1966. The school's Red Guards made Han stand on a stack of benches to be struggled, and although he didn't smoke, the Red Guards lit several cigarettes and stuck them in Han's ears, nostrils and lips. He ultimately died as a result of his torments.

Wang Leng, a thirty-six-year-old language teacher at the Xi'an No. 8 Secondary School, was beaten and tortured by Red Guards from the No. 37 Secondary School, where she used to teach, from 25 August onwards. She died on 2 September.

A former student of the No. 37 Secondary School told me Wang Leng's story when he learned I was carrying out research on the Cultural Revolution. He clearly remembered the details of how she was tormented, but he didn't remember the date, only that it was after the Red Guard movement emerged in August 1966. He remembered the names of the Red Guards who killed Wang Leng, and the official positions their parents held, but those names are outside the scope of this book. Other residents of Xi'an who weren't students or teachers at the school also provided some related material.

I asked another friend to go to the No. 37 Secondary School to look up the date of Wang's death in their files, but the school authorities refused access. Eventually, this friend located Wang Leng's daughter, who was thirteen when her mother was killed, and whose younger brother was eight years old. When her mother was mentioned, the daughter broke down in tears and declined to be interviewed. However, this friend helped me find some records from that time that allowed me to piece together the story that follows.

The Xi'an No. 37 Secondary School had more than 900 students and covered the first three years of secondary school, what would be called middle school in the United States. It was located in Xi'an's southern district, close to the CCP's Northwest China Bureau. Many of the students were the dependents of 'revolutionary cadres', and they became the main force among the Red Guards. In summer 1966, Red Guards from the school beat two teachers to death and injured nine other school staff, and one other person became deranged.

Wang Leng had taught for many years at the No. 37 Secondary School, but she was transferred to the No. 8 Secondary School in February 1966. On the morning of 25 August, two Red Guards escorted Wang Leng back to No. 37, where she was locked up in the school's jail for 'ox demons and snake spirits' and kicked and beaten. That afternoon, Wang was made to serve as a 'secondary target' in a struggle session against a teacher surnamed Zhang. Red Guards made her bend at the waist while holding two iron dumbbells. When Wang fainted an hour later, one of the Red Guards who'd escorted her from the No. 8 Secondary School began beating her with a wooden club.

Around 10:00 at night on 28 August, Wang Leng and another twenty or so 'ox demons and snake spirits' were taken to a 'dictatorship room' where Red Guards forced them to crawl over glass shards scattered under a circle of desks. After torturing her until dawn, the Red Guards tore out and shaved Wang's hair. She was then forced to engage in 'labour reform' for more than ten hours.

The beatings and interrogations continued on 30 August. Wang Leng was beaten for more than two hours in the morning and for another hour in the afternoon, and her eyes were badly injured. In her curriculum vitae, Wang had given her 'family background' as 'office worker'. The Red Guard forced her to confess to being from a 'capitalist and landlord' family.

After two days and nights of non-stop beatings and labour reform, a special struggle rally was held for Wang Leng on 31 August. She arrived in a dunce cap, carrying a placard stating she was a 'reactionary' with her hands tied behind her back. Two tables were place on the stage, with a bench on top of them. The Red Guards ordered Wang to stand on the bench with her head bowed and bent over at the waist, and then beat her with brooms while others yelled slogans at her.

Red Guards hung an iron dumbbell from Wang Leng's neck and then added another. They put another bench on top of the one Wang was standing on and ordered her to climb onto it. When she stood on the highest bench, they kicked it away. Then they told her to put the bench back and climb on top of it again and kicked it out from under her again. They did this several times until Wang passed out.

After Wang Leng lost consciousness, the Red Guards accused her of playing dead, and they picked her up and threw her down. Then they dragged her behind the canteen, where they beat her with iron bars and threw bricks at her and stomped on her while yelling, 'Son of a bitch, you still won't behave!' Wang Leng's back was broken, her skull was fractured, and blood ran from her eyes, ears and mouth. The Red Guards continued to kick Wang and dragged her head-down 400 metres to the classroom building, leaving a bloody trail behind her. In the building, they doused her with cold water.

Wang Leng died on 2 September. By that time, her head was swollen to the size of a winter melon. Her body was quickly cremated. The cremation certificate written out by the No. 37 Secondary School Red Guards stated:

> Wang Leng, thirty-six, was guilty of the most heinous crimes, popular indignation was enormous, and she was extremely unco-operative during the movement. During mass struggle on 31 August, Wang Leng refused to confess her crimes and made vicious remarks like, 'Chiang Kai-shek doesn't deserve to die.' Her obstinate resistance to the people outraged the masses, and sons and daughters of the Five Red Categories beat her unconscious at the scene. She was taken to the hospital, and when emergency measures were ineffective she died on 2 September. Opinion: Cremate, with the cremation fee to be paid by the family. ASAP.
>
> No. 37 Secondary School Red Guards (seal)

This certificate shows not only the Red Guard attitude to Wang Leng's death, but also the brutality of the overall atmosphere at the time.

A retired teacher named **Wang Bogong** who was beaten along with Wang Leng at the 31 August struggle rally died one day later. Formerly a language teacher at the No. 37 Secondary School, Wang was in his sixties and had retired the year before. A former student recalled hearing that he had graduated from the Whampoa Military Academy and had been an army political instructor and translator. After the War of Resistance against Japan ended, Wang had left the military and had become a teacher. The Red Guards accused him of being an 'old counter-revolutionary'.

After Wang Leng and Wang Bogong were killed, the school's Cultural Revolution Preparatory Committee chairman repeatedly warned the other 'ox demons and snake spirits' that 'If you don't behave, you'll end up like Wang Leng.'

At that time, the Cultural Revolution in Xi'an was led by the CCP's Northwest Bureau, along with the Shaanxi Provincial Party Committee and Xi'an Municipal Party Committee. They did nothing to stop the violence. The Party leader for Xi'an, Xu Bu, even directed that the 'experience' of the No. 37 Secondary School be written up in a report.

The Red Guards who enthusiastically took part in beating Wang Leng subsequently became members of the Red Terror Squad established in early September. Half a year later, as the Cultural Revolution developed and its targets expanded, the 'revolutionary cadres' who were the parents of these Red Guards were also struck down, and the Red Terror Squad was disbanded. The Party leader of Xi'an, Xu Bu, was eventually also struck down and killed himself. Zhang Xiao used this opportunity to expose how Red Guards had beaten his wife Wang Leng to death. Some students also spoke out about the injustice of Wang's death because she didn't have any 'problems'. But they didn't dare bring up Wang Bogong's death because he'd had 'historical problems' as a former Kuomintang army instructor. The common view then was that people who had 'problems' deserved to be beaten to death, or at least that it didn't matter.

In the 1990s, this secondary school had several class reunions, but no one apologised or expressed any regrets or qualms about the deaths of Wang Leng and Wang Bogong. A former student who is now a writer said that Wang was very strict with students and seemed very conceited, wearing a *qipao* and perming her hair to accentuate her attractiveness. There's a very misogynistic component in Chinese culture that's reflected in the killing of Wang Leng in the 1960s and in the lack of regret for her killing in the 1990s.

The trend of Red Guards murdering teachers started in Beijing and spread to other parts of China through the 'great networking'. The surge in killings in Xi'an occurred only a few days after the surge in Beijing following Mao's review of the Red Guards at Tiananmen Square, showing how effectively the leaders of the Cultural Revolution were able to promote these violent methods through modern communication and transportation.

One day in spring 1999, after finishing a class at Stanford University, I encountered four elderly Chinese visitors touring the campus, and they asked me to take a photo of them together in front of a flower bed. One husband and wife lived in the US, but the other couple came from Xi'an, and the wife was a retired secondary school teacher. As we struck up a conversation, I asked the teacher if she knew anything about the death of Wang Leng. She said yes, and told me that Wang's husband's name was Zhang Xiao. At that moment, her husband pulled her aside and whispered something to her, after which they quickly took their leave. Seeing them hurry off, I felt perplexed and sad. What were they afraid of? The aftereffects of Wang Leng's death, or of the Cultural Revolution, were still felt so clearly more than three decades later, and on the other side of the world.

Dang Qingfan, born in 1885, a native of Heyang County, Shaanxi Province, was vice-chairman of the Shaanxi Provincial Political Consultative Conference prior to the Cultural Revolution, and lived in Xi'an. From 30 August 1966 onwards, student Red Guards from the Shaanxi Normal University No. 2 Affiliated Secondary School repeatedly ransacked Dang's home, and ultimately beat him to death in his home on 4 September.

Dang Qingfan had passed the county-level imperial examination, but he abandoned the imperial civil service, cut off his queue and began studying at the China Public School run by former overseas students in Shanghai. He joined Sun Yat-sen's Alliance Society and was one of the first members of the Kuomintang, serving as secretary general of the Shaanxi Jingguo Army under commander-in-chief Yu Youren. After Yu Youren left Shaanxi in 1922, Dang Qingfan turned to academic research, focusing on pre-Qin thought and ancient script. During the War of Resistance against Japan, Dang encouraged KMT General Yang Hucheng to make contact with the Communist Party's Zhu De and Zhou Enlai. He published articles criticising the Kuomintang in 1940, and in 1948 he was received at the CCP base in northern Shaanxi by Wang Zhen, one of Chinese Communism's Eight Elders. After the CCP took power in 1949, Dang became a professor at Northwest University as well as vice-minister of education for the Northwest China Military and Administrative Commission that controlled the region at that time. In 1955, Dang was appointed vice-chairman of the Shaanxi Provincial Political Consultative Conference. This was a high-ranking position, but with no real power, and Dang, by then seventy years old, spent most of his time at home.

After the Cultural Revolution began, the secretary general of the Provincial Political Consultative Conference and head of the United Front Department began frequently visiting Dang in his home and asking his views on the Cultural Revolution in a rather strained atmosphere. In early August 1966, Dang was summoned to a meeting at the Provincial Political Consultative Conference, but it turned out to be a 'struggle session' with speeches and big-character posters. Another member of the Consultative Conference, Ru Yuli, who had served as a sernior official under the Nationalist government, was struggled along with Dang. Dang was accused of being an 'anti-Party, anti-socialist element' and was stripped of privileges such as access to a car.

The decision to struggle Dang Qingfan came from the Shaanxi Provincial Party Committee. At this stage, Consultative Conference cadres berated Dang and put big-character posters up on his home, but he wasn't subjected to beating or ransacking. But as the Cultural Revolution continued to develop, beating and ransacking was delegated to young Red Guards, and less than two weeks after Mao's 18 August rally, Red Guards spent serveral days ransacking Dang Qingfan's home. A widower, Dang lived in his own stand-alone quadrangle compound with his youngest son and an elderly housekeeper; his eldest son's family lived in the same compound. Dang Qingfan was locked up in a single room and prohibited from seeing or talking with his family, who could hear him being physically and verbally abused.

The Red Guards who came to Dang's home were students from the Shaanxi Normal University No. 2 Affiliated Secondary School. Many of its students were the children of senior cadres in the CCP's Northwest Bureau and Shaanxi Provincial Party Committee and were particularly brutal in the violence they inflicted on teachers and schoolmates. The geography teacher was a Uyghur woman, and as well as shaving half her hair off, they forced her to drink a mixture of lard and fluid from a spittoon. Then they made her stand on a stack of tables to be struggled, after which they pushed over the tables and sent her tumbling to the ground. A student who was the daughter of a professor was pushed down four flights of stairs. The Red Guards also engaged in violence outside the school, and dozens of them came to ransack Dang Qingfan's home.

Every item in Dang's home was carefully examined. On 3 September, the day before Dang was beaten to death, several trucks came to his home and took away all his books, paintings and furnishings. Dang Qingfan had collected some ancient books, including a valuable woodblock edition of *History of the Southern Dynasties*. He had also collected Shang dynasty bronze rubbings, oracle-bone inscriptions and the like. People who resembled cadres assisted in the ransacking. (After the Cultural Revolution, an exhibition at the Shaanxi Provincial Library displayed Dang's copy of the *History of the Southern Dynasties*, claiming that the book had been 'donated'.)

At noon on 4 September, three Red Guards from the school, including two girls who had taken part in the ransacking, came again to Dang Qingfan's home and entered his bedroom. His family didn't dare stop them for fear of inciting even greater violence. About fifteen minutes later, the three Red Guards left in a hurry. When Dang's family entered his bedroom, they found him lying in bed, his head covered with blood and his face deathly pale, breathing his last. The wall was stained with blood more than a metre above his bed, and blood stained a heavy camphor wood brush pot that had been left in the room. His family believed that Dang was struck in the head with this brush pot, but whether or not other weapons were used is known only to those who were present at the time. Although his family saw that Dang was near death, they didn't dare call for help and didn't know what else to do.

About ten minutes after the first group of Red Guards left, another group arrived from the Affiliated Secondary School. They went straight to Dang Qingfan's room, but when they saw he was dying, they left. One of them was Linghu Jingping, a Red Guard leader whose father was the director of the Northwestern Electrical Power Management Bureau. Linghu Jingping didn't take part in killing Dang Qingfan, but he was an eyewitness.

Dang Qingfan died soon afterwards. That night, two cadres from the Provincial Political Consultative Conference, Zheng Dianhui and He Gang, came to inspect the murder scene and make a record; they told Dang's family not to tell anyone what had happened. In the middle of the night, crematorium staff came to take the body away, clearly under instructions from the Provincial Political Consultative Conference.

The day after Dang Qingfan's death, on 5 September 1966, his youngest and eldest sons, along with his eldest son's wife and children and his elderly housekeeper, were all 'repatriated' to their native villages in a process similar to that carried out in Beijing. Dang's family had no choice but to leave without a fuss, and they lived in poverty in Dang's native Heyang County. In the space of a few days from late August to early September, Dang Qingfan had gone from vice-chairman of the Provincial Political Consultative Conference to victim of the Cultural Revolution, and his family had been expelled to the countryside, the destruction of this household as thorough as it was expeditious under the concerted action of the Red Guards and the government.

Some of the Red Guards who had persecuted Dang joined the Red Terror Squad that was established in Xi'an in September. But once the Cultural Revolution's leaders in Beijing began targeting provincial authorities and propping up the so-called rebel faction, these early Red Guard leaders quickly fell from power. Some of them engaged in conflict with the rebel faction, causing the Central Cultural Revolution Small Group to abandon and even suppress them. Even so, the Red Guards' violent acts in summer 1966 were never truly negated. When the Red Terror Squad and the rebel faction began fighting with each other, the rebel faction at Jiaotong University went to talk with Dang Qingfan's family with the intention of collecting evidence to use as negative propaganda against the so-called Royalists (those who defended the former Provincial Party Committee). But after contacting Dang's family, the rebel faction quickly changed its mind, because Dang was still designated an 'anti-Party, anti-socialist element' and in their eyes killing such a person didn't constitute a crime or error worth investigating against their opponents.

In 1967, Dang Qingfan's son made his way to Beijing and submitted a petition to the Central Cultural Revolution Small Group's 'masses petitioning reception centre'. He wanted to change his family's circumstances and hoped the leaders in Beijing would regard his father's case with sympathy. At that time, the Small Group was in control of the Cultural Revolution, and Mao's wife, Jiang Qing, was its first vice-chairman. Cadres at the reception centre told Dang's son that the case could not be 'definitively handled' until a later stage of the campaign.

After Lin Biao died while attempting to flee China in September 1971, the Cultural Revolution's leaders began to relax their policies towards old cadres who had suffered severe persecution, and the Shaanxi Provincial

Political Consultative Conference delivered the following 'verdict' regarding Dang Qingfan: 'A contradiction between the enemy and us to be handled as a contradiction among the people.' Dang's family was allowed to return to Xi'an, but their home was already occupied by others. They were allowed one small room in the compound the family had previously owned.

Eventually the Provincial Party Committee's United Front Department resumed operations, and given Dang Qingfan's previous high ranking in the province, several united front cadres began investigating his death. They concluded that too much time had passed to clearly ascertain what had happened, but in any case it was blamed on Lin Biao, who by then was considered a traitor and the leader of an anti-Party clique.

After Mao died, and the Gang of Four were arrested, the Shaanxi Provincial Party Committee rehabilitated Dang Qingfan in 1977 and carried out a ceremony to 'lay his ashes to rest' (although like most victims of the Cultural Revolution, his ashes hadn't been retained). The Provincial Party Committee handed the case over to the provincial Public Security Bureau, but the PSB was likewise unable to get to the bottom of Dang's death.

In the 1980s, the Beijing Municipal Party Committee sent two cadres to talk to Dang's family and carry out an investigation. The reason was that the Shaanxi Provincial Political Consultative Conference 'cadre vetting office' had written a letter to the Municipal Party Committee saying that one of the cadres working for the Committee, Wang Shen, had killed Dang Qingfan during the Cultural Revolution. Wang Shen had been a student Red Guard at the Shaanxi Normal College No. 2 Affiliated Secondary School and a mainstay of the Red Terror Team. His father, Wang Lin, was secretary of the CCP's Northwest Bureau secretariat at the time. The purpose of the investigation was to determine whether this cadre could be promoted instead of being prosecuted or punished. Dang's family never knew whether Wang Shen's career was ultimately affected.

By the time Dang Qingfan was killed, he was an old man of eighty-one. It takes a special kind of brutality to beat such an elderly person to death, and he wasn't killed when a mob got out of hand or by accident; he was simply murdered. Dang's family has always hoped to talk with the Red Guards who killed him and hear some form of repentance or apology. How much longer must they wait?

A former student of Dang Qingfan's, **Yuan Xuanzhao**, was another victim of the Cultural Revolution in Xi'an. A teacher at Xi'an's No. 5 Secondary School, Yuan was locked up in the school and beaten and humiliated. A student killed a sparrow with a slingshot and then forced Yuan to eat the entire bird. Another student forced him to eat a box of shoe polish. He tried to escape but was captured and tortured even more. Finally he killed himself.

SICHUAN PROVINCE

Ding Yuying, principal of the Kaixuan Road Primary School in Chongqing's central district, killed herself during the Spring Festival in 1967. She had been struggled by her school's 'revolutionary rebel faction' and was ordered to return to the school on the first day of the Lunar New Year, 9 February, to continue receiving criticism. As she was on her way to the school that day and crossed the Jialing River Bridge, she jumped into the river and drowned herself.

Li Shunying, principal of the South Shore School for Dependents of Employees of the Changjiang Shipping Division in Chongqing, was repeatedly denounced and forced to haul heavy rocks. The 'revolutionary rebel faction' felt she was too slow and shoved her, causing injuries to her back and legs. She became semi-paralysed and died in summer 1968.

TIANJIN

Yao Fude, a worker at the Jinzhong Bridge Primary School in Tianjin's Hongqiao District, drowned himself in the Ziya River behind the school after students repeatedly beat him in late August 1966.

An eyewitness said that the Ziya River had very high banks and was quite shallow, and Yao had to jump a good ten feet to reach the water. He dove head-first, and his head became stuck in the sediment at the bottom of the river, leaving his legs protruding from the water. Many people along the river bank saw him die.

As in Beijing, a great deal of violence occurred in Tianjin in Red August 1966, with some people being beaten to death and others driven to suicide. Tianjin is located along the Haihe River and its tributaries, so drowning became a common means of committing suicide. The place where Yao Fude died was only about 100 metres from where the Ziya River flowed into the Haihe River.

A teacher from the Jinzhong Bridge Primary School said people at the school noticed that Yao Fude was missing half a finger, and during the Cultural Revolution he was 'exposed' as having lost it to frostbite while a soldier in the Nationalist Army. The teacher wasn't sure if that was true or if it was just an excuse the students gave for beating him. She was also not sure how old he was when he died, or if he left family behind. All she knew was that eventually a nephew of Yao Fude's came to the school to negotiate over his death.

The Jinzhong Bridge Primary School was eventually abolished, and the Santiaoshi Secondary School took over the address.

Yang Jingyun, a female language teacher at the Tianjin Xinhua Secondary School, suffered a cerebral haemorrhage and died while being struggled in summer 1966. A female English teacher surnamed Gu was scalded to death around the same time when Red Guards poured boiling water on her head.

The Xinhua Secondary School, located on Machang Road, had been the church-run Shenggong Girls' School before 1949.

A woman surnamed Sun, a nurse and the wife of Fan Quan, the director of the Tianjin Children's Hospital, was beaten to death by Red Guards in late August 1966 at the couple's home at the intersection of Changde Road and Guilin Road.

Fan Quan graduated from Beijing's Xiehe Medical School. In 1965, he was sent to Ji County to work with a 'rural medical team' but after the Cultural Revolution began, he was sent back to the Children's Hospital to undergo struggle. Red Guards ransacked his home in late August 1966 and made a bonfire of his books. His wife was forced to kneel next to the bonfire, and her face was burned. The Red Guards also forced her to eat excrement wrapped in bread. Her neighbours saw her being tortured.

Fan Quan was told to return home and found his wife's body hanging from a doorframe. One of her arms had clearly been broken, and it seemed unlikely that a person with a broken arm could have hanged herself. Fan Quan only saw her from the back, as when he moved forward to look at her face, Red Guards knocked him out. By the time he regained consciousness, the corpse had been removed.

Sun and Fan had three sons. The elder two had studied engineering and graduated from Tsinghua University; the third had graduated from Tianjin Medical School and worked at a hospital. When the Cultural Revolution first began, the third son wrote a big-character poster about his father to prove his loyalty to the revolution. Later when he realised the horror of the Cultural Revolution, he attempted to kill himself by jumping from a window, but survived.

YUNNAN PROVINCE – KUNMING

Ye Zudong, a language teacher at the Kunming Normal College Affiliated Primary School, died of a cerebral haemorrhage while being struggled in late autumn 1966.

Xu Xingqing, head teacher at the same school, hanged herself in a classroom after being denounced around the same time.

Zhang Shouying, a teacher at the primary school of the Lancang Lahu Ethnic Minority Autonomous County in Yunnan Province, was beaten to death during a struggle rally in 1967. Apart from being attacked as a teacher, she also came from a 'bad family background' (her father having been a landlord in Mojiang County). The Lancang Lahu Ethnic Minority Autonomous County was located in the border area, and had only enough primary-aged pupils for a single school. During the Cultural Revolution, 20% to 30% of the county's teachers were 'ferreted out' and brutally struggled as 'ox demons and snake spirits'. Some were also accused of being 'reactionary academic authorities'.

ZHEJIANG PROVINCE

Feng Shikang, a language teacher at the No. 2 Lower Secondary School in Shaoxing, was repeatedly subjected to brutal struggle and denunciation in summer 1966. Apart from the usual humiliation and physical torment, a student picked up a wooden stool and smashed it against Feng's head, knocking him to the floor. Feng drowned himself in a river the next day. After his death, his son was called to the school and told, 'Your father resisted the Cultural Revolution, and even death cannot expiate his crimes.'

A former student of Feng's described him as a short man around fifty years old. He was usually very nice to his students and was a good teacher. The student said he didn't take part in beating Feng, but he was unable to avoid attending the struggle rally, and he shouted some slogans.

The Xiaoxing No. 2 Lower Secondary School was originally called Chengtian Secondary School, and was located near the former home of Qiu Jin, a female revolutionary executed by the Manchus in 1907.

The principal of the school at the time the Cultural Revolution began, Zhang Chengye, was beaten until he vomited blood. A language teacher named **Qu Fuzi** became deranged as soon as the Cultural Revolution began. The Red Guards punished him by making him sweep the floor, and he would sing as he swept. Knowing very well that Qu was mentally ill, the Red Guards still struggled him and accused him of defaming Jiang Qing. He died not long afterwards.

PART THREE

Other Killings Early in the Cultural Revolution

CULTURAL FIGURES

LITERATURE AND JOURNALISM

Like academics and educators, journalists, artists, writers and publishers were all major targets during the Cultural Revolution. In April 1966, the CCP Central Committee issued its 'Summary of the Army Literary Work Seminar Entrusted by Lin Biao to Comrade Jiang Qing', which explicitly stated that the literary and arts circles 'were imposing dictatorship over us through an anti-Party, anti-socialist revisionist line antagonistic to Chairman Mao's thought'. According to this theory, literary and artistic work units had become 'anti-Party, anti-socialist revisionists', and the Cultural Revolution's leaders sent military representatives to manage them, control them, and lead the Cultural Revolution in them. Although these places didn't have student Red Guards berating and beating people to death like the schools did, there were still acts of savage violence.

In the 16 May Circular that the CCP Central Committee issued to launch the Cultural Revolution in 1966, Mao personally wrote the following passage:

> Raise high the great banner of proletarian cultural revolution and thoroughly criticise academics, educators, journalists, writers, artists and publishers as representatives of the bourgeoisie, stripping them of their political power in the cultural realm. In order to do this, it is necessary to at the same time criticise bourgeois representatives

who have infiltrated the Party, the government, the military and the cultural realm, purging them and in some cases removing them from their positions.

Mao not only personally designated a list of 'bourgeois representatives', but also instructed provincial-level organs to create similar lists. Anyone whose name was on the list could have their every action construed as a crime. The ranks of writers had already been purged on a massive scale in 1957, and once the Cultural Revolution began, all but a tiny minority of those remaining came under attack.

Wu Han, born in 1909, was a prominent scholar of history who had also served as vice-mayor of Beijing in the early years of the PRC. The Cultural Revolution began with criticism of Wu's historical play *Hai Rui Dismissed from Office* as an anti-Mao allegory. In summer 1966, Red Guards ransacked Wu's home and then tied him to a tree and beat him with brass belt buckles. He was denounced at struggle rallies more than 100 times and formally arrested in March 1968. He died in prison on 11 October 1969. His wife, **Yuan Zhen**, was also subjected to long-term persecution, and died on 18 March 1969. Their adopted daughter, **Wu Xiaoyan**, became mentally ill in 1973 and was imprisoned in autumn 1975 during the campaign to 'beat back the Right-deviating verdict-reversal wind'. She killed herself in a psychiatric hospital on 23 September 1979 at the age of twenty-one. Wu Han was rehabilitated in 1979.

An interviewee said that in 1968, the Beijing Municipal Party Committee Party School had a 'No. 2 Study Class' especially for persecuting people. Wu Han was struggled at rallies there, and whenever the canteen was open for meals, he had to stand on a table in the doorway for 'public exposure'.

In the 1990s, Tsinghua University built a memorial pavilion in tribute to Wu Han's academic distinction and outstanding character. In comparison, no mention has been made of the nearly fifty people who died on the Tsinghua campus.

In private conversation, some people comment that in the series of campaigns targeting intellectuals starting in the 1950s, especially the 1957 Anti-Rightist Campaign, Wu Han played the role of attacker, and as a result enjoyed a high social standing until he himself came under attack in the Cultural Revolution.

Some say Wu Han 'got what he deserved' because he had persecuted others and had carried out the principles of persecution that were ultimately turned against him and his family members.

To be a victim of the Cultural Revolution is completely different from being a saint or a hero. Pointing out the role that some victims played in creating this disaster is unavoidable in examining historical truth and how things developed.

Lao She (the pen name of Shu Sheyu), born in 1899, was a famous writer who served as chairman of the Beijing Writers' Association and vice-chairman of the Chinese Writers' Association. On 23 August 1966, Red Guards escorted Lao She and twenty-eight others to Beijing's Confucian temple, where they were beaten and humiliated for three hours while kneeling before a bonfire of Peking Opera costumes and stage props. On the night of 24 August, Lao She drowned himself in Taiping Lake in Beijing's Xicheng District.

Understanding Lao She's death requires understanding what kind of action this violent struggle was, and why it became so pervasive in the summer of 1966.

One of the other victims was the writer Xiao Jun, and *Xiao Jun Commemorative Essays*[1] lists the names of others as well: Luo Binji, Xun Huisheng, Bai Yunsheng, Hou Xirui, Gu Senbo, Fang Hua, Hao Cheng, Chen Tiange, Wang Chengke, Zhao Dingxin, Zhang Menggeng, Zeng Bairong, Su Xinqun, Li Ming, Zhang Guochu, Shang Baiwei, Jin Ziguang, Wang Songsheng, Zhang Zengnian, Song Haibo, Zhang Zhi, Zhang Jichun, Duanmu Hongliang, Tian Lan and Jiang Feng. All of these people were writers, artists and cadres with the Beijing Municipal Cultural Bureau and the Federation of Writers and Artists. Xun Huisheng was a famous Peking Opera performer, while Xiao Jun, Luo Binji and Duanmu Hongliang were veteran writers, and Zhao Dingxin was the director of the Cultural Bureau.

The reason the Red Guards beat these people was first of all because back in April 1966, the CCP Central Committee had explicitly stated that the cultural community was 'imposing dictatorship on us through an anti-Party anti-socialist revisionist line antithetical to Chairman Mao's thought', and that these people were to be eliminated. Military representatives were sent to each cultural work unit to lead the Revolution there.

Under the system of that time, writers' associations had a group of 'full-time writers' drawing regular salaries. Not all writers were denounced and struggled. In the Beijing Writers' Association, chairman Lao She 'stepped aside' and the leaders of the newly established Cultural Revolution Committee included writer Hao Ran as well as military representatives. Hao Ran's novel about the rural co-operative movement, *The Golden Road*, became a prototype for 'giving prominence to class struggle' and 'portraying lofty and perfect proletarian heroes'. Although Lao She also endorsed communism and socialism, his works were very different from Hao Ran's. Many writers were criticised and attacked

---

[1] Shenyang chenfeng wenyi chubanshe, 1990, p. 800.

during the Cultural Revolution, but different writers were penalised to different degrees. The difference between who was rewarded and who was punished clearly showed the orientation of the Cultural Revolution in the literary sphere.

In 1980, I spoke twice with the elderly writer Xiao Jun, who was harshly beaten like Lao She, and listened to his recollections of what happened back then.

Before the Red Guard movement began, some literary workers were 'ferreted out' and denounced during meetings in their work units. Xiao Jun was once ordered to stand at a rally, but writers were only verbally abused, and no one beat them.

The violent attacks they subsequently experienced were a direct result of the rise of the Red Guard movement, especially following Mao's prominent support of it in August 1966. As Red Guard attacks spread from the schools to the community at large, they were even more energetically supported by China's top officials. That is why Red Guards from Peking University and the Beijing No. 8 Girls' Secondary School were able to charge into the Cultural Bureau and Cultural Federation organs and inflict violence on the 'ox demons and snake spirits' there. Several girl Red Guards lashed at Xiao Jun with brass-buckled belts, cut off his hair and hung placards around his neck stating 'Reactionary writer Xiao Jun' and 'Counter-revolutionary Xiao Jun' with his name X'd out in red.

At three o'clock in the afternoon on 23 August, under the broiling sun, the twenty-nine targets were called out one by one and had placards hung around their necks stating their names and crimes, after which they lined up in the courtyard. At four o'clock, they were loaded into a truck and driven to the courtyard of the Temple of Confucius at the Imperial College in Dongcheng District. This was once the highest institute of learning in imperial times, but had since become the Capital Library. The Red Guards built a bonfire in the courtyard and began burning Peking Opera costumes, book and so on, the flames raging as they thunderously shouted, 'Down with the counter-revolutionary reactionary gang!', 'Down with anti-Party element XXX!', 'If XXX doesn't surrender, let him be destroyed!', 'Whoever opposes Chairman Mao will have his dog's head smashed!' and 'We pledge our lives to protecting Chairman Mao and the Party Central Committee!'

The victims were forced to form a circle around the bonfire and kneel with their heads touching the ground as hundreds of Red Guards stood behind them. Some Red Guards brought over stage prop swords, rifles and mallets and began randomly beating them, while others whipped them with belts. Sandwiched between the bonfire and the Red Guards, the victims had no way to escape.

Xiao Jun said he felt infuriated while being beaten in front of the bonfire. In his youth he had studied at a military academy and was trained in martial arts, and he thought that if he resisted and used his skills, he could overcome at least a dozen people. But he saw Lao She kneeling beside him, his face pale and blood running from his head, and he realised that if he fought back, he would be hopelessly outnumbered and ultimately beaten to death, and the others along with him. So he suppressed his impulse to resist and endured being viciously beaten for more than three hours.

The victims were then dragged into the truck and taken back to the Cultural Bureau. Xiao Jun was locked in a closet next to the reception office and made to stand without being given anything to eat or drink, and he finally passed out. When he didn't come home, his children went to the Cultural Bureau to look for him, only to be beaten themselves. Xiao Jun was held for more than a month before finally being allowed to return home at the end of September. His son, Xiao Ming, lost consciousness after being beaten, and, mistaken for dead, he was loaded into a truck and sent to the crematorium. Fortunately he revived on the way and was not incinerated.

Xiao Jun had eleven family members, old and young, depending on him. He had been repeatedly denounced since the 1940s and earned only 110 *yuan* per month. There was never enough to eat at home, since all they could afford was fifty cents' worth of pork along with cabbage. If he died, how would his family manage? No matter what, he had to endure his persecution and survive. He felt Lao She was different from him; having always been relatively 'obedient', he'd escaped persecution in previous political movements and maintained a prominent social status, so he might not have been mentally prepared for this brutal treatment. Furthermore, Lao She was older and lame. The ability to endure the torments inflicted by the Red Guards was closely related to a person's physical strength.

After being beaten at the Temple of Confucius, Lao She was taken back to his work unit and beaten some more. The writer Yang Mo, who was present at the time, recalled the events of 23 August in his journal three months later:

> On the stairway in front of the Federation of Cultural Circles, several girl students closed in on him and questioned him, occasionally striking him a couple of times with their belts. We were forced to stand in a circle and watch. I didn't dare walk away but stood there on the side, my heart burning. One of our writers stepped forward and indignantly criticised Lao She for taking American money.[2]

---

[2] *The Journals of Yang Mo*, Vol. 2, p. 5, Beijing shiyue wenyi chubanshe, 1994.

That night, Lao She was taken to the Public Security Bureau and wasn't allowed to return home until very late. He was ordered to report to the Federation the next day to be criticised and struggled, but after leaving home the next morning, he failed to appear. Red Guards went to his home searching for him with their belts ready. Early the next morning, 25 August, Lao She's body was found floating in Xicheng District's Taiping Lake.

After the Cultural Revolution, in June 1978, when Lao She's remains were laid to rest, a news report stated that his urn contained his fountain pen and his glasses but didn't mention the absence of his ashes. In 1994, I had an opportunity to meet Lao She's son, Shu Yi, and I asked why the urn contained only his pen and glasses. He replied that, as in other cases, Lao She's ashes hadn't been retained by the crematorium. Shu Yi was thirty-one years old when his father died, and when he went to the crematorium to deal with the remains, he brought a letter of introduction from the Beijing Federation of Cultural Circles stating that Shu Sheyu (Lao She's real name) had 'separated himself from the people'. Two young women handled the paperwork. The younger one with her hair in braids said that the higher-ups had stipulated that remains would not be retained in such cases. I asked the nature of this stipulation, and on what authority it had been issued. Shu Yi said he didn't know, but only recalled the girl in braids saying it.

Shu Yi also told me that the crematorium employee with braided hair told him that Lao She was the first such high-level cadre whose remains had been discarded in this way. Apart from his position in the Writers' Association, Lao She also held a senior position in the CPPCC, as Shu Yi noted in his essay 'Father's Last Two Days'.[3] Before being publicly denounced, Lao She had a car and driver that took him to and from work, which indicates that his status and ranking were very high. For a high-ranking cadre to have his ashes discarded must have been the result of high-level instructions if there was no written stipulation to that effect.

One explanation put forward is that retaining the ashes was technically impossible given the immense number of dead bodies being processed in Red August.

These technical difficulties were clearly not the main reason, however. The stipulation that the remains of these victims could not be kept was intended as a posthumous insult. According to the logic of the Cultural Revolution authorities, if the victims could be so brutally stripped of

---

[3] See Shu Yi, *The Death of Lao She*, Beijing, Guoji wenhua chubanshe, 1987, p. 62.

their lives, their remains could naturally be subjected to further relentless attack. Their limitless power extended even to the crematorium, and the persecution of the Cultural Revolution continued even to the treatment of the victim's ashes.

Lao She drowned himself following the intolerable physical torments he'd suffered and facing the prospect of further torture and humiliation. He left no suicide note and ended his life in silence.

Why didn't Lao She write a suicide note? Could he have been happy to go to his death, or did he feel so inadequate and dejected that he preferred to die without a word? He had been a writer all his life, with a sharp and prolific pen. Expressing his opinion through his writings had been his profession. He'd kept a journal every day of his life. When he left home on the morning of 24 August, he was carrying a pen and paper. Someone saw him sitting along the lake all day before he drowned himself. That is to say, he had the time as well as the necessary materials to write a suicide note, and he was fully capable of expressing his disappointment, anger and protest. Yet he didn't write a single word before he killed himself. Was it because he'd reached a spiritual impasse? Ending one's own life is the greatest violence a person can commit, but for Lao She to die without writing a suicide note suggests that using words to express himself had become even more difficult than dying in that horrifying August of 1966.

After the Cultural Revolution ended, Lao She was rehabilitated and given a ceremonious send-off by the authorities. His friends and family members published a batch of articles commemorating him, but none of them mentioned any comments he'd made about his brutal treatment or about colleagues or others he knew who'd been persecuted to death. There might have been two reasons for this: Lao She never said anything suitable for publication, or the people writing these essays didn't feel they should set out his actual views.

The writer Ba Jin was an old friend of Lao She's. In his essay 'In Memory of Comrade Lao She', he wrote that he saw Lao She at the Great Hall of the People on 10 July 1966. At that time, Beijing historian and writer Wu Han and others were being viciously attacked in the newspapers, and Wu Han had been beaten and humiliated by students who had burst into his home. Classes had been suspended for more than a month, and Beijing's students had been struggling large numbers of educators on school campuses. At that time, being able to enter the Great Hall of the People was a sign of personal and political status. Ba Jin wrote, 'I had been in Beijing for more than a month attending an emergency meeting of African and Asian writers, and constantly heard people mentioning Lao She's name. I guessed that something would happen to him and was very worried for him. Now, sitting next to him, I heard him say, "Please tell all our friends that I have no problems," and I was extremely happy.'[4]

In his essay 'Father's Last Two Days', Shu Yi wrote that after Lao She was struggled on 23 August, he came home late at night and told his wife, 'The people understand me! The Party and Chairman Mao understand me! The Premier [Zhou Enlai] understands me even more.'[5] Are we to infer from what Ba Jin and Shu Yi wrote that having seen a large number of people severely persecuted in July and August 1966, having seen Mao and Zhou enthusiastically support the Red Guards, having seen the devastating violence inflicted on others and himself, all that Lao She seemed to care about was that he had 'no problems' and that Mao and Zhou 'understood' him? Was his anxiety limited to this and nothing else after being subjected to physical brutality and having his spirit ground to a pulp under the vast millstone of the Cultural Revolution? Had he completely accepted the methods and thinking of the Revolution, and was only able to plead his innocence within that framework?

After Lao She was rehabilitated, a book entitled *Lao She's Writing Career* was published.[6] Its synopsis states, 'This book consists of Mr Lao She's autobiographical writings, including essays he wrote about his own life and works... This book can be read as an autobiography and also as valuable material in studying Lao She.' This book includes an essay entitled 'The New Society is a University', originally published in *People's Literature* on 1 October 1951. The following are some extracts (from pages 247–249):

> Over the past year, every day and every hour something occurs in society that draws my excitement and acclaim: Which should I mention?
>
> I've finally resolved that I cannot keep failing to make up my mind! I'll write about the rally the day before yesterday at the Temple of Heaven to denounce local despots. The venue was the cypress grove in the Temple of Heaven. I arrived quite early, but the grove was already packed with people.
>
> The rally began. From the stage was proclaimed the purpose of the rally and the crimes of the local despots. Below the stage, at the appropriate moment, one group after another, in front, in back and at either side, shouted, 'Down with the local despots!' and 'Support the people's

---

[4] This essay is included in Ba Jin's essay collection *Explorations*; see *The Complete Works of Ba Jin*, Vol. 16, p. 156, Beijing, Renmin wenxue chubanshe, 1991.
[5] *The Death of Lao She*, op. cit., p. 61.
[6] Published by Tianjin baihua wenyi chubanshe, 1981.

government!', after which the whole gathering joined in, their voices like an ocean tide. The voice of the people is the power of the people, and this power was enough to make a villain tremble.

The local despots were brought onto the stage. Beneath the stage, fists and fingers stretched toward the enemies like so many daggers. The local despots, ferocious despots, didn't dare raise their heads. They knelt down. The dynasty of local despots has passed, and the people have taken over.

Old and young, male and female took to the stage and accused them. When the accusations became most distressing, many people below the stage yelled, 'Beat them!' I and the intellectuals beside me also automatically yelled this. 'Beat them! Why aren't you beating them!' Security guards blocked people from going over to beat the local despots, while my lips and those of hundreds of others shouted, 'They should be beaten!'

Shouting this made me into another person!

I've always been a very gentle person. True, I hate local despots and villains, but if they hadn't been on the stage being accused, how would I have yelled out, 'Beat them! Beat them!'? The people's wrath agitated me, and I became part of everyone. Their hatred was also my hatred. I could not and should not 'look on unconcerned from the sideline.' The power and righteous indignation of the masses infected me and taught me to no longer be gentle and timid. In truth, what is the value of being gentle? Hating the enemy and loving one's country is the only valuable and sublime feeling.

This was not merely denouncing a few local despots; we were all learning something. This told the people who had been browbeaten by local despots: Act boldly and confidently, report local despots, denounce local despots, don't be afraid of them any more! With Chairman Mao deciding for us, what have we to fear? Reporting on local despots is not only avenging oneself but also ridding society of evil. This tells me and gentle people like me: Be strong, cast off your sentimentality and refinement, cast it far away; extend your fist, open your eyes, stand with the great masses, confronting and fighting local despots! Local despots are not superhuman, but are quivering fellows kneeling before us. Local despots haven't just browbeaten a few individuals unrelated to us; they are the enemies of society!

An honest old fried cake vendor denounced a local despot for eating his cakes without paying for thirty years!...

It's hard not to feel shocked after reading this essay. First of all, the denunciation rally and the struggle methods he describes are exactly what Lao

She himself experienced fifteen years later at the Temple of Confucius. The two gatherings took the same form: both were mass rallies where the crimes of the targets had been decided in advance. After the meetings, the shouting of slogans stirred up emotion, and the 'exposure and accusation' didn't allow the targets to explain or defend themselves, and didn't allow an evaluation by legal standards, but just whipped up hatred. Then at the climaxes, those attending yelled, 'They should be beaten,' and violence was inflicted on the targets.

The denunciation rally that Lao She wrote about was similar not only in form but also in detail to the one he was subjected to. At the 1951 rally, the one specific crime Lao mentioned was that one of the targets had eaten a vendor's fried cakes for thirty years without paying. This should have been taken to the courts, but in the atmosphere of the denunciation rally, only one side was heard, with no one asking the details or talking about legal criteria, and violence was inflicted on the target as people shouted 'Beat him!' yet Lao She felt that was justified and wasn't disturbed at all. When Lao She was struggled, his accusers said he'd 'taken American money'. They probably referred to his accepting a US State Department invitation to visit in 1946 and being provided with travel expenses. Lao She had written articles about this trip; it was no secret, and the nature of it was clear. But in the process of the struggle described by Yang Mo, it was enough to subject Lao She to beatings by Red Guards. Furthermore, as chairman of the Beijing Writers' Association, he could be accused of being a 'local despot in literary circles'.

Lao She's essay describes the step-by-step process that led a 'gentle' person to finally shout for someone to be beaten, which helps us to understand the psychological mechanism of this kind of struggle rally. What Lao She experienced years earlier was probably what the Red Guards experienced while beating him fifteen years later. His autobiographical account shows us how a group mentality can whip up hatred and rationalise violent actions. This method is very effective, and that is clearly why the struggle rallies of the Cultural Revolution employed the same method.

Of course, the saddest thing is that when Lao She wrote about the struggle rally in 1951, he was full of enthusiasm and didn't consider it further. He was applauding this new way of life, an important part of the new social system. This kind of struggle rally subsequently developed in practice and in theory, and in the Cultural Revolution it became deeper and more wide-ranging. In the ten years of the Cultural Revolution, almost every individual either struggled others or was struggled themselves. These struggle rallies were a horrible invention that violated legal procedures and stirred up irrationality, encouraging violent abuse.

It cannot be said that Lao She was responsible for these thousands of struggle sessions; at the end of the day, he was a victim. But he had at one point accepted, affirmed and extolled the mechanism that ultimately killed him.

After reading this essay of Lao She's, as an ordinary reader, I would rather assume that on the day Lao She sat beside the lake before drowning himself, what he was thinking about was not merely whether he 'had a problem' or whether the highest authorities 'understood' him, but also about other things such as the responsibility he bore for praising this kind of struggle method, which in the intervening fifteen years had affected not only strangers, but even his colleagues and acquaintances, and ultimately himself as well.

Yang Shuo, chairman of the Foreign Literature Committee of the Chinese Writers' Association, killed himself with an overdose of sleeping pills after being denounced at a struggle rally in his work unit on 3 August 1968.

Born in 1913, Yang Shuo was one of China's most famous authors, his essays reprinted in secondary school literary textbooks and memorised by students throughout China, except during the Cultural Revolution.

Yang Shuo was one of the many victims rehabilitated after the Cultural Revolution ended. For a time around 1980, the stories of senior cadres and notables appeared in newspapers, with the length of the article proportionate to their importance. The short news item about Yang Shuo's posthumous rehabilitation stated that he had been 'persecuted to death', a common phrase at that time for people who had committed suicide while being struggled.

The *China Encyclopedia* published after the Cultural Revolution includes an entry of around 1,000 words on Yang Shuo describing his life and works, but doesn't mention how he died, or the events leading up to it. The book's entries on other victims who committed suicide, such as archaeologist **Chen Mengjia**, also leave out such details. A new generation of young students resumed studying Yang Shuo's essays in textbooks, but most of them probably knew nothing about how he died.

Years later, Zhang Guangnian wrote about Yang Shuo's death in his *Xiangyang Diary*.[7] Better known by his pen name Guang Weiran, Zhang Guangnian was the lyricist of the *Yellow River Cantata* and a leader of the Chinese Writers' Association for many years. On p. 259 of his book, the journal entry for 12 November 1975, he writes:

---

[7] Shanghai yuandong chubanshe, 1997.

Tonight Yang Shuo's younger brother Yang Yuwei and daughter Yang Du came to visit, with Yan Wenjing present. Yuwei spoke in detail of how Yang Shuo had died of illness and his investigation and research into it. We talked for two hours.

In the journal entry for 6 December of that year, he writes:

At 9:00 this morning, I drove with Yan Wenjing, Wei Junyi and Wang Zhiyuan to Babaoshan for a ceremony to lay Comrade Yang Shuo to rest...

These journal entries indicate that seven years after Yang Shuo's death, his work unit held a ceremony to lay his remains to rest in Beijing's preeminent cemetery. At that time, one of the main reasons for work units holding such ceremonies was the issuing of a new 'verdict' about the person's 'problems'. With the death of Lin Biao and the re-emergence of Deng Xiaoping, new and more relaxed 'policies' were applied to some people who had been 'dealt with' during the Cultural Revolution. If they were found to have no other 'problems', they were given a new 'verdict' and a memorial ceremony was carried out for the many whose remains had been discarded at the time of their deaths.

Before what Zhang Guangnian referred to as a 'spirit-moving ceremony' (this does not appear to be a term generally used at that time, but one he was personally accustomed to using), Yang Shuo's brother and daughter had come to see Zhang and another leader, Yan Wenjing, probably about the new verdict. Their intention is clear in their saying that Yang Shuo's death from an overdose of sleeping pills should be referred to as 'dying from illness' rather than suicide. Zhang doesn't say whether this version was accepted, but merely records that this conversation took place.

This may be difficult to understand for anyone who didn't experience the Cultural Revolution. Why did Yang Shuo's family take this position seven years after his death? A number of the cases in this book show that even the dead were subjected to posthumous struggle and humiliation for the crime of 'separating themselves from the Party and the people' through suicide.

The family of the victim couldn't blame or take action against the perpetrators, but could only claim that no suicide had been committed in order to save the deceased and themselves from even greater persecution. In the system of the Cultural Revolution, the manner of Yang's death was the only issue his family could contest.

Yang Shuo was famous for his exquisite essays, the finest of which were written in 1961. Included in many literature textbooks, their titles, 'Lychee

Honey', 'Snow Spray' and 'Ode to the Camellia' indicate that they are about things generally considered beautiful and good. At the same time, Yang used descriptions of these things to express his emotions. Yet, if one reads the literary magazines that published these sublime essays in 1961, one would be shocked by the execrable printing quality and by the coarse and unbleached paper. Put bluntly, this paper was little better than toilet paper in the old days.

This was in the middle of the Great Famine, when tens of millions starved to death and many others suffered from oedema. Food shortages naturally had a significant impact, and it was not only food that was lacking, but other basics such as paper, cloth, cooking implements and bowls. Magazines were printed on rough straw paper because that's all there was.

The regime's absurd economic policies and indifference towards human life created a comprehensive economic disaster that caused not only physical death, but also lasting psychological trauma. Families fought over food, and in the wider society people abandoned morality for the sake of obtaining the necessities of life. Yang Shuo's essays during that time suggest that he's often overseas, or that while in China he's enjoying lychees, camellia blossoms and snow in China's most scenic areas – Guangdong's hot springs, or the northern coastal resort of Beidaihe, or Kunming, land of eternal spring. He was clearly a privileged person and may never have known hunger, but he wasn't deaf or blind and must have known about the suffering of the people around him, and that few enjoyed the kind of life he did in high-class guesthouses. There was no honey in 1961, and his starving country was nothing like a dewy camellia blossom.

But the bitter reality of 1961 didn't seem to influence his writing. His sentences would have seemed totally unrelated to the hunger and poverty of real life if not printed on such poor-quality paper.

Using the traditional discourse of criticising literary works, his essays were 'simulations of peace and prosperity'. This critique may be overly simplistic, and there may have been more complex and cautious considerations behind these essays, but he doesn't seem to have left behind any other record of his feelings.

Even more ironic is that it was only at a time of economic hardship, when publishing policies were somewhat more 'relaxed', that he could have been allowed to write such exquisite lies and that his work would have been so highly esteemed and selected for inclusion in literature textbooks. His essays avoided the topics of starvation, deficiency and death, but at least they extolled beauty; they didn't boast of ten-thousand-kilo crop yields, and their praise of Mao was not as grotesque and absurd as in later years, nor did they encourage 'struggle', 'dictatorship' or slaughter.

After the Cultural Revolution began, on 13 June 1966, the CCP Central Committee and State Council endorsed and transmitted the Ministry of

Education leading Party group's 'Report Requesting Instructions Regarding Opinions on the Handling of Political, Language and History Teaching Materials Studied in Secondary Schools in the 1966–1967 School Year'. The report stated that the printing and distribution of the original teaching materials had been suspended, and politics and language classes were using Chairman Mao's works as their basic teaching materials.

Against this background, Yang Shuo's essays were eliminated from textbooks; even sham beauty was no longer wanted during the Cultural Revolution. Its leaders had already thoroughly consolidated power and were engaged in 'continuous revolution', so they didn't care about embellishing reality; furthermore, a simulacrum of peace and prosperity and a yearning for beauty implied endorsement of such concepts. The new Cultural Revolution literary genre was full of exaggeration, violence and uncouth expressions that corresponded to the brutal persecution of people in real life, while also being full of fanatical adoration of Mao that matched his absolute power. Yang Shuo's style could no longer be tolerated and eventually, neither could Yang Shuo.

Tian Han, a native of Changsha, Hunan Province, joined the Communist Party in 1932. He was a writer and vice-chairman of the Chinese Federation of Cultural Circles. At the outset of the Cultural Revolution, his works came under criticism as 'anti-Party poisonous weeds'. He died in prison on 10 December 1968, at the age of seventy.

Cheng Zhengqing, in his forties, was a photographer for the Xinhua News Agency. After Chen was subjected to struggle during the Cultural Revolution, he and his wife, **He Hui**, who was also employed at Xinhua, killed themselves by taking an overdose of sleeping pills on the night of 27 August 1966. They left behind four young children.

Someone who knew Chen Zhengqing said that he had taken pictures at the CCP's inaugural ceremony for the People's Republic of China and had also photographed many historical figures, including Mao Zedong and Chiang Kai-shek. He kept his photographs in an album arranged chronologically, and because Chiang was placed before Mao in his album, he was accused of being 'reactionary'.

It is said that ten people committed suicide in the Xinhua News Agency building in August 1966, but I've been unable to locate a list of the names. It is particularly ironic that even Xinhua, the Party's official news agency, seems unable to clearly recall its own Cultural Revolution history, let alone that of the rest of the country.

Chu Anping, a member of the September 3 Society[8] and former editor-in-chief of the *Guangming Daily*, attempted to drown himself after Red

---

[8] TN: A democratic party named for China's victory in the War of Resistance against Japan on 3 September 1945.

Guards ransacked his home in August 1966, and not long after that he disappeared. No one knows where or how he died. He was fifty-seven at the time.

As chief editor of *Guangcha* (Observation) Magazine in 1946, Chu Anping criticised the Kuomintang government then in power and demanded freedom of the press. He was appointed chief editor of the *Guangming Daily* in April 1957 when Mao launched his campaign to 'let one hundred flowers bloom and a hundred schools of thought contend.' During a meeting on 1 June 1957, Chu gave a speech in which he criticised the Communist Party's uncompromising rule (reported in the *People's Daily* on 2 June). This was the most daring and severe criticism the CCP had faced during the Hundred Flowers campaign. The result was that Chu was designated a Rightist and sent to the countryside for labour reform, and after that he lived off 100 *yuan* a month that he received from the September 3 Society. He had his fame to thank for this at a time when ordinary Rightists were treated much worse.

Red Guards ransacked Chu's home in late August 1966, when attacks were being carried out against 'black elements' and 'ox demons' throughout Beijing and many residents were being killed or expelled to the countryside. Chu went out to the suburbs and attempted to drown himself in the Chaobai River, but it was too shallow, and his failure only subjected him to more derision and abuse. He disappeared a few days later. No one was living with him at the time. His disappearance was investigated, but his body was never found.

Chu's disappearance prompted various rumours. One was that a group of Red Guards had taken him away and beaten him to death. Another circulating in Taiwan had it that Chu drowned himself at Shandong's famously scenic Penglai port. Whoever imagined this had no understanding of Chinese conditions in 1966, which would never have allowed for such a romantic demise.

Fang Yingyang, chief editor of the English edition of the Beijing Foreign Language Bureau's magazine *China Reconstructs*, was beaten to death while under 'isolation and investigation' on 9 January 1969, but his death was falsely reported as a suicide. A 1934 graduate in foreign languages from Nanjing Central University, Fang wrote poetry and essays as well as translating books. His father was a secondary school teacher, and his younger brother, Fang Yingxuan, was a noted tenor.

At the time of his death, Fang Yingyang was being held on the fourth floor of one of the Foreign Language Bureau's buildings. In January 1969, the military authorities controlling the Bureau prepared to hold a 'leniency and severity rally' to 'leniently handle' Fang Yingyang. 'Leniency' at that time meant the closing of the 'investigation' with a relatively mild verdict and the release of the target from the 'ox pen'.

When word of Fang's likely release got out, someone lured him from his room late at night on 9 January, removed his spectacles and beat him to death. His body was then moved elsewhere, with his glasses put back on, and he was declared to have 'committed suicide to escape punishment'. The truth of the case was exposed in April 1971.

Zhang Wenbo, the forty-five-year-old editor of the Russian edition of *People's Pictorial Magazine*, leaped to his death from his fourth-floor home in the residential compound of the PRC External Cultural Liaison Committee on 27 February 1969.

Zhang Wenbo was a graduate of the Harbin Foreign Language Technical School and stayed there to teach for a time. He was transferred to Beijing in 1957 and worked at *Russian Friend News*. When the breakdown in Sino-Soviet relations resulted in that periodical being disbanded, Zhang became Russian editor at *People's Pictorial*.

The son of a neighbour said Zhang was a tall man of solid build who loved swimming, diving and skating and kept largely to himself, reading books at home in his free time. In spring and autumn he always wore a cream-coloured windbreaker. Every day he rode his expensive manganese steel bicycle to work, and after work he carried it back up the four floors to his home. Zhang's son played with other children in the compound, and when making aeroplane and ship models, Zhang would point out spots that the children needed to pay attention to.

This neighbour's son recalled that during the Cultural Revolution, a lot of big-character posters were put up about Zhang Wenbo, accusing him of 'Leftist ideology' (Zhang was said to have a very high professional standard, and was a Class Four translator). The poster also said that Zhang's father had served as head of the Jilin Province Education Bureau before 1949 – i.e. that he came from a 'reactionary family'.

Zhang Wenbo died early in the morning. Someone who had just come out of the downstairs canteen heard a crashing sound, and turned to see someone on the ground below the bathroom window of Zhang's home. People started gathering around and quickly identified the body.

Zhang Wenbo had a fourteen-year-old daughter and a younger son. After he was found dead, children from the building went to the daughter's school and told her to come home. Zhang Wenbo's wife, a music teacher at the Beijing No. 61 Secondary School, died in 2003, and Zhang's son was too young at the time to know exactly how his father was persecuted. He only knew that Zhang was always writing 'confessions'. Most parents didn't tell their children about their persecution, partly because they wouldn't understand, and also because they were afraid the children would talk about it and bring even more trouble on them.

Because Zhang was a 'problematic' person and had committed suicide, his family wasn't allowed to save his ashes after he was cremated. Instead, they gathered up some soil soaked with his blood from where he had fallen and buried it beneath a big pine tree in a courtyard on the eastern side of Beihai Park. The family quietly went to visit him there from then on. During the middle stage of the Cultural Revolution, Jiang Qing and others occupied Beihai Park, and it was closed to the public, so the family was no longer able to mourn there. After Mao died, the park was reopened, and Zhang's children and his neighbour's child were able to visit the 'grave' again. Zhang Wenbo was eventually rehabilitated.

Li Changgong was one of fifty-four staff of the *New Hunan Daily* who were designated Rightists in 1957. He was sent to the Xinsheng Cement Plant in Pingtang to serve his sentence. When the Cultural Revolution began, he was declared a member of an anti-Party, anti-socialist 'Three Family Village' at the plant and was subjected to struggle. He killed himself by leaping from a cliff.

Fu Lei, born in Shanghai in 1908, was a translator of many French works. Fu was designated a Rightist in 1957, and in August 1966 his home was ransacked and he was subjected to struggle. On 3 September, Fu Lei and his wife, **Zhu Meifu**, hanged themselves in their home, leaving a suicide note. Fu was fifty-eight and Zhu was fifty-three.

Fu Lei was rehabilitated after the Cultural Revolution, and *Letters Home*, a book of correspondence between Fu and his sons, was published and became a bestseller. Fu Lei had two sons, Fu Cong and Fu Min, both of whom were born in the 1930s. In 1966, Fu Min was an English teacher at the Beijing No. 1 Girls' Secondary School. He attempted to drown himself during the Red Guard attacks on teachers in August, but survived. Fu Cong became a famous pianist. In 1958, the government sent him to Poland to study, but when he graduated he went to England instead of returning to China, as a result of which he was called a traitor.

Ye Yonglie's essay 'The Death of Fu Lei' doesn't refer to Fu Min's attempted suicide, but mentions something Fu Cong said in 1980:

> I heard many stories about him in Poland [meaning about Fu Lei being designated a Rightist]. When I graduated in December 1958, if I went back, it would certainly be a case of 'father exposing son and son exposing father', but my father and I wouldn't do that. This drove me to flee for the hills, and I naturally feel very guilty about it.[9]

---

[9] *Unnatural Death*, p. 49, Beijing Normal University Publishing, 1986.

There is a rumour that the last portion of Fu Cong's quote was edited out, and that he originally said, 'I naturally feel very guilty about it, because I didn't suffer with them.'

Wen Jie, a leader of the Shanghai Writers' Association and a famous poet, was imprisoned in 1968. His wife, **Du Fangmei**, a forty-year-old cadre at the Shanghai Bank, leaped to her death that summer. The couple had three young daughters. After Wen Jie was 'liberated' from being a target of criticism in the Cultural Revolution, he formed a romantic attachment with the novelist Dai Houying, who was in the inner circle of the Cultural Revolution leadership. Their relationship was severly opposed by Gang of Four member Zhang Chunqiao, and Wen Jie was accused of 'corrupting a revolutionary'. He gassed himself to death in 1971 at the age of forty-eight. After the Cultural Revolution, Dai Houying wrote about Wen in her novel *Death of a Poet*.

Ye Yiqun was the fifty-five-year-old vice-chairman of the Shanghai Municipal Federation of Cultural Circles, and a literary theorist who edited the college textbook *Fundamental Principles of Literature*. He leaped to his death on 2 August 1966, after coming under attack.

Zhao Shuli, born in 1906, was a famous writer, chairman of the Chinese Folksong Association and board member of the Chinese Writers' Association. In 1964, he became deputy Party secretary of Jincheng County, Shanxi Province. During the Cultural Revolution he was accused of being a 'pacesetter for the counter-revolutionary revisionist cultural road', and he was beaten until his ribs and hip were broken. On 23 June 1970, the Shanxi Province Higher People's Court declared him under 'isolation and investigation' and he was taken to Taiyuan's largest assembly hall and struggled on 17 September. He collapsed and fell unconscious during the struggle rally and died on 23 September.

MUSIC

Li Guoquan, born in 1914, was a violinist and orchestral conductor of the China National Opera and Dance Drama Theatre. An overseas Chinese who had returned from Southeast Asia, Li was repeatedly struggled and humiliated once the Cultural Revolution began. A placard was hung around his neck along with an orchestral drum, and he was forced to march through the streets while beating the drum and calling out, 'I am Dayangu.' (The term 'Dayangu' was a special crime applied to members of the arts community, referring to 'large' [da], 'foreign' [yang] and 'traditional' [gu].) He was also forced to lick a urinal. Li Guoquan hanged himself from a water pipe in the bathroom of his home on 26 August 1966.

Li Zaiwen, known by her professional name, Xiao Bai Yushuang, was a famous performer of Beijing Pingju Opera. She killed herself in August 1966 after being beaten and humiliated by Red Guards. In its March 1968 'Request for Instructions Regarding Criticism by Name in Periodicals', the Beijing Municipal Revolutionary Committee listed Li among the twenty-two 'evildoers' to be criticised by name.

Chen Zixin, chairman of the office of the Central Philharmonic Orchestra, was driven to suicide in 1968. Chen and his wife, Zhou Guangren, who was a pianist for the Philharmonic, were denounced separately by their work unit. The 'rebel faction' forced Chen to confess to 'historical problems', but he couldn't remember events from a certain year, no matter how hard he tried. Set for a denunciation by the entire orchestra the next day, Chen killed himself that night.

Gu Shengying, a thirty-year-old pianist with the Shanghai Symphony Orchestra, committed suicide along with her mother, **Qin Shenyi**, and younger brother, **Gu Woqi**, after being beaten and humiliated at a struggle rally on 31 January 1967.

Prior to the Cultural Revolution, Gu Shengying had been one of China's outstanding pianists. She joined the Shanghai Symphony Orchestra in 1954, and in 1958 won the top award for female pianists in the 14th International Music Competition in Geneva.

On 31 January 1967, in a rehearsal room on Hunan Road, the orchestra's rebel faction dragged Gu Shengying to the auditorium stage, and in the presence of the entire orchestra and staff, slapped her in the face and pulled her hair, then made her kneel before Mao's portrait and beg for forgiveness for her crimes. After that, Gu went to her home in Yuyuan Road and committed suicide with her mother and younger brother.

Gu's mother, Qin Shenyi, had graduated from Datong University with a degree in Western literature, and was a housewife. Gu's father, Gu Gaodi, was arrested in 1956 as a counter-revolutionary in the Pan Hannian case[10] and sentenced to twenty years of labour reform.

Gu Shengying's brother, Gu Woqi, was admitted in 1955 to Shanghai Jiaotong University, which was China's first and best modern engineering

---

[10] Pan Hannian was a leader of Shanghai's underground Communist Party prior to liberation. He became vice-mayor of Shanghai in 1949 and led Shanghai's campaigns to suppress revolutionaries, arresting and executing many counter-revolutionaries and attacking many members of the industrial and business communities. Then in 1955, Pan himself was arrested as a counter-revolutionary, and in 1963 the Supreme People's Court sentenced him to fifteen years in prison. He was released on parole soon after that, but after the Cultural Revolution began, he was taken into custody once again in 1967 and was sentenced to life in prison in 1970. He died in 1977. Pan was posthumously rehabilitated in 1982.

school. In 1956, the central government ordered the school to relocate to Xi'an. A group of professors objected, as a result of which they were labelled Rightists in 1957, and no one dared offer any further objections to the move. After Jiaotong University moved to Xi'an, Gu Woqi remained in Shanghai due to illness. After several years, he finally found part-time work as a substitute teacher for several schools.

Gu Shengying and her mother and brother gassed themselves to death at home. While most households in China used coal briquettes for cooking, many buildings in Shanghai were supplied with gas, which was cleaner and more convenient. During the Cultural Revolution, this same gas supply became a suicide tool exclusively used by Shanghainese. East China Normal University professor **Li Pingxin**, Shanghai Conservatory of Music professor **Li Cuizhen** and Shanghai Writers' Association poet **Wen Jie** all used gas to kill themselves.

The bodies of Gu Shengying and her mother and brother were cremated, their ashes discarded, and their home occupied by others. Someone heard that they'd left a suicide note for Gu Gaodi, but no one told Gu about any note after he finished his term of labour reform and returned to Shanghai after the Cultural Revolution. He died soon after that.

Other victims of the Cultural Revolution in the Shanghai Symphony Orchestra included its conductor, **Lu Hong'en**, who was executed, and a viola player, **Zhou Xingrong**, who killed herself in 1968.

A symphony orchestra should be representative of arts and culture, but during the Cultural Revolution era, it became a scene of barbaric cruelty. Of course, it was the Beijing leaders of the Cultural Revolution who directed violence throughout the country, but most of the people who carried out these particular acts of brutality were members of the orchestra.

When Gu Shengying was struggled on 30 January 1967, it was right at the time of Shanhgai's 'January power seizure'. One of the orchestral 'activists' involved in struggling Gu later became leader of the Cultural Bureau under the new organ of authority, the Shanghai Municipal Revolutionary Committee (two members of the Gang of Four, Zhang Chunqiao and Yao Wenyuan, were chairman and vice-chairman, respectively, of this Committee), and in 1972 led the Shanghai Acrobatic Troupe on a European tour. During the Cultural Revolution, there were no opportunities for advancement apart from rising in officialdom, and going on a foreign tour was an even rarer opportunity. Against this background, it can be seen what enormous personal advantages could be gained through 'revolutionary' action.

This leader of the Cultural Bureau eventually fell from power, not as punishment for persecuting others, but because he created a scandal through an extramarital love affair.

Like educators, artists were a focal target of the Cultural Revolution, but it must also be noted that many educators died as the result of violent acts committed by secondary school students, while violence against artists was mainly committed by adults. If not for the Cultural Revolution, the jealousy, ambition and malice of these perpetrators would probably have been limited to petty acts of spite, but with the permission and encouragement of Cultural Revolution policies, rivalries developed into brutal mistreatment of colleagues that frequently resulted in death.

In 2001, in commemoration of the twelfth anniversary of 4 June 1989, Ding Zilin, leader of the Tiananmen Mothers, a group of family members of victims of the massacre, published an article entitled 'In Deeply Cherished Memory of Three People'. One of those three was her seventeen-year-old son, Jiang Jielian, while the other two were her secondary school and university schoolmate, Lin Zhao, a victim of the Anti-Rightist Campaign, and her primary school classmate, Gu Shengying.

Gu Shengying and Ding Zilin were in the same third-grade class in 1944 at the affiliated primary school of Shanghai's famous McTyeire School. Gu, who sat directly in front of Ding, wore her hair in 'butterfly braids' and was already studying piano. Ding Ziling remembers her as a gentle, quiet and intelligent student who got top marks in all her classes and patiently helped Ding when she was having difficulties with English. When Ding Zilin transferred to a different school, her teacher and classmates threw a farewell party for her, and Gu Shengying gave her a chocolate candy shaped like a Jeep, which Ding saved until warmer weather obliged her to eat it.

Ding Zilin's warm and simple story contrasts sharply with the violence and death of the Cultural Revolution, when even a little girl's butterfly braids were not allowed.

There are still people who say that revolution is needed to smash the bourgeois lifestyle so the majority of working people can enjoy new lives. But people like Gu Shenying weren't killed by ordinary people who didn't have the opportunity to play the piano or learn English. Indeed, the vast majority of ordinary people worked diligently to save enough money to buy butterfly clips and chocolate for their children, and maybe even a piano. It was Mao and his wife, Jiang Qing, in the positions of highest power and enjoying the highest material privileges, who launched a movement that destroyed artists such as Gu Shengying and Lu Hong'en and also robbed ordinary people of the opportunity to be educated, to appreciate and learn the arts and to earn enough money to support and improve their lives. We can only mourn for the generation of women represented by Ding Zilin. Starting out as gentle and lovely children and good students, they were then forced to live with such horrible incidents as Rightist labelling, 'contradictions between the enemy and us', arrest, imprisonment, struggle rallies and executions. Lin Zhao was sentenced to death and executed, Gu Shengying was driven to suicide and Ding Zilin's son was shot in the 4 June crackdown. Even the harshest person can find no way to blame this generation, but can only condemn the system, theories and authorities that created their immense misery.

Lu Hong'en, born in 1919, graduated in 1943 from the state-run Shanghai School of Music and in 1950 became a tympanist for the Shanghai Symphony Orchestra. He became its director in 1954, but was hospitalised for 'schizophrenia' in 1965 and suffered a relapse in May 1966. He was arrested on 28 May for 'reactionary speech' while under the influence of his illness. After being detained for two years, he was sentenced to death for counter-revolutionary crime on 27 April 1968 and was executed.

Lu Hong'en was born to a Catholic family in Shanghai. His wife, Hu Guomei, was a graduate of Shanghai's McTyeire School, and was a piano accompanist for the Shanghai Dance School. The Shanghai Symphony was one of China's premier orchestras, and Lu not only had musical talent, but was also an excellent writer.

In January 1965, Lu Hong'en and other people from the orchestra took part in the Socialist Education Movement in nearby rural Fengxian County, and Lu suffered a mental breakdown. His colleagues took him to the county hospital for an injection to calm him down, after which he was taken back to Shanghai.

The Shanghai Symphony arranged for a car to take Lu to the Shanghai Mental Hospital in the company of symphony Party secretary Chen Yanlong, Lu's brother-in-law, Hu Guo'an and others. After an examination, the hospital's best doctors diagnosed Lu with schizophrenia, and he stayed in the hospital for two months until his condition improved. He went back to work at the symphony, but was no longer director.

In spring 1966, Lu Hong'en suffered a relapse; he couldn't sleep, and suspected others of persecuting him. He sent a long letter of complaint to the Vice-Minister of Culture in Beijing, Xia Yan, but then tore it up unsent. His wife asked her brother to get Lu readmitted to the mental hospital. Hu Guo'an, a Russian teacher at the Shanghai Foreign Language Institute, immediately telephoned the Shanghai Symphony, but was told that Lu would not be taken to hospital, and that it was none of his business.

Lu Hong'en had made the mistake of saying that Khrushchev was right. Mao regarded Khrushchev as a revisionist, and that term attracted extreme opprobrium during the Cultural Revolution. Lu Hong'en was mentally unstable, and during the meeting the symphony held to argue the point with him, he became even more intense and extreme in his opinions. His defence of Khrushchev was deemed 'counter-revolutionary speech' and instead of the mental hospital, Lu was sent to the PSB detention centre as a 'current counter-revolutionary'.

Living conditions in the detention centre were poor. A heavy smoker, Lu couldn't get any cigarettes, and the Chlorpromazine that had been prescribed for him was cut off. His illness became worse.

Reportedly, whenever Lu Hong'en saw anything red in the detention centre, he wanted to smash it, and of course during the Cultural Revolution, everything was red to symbolise revolution. He is also reported to have shouted 'reactionary slogans' regarding Mao. After being held for two years, Lu was sentenced to death in 1968 at a televised trial in the Cultural Arena in the middle of Shanghai. The report of his execution was posted on the streets of Shanghai. More than thirty others were executed with him.

Shanghai's *Liberation Daily*'s report on the trial stated:

> In order to defend to the death the proletarian headquarters led by Chairman Mao and vice-chairman Lin, and to defend to the death Chairman Mao's revolutionary road and seize full victory for the Great Proletarian Cultural Revolution, Shanghai's public security, procuratorial and judicial organs yesterday held a 'Public Trial to Hold High the Great Red Flag of Mao Zedong Thought and Resolutely Suppress Current Counter-revolutionary Crime' to harshly sentence a batch of irredeemably evil current counter-revolutionaries... After the public trial, the defendants were sentenced to death, and Liu Youxin and the other infamous current counter-revolutionaries were immediately taken to the execution ground, where their executions were carried out. The revolutionary masses inside and outside the execution ground shouted slogans for a long time, and everyone clapped and cheered.

When Lu Hong'en was sentenced to death, his brother-in-law, Hu Guo'an, was immediately locked up by the opposing mass organisation at the Shanghai Foreign Language Institute. They forced him to 'confess' to his relationship with Lu Hong'en and tried to find errors he'd made in dealing with Lu for which they could punish him. Because Hu Guo'an had always been very cautious, he was released after two days.

Following Lu's execution, a representative of the judicial organs went to Lu's widow and made her pay for the bullet that killed him.

One of the Gang of Four, Zhang Chunqiao, is reported to have said regarding Lu's death sentence, 'Lu Hong'en wasn't mentally ill, he was a counter-revolutionary. He called out "Long Live Khrushchev" – why not cry out "Long Live Chairman Mao"?' Zhang was chairman of the Shanghai

Municipal Revolutionary Committee at the time. I haven't been able to verify the accuracy of this report, but what is certain is that Zhang Chunqiao and his newly established Committee gave final approval to death sentences in Shanghai at that time.

The leaders of the Shanghai Municipal Revolutionary Committee, Zhang Chunqiao and Yao Wenyuan, were both members of the cultural community and must have heard music conducted by Lu Hong'en, or at the very least must have known of his reputation.

Lu was not the only person sentenced to death for 'counter-revolutionary speech' while suffering from mental illness. Convicting and even executing such people was unlawful on many levels.

First of all, their mental instability was often a result of physical and psychological abuse. According to an investigation carried out in Shanghai in 1984, 11,510 people were beaten to death or driven to suicide during its Cultural Revolution.

Second, they spoke the offending words while under the influence of mental illness. Most countries under the rule of law do not allow words or actions spoken by the mentally ill to constitute grounds for conviction of a crime, because the mentally ill are unable to take responsibility for what they say and do. In Lu Hong'en's case, he had already been hospitalised for mental illness just one year earlier, and at the time of his 'crime' he was still taking prescription medication. The failure to take his condition into account was not a matter of ignorance, but of a wilful refusal to acknowledge it.

Third, while Lu Hong'en was mentally unstable, he wasn't a murderer or arsonist, nor had he damaged anything or presented any danger to the public. Given that the Chinese Constitution protected a citizen's freedom of speech, there was even less reason for convicting him of a crime. But the remarks Lu made were considered 'venomous attacks on Chairman Mao and Vice-chairman Lin', one of the most heinous crimes at that time.

Fourth, the death sentences handed down against Lu Hong'en and others didn't go through normal legal procedures, in particular the right to a defence and appeal. If allowed to defend himself, even if Lu's favourable remarks regarding Khrushchev were found to be the basis for conviction of a 'counter-revolutionary crime', Lu or his lawyer could at least have requested a certificate of mental illness from a doctor at the psychiatric hospital. Furthermore, prior to the Cultural Revolution, defendants sentenced to death could appeal to the Supreme People's Court, and the death sentence could only be carried out if the appeal was rejected. During the Cultural Revolution, this final authority over death sentences was delegated to the provinces and to municipalities under the direct jurisdiction of the central government. Under the Party's unified leadership of the procuratorial, judicial and public security organs under the Revolutionary Committees, death sentences were decided by the Communist Party.

Lu Hong'en had brought joy to many through the beautiful music of the Shanghai Symphony Orchestra. If effectively treated, his mental illness might have been alleviated. Instead, he was killed. After his death, his wife, Hu Guomei, lived in a state of deep depression until she died.

He Wuqi, the forty-year-old deputy director of the Shanghai National Minorities Orchestra, was a graduate of the Shanghai Arts Academy. At the outset of the Cultural Revolution, he was repeatedly criticised and struggled as a 'revisionist artist', and in April 1968 he was locked up in an 'ox pen' for 'isolation and investigation' and beaten over an extended period. Late at night on 18 July, he escaped, and while being chased he ran onto a railway line and was crushed by a train. He left behind a wife and two school-aged children.

He Wuqi's elder brother, He Huizhong, had died during the Great Famine in 1960 after being sent to Gansu Province in 1958 for the 'historical problem' of having joined the KMT while a student. His wife, who survived him with three young children, was persecuted during the Cultural Revolution because of his 'problem'.

FILM AND THEATRE

Zheng Junli, born in 1911, was the director of the Shanghai Film Studio when he was arrested during the Cultural Revolution. He died in prison on 23 April 1969. Mao's wife, Jiang Qing, had been a film actress in Shanghai in the 1930s, and while wielding enormous power during the Cultural Revolution, she revenged herself on some actors and directors whom she'd known in those days.

Xu Tao, a fifty-six-year-old director for the Haiyan Studio of the Shanghai Film Studio, drowned himself on 21 June 1966, after being denounced and humiliated during the Cultural Revolution. **Zhang Youliang**, deputy director of the Haiyan Studio, leaped to his death on 19 March 1968, after being persecuted and beaten.

Gu Eryi, born in 1915, was a director at the Shanghai Film Studio. Gu experienced protracted persecution during the Cultural Revolution. His home was ransacked and he was publicly denounced and then sent to a May 7 Cadre School. He hanged himself in a work shed of the cadre school on 18 June 1970.

Shangguan Yunzhu, a famous actress at the Shanghai Film Studio, had her home ransacked in 1966, and during the Cleansing of the Class Ranks in 1968, she was locked up in an 'ox pen' like nearly all of the studio's artists over forty years old. She was beaten while being 'interrogated'. Shangguan Yunzhu leaped to her death on 23 November 1968, at the age of forty-eight.

Xu Lai, born in Shanghai in 1909, was a film actress who knew too much about Jiang Qing's early life in the film industry, having starred in many films in 1933 and 1934 before retiring from public life in 1935. Xu went to Hong Kong in the late 1940s but then moved to Beijing at the end of 1956. She was arrested in October 1967 and died in prison on 4 April 1973. She was rehabilitated on 25 April 1980.

Hai Mo, originally surnamed Zhang, was a screenwriter for the Beijing Movie Studio. In 1960, he was expelled from the Party as a 'Rightist who slipped through the net', after which he was demoted and sent down to the countryside for penal labour under surveillance. In 1962 he was 'screened out' for rehabilitation, and his Party membership was restored. During the Cultural Revolution he was locked up and struggled, and finally died as the result of torture in May 1968, aged forty-five.

Wang Ying, born in 1913, was a film actress and writer who reportedly ran afoul of Jiang Qing when she was given the lead role in the stage play *Sai Jinhua*, about a famous courtesan, a role that Jiang Qing had wanted. While in the US in 1942, Wang had assisted the writer Agnes Smedley with *The Biography of Zhu De*. Wang Ying returned to China in 1955 and became a screenwriter for the Beijing Movie Studio. She was arrested during the Cultural Revolution and died in prison on 3 March 1974.

Ying Yunwei, a twenty-seven-year-old director of plays and films, was seized and struggled by Shanghai's 'rebel faction' on 16 January 1967, and died while being paraded through the streets.

Guo Dun, an actress in her thirties with Shangdong's Yantai Theatre Group and formerly with the Beijing Youth Art Theatre, killed herself in 1966 after being publicly exposed and struggled.

Yan Huizhu, born in 1919, was a famous performer of Kunqu opera and vice-principal of the Shanghai Traditional Opera School. After being brutally struggled, beaten and humiliated in August 1966, she hanged herself in her bathroom on 11 September 1966.

After the Cultural Revolution, someone wrote of 'the death of a famous and beautiful actress', the usual phrase used in newspapers, but no papers reported Yan's death at the time, nor did any media express sorrow for her passing. As both an artist and an educator, Yan Huizhu died as a dual target of the Cultural Revolution.

Yan Huizhu's husband, Yu Zhenfei, was also a famous performer of Kunqu opera and was principal of the Shanghai Traditional Opera School. Both husband and wife were beaten and humiliated by Red Guards, and were forced to 'admit their error and request punishment' and to write 'confessions' as 'representatives of the bourgeois reactionary artistic line at the Traditional Opera School'.

A relative of Yan Huizhu said that shortly before she killed herself, Yan saw a 'general order' posted on the street by the Beijing Xicheng District Red Guard Disciplinary Patrol stating that members of the 'seven black categories' had to be expelled from the cities and sent to the countryside for labour reform. Reading this notice filled her with terror and despair; she realised that the humiliation and torment she'd suffered was going to continue for some time to come.

Yan Huizhu's husband, Yu Zhenfei, survived, and after the Cultural Revolution, in the early 1980s, he led the Shanghai Kunqu Theatre to Beijing for a performance that deeply moved the audience with its elegance.

Han Junqing, a famous performer of virtuous female roles at Tianjin's Hebei Clapper Opera Theatre, was struggled and paraded through the streets during the Cultural Revolution, and was forced to remove her shoes and walk on a cinder road on her bound feet. She killed herself by drinking DDVP pesticide and swallowing a pack of matches in order to hasten her death.

Yan Fengying, a famous performer of the Huangmei opera of Anhui Province, became wildly popular through her performance in the film *The Emperor's Female Son-in-Law*. During the Cultural Revolution she was accused of being a secret agent and was beaten and humiliated. She killed herself with an overdose of medicine on 8 April 1968, at the age of thirty-eight.

RELIGIOUS PRACTITIONERS

Liao Jiaxun, a nun, was arrested because of her religious beliefs and died in Beijing's Banbuqiao Prison during the Cultural Revolution.

An article in the 1 September 1966, edition of the *People's Daily* reported that the Beijing Municipal People's Committee supported the secondary school Red Guards in banning the Franciscan Missionaries of Mary from Beijing and deporting eight foreign nuns on 31 August.

A struggle rally was held outside the order's building, and photos remaining from that time show nearly twenty nuns bent at the waist. Some of them were clearly Chinese. Of the eight deported foreign nuns, one died upon arrival in Hong Kong.

A secondary student at that time recalled that Red Guards from his class ransacked the convent and brought chocolates back to the school to eat.

An artist, Yu Feng, who was once a neighbour of the Liao family, said that Liao Jiaxun's father had been an envoy to France in the 1920s, and her mother was French. Liao Jiaxun was a beautiful woman, well-bred and refined and educated in several languages and in the art and culture of the world; she particularly loved music. Yet she insisted on becoming a nun.[11]

Liang Baoshun, in his forties, was an engineer at the Tianjin Electrical Machinery Factory, and a Christian. Liang was struggled and locked up during the Cultural Revolution and soon died from a head wound. The factory managers said he committed suicide, but his family maintained he'd been beaten to death.

Shen Yaolin, a resident of Gegu Town in what is now Tianjin's Jinnan District, had dealt in images of the God of Wealth before the Cultural Revolution, as a result of which he was accused of 'engaging in feudalistic superstition'. When he learned he was going to be 'seized and struggled', he killed himself. He was around forty years old.

OTHERS

Shu Sai, a resident of East Dafosi Street in Beijing, was arrested on 7 December 1966, for putting up a big-character poster opposing Lin Biao. She died in Xi County, Shanxi Province, on 24 May 1971, at the age of fifty-four.

Born in Jiangling, Hubei Province, Shu Sai joined the CCP in 1938. She worked in the Construction Industry Ministry in the 1950s, but was expelled from the Party and demoted in 1958 for 'willfully stirring up trouble'. She was then dismissed from her official posting in 1960 and sent for re-education through labour as a 'bad element'. She was released on medical parole in 1962.

Late at night on 2 December 1966, Shu Sai put up big-character posters written with gold ink on red paper on walls all over Beijing's busiest areas, including Party and government office buildings and the Beijing Train Station. She was arrested on 7 December, and when a batch of 'prisoners awaiting trial' was sent to Shanxi in October 1969, she was among them.

This information comes from an article entitled 'Record of the Trial of a Persecuted Innocent'.[12] It is worth noting that Shu Sai never went to trial. If she'd lived elsewhere, she might have been handed a death sentence like

---

[11] See Yu Feng, 'Talking of Faded Memories: On Reading Comrade Feng Yachun's Prison Jottings'.
[12] Shu Tiemin, Fan Hui, 'Record of the Trial of a Persecuted Innocent', *Yanhuang Chunqiu*, No. 7, 2000.

Lin Zhao and Lu Hong'en in Shanghai, Lu Lanxiu in Suzhou and Zhang Zhixin in Liaoning. Was she spared because she had joined the CCP? Or was it because the Beijing judicial system already had enough death sentences to deal with? Or is it just an example of the arbitrariness of death sentences at that time? We will only know if the files of Shu Sai and others are made public someday.

Lou Wende, a massive man in his late forties, was the director of the Shanghai Huguang Tool Factory. At the outset of the Cultural Revolution, someone put up a big-character poster criticising him, and finding it unbearable, Lou fled to Beijing, where his son was a university student. His son had no choice but to take Lou back to the factory. A few days after his return, Lou had his son go to the canteen and read the big-character poster, and while his son was away, Lou smashed himself in the head with a hammer. He left behind his elderly mother.

Wang Deming, in his thirties, was a clerical worker in the Shanghai Pharmaceuticals Company. After his father, who worked for the Shanghai Railway Bureau, was 'seized and struggled' in 1966, Wang Deming and his parents committed suicide together.

Sun Huilian, a clerk in the pharmacy of Fengwang Commune in Shazhou County, Jiangsu Province, was regarded as a class enemy because she came from a 'landlord' family. Soon after the Cultural Revolution began, Sun learned that she was going to be 'seized and struggled', and she and her husband, **Miao Zhichun**, a doctor at the commune, drowned themselves in a river.

Wang Shaoyen, a retired teacher from the No. 2 Secondary School in Xiaoshan County, Zhejiang Province, lived in a village in the county's Linpu Township. Designated a 'black element' because of his family background, Wang was ordered to stand in front of a portrait of Mao every day in summer 1967 and 'apologise and appeal for leniency.' One day, Wang and his wife were summoned to the local residents' committee and struggled. Wang's wife was allowed to go home first, where she hanged herself. When Wang found his wife dead, he left the house and was found drowned in a nearby pond the next day.

Du Mengxian, a native of Dajingkou Village in Dalian's Lüshunkou District (now known as Lüshunkou City) committed suicide in 1968 at the age of thirty.

The Du family was categorised as 'rich peasants' during the 1950 Land Reform Campaign, and as a result Du Mengxian was considered a 'rich peasant offspring'. Once the Cultural Revolution began, the Sichuan railway construction team in which he worked was disbanded. He returned home in spite of his family warning him not to do so. Soon afterwards he was subjected to struggle, as a result of which he hanged himself.

Du Mengxian had an elder sister who was a nurse at a maternity hospital in Dalian. The sister's husband, **Wang Maorong**, was a research fellow at the Dalian Institute of Physics and Chemistry. He likewise committed suicide after coming under attack in 1968.

Yu Binghe, an engineer at the Lanzhou Water and Electricity Bureau, was humiliated, beaten and interrogated under torture during the Cultural Revolution because his father had been a KMT official. He leaped to his death in 1967 at the age of thirty-four, leaving behind a wife and three children aged six, three and one. The youngest son, who never knew his father, suffered from bias on several fronts, and became a long-term psychiatric patient at the age of twenty.

CADRES

Liu Shaoqi, born in 1898, was President of the PRC, vice-chairman of the CCP Central Committee and the second most powerful man in China when the Cultural Revolution began. He fell from power in August 1966, and in 1967 Party newspapers were referring to him as 'the biggest capitalist-roader power-holder within the Party.' In October 1968, the Central Committee expelled Liu permanently from the Party as a 'turncoat, hidden traitor and scab', and he was subjected to protracted imprisonment and torture. In February 1980, the Central Committee rehabilitated Liu Shaoqi and announced that he had died on 13 November 1969.

THE DEATH OF SENIOR OFFICIALS AND THE DEATH OF ORDINARY PEOPLE

Before my online Chinese Holocaust Memorial was blocked by Beijing, I received letters from two readers in China. They observed that the website showed ordinary Cultural Revolution victims, including their names and tragic experiences, which the media had ignored for decades, which was an extremely important breakthrough, yet they wondered why the website didn't list high-status victims of the Cultural Revolution, in particular Liu Shaoqi and Tao Zhu.

It's true that Liu Shaoqi, who was China's second most powerful man before August 1966, and Tao Zhu, who became the fourth most powerful after Liu Shaoqi was unseated, were both imprisoned and tortured during the Cultural Revolution, and that both suffered tragic deaths.

Most of the people listed on my website are ordinary people who held no positions in the power structure, and who even after being rehabilitated never had their names or stories recorded.

The concealment or neglect of these ordinary victims has led to a distorted view of the Cultural Revolution, and the failure to record the suffering and long-term persecution of these people has made the crimes of the Cultural Revolution look less serious in the historical record. In my view, it is the deaths of these ordinary people that lie at the core of the Cultural Revolution landscape, and that's why I've spent so many years tracking down their stories.

Liu Shaoqi was not an ordinary man, but he was also a victim of the Cultural Revolution. His special status meant that everyone knew his name. Even so, it has been very difficult to verify exactly what kind of torments he suffered, and how he viewed his own treatment. In democratic countries, leaders who are elected to office are largely understood by the people, and they lose much of the right to privacy that ordinary people enjoy. In countries without popular elections, the situation is just the opposite: the highest reaches of power are kept secret, and ordinary people have no way of gaining an understanding of their leaders as individuals. An air of mystery is used to sustain power that has not been granted by the people, reinforcing this kind of authority. The people in the highest circles of power aren't elected by the people or monitored by the media. They need to maintain their distance from the people.

During the Cultural Revolution, ordinary 'ox demons and snake spirits' were handed over to ordinary Red Guards and rebels for struggle, torture and even killing. But high-level officials such as Liu Shaoqi and Tao Zhu were confined in isolation and placed under the direct control of the supreme centre of power.

That is to say, a person in the top power circle who became an 'ox demon' or 'snake spirit' had to be kept apart from the masses who were being struggled. After Liu Shaoqi was unseated, hundreds of thousands of students and residents staged a month-long 'pluck Liu' movement outside of Zhongnanhai. This movement was encouraged and supported by the Cultural Revolution's leaders, who nevertheless prevented the rebel factions from seeing Liu in person. Liu Shaoqi was handed over to the rebel faction within Zhongnanhai for criticism and struggle, as shown by documentary footage.

To this day, the Chinese government has not granted access to the Cultural Revolution archives; it is impossible to read the files on even ordinary people, much less on senior officials such as Liu Shaoqi.

As Stanford University Professor Emeritus Lyman P. Van Slyke has said, 'Figuring out what Chinese officials are thinking and doing is difficult. It is as though they are standing on a stage with the curtain raised only enough to allow us to see their feet and shoes. From this limited information we must draw our tentative conclusions.'[13]

A Deleted Detail: Paralysed and Tied to His Bed for the Last Six Months of His Life

In spring 1980, four years after Mao died and eleven years after Liu Shaoqi's death, the CCP Central Committee rehabilitated Liu and carried out a solemn memorial service for him. At the same time, official newspapers published a series of articles regarding Liu's life and revolutionary achievements.

During this time, an elderly writer and Party member told me that she went to see the chief editor of the *People's Daily*, Hu Jiwei, regarding an article relating to her that the newspaper had published. She had known Hu since their days in Yan'an decades ago. In Hu's office, she overheard him talking with Liu Shaoqi's widow, Wang Guangmei, on the telephone regarding an article that was about to be published. The article stated that after Liu had been imprisoned in solitary confinement, he had become paralysed and had been bound to his bed for six months before he died. The *People's Daily* was removing that detail from the article, and Hu was asking 'Comrade Guangmei' to agree to it 'for the sake of the Party's image'.

The elderly writer was very upset when she told me about this, saying she couldn't believe that a paralysed person would still be bound to his bed. She felt ashamed of the Party. In fact, the newspaper that edited out that information should also feel ashamed.

I looked at the *People's Daily* articles published around the time of Liu Shaoqi's rehabilitation in 1980, and in fact found no mention of him being tied to his bed for six months.

An essay by Liu's daughter published at the end of that year[14] also made no mention of this detail. But six years later, *Turbulent Decade: A History of the Cultural Revolution*, by Gao Gao and Yan Jiaqi,[15] stated, 'No one changed or washed his clothes or took him to the toilet, and his clothes were covered with excrement. Extended periods lying in bed resulted in his lower limbs atrophying and becoming stick-like, and his body was covered

---

[13] Private communication with the author. Professor Van Slyke has used versions of this quote in his lectures and conversations.
[14] 'The Flowers of Victory Offered to You', *Workers' Daily* (Gongren Ribao), 5–8 December 1980.
[15] Tianjin renmin chubanshe, 1986, p. 178.

with bed sores... They used bandages to tie Liu Shaoqi's legs tightly to the bed so he couldn't move.'

Turbulent Decade was banned from sale before it could appear on the market. The two authors went into exile in 1989. I once asked them the source of their information. They said there was a specific source, but they couldn't look it up because they'd had to leave all their materials for the book behind in China.

Another book published in 1996, *The Cultural Revolution Files*,[16] includes this same detail. Because it was published so long after the fact, this information didn't attract as much notice as it would have done back in 1980; no one was taking much note of Liu Shaoqi by then, so the government censors didn't bother with this detail.

Some people may think that Liu Shaoqi being tied to his bed is a small matter compared with the fact that he was persecuted to death. But by editing out this information, the *People's Daily* did in fact play a role in 'protecting the Party's image'.

There is no practical purpose served by tying a paralysed man to his bed. The only explanation is intentional cruelty and abuse. The article by Liu Shaoqi's daughter does include some other details that are quite horrific. One is that in September 1967, after Liu's wife was arrested and his children were driven from their home, 'that same night, a high wall was built' around Liu's home in Zhongnanhai, and he was no longer allowed to set foot out the door. Other senior officials, including Mao, also lived in Zhongnanhai. To construct an enclosure wall, effectively a prison, in one night allowed Mao and the others to do what they pleased, but could it also be that they enjoyed having Liu Shaoqi suffering so close by? Liu's daughter's article includes another sentence: 'They stopped given Father the vitamins and diabetes medication he'd been taking for years.' Terminating this medication was bound to have serious consequences.

Turbulent Decade states that in October 1969, 'The diabetic Liu Shaoqi had already lost the capacity to look after his own basic needs. He had been bedridden for a long period. No one bathed him, and he became filthy and smelly. Before he was removed from Beijing, the nurse took off his clothes and wrapped him in pink bedding with a white sheet on top.'[17] One of the book's authors, Gao Gao, was a doctor and was especially knowledgeable about illness.

---

[16] Li Songchen et al. (ed.), Beijing, Dangdai Zhongguo chubanshe, 1996, p. 286.
[17] *Turbulent Decade*, pp. 181–182. The English edition translated by D.W.Y. Kwok quoted here (University of Hawai'i Press, 1996, pp. 162–163) omits the sentence about Liu's unwashed state.

Confining Liu behind high walls and stopping his diabetes medication were brutal methods, but they don't provide the same direct, specific and immediately understandable effect of tying a paralysed man to his bed. The *People's Daily* edited out this detail because it was the most horrifying.

The *People's Daily* played a positive role in negating the Cultural Revolution from 1978 onwards. The truth was that in China, only newspapers like this could openly voice their views, while the vast majority of people could only remain silent. But the *People's Daily* could still only go so far, and after so many years of publishing lies, no one would quibble about this minor edit. It is only by chance that I happened to learn of it.

Those of us living outside the Red Wall should ask what other details were edited out, or never written in the first place. No one will answer this question, and as the following narrative shows, this editing of historical truth continues.

Explaining Liu Shaoqi's Death

From material published in official media, we can see how Liu Shaoqi's fate transpired.

During the Eleventh Plenum of the Eighth Central Committee in August 1966, Liu Shaoqi was demoted from the second-highest position in power to the eighth. Soon after that, student rebels began putting up big-character posters attacking Liu and calling for him to be unseated.

In January 1967, Liu Shaoqi was struggled inside Zhongnanhai, and his personal telephone line was cut off. In April, Liu's wife, Wang Guangmei, was struggled by 300,000 people at Tsinghua University. The *People's Daily* referred to Liu (without naming him) as 'the biggest capitalist-roader power-holder within the Party.' In July, hundreds of thousands of revolutionary rebel faction members gathered around Zhongnanhai for more than a month calling for Liu to be 'plucked out'. Liu and his wife were subjected to struggle rallies and beatings inside Zhongnanhai. In September, Liu's wife was sent to prison (she wasn't released until twelve years later), and their children were expelled from Zhongnanhai, while Liu was confined inside his home.

In summer 1968, Liu became seriously ill. In October, the Twelfth Plenum of the Eighth Central Committee declared him a 'renegade, hidden traitor and scab' and permanently expelled him from the Party.

In October 1969, while on the verge of death, Liu was sent to Kaifeng, Henan Province, and remained in custody in a government compound there. He died on 13 November.

Mao died seven years later, in September 1976, and Liu was rehabilitated less than four years after that. All of the accusations against him were withdrawn.

Ordinary people were not allowed to ask why all this had to happen, but the Chinese government quickly offered theories regarding the Cultural Revolution and Liu Shaoqi's death: the main blame fell on Lin Biao and the Gang of Four, and Mao was not at fault.

In 1980, new 100-*yuan* notes included portraits of Mao, Zhou Enlai, Liu Shaoqi and Zhu De. Some people found this line-up very strange: Why did Zhou Enlai come before Liu Shaoqi, when he had ranked behind Liu before the Cultural Revolution? Others said that after Lin Biao died, Zhou became second-in-command, the same as Liu. All of this was just for argument's sake; in pre-Internet times, ordinary people had no way of discussing such topics in writing and could only talk about them.

The government referred to Mao, Zhou, Liu and Zhu as 'great proletarian revolutionaries', 'great Communists' and 'great Marxist–Leninists'. On the bank notes, the four of them are placed close together with no space between them, as if conspiracy, persecution and murder had never occurred among them.

A massive pictorial volume entitled *President of the Republic, Liu Shaoqi* was published in 1988, edited by the CCP Central Committee Research Room and the Xinhua News Agency. The book includes a 'Chronology of Liu Shaoqi's Life', containing only one sentence for 1967: 'On 18 July 1967, while Mao was away from Beijing, Jiang Qing, Kang Sheng and Chen Boda organised an unauthorised rally to denounce Liu Shaoqi and Wang Guangmei.'[18] After so many years, the editors still took pains to manufacture this lie and absolve Mao of responsibility. Why?

As mentioned earlier, unseating Liu Shaoqi was a long-term process, and his persecutors would not hesitate to mobilise a nationwide movement or even a civil war to do so. In the three years from the time Liu Shaoqi lost his second-in-command status until his death, everyone in China was mobilised to shout 'Down with Liu Shaoqi.' Does Mao's absence from Beijing in mid-July 1967 prove he had nothing to do with this plan?

Mao's personal physician, Li Zhisui, said that soon after the struggle rally was held in Zhongnanhai to denounce Liu Shaoqi, Deng Xiaoping and Tao Zhu, Mao had Li flown to Hangzhou and asked him what had happened at the rally.[19] A documentary film was made of the occasion; it has never been

---

[18] CCP Central Committee Research Room, Xinhua News Agency (eds), *President of the Republic, Liu Shaoqi*, Beijing, Zhongyang wenxian chubanshe, 1988, p. 285.

[19] Li Zhisui, *The Private Life of Chairman Mao*, New York, Random House, 1994, pp. 489–491.

shown publicly, and was clearly shot just for viewing by top officials. The scenes of Liu Shaoqi being attacked and forced to stand face down and bent at the waist while being beaten were typical of struggle rallies at that time. After that, Liu Shaoqi was placed in solitary confinement until his death.

In 1999, the new 100-*yuan* note was changed again to include only Mao's portrait. Perhaps after so many years, young Chinese didn't even know who Liu Shaoqi was any more, so what need was there to mention him and conjure up memories and questions about the Cultural Revolution? Mao alone was enough to symbolise power.

If history isn't recorded and analysed, people's recollections will dwindle and disappear or be distorted into a different scenario. As memories fade with time, lies are repeated and dissenting voices are suppressed, and the official version of Liu Shaoqi's fate endures.

A Continuation of Ancient China's Sovereign-Minister Mutual Destruction, or a Chinese Version of Stalinism?

How should the case of Liu Shaoqi, a brutal struggle between China's top two leaders, be explained?

One way of thinking can be traced back to China's ancient tradition of autocracy. In Chinese history, there are many cases of intrigue and murder between emperors and their ministers, especially in the early years of new dynasties.

During the 'Spring and Autumn period', King Wu killed Wu Zixu and King Yue killed Wen Zhong, examples of the idiom that 'when the cunning hare dies, the running dog is cooked.' There is a long list of ministers who were killed after rendering extraordinary service to their emperors.

This new round of killing followed the initial slaughter and usurpation of power, which was carried out among the paramount leader's comrades-in-arms. Unlike factional fighting between bandits, these killings involved certain judicial procedures such as trial and sentencing, and the victim was prosecuted with a written indictment of charges; that is to say, a reason and basis had to be found, or at least manufactured.

The historian Sima Qian's 'Biography of Li Si' states that when Li Si was a young government official, he noticed that rats eating filth in hostel latrines became frightened when humans or dogs approached, but that rats living under the main chamber of the granary were able to fill themselves on grain without any fear of humans or dogs. Li Si sighed, 'So it is with a man's status: it's all a matter of location!' In the time of the Qin dynasty (221–206 BCE), Li Si helped Qin Shihuang attack and annex territories and was appointed prime minister. Later he recommended the notorious burning of books and burying of scholars. After Qin Shihuang died, he helped the late monarch's younger son, Hu Hai, attain the throne. Two years later, Li Si was sentenced to death as a traitor. Sima Qian records that as Li Si made his way to the execution ground on the arm of one of his sons, he said, 'If only it were possible for us to once more take our yellow dog through the eastern gate of Shangcai to hunt the cunning hare!'

Sima Qian records Li Si's words before he died. We don't know where he obtained this information, but since Li Si was executed in public, the report may well be true. No report has been published to date on what Liu Shaoqi said before he died. The last of Liu's words officially reported are, 'Fortunately history is written by the people.' His widow, Wang Guangmei, stated this at the time that Liu was rehabilitated. They had been forcibly separated for two years before Liu died, and nothing has been reported of what Liu said during that time. He was in solitary confinement, and no one who sympathised with him was allowed near him. In this respect, the Cultural Revolution was even crueller than the tyrannical Qin emperor.

In the twentieth century, the most violent slaughter among high-ranking officials occurred in the Soviet Union, China and within Cambodia's Khmer Rouge. Stalin was the originator of this trend. During the agricultural collectivisation movement and campaign against counter-revolutionaries, Stalin caused the deaths of millions of ordinary people, and also purged everyone from the Politburo except for himself. The other six, Leon Trotsky, Grigori Zinovyev, Lev Kamenev, Alexei Rykov, Mikhail Tomsky and Nikolai Bukharin, were either driven to suicide, assassinated or sentenced to death.

Bukharin was imprisoned in 1937. Put on trial as part of a Trotskyite plot, Bukharin confessed his crimes and was executed in 1938. Some say Bukharin confessed because his youngest child was only two years old, and he hoped that by confessing he could protect his family. Others say Stalin tricked him into corroborating his lies with a promise to spare his life. When Liu Shaoqi was taken into custody in 1967, his youngest daughter was only six years old. Liu made two self-criticisms in October 1966 and July 1967. He didn't resist the Cultural Revolution, but that didn't spare him from being struck down.

Another of Stalin's methods was to use one person to purge another, and then use a third person to strike down that person. He repeatedly used this method in the highest circle of power. Stalin united with Bukharin to purge Trotsky, and then purged Zinovyev, Kamenev and finally Bukharin himself. The heads of Stalin's secret police were replaced in the same way.

China's situation was similar. From 4 to 28 May 1966, Liu Shaoqi convened an enlarged Politburo meeting that passed the guiding document of the Cultural Revolution, the 16 May Circular, and purged senior leaders Peng Zhen, Luo Ruiqing, Lu Dingyi and Yang Shangkun. In 1998, Li Xuefeng wrote:

> On the afternoon of 11 May, the Central Committee Politburo enlarged meeting held its first plenum with Liu Shaoqi presiding. Shaoqi, [Deng] Xiaoping and the Premier [Zhou Enlai] were all on the rostrum, but Chairman Mao was away and did not return for the meeting... Someone behind began reading out some kind of report. As soon as he heard it, Peng Zhen became angry and indignant, and he turned around and shouted toward the back, 'Who was the first to shout "Long live"?', to prove that he was the first in history to cry out for the Chairman to have a long life. Shaoqi on the rostrum quickly stopped him, and the quarrel ended.[20]

One year later, it was Liu Shaoqi's turn to defend himself.

According to Liu Shaoqi's children, on 1 April 1967, the *People's Daily* published an article by Qi Benyu attacking Liu Shaoqi entitled 'Patriotism or Treason'. This enraged Liu, who said to his children, 'I'm not a counter-revolutionary and I don't oppose Chairman Mao. I was the one who proposed Mao Zedong Thought at the Seventh Party Congress, and I've promoted Mao Zedong Thought as much as anyone.'[21]

Liu Shaoqi's promotion of Mao Zedong Thought in 1945 greatly enhanced Mao's power and status, but Lin Biao, who replaced Liu as Mao's second-in-command, invented a corpus of language, ceremonies and rules regarding Mao in the 1960s, including the brandishing of Little Red Books and the erecting of gigantic statues of Mao everywhere. In this respect, Peng Zhen and Liu Shaoqi were no match for Lin Biao.

Once Lin Biao came into favour, he was referred to as 'Chairman Mao's close comrade-in-arms' and written into the Constitution as Mao's 'successor'. But he retained this status for only five years before he was ousted by Mao and finally died in Mongolia while attempting to flee from China.

The point is that even though competitive fawning over the supreme ruler only brought disaster, there was no shortage of people willing to give it their all.

This history is astonishing: Mao was not only able to cause the tragic deaths by starvation, violence and humiliation of millions of ordinary

---

[20] Li Xuefeng took over from Peng Zhen as leader of Beijing after Peng was unseated. This was originally published as 'What I Know of the Inside Story of the Launching of the Cultural Revolution', *Bainianchao*, No. 4, 1998, and later included in *What We Experienced*, Beijing shiyue wenyi chubanshe, 2001, pp. 37–38.

[21] 'The Flowers of Victory Offered to You', *op. cit.*

people, but could even cause the deaths of leaders second in power only to him, Liu Shaoqi and Lin Biao, and furthermore do this without any resistance from them. This is a rarity in history.

If Mao hadn't died in 1976, the purges would have continued; it seems that only his death was enough to end the terror. It was the same in the Soviet Union; after the death of Stalin and the most enthusiastic executor of his policies, Lavrentiy Beria, no more Politburo members were killed.

I point out comparisons between Liu Shaoqi's death and Ancient China and Stalinist Russia, not to prove that this sort of thing is widespread and unsurprising, but rather to show that it is not a matter of chance. Killing at the top levels of government is closely related to the social system and prevailing ideology; it is a product of dictatorship and despotism.

Even so, there are differences. China's emperors could kill their outstanding ministers but were never able to mobilise the entire country as Mao did, nor were they able, like Mao, to suspend schooling throughout the country for three to six years so that students could take part in 'plucking out' and denouncing Liu. The enormous economic and moral price that Mao exacted from ordinary people in order to unseat Liu Shaoqi makes ancient emperors and Stalin pale in comparison.

Mao Zedong Micromanaged the Cultural Revolution

Mao was the initiator and leader of the Cultural Revolution. He personally drafted programmatic documents such as the 16 May Circular, reviewed the Red Guards multiple times at Tiananmen Square, promoted the fawning Lin Biao as his successor, established the Central Cultural Revolution Small Group with his wife, Jiang Qing, as 'first vice-chair', launched the campaign to 'strike down Liu, Deng and Tao', supported the 'January power seizure', organised the Revolutionary Committees and launched the Cleansing of the Class Ranks, all of which undeniably constituted overall leadership of the Cultural Revolution. He also, however, showed considerable interest in directing more detailed operations.

On 28 July 1968, Mao received five leaders of rebel faction organisations at five Beijing universities. The main content of the discussion was Mao's sending 'worker propaganda teams' to the universities. Before the conversation ended, Mao suddenly changed the subject to Liu Shaoqi's health. He said: 'I hear Liu Shaoqi's been revived. Liu Shaoqi and Bo Yibo nearly died. They suffer from kidney disease, heart disease, high blood pressure and diabetes. It took four or five doctors and two nurses to save them. Now they're out of danger. Did you hear?'

This part of the conversation had no connection with what came before, and the sudden change of subject to Liu Shaoqi's health suggests that it was a matter of concern to Mao. These remarks, made a year after Liu was placed in solitary confinement and a year before he died, indicate that Mao was closely tracking his condition.

The essay 'The Flowers of Victory Offered to You' by Liu's children mentions that they wrote a letter to Mao in 1972 asking to see their father. Mao sent a memo allowing them to visit their mother in prison, and started it with the sentence, 'Your father is dead.'

When Lin Biao flew out of China in his escape attempt, his daughter, Lin Liheng (Doudou), didn't go along but reported her parents' actions to the higher authorities. Even so, she was subsequently taken into custody. The book *The Ye Qun I Knew*[22] states: 'On 31 July 1974, Chairman Mao received Lin Doudou's letter and issued this memo: "Lift Lin Liheng's surveillance and allow her to contact Zhang Qinglin. She's different from the diehards."' Zhang Qinglin was the prospective husband Lin Biao and his wife had chosen for their daughter before they died. This memo shows that Mao personally controlled the contact between Lin's daughter and her fiancé, even three years after Lin Biao's death.

These details allow us to infer that Mao may have ordered the overnight construction of the wall around Liu Shaoqi's home, the termination of his medication, and his being bound to his bed and sent to Kaifeng festering in his own filth, rather than someone at a lower level making these decisions.

There is one more example. At the end of July 1966, Mao decided to withdraw the work groups from the schools, after which the head of the Peking University work group, Zhang Chengxian, was beaten and humiliated by Red Guards from the university's affiliated secondary school. On 17 August, Mao's directive was transmitted: 'Zhang Chengxian can come out with the work group [i.e. can leave Peking University]. Zhang Chengxian has heart disease and should not be punished to death for his errors.'[23] Zhang's status was lower than Liu Shaoqi's or Lin Biao's; he was only a provincial-level cadre. Even so, Mao directly intervened to ensure that Zhang would not be 'punished to death'.

These examples are merely what we've been able to see in a severely edited historical record. There is little room for doubt that many more dark and horrific details have been covered up or permanently eliminated for fear of damaging the image of Mao or the Communist Party.

---

[22] Guan Weixun, *The Ye Qun I Knew*, Zhongguo wenxue chubanshe, Beijing, 1993, p. 180. Ye Qun was Lin Biao's wife.

[23] See *Chronicle of Peking University*, op. cit., p. 651. Zhang Changxian's own essays after the Cultural Revolution also referred to this matter.

This attention to the details of persecution reflects Mao's personal style. Behind this attention was a relish for the persecution process; Mao enjoyed not only his absolute power over the lives and deaths of ordinary people and his comrades-in-arms and ministers, but also the suffering of his victims' family members.

Many people may enjoy wielding power and inflicting pain on others, but this mentality is normally inhibited and punished by morality and law. Under Chinese autocracy, Mao held paramount power and was not subject to the law or to constraint by other people, so the Cultural Revolution afforded him ample opportunity to brazenly satisfy his cruel and ruthless desires.

When Mao was young, he advocated a philosophy of unrestraint and doing as he pleased. In 1970, he told the American journalist Edgar Snow that he was 'a monk without an umbrella – no hair and no sky' (a pun sounding like the Chinese words 'no law and no Heaven'). Jiang Qing proudly quoted Mao saying this when the Gang of Four were put on trial. Traditional Chinese believed that all behaviour, whether good or evil, was observed by Heaven, and the dread of displeasing the gods constrained people's actions. Mao's yearning for and implementation of a philosophy of 'no law and no Heaven' may be an obvious example of the disintegration of this tradition in China, and helps explain why Mao had no qualms about killing countless ordinary Chinese or persecuting to death the two men who were his seconds-in-command, Liu Shaoqi and Lin Biao.

In *The Gulag Archipelago*, Aleksandr Solzhenitsyn describes people whose profession it was to persecute and eliminate counter-revolutionaries. In one discussion, he said Freud's attribution of basic human desires to eating and sex was not enough; the desire for power should be included as well. He quotes Tolstoy's description of the joy a person feels at wielding the power of life and death, and says this was the joy experienced by functionaries dedicated to eliminating counter-revolutionaries. It is not only the Soviet Union that provides plentiful fodder for this notion; the few examples mentioned here of Mao's trivial memos clearly show that he experienced a similar enjoyment.

Liu Shaoqi and Cultural Revolution Violence

When Liu Shaoqi dropped from the second to the eighth most powerful person in China in August 1966, he was blamed for sending out the work groups, suppressing the student movement and obstructing the Cultural Revolution. Because the history of the Cultural Revolution hasn't been called to account, this explanation continued to prevail.

The essay by Liu's children, 'The Flowers of Victory Presented to You', emphasises that Liu decided to send the work groups to the universities and secondary schools after conferring with Mao. Liu's children wished to show that blaming Liu was inconsistent with the facts, and that Liu hadn't taken the initiative to do something that Mao wouldn't like. The logic they used to defend their father was that if Mao agreed to sending out work groups, it wasn't Liu's fault. They didn't use law or morality as a standard for criticising this act.

The truth is that if we agree that the Cultural Revolution was evil and a crime, then Liu Shaoqi, and Lin Biao after him, acted as Mao's primary aides in promoting it and therefore were the chief accessories to this crime.

The facts are very clear that the work groups were sent in to attack educators and school administrators. If it was only to 'suppress the student movement', relying on the original school leaders would have been enough, as demonstrated in 1957, when university administrators labelled a large number of students as Rightists and imposed harsh punishments on them without obstruction.

As noted earlier, Liu Shaoqi also presided over the enlarged Politburo meeting that drafted the 16 May Circular, which was implemented by work groups dispatched to universities and secondary schools to 'seize power' from 'bourgeois intellectuals' in education circles.

If the work groups hadn't been mobilised to take over leadership of the schools, how would the students have dared attack the school authorities? The schools were led by Communist Party branch committees. It was only with the support of the CCP Central Committee that the students began mass attacks against school leaders and began calling them 'counter-revolutionary revisionist reactionaries'.

Liu Shaoqi's wife, Wang Guangmei, was part of the work group sent to Tsinghua University, which removed Jiang Nanxiang as Tsinghua's leader and as Minister of Higher Education.

Under the leadership of Liu Shaoqi and the work groups, arbitrary percentages of teachers, staff and students were categorised as 'class enemies'. No one has ever been called to account for the mathematics behind this persecution and the cruelty and absurdity it represented.

One of Liu Shaoqi's daughters, a seventeen-year-old student at the Beijing Normal University Affiliated No. 1 Secondary School, was among the first students to attack the school's administrators and lead its Revolutionary Committee.

Beijing's secondary schools suspended classes in early June, around the time the work groups arrived. In a speech to members of the work group at the No. 1 Secondary School on 20 June 1966, Liu Shaoqi said of the school's principal and Party secretary, 'Liu Chao is an anti-Party, anti-socialist element; that is certain... It's still too early to struggle Liu Chao. Start by attacking the enemy's weak spot and then the enemy's backbone. Start by fighting the easiest battles to isolate the main enemy. The people under Liu Chao's command should be made to revolt. Fight to win over the students first, and also the teachers... If Liu Chao is to be struggled, don't do it now. He can be struggled, and active preparations can be made; don't stop, just actively prepare.'

The powerful President of China referred to a secondary school principal as an 'anti-Party, anti-socialist element' and 'enemy', and personally commanded and manipulated a work group and his teenage daughter to 'struggle' that principal, who was never allowed to defend himself or resist.

This process was replicated all over China while Liu Shaoqi was in charge of the Central Committee's work in June and July 1966. Following the 18 June Incident at Peking University, Liu Shaoqi expressed his opposition to 'chaotic struggle'. The Central Committee's endorsement of the 18 June Incident as a 'revolutionary incident' was a turning point in the Cultural Revolution, and marked the fall of Liu Shaoqi as the second most powerful man in China.

Articles published after Liu Shaoqi was rehabilitated say that after he was struggled at Zhongnanhai and then escorted back to his office on 5 August 1967, he took out a copy of the Chinese Constitution and protested his treatment. This dramatic gesture seems entirely justified, but readers might ask, 'What made Liu Shaoqi think of the Constitution then and not earlier?' So many unlawful incidents had occurred, including the struggling of the principal at his daughter's school, but as China's President, what had he said or done? Did he think that the Constitution didn't have to be implemented until the country's President lost his freedom?

The Fate of the Rebels who 'Plucked Out Liu'

The 'pluck Liu movement' occurred on 8 July 1967, outside the red walls of Zhongnanhai. Led by university student 'revolutionary rebel factions', some 200,000 'revolutionary masses' gathered outside Zhongnanhai and demanded that Liu Shaoqi be 'plucked out'.

This movement was launched by rebels of the Beijing Institute of Civil Engineering and Architecture, and they even engaged in a (bogus) hunger strike for more sensational effect.

It made for a grand spectacle, with Fuyou Street, west of Zhongnanhai, thronging with people, a deafening clamour of gongs and drums and constant shouting of slogans, with enormous posters pasted to the walls. The newly created power organ, the Beijing Municipal Revolutionary

Committee, had given the students a large amount of paper to print newspapers and leaflets. All of the rebel factions in the city's work units came over to support the movement. Trucks from suburban university campuses brought food, propaganda materials and loudspeakers.

This movement put the students into the public spotlight as the brutality against Liu Shaoqi escalated behind closed doors. But the students only obtained Liu's written self-criticism and never saw his face; nor did they have the chance to enter Zhongnanhai.

Ironically, during the investigation of the May 16 Clique in 1970, the 1967 'pluck Liu' movement became the 'counter-revolutionary siege of Zhongnanhai', as will be related in Part Six. Some of the 'pluck Liu' activists were placed under 'isolation and investigation' and forced to confess their wrongdoings. In this way, the iron wheel of the Cultural Revolution crushed both China's second most powerful leader, and the young students who had attacked him.

Deng Tuo, born in 1912, an essayist and culture and education secretary for the Beijing Municipal Party Committee, came under criticism at the end of March 1966 for the columns 'Night Chats at Swallow Hill' and 'Jottings from the Three Family Village', of which he was co-author with **Wu Han** and Liao Mosha. Starting in April, the newspapers published a series of essays attacking these works as 'anti-Party and anti-socialist'. Deng Tuo took a drug overdose in his Beijing home on 18 May 1966. He was rehabilitated in 1979.

What degree of criticism was Deng Tuo under at the time of his death? He clearly didn't suffer the kind of physical torment that was inflicted on others after him, but in Beijing, even kindergarten students were taught a new song: 'Wu Han, Deng Tuo, Liao Mosha, three rotten melons on the same vine.'

CENTRAL COMMITTEE PROPAGANDA DEPARTMENT

Yao Qin, deputy director of the Propaganda Department, hanged himself in June 1966. Yao's daughter, Yao Xue, was a student at the Beijing Normal University Affiliated Girls' Secondary School at the time, and because of her father she was attacked in big-character posters. Her position as a student cadre was also used as evidence that she was 'the child of a reactionary in an important position'.

Liu Kelin was a forty-two-year-old leading cadre in the Propaganda Department's international section when he leaped to his death from the fifth floor of the department's office building on the afternoon of 6 August 1966. People inside the building heard a loud crash when he hit the ground.

His family never learned what kind of attacks or persecution he suffered. They heard he'd been accused of being an 'alien-class element', but the background of his death was very unclear. Mao had attacked the Propaganda Department as the Palace of Yama (the King of Hell), and as soon as the Cultural Revolution began, he sent Tao Zhu to be the new director and purge the department. Red Guard violence was also on the rise at just that time. Liu's friend Bian Zhongyun was beaten to death by her students the day before Liu died.

When Liu Kelin died, his wife was working in a Socialist Education Movement work team in Ningxia, so the Propaganda Department authorities asked his eldest daughter whether she wanted to keep the ashes when Liu's body was taken to the crematorium. A secondary school student, she was too afraid to say she wanted the ashes, and Liu Kelin's remains were not preserved. This plagued his daughter's conscience for decades afterwards. Some say, however, that the Propaganda Department authorities had already decided to discard Liu's ashes in accordance with the practice at that time, and that his daughter wouldn't have been given his ashes even if she'd said she wanted them.

When a ceremony was held to lay Liu Kelin's remains to rest after the Cultural Revolution, all that was present was an empty urn. After attending the ceremony, Liu's good friend Liu Shenzhi wrote two poems, one of which included the sentence, 'No tears while facing an empty coffin.' It was a very common situation for victims of the Cultural Revolution.

After Liu Kelin died, his sixty-three-year-old mother-in-law and her eighty-two-year-old mother were expelled from Beijing by Red Guards. Both women died not long afterwards.

Wang Zhongyi was head of the Propaganda Department and vice-chairman of the editorial committee of the works of Mao Zedong. A Grade 10 cadre, Wang had spent time with Mao in Yan'an and was a seasoned revolutionary with a long record of service. After being struggled with other directorate-level leaders, Wang Zhongyi killed himself with an overdose of sleeping pills on 9 September 1966. He was forty-two years old and left behind a sick wife and four children. His ashes were not retained.

At noon on the day Wang died, his daughter, a secondary school student, told a friend that she couldn't wake up her father. The friend accompanied her back home, and found Wang dead in his bed. The father of the daughter's friend was Liu Kelin, who had leaped to his death not long before.

Zhang Linzhi, born in 1908, joined the CCP in 1929. As Minister of the Coal Industry Ministry and an alternative member of the CCP Central Committee, he was beaten to death while being denounced at the Beijing Mining Institute on 22 January 1967.

Before the Cultural Revolution, from 15 December 1964 to 14 January 1965, the CCP Central Committee convened a work conference to summarise the experience of the Socialist Education Movement. During the conference, during a 'very small-scale' enlarged meeting of the Politburo Standing Committee, Mao had the following conversation with Liu Shaoqi:

> Mao: 'This movement of ours was called the Socialist Education Movement... its focus was to rectify the capitalist-roader power-holders within the Party.'
> Liu: 'There are capitalist-roaders, but the capitalist class has been eliminated, so how can such a faction exist? Once you start talking about a faction, too many people are involved, and the contradiction between the enemy and us is everywhere. Who in the Coal Ministry or Metallurgy Industry is a capitalist-roader power-holder?'
> Mao uttered without much thought, 'Zhang Linzhi is one.'[24]

Perhaps not coincidentally, Zhang Linzhi was the first ministry-level cadre to be seized and struggled to death in a school in Beijing, and is probably the only central government official who died while under the control of student Red Guards. As the Cultural Revolution's targets expanded from the schools, senior Communist cadres were also sent to the schools to be struggled after they were 'struck down'. As Minister of the Coal Industry, Zhang Linzhi was struggled at a corresponding educational institution, the Mining Institute.

On 24 December 1966, Qi Benyu of the Central Cultural Revolution Small Group spoke at a mass rally at the Mining Institute, saying that Zhang Linzhi was a 'diehard follower of Peng Zhen' (who had been publicly struck down in June 1966), and that he had to be 'thoroughly struck down and discredited'. After this, Zhang was repeatedly denounced and beaten until he died on 22 January. There were differing claims regarding whether he was beaten to death or committed suicide, but it is beyond dispute that he had been brutally beaten and seriously injured at the time of his death.

---

[24] See Gao Xiaoyan, 'Liu Shaoqi, Mao Zedong and the Four Cleans Campaign', *Southern Weekend* (Nanfang Zhoumo), 20 November 1998. This article was the result of interviews Gao Xiaoyan carried out with He Jiadong and Liu Shaoqi's son, Liu Yuan, on the occasion of the hundredth anniversary of Liu Shaoqi's birth. This conversation is also recorded in the book *The Unknown Liu Shaoqi*, Henan renmin chubanshe, 2000, p. 116.

Nan Hanchen, born in 1895 and the first governor of the People's Bank of China (1949–1954), was a delegate to the National People's Congress and chairman of the Chinese Committee for the Promotion of International Trade when he was accused of being a traitor and a capitalist-roader. Nan killed himself in January 1967 by taking an overdose of sleeping pills that a doctor said could have knocked out an elephant.

Wang Bi was a veteran Party member and cadre in the Ministry of Finance. Her husband, Gu Zhun, served as director of the Shanghai Finance Bureau and Tax Bureau after 1949, but was dismissed in 1952 and designated a Rightist in 1957. After being rehabilitated in 1961, Gu was once again labelled a Rightist in 1965. The couple divorced, but Wang Bi was persecuted during the Cultural Revolution for 'long-term sheltering of a counter-revolutionary husband' and 'destroying evidence of counter-revolutionary crime'. Wang Bi poisoned herself to death on 8 April 1968, at the age of fifty-four. Gu Zhun died on 3 December 1974; two of his books were finally published in the 1990s, *The Greek City-State System* and *From Idealism to Empiricism*, becoming very influential in scholarly circles.

Hu Maode, born in 1923, was a Class 13 cadre at the Central Broadcasting Administration's External Broadcasts Department. On 10 May 1968, the broadcast administration arranged a struggle session for Hu Maode, Qi Yue and other cadres. Before the struggle session was held, Hu jumped to his death from the sixth floor of the administration's office building on Chang'an Avenue, grazing a huge portrait of Mao hanging on the front of the building as he fell. His body was left on the ground for several hours, covered with a plastic sheet. The struggle session was rescheduled because of his death. Hu's friend Li Shenzhi was a cadre with the Xinhua News Agency who had been designated a Rightist in 1957. When he learned of Hu's death, Li went to his home and circled the door three times but didn't go in. Hu left behind a son and daughter, both in primary school at the time.

Xu Guangda, born in 1908, was Deputy Minister of Defence and a member of the Eighth CCP Central Committee. Dai Huang's book *Hu Yaobang and the Rectification of Unjust Cases* reveals that a Central Committee special investigation team tried to force Xu to admit to being 'chief of general staff of the He Long mutiny' and other such crimes, beating him repeatedly until he suffered a heart attack and fell unconscious. After a doctor at the scene revived him, they continued to beat him until he could no longer stand, and then placed him in a cane chair and continued to beat him until the chair toppled over, then righted the chair and continued to beat him until his clothes were covered with blood. Xu Guangda was admitted to the hospital in November 1968, and during his sixty days there, he was interrogated seventy-nine times and forced to write twenty-five confessions. On another occasion he spent eighty-one days in the hospital, during which he was interrogated twenty-nine times and had to write twenty-nine confessions. Xu was reported to be in critical condition on 23 May 1969, but the interrogations continued. Bedridden three days before his death, he was still dragged down to 'admit his crime and appeal for Chairman Mao's leniency'. He died on 3 June.

Jiang Yiping, alias Wang Xuxin, was born in 1922 and joined the CCP in Yantai in 1938. A technical school graduate, he at various times headed up the Dalian Chemical Plant, Jilin Chemical Engineering Company and Taiyuan Chemical Fertiliser Factory, and served as Minister of Chemical Engineering and director of the State Planning Commission's Chemical Engineering Department. Persecuted during the Cultural Revolution, he killed himself in November 1969.

Li Bingquan, head of the Xinhua News Agency's External Affairs Department, died on 2 May 1970, while under 'isolation and investigation'. He was declared to have committed suicide, but the wounds on his body led some to suggest that he had been killed.

Someone told me about Li's death and suggested that I go to Xinhua's 'veteran cadre office' to ask for his wife's address and find out what had happened. Before I could do this, I read an article by Li's old colleague, Li Shenzhi, entitled 'Li Bingquan's Tragic Life during the Cultural Revolution',[25] which provided many details.

The article says that Li Bingquan had spent years doing underground work for the Party, and made an enormous contribution to facilitating talks between the northern military leader Fu Zuoyi and the CCP that led to the 'peaceful liberation' of Beijing, and had even been the subject of a famous documentary film. During the Cultural Revolution, he was persecuted as a 'reactionary man of letters' and forced to move from a high-rise building to a shabby dormitory. Li Shenzhi's essay emphasised that the articles that served as 'evidence' of Li Bingquan's 'crime' were written while Li was writing for the *Pingming Daily* under Fu Zuoyi's government. At that time, he was working underground for the CCP and was obliged to attack it as cover. Furthermore, he had submitted the articles to the Party for approval prior to publication.

Li Shenzhi's essay is clear and powerful, but his comments on his colleague's death have some blind spots. One of them is that while vigorously defending Li, he gives the impression that if Li Bingquan had actually meant what he wrote in those articles, there would have been good reason to subject him to such brutal punishment during the Cultural Revolution without any legal process.

---

[25] *Yanhuang Zisun*, August 2003.

The second blind spot is that Li Bingquan's experience was tragic and deserving of sympathy, but his wasn't an isolated case. These brutal mass purges had been carried out among high-level Communist cadres for decades in the Soviet Union, China and Kampuchea. Large numbers of senior cadres had been brutally persecuted and even killed, while the accusations made against them were subsequently found to be false. The pervasiveness of this phenomenon showed that this was not the result of particularly ruthless individuals, but of the system and basic theory of the countries in which they occurred. Defending Li Bingquan on the basis of his individual circumstances is inadequate.

Fan Changjiang, born in 1909, was a CCP member and a famous reporter in the 1930s. When the Cultural Revolution started, he was vice-chairman and Party secretary of the China Association of Sciences. Fan was subjected to ruthless struggle starting in 1967 and was sent to the May 7 Cadre School of the Chinese Academy of Sciences in Queshan County, Henan Province in March 1969. On 22 December 1970, he was struggled deep into the night. The next morning his naked body was found in a nearby well, and his death was declared a suicide, although no suicide note was found.

A 'Fan Changjiang News Award' was established in 1991. According to the *People's Daily* online, 'The Fan Changjiang News Award is the Chinese Journalists' Association's highest award for young and middle-aged journalists. It is a permanent national award approved by the Central Propaganda Department... The objective of the selection process is to commend and encourage all journalists to learn from and continue the noble spirit of Comrade Fan Changjiang's dedication to the cause of the people.'

Fang Changjiang visited Yan'an in 1936 and interviewed Mao and Zhou Enlai, publishing his reports in *Dagong Bao*. The article about him in the *People's Daily* online is entitled: 'Fan Zhangjiang: A Red Star on China's Frontline of Journalism in the 1930s.' The article said that Fan joined the Party in 1939 under Zhou Enlai's sponsorship, and included a photo of Fan being received by Mao. The luxurious display in the background of the photo indicates that it was taken after Mao assumed power in 1949. The article says nothing about what happened to Fan after 1949.

After the CCP took power, Fan Changjiang served as editor-in-chief of the Xinhua News Agency, publisher of *Liberation Daily*, deputy director of the General Administration of Press and Publication and publisher of *People's Daily*. However, he left journalism in 1952. Clearly, what he wrote in 1936 was beneficial to the CCP, but once the Party came to power, it no longer needed his type of journalism.

How is it that a journalist who had a national award named after him in 1991 did not engage in journalistic work from 1952 onwards? And why was he found dead in a well in 1970? None of this has ever been reported or analysed, and taken together, the contrast is ironic. Perhaps that is why no one is allowed to talk about why Fan left journalism and how he died.

SHANXI PROVINCE

Li Jisheng, director of the Taiyuan Municipal Education Bureau, killed himself on 13 September 1966, two days after being 'seized and struggled'.

SHANGHAI

Lü Xianchun, a Communist Party member and deputy section chief in the Shanghai Municipal Finance Bureau, killed herself in August 1966. During the 'Smashing of the Four Olds', Lü voluntarily handed over valuables and other items to her work unit and requested that her home not be ransacked. Even so, people from the Finance Bureau ransacked Lü's home as well as her mother's. Lü Xianchun then leaped to her death.

Chen Lian, a forty-eight-year-old cadre in the Propaganda Department of the CCP Central Committee East China Bureau, leaped to her death from her home on the eleventh floor of Shanghai's Taixing Building on 19 November 1967, after being accused of being a traitor.

Chen Lian was the daughter of a former senior KMT official, Chen Bulei. She and her husband, Yuan Yongxi, joined the CCP as students in the late 1930s. Both were imprisoned by the Nationalist government in 1947 but were released when Chen's father posted bail. The couple continued to work for the CCP, and both became high-level cadres after 1949. Yuan Yongxi became Party secretary of Tsinghua University, and in 1952 went to Peking University and forced all the teachers, administrators and students to make a 'frank debriefing' of their so-called 'historical problems'. (See the entry on **Pan Guangdan** in Part One.)

In 1957, Yuan Yongxi was designated a Rightist and sent to a labour reform farm in Beijing's suburban Changping County for five years. Chen Lian divorced her husband, after which she was appointed Party secretary of the Beijing Forestry Institute but never took up the position. In 1962 she was appointed to the Propaganda Department of the CCP Central Committee East China Bureau in Shanghai, and she was also a member of the Chinese People's Political Consultative Conference at that time.

Chen Lian had a younger brother who was also designated a Rightist in 1957. Her son wrote in 2002:

> My sixth uncle, Chen Sui, a graduate of Shanghai's Jiaotong University and teacher at the Jianshe Secondary School, was labelled a Rightist. We heard nothing from him after he was sent to Ningxia for labour reform. After the Cultural Revolution ended, the family was notified that my uncle had died during the Great Famine in 1962. At that time, the labour reform team made starving inmates go out to gather their own wild herbs to allay their hunger, and my uncle died after accidently eating something poisonous. He died at the age of thirty-six having never married.[26]

The above account indicates that the family didn't learn of Chen Sui's death until more than ten years later, and that he had no contact with his family after he was sent to labour reform. This kind of 'drawing a clear distinction' was applied not only to Chen Lian and her husband, but also to Chen and her brother.

Before the Cultural Revolution, 'drawing a clear distinction' largely protected Chen Lian's social standing and the living conditions of her three children. But once the Revolution began and its targets of attack further expanded, Chen Lian was unable to escape accusations that she had turned traitor while imprisoned by the Nationalist government.

Sun Lan, director and Party secretary of the Shanghai Education Department, became a key target during the Cultural Revolution. After the department established a Revolutionary Committee in August 1967, it organised a 'Sun Lan Special Investigation Group' that tortured and humiliated Sun more than 100 times. She killed herself on 8 April 1968.

Liu Wang Liming, born in 1896, was a member of the Central Committee of the China Democratic League. She was designated a Rightist in 1957, and in September 1966 she was struggled for three days by Red Guards in Shanghai and then detained at the Public Security Bureau. She died in prison on 15 April 1970.

Born Wang Liming in Taihu County (Liu was her husband's surname), she won a scholarship to study in the US in 1917 and obtained a Master's degree in biology at Northwestern University in Chicago. She was a participant in the Nationalist government's National Assembly in 1928 and 1932, and in 1933 became a member of the China Democratic League's Central Committee. She took part in activities opposing the ruling Kuomintang.

In 1949, Liu joined the Preparatory Committee for the CCP's Political Consultative Conference and was elected a delegate. She then served as a delegate to the second, third and fourth CPPCCs, and was a member

---

[26] Chen Bida, 'In Memory of My Father', published on Tao Shilong's Five Willow Village website, 2002.

of the Standing Committee for the second and third. She was also on the Standing Committee of the Chinese Women's Federation.

After Liu was designated a Rightist in 1957, her son Liu Guanghua, a *Wenhui Bao* reporter stationed in Beijing, was also designated a Rightist.

Half a year before the Cultural Revolution began, Liu broke her wrist and began living with her daughter in Shanghai. In September 1966, the Red Generation Red Guards of Shanghai Jiaotong University targeted Liu and subjected her to mass struggle, ransacking her home and taking away photos and other materials. The Red Guards required no official documents to confiscate these items, and their targets couldn't ask who authorised the search and seizure, but Liu's family knew the action had been taken with the agreement of the Shanghai authorities.

After being struggled for three days, Liu was sent to Shanghai's No. 2 Detention Centre along the Huangpu River. Her family was notified to bring clothes for her, and much later she was formally arrested and transferred elsewhere; her family was never told where she was.

Liu was arrested on the charge of being an 'American agent' because she had studied in the US and her eldest son had remained in the US after also studying there. From a legal standpoint, this doesn't make sense, but in terms of the authorities' intentions, it was easy to understand. The authorities wanted to cut off all Western influence in China, which meant attacking and purging anyone who had been educated abroad or who had family in the West.

Liu was never formally tried but remained in prison, as was common during the Cultural Revolution, since the legal system had been completely dismantled. Three years and eight months later, in 1970, Lu's daughter was informed verbally that Liu had died in prison of heart disease, and that her body had been disposed of. The family never received any formal death certificate or their mother's ashes.

After Liu's son Liu Guanghua was labelled a Rightist, he was sent to Qinghe Farm for Re-education through Labour. Qinghe Farm was an enclave located 150 kilometres from Beijing but which was still under the capital's jurisdiction and was used as a labour farm for its residents. More than three years later, Liu Guanghua was 'released from re-education', but he remained on the farm and was later transferred to another farm even farther from Beijing but still under the city's jurisdiction. Later yet he was sent to an ordinary village in the northeast, where he laboured until 1978. By the time he learned of his mother's death, she'd already been gone for two months.

Liu Guanghua was labelled a Rightist because he wrote an article about the big-character posters students at Peking University had put up to 'air their views' on 19 May 1957. Liu said he arrived at Peking University on 22 May, just three days after students there began putting up posters criticising the government. The university's deputy Party secretary, Cui Xiongkun, had the posters taken down. Liu Guanghua reported these matters as a journalist who had been trained to believe that his first responsibility was to report the truth. His article was published in *Guangming Daily* and *Wenhui Bao*. The situation changed rapidly, and those who had aired their views suddenly became 'Rightists', as did Liu Guanghua thanks to his article.

When I interviewed Liu Guanghua in 2000, he said he no longer had a copy of the article and couldn't recall its exact date of publication. Hearing this made me feel the seriousness of the loss of information; a reporter wasn't even able to save a copy of the item that had caused him so much hardship. Later I read an article regarding that news report in the Peking University student magazine *Forum* from 1957, and I copied it down. It's not Liu's original piece, but rather the written attack on him, but it gives some idea of what he wrote.

Reactionary News Report – Liu Guanghua, Writer of 'Peking University's Democracy Wall'

This reactionary article was published in *Wenhui Bao* on 25 May. It is an article of political incitement in which he not only vilifies the Party but also holds that the students' spectacular and righteous actions attacking the frenzied assault by Rightists were 'groundless fears', and extolled Rightists as 'young people full of vigour and vitality'. He described the Rightists' attacks against the Party and socialism as 'a tonic and restorative to cure the ills of the Peking University leadership.'

Who is Liu Guanghua, the author of this article? He is a young reporter with *Wenhui Bao* and the son of Liu Wang Liming, a member of the Luo Longji Clique, and he graduated from the Journalism Department of Yenching University. In college he edited *Survey*, his head full of bourgeois thought, and at the university he was struggled and was unhappy about it, so he wrote a letter of complaint that he wanted to publish in a Hong Kong newspaper.

While Liu Guanghua was at the labour farm, the Peking University administrator **Cui Xiongkun**, whom he'd written about in his article, drowned himself at the university in 1968. Not many people would have imagined this back in 1957.

After Mao's death, there was a gradual easing, and back in Shanghai, Liu Guanghua and his sister wrote a petition on behalf of their mother and sent it to the Shanghai municipal government in 1978. The reply was that the government 'upheld the original verdict of a contradiction between the enemy and us handled as a contradiction among the people'.

Liu's daughter petitioned the Organisation Department of the CCP Central Committee in Beijing, where the director, Hu Yaobang, was actively promoting rehabilitation work. The Organisation Department replied through the Shanghai Municipal Party Committee, stating that the problem would be resolved.

The day after Liu's daughter received the letter, she was called to the Shanghai Public Security Bureau, where two men who looked like section chiefs told her, 'We've looked into it, and we're upholding the original verdict.'

At that point, Liu's daughter took out the letter from the Organisation Department, and the two men immediately said, 'What was declared just now doesn't stand. You'll be notified later.'

The problem still wasn't resolved, however. Liu Guanghua and his sister asked someone to make inquiries in Beijing, and Hu Yaobang's secretary said a phone call had been made to Shanghai. After Hu's secretary called Shanghai twice, the Municipal Party Committee sent someone to look into Liu's case with the deputy director of the PSB. Liu Wang Liming was rehabilitated in 1979, and in March 1981 the CPPCC held a memorial ceremony for her and placed her urn at the Babaoshan Revolutionary Cemetery. It was empty, since Liu's ashes hadn't been retained.

In this exhausting process of getting Liu rehabilitated, analysis and introspection on the political thinking of Liu Wang Liming and others who shared her experience was completely neglected.

The *Taihu Gazetteer* published in 1995 includes a 2,000-word account of Liu Wang Liming, describing how she'd taken a stand against the Nationalist government in the 1930s and 1940s and emphasising her work for the CCP after 1949, which had earned her the praise of Mao and Zhou Enlai. However, the *Gazetteer* contains only a single sentence regarding her imprisonment and death. This was typical of the trend in the 1990s of expunging the bloodstains of the Cultural Revolution in an effort to bolster Mao's prestige.

SICHUAN PROVINCE

Yao Su, county head of Suining County, Sichuan Province, was brutally seized and struggled and locked up during the Cultural Revolution. He drowned himself in a river on 27 July 1967.

CHONGQING

Sun Bin, deputy director and deputy Party secretary of the Chongqing Municipal Public Security Bureau, hanged himself on 15 June 1967, after being denounced at a mass rally.

Xia Zhongshi, born in 1889, had been a delegate to the CPPCC, and at the time of the Cultural Revolution was chairman of the Chongqing Municipal Party Committee. He had been a lieutenant general of the KMT's 78th Army, but surrendered to the Communists during the Civil War. Xia was arrested on 14 September 1968, and locked up in a training team set up by the Revolutionary Committee's people's defence group. He was accused of being the 'deputy commander-in-chief and chief-of-staff' of the 'National Revolutionary Army First Army Group Counter-revolutionary Clique'. Nearly eighty years old, Xia was interrogated under torture for more than two months, and finally died in January 1969.

TIANJIN

Li Liang, born Lin Zengtong in 1918, was the great-grandson of Lin Zexu, the Viceroy of Canton who attempted to end the opium trade in the 1800s. At the time of his death, Li was a cadre in the Tianjin Public Security Bureau's Third Department. Accused of 'illicit relations with a foreign country' in 1968, Li was struggled and interrogated under torture and was formally arrested at a 'smash the public security, procuratorial and judicial apparatus' rally on 22 April. Li died in prison on 27 February 1969. He was rehabilitated after the Cultural Revolution.

Zheng Enshou, a nationally renowned fisheries expert, deputy director of the Tianjin Fisheries Bureau and director of the Hebei Fisheries School, was accused of being 'head of a spy ring', as the pre-1949 Chinese Fisheries Construction Association was called. Zheng Enshou was beaten to death during the Cleansing of the Class Ranks on 14 November 1968, and ten other former members of the association were permanently disabled. The victims were rehabilitated in 1979.

SHAANXI PROVINCE

Xu Bu was vice-mayor of Xi'an and secretary of the Municipal Party Committee secretariat. Xu had been vice-mayor of Nanjing, but soon after the Cultural Revolution began, he was transferred to Xi'an and led Cultural Revolution activities there. He leaped to his death after being struck down in 1967.

Hai Tao, a native of Henan from the Hui ethnic minority, was chair of the Shaanxi Province Women's Federation when she took an overdose of medicine after being struggled during the Cultural Revolution. Hai had joined the CCP at a young age, and her husband, Song Youtian, was a high-level Party cadre who became vice-governor of Shaanxi Province after the Cultural Revolution.

FUJIAN PROVINCE

Liu Peishan, a lieutenant general and second political commissar of the Fuzhou Military Region, was criticised for his leadership of a work group sent to Nanchang for 'support-the-Left' work. After making a self-criticism before the masses in Nanchang's People's Square on the evening of 7 June 1967, he was sent to a 'Central Committee Study Class' in Beijing, where he killed himself on 8 May 1968.

Chronology of Zhou Enlai[27] records that Zhou expressed the following opinion on how to handle this: 'Comrade Liu Peishan should be held responsible for his suicide. But due to objective reasons, he cannot be said to have committed suicide to escape punishment or to have been a traitor. Comrade Liu Peishan was a revolutionary warrior for decades, and his family should enjoy the treatment of the family of a revolutionary cadre. I agree to his ashes being placed at the Yuhuatai Martyrs Memorial Hall in Nanjing.'

LIAONING PROVINCE

Zhang Zhixin, a thirty-nine-year-old cadre in the Propaganda Department of the Liaoning Provincial Party Committee, was arrested as a 'current counter-revolutionary' on 24 September 1969, after expressing alternative views regarding the methods used in the Cultural Revolution. Sentenced to life in prison, Zhang Zhixin was tortured extensively and became deranged, after which she was further charged with 'maintaining a reactionary standpoint'. Zhang was sentenced to death and summarily executed on 3 April 1975. Before she was taken to the execution ground, her windpipe was cut so she couldn't speak.

Taking special precautions to prevent a condemned person from speaking at the execution ground was common at the time, especially for those

---

[27] *Chronology of Zhou Enlai*, CCP Central Committee Documentary Research Room, 1997, pp. 235–236.

sentenced at 'public trials'. Severing the windpipe was the most brutal of these methods. The Liaoning Provincial Revolutionary Committee, headed by Mao's nephew, Mao Yuanxin, authorised Zhang Zhixin's death sentence.

NINGXIA HUI ETHNIC MINORITY AUTONOMOUS REGION

Tian Tao, Party secretary of Sishilidian Commune in Helan County, joined the CCP in 1939 and at one point served as a cadre in its Central Committee's Northwest China Bureau. During the Cultural Revolution, he put up a big-character poster in Yinchuan City opposing the leaders of the autonomous region's Revolutionary Committee. He was arrested on 12 February 1970, during the campaign against counter-revolutionaries, and on 15 March the 'Revolutionary Committee Defence Department' sentenced him to death, suspended for two years, as a current counter-revolutionary. Tian died in prison on 9 November 1971. He was eventually rehabilitated.

PART FOUR

Victims of Factional Struggle

By 1968, the officially sponsored 'conservative' Red Guards had been largely disbanded, and rebel faction mass organisations (also an outgrowth of the Red Guard movement) were the most active elements in the Cultural Revolution. Although calling themselves rebels, these groups were invariably loyal to Mao Zedong and supported the Revolution he had created. The rebel organisations vied for power among themselves, each attempting to establish its revolutionary credentials through violent conflict with rival groups.

Deaths in such battles were different from other kinds of deaths in which the victim was persecuted without being able to retaliate or even talk back. In armed battles, two sides faced off and berated and attacked each other. Furthermore, victims of persecution had no way out, while there was usually a choice of whether or not to participate in an armed battle, and an element of personal responsibility. But it was the Cultural Revolution that created the opportunity for them to fight and also gave them the chance to kill others. Both sides vied to prove their loyalty to Mao and their enthusiastic execution of the order to attack 'class enemies', which clearly facilitated Mao's implementation and promotion of the Cultural Revolution. In a sense, those who died participating in these battles were also its victims.

BEIJING

TSINGHUA UNIVERSITY

The rebel faction that dominated Tsinghua University was the Jinggang Mountain Corps, named after the place where Mao launched his armed rebellion. The leader of the Jinggang Mountain Corps, Kuai Dafu, was a Tsinghua student who had come under attack from President Liu Shaoqi's wife, Wang Guangmei, on 7 June 1966. Mao subsequently voiced support for Kuai and made him a vanguard of the Cultural Revolution famous throughout the country.

Beginning in January 1967, Kuai Dafu took charge of the Tsinghua campus and also established 'liaison stations' to promote the Cultural Revolution in every province and major city. From the perspective of its victims, the rebel faction committed many evil acts, but from the perspective of the Cultural Revolution's leaders, the faction rendered extraordinary service.

From early April until 27 July 1968, the Jinggang Mountain Corps engaged in armed battle for more than 100 days with a smaller organisation known as 4–14. According to *Tsinghua University Annals*,[1] twelve people were killed during this time, hundreds were wounded, and school buildings and other facilities were destroyed. Among the victims during this time was **Luo Zhengfu**, a twenty-eight-year-old worker at the Beijing No. 1 Machine-tool Factory who was the younger brother of Luo Zhengqi, a cadre at Tsinghua University. When Tsinghua's Jinggang Mountain Corps Public Security Group attempted but failed to seize Luo Zhengqi on 4 April 1968, they abducted Luo Zhengfu instead, even though he had nothing to do with the university. They stuffed up his mouth with cotton yarn used for buffing vehicles and loaded him into the trunk of a vehicle to take him back to Tsinghua. Luo choked to death on the way. Others killed included **Bian Yulin**, a student of chemical engineering, and **Duan Hongshui**, a nineteen-year-old construction worker, both of whom were stabbed to death during a factional battle at the university on 30 May 1968. **Qian Pinghua**, a twenty-five-year-old student in the Automation Department, was fatally struck by a stray bullet while returning to school at noon on 18 July 1968.

On the morning of 27 July 1968, more than 30,000 members of the Capital Workers and Peasants Mao Zedong Thought Propaganda Team invaded the Tsinghua campus to re-establish control. They consisted of workers from sixty-one factory and mining enterprises, under the command of military personnel. Eyewitnesses say that the Propaganda Team arrived in large trucks that created a convoy of awe-inspiring length on the highway leading to the school.

The Jinggang Mountain Corps believed that 'black hands' had sent the Propaganda Team to Tsinghua to attack them, and they fought back, killing four members of the Propaganda Team and injuring hundreds

---

[1] Tsinghua daxue chubanshe, 2001.

of others. Three members of the Propaganda Team were killed with a home-made hand grenade over by the dormitories around 6:00 that evening: **Pan Zhihong**, a thirty-year-old worker at the Beijing Power Supply Bureau, **Wang Songlin**, the thirty-six-year-old deputy section chief of the Beijing No. 2 Machine-tool Factory, and **Zhang Xutao**, a thirty-nine-year-old worker at the Beijing No. 541 Factory. Two more members of the Propaganda Team were killed at 10:00 that night: **Li Wenyuan**, a thirty-six-year-old worker at the Beijing No. 4 Rubber Factory, was shot, and **Han Zhongxian**, a thirty-six-year-old worker at the Beijing No. 1 Foodstuff Factory and a member of its Revolutionary Committee, was stabbed with a spear while he was resting in a building.

At 3:00 a.m. in the morning on 28 July, Mao, Lin Biao, Zhou Enlai and other top leaders of the Cultural Revolution summoned Kuai Dafu and four other famous university rebel leaders and told them that the 'black hand' behind the Propaganda Teams was in fact Mao. From then on, Kuai Dafu gradually lost power, and military representatives and the Propaganda Team controlled Tsinghua until Mao's death in 1976.

The '100-day war' at Tsinghua University is recorded and described in the *Tsinghua Annals* and in an essay by Professor Tang Shaojie entitled 'A Review of Tsinghua University's 27 July Incident'. But no articles to date have touched on the question that should be asked regarding the five victims who died at that time: Given that it would have been possible to avoid the violent confrontation when the Propaganda Team entered Tsinghua, who was responsible for their deaths?

Mao chose to dispatch the Propaganda Team; no one but him could make such a major decision. At the same time, it's very clear that when the Propaganda Team entered the school, Kuai Dafu was in telephone contact with people outside and was told that the Propaganda Team was being sent to Tsinghua. But no one told Kuai that this decision had been made by the Cultural Revolution's supreme power organ, and that's why the Jinggang Mountain Corps violently resisted.

If Kuai Dafu had known that Mao had made this decision, there's no way he would have dared to openly oppose it. His rise from an ordinary student to the famous 'Commander Kuai' had been fostered entirely by Mao's support. He had no resources or ability to resist Mao; he merely misunderstood who was backing the Propaganda Team. This misunderstanding was to a considerable degree created by Mao's strong support for Kuai over the preceding two years.

This can be seen from the conversation Mao had with the five student leaders in the early hours of 28 July. The meeting started before Kuai Dafu arrived.

MAO: [NIE YUANZI, TAN HOULAN, HAN AIJING and WANG DABIN enter the meeting room, MAO stands and shakes their hands] You're all so young!
[MAO shakes hands with HUANG ZUOZHEN] Your name is Huang Zuozhen? We haven't met, you weren't killed?
JIANG QING: It's been a long time.
MAO: Didn't we see you at Tiananmen Square? But we didn't speak, that's no good! You wouldn't 'ascend to the temple' for no reason, but I've read about you and I know about your situation. Why didn't Kuai Dafu come? Was he unable to get away, or didn't he want to come?
XIE FUZHI: It could be he didn't want to come.
HAN AIJING: That's not so. How would he not come if he knew the Central Cultural Revolution Small Group wanted to see him? He would cry if he didn't get to see the Chairman. It has to be that he was unable to get away.
MAO: Kuai Dafu wanted to catch the black hand. So many workers were 'suppressing' and 'oppressing' the Red Guards, but who was the black hand? No one's been caught. The black hand was me! He didn't come. He should come to catch me! The Xinhua Printing Factory, Knitting Factory and Central Security Unit were sent by me. I said, how can we resolve the armed fighting at the university? You go in and do some work and see what's happening, and it turned out 30,000 people went. The fact is that they hate Peking University but not Tsinghua. [To NIE:] What are the workers and students up to, tens of thousands marching in the streets? I hear you received them pretty well – was it you or Jinggang Mountain?
NIE YUANZI: We stood at the main entrance and passed out water...
WEN YUCHENG, HUANG ZUOZHEN: It wasn't them. What unit did Peking University fight with?
NIE: It was with the Agricultural School. They berated us as old fogeys.
MAO: You didn't fight with them?
NIE: We fought each other.
MAO: Peking University caught its black hand, but that black hand wasn't me, it was Xie Fuzhi. I'm not that ambitious. I said, a few of you go and discuss things with them. Kuai Dafu said there were 100,000.
XIE: It was fewer than 30,000.
MAO: What do you all think about the fighting at the universities? One possibility is a full withdrawal and leaving the students alone and letting them fight as they want. In the past, the Revolutionary Committee and garrison command didn't care about the fighting at the universities and didn't worry about it or try to suppress it, but it seems that wasn't right. The other possibility is to give some help, and the workers were

in full agreement with this, as were the peasants and most of the students. There are more than fifty universities and colleges, and about five or six have been having intense fighting, testing your abilities. As to how to solve this, one lives in the south and another in the north, both known as New Peking University with parentheses, (Jinggang Mountain) or (Commune), like the Communist Party of the Soviet Union (Bolshevik). How about military control, asking Comrade Lin Biao to assume command along with Huang Yongsheng – we still need to solve the problem! You've been engaged in the Cultural Revolution for two years. Struggle-criticism-transformation, now it's no struggle, no criticism, no transformation. Struggle is struggle, you're engaged in armed struggle. The people don't like it, the workers don't like it, the peasants don't like it, the local residents don't like it, the students at most of the schools don't like it, and most of the students at your schools don't like it. Even the faction that endorses you doesn't like it. Is that how you unite the country? You at New Peking University, most of you are old Buddhas, philosophers. Are there none who oppose you in the New Peking University Commune, in the school's Cultural Revolution Committee? I don't believe it! If they don't say it to your face, they're sure to be complaining behind your back. Wang Dabin, are things going a little better for you?

[KUAI DAFU arrived in the middle of the meeting. The record continues as follows...

HUANG ZUOZHEN reported that KUAI DAFU arrived. KUAI came in crying. MAO stood up and walked forward with his hand extended, JIANG QING smiling. KUAI wept as he reported an emergency situation at Tsinghua, saying black hands had manipulated workers to invade Tsinghua and suppress the students, and it was a major conspiracy.

Someone commented that KUAI DAFU's behaviour at this point was like a spoiled child tattling to his parents. After this, MAO spoke.]

MAO: If you want to catch the black hand, the black hand is me. You've got me. We're inclined toward your side. I can't accept the idea that 4-14 must triumph. But we need to win over the masses among them, including some of the leaders. Zhou Jiaying's main viewpoint is that conquerors can't rule, and that Kuai Dafu has to hand over his power to 4-14.

We told the workers to go and do propaganda work, but you rejected them; Huang Zuozhen and Xie Fuzhi spoke but they couldn't do anything. The workers were unarmed, and you rejected them and injured and killed workers. It's like at Peking University, and how we're inclined toward Nie Yuanzi; we're partial toward you five main leaders. Don't you know why tens of thousands of people went to Tsinghua? Would they dare to go without the Centre's decision? You're at a big disadvantage – 4-14 welcomed them but Jinggang Mountain didn't, and that wasn't proper. Today the people that came didn't include 4-14 or [Peking University] Jinggang Mountain. 4-14 has incorrect ideology. Jinggang Mountain and Red Flag Waving have more bad people, while there are more good people with Nie Yuanzi.[2]

Kuai Dafu and his Jinggang Mountain unit were naturally unhappy with Mao's abandonment, but they wouldn't use armed resistance. Even if they were blinded by ambition, and didn't think it a crime to kill people in the course of 'armed struggle', and wouldn't let up even after twelve people were killed, they would absolutely never dare to openly oppose Chairman Mao. The situation is clear: if someone had told Kuai Dafu early on who had dispatched the Propaganda Team, Han Zhongxian and the others would not have been killed.

In addition, although Han Zhongxian and the other four Propaganda Team members were perfectly willing to take part in the 28 July 1968 movement, they probably had no idea that they would be resisted with violence resulting in loss of life. If given the choice, they would surely have asked higher-ups to ensure their safety by informing people on the Tsinghua campus that they were coming on orders from Mao.

So why did five people have to die? I posed this question to Tang Shaojie, who once interviewed Kuai Dafu in Shenzhen. Tang said that Kuai Dafu's explanation was: the Chairman dealt with the big picture, not with the details.

This explanation of the Chairman dealing 'with the big picture' resulted in no one asking, even after the Cultural Revolution, who should be held accountable for the Propaganda Team deaths. Not only was Mao's responsibility not pursued, but Kuai Dafu never apologised to the families of those five people.

The saying that 'the Chairman dealt with the big picture' was a product of Cultural Revolution thinking. In fact, in any civilised society, even with divisions between rich and poor and between people of higher and lower status, no one has the power, outside of the courts, to strip any other person of their life; that is a basic principle. The Cultural Revolution shattered this principle, and established the concept of the 'big picture' to make allowances for this, especially in the case of 'great' personages.

---

[2] The students present at a meeting compiled notes of the meeting and circulated them. The text can be found in Yongyi Song and Guo Jian (eds), *Chinese Cultural Revolution Database*, University Services Centre for China Studies, Chinese University of Hong Kong, 2002.

While I was constructing my online memorial, more than one person asked what was the point of writing about these ordinary victims? This question has an essential link to the concept of the Chairman's 'big picture'. When the person saying this is powerful, it shows that power has caused them to overlook the ordinary person. When it is an ordinary person saying this, it's the result of long-term spiritual enslavement.

During the Cultural Revolution, Mao mobilised the Red Guards, the Cleansing of the Class Ranks and other such movements that killed countless educators, writers, 'current counter-revolutionaries' and 'theoretical counter-revolutionaries' that his Revolution had established as its targets. It was a crime of massive proportions. Mao also treated loyal followers like Han Zhongxian as sacrificial lambs and allowed them to be killed. That is likewise a crime.

PEKING UNIVERSITY

Wen Jiaju, a nineteen-year-old student at the Beijing Institute of Geology Affiliated Secondary School and the son of a teacher at the institute, was beaten to death during factional struggle at Peking University on 19 April 1968. Wen had gone to the Peking University library to brouse the periodicals because the Institute of Geology's library had closed down during the Cultural Revolution. Students from one of the battling factions, the New Peking University Commune, discovered Wen Jiaju at the library and took him to the biology building, where they beat him to death while interrogating him.

According to the *Peking University Chronical of Major Events*, Sun Pengyi, a member of the Standing Committee of the Peking University Cultural Revolution Committee and also vice-chariman of the university's new leading group, arranged a fake investigation into Wen Jiaju's death, saying that Wen was a 'political pickpocket who had been beaten by the masses... Don't worry, the university's Cultural Revolution [Committee] will deal with it.' Sun Pengyi was one of the writers of 'China's First Marxist–Leninist Big-character Poster', which played a key role in launching the Cultural Revolution.

CHINESE UNIVERSITY OF SCIENCE AND TECHNOLOGY

Zhou Jincong, a mathematics teacher, had a relatively privileged background because his father was an overseas Chinese from Singapore. During the Cultural Revolution, the university's 'East is Red' faction seized power first and occupied the university's broadcasting station. The opposing 'Yan'an' faction was smaller and had no resources, so Zhou donated several hundred *yuan* for Yan'an to buy a loudspeaker. One day, people from East is Red stuffed him in a burlap sack and beat him to death.

BEIJING INSTITUTE OF GEOLOGY

Yang Yuzhong, a student in the institute's Exploration Engineering Department, was a leader of its East is Red organisation. He leaped to his death in April or May 1967 after coming under investigation because of his association with Zhu Chengzhou, the head of East is Red, who had become critical of the Central Cultural Revolution Small Group in early 1967.

Sun Mingzhe, formerly a teacher of politics at the Beijing Institute of Geology, was designated a Rightist in 1957 and sent to the countryside for 'labour reform'. After having his Rightist cap removed, he was assigned work in the Educational Administration Department. He and two other 'Rightist' teachers, Wu Hongbang and Li Jincai (one of whom was not yet rehabilitated) worked together to use mathematical methods to study problems with national economic planning. When the Cultural Revolution began, they were accused of being the institute's 'Three Family Village Anti-Party Clique'. After a propaganda team came to the institute in August 1968, Sun Mingzhe killed himself.

Lin Moyin, a native of Pingyang County, Zhejiang Province, graduated from Peking University in 1952 and was a teaching assistant and lecturer in the rock teaching and research section of the Beijing Institute of Geology before being designated a Rightist in 1958. After three years at the Qinghe labour reform farm, he began working in the laboratory of the Beijing Municipal Geology Bureau. When two factions began fighting at the Beijing Institute of Geology during the Cultural Revolution, the Revolutionary Committee faction in control of the institute brought Lin back by force to interrogate him for evidence disadvantageous to the opposing faction. Lin killed himself while in custody on 27 September 1968, aged thirty-nine. He was rehabilitated in July 1979.

CHONGQING

Luo Guangbin, forty-three years old, was a writer and member of the Chongqing Federation of Cultural Circles. Luo was one of the authors of the famous revolutionary novel *Red Cliff*, so he was not struggled like so many other writers during the Cultural Revolution, and actively took part in the activities of revolutionary rebel organisations. After these organisations divided into factions, an opposing faction abducted and locked Luo up, and he fell from a window on 10 February 1967. His faction said Luo had been killed; the opposing faction said he'd killed himself.

Liu Zongqi, around nineteen years old, was learning industrial production at the Yangjiaping Machine Factory (later renamed the Mine Machine Factory, which ultimately went bankrupt) in Chongqing's Jiulongpo District when an armed conflict developed between two factions. Liu was struck by a bullet on 1 August 1967, and died on a hillside near the factory. He was buried under Wutai Mountain near the factory.

Liu Zongqi's father was an engineer at the Chongqing Iron and Steel Company who was labelled a Rightist in 1957, as a result of which Liu was not allowed to advance to upper secondary school. He loved drawing and basketball and had many friends. His younger brother, Liu Zongping, later took his place at the factory.

Yao Daogang, a captain with the Chongqing Changjiang Shipping Company, set off in its No. 32 steamer on 7 August 1968. Upon reaching Wan County, the steamer came under a surprise attack by the county's revolutionary rebel faction. Several passengers were wounded, and Yao was shot dead.

CHENGDU

Geng Ligong, a fifteen-year-old lower secondary student at the Chengdu Railway No. 1 Secondary School, was killed during a factional battle. In 1967, mass violence broke out between two factions: the Red Guard Chengdu Troops (known as Hongcheng) and '8–26', an organisation established at Chengdu University on 26 August 1966. Geng Ligong belonged to neither organisation, but his school was occupied by Hongcheng, and the opposing 8–26 group wanted to gain control. On the night Geng was killed, he had gone to the school to see a friend who was a member of Hongcheng, not knowing that it had been surrounded by 8–26. As he prepared to enter the building, someone fired a gun and killed him. His body was left at the school entrance and only discovered the next day.

Geng Ligong's family lived in the railway compound. His father was a railway engineer, and an elder brother was at a university in Beijing. His mother had died before the Cultural Revolution. A younger childhood friend said that Geng was an outstanding student, a kind, helpful and polite boy who was held up as an example to other children. Geng's death was a major trauma to this friend.

Jiang Zhong, a third-year student at the Railway Ministry's Second Department Chengdu Secondary School, lived in the railway residential quarters. During an armed struggle between two factions in 1967, he was struck by ten bullets and died on the spot.

Li Quanhua was a third-year student at the Beijing Institute of Geology. A fight broke out between two factional organisations at the Chengdu Munitions 132 Factory (for assembling fighter planes) in December 1967, with one group holed up in the building and the other trying to enter. After an impasse developed, the group outside decided to set fire to the factory, while those inside began shooting at them. Li Quanhua, supporting the group attacking the building, was struck by a bullet fired from inside. These kinds of armed battles continued to occur in Sichuan and became a major cause of deaths and destruction of public property.

Wang Nianqin, an upper-classman at the Chengdu No. 8 Secondary School, lived in Chengdu's Railway New Village. During the city's armed factional warfare in 1967, a stray bullet struck Wang in a classroom, severing an artery in his thigh. His classmates didn't know how to bandage the wound, and the vehicle taking him to the hospital took a lengthy detour to avoid a checkpoint set up by the other faction. Wang Nianqin died at the entrance to the hospital. He was in such pain that his last words were to ask his classmates to finish him off.

GANSU

Li Shibai, a forestry worker at the Liancheng Tree Farm in Gansu's Yongdeng County, had been a soldier while the KMT was in power, but he went over to the Communists in 1949. In 1958 he was designated a Rightist and sent to a *laogai* camp. He was beaten to death in December 1967 by someone who falsely claimed to have 'wrestled with counter-revolutionaries to protect a bridge' and thereby became 'a hero defending the Cultural Revolution'.

When Yongdeng County established its Revolutionary Committee on 17 December 1967, forestry workers went to take part in the celebrations. The deputy squad leader of the Lanzhou 8110 Army 'support-the-Left' unit, Liu Xuebao, stayed at the tree farm and tricked Li Shibai into going over to the Chimuha Bridge, where he fractured Li's skull with an ax and rocks. Liu Xuebao then injured his own hand by exploding a detonator cap to create the false impression that he had fought with a counter-revolutionary who was trying to destroy the bridge.

Liu Xuebao was named a 'heroic warrior' who had 'risked his life to protect the bridge' and became a delegate to the CCP's Ninth Party Congress and a member of the Provincial Military Region Party Committee. On 24 April 1968, the *PLA Daily* published a headline story entitled 'Only the Red Sun in His Heart, Offering All to Chairman Mao: Defender of the Great Proletarian Cultural Revolution, Heroic Warrior Liu Xuebao', along with a commentary entitled 'Never Forget Class Struggle'. The *People's Daily* reprinted the story on its front page the next day and called for everyone to 'learn from hero Liu Xuebao'.

After the Cultural Revolution, an investigation found that Liu Xuebao's story was bogus. The Lanzhou City Intermediate People's Court found him guilty of 'intentional homicide' in July 1985 and sentenced him to life in prison.

ANHUI PROVINCE

Lou Hedong, a native of Huaiyuan County, Bengbu City, Anhui Province, graduated from the Huaiyuan No. 2 Secondary School and was admitted to Anhui Normal University (then known as Wannan University) in 1962. He was still a student when the Cultural Revolution began. In 1967, Anhui's rebel faction split into two sub-factions that began fighting each other, and Lou took on a leadership position in one of them before gradually withdrawing. At a mass rally attended by both sides, Lou gave a speech calling on them to end the senseless violence. As he left the rostrum, a member of his own sub-faction shot him in the back of the head. Lou was about twenty-five years old at the time and married. The man who shot him was subsequently paraded through the streets of Bengbu, but it is not known if he was brought to justice.

HENAN PROVINCE

Sun Keding, a Shanghai native in her thirties employed in the intelligence office of the Metallurgy Ministry's Refractory Material Institute in Luoyang, was married to the institute's deputy director, Lü Guolin. Sun was drawn into factional conflicts in 1967 and 1968, and was tied up and flogged to death in the institute's production workshop by the opposing 'Proletarian Revolutionary Committee'. Her post-mortem found Sun Keding's whole body covered with wounds and bruises. After the Cultural Revolution, the person who ordered the flogging was given a suspended sentence.

JIANGXI PROVINCE

Sun Weidi, an eighteen-year-old student at the Jiangxi Province Dexing County Dexing Secondary School, was a member of the school's '3–7' organisation, named after Mao's directive issued on 7 March 1967, regarding the Cultural Revolution in the schools. The school had another faction called East is Red that opposed 3–7. Sun Weidi was captured by East is Red in July 1968 and beaten to death.

JIANGSU PROVINCE

Zhou Hexiang, a native of Nanqiao Town, Wuxi County, became embroiled in a struggle between two factions in 1967. He leaped to his death from a third-floor window after being abducted by the opposing faction, and locked up and beaten in a building that locals called the 'Western-style house'.

ZHEJIANG PROVINCE

Wang Zhixin, around thirty years old, was a postman in Siwu Village, Chongren Township, in Zhejiang's Sheng County. Wang belonged to one of two factions that engaged in armed battles during the Cultural Revolution. One day after work, he was kidnapped and shot by the opposing faction. He was survived by his wife and two young children.

PART FIVE

1968 Cleansing of the Class Ranks

The year 1968 brought a new campaign called the 'Cleansing of the Class Ranks'. The basis for the campaign had already been established a year earlier with a document criminalising thought and speech that 'attacked and vilified' Mao, Lin Biao, and other top leaders. Another document in spring 1968 stated that the objective was to 'unearth concealed class enemies', with a focus on vetting the personal records of cadres and teachers. By then, trial campaigns had been going on since 1967. The Cleansing of the Class Ranks was the fiercest and most protracted operation of the Cultural Revolution, and persecuted the greatest number of people, mainly because it was carried out in a fairly organised top-down fashion. At the very top, Mao personally issued a series of notices and documents that provided detailed guidance on how to conduct it.

On 19 May 1968, Mao wrote the following memo on a report sent to him by Yao Wenyuan:

Comrade Wenyuan:
    I suggest that this document be distributed throughout the country. First print off a number of copies and distribute it to the relevant comrades, then read it out in an informal meeting, make revisions and issue it with annotations. Of the similar material in hand, this is the best written.
    Mao Zedong

This subsequently became known as Mao's '19 May Directive'. The title of the report Yao Wenyuan sent to Mao was 'Experience of the Beijing New China Printing Plant Military Control Committee's Mobilisation of the

Masses to Launch a Struggle against the Enemy'. The memo and report were issued together as Central Committee Document No. [1968] 74. The report, which mentioned dozens of 'class enemies' at the printing factory, was compiled by Mao's Central Security '8341 Unit'. It was transmitted down to the lowest level of the Party organisation, and every work unit was involved in the campaign. The Revolutionary Committees, new power organs established in every locality during the Cultural Revolution, decided whom to investigate, detain and struggle, as well as the ultimate verdict and 'handling'. It was Mao who named the Revolutionary Committees and assigned them to carry out a 'centralised' leadership that made no distinction between Party and government, between administrative, legislative and judicial departments, or between prisons and administrative organs. These boundaries had already been blurred, but the degree of integration reached unprecedented levels during the Cultural Revolution, to the point where a secondary school's Revolutionary Committee could incarcerate its teachers and staff.

During the Cleansing of the Class Ranks, two particular expressions came into common usage: one was 'special investigation group' and the other was 'isolation and investigation'. Every work unit established special investigation groups and carried out 'investigations' on 'targets'. A substantial number of people became members of special investigation groups assigned with interrogating and investigating targets for 'cleansing'. The special investigation groups could incarcerate targets in their work units and prevent them from moving freely or returning home in a process known as 'isolation and investigation'. Many people put under 'special investigation' were locked up in work unit jails for months or even years.

There were two kinds of 'hidden class enemies'. One was 'historical counter-revolutionaries', which meant people who sometime in their past had engaged in 'counter-revolutionary' activities, and the other was 'current counter-revolutionaries', which meant people who were still engaged in 'counter-revolutionary activity' at that time. School and work were suspended to engage in 'unearthing' these two kinds of 'counter-revolutionaries'. Each 'unearthing' was reported as a 'great victory of Mao Zedong Thought'. The more 'enemies' unearthed, the greater the credit, so every Revolutionary Committee expended massive energy on unearthing as many as possible to demonstrate their revolutionary spirit and gain credit for their achievements. Any petty matter could be investigated as possible 'counter-revolutionary activity'.

Under the Cultural Revolution's high-pressure terror and strict control, it was out of the question for anyone to publicly express criticism of the Cultural Revolution or take any action to oppose it. Consequently, the 'current counter-revolutionaries' unearthed during that time were of two main types: one consisting of people who had said things in private conversation or letters or had written something in a diary that could be construed as 'counter-revolutionary'; the other consisting of those who tried to have previous punishments mitigated or rescinded, referred to as 'verdict reversal'. Interrogated under torture, many people admitted to completely fictional crimes and were imprisoned or executed, while others died while under investigation. Confidential government documents show that nearly 10,000 Shanghai residents killed themselves during the Cleansing of the Class Ranks, while in Beijing 3,000 people committed suicide and another 200 were beaten to death. The actual numbers are almost certainly much greater.

Lin Zhao, born in 1932, was a student of Chinese in the Peking University class of 1954. Designated a Rightist in 1957, Lin was sentenced to twenty years in prison as a counter-revolutionary in 1960. She was then sentenced to death and executed on 29 April 1968. Her family was never given a notice of her death sentence, but was charged the cost of the bullet that killed her. Soon after Lin's death, the Cleansing of the Class Ranks was formally launched nationwide.

I first heard Lin Zhao's name in 1980. At that time, students at Peking University had a literary magazine called *Weiming* [Nameless] *Lake*. The last editorial meeting for this magazine discussed how some university teachers had just held a memorial ceremony for a person called Lin Zhao, who had been labelled a Rightist while a student and then executed during the Cultural Revolution. While a student, she had been an editor of the student literary magazine *Honglou* (Red Building).

The fact of Lin Zhao having been an editor of *Honglou* caused the editors of *Weiming Lake* to cry out in surprise. Honglou and Weiming Lake were both places on the university campus, and although *Weiming Lake* was unable to continue as a student publication, it still fared better than *Honglou* because of changes in the political environment.

Lin Zhao's schoolmates, younger sister and a friend of her mother had all written essays commemorating her after the Cultural Revolution. The Lin Zhao they describe was young, clever, a talented poet, a seeker of truth, unyielding and full of character, and had met an extremely tragic fate. They focused on her as an individual rather than on the era that provided the background to her tragedy.

As an individual, Lin Zhao was truly someone who stood out from the crowd, but as a victim, her experience was identical to that of numerous other victims, in that it was brought about by the policies of the top leadership.

Lin Zhao was one of 714 people (including 589 students) designated Rightists at Peking University out of a student body of 8,983.[1] All of them suffered long-term persecution and some, like Lin Zhao, were sentenced to death during the Cultural Revolution. Two years after Mao died, these Rightists had their status 'corrected'.

The large number of Rightists resulted from a quota set at the upper levels of government. There would have been an explanation for this in the relevant high-level internal directive, but it has not been made public. However, this point can be found in *Selected Works of Mao Zedong*, published after Mao's death.

Peking University students didn't begin putting up big-character posters 'airing their views' until 19 May 1957, but as early as 15 May, Mao had written his essay 'Things are Changing', which was circulated only among the Party's high-level cadres. In this essay, Mao proposed that Rightists made up 'around 1%, 3%, or 5 to 10%'. This is what Mao subsequently spoke of as 'open conspiracy'.[2]

In a speech at a Shanghai cadre conference on 9 July 1957, Mao said again, 'Rightists are only a tiny minority, like we were saying about Peking University, just 1, 2 or 3%. This is for students. In terms of professors or associate professors, it is slightly different; around 10% are Rightists.'[3] Around 10% of the university's teaching and administrative staff were consequently designated Rightists.

Two of the students who edited *Honglou* also edited another magazine called *Forum*, and they were both Lin Zhao's schoolmates and friends. The *Honglou* editorial department quickly dismissed the two *Forum* editors, and even though *Forum* published only one issue, it became major evidence used against many students. Lin Zhao's relationship with *Forum* was one of the reasons she was designated a Rightist.

Rightists were dealt with gradually. In summer 1957, they were still attending classes, but by the end of the year, some had been arrested and sentenced and others were punished in various ways. The chief editor of *Forum* was sentenced to eight years in prison. After being punished with physical labour in the library, Lin Zhao made an unsuccessful suicide attempt.

While in Shanghai in 1962, Lin Zhao was sentenced to twenty years in prison. The reason for this was that while recuperating from an illness in her mother's Shanghai home in 1960, she met a Rightist student from Lanzhou at the library. He edited a magazine called *Meteor*, and Lin Zhao

---

[1] See *Chronicle of Peking University (1898–1997)*, Beijing daxue chubanshe, 1998.
[2] *Selected Works of Mao Zedong*, Vol. 5, 'Things are Changing'.
[3] *Selected Works of Mao Zedong*, Vol. 5, 'Assault to Beat Back the Bourgeois Rightists'.

published poems in it. The magazine's editors printed a few dozen copies but hadn't yet distributed them when they were arrested in Gansu, and the magazines confiscated by the PSB. Lin Zhao was arrested in Shanghai at the same time, and she and the Lanzhou students were sentenced to lengthy prison terms.

According to Lin Zhao's younger sister, she spent time at a psychiatric hospital in Shanghai, and a famous psychiatrist, **Li Zonghua**, diagnosed her as mentally ill. During the Cultural Revolution, Li Zonghua was accused of protecting counter-revolutionaries by diagnosing them as mentally ill. Placed under long-term 'isolation and investigation' and physically abused, he died in August 1970.

Lin Wuling, author of *The Time of Weeping Blood*, was locked up in the same prison as Lin Zhao, but at a later time. Lin Wuling helped me interview someone who was imprisoned in Shanghai's Tilanqiao Prison at the same time as Lin Zhao. This interviewee had also been labelled a Rightist in 1957, and had been upgraded to counter-revolutionary and imprisoned in 1966. In prison he was assigned 'general affairs' tasks, and through reading the prison intake forms, he knew quite a lot. He said Lin Zhao was sent to the – usually male – fifth floor of the No. 3 prison block after becoming deranged from her persecution and constantly yelling in the female prison block. At that time, there was no one else on the fifth floor, and few people in the No. 3 block, because it was mainly used for prisoners in transit to labour reform farms. When Lin Zhao shouted upstairs, she was made to wear a rubber headpiece that covered her mouth and left only the eyes and nose exposed. My interviewee saw Lin Zhao when he was making deliveries upstairs. He noticed that her eyes were completely red.

He said that prisoners were obliged to attend a rally during which Lin Zhao was sentenced to death; the execution was carried out immediately afterwards. As her death sentence was delivered, Lin Zhao was on the stage and unable to speak. My interviewee said the prison authorities may have done something to her as they had to Zhang Zhixin, whose windpipe was cut so she couldn't speak before she was killed. He heard at the time that Lin Zhao was executed in a small courtyard behind the auditorium. She died on 29 April 1968 for offending the authorities with her remarks while mentally ill.

Some of Lin Zhao's teachers and schoolmates subsequently erected a memorial for her in Suzhou, which in recent years has drawn so many admirers that a police guard has been placed there to discourage these visits, and some of those making pilgrimages have been detained.

BEIJING

BEIJING AGRICULTURAL UNIVERSITY[4]

On 16 February 1968, the university's Revolutionary Committee held a 'university-wide mass rally to open fire on the class enemy', during which targets were dragged to the stage and subjected to struggle and then marched through the streets. This rally marked the full-scale launch of the Cleansing of the Class Ranks at the university. From then on, teachers and cadres from every department were 'seized and struggled' to carry out the 'dictatorship of the masses'. Many 'special investigation groups' were established, and they placed their targets under 'labour reform' and long-term 'isolation and investigation' while subjecting them to all kinds of brutal physical abuse. Thirty people died at this university during the Cultural Revolution, including sixteen during the Cleansing of the Class Ranks. Most of the victims I have identified died before the nationwide launch of the campaign.

An Tiezhi, an administrative cadre and vice-chairman of the university's labour union in his forties, leaped to his death from a smokestack on campus on 19 February 1968, three days after the university-wide rally.

Wu Weijun, associate professor in the Crop Protection Department, slit his wrists on 6 March 1968.

Guo Shiying, a student, leaped to his death on 22 April 1968. Guo had been a student of philosophy at Peking University, and in 1963 he joined with other students in forming an association to write poetry and discuss politics. They used loose-leaf note paper to circulate their poems, referring to themselves as the 'X Society'. When the Public Security Bureau learned of their activities, they were arrested. After being interrogated, some members spent years in 're-education through labour' at the Chadian Labour Farm. But Guo Shiying was the son of Guo Moruo, one of the most important 'candidates for united front recruitment' at that time. After a year at a labour farm in Henan's Yellow River flood plain, Guo wasn't allowed to return to Peking University, but continued his studies in 'plant cultivation' at Beijing Agricultural University. Due to his 'criminal record', he was designated a 'reactionary student' during the Cultural Revolution and was locked up on 19 April 1968. He committed suicide three days later.

Two associate professors also killed themselves on 22 April. After **Zhao Xibin**, an associate professor of animal husbandry, killed himself, someone

---

[4] Now China Agricultural University.

used whitewash to write on the ground, 'Zhao Xibin isolated himself from the people and deserves 10,000 deaths.' **Liu Shiqin**, an associate professor of veterinary medicine, killed himself in a basement while under investigation.

Liu Zhongxuan, a lecturer in agriculture, died on 2 May 1968, while under 'isolation and investigation'. He was declared to have 'committed suicide to escape punishment'. Another teacher held in the same building said he heard Liu being beaten and screaming in pain for several hours before he died, but he wasn't able to see what happened. This teacher believes that Liu didn't commit suicide, but was pushed out of the window after he died.

Luo Zhongyu, an associate professor of veterinary medicine, who had returned to China in the 1950s after studying in the United States, killed himself by slitting his wrists while under 'isolation and investigation' on 6 June 1968.

RENMIN UNIVERSITY OF CHINA

He Sijing, a seventy-two-year-old professor and member of the university Party Committee, was beaten to death on campus in April 1968. Like other universities, Renmin experienced a number of fatal beatings during this time.

Another Renmin University professor, Liu Lian, wrote:

> [He Sijing] was wantonly humiliated and beaten by a crazed mob and denounced in a washroom. They surrounded him and pushed him back and forth among them. The elderly man suffered from high blood pressure and was extremely nearsighted, and while being shoved around he became unsteady on his feet and fell against the concrete sink. His glasses were shattered and his eyeball popped out of its socket, blood flowed unceasingly, and he soon died of a cerebral haemorrhage.[5]

Liu Lian and her husband, He Ganzhi, were also subjected to brutal beating and torture at this time. Liu's book describes their experiences and their observation of the violence at Renmin University.

He Sijing was a veteran Party member, and his daughter and son-in-law also occupied high positions. Perhaps because of this, his death was reported to the top levels of the Party and is recorded in *Chronology of Zhou Enlai*:[6]

---

[5] Liu Lan, *Together Through the Storm: My 20 years with He Ganzhi*, Nanning, Guangxi jiaoyu chubanshe, 1998, p. 234.
[6] CCP Central Committee Documentary Research Room (ed.), *Chronology of Zhou Enlai*, Zhonggong zhongyang wenxian chubanshe, 1997, p. 244.

10 July [1968]. Memo to Minister of Public Security, Xie Fuzhi, on the report on the fatal beating of He Sijing, member of the former Party Committee of the Renmin University of China, head of the Law and Philosophy Departments and national senior grade professor: Renmin University has had the largest number of these kinds of fatal beatings, suicides or silencings. I recommend that the Ministry of Public Security transmit the message to the [Beijing Municipal] Public Security Bureau Military Control Commission to establish a special agency to investigate these cases and get to the bottom of them. It is not good policy to have any mass organisation arrest and interrogate on their own and beat people to death without the organs of dictatorship looking into it.

In fact, mass organisations had been arresting, interrogating and beating people to death since August 1966, when the worst of such episodes in Beijing occurred, without Zhou Enlai issuing any memos about it. His 1968 memo shows that this kind of situation, which had been ongoing for two years by then, was still being resolved through 'recommendation'.

The 'special agency' that Zhou Enlai recommended for investigating these cases was never established. Several weeks after Zhou wrote this memo, Mao sent Worker and PLA Mao Zedong Thought Propaganda Teams to each university, and when these teams led the Cleansing of the Class Ranks, they merely systematised and formalised the violence and persecution carried out by the mass organisations.

BEIJING COLLEGE OF AERONAUTICS

The Beijing College of Aeronautics made a name for itself during the Cultural Revolution, not only in Beijing but throughout the country, due to its famous 'revolutionary rebel faction' called the Beijing College of Aeronautics Red Flag Red Guards, abbreviated as BeiHang Red Flag. The leader of BeiHang Red Flag, Han Aijing, was known as one of the 'five great leaders' in 1967 and 1968. The other four 'great leaders' were at Peking University, Tsinghua, Beijing Normal University and China University of Geosciences. The Beijing College of Aeronautics was much smaller than the first three of these universities, and the ability of BeiHang Red Flag to win such plaudits was clearly due to its unusual level of activism, not only on campus but also in driving forward the Cultural Revolution throughout China. When the Revolution established new organs of power called 'Revolutionary Committees' in 1967, the head of BeiHang Red Flag, Han Aijing, became chairman of the college's Revolutionary Committee, and therefore the most powerful person at the school. Han Aijing was also vice-chair of the 'core group' of Beijing's University Red Guard Congress (abbreviated as 'Red Congress').

After BeiHang Red Flag stirred up trouble for a while, it lost its favoured status with Mao at the end of July 1968, and the organisation's members, including some who had been appointed to official positions, were gradually abandoned. After the Gang of Four went on trial in 1980, Han Aiqing was sentenced to fifteen years in prison. But the reason for his sentence in public documents was that he was an associate of the Gang of Four and had persecuted 'revolutionary cadres', without mentioning the persecutions he had been involved in at the Beijing College of Aeronautics.

In the 1990s, someone wrote a report about the 'stars' of the Cultural Revolution, including Han Aijing. He acknowledged what he'd done back then, and said he'd been wrong to participate in struggling former Defence Minister Peng Dehuai, but he offered no apology for his part in the persecution and death of ordinary teachers at the college.

This is typical of people who joined revolutionary rebel factions as university students, many of whom have written about the fascinating adventures of their youth, how Mao took a special interest in them, how they became a focus of public attention and basked in the limelight, or how they were unfairly blamed after joining the Revolution full of ideals, but completely ignoring the pain and torment they caused by beating and struggling others. Of course, the top leaders of the Cultural Revolution must be called to account for leading college students to persecute others, but that doesn't give these former students an excuse to deny personal responsibility for the evil they committed. The example of the Beijing College of Aeronautics clearly shows the responsibility the Red Guards and rebel faction bear for the persecution of teachers and staff.

In the first half of 1968, while Beihang Red Flag was in control of the college, the number of people persecuted there outnumbered those at Tsinghua University, even though it was a much smaller school. One obvious reason is that Han Aijing rose to power at the Beijing College of Aeronautics in January 1967 and maintained control of the situation, not allowing Beihang Red Flag to develop splits while it swallowed up other organisations. This gave it even more power to engage in class struggle and 'dig deep to unearth class enemies', and that much more strength to torture and humiliate college teachers and other staff during the Cleansing of the Class Ranks.

Someone told me that more than twenty people were persecuted to death at the college in spring and summer 1968. One interviewee who studied there after the Cultural Revolution said that even then, the saying still circulated that someone had jumped to their death from nearly every window in the school's main building. The rumour made him shiver in horror, but he never knew who jumped to their deaths, or why. I've been able to identify eight of the victims, all of whom died before the propaganda team arrived, while the revolutionary rebel faction was in control of the school.

Hu Shuhong, a forty-five-year-old lecturer in the university's mathematics teaching and research group, leaped to her death from the school's main building in May 1968 after being put under 'isolation and investigation'. Hu Shuhong's husband, surnamed Li, was a teacher at the Beijing Institute of Mechanical Engineering, and was also put under 'isolation and investigation' at his school. After Hu Shuhong died, the College of Aeronautics brought her husband to the school in a truck but didn't allow him to see her body. Li leaped to his death the next day.

Hu Shuhong was one of two victims in the college's mathematics reaching and research group, which had only thirty teachers at that time.

The first to be put under 'isolation and investigation' were seven older members of the teaching and research group who had graduated from college before 1949 and were therefore assumed to have 'historical problems'. The teachers were expected to provide detailed 'debriefings' of their personal histories, which had already been exhaustively covered in previous political campaigns. Now the interrogations were even more brutal, and the school's Revolutionary Committee did not allow the teachers to return home, see their families or talk with others.

Three teachers were detained first. The fifty-year-old head of the teaching and research group and its only professor had been sent to study in the United States by a church organisation, on top of which he was accused of being a 'landlord who slipped through the net'. He was ultimately cleared of being a landlord, but died of cirrhosis of the liver in his sixties, possibly due to his mistreatment.

Another of the three was associate professor Xiong Zhenxiang, who had never been anything but a mathematics professor. There were two main 'reasons' for locking her up. The first was that she had a 'relationship' with Liu Shaoqi's wife, Wang Guangmei. Both women graduated from Furen University, but Xiong graduated a year earlier, and Wang studied physics rather than mathematics, although both subjects came under the same university department. They'd had no contact with each other after graduation, and once Wang Guangmei became the wife of China's President, such contact was even less likely, but that didn't keep Xiong Zhenxiang from being interrogated for an entire day about this relationship. The second reason was that she had 'concealed her family's class status'. She had described her 'class status' as 'office worker', but the special investigation group forced her to admit to being from a 'landlord' family. Xiong was placed under 'isolation and investigation' late in April 1968, and she was held for eight months, which was the shortest time of the three.

Xiong's husband, an editor at Higher Education Publishing, was also put under 'isolation and investigation' and not allowed to return home. Xiong's oldest child was a secondary school student, and the youngest was nine. Their home was ransacked five times; once by each of the College of Aeronautics 'rebel factions', another time by secondary school students, and once more by people from Higher Education Publishing.

During the eight months Xiong was held, she underwent many interrogations and 'external inquiries' without any evidence being uncovered of a relationship between her and Wang Guangmei, nor was there any evidence that her father had ever owned property of any kind. She also couldn't be counted as a 'reactionary academic authority', so finally the college authorities released her with the declaration: 'No verdict and nothing added to her file,' which seemed to leave open the possibility of another 'investigation' at a later time.

Hu Shuhong was the third of the first group taken in for 'isolation and investigation'. She was held in the office of the mathematics teaching and research group in one arm of the U-shaped main building of the college, and that's where she leaped to her death.

The other teacher in the mathematics teaching and research group who was killed during the Cleansing of the Class Ranks was **Yang Wenheng**. While Hu Shuhong was accused of being a 'historical counter-revolutionary', Yang Wenheng, who was only in his thirties and had graduated from Sichuan University in 1953, was attacked for a 'current problem'. Yang Wenheng was a member of the CCP and the college's Party branch; he should have been one of the safer teachers, yet he still came to grief.

Something caused Yang to become dissatisfied with the Cultural Revolution a little more than a year after it began. Jiang Qing was one of the Cultural Revolution's most powerful and active leaders, but she often said things that didn't make sense. In a private conversation with friends, Yang Wenheng said, 'Jiang Qing shoots off her mouth,' or something to that effect, and as a result, he was accused of the 'current counter-revolutionary' crime of 'venomously attacking the esteemed and beloved Comrade Jiang Qing'.

The methods for 'investigating' such crimes were particularly brutal. Since this counter-revolutionary crime involved speech, and there were no tape recordings or any written text as evidence, the 'special investigation group' had to rely on obtaining a confession through torture or else choose conspiratorial methods of sowing dissention, intimidation and bribery or forcing someone to 'expose' the suspect. The last time that the special investigation group interrogated Yang Wenheng, it arranged for several people to struggle him in shifts to force him to admit to 'counter-revolutionary speech'. One group would spend several hours threatening and insulting him, then another group would take over. Yang Wenheng had to stand for more than thirty hours without being given anything to eat or drink.

This method, which was also used at other schools at the time, was referred to as 'stewing the eagle'. The interrogators on the night shift were given free food from the canteen, usually a bowl of noodles, which signified the political trust and the honour of being used for this purpose, while also constituting a significant material reward at a time of economic shortages.

After this marathon struggle session, Yang Wenheng was allowed to go home, where he wrote a suicide note. He then went to the Western Hills, where there were several military units. When a military truck began driving past, Yang ran in front of it and was killed. He was identified by a receipt from a medical consultation that he was carrying in his pocket.

Yang Wenheng's wife didn't work at the College of Aeronautics, but had graduated from there. They had a child who was only four or five years old.

Ten of the mathematics teaching and research group's teachers were 'investigated'. Whenever one was struggled, the others were escorted to be present as 'secondary targets', standing bowed over at a ninety-degree angle to signify 'hanging their heads and admitting their guilt'.

A foreign language teacher at the college, **Li Keng**, also killed herself around this same time. The foreign languages teaching and research group, and mathematics teaching and research group, both came under the 'Basic Teaching Department'. After being put under 'isolation and investigation', Li Keng leaped to her death from the fourth floor of the college's main building.

The death of **Li Guorui** and his family in July 1968 was even more shocking. Li was a teacher in the college's mechanical principles teaching and research group, while his wife, **Yang Yaqin**, was a preventative health doctor at the university hospital. Li Guorui was only a secondary school student before 1949, but in summer 1968 he was forced to 'confess' that he was part of his school's collective recruitment into the KMT's Three People's Principles Youth Corps. While being questioned, he saw others being tortured. He and his wife and mother talked things over and decided to commit suicide, along with Li and Yang's two children, eight and ten years old. The whole family put on clean clothes, took poison and then lay down on their beds and died.

PEKING UNIVERSITY

According to statistics gathered by the Peking University Party Committee after the Cultural Revolution, twenty-four people committed suicide at the university during the Cleansing of the Class Ranks alone. However, the government has been unwilling to release the names of the victims. *Chronicle of Peking University (1898–1997)*[7] records the names of some people who were persecuted to death, along with the dates of their deaths, but only full professors and high-level cadres; even associate professors were excluded. After years of inquiries beginning in the 1980s, I have been able to identify sixty-three victims of the Cultural Revolution at Peking University, including at least thirty-five who died during the Cleansing of the Class Ranks.

Name	Age	Sex	Status	Department	CCP member	Died	Cause of death*
Wang Qian	48	M	professor	history	x	11-Jun-66	poison
Zhang Yongxin	25	M	canteen cashier	Hanzhong branch	x	22-Jul-66	hanging
Dong Huaiyun	39	M	lecturer	mathematics and mechanics	x	28-Jul-66	hanging
Wu Xinghua	45	M	professor	Western languages		3-Aug-66	illness from being forced to drink contaminated water
Yu Dayin	61	F	professor, CPPCC delegate	Western languages	other	15-Aug-66	poison
Wu Suzhen	60	F		family member		22-Aug-66	beating by Red Guards
Chen Yanrong	37	M	worker	Academy of Sciences gas plant		27-Aug-66	beating by Red Guards
Nameless		F	alleged landlord	neighbourhood resident		27-Aug-66	beating by Red Guards
Kong Haikun		M	father of legal department administrator	family member		29-Aug-66	beating by Red Guards

---

[7] Beijing daxue chubanshe, 1998.

Chen Xiance	38	M	Party cadre	Chinese literature	x	2-Sep-66	poison
Yang Mingai	29	M	student	economics	CYL	11-Sep-66	hanging
Xiang Da		M	professor	history		?-Oct-66	illness during forced labour
Shen Naizhang	55	M	professor	philosophy		6-Oct-66	poison
Chen Shuzhen	23	M	student	Chinese literature	CYL	21-Nov-66	leaping from height
Shen Dali	20	F	student	Chinese literature		18-Mar-67	poison and drowning
Liu Changshun		M	canteen manager	logistics department		?-Nov-67	illness under investigation
Cheng Yuan	64	F	typist	Western languages		9-Jan-68	hanging
Meng Fudi	36	M	lecturer	Western languages		27-Mar-68	hanging
Wen Jiaju	20	M	student	Institute of Geology Affiliated Secondary		19-Apr-68	beating
Li Yuan	40	M	teacher	history		21-Apr-68	hanging
Yin Wenjie		M	student	radio		27-Apr-68	shot in crossfire
Wang Hou	50	M	cook	PU Affiliated Secondary		7-May-68	drowning
Lu Xikun	45	M	assistant professor	chemistry	x	24-Jun-68	poison and vein cutting
Lin Fang	41	F	deputy director, equipment room	chemistry		16-Jul-68	drowning
Liu Wei		M	student	geology & geography		20-Jul-68	leaping from height
Xu Shihua	48	M	librarian, lecturer	library	x	?-Aug-68	drowning
Chen Tongdu	65	M	professor	biology		28-Aug-68	poisoning
Li Jie	50	F	administrator	PU Affiliated Secondary		?-Sep-68	beating by Red Guards

Zhu Qiquan	36	M	teaching assistant	Russian		15-Sep-68	leaping from height
Wu Lianqin	24	M	student	international relations	CYL	6-Oct-68	hanging
Rao Yutai	77	M	professor	physics		16-Oct-68	hanging
Cui Xiongkun	49	M	deputy Party secretary and dean of studies	adminstration office	x	17-Oct-68	drowning
Dong Tiebao	52	M	professor	mathematics and mechanics		18-Oct-68	hanging
Liao Ying	42	M	lecturer	physics		21-Oct-68	vein cutting
Li Dacheng	32	M	teaching assistant	biology		23-Oct-68	leaping from height
Wu Weineng	41	M	CRC office staff	history	x	4-Nov-68	drowning
Gong Weitai	36	M	lecturer	Russian	x	7-Nov-68	vein cutting
Qian Rongpei	57	M	purchasing agent	instrument plant		7-Nov-68	drowning
Zhang Jingzhao	49	F	lecturer	mathematics and mechanics		9-Nov-68	sleeping pills
Chen Yonghe	33	M	lecturer	mathematics and mechanics		11-Nov-68	leaping from height
Guo Xiangxian	47	M	deputy director	university hospital	x	16-Nov-68	vein cutting and hanging
Tang Jiahan	38	M	lecturer	Oriental languages	x	23-Nov-68	hanging
Xie Debin	54	M	cook	canteen		?-Dec-68	hanging
Liu Ping	23	F	student	Chinese literature	CYL	4-Dec-68	poisoning
He Yitang	32	M	teaching assistant	biology	x	6-Dec-68	leaping from height
Li Qichen	34	M	teacher	geophysics		8-Dec-68	leaping from height
Xu Yueru	39	F	department head	Western languages	x	10-Dec-68	hanging
Liu Youwen	32	M	teaching assistant	radio	x	17-Dec-68	lying on railway line

1968 CLEANSING OF THE CLASS RANKS | 365

Jian Bozan	71	M	professor, university vice-president	History	x	19-Dec-68	sleeping pills
Dai Shuwan	68	F	wife of Jian Bozan	family member		19-Dec-68	sleeping pills
Wei Bi		F	wife of Zhou Binlin (economics department)	family member		17-Feb-69	sleeping pills
Li Renjie	23	M	student	chemistry		23-Feb-69	hanging
Yan Kaiwei		M	lecturer	geophysics		?-Oct-69	illness under investigation
Cui Zhilan		F	professor	biology		2-May-70	illness during struggle
Yan Huatang		M	professor	physical education teaching & research		24-May-70	illness during forced labour
Wang Aiqing	32	M	office staff	physics		11-Aug-70	poison
Jiao Fuju	51	M	worker	general services		?-Nov-70	poison
Chen Xinde	65	M	lecturer	Oriental languages	other	20-Dec-70	died in prison
Jiang Xiaoguan		M	intern	university hospital		Feb-71	vein slitting
Liu Changhe	44	M	lab technician	chemistry		9-Aug-71	sleeping pills
Zhou Shanfeng	28	M	teaching assistant	mathematics and mechanics	CYL	12-May-73	vein slitting
Wang Zhongmin	72	M	professor	Library	other	16-Apr-75	hanging
Li Geliang		M	office staff	university hospital		Oct-75	poison

* Except for beatings, illness, shooting, and death in prison, all of these deaths were suicides.

CRC=Cultural Revolution Committee. CYL=Communist Youth League. 'Other' refers to political parties other than the Chinese Communist Party.

The following are further details regarding some of the victims of the Cleansing of the Class Ranks at Peking University.

Cheng Yuan, a sixty-four-year-old speciality typist and former teacher of German language studies in the Department of Western Languages, hanged herself on 9 January 1968.

A native of Sichuan, Cheng was a single woman who had studied in Germany. A former colleague said she liked to wear cheongsams and held herself aloof from the world. During the Cultural Revolution, someone put up a big-character poster saying she was a 'Miss Mary-type person'. 'Miss Mary' was famous character in the revolutionary novel *Red Cliff*, a KMT spy and seductress who knew foreign languages.

After the Cleansing of the Class Ranks started, Cheng Yuan was detained in Peking University's Langrun Park. She tied a rope to her steel bed frame, looped it around her neck, lay down and strangled herself. A colleague said, 'She died like a blade of grass.'

Two teachers and a cadre in the Western Languages Department committed suicide during the Cleansing of the Class Ranks. One of them was **Meng Fudi**, a Spanish specialist who hanged himself at home in 1968 after being accused of having been a member of the Three People's Principles Youth Corps.

Another victim in the Western Languages Department was **Xu Yueru**, born around 1930 and head of the department office, who hanged herself in Red Building No. 3 on 10 December 1968.

Xu Yueru became a 'cadre college student' in 1956 and majored in German in the Western Languages Department. (Unlike ordinary undergraduates, such students were cadres before beginning their university studies, and while studying they enjoyed different treatment from the other students.) She didn't finish her university studies or graduate, but in 1958 became head of the department's office and its Party secretary. When the Cleansing of the Class Ranks was launched in 1968, she was accused of being an 'alien-class element' who had 'infiltrated the Communist Party'.

During the Cleansing of the Class Ranks, the Worker and PLA Mao Zedong Thought Propaganda Team that was in control of Peking University called for all of the school's personnel to live collectively at the school, and to expose and criticise each other on a regular basis. Groups of about fifteen people would take turns giving 'debriefings' of their own histories from birth to the present day. After one person finished 'debriefing', he or she had to leave the group and go into another room while the others began to 'expose' his or her problems.

Xu Yueru normally lived in the unmarried women's quarters in Red Building 3. (The Peking University campus originally had seven buildings used as teacher dormitories, and during the Cultural Revolution they were renamed Red Building 1, Red Building 2, and so on.) The teachers were allowed to go home one weekend, and after Xu Yueru returned to her quarters, she hanged herself.

Li Wuling, a relative of Xu Yueru, saw her name on my website and wrote to me saying that Xu's father had once worked for the Central Bank and had died before 1949. After the father's death, the family became impoverished and lived in a tiny room in Shanghai's Yongjia Road, along with two widows. Li recalled that Xu Yueru's childhood nickname was Xiao Mei.

Li Wuling wrote an autobiographical book, *The Years of Weeping Blood*,[8] describing how he was designated a Rightist in 1957 and underwent twenty-two years of 'reform through labour' and 're-education through labour'. He heard that Xu Yueru had joined the CCP and become a leading cadre at Peking University, so he had fallen out of contact with her, as was common during that time. Division into political classes inevitably destroyed relationships within families and between friends. Li Wuling said he never guessed that Xu would die so tragically.

Li Yuan, a forty-year-old teacher of ancient Chinese history, was accused of being a 'spy for KMT central intelligence' and locked up in the university's administrative building on 20 April 1968. He died that night after being harshly beaten. The university's Cultural Revolution leaders declared he had hanged himself, but his wife believed he was beaten to death. Someone who saw where Li died said the room had a very low ceiling, making it impossible for a person to stand upright, but the Public Security Bureau claimed that Li managed to strangle himself while sitting down.

Li Yuan's wife, Jin Xiangrong, worked at the Dalian Postal and Telecommunications Office; Li had been unable to bring her to the capital when he began teaching at Peking University in 1959. The couple had three children who were four, six and nine years old when Li died. Apart from the configuration of the room, Jin Xiangrong had other reasons to suspect foul play. She said that her husband had been very positive and optimistic in letters before his death, and that his body was covered with wounds. She added that Li Yuan was never a KMT agent, but while in secondary school he had filled out a 'Central Bureau of Investigation and Statistics' form to obtain relief services that he never ended up receiving. He 'confessed' to this issue in 1950, and it had been designated a 'routine historical problem'.

After the Cultural Revolution, Jin Xiangrong demanded that Li's killers be brought to justice. The Peking University authorities were unable

---

[8] Hong Kong, Bosi chubanshe, 2002.

to pursue the matter, but they did provide one of his children with a job at the university.

Lu Xikun, associate professor and deputy director of the Chemistry Department, graduated from Southwestern Associated University and joined a student volunteer unit during the War of Resistance against Japan, helping the war effort by serving as a translator for the US Army. This was considered a 'serious historical problem' during the Cultural Revolution, and Lu Xikun was forced to 'confess'. He killed himself by drinking insecticide on 24 June 1968. Less than a month later, on 19 July, his wife, **Lin Fang**, who worked in the Chemistry Department's equipment room, killed herself. The couple had three juvenile children.

Zhu Qiquan, a thirty-year-old teacher in the Russian Department, leaped to his death on the night of 15 September 1968, after being locked up in a small room in the student dormitory for 'venomously attacking' Lin Biao.

A native of Shanghai, Zhu graduated from college in the late 1950s, but because there were almost no opportunities for advancement after 1956, he was still a teaching assistant in 1966.

Zhu Qiquan was too young to have any 'historical problems', but was considered a 'current counter-revolutionary' based on criticisms he'd allegedly made of Lin Biao. The kind of 'reactionary speech' serving as 'evidence' couldn't be made public for fear of 'spreading toxin', so Zhu Qiquan's colleagues took part in rallies 'exposing' and criticising his 'reactionary crimes' without knowing what he'd actually said.

Zhu Qiquan was unmarried, and his colleagues knew little about his family except that his father was named Zhu Wuhua and was a prominent professor of engineering who later served as the president of Shanghai Jiaotong University. People from the university say they couldn't recall him ever talking about his son's death; that kind of pain remained buried deep in people's hearts and was never touched upon.

Another lecturer in the Russian language teaching and research section, **Gong Weitai**, was put under 'isolation and investigation' and brutally struggled for being a 'traitor'. While locked up in the university's No. 1 classroom building on the night of 7 November 1968, Gong slit the arteries in his thighs with a razor and bled to death. He was thirty-seven and left behind a pregnant wife.

At the time of his death, Gong was lying on an improvised bed with two students assigned to 'keep watch' over him sleeping nearby. Gong managed to cut himself and bleed to death without waking his guards, who only realised Gong was dead when they were unable to wake him up in the morning and found the floor soaked with blood.

A relative of Gong's was also a teacher at Peking University and was living in the same building. On the day that Gong Weitai died, she passed that room on the way to the bathroom and saw that the floor was freshly scrubbed, only hearing later, to her great horror, that Gong had died there.

Teachers were living in that classroom building because the university's Worker and PLA Mao Zedong Thought Propaganda Team had ordered all staff to live in specified areas of the university, even those who already occupied its dormitories. Teachers in the Russian Department were ordered to live in the No. 1 classroom building. All of the male lecturers, from department head Cao Jinghua to the young teaching assistants, lived in one classroom, while the female lecturers shared another classroom. Even one female teacher who didn't have 'problems' and had a one-year-old child was forced to stay there. Rice straw was spread on the floor, and the residents brought quilts from home. Only a handful with fewer 'problems' were allowed to go home on weekends. The teachers were held like this for more than a month.

There were meetings in the morning, at noon and at night for mutual 'exposure' and to hear 'debriefings' of each other's 'problems' as well as to hold 'struggle sessions'. The teachers had to study Mao's works and pay their respects to Mao's portrait every morning and evening. Everyone had to get up together early in the morning and wash.

People were struggled constantly in the No. 1 classroom building. Another teacher in Gong Weitai's department said that the building was filled with the wails and howls of people being struggled and beaten. Russian Department head Cao Jinghua had a 200-watt lightbulb hanging over his head, preventing him from sleeping. When he asked to be moved, he was told that wasn't allowed to sleep until he gave a 'frank debriefing of his problems'.

Everyone was ordered to 'expose' each other 'face-to-face' or 'back-to-back'. If anyone refused to speak during a meeting, they would immediately be criticised or be given a 'private talk'. Some still clung to concepts of 'old' morality and felt that 'exposing' others was shameful and horrible. One teacher told me that although he himself didn't suffer very harsh struggle, he was obliged to expose and struggle others, and he considered this 'the blackest time of my life'. He had a conscience, in stark contrast to those who to this day deny that they ever did anything wrong.

Gong Weitai was a 'focal investigation' target in the Russian Department, which meant he was shut up in a small room and slept on the floor with two students who slept in beds whilst keeping watch over him. Slogans such as 'Leniency for frankness and harshness for resistance, stubborn resistance is a dead end road' were pasted all over the room. Gong had been dragged there after being attacked in his home in the middle of the night, and he had already been locked up for some time when the rest of his colleagues were ordered to live in the classroom.

Gong Weitai was struggled repeatedly. During the day on 7 November 1968, he was struggled by the entire department while he 'flew the aeroplane'. What Gong endured inside his room will never be known if his torturers never speak.

It's hard to imagine the depths of despair that drove Gong Weitai to kill himself, his life draining from him without complaint or protest or so much as a moan to alert those sleeping near him. One can only imagine the horror of his colleagues, who didn't dare mourn him but had to hold a meeting to denounce him for 'committing suicide to escape punishment', 'isolating himself from the people' and becoming 'more despicable than a pile of dog shit'.

Gong had studied in the Soviet Union and was one of the best teachers in the Russian Department. His colleague said his literary and music training were also excellent, and he was a man of good character who got on well with others.

Gong Weitai was accused of being a 'traitor'. While in secondary school, he had once been a member of the National Liberation Youth Vanguard, a Communist youth organisation, and had been arrested at one point by the Kuomintang government and then quickly released. In 1968, the Peking University Worker and PLA Mao Zedong Thought Propaganda Teams interpreted that as indicating that he'd turned traitor. Gong's colleagues felt this made no sense whatsoever, but all they could do was raise their hands at the meeting and call for him to be 'struck down'. **Cui Xiongkun**, forty-nine years old, who had been dean of studies and a member of the university's Party Standing Committee before the Cultural Revolution, drowned himself in the campus swimming pool on the evening of 16 October 1968, after escaping from the building where he was being held.

When other Peking University leaders were 'overthrown' in June 1966, Cui Xiongkun was an exception. Since he wasn't considered part of university president Lu Ping's 'reactionary gang', he was recruited as a leader of the work group that managed the Cultural Revolution at the university. In April 1967, he became a leader of the Administrative Committee under the Peking University Cultural Revolution Committee, then a member of its Standing Committee and leader of the 'struggle-criticism-transformation committee'. He was also involved when the university's 'revolutionary mass organisations' split into two factions.

After the university's 'Workers and PLA Mao Zedong Thought Propaganda Team' launched its 'Cleansing of the Class Ranks' in the latter half of September 1968, Cui Xiongkun became a target, and he killed himself. His experience was unusual, but his fate was no less tragic for it.

On that same day, **Rao Yutai**, a physics professor and one of the founders of physics education in modern China, hanged himself from a water pipe in a campus building after being put under investigation.

One of the university's teachers, who was not in the Physics Department, heard that Rao was accused of 'illicit relations with a foreign country'. It was well known that Rao, who was born in 1891, had studied physics in the United States and had obtained degrees at Princeton and the University of Chicago, but no one knew what he had done to draw accusations of 'illicit relations'. One day, my interviewee saw Rao Yutai walking very slowly and bent deeply at the waist, suggesting that he had been badly abused. Old and ill as he was, he was not spared.

Dong Tiebao, a fifty-one-year-old professor of mathematics and mechanics, had obtained a PhD in the US before he began teaching at Peking University in 1956. Locked up for 'isolation and investigation' as a suspected spy, he hanged himself on 18 October 1968.

According to the *Chronicle of Peking University 1898–1997*:[9]

> On 7 November 1956, the ninety-sixth issue of the school journal reported that since the beginning of the school term, seven teachers, breaking through various barriers, had come to work at Peking University after returning from capitalist countries. They were mathematics PhD Liao Shantao, mechanics PhD Dong Tiebao and his wife, horticulture PhD Mei Zhen'an, all of whom returned from the US...

They had come home because Zhou Enlai sent letters to Chinese studying in America inviting them to return to China to work. That was in the relatively relaxed year of 1956. When the Anti-Rightist Campaign was launched in summer 1957, Dong Tiebao wasn't designated a Rightist, but during the 1958 'campaign to pluck out white flags', the Mathematics and Mechanics Department assembled students to denounce him. One of the young teachers who attended that denunciation meeting told me he heard that afterwards, Dong Tiebao went home and said nothing, but just kept chewing on his fingertips. This teacher said he was deeply ashamed of his behaviour at that time.

Ten years after Dong Tiebao returned to China, the Cultural Revolution began, and he became one of more than 900 staff put under 'focused investigation'. He was held in Building No. 28 and not allowed to go home

---

[9] Peking University Publishing, 1998, p. 509.

or have his family visit him while he was forced to give a 'debriefing on his problems'. Since Dong Tiebao is dead, we can only surmise that he experienced the kind of beatings and non-stop interrogation that others endured at this time.

Dong's wife, Mei Zhen'an, who worked in the Horticulture Department, was also 'investigated'. Her elder brother, a research fellow at the Chinese Academy of Sciences, was accused of being their 'confederate'. On the night of 18 October 1968, Dong Tiebao slipped out of Building 28 while his guard was distracted, but apparently feeling he had nowhere to go, he hanged himself from a tree near the school.

After Dong's death, one of the members of his 'special investigation group' mysteriously and vividly told others in the department that Dong had chosen that place to kill himself because it was close to his brother-in-law's work unit, and that he must have been trying to make contact with his brother-in-law, but didn't succeed, and so on. None of the people in the special investigation group showed any sympathy for Dong.

Dong Tiebao had two sons and a daughter. His elder son and daughter, both secondary school students, were sent down to the countryside with other 'educated youth'. Later, Dong's wife sent a letter to Zhou Enlai explaining how they'd come back from the US and requesting his help in getting her children transferred back to Beijing. Her letter had some effect. While other students of the same age remained separated from their parents in the countryside, Dong Tiebao's two children returned to Beijing as 'preferential treatment' given to 'returned overseas Chinese'.

The *Chronicle of Peking University* records that Dong committed suicide, but doesn't state how he killed himself or that he was under 'isolation and investigation' at the time, leaving the circumstances behind his death very vague.

Three weeks after Dong Tiebao's death, his department colleague, thirty-three-year-old **Che Yonghe**, leaped to his death on 11 November 1968 following 'isolation and investigation' for being a member of a 'counter-revolutionary clique'.

Chen Yonghe began studying mathematics at Peking University in 1952. He was too young to have any 'historical problems', but it appears that he voiced some complaints while playing bridge and chatting with colleagues. These remarks were classified as 'counter-revolutionary speech', and he and the people he played cards with were accused of being a 'bridge club' and a 'counter-revolutionary clique' and were interrogated under brutal physical and mental torture.

Chen Yonghe was held on the fourth floor of one of the university's buildings under the supervision of students who accompanied him even when he went to the canteen for his meals. It appears that on the day of his death, he had opened his window before going for lunch, and after he came back to the room, he went to the window and jumped out while the students guarding him watched.

A colleague of Chen's said that he was an outstanding teacher who had attracted envy, and that was a reason for his persecution. The Cultural Revolution provided plentiful opportunities for people to vent their jealousy.

Chen Yonghe's wife was a mathematics teacher at the Peking University Affiliated Secondary School, and they had a four-year-old son.

Li Dacheng, a teaching assistant in zoology in the Biology Department, leaped to his death on 23 October 1968 after being accused of being a 'current counter-revolutionary'. He was in his thirties when he died.

Li Dacheng enjoyed doodling in his spare time. There were constant meetings during the Cultural Revolution, including group reading of articles in Party newspapers that guided the entire process of the Cultural Revolution. One time during a meeting in 1968, Li Dacheng wrote the words 'Long live Chairman Mao' on a newspaper. Someone discovered that the words 'down with' were printed in the newspaper next to the words 'Chairman Mao' that Li had written. Added to the fact that Li had relatives in Hong Kong, this was enough to qualify him as a 'current counter-revolutionary'.

The propaganda team in control of Peking University announced that Li was to be struggled. The day before the struggle session was to be held, Li Dacheng leaped to his death from a window in the university's biology building. Biology professor He Duxiu, standing outside, witnessed Li's death.

The Peking University propaganda team was acting under the guidance of the Cultural Revolution's top leadership. Central Committee Document No. [68] 74, Mao's '19 May Directive', included the following paragraph:

> Military control personnel of the Beijing Xinhua Printing Factory, while mobilising the masses to struggle against the enemy, have been very resolute; whether secret agents, traitors or the smidgen of capitalist-roaders, they have led the masses to ruthlessly criticise them. Especially those who venomously attack the Great Leader Chairman Mao and Vice-Chairman Lin Biao, or who venomously attack the Central Cultural Revolution Small Group, and current counter-revolutionaries opposing the Proletarian Headquarters, once discovered, have been ruthlessly attacked without mercy.

During the Cultural Revolution, brutal persecution of others was carried out in concert with worship of Mao. The degree of this worship is hard for people in other eras to imagine. Every space was covered with Mao's portrait and quotes, and newspaper articles repeated Mao's name constantly. But even this was not enough. Defiling any such materials was considered an attack on Mao himself and constituted an act of 'current counter-revolution'. An enormous number of such 'counter-revolutionaries' throughout the country were subjected to severe persecution and abuse.

We have to wonder whether Mao and his followers genuinely believed that people such as Li Dacheng actually opposed Mao. Did they have a persecution complex, fabricating enemies, or were they conscious revolutionaries who wanted to use this horrific persecution to establish absolute power and rule? It appears that both were the case. When a group of powerful people loses all restraint, they will not only abuse their power but also become psychotic.

Li Dacheng graduated from Peking University's Biology Department in 1958 and then stayed on to teach. A colleague of Li's said, 'He was a particularly honest man.' When Beijing people use the word 'honest', this refers to someone who obeys the rules and minds his own business. Although he was an honest man who had offended no one, the Revolution descended upon him and destroyed his young life.

Li Dacheng had been a head teacher; one of his students said that Li was a short man but good at the high jump and had done well in school competitions. He was even able to jump straight up into the upper berth of the bed where he slept in the dormitory. Such a vital young man who was kind to his students died in this way.

Li Dacheng's colleagues and students remember his death, and that he killed himself, but they can't recall the exact date. Peking University has a list of people who died of unnatural causes during the Cultural Revolution and the dates of their deaths, but these records have been classified as 'secret' and can only be accessed with the special authorisation of the university Party Committee. *Chronicle of Peking University 1898–1997*[10] records the names of some people who were persecuted to death during the Cultural Revolution, but only full professors and instructors. Li Dacheng graduated in 1958, only eight years before the Cultural Revolution, so he never had a chance to be promoted. As a result, his death was not included in the university chronicle.

In investigating the history of the Cultural Revolution at Peking University, I have only been able to gain an understanding of victims' deaths by going to each department individually, and it has been difficult to

---

[10] *Op. cit.*, pp. 447–448.

obtain complete information. From what I understand, three teachers were persecuted to death in the Biology Department in 1968. The names of the other two people are **He Yitang**, who leaped to his death on 6 December, and **Chen Tongdu**, who poisoned himself on 28 August.

Chen Tongdu studied in the United States, and after returning to China taught at Nankai and Peking Universities. He wrote a textbook on biology and was known as an excellent lecturer and a great favourite with students. During the Cultural Revolution, he was attacked over an extended period, first with accusations of having 'complicated social relations' and later with being a spy.

I was unable to learn the details of the treatment Chen Tongdu and He Yitang suffered, but the experience of Hu Shouwen, detailed earlier in Part One, sheds light on the acts of violence prevalent in the Biology Department. Hu's wife, who also worked in the Biology Department, was once interrogated for twenty hours non-stop during the Cleansing of the Class Ranks, until she was so exhausted that she said she confessed to committing a 'capital offence' and said she should be executed.

Wu Weineng, director of the History Department office, drowned himself on 4 November 1968. When the Cultural Revolution began, Wu actively participated in exposing and criticising the university's original leaders, and at one point became leader of the History Department's Cultural Revolution Committee. After the Workers' Mao Zedong Thought Propaganda Team took control of the university in August 1968, Wu was put into a 'study group' in which members exposed and criticised each other. Something Wu Weineng had said in 1959 was 'exposed'. Wu's father, a member of the Xingfu (Happy) People's Commune in northern Jiangsu Province, had starved to death during the Great Famine, and Wu had remarked that 'the Happy Commune wasn't happy.' For that he was accused of 'venomously attacking the People's Communes'. He drowned himself in a pond in the northern corner of the Old Summer Palace.

When Wu Weineng's body was discovered, there were three other corpses in the pond. Two of them were a husband and wife from the Beijing Institute of Geology, and the other was a teacher from Tsinghua University. This was at the height of the Cleansing of the Class Ranks.

The day after Wu died, the History Department held a criticism meeting during which he was posthumously accused of being a counter-revolutionary and betraying the Party (by suicide) among other crimes.

Zhang Jingzhao, a forty-nine-year-old mathematics teacher, killed herself while locked up in a toilet on 9 November 1968. A former student said she was a wonderful teacher who made the textbooks come alive.

Tang Jiahan, a teacher of Indonesian and head of the Indonesian teaching and research section of the Asian Languages and Literature Department, hanged himself in his campus lodgings on 23 November 1968, after being put under investigation in October.

Tang Jiahan graduated from college in the early 1950s and had previously taught at the Nanjing School of Asian Languages. When China's colleges were reorganised, he was transferred to Peking University and was sent to Indonesia to study for one year. Although his home was in the teachers' living quarters, very close to the school, once the Cleansing of the Class Ranks began, Tang had to live collectively with his department colleagues on campus for the regular debriefing and criticism sessions.

One Saturday, Tang Jiahan was allowed to return home, and he went to bed in one of its two small rooms. Late on Sunday morning, when he hadn't got up, his wife tried to go into the room, but found it locked from the inside. The couple's ten-year-old son climbed through the transom above the door and opened it from inside, and Tang's wife found him lying on the bed with a rope around his neck, strangled to death.

When the family reported Tang's death to the school's propaganda team, someone from the team told his son, 'Your father was a counter-revolutionary who committed suicide to escape punishment.' The boy was too afraid to cry.

A professor in the university's Government Department, Zhao Baoxu, told me that at that time he was locked up in the 'custody and reform compound', going out during the day for 'labour reform' – sweeping streets and cleaning toilets. One day he saw a poster pasted on the wall: 'Tang Jiahan's death will not expiate his crimes!' That's how he found out that Tang had died.

Tang Jiahan had two main 'problems': One was his 'family background' – his father was a landlord who had been executed in 1950. The other was 'Leftist ideology'. There weren't many people studying the Indonesian language, and he was very diligent and professional, one of the best people fostered in the Asian Languages Department before the Cultural Revolution, but he was referred to as a 'black sprout'. At the outset of the Cultural Revolution, he 'exposed' problems in the Asian Languages Department, but eventually he himself came under persecution.

Tang Jiahan and his wife, Xu Xiaoyang, were known to be devoted to each other. Xu Xiaoyang eventually died of cancer, and their son now lives in the United States.

Li Qichen, a thirty-four-year-old graduate of Peking University who remained there to teach geophysics, killed himself on 8 December 1968, after being brutally tortured under 'isolation and investigation' on accusations of being a member of a counter-revolutionary clique.

Jian Bozan, a professor of history, was subjected to criticism and struggle after the Cultural Revolution began. He was detained, and his home was ransacked. Jian and his wife, **Dai Shuwan**, committed suicide together on 18 December 1968. Jian was seventy, and Dai was sixty-eight.

Jian Bozan and Dai Shuwan are quite unique among the victims of the Cultural Revolution in that they had already gone through the stage of being tortured and humiliated, and it was only after they were released and their living conditions improved somewhat that they committed suicide.

Wu Ningkun, living in the US, was invited to return to Beijing in 1951 to teach English at Yenching University. At that time, Jian Bozan was head of Yenching's History Department. In his book *A Single Tear*, Wu describes being summoned to Jian's home after writing his detailed 'autobiography' during the Loyalty and Honesty campaign in 1952:

> 'I have been asked by the party organisation to have a word with you about your autobiography,' he began in a condescending tone of voice. 'You have given a broad outline of your life. Quite a complicated life, I must say, for a man of your age. It is against the party's policy to force a confession, but you still have time to add to what you have written, especially crucial ommissions. It will be in your own best interest. I hope you will take advantage of this opportunity...' Then he lit a cigarette and started puffing smoke at me.
>
> Taken by surprise, I bristled at the brazen insult and the implied threat from a fellow professor. 'I have nothing to add,' I said shortly.
>
> 'No don't hasten yourself and don't let your feelings run away with you. We all have a past to deal with, whether we're willing to face it or not. As Marxists, we believe in facing the facts and relieving the load on one's mind by telling the party all. You must be able to recall the important things you experienced in your adult years, especially what happened recently. For instance, it was certainly a good thing that you returned to China from America, but why and how? What were the real circumstances of your return? The real motives?'
>
> 'I already gave a detailed account of them in my autobiography.' Again, I answered briefly.
>
> 'Indeed you did. But could you go over them, check on their accuracy and fullness, and perhaps supplement them with significant details?'
>
> 'I have nothing to add,' I repeated.
>
> 'It's up to you. There is also the question of what you really did in the Nationalist Air Force, besides what you have put down.'
>
> 'I have nothing to add.'
>
> 'I leave it up to you. You may or may not add anything of your own free will. As I said, it's against the party's policy to force a confession, but there is still time for you –'

'I have nothing to confess. And I did not return to my own country to make a confession, Professor Jian.'[11]

After the Loyalty and Honesty Campaign, Peking University relocated to the Yenching campus, and Yenching University was abolished. Jian Bozan became chairman of Peking University's History Department and a grade-one professor. In the early 1960s, he was appointed vice-chairman of the university. Prior to the Cultural Revolution, he was one of China's most authoritative historians.

Wu Ningkun was designated a Rightist in 1957 and sent to the Great Northern Wilderness for 'labour reform'. During the Cultural Revolution he was also subjected to brutal struggle. He returned to the US in the 1980s. What he describes in his book seems very realistic. At that time, Jian Bozan was a senior Party member and Marxist historian, and he was in a position to talk to someone like Wu Ningkun in that way. Compared with other cadres who led the Loyalty and Honesty Campaign, Jian Bozan's manner of speaking can be considered courteous.

The Cultural Revolution thoroughly changed Jian's status. Mao's remarks regarding the Revolution repeatedly mentioned Jian Bozan by name.

In a speech in Hangzhou on 21 December 1965, Mao said:

Some intellectuals, Wu Han and Jian Bozan, for instance, are increasingly unreliable. Now there's that Sun Daren who wrote an essay targeting Jian Bozan's claims of the feudalist landlord class's 'policy of concessions' to the peasants. After the peasant wars, the landlord class only retaliated – where were there concessions?

During an enlarged Politburo Standing Committee meeting from 17 to 20 March 1966:

Now the academic and education communities have come under the control of bourgeois intellectuals. The deeper the socialist revolution, the more they resist and expose their anti-Party, anti-socialist aspect. Wu Han, Jian Bozan and others are Communist Party members, but also oppose the Party; in fact, they're Kuomintang. Recognition of this problem is still very poor in many places at present, and academic criticism has not yet been developed.

---

[11] Wu Ningkun, *A Single Tear*, London, Hodder & Stoughton, 1993, pp. 221–22.

On 23 April 1966, the *People's Daily* published an article nearly two pages long entitled 'Comrade Jian Bozan's Anti-Marxist Historical Views'.

On 21 July 1966, Mao mentioned Jian again in a speech: 'The Cultural Revolution can only rely on the masses. Someone like Jian Bozan who wrote so many books – can you read or criticise them? Only they can understand the situation; even I can't.' He also said: 'The Cultural Revolution, criticising bourgeois thought, how much struggle has Lu Ping faced, or Li Da? Jian Bozan has published so many books, but can you struggle him? The masses write antithetical couplets saying he's a big god in a small temple, and too many turtles in a shallow pond. Can any of you deal with him? I can't, and neither can the provinces.'

Mao's 21 July remarks are not coherent, but the meaning is clear: he wanted more people to struggle Jian Bozan, and that included verbal and personal attacks.

Chronicle of Peking University (Beijing daxue chubanshe, 1998) states that on 7 April 1966, the Peking University Party Committee decided to 'now emphasise dealing with the Jian Bozan problem'. After playing a role in pushing forward the Cultural Revolution, the university Party Committee was itself 'struck down' on 1 June.

Jian Bozan was struggled at all kinds of denunciation rallies, and he was paraded through the streets on a horse cart. He was thoroughly humiliated as well as physically beaten.

On 24 August 1966, Red Guards from the Beijing Normal University Affiliated Girls' Secondary School joined with Red Guards from other secondary schools in going to Tsinghua University to smash things. They then ransacked Jian Bozan's home on Yenching's eastern campus – the home that Wu Ningkun describes in his book as having such a large library that the university was building an addition to the house. The Red Guards tore up the paintings and books in Jian's home and then sealed off his study. Returning to their schools late that night, they excitedly told their classmates how they had harangued Jian, and they imitated and ridiculed Jian flinching in horror, a completely different image from the haughty demeanor Wu Ningkun described.

I have no intention of belittling Jian Bozan. The terror created by the Red Guards was unprecedented. They were not like the police; they could arbitrarily beat and even kill people. The Red Guards of the BNU Girls' School had killed their vice-principal, Bian Zhongyun, only three weeks earlier. Although only secondary school students, they were capable of thinking up all kinds of strange torments, and victims who didn't submit to them could be beaten to death on the spot. There were many besides Jian Bozan who shrank in terror before them. Our reluctance to infringe the dignity of the victims mustn't make us avoid describing the brutality and viciousness of the Red Guards Mao used to carry out his persecution.

After that, Red Guards from Peking University also ransacked Jian's home, and the family was forced to move into a small, dark house in Haidian. It had no kitchen, and they had to cook their meals on a stove placed in the doorway. Nearby children knew that Jian was a 'reactionary' and 'ox demon and snake spirit' and constantly jeered at him and spit and threw filth at his cooking pot.

The *Chronicle of Peking University* (which provides little detail on the Cultural Revolution) records that Jian Bozan was struggled at mass rallies twice in 1967, on 4 April and 16 May. At the struggle rally, the targets stood on the stage with their heads bowed and bent at the waist and their arms pulled backward in the stance known as 'flying the jet'.

Two years later, in November 1968, at the Twelfth Plenum of the Eighth Central Committee, Mao once again mentioned Jian:

> There is one Jian Bozan, a professor and historian at Peking University, a bourgeois historical authority. It would be hard for him not to get mixed up with emperors, generals and ministers. Toward these people you can't use methods that don't respect their dignity. Like only paying them 24 *yuan* per month, or at most 40 *yuan* – you can't cut it too much. These people aren't very useful. Then there's Wu Han – he might still be somewhat useful. If you need to ask about idealism or emperors, generals and ministers, they're the ones you have to ask.
>
> Jian Bozan and Feng Youlan spread poison, so we have to criticise them. We have to criticise them, but also protect them and give them something to eat, and have them be reeducated by the workers, peasants and soldiers.

Because of this 'highest directive' from Mao, the leaders of the Mao Zedong Thought Propaganda Team headquarters that controlled Peking University immediately went to the university's 'ox pen' – or 'supervision and reform compound' – and released Feng Youlan and Jian Bozan. They also declared that Feng Youlan would be paid a living allowance of 125 *yuan* per month, and that Jian Bozan and his wife would be paid 120 *yuan* per month. They said this was in accordance with Mao's instructions to 'support' them as 'negative examples'. As for the other people held in the compound, they remained imprisoned. More than 200 of the university's teachers and staff were held in that compound.

Jian Bozan and his wife were moved from their little dark house back to the campus and were allocated one of the university's better quarters in Yenching's southern campus. Their living allowance of 120 *yuan* per month, while much lower than Jian's original pay, was still a very decent amount, given that young teachers who had been working at Peking University for seven or eight years were paid only 56 *yuan* per month.

Peking University professor Zhao Baoxu says that at one point, someone from Zhou Enlai's office asked Jian Bozan if he needed anything, and Jian said, 'The only request I would make is that when I'm struggled, it should be by adults and not by children.'

After receiving 'preferential treatment' for a month on Mao's instructions, Jian Bozan and his wife, Dai Shuwan, took an overdose of sleeping pills in their campus home on the night of 18 December 1966.

Some say that the couple killed themselves because military representatives were once again forcing them to 'expose' and 'confess' their 'problems'. This may have been a reason, but it wouldn't have been the only reason. The Cultural Revolution had been going on for more than two years, and Jian Bozan had already endured a great deal. Furthermore, when he was released he had been clearly told that he was to serve as a 'negative example' and would not be treated as a guest of honour, so he wouldn't have had great expectations. In fact, after Mao handed down his 'highest directive', Jian's conditions improved – at the very least he didn't have children spitting into his wok. In my opinion, the suicide of Jian and his wife expressed their refusal to play the role of 'negative example' that Mao had assigned to them.

We might wonder if anyone told Mao of the deaths of Jian Bozan and his wife. Up to now, no document has been found reflecting any reaction on the Chairman's part. It's possible that no one ever dared to tell him for fear of infuriating him. The suicide note that Jian Bozan left reportedly included the sentence 'Long live Chairman Mao,' but their suicides demonstrated that Jian and his wife were unwilling to co-operate by serving as struggle targets or otherwise being toyed with.

Of course, this was also because Jian Bozan was not an ordinary man. Other people, the little people, were never given the opportunity to demonstrate their personal will. I've heard of no other instances during the Cultural Revolution when someone killed themselves after obtaining such 'favour' and 'leniency'. History should take note of the actions of Jian Bozan and Dai Shuwan, and also of why such actions were so rare.

TSINGHUA UNIVERSITY

The methods Tsinghua University used to persecute intellectuals were summarised in a report and became a Central Committee document that was distributed throughout the country as a model to emulate.

Liu Chengxian, deputy director of the university's United Front Department, was locked up with other mid-ranking cadres and tortured by the university's Jinggang Mountain Corps. She leaped to her death on 12 June 1968.

Chen Zudong, a fifty-five-year-old professor of Hydraulics, hanged himself on 20 September 1968, while under investigation for 'historical problems'.

Chen Zudong graduated from Tsinghua University in 1935 and was sent to the US and India for observation and study. During the War of Resistance against Japan, he managed an arsenal in Guizhou, and in 1949 he was chief engineer at the Shanghai Longhua Airport. He became a professor and chairman of Tsinghua's Hydraulics Department in 1956.

Chen Zudong had gone without pay for three months before his death as a penalty for being an 'ox demon and snake spirit' and a 'target of investigation'. He was repeatedly interrogated and denounced and forced to give 'debriefings' on his 'historical problems'. Before 1949, he had signed up to join the Kuomintang, and when the Nationalist government left China in 1949, he'd been given a plane ticket, but remained in Shanghai. He'd already been purged because of his old KMT connection during the 1955 Campaign to Eliminate Counter-Revolutionaries. He avoided being designated a Rightist in 1957 because he didn't dare speak out, but in 1968 he came under heavier persecution than ever before.

In his 'highest directive' issued in April 1968, Mao declared the Cultural Revolution to be a 'great proletarian cultural revolution, a great political revolution carried out under the conditions of socialism in which the proletariat oppose the bourgeoisie and all exploiting classes. It is a continuation of the long struggle of the vast revolutionary masses under the Chinese Communist Party and its leaders against the Kuomintang reactionary dregs, and a continuation of the class struggle between the proletariat and the bourgeoisie.' The phrase 'Kuomintang reactionary dregs' was already in common usage in the guiding documents of the Cultural Revolution in 1967. It was under this theoretical guidance that Chen Zudong became a target of persecution.

What put him under even greater pressure was that he was also forced to 'expose' what his schoolmates and colleagues had done before the CCP took power in 1949. Chen told his family that he was willing to frame himself, but he couldn't testify against others.

After the Cultural Revolution, some writers published articles and books about their experiences. I've noticed that some of these people mention reporting the content of private conversations with others, and so on, which brought trouble and even calamity to those involved, but they write about it calmly as if they'd done nothing wrong. They seem to think that as long as what they reported was true and not manufactured, it was perfectly all right to inform. To a certain extent, this is because under the horrendous pressure and drive to seek reward and escape punishment during those years, false witnesses were ubiquitous, and few of them were punished or even morally censured after the Cultural Revolution.

Against this background, the pain Chen Zudong described left a deep impression on me. He obviously regarded informing against others as a breach of his ethical standards that caused him anguish. The Cultural Revolution was not only physically punishing, but also devastating to the conscience of people like Chen who persevered in their moral outlook.

On the night of 20 September, Chen Zudong told his wife that the school had told him to make a 'debriefing of his problems'. This had happened before, so his wife didn't think anything of it. After Chen went out, his wife left on the light and waited for him, but instead of going home, he went to the ruins of the Summer Palace and hanged himself.

The next day, the school told Chen's wife to come and identify his body. Three of the couple's children were already working elsewhere, so Chen's wife and one daughter went to the palace grove where the body had been found hanging from a tree.

Soon afterwards, Chen's daughter in Beijing was assigned work on a farm in the northwest. Chen's wife had retired from her job as a factory accountant, so she went to live with another daughter in the northeast. In that way, the family was scattered to the winds.

After Chen Zudong died, a loudspeaker broadcast at Tsinghua University proclaimed that he had 'committed suicide to escape punishment', had 'isolated himself from the Party and the people', that he 'deserved to die ten thousand deaths' and had 'become a despicable pile of dog shit'.

Chen Zudong was rehabilitated in 1978. Prior to the Cultural Revolution, Tsinghua University had 108 professors who had been jokingly referred to as the '108 heroes' of the classic *The Water Margin*, and Chen was one of them. His family later heard that by 1978, only forty-odd of those 108 heroes were still alive.

Another professor of Hydraulics, **Li Piji**, leaped to his death from the Water Conservancy Building less than two months after Chen Zhudong died, on 29 November 1968. Born in 1912, Li Piji had studied in Germany. He had been chief editor of a textbook on his subject and had made models and experiments for many major reservoirs. When Professor Zhang Wei was struggled, Li Piji had consoled him by saying, 'You'll be all right, just try to get past it.' The fact that he himself later committed suicide suggests what he must have gone through while in custody.

Tsinghua University had new and old water conservancy buildings, with key teaching facilities and important research. Li Piji died in the old building. As for the new building, in May 1970, PLA and Mao Zedong Thought Propaganda Team commander Chi Qun, who was also propaganda head of Mao's security team, ordered the destruction of the equipment in its experimentation hall for conversion into an automotive assembly workshop. Two months later, on 27 July, the workshop 'manufactured' ten vehicles under the '727' brand to commemorate 27 July 1968, when Mao sent the propaganda team to take control of Tsinghua University.

Yin Gongzhang, a forty-two-year-old lecturer in basic courses, and his wife and fellow lecturer, **Wang Huichen**, went to the Fragrant Mountains outside of Beijing and hanged themselves on 6 November 1968. On that same day, **Yang Jingfu**, a thirty-six-year-old teacher of foreign languages, leaped to his death.

Cheng Guoying, the forty-six-year-old vice-chairman of the Architecture Department's fine arts research section, hanged himself on a slope next to the university's lotus pond on 12 November 1968.

Cheng Yingquan, a forty-nine-year-old 'Rightist' lecturer in civil engineering, drowned himself on 13 December 1968.

Cheng Yingquan was the first person to establish architectural studies at Tsinghua University. He was engaged in urban planning research. During the debate during the 1950s over whether or not to preserve Beijing's old city and its walls, he was one of the people who advocated preservation. This was the main reason he was designated a Rightist in 1957.

After the designation, Cheng's wife divorced him and took their two children, so Cheng lived in a dormitory for unmarried staff. During the Great Famine in the early 1960s, he sometimes saved up portions of his own grain ration, baked some buns and invited his children over for dinner.

Like other instructors who had graduated from college before 1949, Cheng was required to repeatedly give 'debriefings' on his 'historical problems' – and he was a Rightist on top of that. A colleague who spoke of his suicide was very distressed and said it 'wasn't worth it', meaning that being persecuted to death wasn't worth it. At that time, some people bore up under torture and survived by despising their persecutors; others were unable to do so.

Cheng Yingquan drowned himself in the university swimming pool, and his body was discovered the next morning during a routine patrol. Cheng knew how to swim, so it must have taken great willpower to kill himself this way.

Cheng Yingquan had an elder brother living in Shanghai and visited him during the period between the Anti-Rightist Campaign and the Cultural Revolution. His niece formed a deep impression of him at that time. When she saw Cheng's name on my website, she wrote to me saying that was the first she'd heard of how her uncle died.

Zou Zhiqi, a fifty-seven-year-old mechanics professor, leaped to his death on 10 December 1968.

Lu Xueming, a forty-one-year-old physical education teacher, leaped to his death on 8 February 1969.

Li Yuzhen, a fifty-eight-year-old staff member of the university library, leaped to her death on 23 April 1969.

Wang Dashu, a thirty-one-year-old teaching assistant in the Department of Electrical Engineering, poisoned himself to death on 4 May 1969.

CHINESE ACADEMY OF SCIENCES

Yao Tongbin, director of the Academy's Aerospace Institute, was beaten to death on 8 June 1968.

Lin Hongxun, an associate research fellow at the Mechanics Institute, killed himself after being subjected to a brutal 'investigation' in 1968. Lin Hongxun had studied in the US and joined the Mechanics Institute after returning to China. He had taught fluid mechanics in Peking University's Mathematics Department in the 1950s.

Another associate research fellow in the Mechanics Institute who had studied in the US, **Cheng Shihu**, likewise killed himself after being subjected to brutal 'investigation' in 1968. He had taught vibration theory at Peking University in the 1950s.

Zhao Jiuzhang, born in 1907, was a meteorologist and director of the Institute of Geophysics of the Chinese Academy of Sciences. After graduating from Tsinghua University, Zhao obtained his PhD at the University of Berlin in 1938. During the Cultural Revolution, his home was ransacked, and he was struggled with a placard around his neck. Zhao took an overdose of sleeping pills on 25 October 1968.

BEIJING BROADCASTING INSTITUTE

Chen Yinglong, in his thirties, was a teacher in the Radio Department of the Beijing Broadcasting Institute. Chen leaped to his death after being locked up in 1968.

When Chen had previously filled out the required curriculum vitae form, he had given his class status as 'landlord'. This CV was brought out during the Cultural Revolution, and the school put up many big-character posters saying that Chen was a 'target of dictatorship'. Chen Yinglong's colleague said that Chen wasn't a landlord himself, but came from a landlord family, a distinction that wasn't made clear on his CV.

One day in summer 1968, when it was time for the department's teachers to go home after a meeting, Chen was told to stay behind. There is no further information on what transpired, only that he killed himself by jumping from the third floor of the school. Chen left behind three children, all below school age.

BEIJING INSTITUTE OF MECHANICAL INDUSTRY

Dong Jifang, a forty-three-year-old teacher and head of the institute's teaching and research section, killed herself after being humiliated in the course of 'struggle' and 'investigation'.

BEIJING NORMAL COLLEGE

Li Xin, a teacher in the Foreign Languages Department, leaped to his death from the window of the college's main building while under 'isolation and investigation' in 1968. He was not yet forty years old.

Li's colleagues described him as a learned and mild-mannered person. Prior to the Cultural Revolution, Li had served as a substitute teacher at the Normal College's Affiliated Secondary School, so the teachers there knew him. After Li died, his body was left on the ground for a time and covered with a tattered straw mat. A teacher from the secondary school who saw Li's body on the ground said that she subsequently took a different route to avoid that spot, because it was too painful to look at the place where someone she knew had met such a horrible end and their remains had been treated that way.

CENTRAL UNIVERSITY FOR NATIONALITIES[12]

Xu Yin, a cadre and chairman of the Han Language Department, leaped to her death from the third floor of a school building after being put under 'investigation' in the school in 1968. Soon afterwards, Xu's husband, **Tang Hai**, chairman of the university's Art Department, also came under 'investigation' and committed suicide.

BEIJING INSTITUTE OF TECHNOLOGY

Xu Youfen, a staff member in the institute's library, was put under investigation in 1968. The people interrogating her had prepared a thick dossier, and

---

[12] Now Minzhu University of China.

they pulled out a sheet of paper and let her quickly see her name on it, then placed it back in the file and forced her to 'honestly confess her crimes'. In fact, they were bluffing and hoping to trick her into incriminating herself. Xu Youfen was so terrified by her experience that after returning home she suffered an acute attack of illness and died.

BEIJING INSTITUTE OF CHEMICAL ENGINEERING[13]

Fu Guoxiang, a student of chemical engineering, began studying at the institute in 1963 and should have graduated in 1968, but instead he was purged as a 'reactionary student' and subjected to struggle. Fu leaped to his death from the sixth floor of a school building at the age of twenty-three.

BEIJING RAILWAY INSTITUTE[14]

Wu Xiyong, a fifty-seven-year-old professor, was accused of being a secret agent and brutally beaten because he had studied economics and obtained his PhD in France. He poisoned himself on 21 September 1968.

TSINGHUA UNIVERSITY AFFILIATED SECONDARY SCHOOL

Zhao Xiaodong, a fifty-nine-year-old physical education teacher, leaped to his death on 9 August 1968, after being locked up and struggled.

Apart from being a teacher, Zhao Xiaodong was also head of the physical education teaching and research group. A graduate of Northeast University's Sports Department, Zhao was among the first batch of Chinese athletes with a college degree, and he once won the male all-around sportsman trophy for the Northeast Region. Before the Cultural Revolution, the Tsinghua University Affiliated Secondary School team was the most outstanding in Beijing, and this was clearly related to the effort and ability of Zhao Xiaodong.

A former student of the school said that he recalled Zhao getting up every morning at 5:00 and arriving at the dormitory at 6:00 sharp to get students up for their morning exercises. Thinking back, he was moved by the realisation of how difficult this was, but as a young student he didn't know enough to feel grateful. After the Cultural Revolution began, class struggle

---

[13] Now Beijing University of Chemical Technology.
[14] Now Beijing Jiaotong University.

theory made persecuting teachers a revolutionary act, and no one felt any sympathy when Zhao died; recalling this made the former student very sad.

Zhao Xiaodong was put under 'isolation and investigation' in the school's 'ox pen' at the outset of the Cleansing of the Class Ranks in early 1968, and he was only allowed to go home occasionally to fetch clothing, while his son delivered medicine to him once.

Zhao was accused of 'historical problems'. A former student recalled hearing that Zhao had once been a member of the Three People's Principles Youth League, and had been a travelling salesman, major crimes at the time. Nowadays this would be considered just a stage in growing up or making a living, but it became a reason for locking Zhao up and struggling him twenty years after the fact.

After Zhao was struggled in a classroom on the school's fifth floor, he took the stairs to the corner landing between the fourth and fifth floors, where there was a small window. A student named Gao Wangling was on the stairs at the time and saw Zhao jump out of the window. Gao said that he'd always wished he'd pulled Zhao back, but he also knew that Zhao was a tall, strong man, and that even if he'd reacted more quickly, he wouldn't have been able to stop him.

The Tsinghua Affiliated Secondary School was one of the points of origin of the Red Guard movement, but by 1968, the first group of Red Guards who had controlled the school in 1966 had lost power and had been replaced by the Jinggang Mountain Red Guards and their extension, the Jinggang Mountain Corps. A former member said that Zhao Xiaodong's suicide initially caused tension in the faction, but since Zhao had been a member of the KMT's Three People's Principles Youth Corps, the rebels decided he was a 'class enemy' who 'deserved what he got'.

When I spoke to former teachers and students of the Tsinghua Affiliated Secondary School, most of them still remembered Zhao Xiaodong's suicide, but students who later became writers made no mention of the deaths of Zhao or any of the other victims in their published works.

A former student was able to confirm the date of Zhao's death as 9 August 1968. That was at the height of 'intensified struggle against the enemy' – another of the repeated upsurges in violence during the Cultural Revolution.

BEIJING NORMAL UNIVERSITY AFFILIATED GIRLS' SECONDARY SCHOOL

Hu Xiuzheng, a thirty-five-year-old chemistry teacher, leaped to her death on 11 August 1968, after being detained at the school for 'attempted verdict reversal and opposing the Cultural Revolution'.

A photograph of Hu Xiuzheng shows a plain, serious and proper woman, the image of a typical and ordinary female secondary school teacher, and indeed, that's what she was. Hu graduated from BNU Girls' Secondary in 1951, but was unable to further her studies due to her family's economic hardship. After graduating, she became manager of the school's laboratory while taking classes part-time. She had been teaching chemistry at the school for twelve years when the Cultural Revolution began.

In 1958, Hu Xiuzheng married Zhang Lianyuan, who was a physics teacher at the Beijing No. 8 Secondary School, located about one kilometre from BNU Girls' Secondary, also in Xicheng District. They lived in the staff quarters of BNU Girls' Secondary, and their young daughter boarded at a nearby nursery. Hu's salary at the time was 64 *yuan* per month, and Zhang earned 68 *yuan* per month. The couple also supported Hu's widowed mother and maternal grandparents.

Hu Xiuzheng shouldn't have been a particular focus of attack, because she was an ordinary teacher and not a 'reactionary academic authority'. In addition, she was too young to have 'historical problems' and not an outspoken person who would be accused of 'reactionary speech'. Her problem arose from the class ranking assigned to her husband's father.

Zhang Lianyuan's father lived in a village in Gu'an County, Hebei Province. During the Socialist Education Movement in 1964 (known as the 'Four Cleans Movement' in the countryside), the father was designated a 'landlord who had slipped through the net' and was ordered to attend a 'scoundrel rally', making him a 'class enemy' and 'target of dictatorship'.

Twenty-eight years after Hu Xiuzheng's death, I interviewed her widower, Zhang Lianyuan, and asked him whether his father was a landlord or a 'scoundrel'. Zhang was still able to fluently and in detail recount his father's history and why he should not have been designated a 'landlord'. Since his father was rehabilitated on his class background issue in 1979, the specifics of his pre-1949 history were no longer relevant, but Zhang was still able to detail them exhaustively and with considerable agitation, because back during the Cultural Revolution, they actually did matter. Because of his father's history, Zhang had been detained and struggled and had even lost his wife, and he had clearly pondered these stories countless times, even apart from the many times he'd been forced to write out 'confessions' regarding his father's affairs, so it was hardly surprising that he could still recall them in such detail.

Anyone listening to this narrative now would wonder why the question of whether Zhang Lianyuan's father was a landlord or a scoundrel would have anything to do with Hu Xiuzheng. She was merely his daughter-in-law, and whatever made him controversial occurred before she had even met his son. But during the Cultural Revolution, these remote matters became mortal crimes and the direct cause of Hu's persecution and death.

After Zhang Lianyuan's father was designated a 'landlord who slipped through the net' in 1964, Zhang reported the matter to the Party branch of his school, which in turn reported it to the Xicheng District Party Committee. Reading the relevant Party regulation, Zhang found that a person's class status was supposed to be determined in accordance with his economic circumstances three years before the PRC's founding in 1949. According to that standard, his father shouldn't have been considered a landlord, and Zhang Lianyuan sent a letter to the CCP's North China Bureau requesting a 're-examination' of the case.

When Red Guard violence commenced in Beijing's secondary schools in August 1966, the vice-principal of Hu Xiuzheng's school, **Bian Zhongyuan**, was beaten to death by student Red Guards on 5 August, and the secretary of the Party branch of Zhang Lianyuan's school, **Hua Jin**, was beaten to death on 22 August, while history teacher **Shen Xianzhe** committed suicide after being beaten, and violence spread outside of the schools as well. By early September, Red Guards at Zhang Lianyuan's school had already killed eight people.

On 3 September 1966, two cadres from the production team Zhang Lianyuan's father belonged to came to Beijing demanding to bring Zhang and Hu Xiuzheng back to the village. The reason they gave was that the two teachers were 'settling old scores' by demanding a 'verdict reversal' for Zhang's father and making a 'vain attempt to reverse a Four Cleans Movement case', referring to Zhang Lianyuan's 1964 letter. Zhang was summoned to the school, where he was promptly beaten and interrogated by cadres from his father's village. Student Red Guards then took turns beating Zhang with clubs, belts, ropes and brooms.

Two teachers who saw Zhang being beaten tried to intervene. One was a laboratory technician named Zhang Liangyin, who told the students, 'You need to get the facts straight first,' but the Red Guards pushed him out of the office. The other was physics teacher Zhou Guozheng, who was a Catholic and therefore also in a disadvantaged situation. Even so, when he saw the beating going on, he told the students, 'You can't beat people like this,' and tried to stop them.

By then everyone knew how many people had been killed or injured by student Red Guards from the No. 8 Secondary School, and it required enormous courage for Zhang Liangyin and Zhou Guozheng to speak up in that atmosphere of terror. No wonder that twenty-eight years later, Zhang Lianyuan still remembered their names and what they said, and still felt so profoundly grateful to them. Although today we may admire these two men immensely, we can only regret that there were not more like them. It is their rarity that obliges us to remember their names. In a time of horror, they acted with extraordinary courage and a sense of justice and reached out to help a colleague in trouble.

Zhang Lianyuan was beaten all day long on 3 September. The Red Guards forced him to eat a steamed bun pungent with mould. That night, he was locked up in the school and expected to be beaten to death like his colleague Hua Jin and the other 'ox demons' outside the school whose names he didn't know. But after beating him for a while, the Red Guards said, 'Don't kill him. Leave him for the people in the village to beat.'

Student Red Guards from the No. 8 Secondary School ransacked Zhang Lianyuan's home again and then completed the paperwork to have Zhang and his wife expelled from Beijing. The next day, 4 September, they used Zhang's own money to hire a truck to take the couple, along with their belongings, to the village where Zhang's father lived, now known as the Wucun production brigade of Niutuo Commune in Hebei's Gu'an County. Upon their arrival, the production brigade's cadres ordered them to hand over all of their valuables, including cash, watches and fountain pens.

Zhang Lianyuan and Hu Xiuzheng were locked up separately under round-the-clock surveillance and weren't allowed to see or speak to each other. They were beaten, marched through the streets, taken to public criticism rallies and subjected to all kinds of other punishments. They were also threatened: 'If you don't behave, we'll hand you over to the secondary school's Red Guards.' The couple were compelled to write self-criticisms and confessions according to the specifications set by the production brigade cadres. After a week, they were allowed to work in the fields with other commune members, but they still had no freedom of movement. Zhang's father was beaten even more harshly and subjected to brutal punishment. One time he was ordered to kneel on an upended bench for an entire night, and was not allowed to move or go to the toilet. He attempted suicide several times.

Zhang Lianyuan and Hu Xiuzheng attempted to use Hu's younger sister as a conduit to send letters and telegrams to the CCP Central Committee, State Council, Central Cultural Revolution Small Group and the new Beijing Municipal Party Committee, asking for help. However, their letters were just handed over to the North China Bureau, which passed them to the Tianjin Prefectural Party Committee, which in turn passed them down to the Gu'an County Party Committee. Zhang and Hu asked the Gu'an County Party Committee not to pass their letters along to the commune, but they did so anyway. It doesn't take much imagination to guess the result of their petitions being handled that way.

Zhang and Hu's daughter remained at her boarding nursery in Beijing; they were forbidden to visit her. Finally, after two months of repeated requests, Hu Xiuzheng was allowed to return to Beijing to visit her child on 3 November. After that she reinstated her Beijing household registration and began looking for ways to bring her husband back from the village. At one point she went to the powerful 'People's Visits and Letters Reception Office' to ask for help, but to no avail. She thought of another method. The materials that remain include a medical certificate issued on 13 January 1967, by the Beijing Post and Telecommunications Hospital Outpatient Clinic. Hu Xiuzheng wrote a letter to the two Party branch secretaries at the production brigade saying that she was ill, her mother was in the hospital with a serious illness, and her child was also ill, and because the school's teachers were all busy with the Cultural Revolution, she could not get help from her colleagues. Hu used this as an excuse to request that the Party secretaries allow Zhang Lianyuan to take a few days' leave to return to Beijing and bring their daughter back to the village. After repeated negotiations, Zhang was granted five days' leave and returned to Beijing, and he didn't go back to the village after that. However, his household registration remained at the village, as did all of the family's belongings. The Beijing authorities refused to issue him a *hukou* card or to return the belongings that were seized when the family's home was ransacked.

At this point, the high-ranking cadres who were the parents of many of the original Red Guards were purged in a new campaign to 'criticise the bourgeois reactionary line', and this first batch of Red Guards fell from power and came under criticism for the violent acts they'd committed in summer 1966. In November, the Beijing Municipal Party Committee issued a directive forbidding kangaroo courts and unauthorised jails. Under these conditions, some Beijing residents who had been expelled to the countryside in summer 1966 attempted to return home. However, on 18 March 1967, the Beijing Municipal Public Security Bureau Military Control Commission issued a 'notice' reaffirming the 1966 Red Guard 'repatriation' campaign, and the expelled persons were not allowed to return. The notice stated:

> Our Great Leader Chairman Mao instructs us: Toward the reactionary faction, it is essential to 'implement dictatorship to suppress these people; they must be kept in line and must not be allowed to engage in irresponsible talk or actions. If they talk or act irresponsibly, punish them immediately.'
>
> The Capital Red Guards and the revolutionary masses, raising high the great red banner of Mao Zedong Thought in the production class's Cultural Revolution, have repatriated a batch of persistently reactionary landlords, rich peasants, counter-revolutionaries, bad elements, Rightists and dregs of society to the villages for penal labour under surveillance.

This is of great significance in consolidating the dictatorship of the proletariat. In recent months, some repatriated landlords, rich peasants, counter-revolutionaries, bad elements and Rightists have secretly returned to Beijing in a vain attempt to reverse their verdicts, willfully stirring up trouble, engaging in sabotage and disturbing social order.

In order to strengthen dictatorship over the enemy and safeguard the revolutionary order of the capital, and in accordance with the demands of the vast revolutionary masses, this 'Methods for Handling Persons Repatriated during the Cultural Revolution Who Have Returned to Beijing' is issued for immediate compliance and execution.

This notice was posted all over the streets. At this time, Zhang Lianyuan was living in Beijing without an official household registration, and his situation was perilous. In early May, the authorities at Zhang's school declared that he was to be repatriated. Zhang went to the Xicheng branch of the Beijing PSB to discuss his situation and handed over his materials, requesting that he be allowed to stay. The PSB branch stressed that he lacked a Beijing *hukou* and had to leave.

Anyone in the capital without a *hukou* was not allowed to reside there or obtain food rations, and even more importantly, having his Beijing *hukuo* nullified and being expelled marked him as a 'class enemy', making him a target of dictatorship wherever he went. Under threat of a possible second 'repatriation', Zhang Lianyuan wrote up a report in May 1967 recounting his unfortunate situation. Both he and Hu Xiuzheng signed the report, which employed Cultural Revolution logic to point out that they were both ordinary teachers and belonged to the 'masses' and that refusing to restore their *hukous* was a manifestation of the 'bourgeois reactionary line'.

Furthermore, by then recent developments in the Cultural Revolution had caused the Party secretaries of the production brigade where Zhang Liangyuan's father lived to come under criticism, so Zhang and Hu accused the 'capitalist-roader faction in power within the Party' of persecuting their family. The couple went to the Central Cultural Revolution Small Group reception office to talk with officials there and submit the report, and they even wrote letters to Jiang Qing and other leaders of the Cultural Revolution, desperate to identify a rationale within the Revolution's own propaganda that would allow Zhang to transfer his *hukou* back to Beijing. Rather than negating or reversing a verdict of the Cultural Revolution, they were only trying to show that the punishment didn't apply to them. Indeed, there had never been any formal case against them. Even in the case of Zhang Lianyuan's father, it was said that the 'Four Cleans' work group had decided after three rounds of discussion that he was not a landlord, but the night before the work group left the village, he was declared a landlord. Under those circumstances, many such individuals or their family members would propose that this verdict was improper. It wasn't a matter of questioning the standards for the verdict, but to suggest that their case didn't meet those standards. In terms of legal process, this was a completely natural thing to do. In practice, however, all but a tiny minority of such supplicants were harshly suppressed for attempting to clear their names.

On 25 October 1967, the CCP Central Committee issued its document No. [67] 325, entitled 'CCP Central Committee Stipulations Forbidding Reversal of Verdicts against Landlords, Rich Peasants, Counter-Revolutionaries, Bad Elements and Rightists', stating:

> At present there are some landlords, rich peasants, counter-revolutionaries, bad elements and Rightists who during the Cultural Revolution movement are going around filing appeals and willfully stirring up trouble as they seize the chance to negate their past crimes. The Central Committee reiterates its past stipulation that landlords, rich peasants, counter-revolutionaries, bad elements and Rightists are not allowed to seize the opportunity to reverse their verdicts during the Cultural Revolution. Exceptional cases that genuinely deserve re-examination must be left until after the movement. Criminals in custody or in labour reform factories or farms must remain under supervision without exception and are forbidden to engage in irresponsible speech or action.

From then on, 'verdict reversal' became an actual crime, and once the Cleansing of the Class Ranks was launched, it was categorised as a 'current counter-revolutionary' crime.

It was against this background that in spring 1968, Zhang Lianyuan and Hu Xiuzheng came under attack in their respective schools for 'verdict reversal'. Hu became one of the main targets of attack in the Cleansing of the Class Ranks carried out by the Revolutionary Committee of the Beijing Normal University Affiliated Girls' Secondary School. Big-character posters were put up around the school attacking her for 'verdict reversal for a reactionary landlord', 'reversing the verdict on the Four Cleans Movement' and 'reversing the verdict on the Cultural Revolution'. Just as in summer 1966, her husband had become implicated in his father's case, she now became implicated in her husband's case and became the target of a new round of persecution.

Apart from being interrogated around the clock by members of the special investigation group, Hu was required to go to classrooms and repeatedly 'confess her problems' while the students constantly called out slogans such as 'Hu Xiuzheng needs to make an honest confession,' and 'Frankness is treated with leniency and resistance with harshness.'

Zhang Lianyuan was never allowed to see his wife, and had no way of finding out what was happening to her. But everyone at the school knew that the Workers and PLA Mao Zedong Thought Propaganda Team had organised students to struggle the school's vice-principal, Hu Zhitao, for forty-eight hours around the clock in shifts. This struggle rally was publicised as an achievement and a credit to the school. Unlike in 1966, people were normally not beaten to death in public during the 1968 Cleansing of the Class Ranks, but this kind of protracted struggle and interrogation was still carried out on a grand scale. Furthermore, it was an open secret that a great deal of physical abuse occurred behind closed doors. Late at night, interrogators routinely employed methods that they believed would effectively elicit a confession. Two teachers who couldn't bear it any more finally admitted to doing everything they were accused of, and even embellished their crimes with various stories such as how they had worked as secret agents and engaged in espionage. They were then finally allowed to sleep. (They subsequently retracted their confessions.) One nineteen-year-old student who took part in one of these late-night interrogations passed out from exhaustion and fear, even though she was on the giving rather than the receiving end.

In June 1968, Zhang Lianyuan wrote a self-criticism admitting his failure to 'draw a clear distinction from reactionary family members' and admitting his 'motivation and objective' in writing a letter to the upper level. Hu Xiuzheng also wrote several lengthy self-criticisms admitting her error in questioning the political verdict the production team had reached on her father-in-law and writing a letter asking for help. She repeatedly expressed her admission of guilt and criticised her own 'class standpoint errors' in sincere and careful wording. Even so, the struggling against her escalated.

Zhang Liangyuan was put under 'isolation and investigation' first, and as soon as he was granted permission to return home in early August, Hu Xiuzheng was taken away for 'isolation and investigation'. That night, a neighbour who was also a colleague of Hu's came and notified her husband that she wasn't being allowed to come home, and asked him for a ration coupon and money for Hu to buy food at the school.

I interviewed a teacher of Russian named Pei Jingying who was locked up like Hu Xiuzheng at the school. In 1957, her husband was designated a Rightist and expelled from Beijing for 'labour reform', at which point the couple divorced, and she sent their only daughter to live with her older sister. During the Cultural Revolution, the sister's family were also designated 'ox demons and snake spirits' and had no money, so Pei took some gold jewelry to the Chinese People's Bank to exchange for cash, and that was the 'reason' for her being put under 'isolation and investigation'. No one kept diaries during the Cultural Revolution, especially people like her who were locked up, so Pei Jingying can't remember which day Hu Xiuzheng died, but she remembers it was a Sunday, because the canteen only served two meals on Sunday. I checked the calendar, and in fact 11 August 1968 was a Sunday.

Around five o'clock in the afternoon on 12 August, the leader of the Beijing No. 8 Secondary School students notified Zhang Lianyuan that Hu Xiuzheng had killed herself. They said she died the night before by leaping from a fifth-floor window of a student dormitory at the school.

Zhang took their child to the school, where Hu's body had been moved to a secluded corner next to the enclosing wall and covered with a shabby hemp bag from which one of her feet protruded.

After the authorities of the Affiliated Girls' School held a meeting and condemned Hu Xiuzheng for 'alienating herself from the Party and the people', several teachers took her body to the crematorium. Zhang Liangyuan received some items that Hu had left behind while under 'isolation and investigation' – some notebooks of her study of Mao's works and some draft self-criticisms. There was no suicide note among the items, and no writings expressing despair or the intention to kill herself; Zhang believes that if she had actually committed suicide, she would have left a note for him and their daughter, who was not even five at the time. After ten years of marriage, he felt he completely understood his wife; she was a strong-willed woman who had begun working independently at a very young age to support her family. Since the Cultural Revolution's launch in 1966, the couple had endured violence and terror together, had been sent to the countryside together and suffered torture there. After two months she had found a way to leave the village and then a way to get Zhang back to Beijing as well. She was a brave and resilient person. After all the hardship she'd already experienced, Zhang was sure she could press on. He found no evidence of an inclination towards suicide.

However, he was in no position to look for evidence of foul play. After his wife died, Zhang Lianyuan was put under 'isolation and investigation' a second time at the No. 8 Secondary School, where he was locked up with at least eight other teachers. His daughter was kept at the nursery, even at the weekends.

Zhang was held until one day in spring 1969, when the propaganda team that controlled the school announced that he could return home and resume his teaching duties. In the words used at that time, he'd been 'liberated'. In accordance with the rules of that time, before being 'liberated' he had to write a very long self-criticism, the first draft of which he has retained to this day. In the self-criticism he confesses his 'family problem' and 'verdict reversal problem' and thanks the Party and Chairman Mao for 'rescuing' him.

The sum total of Zhang Lianyuan's offences consisted of the letters of appeal he'd written to explain to the Party's upper levels that his father had not been a landlord in the three years preceding 1949, and later to explain why he shouldn't have been expelled to his father's village. Because of these letters that he'd sent from 1966 to 1969, Zhang had been beaten, humiliated, and jailed for an extended period, and worst of all, his wife had been persecuted to death and would never come back, while his young daughter had been traumatised and would never see her mother again. Yet when he was finally 'liberated', he had to thank the Party and Chairman Mao.

Hu Xiuzheng's death was referred to as 'committing suicide to escape punishment' and 'alienating herself from the Party and the people'; she was expelled from the Party, which she had joined in 1960. After Lin Biao's death in 1971, policies for handling people underwent some changes. In 1973, the CCP Central Committee issued a document saying that Party members who killed themselves during campaigns would no longer be punished for 'betraying the Party'. This resulted in a new 'verdict' stating that Hu Xiuzhen did not have any problems and was 'not to be expelled for betraying the Party'. Two years after Mao's death, Hu's crime of 'verdict reversal' was also overturned, and she was 'rehabilitated'. Her memorial ceremony was carried out at the BNU Affiliated Girls' Secondary School in July 1978, ten years after her death.

Zhang Lianyuan's father also had his issue resolved in 1979. He was first rehabilitated, and then, after a number of twists and turns, his class was changed from 'landlord' to 'worker'.

During the 'implementation of policy' in 1978, the various files, reports and conclusions of inquiries compiled by the special investigation groups during the Cultural Revolution were removed from personnel files and destroyed. The subjects of these materials had never been given copies and never had a chance to read the texts that determined whether they would live or die. At the Beijing No. 8 Secondary School, Zhang Lianyuan was one of two teacher representatives who served as witnesses to the destruction of those materials. Packed into two standard burlap bags, these documents that had caused the death and suffering of so many were pulled out and stuffed straight into a furnace, where they quickly turned to ash.

Zheng at one point went to his wife's school and requested to see her file, but the cadre in the personnel department told him the files had been destroyed in order to 'avert further trouble'. As a result, all Zhang Lianyuen obtained was 'Hu Xiuzheng's Notification of Rectification Decision', a single piece of paper bearing the red stamp of the CCP branch of the Beijing Normal University Affiliated Secondary School. Dated 15 June 1978, it stated: 'On 11 August 1968, Comrade Hu Xiuzheng unfortunately passed away as the result of persecution by the Lin Biao and Gang of Four Reactionary Line. The erroneous decision and all false accusations imposed on Comrade Hu Xiuzheng are hereby completely overturned, and she is thoroughly rehabilitated.'

Hu Xiuzheng's decision made no mention of what had led to her persecution, nor was any record retained of how she was persecuted to death.

Zhang Lianyuan eventually remarried a woman who was a descendant of Lin Zexu, the Guangzhou viceroy who tried to halt the British opium trade in 1839, and the two of them raised his child together. The end of the Cultural Revolution allowed Hu Xiuzheng's daughter to avoid Hu's fate; in 1997, she obtained a PhD in biology from a British university, and she married and became a mother at around the same age that her own mother died.

Three other teachers at the Beijing Normal University Affiliated Girls' Secondary School killed themselves after Hu Xiuzheng.

Language teacher **Zhou Xuemin** was gentle and cultivated, and before the Cultural Revolution, her teaching methods had been praised and promoted; that was the reason for her being labelled a 'reactionary academic authority'.

Geography teacher **Zhao Shouqi**'s husband had been labelled a Rightist in 1957 and sent to Shanxi Province for hard labour, leaving her to raise their four children alone. She killed herself after being attacked and humiliated in big-character posters.

History teacher **Liang Xikong**, thirty-eight years old, was a graduate of Beijing Normal University. Students who took his class said he was jocular and witty, a learned man and an engaging lecturer. One day while teaching Ancient World History, he came to class with nothing in his hands and flipped through a student's textbook, as if he'd forgotten where he'd left off last time. Then he began recounting a Greek legend, and the students listened with rapt attention. When the story ended, he picked out several points, such as whether it demonstrated if people knew how to make iron implements at that time. He presented what could have been a dry and boring lecture in a way that allowed students to genuinely learn history. He hanged himself after being accused of 'historical problems'. There's no way of knowing what kind of torture Liang suffered before he died, but it must have been horrendous in order to make a man with such a strong sense of humour kill himself, abandoning his wife and child.

Liang's wife, Jiang Peiqi, was an agriculturalist who didn't live in Beijing. They were only able to see each other for seven days each year during the

Spring Festival. They had one child who was still very small and lived with Jiang.

In July 1978, a memorial ceremony was held at the school for the teachers who committed suicide during the Cleansing of the Class Ranks, the equivalent of 'rehabilitating' them. After Liang Xikong was rehabilitated, the school helped his wife relocate to Beijing and provided her with housing in the school's living quarters.

Also, at the No. 8 Boys' Secondary School where Zhang Lianyuan had taught, a young teacher named **Gao Jiawang** was locked up as a 'current counter-revolutionary' and killed himself in autumn 1968. Gao had graduated from the school and continued working there, supervising the dormitory and the workshop where students studied industrial topics. Born to a landlord or rich peasant family in a coastal area, he was accused not only of being a counter-revolutionary but also of drawing coastal defence frontline maps to send to Taiwan. At the time of his death, Gao Jiawang was newly married to a primary school teacher.

ERLONG SECONDARY SCHOOL

Zhang Fang, a forty-year-old English teacher, was viciously beaten by student Red Guards in summer 1966, then came under 'investigation' during the Cleansing of the Class Ranks in 1968. Unable to bear the torment, she sought refuge with the family of a student in Xinxiang, Henan Province. After being discovered by members of the local 'rebel faction', Zhang hanged herself in Xinxiang on 19 May 1968.

The first time I heard Zhang Fang's name was in a telephone call with the late writer Wang Xiaobo. It was in 1996, the thirtieth anniversary of the launch of the Cultural Revolution. I hadn't read any of Wang's books, and I had telephoned to talk to his wife rather than to him, as part of my ongoing effort to talk to as many eyewitnesses of the Cultural Revolution as possible and gather more facts about victims. As it happened, Wang Xiaobo's wife wasn't at home, but when I told Wang the purpose of my call, he asked if I'd looked into the Erlong Secondary School, and when I said that school wasn't among the 100 I'd looked into so far, he told me about the suicide of Zhang Fang while he was a first-year student there.

Wang Xiaobo said (erroneously) that Zhang Fang was a physics teacher, and was beaten along with other teachers and the school's administrators at the time when violence surged up in schools throughout Beijing in Red August 1966. The head teacher, whose parents were said to be capitalists, hanged himself after being beaten. Zhang Fang was badly beaten, but she didn't die until she was purged again during the Cleansing of the Class Ranks in 1968.

I immediately added Zhang Fang to the list of victims on my website. The fact is that investigating the history of the Cultural Revolution is difficult and painful work. It often takes enormous effort just to determine basic information such as a name or a date of death – not only because it involves incidents that occurred decades ago, but also because many people block access to this information. And when one finally does clarify the facts behind the death, the tragedy and horror plunges one into grief rather than bringing the joy and satisfaction that rewards other kinds of research.

Wang Xiaobo's recollection and recounting of Zhang Fang's story left a deep impression on me, even though I never met him. I've talked with a number of authors who were secondary school students during the Cultural Revolution, and more than one of them has professed no memory of brutal incidents that occurred around them, while others have claimed that the situation 'wasn't all that serious'. This ability to overlook the suffering of others is unfortunately much more common than the sensitivity to suffering exhibited by Wang Xiaobo.

I later read Wang's essays, and felt that their social and cultural criticism, including his boycott of the upsurge in nationalism in 1996, was consistent with his views on the Cultural Revolution and his memories of and sympathy for its victims. Unfortunately, he died before I had a chance to meet him.[15]

At the request of Wang Xiaobo's wife, I wrote an afterword for a collection of his essays in 1997. I started with how he'd told me about teacher Zhang Fang's death, and I expressed my gratitude for his support for my research. I felt there was a connection between his memories of the Cultural Revolution and its victims and the accomplishment of his essays.[16]

The Erlong Secondary School was located near Xidan, only about one kilometre from Tiananmen Square and right next to the PRC's Ministry of Education and Ministry of Higher Education.

A former colleague of Zhang Fang's said her beating on 9 August 1966 was 'too painful' and impossible to describe. It is in fact very painful for people who shared the horror of this time to recall and describe what happened to other victims. Through further questioning, I learned that Zhang had been buried alive three times, only being dug out after the earth reached her chest; that she had been thrown into a septic pool; that she had been poked with needles at night so she couldn't sleep; and that her hair had been shaved off and her scalp burned.

---

[15] TN: Born in 1952, Wang Xiaobo died of a heart attack in 1997.
[16] My essay didn't end up being used as an afterword for the book, but it was published in *Fangfa Magazine* (No. 3, 1998), which was banned not long afterwards.

When the second round of persecution began with the Cleansing of the Class Ranks, Zhang Fang was tortured again. Unable to bear it any more, she took refuge with the family of her student Li Xueli in Xinxiang, Henan Province. The harsh 'struggle' of the Cultural Revolution years was naturally accompanied by strict control of personal movement, and escaping from one's work unit was regarded as a serious act of resistance. The only way to escape completely was through suicide.

The 'rebel faction' heading up Xinxiang City's Revolutionary Committee discovered Zhang Fang, apprehended her, interrogated, tortured and raped her. They also notified the Erlong Secondary School authorities of her whereabouts. The school sent a personnel cadre and a Red Guard leader to Xinxiang to escort Zhang Fang back to Beijing. The Red Guard leader was one of the students who had beaten her in 1966, and he later became a member of the Revolutionary Committee that took control of the school. In Xinxiang, he smacked Zhang in the face and savagely kicked her. Unable to bear the torment, Zhang Fang wrote a suicide note describing her maltreatment and then killed herself. That suicide note was still preserved at the Xinxiang PSB in 1979.

When victims were rehabilitated in 1979, the school sent a young teacher named Zhang Xiaosong to accompany Zhang Fang's daughter, Tang Jinjin, to Xinxiang to recover her mother's remains. In a desolate graveyard, they found the only unnamed grave from that period, and guessing that Zhang Fang must be buried there, they paid 50 *yuan* to have it dug up and the coffin opened. Zhang was a petite woman, and when Tang Jinjin was able to identify the corpse from her mother's small plastic shoes, her distress can only be imagined. Zhang Xiaosong helped Tang Jinjin take the remains to the crematorium, and Zhang Fang's ashes were brought back to Beijing.

Because the Red Guard leader who had beaten Zhang Fang now occupied a leading position at the school, her family objected to holding a memorial ceremony there. The Xicheng District Education Bureau transferred the former Red Guard to a different secondary school.

Wang Xiaobo and the colleagues at the school who witnessed her suffering still remembered Zhang Fang thirty years later: a victim of the Cultural Revolution, a petite woman, a mother, an ordinary teacher at a secondary school in the middle of a city with a 3,000-year history. We can't overly blame the people who have chosen to forget the death and violence in the schools at that time, but at least we should praise those who have remembered the unfortunate victims around them.

In March 2007, Zhang Fang's daughter read what I'd written about her mother on the Internet and contacted me, providing me with a photocopy of her mother's suicide note and the court judgment of the local Revolutionary Committee leader, who was tried after the Cultural Revolution.

Suicide note

I began taking part in the revolution in my youth and never did anything wrong; I just had some different thinking on some issues, and yet you have persecuted and humiliated me this way! Chairman Mao said, 'Ideological problems should be solved through the methods of persuasion and education, discussion and criticism, and cannot be solved through coercion.' How have you been obeying Chairman Mao? You enjoy using methods that look Leftist but are really Rightist. My death is very unjust! But when even a member of the Revolutionary Committee beats people, how can I bear to go back? If there is any humanity left in you, you should send the 290 *yuan* and seventy kilos of national grain coupons along with my clothing back to my home. I earned all of this through my hard labour and not through exploitation, and you shouldn't misappropriate it.

My two children will lose their mother before they're grown. Their father's health is very poor. Please don't persecute my family, and don't persecute Li Xueli; she's only a child, after all, and all guilt (if there is really any guilt involved) should be borne by me alone.

Zhang Fang
The night of 19 May 1968, in Xinxiang

Xinxiang City Hongqi District People's Court
Criminal Judgment
(79) Hongqi Criminal Case No. 26

Prosecuting organ: Xinxiang Public Security Bureau
Defendant: He Tingzhi, male, forty-eight years old, from a poor peasant family, worker, illiterate, Han, native of Fengqiu County, Henan Province, arrested at Minzu West Road No. 324, Xinxiang City; the defendant has been a farmer since his youth and was an apprentice. In 1947, he served as a puppet soldier in the Fengqiao County puppet security team for more than one month. From 1954 to 1966, he was a worker. In 1967, he was integrated into the Xinxiang City Property Company Revolutionary Committee as vice-chairman. He was detained for questioning on 6 April 1977, and was arrested in accordance with law on 28 April of that year, and is now in custody.

The hearing of this case has concluded, and it has now been proven through investigation:

The defendant He Tingzhi on 15 May 1968, unlawfully imprisoned Zhang Fang, a female teacher at the Beijing Erlong Road Secondary

School who was passing through our city, in the Sinxiang City Property Company, and in collusion with the criminal Zhao Baoxu (at that time chairman of the property company's Revolutionary Committee, and who has already been sentenced to reform through labour) set up a kangaroo court, carrying out unlawful interrogation, and then notifying Ji Zehua, Zhang Hongbao and another from the Beijing Erlong Road Secondary School to write to the property company, and carried out unlawful interrogation and beating, using their official power and the pretext of arranging housing and assisting with a work transfer and other measures, to commit four counts of rape and taking advantage of their work to corruptly obtain public funds of 665 *yuan* (all returned) and bribes of white rice, peanuts, grain coupons, cotton, sesame oil, etc.

Based on the above facts, the defendant He Tingzhi committed the serious crimes of illegal imprisonment, setting up a kangaroo court, illegal interrogation and homicide, rape, corruption and graft. After being arrested he confessed his crimes, and in accordance with law this court sentences He Tingzhi to a prison term of ten years (commencing from 6 April 1977, and ending on 6 April 1987).

If the defendant is not satisfied with this judgment, he may submit an appeal within ten days to the Xinxiang City Intermediate People's Court.

9 October 1979

These two documents allow a further understanding of the brutality and repulsiveness of the Cultural Revolution.

JINGSHAN SECONDARY SCHOOL

Yu Gongsan, a language teacher, leaped to his death from the fifth floor of the school building on 10 August 1968 after being put under 'investigation' for 'historical problems'.

A former student of the school said that Yu was especially good at teaching classical literature. When he was labelled an 'ox demon and snake spirit' during the Cultural Revolution, he was beaten and humiliated and walked around with his head bowed. On 9 August 1968, while this student was riding his bicycle with his younger brother on the back, they saw teacher Yu walking along with his head bowed, and as they passed, his younger brother spat at Yu. At that time, the student felt it was normal to treat 'class enemies' this way, but when he learned the next day that Yu was dead, he was distressed to think that he and his brother had contributed to Yu's persecution and death.

After Yu died, his wife, who was unemployed, was expelled from Beijing to the countryside.

PEKING UNIVERSITY AFFILIATED SECONDARY SCHOOL

Wang Hou, around fifty years old, was a cook at PU Affiliated. After being interrogated about 'historical problems', he killed himself in the Baishiqiao River near the school in July 1968.

At a 'rehabilitation meeting' at the school after the Cultural Revolution, Wang Hou's younger brother asked, 'Why did they kill him? Wouldn't it have been a good thing if he had lived and kept cooking for the teachers and students?'

Wang Hou's 'problem' was that he had been a police officer before 1949. When someone tried to save him after he leaped into the river, he said, 'Don't save me. I can't take it any more.'

Li Jie, a teacher, had been harshly beaten by the school's Red Guards in summer 1966. She died of a ruptured spleen after being beaten again during the Cleansing of the Class Ranks in September 1968.

As with other victims, writing Li Jie's story is painful and depressing, but in the process of looking into it, I encountered a teacher named Guan Qiulan who inspired me with a glimpse of radiant morality. While helping me understand Li Jie's situation, Guan also expressed her guilt and regret over what happened, showing me the capacity human beings have for introspection and the pursuit of virtue.

I knew from the outset that investigating and recording the history of the Cultural Revolution would not be easy and would require great mental and physical effort. But I didn't expect this research to cause me so much anguish. Perhaps the word 'anguish' is inappropriate, because it's not a matter of clear-cut pain, but rather a feeling of depression during and after my writing.

My research method is to collect as many textual and photographic materials as I can find, and then to interview as many people as possible who experienced the Cultural Revolution, because I maintain the view that many of its events, especially those that befell ordinary people, lack records and reports and require investigation. I'm grateful to many interviewees who spent so much valuable time recalling and bearing witness to the Cultural Revolution. They told their stories and I compiled them into a record, writing out what happened to each individual. For example, PU Affiliated was one of the schools where the Red Guard movement began, and is also a place where Guan Qiulan taught for forty years. I discovered stories that had never been reported before.

One story involves PU Affiliated as the place of origin of the famous antithetical couplet 'The son of a hero is a good fellow, the son of a reactionary is a bastard.' The father of first-year student Wan Hong had been designated a Rightist in 1957, as a result of which she was labelled a 'bastard'. When some male Red Guards wanted to beat her, she tried to hide in the girls' restroom. One of the Red Guard leaders, Peng Xiaomeng, was in the restroom at the time. Wan Hong begged her, 'You've been received by Chairman Mao [when Mao reviewed the Red Guards on 18 August 1966], you know the policy. Please tell them not to beat me.' Peng Xiaomeng just pulled her out of the restroom. Wan was ordered to stand on a stool while schoolmates beat her with their belts. Another student kicked the stool out from under her so she crashed down onto the cement floor.

When one of Wan Hong's schoolmates told me how Wan was struggled and abused, her fifteen-year-old daughter, sitting nearby, became so distraught that she wept. I didn't allow myself to cry, but it took me a long time to overcome my feelings of depression over the darkness of human nature. A friend who has always supported my research on the Cultural Revolution became worried about me at this time and kept saying, 'Why do you have to write these stories? It's too painful for you.'

I'm grateful for her concern and kindness, but now that I've started, I have to continue, even if it tears at my soul like a wire brush. Fortunately, this apparently simple investigative work is in fact very time-consuming, and occupies and diverts my attention. Also, at times like these I'm reminded of related but different matters. One of them is the repentance expressed by teacher Guan Qiulan.

When I was in Beijing in summer 1997, someone told me that Guan had read my essay '1966: The Revolution in which Students Beat Teachers', and that she wanted to talk with me. Naturally I was very willing. I'd heard her name long before as a model teacher loved and respected by her students. By the time I finally met her, she had retired from PU Affiliated but was working as the principal of a private vocational secondary school. Although no longer young, she was still vigorous and nimble, candid and quick-thinking.

The day we met was hot and humid, and I was moved that an elderly person would agree to meet me under such oppressive conditions. Guan had grown up in Indonesia, but had come to Beijing in 1949 and attended secondary school there, after which she studied history at Peking University. Her father had been a teacher in Indonesia, and after graduating she also wished to devote herself to this 'most sacred enterprise under the sun'. Because she'd come from overseas, she had been placed in the 'restricted use' category, although she didn't know it at the time. Once the Cultural Revolution began, she was sent to one of PU Affiliated's three 'labour reform teams', which were divided up according to the seriousness of the 'crime'; Guan and Li Jie were among the twelve teachers in the No. 2 team.

One day, the Red Guards locked up Guan Qiulan and some other teachers from the labour reform team in a small room downstairs. A Red Guard picked up a knife, grazing Guan's face and then jabbing vice-principal Liu Meide's face, saying, 'Liu Meide, I'm itching to kill you.' They then shut the door tight. That night, Guan Qiulan knocked on the door and told the Red Guards that she had to go home and take care of her three-year-old daughter. The Red Guards didn't permit this, but they opened the door for a few minutes before closing it again. After a short time, Guan knocked on the door again, saying, 'Please let me go home. I have a child!' Still she was not allowed to go. She wasn't even thinking of getting fresh air, but only of getting home to her child, but the fact was that by continuing to knock at the door, she brought in fresh air for all of the people locked up in the small room. Near dawn, perhaps when the Red Guards changed shifts, Guan knocked again, and the Red Guard said, 'Get out of here!' She went home right away. Only later she learned that because the room was so small and unventilated and contained chemicals, the 'ox demons and snake spirits' might well have suffocated in that hot weather.

The No. 2 team included a physical education teacher named Zhang Min, and one day she and Guan were assigned to move sand. Two Red Guards came over and said, 'Stop there. Zhang Min, do you earn 126 *kuai* per month?' Then without giving any reason, they took off their belts and one began beating her while the other counted. They said they would lash her 126 times, but in fact they continued for 200 strokes before stopping. After that, Zhang and Guan went into the restroom. Zhang Min was physically robust, and she supported herself against the wall while Guan pulled the shirt off her back, breaking down in tears at the sight of her mangled flesh.

Another teacher in the No. 2 team, Chu Zaisheng, had his hair shaved off. While he was labouring in the vegetable cellar, a Red Guard came over and began lashing his bald head with his belt, raising a welt with every stroke.

The Red Guards also ordered members of the labour reform teams to beat each other. Most of the teachers in the No. 2 team refused, but there was one person who beat others.

Guan Qiulan said, 'At that time, people lost all dignity.'

Guan remembered that the young Li Jie had run off to Beijing to escape an arranged marriage. That was during the Japanese occupation, and Li Jie married a Japanese businessman. Later that man left China, and their child died. During the 1950 Campaign to Eliminate Counter-Revolutionaries, Li Jie 'confessed' this period of her history, and the authorities issued a 'verdict'. She subsequently handled the books and reference materials at PU Affiliated and did ordinary clerical work. She was tidy and industrious.

When the Cultural Revolution began, a big-character poster entitled 'Liu Meide's heinous crimes at the Peking University Affiliated Secondary School' attacked not only Liu Meide, but also several teachers and staff who worked under her, including Guan Qiulan and Li Jie.

When the Red Guard movement began, Li Jie was harshly beaten. She was ordered to kneel inside a cabinet, where she couldn't move an inch, and beaten with an iron bar. When rummaging through Li's belongings, the Red Guards found she'd saved a document relating to her family's gravesite; they said it was a 'land deed' and that she was saving it for when the 'regime changed'. They nearly beat her to death.

There was a small change in the course of events in November 1966 as the targets of attack were expanded and the first group of student Red Guards fell out of favour. The Cultural Revolution's leaders called for the 'spearhead of struggle' to be aimed at high-status individuals referred to as 'the capitalist-roader faction in power', and members of labour reform teams who had no special status and whose 'problems were not great' were allowed to leave. Under those circumstances, Guan Qiulan furtively went to the State Council Letters & Visits Reception Office and submitted a written report stating that she was a returned overseas Chinese and had no 'problems'. She also reported that members of No. 2 Team were also not part of the 'faction in power' or 'reactionary academic authorities' and didn't have any 'major problems'. But she left out Li Jie and didn't say anything on her behalf.

Eventually, members of No. 2 Team were released one by one, but Li Jie was upgraded to No. 1 Team and was subjected to long-term labour reform and torture.

Two years later, during the Cleansing of the Class Ranks, Li Jie was once again targeted because of her 'historical problems' and was harshly beaten by a new group of student Red Guards. Unable to walk after the beating, Li Jie crawled back to the room where she was being held. When the school authorities saw she was in bad shape, they sent her to Haidian Hospital, where she died. The death certificate issued by the hospital said she'd died of a ruptured spleen.

Guan Qiulan said she felt guilty about Li Jie. I told her that even if she had included Li in the material she submitted to the State Council Reception Office, it might not have done any good and may have even made things worse, giving examples that I knew of.

Guan didn't see things that way, though. She said that after the Cultural Revolution, she looked up Li Jie's younger sister, hoping to do something for her. But in 1966 she didn't mention Li's name. On the surface, this was because she felt that she and others in the No. 2 Team genuinely had 'no problems', while Li Jie was problematic because she had married a

Japanese during the occupation. Guan knew what Li Jie's 'problem' was, but it shouldn't have been grounds for her to be put into a labour reform team and brutally beaten twenty years later. Guan felt that allowing Li to be beaten when she knew she didn't deserve it had contributed to her death: 'I feel I wronged her.'

I wanted to reassure her that this was the fault of the system and not of any individual, but I realised that she understood this and was speaking on a different level.

Suddenly I remembered a story from the Bible. When people wanted to stone a prostitute, Jesus said, 'He that is without sin among you, let him cast the first stone.' As a result, everyone dropped their stones and went away. This story is profoundly meaningful, and I don't think I'm forcing the analogy by applying it to Li Jie.

There were many such situations during the Cultural Revolution in which someone was deemed to have a 'problem', and then everyone 'exposed' and 'struggled' them, throwing stones at them or watching from the sidelines with a clear conscience while others did so. Afterwards, many people insisted that they only took part in persecuting others out of 'revolutionary idealism', and on this basis they saw no need to apologise, reflect or repent: 'At that time we were responding to Chairman Mao's call for revolution.' But Guan was not of this mind.

Guan said that for a long time she would wake up with a start every morning and ask, 'What's going on?' Walking across the lawn of the school, she would suddenly shudder, because this was where Red Guards had beaten people. She didn't recover until the 1990s.

Before we parted, Guan talked of her philosophy of life and her moral viewpoints. I quickly realised that this apparently carefree, plump, elderly teacher was engaged in an ardent and acute moral pursuit. Her profound memories of the past, her sympathy for the sufferings of others, her clear self-analysis and her regret for what she'd done were all part of it. I've discovered the relationship between these four qualities in others as well, such as the writer Wang Xiaobo.

The best way to deal with the Cultural Revolution is to speak the truth, admit error, apologise to the victims and feel repentance. All are interrelated, but are on different moral planes. Repentance falls within the moral realm, and people outside that realm will have difficulty understanding it. Using a somewhat inappropriate analogy, it may be like trying to install high-powered software in a low-grade computer.

Unfortunately I didn't have the opportunity to talk more with Guan Qiulan. But in the days that followed, as I recorded stories of the Cultural Revolution, even when I felt depressed and discouraged, I kept thinking of my conversation with her on that sultry afternoon. She showed me the power of the human struggle towards goodness. Her repentance gave me the courage and confidence to carry on.

Thank you, Teacher Guan.

RENMIN UNIVERSITY AFFILIATED SECONDARY SCHOOL

This school was located in Beijing's Haidian District, very close to the affiliated secondary schools of Tsinghua and Peking Universities, where the Red Guard movement originated.

Many teachers were persecuted at this school in 1966, and during the Cleansing of the Class Ranks in 1968 those who had been 'ferreted out' in 1966 were hauled out again and locked up in a school building for 'isolation and investigation'.

Yang Jun, a forty-year-old language teacher, hanged himself after being beaten by students in November 1968. Yang had two main 'problems'. The first was that before 1949 he had been a war correspondent for a newspaper, which meant he had a 'reactionary history'. The second was that after 1949 he had published some informal essays, and some unpublished essays discovered when his home was ransacked were interpreted as 'anti-Party and anti-socialist'. For example, one essay described a blind man who played the flute very well, and this was interpreted as an attack on the CCP for heedlessly promoting the Great Leap Forward (using a term that combined the words for 'blind' and 'blow'). One day students thrashed him in a classroom, and Yang Jun hanged himself with a belt that same night.

BEIJING NO. 1 GIRLS' SECONDARY SCHOOL

Wang Yuzhen, vice-principal, was beaten, humiliated and locked up in 1966. After she escaped from the school's 'ox pen' in October 1968, she and her husband drowned themselves in a river outside Beijing.

Wang Yuzhen's husband was a cadre in the Ministry of Water Conservancy and Electric Power. I haven't been able to find out his name, but he appears to have been surnamed Gu, given that an interviewee told me the couple had two children named Gu Yi and Gu Jiaqi, both secondary school students.

The No. 1 Girls' Secondary School was separated from Zhongnanhai only by a wall, and some of the school's students were the daughters of senior cadres. Among the photos that the *People's Daily* published of Mao posing with Red Guards on 18 August 1966, is one of him standing near a senior cadre's daughter from the No. 1 Girls' School.

Not long after Mao reviewed the Red Guards at Tiananmen Square, the school changed its name to 'Big Red One Affiliated Secondary School'. An article in the *People's Daily* on 1 September mentioned the school as one of four involved in expelling Catholic nuns from Beijing, and reported its name change. Former teachers and students said beatings by Red Guards became serious at the school after 18 August. I've described some of the horrors that occurred in the section about Beijing secondary schools in 1966. At that time, Wang Yuzhen had half her hair shaved off and was severely beaten. She was locked up in a room next to the sports ground with several other female 'ox demons and snake spirits' including another vice-principal, Tong Peizhen. The women's families didn't know where they were being held, and they didn't know when they might be beaten to death. Tong Peizhen said, 'There was absolutely nothing we could do. No one dared to come forward and stop the beatings. We couldn't find a higher-level authority to go to, and didn't even know who was in the higher-level position.' Red Guards warned them, 'If you don't behave, you'll end up like Bian Zhongyun,' referring to the vice-principal beaten to death at the Beijing Normal University Affiliated Girls' Secondary School on 5 August.

All of the 'ox demons and snake spirits' were given insulting nicknames, and they had to respond to them at roll call. Tong Peizhen told me, 'It was hard to bear.'

In autumn 1966, the Red Guards sent the 'ox demons and snake spirits' to Shunyi County in the Beijing suburbs for 'labour reform'. Vice-principal Tong Peizhen fell down and was run over by a cart. The people in the cart said, 'It's a reactionary – crush her!' Fortunately, the cart-driver stopped, but Tong's right arm was shattered.

When the Cleansing of the Class Ranks began in 1968, Wang Yuzhen's 'historical problems' were 'investigated'. Wang had joined the CCP before 1949, but in 1968 she was accused of being a 'fake Party member' and placed under 'isolation and investigation'. One day, she managed to escape. She and her husband reportedly sought refuge in a relative's home, but finally went to a western suburb of Beijing and drowned themselves in a river. A few days later, someone found their bodies and reported it to the PSB. The PSB took Wang Yuzhen's clothing to the No. 1 Girls' School, where colleagues identified it as hers.

Wang and her husband had three children, all of whom were in secondary school when the Cultural Revolution began and were sent down to the countryside as educated youth. When their parents were eventually rehabilitated, their father's work unit arranged employment for them at one of its worksites.

BEIJING NO. 3 GIRLS' SECONDARY SCHOOL

Fang Tingzhi, a teacher, was locked up in the school for 'isolation and investigation'. One day at noon she went to the school entrance and threw herself in front of a car.

Not long after Fang Tingzhi's death, another female teacher, **Sun Lisheng**, hanged herself in the school on 12 July 1968, after being locked up for 'isolation and investigation'. Born in 1934, Sun Lisheng had been designated a Rightist in 1957 and brutally beaten and tortured by Red Guards at her school in summer 1966.

A character in the novel Butterfly

While I was carrying out my investigation in 1996, an interviewee who had been a student at the Beijing No. 3 Girls' School in the 1950s told me that a teacher named Sun Lisheng had killed herself during the Cultural Revolution. My interviewee didn't learn of Sun's death until many years later, and didn't know when she had died or where, but she still remembering how beautiful her face was while teaching students how to sing. She'd heard that Sun had been friends with the younger sister of the writer and former Minister of Culture Wang Meng, and that a character in Wang's novel *Butterfly* was based on Sun Lisheng.

Butterfly was a famous example of the 'scar literature' of the early 1980s. One of the novel's main characters was a veteran Party cadre who was struggled during the Cultural Revolution and then resumed his high position in the government. One of the three women involved with him, Haiyun, had been a secondary school student in 1949, pure and passionate and yearning for revolution, and she married this senior Party cadre after the CCP took power. The couple had a child, but then Haiyun was labelled a Rightist in 1957 on the basis of something she'd said, and her husband divorced her and married another woman. Haiyun killed herself during the Cultural Revolution.

The book's title, *Butterfly*, comes from the famous story of the philosopher Zhuangzi dreaming that he had turned into a butterfly, and then, after awakening, being unsure if the butterfly had existed in his dream, or if he was existing in the dream of the butterfly. In terms of the protagonist of the novel, the senior Party cadre, this reflected his thoughts and feelings regarding the contrast between being struggled in the Cultural Revolution and then being restored to his senior position. The novel didn't describe Haiyun's suicide in detail, but said that she killed herself after being beaten.

Anyone who wanted to describe the Cultural Revolution during that period had to avoid mentioning too many details. Articles about rehabilitation all focused on people at the level of deputy minister or above, like the protagonist of *Butterfly*, while ordinary school teachers like Sun Lisheng were ignored. Looking at the novels of that era, we can see that even within the fictional domain, the authorities imposed tight restraints regarding the official verdict on the Cultural Revolution.

1957: Labelled a Rightist, Divorced and Sent to Forced Labour

I had heard about the death of principal Sha Ping at the Beijing No. 3 Girls' School in August 1966, but I knew nothing about other victims there. Later, through talking with other teachers at the school, I learned of three of their colleagues who had been persecuted to death: **Zhang Meiyan** in 1966 and **Fang Tingzhi** and **Sun Lisheng** in 1968. But I wasn't able to find out exactly when Sun Lisheng died, and the school wouldn't allow me to view its files.

After searching long and hard for someone who had known Sun Lisheng, I finally found her daughter and had a long conversation with her. From various people's accounts about her life before and during the Cultural Revolution, Sun Lisheng gradually emerged from the fog.

Sun was born on 24 May 1934. Her father was a secondary school teacher and her mother was a homemaker. The family owned their own small but comfortable home in the maze of Beijing's *hutongs*, and Wang Meng's family live nearby. Wang was in the same class as Sun Lisheng from first grade onwards, and it is because of this relationship that she eventually became a character in his novel *Butterfly*.

Sun Lisheng was a student at the No. 3 Girls' School in 1949, and after encountering members of the CCP, she quickly became the school's first Party member. A senior Party cadre became acquainted with Sun after giving a talk at the school. When Sun was eighteen years old, she married that cadre, who was more than twenty years her senior, and they soon had two daughters. After graduating in 1952, Sun stayed on at the school as a teacher of politics, and in 1956, she was admitted to the Central Party School, an opportunity for fast-track promotion. When the Anti-Rightist Movement began in 1957, her husband was visiting the USSR, so Sun was in the dark about Mao's intentions of 'luring snakes from the den' when inviting people to voice criticism. As a result of her remarks, she was labelled a Rightist and expelled from the Party, and her husband obeyed the Party by divorcing her. Sun signed her divorce papers while heavily pregnant, and the Party arranged for her ex-husband to marry another woman.

In Wang Meng's *Butterfly*, Haiyun requests a divorce after being labelled a Rightist, and there's nothing about the Party or her husband demanding it. This makes Haiyun's misfortune a matter of her own choice rather than the Party's coercion. Of course, the author of a novel isn't obliged to stick to the facts, but given that he was writing about the experience of an actual person during a historical incident, changing anything about the prototype reflects the writer's awareness of that period of history.

Like many female Rightists, Sun Lisheng was sent to labour at the Tiantang (Paradise) River Farm in a distant suburb of Beijing. Sun's third daughter was born there in January 1959. This child never knew her father and was sent with her two sisters to be raised by Sun's mother.

Sun Lisheng's eldest daughter once visited the *laogai* farm where Sun had been held. She recalls that her mother lived in a dark, filthy shed full of cobwebs, and that her bed consisted of several pieces of unplaned wooden sticks nailed together. At the time, Sun was feeding another person lying in the bed, who had been badly injured after falling into a machine. Sun herself developed pericarditis while at the *laogai* farm.

Sun was finally allowed to return to the No. 3 Girls' School just in time for the worst of the Great Famine in 1961. Even in the nation's capital, where people enjoyed relative privilege, many suffered from oedema brought on by malnutrition. Sun wasn't allowed to resume teaching, but grew mushrooms in the school's cellar, a typical task assigned to Rightists when alternative sources of nourishment were needed. After Sun was rehabilitated, she was allowed to work in the school's reference room until the Cultural Revolution began.

While at the *laogai* farm, Sun Lisheng had met a male Rightist of the same age who was also a secondary school teacher, and the two married. Sun gave birth to another daughter, and after she returned to the school to work, she and her husband and fourth daughter lived together not far from her mother's home. Her husband, Nie Baoxun, worked at the Beijing No. 31 Secondary School.

1966: Crawling on Broken Glass with a Brick Hanging from Her Neck

After the Red Guard movement began in August 1966, Beijing residents were mobilised to look after Red Guards from around the country who came to the capital for the 'great networking'. Red Guards from the Jiamusi No. 6 Secondary School ate steamed buns made by Sun Lisheng's mother and then ransacked the mother's house. After finding the family's title deed, they said it was a 'restoration record', cut off Sun's mother's hair and beat her. Then they brought Sun over from the No. 3 Girls' School and beat her as well. Searching for 'hidden gold', the Red Guards destroyed the family's furniture, broke through the roof and dug holes in the ground. When Sun's youngest daughter saw Red Guards digging a hole nearly as tall as she was, she was terrified that they planned to bury the family alive.

Sun Lisheng's mother was a kindly old woman, but just because she owned her home she was beaten so severely that she couldn't walk. With all of the furniture smashed and holes dug in the floor, she and her granddaughters had to sleep on wooden planks placed over the holes. They weren't the only family to suffer such treatment; in another home in the same *hutong*, the parents of a ten-year-old girl named Meimei were beaten to death by Red Guards. In that not very large *hutong*, nearly ten people were killed in summer 1966.

When the principal of the No. 3 Girls' School, Sha Ping, was beaten to death on 22 August, Sun Lisheng was one of the 'secondary targets' because she was a teacher and a Rightist. 'Ox demons and snake spirits' living near the school were also brought in and beaten to death.

During summer 1966, Red Guards at one point tied four bricks to thin wire and hanged them from Sun Lisheng's neck, and then spread the shards of broken bottles on the floor and made her and other teachers crawl over them. The glass cut into their knees and palms and drenched the floor with their blood.

These are the kinds of details that have been avoided, neglected and covered up in histories of the Cultural Revolution. When I began to publish essays about school violence in 1995, some Western scholars who had been researching the Cultural Revolution for many years were shocked. One professor told me he'd done his own investigations and had never heard of such incidents. Another professor asked me how many people I'd interviewed, and how reliable these stories were. The dearth of information had given Western scholars the misleading impression that the Red Guard movement was something like student movements in the West in the 1960s.

Some perpetrators of beatings were shameless enough in 1998 to criticise my accounts of campus violence as 'slandering' the Red Guards. They dared to make these allegations because if I was the only one recording these stories, they could get away with denying that such things ever happened. The lack of historical accounts of the brutal violence of the Cultural Revolution results in the lack of a fundamental platform for appraising and debating it.

It's truly hard to imagine how Sun and her mother survived the Red Terror of summer 1966. Yet there were countless others like them who were similarly tortured in *hutongs* and schools all over the country.

1968: Hanged from the Window of an 'Ox Pen'

Sun Lisheng didn't survive the second round of Cultural Revolution violence. When the Cleansing of the Class Ranks began in 1968, Sun once again became a focal target. She was locked up in the school and wasn't allowed to return home. On 12 July 1968, Sun was found hanged at the school, and the school's authorities declared it a suicide.

Sun Lisheng's mother was always suspicious about her death, because the day before she died Sun had secretly left the school and come to her mother's home for a brief conversation before hurrying back. Sun Lisheng told her mother that she was being treated very harshly, and that her persecutor was a colleague who had previously been her good friend. Now this person had the upper hand in the Revolutionary Committee and was going all out to purge and 'expose' her. She told her mother that her colleague Fang Tingzhi had already been run over by a bus. (This is how we know that Fang Tingzhi died before Sun Lisheng.)

On the day that Sun Lisheng escaped from the isolation room and spoke with her mother, her third daughter was present, and she curled up in bed and pretended to sleep so she could hear fragments of what her mother and grandmother said. She remembered hearing Fang Tingzhi's name, and that her mother mentioned the guava tree near the door of her home. The girl was nine years old at the time. After her mother left, she wept quietly under her quilt.

The next day, Sun Lisheng was found dead. There was no mention of a suicide note.

Sun Lisheng's mother and daughters doubt that she committed suicide because she mentioned no such intention when she snuck back to her mother's home. Most importantly, they say, she was the loving mother of four daughters who were not yet grown, the youngest only seven years old. Her children needed her. She wouldn't abandon them this way.

They also said that from the time she was labelled a Rightist in 1957 until 1968, Sun had gone through a divorce, a *laogai* farm and Red Guard torture. She wasn't a pampered woman who had never known suffering, and she wouldn't take her own life so easily. They wanted to know what actually happened before Sun died.

Sun's youngest daughter saw her for the last time when she was allowed a brief visit home, probably to fetch her ration card. This daughter remembered that her father made fried rice with egg and put it in an aluminium rice box for Sun to take back to the school. Life was very hard for ordinary people in Beijing at that time, let alone Rightists, and fried rice with egg was a very good meal, as well as something that could be made quickly during a short visit. Sun's first three daughters said their stepfather was very good to their mother; another reason why they don't believe she killed herself.

Even with these suspicions, Sun's family had no way of investigating her death. When she was cremated, her husband managed to secretly grab a handful of ashes to take home, but he died not long afterwards, and no one knows what became of them.

A month after Sun Lisheng's death, her younger sister's husband also fell victim to the Cultural Revolution. His name was **Gao Jingguo**, and he was a twenty-seven-year-old research fellow at the Seventh Machine Industry Department's No. 2 Research Institute. While under 'investigation', he fell from a sixth-floor window and died seven or eight hours later. His wife rushed over as soon as she heard what happened, but wasn't allowed to see him. Gao had grown up in rural Sichuan province; his parents had seven children, but only two survived infancy. Gao Jingguo was admitted to university and after graduation was given a job in Beijing, and he and his wife lived with Sun Lisheng's mother. When the home was ransacked in 1966, the younger daughter had just had a baby, but the Red Guards made her stand as a punishment while they ransacked the house. When the new round of persecution led to Gao Jingguo's death in 1968, his child was only two years old, and his parents died of sorrow within months.

Who Killed Sun Lisheng?

Sun Lisheng died while under 'isolation and investigation'. Friends and family had no way of seeing or knowing what people were going through during that process, and that made it possible for unlawful punishment and torture to be carried out. Only those who survived the 'ox pens' can give us an idea of what went on inside.

Sun Lisheng's mother knew the colleague Sun mentioned who was purging her – the two had been classmates and friends. When Sun Lisheng married the senior cadre, her financial situation improved, and she often used her own salary to provide material assistance to this friend. Later a conflict arose between them. In 1968, that person was appointed to the Revolutionary Committee and began ruthlessly purging Sun Lisheng when the Cleansing of the Class Ranks began in 1968. Years later, Sun's mother heard that person was seriously ill. By that time, Sun Lisheng's eldest daughter closely resembled her. Sun's mother took out some clothes that Sun used to wear and had the daughter put them on. She wanted the girl to go to that person's house so it would appear that Sun Lisheng had come back to haunt her persecutor.

She never actually carried out the plan, but it's easy to understand the mentality of victims' family members, who almost never saw any justice carried out on behalf of their loved ones. They were left to get revenge in their imaginations alone.

In 1978, after Mao was dead and victims of the Anti-Rightist Movement and Cultural Revolution began to be rehabilitated, work units held memorial services for their dead colleagues. Sun Lisheng's daughters managed to have a memorial service held for their mother at the Babaoshan Revolutionary Cemetery, even though Sun didn't qualify under the regulations at that time. They mailed out 100 invitations, but hundreds of people came, including Sun Lisheng's childhood teacher, by then more than eighty years old, who tearfully recalled the passionate and beautiful young girl. Several educators who had been brutalised during the Cultural Revolution attended, including Gao Yun, the principal of the Beijing Normal University No. 2 Affiliated Secondary School who had barely escaped the crematorium oven. After the memorial service, Gao Yun went to see Sun Lisheng's daughters out of sympathy for their shared suffering. Sun's first husband didn't attend.

In the decades that followed, only one person expressed an apology, and that was Lu Dingyi. Before the Cultural Revolution, Lu was head of the CCP Central Committee's Propaganda Department and Vice-Premier of the State Council. One of the things that caused Sun Lisheng to be labelled a Rightist in 1957 was that she had said that Lu Dingyi had a 'rude work style'. She thought she was criticising a colleague of her husband, but in 1957 it was construed as opposing the Party. Lu Dingyi apologised to Sun Lisheng's daughters for this.

Lu had been labelled a member of an anti-Party clique and was one of four high-ranking cadres who were struck down during the Cultural Revolution. He was locked up for a long time and suffered terribly. It is extremely rare for persecution victims like him to apologise to people they themselves had persecuted. This is a phenomenon worth noting and studying.

An apology doesn't bring the dead to life or turn back an event that has already occurred, but apart from clarifying right and wrong, it serves as moral redemption. The lack of apology from people who carried out persecution before and during the Cultural Revolution indicates the extent to which it destroyed not only lives, but also moral standards. That's why we should acknowledge and affirm the few who have expressed regret.

No one from the No. 3 Girls' School who hung bricks from Sun Lisheng's neck and made her crawl on broken glass or tortured her under 'isolation and investigation' came and apologised to her family. The interviewee who first told me Sun Lisheng's name said she knew some people who had inflicted cruel torment on others, and who after the Cultural Revolution said without the slightest regret, 'At that time we were following Chairman

Mao's revolution.' The Anti-Rightist Campaign and the Cultural Revolution turned Sun Lisheng and millions of others into 'class enemies' and then allowed them to be arbitrarily humiliated and tortured until they died. This kind of long-term and massive persecution is not only the tragedy of these millions of victims, but also reinforced the belief that a regime was justified in persecuting people this way, and that as Wang Meng wrote, it was like parents spanking their children.

This obviously inappropriate comparison wasn't meant to explain the history of the Anti-Rightist Campaign and the Cultural Revolution, but rather to persuade people to submit to the authorities. Writers who proposed and promoted this formulation were encouraged and rewarded with official positions and special privileges.

Sun Lisheng's children will never get over her death, and many years later, a new incident reopened their wounds. In 2000, Beijing's banks disposed of savings accounts that no one had claimed for a long time, and one was in Sun Lisheng's name. The bank couldn't find her family, but when it learned that her ex-husband was a prominent cadre, it informed him of Sun's savings account through the Chinese Academy of Social Sciences Marxism–Leninism Institute.

Sun Lisheng's savings account held a considerable amount of money. Wouldn't she have arranged for it to be given to her family to support her four young daughters if she had intended to kill herself? This would have required no more than a brief note. Even if she was in such despair that she no longer wished to live, it's hard to believe that she would have deprived her children of this badly needed money. But Sun left no suicide note and didn't tell her family that she had those savings. Did she really not write a note, or did she write one that was destroyed because it exposed the crimes of those who were tormenting her? Or, is it possible that she didn't kill herself in the first place?

The discovery of this bank account was an enormous shock to Sun Lisheng's daughters and led them to once again wonder if their mother had been killed, and if so, by whom?[17]

Sun's eldest daughter remembers that once when she was small, and the weather suddenly turned cold, Sun Lisheng stayed up all night to knit a pair of woollen mittens for her. The guava tree that her third daughter overheard Sun mention while talking to her grandmother the night before she died

---

[17] It is worth noting here that in May 1985, *Beijing Daily* published the names of 857 bank deposit holders at the Beijing Industrial and Commercial Bank whose accounts had gone unclaimed since 1966. This list of names was published again in the December 2008 issue of the Hong Kong-based *Open Magazine* in an article by Yao Guifu. The account-holders include He Dinghua, one of the victims in this book.

really had grown outside her home, she later learned. Their mother was not a dream, but a flesh-and-blood human being who loved them dearly. When the loss of their mother was brought back to them thirty years later, the pain was almost unbearable.

BEIJING NO. 4 SECONDARY SCHOOL

Liu Chengxiu, a language teacher, cut her throat in 1968. Liu had been denounced during the 1957 Anti-Rightist Campaign, but was not made to 'wear the Rightist cap'. During the Cultural Revolution she was attacked as a 'Rightist who slipped through the net'. She died in a narrow passageway behind the school assembly hall where very few people went.

A foreign language teacher, Liu Yuehua, attempted to kill herself by swallowing gold, but didn't succeed. As detailed earlier, a married couple at the school, **Wang Hanying** and **Su Tingwu**, committed suicide in 1966.

BEIJING NO. 5 SECONDARY SCHOOL

He Guanghan, a teacher of Russian, killed himself while being 'investigated' during the Cleansing of the Class Ranks. His 'problem' was that he had visited Taiwan once as a student, and had an uncle living there.

BEIJING NO. 6 SECONDARY SCHOOL

Jiao Tingxun, a history teacher and head of the teaching and research group, was accused of having been a member of the Kuomintang and was denounced during a 'study class' in the latter half of 1968. He subsequently killed himself by sticking his head into a bucket of paste used to put up big-character posters.

'Study classes' were a method used during the Cleansing of the Class Ranks, originating with a directive from Mao in early 1968: 'Running study classes is a good method; many problems can be solved during study classes.'

The study classes at the No. 6 Secondary School were composed of half students and half teachers. The teachers had to 'frankly confess their problems' while the students typically cursed, beat and kicked them. The study classes were broken down into groups with a 'focal target', and Jiao Tingxun was one of them. An 'informant's report' said he'd been a member of the KMT, but Jiao denied it.

The night before Jiao Tingxun died, the study class struggled him and threatened, 'Tomorrow we'll escort you to the street and struggle you there.' He was not allowed to return home that night.

At that time, all schools had large vats of paste prepared by school administrators for putting up the posters that proliferated at that time. The paste was fetched from the vats in smaller buckets when needed. The vat was half filled with paste when Jiao Tingxun pushed his head into it and killed himself in the early hours of the morning.

Jian Tingxun's death was deemed 'alienating himself from the Party and the people'. He had joined the Party during a 1956 recruitment drive aimed at intellectuals, but upon his death he was expelled.

BEIJING NO. 11 SCHOOL

Ruan Jieying, a mathematics teacher, leaped to her death after being persecuted in 1968. She left behind a son who was around three years old.

BEIJING NO. 25 SECONDARY SCHOOL

Wang Shouliang, a language teacher, had developed the hobby of collecting tabloids and leaflets that Red Guards and other 'revolutionary mass organisations' were allowed to print from 1966 to 1968. Because Wang's wife worked as a domestic servant in the Soviet Embassy, the couple was accused of selling the tabloids and leaflets to the Soviets, and both of them were executed.

BEIJING NO. 51 SECONDARY SCHOOL

Tang Pinsan, a physical education teacher, was locked up in a shed for 'investigation' in 1968. Tang killed himself by drinking pesticide just before the Ninth National Party Congress began its session in April 1969.

BEIJING FOREIGN LANGUAGE SCHOOL

Mo Ping, the school's principal, was brutally beaten by Red Guards in 1966 and then put under 'isolation and investigation' during the Cleansing of the Class Ranks. He hanged himself in May 1968.

Mo's colleague, head teacher **Yao Shuxi**, was unable to bear the torment during the early days of the Cultural Revolution and killed herself, but Mo

Ping survived 1966. When the next round of persecution began in 1968, Mo was put under 'isolation and investigation' and interrogated about his 'historical problems'. Mo Ping had joined the Party while serving as an English interpreter for the Communists during negotiations between the KMT and CCP in 1947 that involved American personnel. Besides that, his father had been a diplomat posted to France by the Kuomintang government, and his maternal grandmother owned land in Nanhui County that had been deeded to Mo Ping.

The school's Revolutionary Committee sent someone to Mo's native village in Shanghai's Nanhui County for 'external inquiries', which in April 1968 unearthed a deed revealing that Mo Ping's original name was Wang Fazu. After this was reported to the school, a 'special investigation team' brought him to trial and designated him a 'landlord element' and 'class enemy'.

During the May Day holiday, Mo Ping was granted permission to go home with his household registration booklet so he could divorce his wife. Instead, he went to a mountain near the Ming Tombs in Changping County and hanged himself from a tree.

BEIJING JINGSHAN SCHOOL

Ji Xinmin, head teacher and language teacher in the primary school section, was brutalised by Red Guards in 1966 and forced to eat excrement. During the Cleansing of the Class Ranks, she was accused of having belonged to the Three People's Principles Youth League. She leaped to her death in early 1969.

Another language teacher at the same school, **Yu Gongshan**, also committed suicide.

BEIJING PRIMARY SCHOOL

Zhang Yanqing killed herself by drinking caustic soda after being seized and struggled during a 'leniency and severity rally' in November 1968.

During the rally, Zhang sat among the ordinary participants, not knowing what was going on below. Suddenly, the leader of the meeting loudly proclaimed that someone wasn't being 'candid' and shouted, 'Pull out the old grey-hair!' The grey-haired Zhang Yanqin was shoved onto the stage. After that, she killed herself.

Another grey-haired female attendee, fearing she would be treated the same at the next rally, went that night to Xuanwu Park, across from the school. It was a desolate place at that time, and she paced back and forth in the night. Just as she decided to hang herself from a beam in the toilet, she heard the footsteps of the park's night watchman, so she tucked the rope into her jacket and hobbled off to Xuanwu Hospital. She was suffering from abnormal uterine bleeding at the time, and sought treatment in the emergency room, where she stayed until dawn. Ultimately, she survived, and many years later she told the story to her daughter.

OTHERS

Fu Qifang, a coach for China's national table tennis team, was beaten and humiliated after being accused of being a spy. He hanged himself in Beijing's sports training centre on 16 April 1968.

Fu Qifang started out playing table tennis and then became a coach, helping to lead his team to a series of world championship victories. After Fu killed himself, another coach, **Jiang Yongning**, and a member of the table tennis team, **Rong Guotuan**, also hanged themselves after being beaten and humiliated in struggle rallies. All three men were athletes who had come to mainland China from Hong Kong in the 1950s. Table tennis would not seem to have any direct relationship to politics or ideological viewpoints. Why would the Cultural Revolution destroy these athletes along with writers, teachers and performers? None of China's tyrants had ever done such a thing, and even Hitler and Stalin didn't victimise their countries' athletes.

The following is an order issued by the CCP Central Committee not long after Fu Qifang's death. This document clearly shows how the Cultural Revolution's targets of attack expanded in 1968. The 16 May 1966 notice that the Central Committee issued to launch the Cultural Revolution had designated academics, educators, journalists, artists, writers and publishers as focal targets for attack. Athletes were formally added to the list in 1968. The diction and tone of the order shows how brutal and frenzied the Cultural Revolution had become by then:

> **CCP Standing Committee, State Council, Central Military Commission, Central Cultural Revolution Small Group Order Regarding Military Control of the State Physical Culture and Sports Commission**
>
> 12 May 1968; Central Committee Document [68] No. 71
>
> The State Physical Culture and Sports Commission apparatus (including the National Defence Sports Club) was the concoction of the Party's number one capitalist-roader power-holder in collusion with the counter-revolutionary revisionists He Long, Liu Ren, Rong Gaotang et al. in

accordance with Soviet revisionist methods. It has long separated itself from the Party's leadership and the rule of the proletariat and has been infiltrated by a number of scoundrels to become an independent kingdom. In order to thoroughly lift the lid off of class struggle in the sports apparatus, ferret out scoundrels, manage struggle in all work units, criticise, reform and carry the Great Proletarian Cultural Revolution to its end, it has been decided to put the national sports apparatus under the management of the Chinese People's Liberation Army.

1) Greater military regions and provincial military regions will take over management of all levels of the Physical Culture and Sports Commission organs and teams in their jurisdictions.
2) Aviation clubs (including aircraft and equipment) and glider manufacturing plants will come under the management of the air forces of their military regions.
3) All maritime and diving clubs (including vessels and nautical apparatus) will come under the management of the respective naval fleets.
4) All radio clubs (including communications equipment and apparatus) will come under the management of the communications departments of their respective military regions.
5) All shooting and motoring clubs (including shooting ranges, weapons, ammunition and motorised sports equipment) will come under the management of the designated military training and ordnance departments of their respective greater military regions and provincial military regions.

The management of the state physical culture apparatus will be uniformly implemented by the greater military regions. In accordance with practical requirements, the Army, Navy and/or Air Force will dispatch military control committees or military representatives.

After receiving this order, all work units are to immediately comply in executing it and promptly report to the upper level regarding their management conditions.

Jiang Yongning, accused of being a 'Japanese spy', was locked up and his home was ransacked on 15 May 1968. Brutally beaten and humiliated, he hanged himself the following day. Winner of the table tennis championship in Hong Kong in 1952, and then the national championship in 1953, Jiang had contributed to the Chinese team's subsequent victory in the world championship.

The third table tennis champion to kill himself, **Rong Guotuan**, was born in 1937, a native of Zhuhai, Guangdong Province, and moved to mainland China from Hong Kong in 1957. He became the first Chinese athlete to win a world championship when he won the men's singles title at the 1959 World Table Tennis Championship. Accused of being a 'secret agent' and subjected to struggle, Rong hanged himself from a tree by Longtan Lake behind the State Physical Culture and Sports Commission's Training Department. He left behind a daughter less than two years old.

Athletes are typically strong-willed and cool-headed individuals, which is what allows them to triumph in intense competition before vast audiences. Driving outstanding athletes like Fu, Jiang and Rong to their deaths must have involved immense physical and psychological torture.

In the 1980s, Rong Guotuan's native Zhuhai erected a bronze statue in his honour, but the statue included only his name and not how he died.

SHANGHAI

EAST CHINA NORMAL UNIVERSITY

Li Jigu, a history teacher born in 1895, was struggled and locked up in an 'ox pen' for an extended period during the Cultural Revolution. On 25 July 1968, student Red Guards interrogated him for an entire day while forcing him to kneel and burning his back and neck with cigarettes. After the interrogation, Li drowned himself in the Liwa River, which ran through the university campus.

A native of Shaoxing, Li Jigu graduated from the Zhejiang Provincial No. 1 Normal School in 1917 and was then sent to Japan for overseas study on a government scholarship in 1918. He became a professor at Peking University in 1926 and joined the Kuomintang. In 1928 he went to England as a graduate student at Cambridge University, where he obtained his Master's degree. After returning to China, he continued as a professor at Peking University and served as head of the Literature and History Department at the university's Women's College of Arts and Sciences. In 1938 he became head of the History Department at Northwest Union University. After China's victory in the War of Resistance against Japan, Li became the first president of Taiwan Normal University. He became director of the Zhejiang Province Department of Education in 1948, and secretly remained in Shanghai in 1949 when the Kuomintang government retreated from Hangzhou to Ningbo. He served as president of East China Normal University from 1949 onwards and was the author of many historical works. However, his experience prior to the founding of the PRC resulted in his being labelled an 'uncapped historical counter-revolutionary' in 1955, and he was dismissed from his position as head of the ancient history teaching and research section.

Originally a 'historical counter-revolutionary', once the Cultural Revolution was launched, Li Jigu was accused of the additional crime of being a 'reactionary academic authority'. He was subjected to protracted struggle, including beatings, being marched in the street, labour reform and various forms of physical abuse.

On 4 August 1966, more than 100 teachers and cadres at East Asia Normal University, including Li Jigu, were paraded through the streets wearing dunce caps and placards around their necks, after which they were forced to kneel in the school's Communist Youth Sportsground and be struggled.

After that, the struggle targets were sent to 'dictatorship teams' for 'labour reform'. A history teacher who was under labour reform with Li in summer 1966 said they were assigned various tasks, the easiest being cleaning and plucking weeds and the hardest being transporting sewage and water.

Right next to East China Normal University was the Nanhai Secondary School, where student Red Guards ordered the teachers to run up to the top floor every morning, and then push their heads into the chimney to get 'smoked'. They also ordered teachers to read out a passage from *Quotations from Chairman Mao*: '"Dropping a stone on your own foot" is a folk saying the Chinese use to describe a stupid person. The reactionaries in all countries are just such stupid people.' After reading out this quote, the teachers were ordered to drop stones on their own feet until they bled.

Dai Jiaxiang was an expert on ancient history who was designated a Rightist in 1957. (Nine teachers in the university's History Department were designated Rightists and continued to be persecuted in political movements, which according to the black humour of the Cultural Revolution made them 'campaign veterans'.) No matter how he was cursed or humiliated in 1966, he didn't respond with words or even facial expressions. A colleague who was subjected to 'dictatorship' with him said he didn't understand the Red Guard mentality. The Red Guards wanted some kind of reaction; they wanted the people they were cursing or beating to show their terror and submission, wanted them to say, 'I'm guilty, I deserve to die' to demonstrate the power of the Red Guards. When Dai Jiaxiang refused to react, his attackers were enraged and called him an 'old bastard' or an 'old ox demon' and threatened to throw him in the river, at which point Dai finally responded by pleading, 'Young militants, please don't!' This finally satisfied the Red Guards.

In 1967, a statue of Mao was erected at the school. Because the university's Red Guards had been received by Mao in Beijing on 15 September 1966, they named the statue site '915 Square'. They ordered the 'ox demons and snake spirits' to humbly apologise before the statue first thing every morning. (Normally people were merely required to 'request morning instructions' or 'give the evening report' to statues or portraits of Mao.) In order to avoid encountering others, the teachers began going even earlier to the statue, standing before it just as day broke, hanging their heads, admitting their 'guilt', and then reading out one of Mao's quotes. The Red Guards were still in bed at that time and wouldn't harass them.

When the Cleansing of the Class Ranks was launched in 1968, East China Normal University's History Department set up its own 'ox pens' that divided up targets according to their type of 'problem'. The 'big ox pen' for the most serious 'problems' contained twenty-six people, all teachers except for three cadres. The 'medium ox pen' contained twelve people, most of them younger teachers along with a few students. The third makeshift jail was called the 'study class' and contained ten people. Nearly half of the department's ninety-six teachers and staff were held in the its classroom jails. One time, a former school administrator, Chang Xiping, was taken to the History Department's 'ox pen' and beaten on allegations that he was a 'big black umbrella' for the department's 'ox demons and snake spirits'. After being beaten, Chang left the history building and tumbled to the ground, unable to walk. Another administrator was grabbed and beaten, and he covered his head with his arms. The next day, he put up a note on the wall saying that he deserved to be beaten, but he asked that his head not be beaten and that he be sent to the countryside for labour reform instead.

The head of the university's Mathematics Department, Cao Xihua, was married to the History Department's Party secretary. When he saw his wife being beaten, Cao muttered the word 'hooligans', and for that was dragged to the History Department and beaten. The first stroke of a Red Guard's club sent Cao's wristwatch flying through the air, and he was beaten until a mop handle that was being used on him broke in half. His eardrum was punctured and his face swelled like a melon.

Lin Biao had been pronounced Mao's successor in 1966, by dint of having started the trend of constantly proclaiming 'Long live Chairman Mao!' One of the university's history instructors remarked in private, 'Lin Biao wishes Chairman Mao long life, but then how can he ever be his successor?' Someone informed on him, and he was struggled.

The Red Guards ordered every 'ox demon and snake spirit' to keep a daily 'labour reform journal'. Every person had a notebook hanging on the wall, and the Red Guards would come and inspect them. They had to write down all the work they did and every time they were struggled. At first, everyone bought different kinds of exercise books, but one day the Red Guards ordered them to blacken the covers of every notebook, so the wall of the 'ox pen' was lined with black-covered 'labour reform journals'.

When 'ox demons and snake spirits' lined up to eat in the canteen, they had to first apologise before the statue of Mao, while other people simply had to wave their Little Red Books and wish long life to Mao and health to Lin Biao.

On 20 June 1968, just before the 1 July anniversary of the founding of the CCP, the Red Guards ordered everyone in the 'ox pens' to write a confession and then take it home and post it on their doors. But just before the prisoners were about to go home for the night, Red Guards kicked open the door of the big 'ox pen', and the leader said, 'What kind of confessions are you writing? All of you are hoping for regime change. You need to be sanctioned.' Four students used clubs and wire whips to beat the twenty-six people inside until deep into the night. Some of the teachers were beaten so badly that their faces were too swollen to wear glasses. Some had their clothing beaten to shreds, and some couldn't walk, but had to lean against walls as they made their way home.

One teacher who was beaten said that he didn't get home that night until two or three in the morning. His wife hadn't gone to bed, but was sitting there waiting for him. After he entered the house, he laughed sardonically that today the 'halls had been painted red'.

In the 'ox pen', Li Jigu sat at the same table as a teacher thirty years his junior who had been designated a Rightist in 1957. The Red Guards made them memorise Mao quotes every day and required the pairs sharing tables to test each other. A few days before Li Jigu died, a 'special investigation team' came every day to 'interrogate' him (reflecting the arrogance of the student Red Guards in exercising their power and their chance to employ violence). One day, Li Jigu asked his tablemate, 'I'm feeling confused and light-headed today. Can we skip the memorisation?' He also said, 'I'm seventy-three years old and I have cataracts. The doctor says I'll be blind in two or three years.' His tablemate couldn't think of any way to help him, but just said, 'It's not easy to memorise. Try reciting it a few more times.'

On 25 July 1968, the special investigation team came again to interrogate Li Jigu and didn't let him leave until nearly midnight. Instead of going home, Li drowned himself in the Liwa River that ran through the campus.

Before then, Li Jigu had always arrived very early to the 'ox pen' in order to 'apologise' before the statue of Mao. His umbrella and water cup were still on the table, but when he didn't appear after three or four days, the others in the 'ox pen' knew something must have happened to him. When they learned that a corpse had been dredged from the river, none of the prisoners said anything.

Later the Red Guards kicked open the door of the 'ox pen' and shouted as the remaining twenty-five captives leaped to their feet. 'You're all incorrigible die-hards!' and 'Li Jigu has alienated himself from the Party and the people, and that's the fate of die-hards.' They then announced that a struggle rally would be held to denounce Li Jigu.

Since Li was already dead, the Red Guards drew a caricature of him with his name written on it and crossed out with a red X. At the struggle rally, two former administrators of the History Department were ordered to hold the caricature of Li and stand at the front while the department's other 'ox demons and snake spirits' stood next to the portrait as secondary targets of criticism. The struggling of dead targets occurred in several other places, including Peking University's History Department.

One of the professors in the 'ox pen' was reported for muttering the word 'tragic' regarding Li Jigu's death, as a result of which he was denounced and beaten until he admitted saying it, and then was beaten some more, because the Red Guards insisted he'd said the word three times.

A history teacher said that more than seventy people at East China Normal University were persecuted to death during the Cultural Revolution, but a report published by the school after the Cultural Revolution said there were only thirty-odd; it is not known how they derived this figure. Nan Linyue, a manager at the university who had been labelled a Rightist years earlier, said, 'Bad people can do bad things, but they can only do one bad thing at a time. This kind of mass persecution carried out over such a long period of time could only have been accomplished by the Cultural Revolution's leaders who were in power at the time.'

I've been able to identify the following additional victims at East China Normal University:

Ma Youyuan, a lecturer in physics, leaped to his death on 10 March 1968, while under 'isolation and investigation'.

Hao Li, a language teacher, threw himself from a window on 25 March 1968, while under 'isolation and investigation'.

Yin Damin, a lecturer in physics, drowned himself on 21 April 1968.

Huang Yaoting, a lecturer in education, was designated a 'current revolutionary' by the school's authorities. Huang killed himself before he could be arrested on 10 May 1968.

Yao Bingyu, acting Party secretary of the Biology Department, killed himself on 25 May 1968, while under investigation.

Xiao Chengshen, a professor of education, was arrested in July 1968 and accused of being the head of a spy ring. He died in prison on 7 July 1970.

Sun Ruojian, a language teacher, was struggled for 'historical problems' and hanged himself on 21 July 1968.

Jin Danan, a language teacher, took part in the 1968 'education revolution' in the northern Jiangsu countryside. She became pregnant and took leave to go to Shanghai for a physical examination, but failed to return within the prescribed period and so was subjected to struggle for 'serious bourgeois thinking'. After she was denounced, she poisoned herself on 29 August 1968, and died along with her unborn child.

FUDAN UNIVERSITY

Yang Leisheng, a student of English in the Foreign Languages Department, was accused of being a 'reactionary student' in early 1968. After being locked up, he leaped to his death. He was around twenty-one years old.

On the night before Yang committed suicide, the students in his intake year held a struggle rally during which they said he was a 'reactionary student' and a 'reptile' (a term applied to political opportunists at that time), apparently because someone had exposed 'reactionary language' that he'd used in private conversation. He was put under 'isolation and investigation' in a room in a student dormitory. The next morning, the student assigned to watch over Yang escorted him to the canteen for breakfast. As they reached the side door of the dormitory, Yang suddenly turned and ran up the stairs and leaped from a window at the end of the third-floor corridor before the other student could grab him.

An eyewitness said that he and other students had gone out for morning exercises, and were returning to the dormitory to get their bowls to take to the canteen for breakfast when they saw Yang Leisheng's body on the ground with a fractured skull.

Yang was not the only student in the Foreign Languages Department to attempt suicide around that time.

Ye Feng, an English student, was deemed a 'reactionary student' because of something that happened while she was a first-year, before the Cultural Revolution. Ye was somewhat absent-minded, and one day after finishing evening study, she left her exercise book in the classroom. The male student who sat behind Ye Feng was the son of a revolutionary cadre and a member of the class's Youth League branch. He leafed through the notebook, and finding some of Ye Feng's questions and reflections problematic, he handed it over to the political instructor. As a result, Ye Feng was criticised for her 'complicated' thinking, which wasn't the same as 'reactionary' but still a derogatory term at the time.

When the Cultural Revolution began, Ye Feng was a fourth-year, and this past incident resulted in accusations that she was a 'reactionary student'. In March 1968, she was held under 'isolation and investigation' in a room on the third floor of a student dormitory. She leaped from the window of her room, but because the ground below wasn't cement, she didn't die and only broke her femur.

After Ye Feng was sent to the Shanghai Hospital under the No. 2 Army Medical School, Fudan University's Foreign Languages Department organised a struggle session at her bedside. At first, the hospital wouldn't agree to it, saying it would affect other patients, but the university insisted, so finally the hospital relented and provided a large room where all the students from

Ye Feng's year struggled her as she lay helpless. After Ye Feng was discharged from the hospital but still bed-ridden, another struggle rally was held in the dormitory. Her classmates, including her boyfriend, had to take turns reading out and criticising portions of her 'reactionary' notebook that the special investigation group had selected.

One interviewee told me that in the portion he was given, Ye wrote about a movie in which a Russian criminal was sent into exile in Siberia, and she felt that this kind of thing was still happening. The student was ordered to criticise this remark without knowing what was written before or after.

It was in fact very common for quotes to be taken out of context or completely fabricated. During my investigations, I heard a story about students at Sichuan University who on the eve of the Cultural Revolution were organised to criticise a book by a literary theorist. They only had one copy of the book, and since there were no photocopiers back then, they tore out pages and passed them out so they could prepare their speeches. When one student had nearly finished reading out his speech, someone discovered that the section he was criticising was a quote from Lenin. Because 'Lenin said' had been printed on a page given to a different student, he had treated the quote as the 'reactionary viewpoint' he was meant to criticise.

Even more unfortunate than Ye Feng was a younger student from the Foreign Languages Department, Zhang Xiaomei, who was also placed under 'isolation and investigation'. She jumped from a window onto cement, and her bones were so badly broken that she spent the rest of her life in a wheelchair.

Teachers in the Foreign Languages Department were also among the victims.

Fan Ying, a sixty-four-year-old teacher of foreign languages, was driven to suicide in 1968.

Yang Bi, an associate professor in the Foreign Languages Department, killed herself in 1968. Yang's translation of the novel *Vanity Fair* gained wide distribution. She hadn't studied overseas, but she was clever and hardworking and had studied foreign languages with foreign nuns, so her linguistic skills were excellent. But this 'social relationship' became the reason for her being attacked during the Cultural Revolution.

Her elder sister, Yang Jiang, was also a translator. Yang Jiang and her husband, Qian Zhongshu, lived in Beijing, and she eventually wrote a book about the Cultural Revolution entitled *Six Records of the Cadre School*. She also wrote an essay in memory of her younger sister, claiming that Yang Bi died from a weak heart and an overdose of medicine. However, Yang Bi's colleagues in the Foreign Languages Department of Fudan University knew she killed herself after suffering persecution. They said that her sister may have written what she did because she was unclear about the truth, or perhaps because suicide was considered a crime of 'opposing the Cultural Revolution'.

I was able to identify a few other teachers who died at Fudan during this period:

Yan Zhixian, a professor of chemistry, was beaten to death on 15 May 1968. Student Red Guards carried him, still breathing, to his home, pounded on the door, dumped him in the doorway and left. His wife said that Yan died before he could be carried over the threshold.

Jiao Qiyuan, a sixty-seven-year-old biology professor, carried out specialised research on aromatic plants and lived in Fudan's residential quarters. He drowned himself after being placed under 'isolation and investigation' in 1968.

Cheng Xiandao, a teacher of history in his twenties, had stayed at Fudan to teach after graduating from the university in 1965. Cheng became deeply embroiled in the Red Guard movement, and when conflicts began to develop among Cultural Revolution activists, he was accused in 1968 of taking part in 'bombarding Zhang Chunqiao', the top leader of Shanghai's new power organ. After being put under 'isolation and investigation' in the school, Cheng killed himself.

Another history teacher, **Fan Mingru**, also killed himself during the Cultural Revolution.

Zou Lianfang was the sixty-eight-year-old wife of Zhu Dongrun, a professor of Chinese who was struggled as a 'reactionary academic authority'. Zou was also struggled by her neighbours and punished by being forced to sweep the courtyard of the university dormitory, even though she was ill. One of her crimes was that before 1949, she had joined with others in running a workshop. Zou Lianfang hanged herself at home on 30 November 1968.

Li Xiuying, the thirty-seven-year-old director of the Shanghai Fudan University Attached Nursery School, reportedly hanged herself in its general services office in August 1968.

SHANGHAI FERROUS METALLURGY INSTITUTE OF DESIGN

Weng Chao, a civil engineer who had graduated from Shanghai Tongji University in the early 1940s, died after throwing himself on a railway track during the Cleansing of the Class Ranks in 1968.

A university classmate and friend had tried to maintain contact with Weng Chao during the Cultural Revolution by writing him a letter every three months. Weng's wife wrote to this friend to inform him of Weng's death more than a year later.

TONGJI UNIVERSITY

Chen Haoxuan, an associate professor in his forties in the cement research section of the Construction Materials Department, was locked up at the university for 'isolation and investigation' and tortured into admitting that he was a 'secret agent'. He jumped to his death from the window of the student dormitory where he was being held in July 1968. His widow, Song Wenmao, a mathematics lecturer, was not allowed to view his remains. When she demanded the return of his clothes and shoes, she was accused of 'intending to clear accounts upon restoration of the old order'.

Zhang Jian, a young teacher in the water supply and heating teaching and research section, came from a 'landlord' family. After seeing other people being brutally struggled in 1968, Zhang panicked and hanged himself from a tree along the Sandaoqiao Bridge near the university.

Sun Guoying, a mathematics lecturer in his thirties, was designated a Rightist in 1957. He occasionally listened to news on a short-wave radio, and when he mentioned this to someone, he was accused of 'listening to an enemy radio station'. He was locked up and struggled in 1968. At one point he fled to Hangzhou but was caught and brought back. While locked up in the university's auditorium, he leaped to his death from the second floor.

SHANGHAI FOREIGN LANGUAGES INSTITUTE

Ma Siwu, a sixty-three-year-old French professor in the institute's Overseas Study Preparatory Department, killed himself on 11 July 1968, after being tortured for allegedly helping his brother, Ma Sicong, 'betray the country and go over to the enemy'.

Ma Sicong, also known as Sitson Ma, was director of the Central Conservatory of Music, when he was sent to a labour camp in 1966. On 16 January 1967, he made his way to Hong Kong and from there to the United States, where he was granted political asylum. Ma died in Philadelphia in 1987.

After Ma Sicong's escape, the Cultural Revolution authorities immediately carried out highly publicised mass searches throughout the country, not only to mobilise support in pursuing those who had assisted him, but also to create psychological pressure to prevent anyone else from thinking they could escape.

Accused of helping his brother, Ma Siwu was struggled on 10 July 1968, in the institute's main building and tortured until eleven o'clock that night. The next day, he jumped to his death from the roof of the building.

Ma Siwu had studied in France and lived in the Western fashion, dressing neatly and maintaining his self-respect even during the Cultural Revolution. After his death, his sixty-five-year-old French wife left China and died in France two years later.

According to *The Biography of Ma Sicong*,[18] after US Secretary of State Henry Kissinger came back from visiting China in July 1971, he said at a press conference that Premier Zhou Enlai had asked him about Ma Sicong, who by then was living in Philadelphia. Zhou Enlai said, 'I have two regrets in my life, and one of them is that Ma Sicong left his native land while in his fifties. It makes me very sad.'

The author put this quote of Zhou Enlai's on the flyleaf of his book. Zhou was saying this to people in the US, and it was not reported in China at the time. It was typical of Zhou Enlai to say something different to the Americans than to Chinese, and indicates nothing about the policies he carried out in China. Ye Yonglie also wrote in the book, 'Ma Sicong once said, "The person I most admired in all my life was Premier Zhou Enlai."'[19] Ye Yonglie was moved by Zhou Enlai's words and wanted readers to be as well, but a closer understanding of the truth of the Cultural Revolution and how harshly other attempted escapes were punished shows how hollow and hypocritical the Premier's words actually were. The truth was that people who attempted to escape were arrested and then penalised with death sentences or prison terms of at least ten years. Every province handled such cases in this way, reflecting the unified leadership of the Party Central Committee. If Zhou Enlai truly regretted Ma Sicong fleeing China, what did he feel about those executed for trying to do the same thing? With so many people persecuted to death during the Cultural Revolution, how could he say there were only two things he regretted? We now know that while Zhou Enlai was expressing his regret, several people who had helped Ma Sicong escape were in prison. Yet, twenty years after Ma fled China, Zhou's words were being held up as an example of his 'virtue'.

Ding Suqin, a teacher publicly denounced in 1968 as a spy and a 'historical counter-revolutionary', killed herself with an overdose of sleeping pills.

Zhu Shunying, employed in the institute's health section, leaped to her death from the ninth floor of a building after learning that she was about to be denounced.

Fang Shicong, a forty-year-old teacher, electrocuted himself while being persecuted.

---

[18] Ye Yonglie, *The Biography of Ma Sicong*, Taipei, Xiaoyuan chubanshe, 1989.
[19] Ibid., p. 11.

OTHER UNIVERSITIES

Gu Yuzhen, a professor at East China Institute of Chemical Technology (now East China University of Science and Technology), was accused of being a spy and interrogated under torture for three days straight. He killed himself in July 1968.

Zhang Shen, a professor around fifty years old at the Shanghai Institute of Foreign Trade, killed herself in 1968 after being struggled, made to 'fly the jet', and having her hair shaved off. Her students said she was an excellent teacher and often invited them to her home.

Wang Guanghua, in his fifties, was transferred from the Shanghai Railway Institute to the Machinery Department of Shanghai Work-Study Polytechnic University (since renamed the Shanghai No. 2 Polytechnic University). He leaped to his death from a third-floor window while under 'isolation and investigation' for 'historical problems' in 1968.

SECONDARY SCHOOLS

Zhang Jingfu, an English teacher at Shanghai's Fuxing Secondary School, poisoned himself to death in the latter half of 1968.

Zhang's students said he was a hard-working teacher, humorous and mild-mannered, but he attempted suicide twice during the Cultural Revolution, succeeding the second time.

Zhang Jingfu first came under attack in 1966, for taking a 'counter-revolutionary revisionist educational line' and for endorsing 'Trotskyite' viewpoints. Trotsky's works had been published legally in Shanghai in 1930, so he would have had no reason to expect that sharing such views would get him into trouble decades later.

The Red Guards at Fuxing Secondary School were very violent in summer 1966 (see Part Two). It was under those circumstances that Zhang Jingfu took his first overdose of sleeping pills. His eldest sister discovered him and sent him to the Shanghai No. 4 People's Hospital. The hospital said they couldn't treat a 'class enemy who had committed suicide to escape punishment', so the sister went weeping to the school. The school's Party Committee issued a certificate and sent a teacher to the hospital to testify that Zhang's 'problems' were not serious, at which point he was finally treated and saved.

In August 1968, a Mao Zedong Thought Propaganda Team was sent to Fuxing Secondary School to lead the Cleansing of the Class Ranks. At a terrifying 'mobilisation rally' on the school sports field, the leader of the propaganda team loudly ordered that 'problematic' teachers stand up within three minutes and 'frankly admit their wrongdoing'. Everyone present was silent, and after three minutes the leader of the rally announced, 'Now ferret out the hidden class enemies!' Red Guards that the propaganda team had put in place in advance seized two teachers and pulled them to the stage, where they were declared under 'isolation and investigation'. These teachers were subsequently brutally beaten. The propaganda team then announced that within twenty-four hours, everyone had to go to a designated place to register their 'historical problems' or they would meet a similar fate.

After the rally, meetings were called at all the teaching and research sections requiring each person to declare a stand and take the 'proper attitude'. Zhang Jingfu said nothing at the meeting, and others accused him, 'You're not saying anything. What are you hiding?' That night he took another overdose of sleeping pills, and this time he died.

It should be pointed out that everything done at the Fuxing Secondary School was under the specific directions of Mao and the CCP Central Committee and Central Cultural Revolution Small Group. The report 'Experience of the Beijing New China Printing Plant Military Control Committee's Mobilisation of the Masses to Launch a Struggle against the Enemy', which was part of Mao's 19 May Directive, includes this passage:

> During a factory-wide rally to struggle against the enemy, three of the five workers took the initiative to run up to the stage and criticise their own serious errors, and in great distress admitted their errors to Chairman Mao. At the same time, before the great revolutionary masses, they exposed the backstage instigator who had incited their evil acts, the current counter-revolutionary element Yu Donghai. At that time, the other two of the five, who were standing behind that counter-revolutionary element, waited for the three on stage to call out, at which point the two of them pulled that heinously evil fellow to the stage and handed him over to the masses for criticism and struggle.

A few months after this document was issued, Zhang Jingfu suffered that same treatment in Shanghai.

In that same year, another teacher at the school disappeared after being accused of being a 'current counter-revolutionary'. **Chen Buxiong**, a cartography teacher, disappeared a day before he was scheduled to appear at a public denunciation rally.

Chen had a 'good family background', so came under little attack during the initial stage of the Cultural Revolution, and in 1967 he was allowed to join the school's Revolutionary Committee. In 1968, the school conducted a 'three loyalties and four limitless'[20] campaign, during which Chen created a paper cutting depicting Chairman Mao's image above a January Revolution torch. Student Red Guards on the Revolutionary Committee interpreted it as meaning 'burn Chairman Mao', and then someone revealed that before the Cultural Revolution Chen had used thumbtacks to fasten an unframed portrait of Mao to the blackboard, and had inserted thumbtacks into Mao's eyes to make them shinier. The two incidents led to Chen being exposed as a 'current counter-revolutionary'. The day before Chen was set to appear at a public criticism rally, he fled from the school and disappeared. He was a diabetic who required refrigerated insulin injections to stay alive, and it is unlikely that he survived for long without his medication. The school later decided that Chen had died while on the run.

Shi Jimei, a language teacher and head of the language teaching and research group at the Shanghai Jing'an District No. 71 Secondary School, hanged herself at home in May 1968. Committing suicide with her was her roommate, **Lin Lizhen**, a language teacher at the Shanghai Yucai Secondary School.

Shi Jimei graduated from Suzhou University. She became a secondary school teacher in the 1940s and wrote in her spare time, publishing fiction and essays. She withdrew from literary circles in 1949. Prior to the Cultural Revolution, she was considered one of the best teachers at the No. 71 Secondary School. At the outset of the Cultural Revolution, the school's Party branch designated her an 'ox demon and snake spirit' and a big-character poster exposed her as a writer of the 'romantic literature school'. Her students, who had never read her works, believed she was a bad person who wrote bad novels. She was also humiliated and beaten by Red Guards. She was subjected to 'labour under surveillance' from 1966 to 1968. When the school decided to once again 'seize and struggle' her during the Cleansing of the Class Ranks, she hanged herself.

In 1999, Shi Jimei's 'Fengyi Park' was included in an anthology of classic fiction by female writers of the Republican era, *The Rainbow Series*.[21]

Former students of the No. 71 Secondary School say that many of its teachers were beaten, along with some students with 'bad family backgrounds'. Apart from Shi Jimei, a school handyman, name unknown, also killed himself after being accused of being a 'KMT military and police agent'.

Lin Lizhen, the language teacher at Shanghai Yucai Secondary School who hanged herself with Shi Jimei, had also been seized and struggled

---

[20] TN: Limitless worship, love, faith and loyalty to Chairman Mao, to Mao Zedong Thought and to Chairman Mao's proletarian revolutionary line.
[21] Published by Shanghai Guji chubanshe.

and had half her hair shaved off. A former student of hers provided the following account:

> Lin Lizhen was our head teacher from September 1963 to June 1966, and also our language teacher. Because I was good at composition, she gave me special attention and praise and visited my home several times.
>
> She lived near the Guotai Cinema in Huaihai Central Street, which was near my home, and several schoolmates and I visited her. She was single and shared an apartment with a female teacher from the 71 Secondary School. We liked her very much, and her smiling face often appears before my eyes. Before the Cultural Revolution, she was a model of educational reform at the Yucai Secondary School, and there were many articles about our class in newspapers and magazines, accompanied by her photo. During the Cultural Revolution, after principal Duan Lipei was denounced, teacher Lin was also persecuted. She was a native of Fujian, possibly an overseas Chinese, and very beautiful. Big-character posters said she had been the beauty queen at the church school she'd attended, and many caricatures were drawn of her.
>
> I remember one time she had half her hair shaved off. I was very sad, and when she went home, I secretly followed behind to see her onto her bus. I saw her off several times.
>
> When she and Teacher Shi hanged themselves in their apartment, I cried in secret.
>
> *Wenhui Bao* previously published a photo of our classroom with Teacher Lin standing beside me while I asked her a question. But now I can't find this precious old photo among Yucai Secondary School's files, although there are some other photos.
>
> When I took the university entrance exam in 1977, the essay topic was 'Someone I Can't Forget' and I wrote about Teacher Lin Lizhen. I will never forget her.

Zhou Xinghua, originally principal of the Shanghai Jiguang Secondary School and later transferred to the newly established Shanghai Model Secondary School, leaped to her death in 1968 while under 'isolation and investigation'.

Zhu Benchu, a head teacher in his forties at the Fudan University Affiliated Secondary School, fell to his death from the second floor after being locked up in the school and beaten in 1968. The students beating him declared that he'd committed suicide, but teachers at the school believed he was thrown out the window after being beaten to death. Two of the students who beat him were members of the school's Revolutionary

Committee. After the Cultural Revolution, one of them was sentenced to two years in prison in connection with Zhu's death.

Liu Jingxia, vice-principal of the Fudan University Affiliated Secondary School, committed suicide in 1970 after she was struggled along with her husband, who was a teacher at the Shanghai Foreign Languages Institute.

Zhu Zhenzhong, a history teacher at Shanghai's Lingling Secondary School, leaped to his death from the fifth floor of a building in 1968. Zhu had been a forward for the Red Flag Football Team and later served as a physical education teacher at Rihui Secondary School before contracting asthma. The Cultural Revolution authorities 'investigated' him for possibly joining the Three People's Principles Youth League while a college student.

Sun Jingxiang, a teacher at Shanghai's Hongqi (Red Flag) Secondary School, leaped to her death from the third floor of the education building during the Cleansing of the Class Ranks. A former student said she saw Sun's body in front of the building covered with a burlap sack. This student didn't know Sun's name. A former teacher knew her name, but no other details surrounding her death.

Huang Jiahui, a language teacher at Hongqi Secondary since the 1950s, was transferred to the newly established Changying Secondary School in Shanghai's Hongwei District. As soon as the Cultural Revolution began, Huang Jiahui came under criticism, but she bore it quietly. Because she had 'complicated social relationships' such as a brother teaching in France, she was locked up in the school's makeshift jail in 1968, and killed herself there. Two weeks earlier, one of her daughters had been sent to the Dafeng Farm in northern Jiangsu, and another daughter had also been 'settled in the countryside' in Jilin. Soon after Huang's death, the elderly housekeeper who was the only one left at home also killed herself.

Chen Boming, an accountant at the Shanghai No. 6 Girls' Secondary School, was accused of being a member of a counter-revolutionary clique and was put under 'isolation and investigation' in 1968. He disappeared in February 1969 at the age of fifty.

Chen Boming began working at the school in the early 1950s. At the time of the 'great link-up' in 1966, it provided food and accommodation for Red Guards from elsewhere. One time a kitten was found dead in the canteen food steamer used to prepare steamed buns. When a workers' propaganda team was sent to the school in summer 1968, this incident was brought up again as a counter-revolutionary incident 'persecuting revolutionary young militants' and 'opposing Chairman Mao' (whose surname sounds like the Chinese word for cat). Chen Boming was one of more than a dozen people named as members of a counter-revolutionary clique, and he was placed under 'isolation and investigation'. During the Spring Festival of 1969 (which that year fell on 17 February), he was allowed to leave the 'ox pen' and spend the festival with his family. He disappeared on the way back to school a few days later. It is believed that he drowned himself in the river.

Two other members of the 'counter-revolutionary clique', a cadre in the rear-services department and a canteen cook, also killed themselves. Half a year later, Chen Boming's handicapped younger brother also disappeared; four years later, his wife died of cancer. Chen was rehabilitated in 1978.

Fan Gengsu, a teacher at the Shanghai Songjiang No. 2 Secondary School, had published 'Teahouse Ditties' and other works during the War of Resistance against Japan. He killed himself while under investigation in 1968.

Zhou Shaoying, the principal of the Shanghai Datong Secondary School, was repeatedly struggled during the Cultural Revolution. Zhou drowned herself in the Huangpu River in 1968. She was in her thirties.

An elderly kitchen worker whose family lived in the countryside killed himself after the propaganda team in control of the school had a 'talk' with him. His name and further details of his case are unknown.

Li Dashen was a student at Shanghai's Beijiao Secondary School when his father, an office worker, threw himself in front of a train after being attacked. After writing a letter to the Central Cultural Revolution Small Group criticising the Cultural Revolution, Li Dashen was sentenced to eight years in prison as a counter-revolutionary. When released in 1975, he joined a production team in Shanghai's Hongkou District. Soon afterwards, he was coerced into admitting to theft and leaped to his death from the seventh floor of the Zhapu Building. He was twenty-six years old.

SHANGHAI THEATRE ACADEMY

The ugly violence at the Theatre Academy actually began much earlier than the Cleansing of the Class Ranks. The Cultural Revolution Museum[22] includes a photo taken inside the Shanghai Theatre Academy of Red Guards from the academy and the Shanghai Fine Art School jointly struggling their school presidents and teachers. The targets are kneeling in a line with their foreheads touching the floor. Red Guards stand behind them, raising Mao's Little Red Book in their right hands while resting their left feet on the backs of the educators in front of them. This is a concrete image of what Mao referred to as 'knocking them down and then stomping on them'. Such photographs were not staged but showed the actual brutal and evil acts that occurred during the Cultural Revolution at the Shanghai Theatre Academy.

---

[22] Kelin Yang, *Cultural Revolution Museum*, 2nd edition, Hong Kong, Cosmos Books, 2002, p. 180.

Dong Youdao, a teacher of dramatic literature, was exposed in 1968 after private conversations he had with another teacher in his department, Xie Zhihe. Accused of a 'venomous attack on the Great Leader Chairman Mao and Vice-chairman Lin', Dong and Xie were locked up separately in the academy's basement for 'isolation and investigation', and confessions were extracted under torture. Dong Youdao swallowed iron thumbtacks and other objects to kill himself. Xie Zhihe was subsequently arrested by the 'organs of dictatorship' and sentenced to ten years in prison for counter-revolutionary crimes.

A 'venomous attack' against Mao and Lin Biao was the most serious of all counter-revolutionary crimes during the Cultural Revolution. A student at the Theatre Academy at the time recalls a big-character poster stating the content of the conversations that constituted the crime Dong and Xie had committed:

Conversation No. 1:
  'What do you think is the point of the Cultural Revolution?'
  'It's all because "three points of water" was unhappy about Wang Guangmei wearing a pearl necklace.'

'Three points of water' was code for the Chinese surname of Jiang Qing, Mao's wife. On 28 December 1966, Jiang Qing and Chen Boda, the vice-chair and chairman, respectively, of the Central Cultural Revolution Small Group, had convened a symposium for the Red Guard organisations of some colleges and universities. From their remarks, it was clear that they were arranging for the Red Guard organisations to engage in struggling President Liu Shaoqi and his wife, Wang Guangmei. In her speech, Jiang Qing said that just before Wang Guangmei accompanied Liu Shaoqi to Indonesia in 1963, Jiang Qing had told Wang not to take her necklace, but Wang had worn it anyway.

What Jiang Qing said about the necklace was written on big-character posters and circulated everywhere. When Tsinghua University's rebel faction held a mass rally to struggle Wang Guangmei in April 1967 and forced her to wear a string of table tennis balls around her neck, it was directly related to what Jiang Qing had said. A documentary about Liu and Wang's 1963 trip to Indonesia was shown in 1967 as a classic negative example of the couple's 'bourgeois' and 'revisionist' mentality.

What Dong Youdao and Xie Zhihe said was factual, but the way they said it was considered disrespectful towards Jiang Qing, who at that time was referred to as the 'standard-bearer' of the Cultural Revolution. Any criticism of Jiang Qing and the Cultural Revolution was tantamount to criticising Mao and constituted a counter-revolutionary crime. What Jiang Qing said about the necklace was recorded verbatim at the time:

> Summary of the Symposium for Revolutionary College and University Teachers and Students Convened by the Central Cultural Committee Small Group Comrades Jiang Qing and Boda
>
> 28 December 1966
> ... Someone mentioned Liu Shaoqi's self-criticism.
> Comrade Jiang Qing said, 'His [Liu Shaoqi's] self-criticism is absurd and will never pass muster with the cadres. Our nation's people have a process of knowing. I've known Comrade [Deng] Xiaoping for more than ten years, and I've known Liu Shaoqi since 1964. At the time, I felt our Party was in danger, and I heard him give a report for seven hours. It was all in the style of Khrushchev, opposing the Chairman's investigative methods and advocating Wang Guangmei's on-site work experience.[23] In fact, Wang Guangmei's on-site work experience was fake.'
> Comrade Jiang Qing said Wang Guangmei was dishonest. 'Before going to Indonesia, Wang Guangmei came to see me while I was sick in Shanghai. She said she would be wearing a necklace and a flowered dress. I said, 'You're the wife of the president of a major country. You can wear a few different outfits, but as a Communist Party member, you can't wear a necklace.' She was sleepless for several nights over this, but eventually promised, saying, 'I accept your opinion, and I won't wear the necklace.' But then when I saw the film, she was wearing it. She lied to me. Why wasn't the film shown at Tsinghua? Comrade Liu Zhijian,[24] does the 1 August Film Studio have the film? Show it at Tsinghua. It's a great poisonous weed. If you want to pull Wang Guangmei back here, I'll support you.'

The poster continued:

> Conversation No. 2:
> 'What other world leader loves having his photo taken so much?'
> 'Adolf Hitler.'

During the Cultural Revolution era, the Red Guards ordered Mao's image and quotations to be posted everywhere, and newspapers also published

---

[23] TN: Referring to Wang's famous 'Taoyuan experience'.
[24] TN: Vice-secretary of the PLA Political Department and the military representative on the CCRG.

multiple photos of him every day. A six-page edition of the *People's Daily* was likely to include a dozen photos and portraits of Mao. Hitler was also someone who engaged in a personality cult, but even he didn't go as far as Mao. What Dong Youdao and Xie Zhihe said was fact.

After these two snippets of conversations were published on posters as evidence of Dong and Xie's crimes, the Cultural Revolution authorities made a 'stipulation' to treat this kind of critical comment about the top leaders as 'anti-proliferation material' that couldn't be repeated or quoted in public. The Shanghai Theatre Academy's publication of these comments by Dong and Xie subsequently came under criticism by the movement's leaders because it effectively 'spread' the men's remarks.

This kind of 'anti-proliferation material' became the basis for punishing someone for a serious crime but could also absolutely not be repeated or 'spread'. Under these circumstances, regardless of whether or not such comments should be considered a crime, this practice opened up the very real possibility of fabricating accusations against someone.

Because of this 'anti-proliferation material' policy, many people accused of 'ongoing counter-revolution' during the Cultural Revolution had no idea what 'reactionary remarks' they'd made. In the case of Dong and Xie, people at least knew that it was because of these two exchanges that the men were taken into custody, tortured, driven to suicide (in Dong's case) and sentenced to ten years in prison (in Xie's case). As to whether the two of them actually said exactly those words, there is room for suspicion, because there was no recording of their voices, and they were convicted on the basis of someone's 'exposure'. Their words could have been exaggerated or even concocted by someone seeking to score points.

It can only be imagined what would drive someone to swallow thumb tacks. In 1968, the basement of the Shanghai Theatre Academy was turned into a prison. The people held there for 'investigation' included female students, and everyone was beaten. The most common method used fists and clubs as well as belt buckles. Some of the assailants practised 'kung fu' – they would kick someone to the ground, pull them upright and then kick them over again, dozens of times non-stop. I was able to identify four other people who committed suicide at the Shanghai Theatre Academy after being struggled and locked up in 1968:

Tan Liping, a student of directing at the Shanghai Theatre Academy, was accused of being a secret agent in 1968 because his parents lived in Hong Kong. He hanged himself after being locked up in the school's basement, where he was beaten and humiliated.

Tan Liping's former classmates describe him as suave and urbane. Once he and his schoolmate Chang Ge, who later became a director at Shanghai

Television, went on an excursion to Zhou Mountain, not far from the city. Back then it was uncommon for people to own cameras, but Tan had one, and he took pictures on Zhou Mountain, including some along the water. The people in control of the academy at that time said that these photographs, when put together, depicted the coastline, which was a military secret of the Chinese Navy, and they claimed that Tan planned to send them to military intelligence operatives in the US and Taiwan. Taking pictures was an act of espionage, and since Tan came from Hong Kong he must be a spy for the US and Taiwan. Using that logic, the people in control of the school locked him in the basement for investigation and tormented him along with the other captives.

Tan's suicide was distinctive in that he hanged himself in a prone position. He ripped his bedding into strips and twisted them together to form a rope, tied the rope into a slipknot and tied it to the window frame, but the window was too low to the ground to hang himself in the usual way, so Tan dropped his body into a horizontal position that tightened the rope enough to strangle him to death. The difficulty of this method indicates how determined he was to end his life.

Since Tan Liping had no family in Shanghai, he wrote a suicide note asking two schoolmates to deal with his belongings. It took quite some time for his family to be notified of his death and to arrive at the school from Hong Kong.

Feng Wenzhi, an administrative clerk, hanged himself in the bathroom after being locked up in the academy's basement for 'isolation and investigation' in April 1968.

Luo Sen, a teacher in the Directing Department, killed himself while under 'isolation and investigation'. He was in his forties.

Wang Huimin, Party secretary and head of the Stage Arts Department, was locked up for 'investigation' in 1968. One night, Wang was savagely beaten with a leather whip; some of her protégés took the lead in beating her in order to show that they'd 'drawn a clear distinction' from her. Wang leaped to her death in the middle of the night. Her husband, Jiang Zunfeng, also worked at the academy.

SHANGHAI CONSERVATORY OF MUSIC

He Xiaoqiu, a student of composition, came under attack after she objected to her father's persecution and killed herself in April 1968. She was around twenty-five years old.

He Xiaoqiu's father was He Lüting, a composer and the director of the Shanghai Conservatory of Music. As soon as the Cultural Revolution began, on 10 June 1966 the Shanghai Municipal Party Committee convened a Cultural Revolution Mobilisation Meeting, during which Shanghai mayor Cao Diqiu presented a mobilisation report accusing He Lüting and seven other artists, writers, editors and professors of being 'anti-Party, anti-socialist elements'. He Lüting was also criticised and attacked by name in national newspapers. Educators and artists were key targets of attack in the Cultural Revolution, and He Lüting was both, so there was no escaping his fate.

After the Red Guard movement was launched, He Lüting suffered physical attacks and torture. On 16 September 1966, Red Guards took He and his wife, Jiang Ruizhi, by force to the school. He Lüting was blindfolded and beaten with leather belts until his clothes were ripped and became embedded in his flesh, while Jiang Ruizhi was forced into a corner and beaten until she was covered with wounds. Other groups of Red Guards then took them away separately and tortured them all night. The family's home was ransacked and all of their possessions were destroyed. The Shanghai Conservatory of Music, which had only around 300 people, experienced at least seventeen 'unnatural deaths' during the Cultural Revolution.

The Shanghai authorities formally imprisoned He Lüting on 21 March 1968, and he was not released until 1973. During those five years, he was repeatedly escorted to struggle rallies and was even struggled on television. Televising a struggle rally was Shanghai's particular use of modern technology, even though very few people owned televisions, and the programmes were not broadcast outside the city.

After He Lüting was arrested, his daughter, He Xiaoqiu, was accused of 'reversing He Lüting's verdict'. She did not obey the Cultural Revolution dictate of 'drawing a clear distinction' from her father, but rather expressed her disagreement with how he was treated. At that time, 'verdict reversal' only involved expressing dissatisfaction with a judgment, but it could still be regarded as an act of 'current counter-revolution'. When the school authorised criticism and struggle against He Xiaoqiu, she gassed herself to death in her kitchen.

After the Cultural Revolution, someone wrote an article saying that He Lüting was released in 1973 because his elder brother went to Beijing to see Mao. Like Mao, the family came from Hunan Province, and He Lüting's brother had become acquainted with Mao during his early involvement with the Communist movement. The brother gained access to Mao in 1973 through a personal contact, Wang Hairong, a woman who was very much in favour as Mao's interpreter, and who was also the progeny of an old acquaintance from Mao's home village. He Lüting was released from prison after his brother raised his case with Mao, but by then his daughter had been dead for six years.

Shen Zhibai, born in 1904, was a professor and head of the Folk Music Department. He killed himself in 1968 after being accused of being an American secret agent in 1968.

Chen Youqin, born in 1913, was chairman of the Wind and Stringed Instruments Department. A graduate of the institute (then known as the Shanghai School of Music), Chen had obtained his Master's degree in England before returning to China in 1951. Accused of being a foreign spy, he leaped to his death from a building at the end of 1968.

Wang Jia'en, a professor in the Piano Department, is also believed to have died during the Cleansing of the Class Ranks.

CRAFTSMEN AND TECHNICIANS

Zhang Guoliang, a plaster mould-maker at the Shanghai Oil Painting and Sculpture Workshop, hanged himself in summer 1968 while locked up in a toilet for 'isolation and investigation'. He was in his twenties.

During a private conversation with several friends, Zhang said, 'I'd like to go to Hong Kong once and breathe the free air and eat a steak.' When that comment was exposed, he was labelled a 'current counter-revolutionary'.

The Shanghai Oil Painting and Sculpture Workshop was a small work unit of only fifty-odd people, occupying a Western-style former residential building. Zhang Guoliang was locked up in the tiny bathroom with all the windows closed tight in the stifling summer heat. He hanged himself after a few days.

Yan Yuyou, a native of Jiangxi Province in his forties, was a worker at the Shanghai Xingguang Tool Factory. He killed himself on 21 August 1968.

The Xingguang Tool Factory was created by merging the workshops of master craftsmen. In 1968 it had around seventy staff, nine of whom were 'ferreted out' during the Cleansing of the Class Ranks. For example:

Small proprietor Fu Bingqian, originally the owner of a blacksmith's shop, was accused of being a 'bad element'.

Wuxi native Bian Yuliang's crime was that before 1949 he had been a soldier for the Kuomintang. He had worked for the Telegraph Office, but had been sent to work at the factory because of this 'historical problem'.

Chen Shouzhang was accused of being a 'bad element' because he had been a Class 2 cadre in the Telegraph Bureau's Workers' Welfare Committee before 1949. (During the Cultural Revolution, the KMT-founded Workers' Welfare Committee was declared to be a 'reactionary organisation', but afterwards it was said to have 'helped the Communist Party' and its members were allowed to 'retire with special honour'.)

Wu Yuekuan, a native of Nantong, Jiangsu Province, had joined the PLA when he was fifteen or sixteen years old, but in 1957 he was designated a Rightist and expelled from the Party. In 1960 he had his Rightist cap lifted, and in 1965 he had applied to join the CCP again. His crime was being a 'rehabilitated Rightist attempting to infiltrate the Party'.

Zhang Wenyue, a native of Anhui Province and former proprietor of an iron shop, was accused of being a 'bad element'. And so on.

Apart from being required to 'give debriefings of their problems', these nine people had to line up before work every day and kneel before a portrait of Mao at the door of the factory and admit their error and appeal for leniency. At the end of the workday, they had to do overtime feeding the pigs the factory reared, and carrying out sanitation work, and when they finished that they had to kneel again for half an hour before they could go home. In the winter the kneeling was changed to standing, but the whole process continued for nearly a year.

Yan Yuyou was normally a man of few words. When all of the craftsmen were required to 'give a debriefing of their problems', Yan also reported his history to the factory's Party secretary. The Party secretary subsequently claimed that he didn't say anything to Yan Yuyou that day, but Yan was so nervous that he became incoherent. That night, he hanged himself in the factory's unmarried residential quarters.

Ma Guifang, a fifty-four-year-old technician at the Shanghai Xinhu Glassworks, had at one point collaborated with the Fudan University Xinguang Laboratory because of his outstanding abilities with vacuum glass technology. During the Cleansing of the Class Ranks, he was accused of being a capitalist and was put under 'isolation and investigation' in the factory. He leaped to his death three days later, on 7 September 1968.

Prior to 1949, Ma had joined his five brothers in opening a family-run workshop that refined silver from industrial waste. They ran the factory themselves and had no hired workers. Ma Guifang was the eldest of his brothers, so he was the workshop's legal representative.

After Ma killed himself, the glassworks still designated him a 'capitalist'. He left behind a sickly wife and two juvenile children, who lost their economic support and were forced to survive on a living allowance of 15 *yuan* per person per month. Ma's widow didn't have enough money to buy medicine for her illness, and the family was in dire straits. A new 'verdict' was reached on Ma Guifang in 1970, acknowledging his case as one of 'a contradiction among the people', but his family still received no more than their original living allowance. It was only after they made further representations that one of Ma's children was allowed to 'replace' him at the glassworks in 1975.

Huang Wenlin, an engineer in his forties at the Shanghai cable factory, had been sent by the government to study in the Soviet Union in the

1950s. During the Cultural Revolution, he was accused of 'illicit relations with a foreign country' and put under 'isolation and investigation'. While attempting to escape from custody, he fell to his death, leaving behind young children and an aged mother. A family friend said sadly, 'The mighty tree of a family was felled in this way.'

OTHER SHANGHAI RESIDENTS

Cui Shumin, around sixty years old, was a resident of Qinren Lane on Shanghai's Huashan Road. Cui's son was accused of 'venomously attacking Chairman Mao and Vice-chairman Lin' and was subjected to struggle. In May 1968, Cui and her son, daughter-in-law and six-year-old granddaughter died at home in a case of murder-suicide.

Cui Shumin's son, around forty years old, was surnamed Xu and was addressed by his neighbours as 'Big Brother'. Xu was struggled in his work unit for 'venomous attacks' in the form of stories and jokes, a serious offence that could bring the death penalty. One morning in May 1968, a neighbour found that no one had opened the door at Cui's home, and this was reason to fear that something bad had happened; suicides were common at the time among those who were subjected to public denunciations. A neighbour climbed into a window of the house and found Cui Shumin and her son hanging from a rafter. In a downstairs room, Cui's daughter-in-law was lying strangled on a bed, and the granddaughter was found dead in another room.

The neighbours noticed that Xu had left a long letter tacked on the wall, stating that Cui Shumin and her son had discussed the matter with Xu's wife, and she had agreed to die with them. The six-year-old girl had been adopted by Xu and his wife. Her name was Mu Yun. According to the suicide note, the couple had fed the child some poisoned bread and then suffocated her in her bed, fearing that she would suffer otherwise. The police took the suicide note away.

Zhu Heming, a man around seventy years old who also lived in a lane off Huashan Road, killed himself in June 1968 by striking himself in the temple with tongs.

Zhu had run a billiards hall in Hongkou District before 1949. This made him a 'capitalist' and subjected him to struggle during the Cultural Revolution. He tried to kill himself with an overdose of sleeping pills in May 1968, but survived. In early June, he cut open his thigh in an attempt to bleed to death, but again he was discovered and saved. It was soon after that that he struck himself in the temple with the tongs, and this time he died a week later. Struggling in agony before he died, he bent the iron bars on his bed.

OTHER PROVINCES AND MUNICIPALITIES

TIANJIN

Zhang Fuyou, around thirty years old, was a worker at the Gegu Iron Forging Factory in what is now Tianjin's Jinnan District. After being struggled as a 'current counter-revolutionary' in 1968, Zhang weighed himself down with rocks and drowned himself in the Hai River near his home.

Zhang's neighbour, Wang Peizhong, provided the following testimony:

> During the Cultural Revolution, especially in 1968, the Hai River became a tool for many people to escape, protest and ultimately extricate themselves from the Cultural Revolution. Tianjin is located on the upper stretches of the Hai River, while the southern suburb of Gegu Town is on the lower reaches. The corpses of people who drowned themselves in Tianjin City usually drifted downriver. I didn't count how many passed through Gegu Town, but the memories remain fresh; at that time, we referred to the corpses as the 'big dead fellows'. Whenever a corpse floated past, a policeman from the local police station would order a 'black element' to haul the bodies ashore, and the policeman would look for identification. The body would then be wrapped in a straw mat and buried nearby. At first such sightings drew crowds, but once they grow more common, they received little attention.
>
> There were a dozen or so households in my lane, which went straight through to a ferry pier on the river, and was therefore called Dukou (ferry pier) Hutong. We used to play at the ferry pier, but during the Cultural Revolution, it became a place where victims of the Cultural Revolution killed themselves. In order to prevent their bodies from being carried away by the current, some suicides tied themselves to the wood pilings of the pier and then weighed themselves down with rocks. One morning, some playmates and I could see from afar several grown-ups standing on the pier and pointing at some clothing floating in the water. On drawing closer, we saw that the body of a drowned person had been found below the pier. A lot of people quickly gathered there to look. When the corpse was finally hauled in, they discovered it was a worker from the local wrought iron factory, Zhang Fuyou, who had recently been struggled at a rally as a 'counter-revolutionary'. They took him away that afternoon on a flatbed tricycle. His wife ran after the cart, weeping and wailing... More than thirty years have passed, but whenever I think back on that scene, I still have a hard time calming myself. I always wonder, who were all those nameless victims of the Cultural Revolution? Did their families know they'd died in the

Hai River? Did they know that they were buried in straw mats along the river bank? Someday in the future, when people discover all those bones buried along the river, will they connect them to the Cultural Revolution of 1966–1976?

Nankai University

Chen Tianchi, a fifty-year-old chemistry professor who had obtained his PhD at Louisiana State University in 1949, hanged himself on 20 December 1968.

Sun Zhaolu, a fifty-year-old lecturer in economics who had graduated from Yenching University in Chengdu in 1946 and obtained his graduate degree from the Nankai Institute of Economics in 1951, leaped to his death on 24 January 1969.

Sun Fengchi, a forty-one-year-old lecturer in mathematics who had graduated from Nankai University in 1956, hanged himself on 25 April 1971.

Bian Jiannian, the forty-three-year-old head of the university's Biology Department, drowned himself in a lake after being horrifically abused during the Cultural Revolution, probably during the Cleansing of the Class Ranks, but I have been unable to confirm that.

Tianjin Electrical Transmission Design Institute

An Daqiang, an engineer, threw himself from the fourth floor of a building at the institute after being repeatedly struggled and beaten in the summer of 1968. He was thirty years old.

An Daqiang was a brilliant student who had graduated from Tsinghua University at the age of nineteen, but he became one of the 571 people designated Rightists there, and was sent to the countryside for labour reform. He was working at the institute by the time the Cultural Revolution began. Because of his 'political problems', An had never married. His colleagues remember An buying a piece of pork to prepare himself a farewell dinner just before he died.

The Tianjin Electrical Transmission Design Institute was under the No. 1 Machine Industry Ministry. Many people were persecuted to death at the institute during the Cultural Revolution, but I have only been able to learn the names of two of them, and I was unable to ascertain the exact date of An Daqiang's death.

The other victim at the institute, **Shang Hongzhi**, was a cadre around forty-five years old. He hanged himself in a restroom in 1968, leaving behind a mentally ill wife and five dependent children. His eldest daughter killed herself not long afterwards.

JIANGXI PROVINCE

Chen Fuzhong, head teacher at the Dexing Secondary School (now Dexing No. 1 Secondary School) in Dexing County, was 'ferreted out' as a 'historical counter-revolutionary' in July or August 1968 and was harshly beaten, after which he committed suicide.

Teachers at the school were routinely beaten and tortured by members of the student rebel faction in 1968. Chen Fuzhong had been a member of the Kuomintang before 1949, as a result of which he was persecuted as a 'historical counter-revolutionary'.

Wu Jindeng, a geography teacher at the school, had been designated a Rightist because back when he was studying at Nanjing University, he had casually remarked that he would rather study in the United States than in the Soviet Union. After hearing of Chen's death, Wu Jindeng left the school and begged in the streets for two years before going back.

Wu Xiaofei, born in 1949, was transferred from a school in Fujian Province to the Nanchang No. 1 Secondary School in Jiangxi Province just as the Cultural Revolution began. He began writing an essay that systematically criticised it in October 1966. On 6 May 1968, his father, **Wu Yaxiong** (director of the Nanchang Railway Bureau) was seized and struggled, and Wu Xiaofei's essay was found when the family's home was ransacked. Wu Xiaofei was reported to the provincial Revolutionary Committee, and his case was designated 'a counter-revolutionary case of rare proportions in the province.' The entire family was arrested, and Wu Yaxiong died under torture. More than twenty family members and friends were persecuted on the basis of the essay, and Wu Xiaofei was executed as a 'current counter-revolutionary' on 27 February 1970. He was rehabilitated in 1980.

SHANXI PROVINCE

Zhai Yishan, a teacher around sixty years old at the Quwo No. 1 Secondary School, was arrested and struggled as a 'current counter-revolutionary', and was quickly tortured to death. Slogans were always shouted when meetings were held during the Cultural Revolution, and during one meeting in 1968, Zhai mistakenly reversed the slogan 'Down with Liu Shaoqi, support Chairman Mao.' That was the basis for the accusations against him.

Cai Qiyuan, a fifty-nine-year-old primary school teacher in Zhang Village, Pinglu County, died on 25 May 1968. His family were told it was suicide, but after the Cultural Revolution, they learned Cai had been beaten to death. Cai Qiyuan had at one point studied at the Huangpu Military

Academy and had taught at the Kuomintang's military school before leaving the army. A native of Chengdu, he had been recruited to teach secondary school in Taiyuan in 1925, and he was later transferred to Pinglu County to teach at the Zhang Village primary school. His wife and children continued to live in Chengdu.

Cai's wife, **Qiu Shupei**, employed at the Sichuan Province Postal and Telecommunications Management Office, had killed herself in Chengdu on 8 July 1967 at the age of fifty. The couple had five children, only one of whom was working at the time. After his wife's death, Cai sent money to his four dependent children every month. In August 1968, they didn't receive their usual remittance, and when they wrote to inquire, they received the reply, 'Cai Qiyuan is a historical counter-revolutionary as well as a current counter-revolutionary, and on 25 May 1968, he took sleeping pills to separate himself permanently from the people.'

After the Cultural Revolution, in 1982, the Zhang Village school informed Cai's children that he had in fact been beaten to death during a struggle session at the school, and the suicide had been faked. Since the body had been disposed of without a casket or gravestone, there was no way to determine where he had been buried.

Cai Qiyuan's children demanded that the school take action against the killers. The reply they received was that the debt should be added to the account of Lin Biao and the Gang of Four.

GUANGDONG PROVINCE

Pang Chengfeng, general affairs director at the Guangzhou No. 17 Secondary School, was beaten to death by student Red Guards in April 1968. At the end of that year, **Yang Aimei**, a language teacher at the school, came under investigation and killed herself. Her husband had been deputy director of the propaganda bureau of the Guangzhou Municipal Party Committee prior to the Cultural Revolution, and he was also 'struck down' and held in the garrison headquarters.

HEBEI PROVINCE

Wang Zhicheng, a biology lecturer at Hebei Normal University in Shijiazhuang, was accused of being a KMT agent and beaten in 1968. One day he was dragged from his home to his office, where he died.

Ma Ying, in her thirties, was an educational administrator at the Hebei Normal University Affiliated Secondary School. Accused of political problems, she was locked up in the school and repeatedly beaten by students. She died in custody in June 1968 and was declared to have poisoned herself.

Ma Ying's colleagues didn't believe she had committed suicide. One teacher heard students say, 'That isn't even a human being and needs to die sooner or later.' They were beating Ma at the time.

Ma Ying knew the situation she was in and told the school's music teacher, 'I'm not going to survive this time.' Early one morning a few days later, the other teachers who were locked up heard a pounding on the door, and someone called Ma Ying to come out to work. They then heard someone shout that she was 'playing dead', while someone else went for the school doctor. Shortly after that, people came from the crematorium to take Ma Ying's body away.

Three other people died at this school during the early years of the Cultural Revolution:

Gao Jingshan, a mathematics teacher who had taught at the Normal University before being sent down to the secondary school, was put into the school's 'dictatorship team' for 'labour reform'. One day in August 1968, he was bound to a tree at the school's sports ground and beaten to death.

Zhu Qi, the school's Party secretary, fell to her death after being struggled and taken to the tower of the school's chemical plant. It is not clear whether or not she killed herself.

Chen Chuanbi, a mathematics teacher designated a Rightist in 1957, was beaten regularly during the Cultural Revolution. One morning after a workers' propaganda team arrived at the school in 1968, someone saw Chen Chuanbi come out in new clothes. He disappeared after that, and no one knows what became of him.

CHONGQING

Zhang Kezhi, a professor at Chongqing University, was locked up in an 'ox pen' in 1968 by the university's 'Revolutionary Committee struggle against the enemy leading small group' and tortured to death.

Mu Shuqing, a native of Hejiang County, Sichuan Province, was a teacher of handicrafts at the Dongshenglou Primary School in Chongqing's Central District. Following the death of Mu's father, her mother remarried, but in order to keep her son and daughter from suffering loss, she transferred her father's land into their names, although she still controlled the income from the land. In 1968, Mu Shuqing was 'ferreted out' and struggled as a 'landlord', and she jumped off a cliff.

Mu Shuqing was a person of strong character, and when ordered to kneel in front of Mao's statue and request pardon for her crime, she refused, saying she'd committed no crime; for that she was harshly beaten and then paraded through the streets of downtown Chongqing. By the time she came back, she'd been beaten black and blue.

Mu Shuqing's two daughters took her to a hospital under the Chongqing Medical School, but doctors refused to treat her after hearing she was an 'ox demon and snake spirit'. Mu told her younger daughter to take her to the No. 1 Hospital of Traditional Chinese Medicine, but it appears she'd already decided to kill herself by then. Going from the Medical School hospital to the Hospital of Traditional Chinese Medicine required taking a hilly road along the Jialing River and crossing a bridge. On the way, Mu said she couldn't go any further and told her younger daughter to go back and get her elder daughter to help her. After the daughter left, Mu jumped from the river bank near the bridge and killed herself.

Jiang Cheng, a physical education teacher at the Chongqing No. 37 Secondary School, was locked up on 14 September 1968, in a 'supervision team' established by the Municipal Public Security, Procuratorial and Judicial Military Control Commission. He died whilst being beaten into making a confession.

I know of three other people who died while in the custody of this 'supervision team':

Yun Liangchen, a doctor of traditional Chinese medicine at the Chongqing Cement Plant, was accused of being the ringleader of a 'counter-revolutionary clique'. He died on 14 September 1968, after being brutally tortured and beaten. **Han Zhen**, a doctor at Chongqing's Public Security Bureau training school, and **Zhang Yonggon**, a PSB cadre, both killed themselves in early January 1969.

CHENGDU

Yuan Lihua, a thirty-eight-year-old teacher and deputy Party secretary at the Chengdu Longjiang Road Primary School, was placed under 'isolation and investigation' on 8 November 1968, by the school's Revolutionary Committee. After being continuously struggled and beaten, Yuan wrote a suicide note and killed herself on the night of 27 November.

Liao Peizhi, a teacher at a commune secondary school in Mata Township, Jingyan County, Sichuan Province, was denounced and dismissed from his job during the Cultural Revolution. When he returned to his home in the village, his son accused him of hurting the family by becoming a counter-revolutionary, and Liao dropped dead, possibly from a cerebral haemorrhage. Another teacher, Zhang Pide, was also dismissed and returned to his village for nine years before being rehabilitated and allowed to resume teaching. Of the school's thirty-odd teachers and staff, ten were locked up during the Cleansing of the Class Ranks; one committed suicide and two were dismissed. **Zhong Xianhua**, accused of being a 'secret agent', wrote a letter to Zhou Enlai denying the allegation and asking for help in clarifying the situation. When the letter was returned to local officials, Zhong was additionally accused of 'verdict reversal'. He was paraded through the streets, and when he fell he was dragged until his wrists were dislocated and his face scraped raw. He hanged himself soon afterwards.

SHANDONG PROVINCE

Tang Guoquan, a teacher at the Shandong Province Zibo City No. 6 Secondary School, hanged himself in summer 1968 because he couldn't bear the humiliation he'd been subjected to. The school then called a rally of all teachers and students to declare Tang a 'current counter-revolutionary'.

WUHAN, HUBEI PROVINCE

Zhu Ningsheng, head of the fish physiology research room of the Wuhan Aquatic Organisms Institute of the Chinese Academy of Sciences, was locked up and 'investigated' as an alleged 'secret agent' in 1968. He killed himself in a laboratory.

This institute had 400 personnel, of whom 108 were 'ferreted out' as 'secret agents'. Four people died as a result of being struggled and investigated. One of them was **Li Yushu**, a switchboard operator around fifty years old, who was accused of being an agent of KMT 'central intelligence' and 'military intelligence'. His wife was a cleaner who had formerly been a prostitute, and after the big-character poster about Li exposed this fact, she was also struggled. Li drowned himself in East Lake in Wuchang, which was located near the institute.

Wuhan University

Zhang Zigong, a sixty-four-year-old chemistry professor, had studied in the US on a government scholarship and obtained his PhD at John Hopkins University. While at Wuhan University in 1957, he was designated a Rightist, demoted and assigned smaller living quarters. On 3 January

1968, a 'reactionary leaflet' purportedly opposing the Cultural Revolution and the CCP was discovered in Wuhan, and a major investigation was carried out. The investigators decided that it must have been written by 'an educated person fluent in both Chinese and English'. On this basis, Zhang Zigong was locked up in the university student dormitory and beaten and tortured by students. He died after several days of this abuse.

Liu Shousong, a professor of modern literature in the university's Chinese Department, was placed under 'isolation and investigation' in 1968 along with his wife, **Zhang Jifang**, who was a clerical worker at the university. The couple hanged themselves together on 16 March 1969. Liu was in his forties at the time.

During the War of Resistance Against Japan, Zhang Jifang had served as a radio announcer in Chongqing and had also joined the Three People's Principles Youth Corps, as a result of which she was accused of being a 'historical counter-revolutionary'. Liu Shousong was accused of being 'dishonest in confessing his problems', and the Mao Zedong Thought Propaganda Team threatened to treat him harshly as a 'typical bad element'. When Liu was struggled, his students and colleagues beat him.

On Sunday 16 March 1969, Liu Shousong and Zhang Jifang were granted permission to go home. After returning to their university residential quarters, they erected a small bed in the attic, and then each stood on either end of it and hanged themselves.

Liu and Zhang left behind children in secondary and primary school and Zhang's elderly mother. After they died, the university took back their residential unit and their children were dispatched to the countryside as 'sent-down educated youth'. Zhang's elderly mother, rendered homeless, could only accompany the children to the countryside, and died while moving from place to place. After the Cultural Revolution, Liu and Zhang were rehabilitated, and Wuhan University 'looked after' their youngest child with a clerical position in the Chinese Department in lieu of compensation.

Huang Zhongxiong, a professor of economics, killed himself by drinking pesticide after being struggled and investigated in 1968.

JIANGSU PROVINCE

Nanjing

Yang Shijie, in his fifties, was vice-president of Nanjing University, in charge of scientific research when he killed himself after being put under 'isolation and investigation' in 1968.

Song Liwu, born in 1917, graduated from Tsinghua University in 1939 and was a professor and chairman of the PLA Meteorology Institute in Nanjing. Song's home was ransacked on 30 December 1966, and in 1968 he was placed under 'isolation and investigation'. He was beaten by students and teaching assistants with nail-studded wooden sticks until his head was full of holes. Song died on 27 May 1969, in what the authorities said was a suicide. His only daughter was a secondary school student, and his wife, originally a secondary school teacher, was not working because of health problems. The daughter, wife and Song's eighty-six-year-old father were forced to move from Nanjing to the countryside.

Wu Shuqin, principal of the Nanjing Gupinggang Primary School, killed herself after being struggled in 1968.

Suzhou

Zhou Shoujuan, a sixty-seven-year-old writer and horticulturist, drowned himself in the well of his home on 12 August 1968.

After earning some money from his writings in the 1930s, Zhou bought land on the outskirts of Suzhou and built a garden. He wasn't a 'revolutionary writer', and he published little after 1949. Zhou spent all his time in his garden and achieved a high standard of artistry in creating bonsai. His garden, famous for its many plum blossoms, was known as Plum Hill.

In 1966, Red Guards smashing the 'Four Olds' destroyed many of Zhou's bonsai creations. When he was ordered to write a confession during the Cleansing of the Class Ranks in 1968, he killed himself.

XI'AN, SHAANXI PROVINCE

Shaanxi Normal University

Fourteen staff, including ten teachers, died at the university in 1966 and 1968. The following were among the seven who died in 1968:

Tan Huizhong, a lecturer in history, died after being repeatedly beaten to extract a confession.

Cao Shimin, deputy director of the university library, was driven to suicide.

Sun Rongxian, a lecturer in the foreign languages teaching and research section, killed himself after being tortured into a confession.

Kang Zhaoming, a lecturer in the foreign languages teaching and research section, killed herself while being interrogated under torture.

Xi'an Jiaotong University

As noted previously, this university had a particularly large number of victims, not only during the initial Red Guard period, but also during the Cleansing of the Class Ranks and the One Strike and Three Antis Campaign that followed in 1970.

Qian Xianlun, born in 1909, a native of Wuxi, Jiangsu Province, was a lecturer in the chemistry teaching and research section. He returned to mainland China in February 1950 with the former Kuomintang-run China and Central airlines, and this 'historical problem' came under investigation during the Cleansing of the Class Ranks. Qian gassed himself to death on 3 April 1968 along with his wife, **Yuan Yunwen**, and his mother-in-law, **Zhang Shuxiu**.

Tao Zhong, a forty-year-old lecturer in the university's foreign languages teaching and research section, gassed herself to death on 19 May 1968, after being accused of becoming a 'turncoat' while serving in the underground Communist Party before 1949.

Wang Hailian, employed in the university's General Affairs Department, leaped to his death on 3 July 1968, after being locked up for 'investigation' because he had once been a member of the Kuomintang's Self-Defence Corps.

Fan Bugong, a twenty-four-year-old student from Qian County, was locked up for 'investigation' after he objected to his family being dealt with as 'landlords', and poisoned himself to death on 21 July 1968.

Wang Dehong, a sixty-year-old repairman in the university's Machinery Department, was locked up for 'investigation' because he had once been a member of the Green Gang secret society and had served as a lower-middle ranking military technician in the Kuomintang's arsenal. He leaped to his death on 3 August 1968.

Ren Fuyan, a student of foundry work from Lu County, was locked up for protesting his father being denounced as a 'landlord'. He leaped to his death on 10 August 1968.

Huang Zhongxiu, a forty-six-year-old teacher and vice-chairman of the university's foundation engineering design teaching and research section, was put under 'isolation and investigation' because he had served as a deputy inspector in the marine police under the Nationalist government. Huang hanged himself on 21 August 1968. His widow, **Zhang Yingling**, head nurse at the university health centre, leaped to her death on 15 September that year after being harshly beaten.

Mao Yiming, a native of Suzhou, was a family member of a university employee, and had been interrogated by Red Guards and her residential committee about 'historical problems'. Mao hanged herself on 4 September 1968.

Wang Shu, a forty-two-year-old lecturer in the university's Marxism–Leninism teaching and research section, leaped to her death on 24 September 1968, after being locked up and investigated because she had joined the Three People's Principles Youth League in her youth.

Tang Xingheng, a forty-seven-year-old employee in the university's benefits department, was locked up and investigated in 1968 after being implicated in the case of an 'Anti-Party National Salvation Corps'. Tang hanged himself on 2 November 1968, after which his wife became deranged.

Lu Guyu, a lecturer in the industrial enterprise teaching and research section, was denounced at the outset of the Cultural Revolution for some 'inappropriate political remarks'. He hanged himself on 2 December 1968.

Wang Guopang, a forty-year-old lecturer in the university's No. 350 teaching and research room, hanged himself on 5 December 1968, while under investigation for 'historical problems'.

Wang Zhenguo, a thirty-two-year-old teaching assistant in the university's spare parts teaching and research section, was investigated because at the outset of the Cultural Revolution he had held onto an inspection report for a relative at the Xi'an Electrical Power Design Institute. Wang leaped to his death on 18 December 1968.

Zhou Shougen, a worker in the university factory, leaped to his death on 24 December 1968, after being locked up and 'investigated' for 'taking part in a spying organisation'. The allegation was subsequently found to be bogus.

Shen Zongyan, a thirty-one-year-old laboratory technician in the university's No. 230 teaching and research room, leaped to his death on 31 December 1968, after being placed under investigation in connection with a 'reactionary poster'.

Shen Jiaben, a forty-six-year-old senior lecturer in the university's enterprise and labour teaching and research section, was locked up after Red Guards discovered 'reactionary language' in his journal. After managing to escape on 19 January 1969, Shen drowned himself in a well in Lantian County, Shaanxi Province, on 21 January.

Liu Jihong, the forty-five-year-old head of the university's teaching and scientific research section, leaped to his death on 4 February 1969, after being locked up for 'investigation' of his employment with the Kuomintang before 1949.

The following victims died during the One Strike and Three Antis Campaign (described in greater detail in Part Six):

Yang Wen, born 1920, was vice-chairman of Xi'an Jiaotong University's political department and a Grade 13 cadre before the Cultural Revolution; he later became vice-chairman of the university's Revolutionary Committee. In early 1970, Yang Wen was locked up and put under investigation for issues relating to his time in the northeast in 1939; his convalescence in his home province, Shandong, in 1942–1943; and, especially, during the KMT's attack on Yantai in 1947. Yang Wen hanged himself in a plant nursery in the eastern suburbs of Xi'an on 29 March 1970.

Yao Peihong, a thirty-eight-year-old lecturer in the insulation teaching and research section, leaped to his death on 19 May 1970, while locked up for 'isolation and investigation'.

According to records in the school's files, there were allegations that Yao had participated in a reactionary organisation, that his performance was unsatisfactory, that he had engaged in vilifying speech, and that he stole state secrets with the intention of betraying his country. The 're-examination verdict' reached after the Cultural Revolution stated that Yao had merely engaged in political discussion during a time of economic difficulty. The 'time of economic difficulty' referred to the Great Famine that occurred as a result of the 1958 Great Leap Forward. No one was ever called to account for the famine, but ordinary people who expressed criticism during that time often found themselves persecuted during the Cultural Revolution.

Yuan Guangfu, born in 1947 in Linfen, Shanxi Province, was a student of thermal energy at Shaanxi Polytechnic University (later merged into Xi'an Jiaotong University). Accused of 'counter-revolutionary speech' and involvement in a 'counter-revolutionary case' in Xi'an, Yuan Guangfu hanged himself in custody on 27 June 1970. A review of his case after the Cultural Revolution concluded that all of the allegations against him were false.

Chen Ziqing, a forty-four-year-old associate professor in the university's stress research section, hanged himself on 4 July 1970, after being struggled and locked up for 'slandering and attacking the Great Leader Chairman Mao and Mao Zedong Thought'.

The 're-examination conclusion' regarding Chen's death after the Cultural Revolution stated that he had admitted to some erroneous speech but unfortunately died during the investigation, and was to be treated as a revolutionary teacher. It must be emphasised that confessions were typically extracted under physical and mental torture.

Wang Yuxiu, a thirty-eight-year-old laboratory technician in the university's turbine teaching and research section, hanged herself on 5 July 1970, after being placed under 'investigation'.

Li Xiqin, a fifty-four-year-old professor in the electrical engineering teaching and research section, was labelled a Rightist in 1957 and had his salary reduced. During the Cultural Revolution he was put under 'isolation and investigation', and was interrogated about 'participation in the Kuomintang's Industrial Construction Association', 'sabotaging the student movement', 'assisting special agents to go to Hong Kong' and 'writing reactionary slogans'. Li hanged himself on 12 July 1970.

Li graduated from the Northwest College of Engineering in 1941, after which he studied in the US from 1945 to 1947, first at Oberlin College and then obtaining his Master's degree at Ohio State University. After Li returned to China in 1947, Sichuan's Mingxian Academy hired him as a professor and department head in Mechanics, and he also served as professor of mechanical and electrical engineering at Sichuan University's College of Engineering. In 1950, the Northwest College of Engineering hired him as professor and deputy director of its Electrical Engineering Department. He became professor and deputy director of the Electrical Engineering Department of the Xi'an Dynamics Institute in August 1956, and then a professor of electrical engineering at Xi'an Jiaotong University in September 1957.

The 'verdict' reached in 1978 follows. From this we can see what his 'problem' was during the Cultural Revolution, and what changed afterwards.

Xi'an Jiaotong University 'Conclusion of Investigation into the Political Historical Problems of Comrade Li Xiqin'

Li Xiqin, male, b. 1916, native of Lingqiu County, Shanxi, family background self-employed, personal status functionary.

Joined the China Democratic League in 1954. On 11 July 1970, during the 'One Strike and Three Antis' campaign, he was persecuted to death by the ultra-Leftist line of Lin Biao and the Gang of Four.

While studying at the Northwest College of Engineering, Li joined the Kuomintang in May 1940. He took part in routine activities and was an ordinary member.

In 1941, while at Northwest College of Engineering, he helped launch the China Industrial Construction Association and served as one of the association's academic leaders. He was not found to have taken part in reactionary activities. In 1949, when progressive students at the Mingxian Academy in Chengdu boycotted exams to oppose civil war, hunger and oppression, Li, in his capacity as department head, took the side of school administrators in obstructing the boycott. Li himself provided full details of this incident in 1952, and it is regarded as a routine political historical problem.

Xi'an Jiaotong University Party Committee
9 April 1978

Xu Zhizhong, a thirty-nine-year-old teaching assistant in the condensation teaching and research section, poisoned himself to death on 30 September 1970, after being placed under 'isolation and investigation' as an 'ideological reactionary'.

A 're-examination' of his case after the Cultural Revolution concluded that Xu had been hospitalised for illness twice, in 1965 and 1967, and a doctor at the Shanghai Psychiatric Hospital had diagnosed him with 'delusional schizophrenia' It concluded that Xu was mentally ill and should not be held responsible for anything he had said. However, that assumed that his speech would have made him guilty of a crime had he been sane.

HARBIN, HEILONGJIANG PROVINCE

Han Liyan, a forty-four-year-old teacher and head of the teaching and research group at the Harbin Railway Secondary School, had graduated from Peking University with a degree in history, and taken part in the school opera troupe. He was murdered on 12 May 1968, but the rebel faction controlling the school at the time claimed that he had killed himself. After divisions arose within the rebel faction, someone revealed that Han Liyan had been beaten to death and then thrown from a window to make it look like suicide. Han was rehabilitated after the Cultural Revolution, but no one investigated how he came to die, even though his wife petitioned various departments.

Zhao Fuji, a fifty-seven-year-old professor at Harbin Jiaotong College, was subjected to sustained struggle. In summer 1968, the college authorities suddenly informed his family in Shanghai that Zhao had 'committed suicide to escape punishment'.

Following the Japanese occupation of the northeast in 1931, Zhao Fuji fled his native Liaoning Province and ended up in Jiangtianshan, Zhejiang Province, where he became director of the Western Zhejiang Cultural Centre and joined the KMT. He served as an interpreter for the US Flying Tigers Brigade, which was carrying out pararescue operations in China during the war with Japan. After the war, he obtained his Master's degree in economics at New York University, returned to China in 1949, and taught in Suzhou and then Shanghai. When China underwent its 'restructuring of colleges and departments', the Shanghai Law School and other liberal arts institutions were forced to merge and form the Shanghai College of Finance and Economics, and Zhao Fuji became a professor there. But under China's implementation of the 'planned economy' he was unable to use the knowledge he'd obtained in the US.

In 1958, the Shanghai College of Finance and Economics expelled a group of 'politically unreliable targets of internal control' from the city and transferred them to Anhui, Heilongjiang and other such places. Zhao Fuji was sent to Heilongjiang, and after working in the countryside for a time, he was transferred to Harbin Jiaotong College, where he became a target of struggle once the Cultural Revolution began. His family remained in Shanghai, but he was not permitted to visit them for quite a long time.

Zhao left behind four children who were still in school, the youngest daughter only eight years old. The family subsequently had to live off of his widow's meager pay as a primary school teacher. Since suicide was a crime at that time, when the three older children graduated from secondary school, they were sent to the countryside as farmers instead of being assigned jobs in the city.

Zhao Fuji's family had no way of finding out how he died. Everyone who knew him had been deeply impressed by his positive and cheerful character, which made his death all the more shocking and suspicious.

Tao Qian, associate professor and chairman of the Metal Cutting Department of Harbin Polytechnic University, was placed under 'isolation and investigation' in 1968. His family was informed that he had used his eyeglass lenses to slit his own throat, but they didn't believe he could do such a thing to himself, and suspected that he had been murdered.

DALIAN

Xin Zhiyuan, a handyman at the Liaoning Normal University Affiliated Secondary School, killed himself after coming under the 'dictatorship of the masses' in 1968. Two other people at the school died under similar circumstances at that time: **Tong Mingyuan**, a clerical worker in the dean's office, and a physical education teacher surnamed **Deng**.

Yu Qiyun, a forty-three-year-old physics teacher at the Dalian Engineering Institute, killed herself on 15 June 1968, while under 'isolation and investigation'. Her husband, **Huang Bixin**, a teacher in the college's Radio Department, had been persecuted to death two years earlier. (See Part One.)

Wang Maorong, born in 1933, graduated from the Chemistry Department of Peking University in 1960 and then worked in Room No. 2 of the Dalian Institute of Chemical Physics. After coming under attack during the Cultural Revolution, he took an overdose of sleeping pills, and his body was found in Dalian's Xinghai Park on 31 July 1968. Thirteen days later, his wife gave birth to the couple's only child.

Wang Maorong had chosen a name for the child, Jianqin, but because of the way he had died, his widow never told their daughter anything about him, and after she remarried, she changed the child's given name as well as her surname. That's how many family members of victims tried to protect themselves from social bias and attacks. In fact, they still suffered the consequences of this 'social relationship' and constantly had to engage in 'self-criticism' over whether their thinking retained any of the 'bad influence' and 'poisonous roots' of the dead family member. Wang Maorong's daughter lived with her maternal grandmother for a period of time, and when she was three or four years old, she heard her grandmother sigh, 'Why is fate so cruel? My son and my son-in-law are both dead!' The girl wondered to herself about this, but she was sensitive enough to realise that something had happened that her family didn't want her to know about, and she never dared to ask. The son that Wang Maorong's mother-in-law spoke of was **Du Mengxian**, whose story is told earlier in this book.

When Wang Maorong's daughter was a little older, she came across the family's residential permit in a drawer that had been left unlocked, and she saw that her permit had a different name in it, Wang Jianqin, that had been crossed out. She felt afraid, as if she'd done something wrong that no one could know about. One day while she was in secondary school, her birth father's brother came to the school entrance to look at her. Seeing him from a distance, she was afraid and quickly turned away.

Eventually she was admitted to Peking University as a student of chemistry, and when family members came to see her off, some older relatives told her that her father had studied there too, and that they were proud of her. When she arrived at Peking University, her father's sister visited, and that was the first time someone sat down with her and told her about him. After graduating, she went to the US to continue her studies.

When Peking University celebrated its 100th anniversary in 1998, it created a CD-Rom including the names of all of its graduates over the past 100 years. That's how Wang Maorong's daughter learned that Wang had studied mathematics at the university from 1955 to 1960, and she realised that he had actually existed. When the university's No. 1 student canteen was renovated into a lecture hall and donations were solicited from former students to replace its chairs, Wang Maorong's daughter donated the money for a chair in his honour. It was now a different era from the time when his memory had to be expunged; now his name could be permanently engraved on a chair at his alma mater.

Even so, no one knew how or why Wang Maorong had died, nor had anyone made an effort to seek justice on his behalf. Having his name on a chair wasn't enough.

Wang Maorong's daughter came to me. She wanted to know what the Cultural Revolution was and why her father had died before she'd ever seen him. On my website she learned about **Xiao Guangyan**, who worked in the same institute as her father, and who had been persecuted to death there just a few months later. The two families had been neighbours, and the two men had often played tennis together in the nearby Laodong Park.

Xiao Guangyan, born in 1920, was a research fellow at the Dalian Institute of Chemical Physics under the Chinese Academy of Sciences. He received his PhD in chemistry from the University of Chicago. During the Cultural Revolution he was accused of being a 'secret agent' and was locked up in an 'ox pen' in October 1968. Beaten and tortured, he died in custody on 11 December. He was declared to have taken an overdose of sleeping pills. Two days later, his wife, **Zhen Suhui**, and his fifteen-year-old daughter, **Xiao Luolian**, were found dead in their home.

I was able to retrieve Xiao's 1946 doctoral dissertation on chlorophyll and photosynthesis from the University of Chicago library. Science advances by the day, but this dissertation will be preserved as part of the endless flow of human knowledge.

After obtaining his PhD, Xiao Guangyan returned to China in 1950 and worked as a Grade 2 research fellow in the Dalian Institute of Chemical Physics, engaged in long-term research on catalysts. His wife, Zhen Suhui, had grown up in the United States, her father having been a secretary to Sun Yat-sen. She followed Xiao to Dalian and taught English at the Haiyun Institute.

Xiao Guangyan was denounced and forced to write a self-criticism during the Intellectual Thought Reform Campaign in 1952. Then he was denounced during the 1958 campaign to 'pluck out white flags'. When the Cleansing of the Class Ranks was launched in 1968, he was locked up in the institute's 'ox pen' and died there two months later. When neighbours noticed that there had been no sign of movement at his home for two days, they went inside and found Xiao's wife and daughter in bed, dead of an overdose of sleeping pills.

At that time, more than a hundred of the institute's staff were accused of being secret agents, and anyone who had studied overseas was accused of being a member of a spy ring. Seven of them died while under long-term 'isolation and investigation'; all were declared to have committed suicide, but their family members believed they were fatally beaten or pushed to their deaths.

Xiao's home was ransacked seven times. The floorboards were ripped out, and everything was dumped out of the cabinets. Xiao had been quite well paid at more than 200 *yuan* per month, but because he had so many children, and had bought many books and government bonds, he had saved very little. The Red Guards ransacking his home couldn't find his bank book and interrogated him: 'Why don't you have a savings account? You must have paid it all out for espionage expenses!' Xiao's twelve-year-old son was told to expose him. The Red Guards said, 'Your father is a spy.' The child asked, 'What's a spy?' and they replied 'Don't you go to the movies?'

Zhang Cunhao, a survivor of the 'espionage case', was also a research fellow at the institute who had studied in the US. He was thirty-eight years old in 1968, when Red Guards took him from his home and fractured his wife's collarbone. Once in custody, he wasn't paid a penny, and his four children and elderly sister all had to live off of his wife's monthly pay of 60 *yuan*.

Zhang was held in the 'ox pen' for a year, but after the Cultural Revolution, he seldom mentioned the torture and humiliation he'd suffered, even to his family. He just told them about one incident, perhaps because while tragic, it was also quite ridiculous:

After being sent to the 'ox pen', Zhang Cunhao was given a long list of names. The 'special investigation group' told him to admit that all of these people were members of his espionage ring. One of the names on the list was Zhang Jie, his twelve-year-old son. At that time, Zhang was so bewildered at the thought of his young son being included on a list of 'secret agents' that he adamantly refused to admit that he knew anyone named Zhang Jie. Because of this, he was slapped in the face all night for his 'dishonest attitude'. He said it was truly hard to bear, but thinking of his wife and children kept him from killing himself.

When policies changed after the Cultural Revolution, Zhang Cunhao became head of the Institute of Chemical Physics. His seven dead colleagues could never benefit from rehabilitation, however, nor could they speak of what they'd experienced in the 'ox pen'.

ANHUI PROVINCE

Jiang Nan, a teacher of Russian at Anhui University, was born into an overseas Chinese family in Indonesia and came to China in the early 1950s. After being persecuted during the Cleansing of the Class Ranks, Jiang hanged herself in Wujiang Commune in Anhui's He County in 1969.

Wu Ningkun, who was sent to Anhui University to teach English after being designated a Rightist in 1957 and serving labour reform in the Great Northern Wilderness, tells Jiang Nan's story in his book *A Single Tear*.[25]

Wu Ningkun told me that Jiang Nan's husband, Lin Xing, had collected military intelligence on the Kuomintang for the CCP, as a result of which he was given a posting in the Foreign Ministry, working in the Bulgarian Embassy in the 1950s. After being labelled a 'Right-deviationist' in 1959, Lin was sent to Anhui University, where he became chairman of the labour

---

[25] TN: Wu Ningkun, *A Single Tear*, pp. 217–218, 247–249.

union. During the Cultural Revolution, the couple were locked up under 'isolation and investigation'.

In December 1968, in accordance with a 'highest directive' from Mao, Wu Ningkun, Lin Xing and Jiang Nan were among those ordered to leave Anhui University and go to the villages for 'struggle-criticism-transformation' and to 'continue the Cleansing of the Class Ranks campaign.' One night, Jiang Nan hanged herself in the home of a peasant family she was staying with in Dongying Village. After she died, the propaganda team in control of their university put up a poster saying she had 'committed suicide to escape punishment'.

Wu Ningkun relates that Jian Nan's body was rolled up into a reed mat and buried. Her grave was dug up by thieves who stripped the woollen sweater from her body, and after the body was hastily reburied, a wild dog dug it up and tore it to pieces. The peasants in the village were enraged and said, 'What had the woman college teacher done that she deserved to be devoured by a wild dog? What have we done to deserve such bad luck?'

The propaganda team held a meeting to announce that 1) Jiang Nan's suicide was resistance to the Cultural Revolution and an act of 'current counter-revolution'; 2) this matter had to be kept secret, and leaking it to her husband would be treated as an act of 'current counter-revolution'; 3) the Red Guards and revolutionary teachers had to use Mao Zedong Thought to help the peasants overcome their superstitious thinking; 4) any conjecture or gossip would be treated as a 'serious breach of revolutionary discipline'.

Eventually the truth came out: Jiang Nan had been raped by at least one member of the propaganda team, and the rapist threatened that if she reported it, her husband would be tortured even more severely. Jiang became pregnant as a result of the rape, and going to the hospital to have an abortion required proof of who the father was. She spoke to the leader of the propaganda team about this matter, only to be accused of 'corrupting the working class'. Jiang Nan felt she had no way out and hanged herself.

Her husband, Lin Xing, had been under 'isolation and investigation' for a long time. Before Jiang Nan died, her husband was allowed to eat at the communal canteen with someone watching over him, but afterwards he was placed under strict watch and was not allowed to leave his room under any circumstances. He didn't find out what happened until the Revolution was over.

After the Cultural Revolution, Jiang Nan's rape was investigated, but the members of the propaganda team had all returned to the Ma'anshan Steelworks by then, so the investigation bore no results. A small amount of money was sent to her daughter as compensation.

YUNNAN PROVINCE

Xie Mang, an engineer at the Yunnan Province Electrical Power Bureau, was denounced in a 'Mao Zedong Thought Study Class' held at the Shilong Dam Power Plant in Kunming's Haikou Township in 1968. After making several self-criticisms without passing muster, he leaped to his death at the plant. He was around forty years old. After Xie died, a straw man was created with his name written on it to be struggled in his place that night. His family didn't dispose of his corpse, and he was buried in a shallow grave in the hills without a marker.

FUJIAN PROVINCE

Huang Xinduo, director of the Mathematics Department at Fujian Normal University, was beaten to death while under 'isolation and investigation' in 1968. The day before, he'd been told that his 'investigation' was finished and that he'd be released and allowed to return home, but the next day his family was notified to collect his corpse.

Chen Jing, a forty-four-year-old employee of the supplies department of the Fujian Province Postal and Telecommunications Management Bureau, was put under 'isolation and investigation' and subjected to protracted and brutal 'criticism and struggle' in 1968. He drowned himself in a well on 24 May 1969, leaving behind a wife and five children.

During the War of Resistance against Japan, Chen Jing was a student at the Fuzhou No. 31 Secondary School, and as chief editor of the school magazine he wrote articles against Japan. He joined the Three People's Principles Youth League at the age of sixteen. After graduating from secondary school, he was unable to attend college due to his family's straightened financial circumstances. When the Postal and Telecommunications Bureau recruited workers in 1947, Chen took the examination and was hired after receiving the second highest score.

After the CCP took control of Fuzhou in August 1949, Chen Jing retained his job in the bureau's supplies department. His diligence led to his work unit naming him a 'model worker', but his youthful participation in the Three People's Principles Youth League brought him under varying degrees of examination and criticism in every political movement from 1949 onwards, culminating in particularly harsh attacks during the Cultural Revolution.

Once the Cleansing of the Class Ranks began, Chen became an 'investigation target' and was isolated in a jail operated by his work unit. Repeated criticism and struggle sessions devastated his physical and mental health until he finally killed himself.

HENAN PROVINCE

A cook at the Zhengzhou University Affiliated Secondary School committed suicide in 1968 after being denounced for accidentally ripping a portrait of Mao. A former student of the school said that during the Cleansing of the Class Ranks, the cook had finished fetching water and was placing his carrying pole against the wall when it ripped a portrait of Mao that was hanging there. Added to his 'bad family background', this subjected him to being struggled in shifts by each class. When it was time for this student's class to struggle the man, he didn't appear, and they learned that he had killed himself.

XINJIANG PROVINCE

Mei Fenglian, principal of the Shihezi No. 1 School for Dependents of the Xinjiang Production and Construction Corps, hanged himself in the school's vegetable cellar after undergoing long-term beatings and humiliation in 1968. He was in his forties, and left behind a wife and five children.

JILIN PROVINCE

Xue Shimao, a teacher at Jilin Polytechnic University, was beaten to death one night in the latter half of 1968.

Xue had been a teacher at Shanghai Jiaotong University, but was transferred to Changchun during the Cleansing of the Class Ranks to prepare for the establishment of the Changchun Automotive Tractor Institute. On the night that he was beaten to death, someone summoned him to the 'special investigation group' while he was eating dinner. Xue put down his bowl and went, and he never came home. The next morning, the school's 'propaganda team' told his wife that he was dead, and they closely questioned her about what she had fed him that night. 'Did you poison him?' They also arbitrarily alleged, 'Xue Shimao definitely had a major problem he wasn't willing to confess.'

Xue's wife began vomiting blood and spent more than a month in the hospital, after which she was sent to a village in the countryside. After the Cultural Revolution, she went to the Public Security Bureau and reported the case, and the medical examiner's report at the time showed that Xue Shimao had been beaten to death. It turned out that after Xue was summoned, the 'special investigation group' turned over a bench and told him to stand on the legs and then pushed him over, causing his skull to fracture on a radiator. His cap and clothing were covered with blood.

On the basis of this report, Xue's widow carried out further inquiries and learned that four students and a worker on the Mao Zedong Thought Propaganda Team had taken part in beating him. The worker had since been transferred to the Nubei No. 2 Automotive Factory and had joined the CCP, becoming director of the factory. She petitioned Beijing for two years, and eventually the killer was sentenced to three years in prison.

THE MEDICAL PROFESSION

People who received higher education overseas or from foreign-funded schools in China often came under suspicion for their 'foreign ties', especially during the Cleansing of the Class Ranks. The destructive effects of this paranoia were nowhere clearer than in the medical profession.

A physician's work goes beyond party, class, race and ideology and focuses on sick people. Everyone gets sick and needs a doctor's help at one time or another. No sane person would treat them as a hostile force. But in the Cultural Revolution, many doctors were struggled and persecuted.

Wang Zhongfang, the fifty-five-year-old head of the Internal Medicine Department at the Fujian Medical School Hospital, was placed under 'isolation and investigation' in July 1968 on allegations of 'illicit relations with a foreign country' and being a 'secret agent'. He died in custody on 28 April 1969. His family was informed that Wang had committed suicide, but they didn't believe it.

Wang Zhongfang was a graduate of one of China's best modern medical schools, Beijing Xiehe Medical School, which was founded by Americans. After the Pearl Harbor incident in 1941, when Japan and the US went to war, the Japanese authorities who had occupied Beijing seized the American doctors at Xiehe Hospital and put them in a concentration camp. Wang escaped to Tianjin and practised medicine in Bayannur, Inner Mongolia, before making his way back to his native Fujian and becoming the director of the Shengjiao Hospital in rural Majiang Township. This was a hospital run by Christian missionaries; Wang Zhongfang and his wife were both Christians.

Soon after the CCP took control of Fujian in August 1949, the government locked up Wang Zhongfang. The situation was that in 1949, the US Army shipped some Red Cross relief supplies to Fujian Harbour. Wang Zhongfang's hospital received part of the supplies, mainly milk powder, clothes and other such items, which it then distributed to needy local people. The new Communist government detained Wang and demanded that he hand over the relief supplies or their equivalent cash value. Wang was naturally unable to hand over the goods, because they'd already been distributed, nor did he have enough money to hand over the cash value. He was forced to request money from relatives in China and overseas to collect enough to gain his release.

Wang Zhongfang's experience was not unique. A large number of doctors were locked up, investigated and forced to write 'self-criticisms'. Through these intimidation tactics, the Communist government was able to take control of all hospitals. Leadership positions formerly held by doctors now went to Party members, significantly altering the hospital management system imported from the West.

Although there were changes at the management level, trained doctors still dealt with patients. In 1952, Wang Zhongfang became director of the Internal Medicine Department at the Fujian Medical School. The deputy director was the wife of the medical school's Party secretary, who was also Party secretary of the Internal Medicine Department. The CCP obviously wielded enormous power on the political side, but doctors who were not Party members still had status at the departmental level. This was the basic setup at hospitals before the Cultural Revolution.

In 1966, the Fujian Medical School's Party Committee tossed out doctors such as Wang Zhongfang and denounced them as 'reactionary academic authorities'. As Red Guard violence developed, Wang's home was ransacked and his head was shaved. In 1967, the violence abated somewhat. As a 'reactionary academic authority', Wang Zhongfang was sent to handle outpatient treatment as a kind of punishment; before that, directorate-level doctors normally handled seriously ill patients in the inpatient department. Wang Zhongfang 'did a booming business' in the outpatient clinic, with patients lining up to benefit from his expert skills. No patient is stupid enough to choose a doctor on the basis of whether or not they are a 'class enemy', nor would ordinary people have struggled well-trained doctors such as Wang Zhongfang if given the choice.

Wang was placed under 'isolation and investigation' in July 1968 and locked up in the Fujian Medical School's internal jail, which inflicted torture just as others did. The deputy director of the provincial health bureau reportedly found the torture so unbearable that he falsely implicated more than 200 people as members of an 'Anti-Communist National Salvation Army'. These people were promptly arrested and interrogated, and Wang Zhongfang was one of them. He was accused of an additional crime, 'illicit relations with a foreign country', because his elder brother lived in the US. Before and during the Cultural Revolution, ordinary people weren't even able to communicate with overseas relatives by mail or telephone, and there was no evidence that Wang Zhongfang had imperilled his country by assisting a foreign power. But the normal method during the Cultural Revolution was to lock a person up first and then look for evidence, and if evidence couldn't be found, to continue holding that person and interrogate them under torture. Tactics such as 'following the vine to find the melon', 'divide and demoralise' and 'crushing one by one' were also employed. After Wang Zhongfang was placed under 'isolation and investigation', the medical school's 'rebel faction' went to ransack his home in its staff residential quarters. The rebels ripped up his floor and dug down six feet deep without finding anything. Wang Zhongfang's home didn't even have a radio. But a radio was found in his neighbour's home, so the rebels announced that the neighbour was Wang's 'dispatcher' for espionage activities. An engineer was called over from the Fujian Broadcasting Station to appraise the radio and certify that it was a transmitter-receiver for espionage purposes. The engineer could see that it was an ordinary radio for civilian use, but refused to say anything. The people ransacking the homes refused to admit their error, so they sealed the radio with tape and left.

While Wang Zhongfang was locked up on the 'ox pen', his family didn't know where he was or even whether he was alive. After nine months, on 29 April 1969, they were suddenly notified that he had committed suicide. Wang's wife was summoned to where his body was being held, but wasn't allowed to examine it closely. She asked how he had killed himself, and the hospital authorities said he'd used a shaving razor to cut his carotid artery and had bled to death.

Wang Zhongfang's wife wanted to bury him, so the hospital authorities told her to buy a coffin, but she didn't have enough money. She was a homemaker, and her eldest son, a student at Tsinghua University, had only recently been assigned a job, while the other children were still in school. She quickly telephoned her eldest son in faraway Shenyang, and he sent all the money he had, 86 *yuan* and change, but soon after that, Wang's wife was notified that he had already been cremated. She had hoped to see her husband one last time, dressed and in a coffin, but in the end she was denied even that.

Wang Zhongfang's wife never believed that he killed himself. The couple were devout Christians, and Christians aren't allowed to commit suicide. Furthermore, Wang had already been held for nine months; if he was disposed to take this way out, why wouldn't he have done it much sooner? Why wouldn't he have left a letter for his wife and children? Why hadn't his wife been allowed to view his body up close? She was convinced that he'd been tortured to death. Nevertheless, Wang was accused of 'committing suicide to escape punishment', so his widow was unable to insist on an investigation.

After the Cultural Revolution, Wang Zhongfang was given a 'rehabilitation certificate', but the written record of the examination of his case wasn't released to his family, and no further investigation was carried out.

Wang Zhongfang was not the only person to fall victim to accusations of 'illicit relations with a foreign country'. His friend – a younger doctor in charge at the Fujian Medical School hospital, **Lin Qinglei** – was also implicated in the case, and like Wang, he was declared to have committed suicide.

Two other doctors implicated in the same case were also persecuted to death: **Liu Junhan**, a fifty-year-old neurosurgeon, had graduated from Fujian Medical School in 1949, when it was still called Xiehe Medical School, and was considered one of the best doctors in this demanding specialist field. After being placed under 'isolation and investigation', he leaped to his death on 6 May 1969. **Zheng Wenquan**, head of the hospital's dermatology department, who graduated from the Fujian Medical School in the 1940s, was declared to have committed suicide in spring 1969.

Another hospital worker was persecuted to death in connection with the same case, but unfortunately I've been unable to learn his name.

In 2002, a friend found out the telephone number of Dr Liu Junhan's wife, Dr Wang Xijuan, and called to ask her the date of Liu's death, how old he had been and other details. Dr Wang had retired some years earlier, but had been rehired on a part-time basis due to a shortage of medical personnel. Only after obtaining permission from the Fujian Medical School's Party Committee was she willing to provide this basic information about her husband, and nothing more. Dr Wang wasn't providing any information that could be considered controversial, but her response shows how the unfounded accusation of 'illicit relations with a foreign country' not only caused the deaths of five innocent people in 1968, but left scars on the survivors that still hadn't healed thirty-four years later.

I have been unable to determine how many others were persecuted to death at this medical school in connection with this case. In any event, China lost four experienced specialists at a time it lacked qualified medical professionals.

Wang Zhongfang's younger brother, Wang Yue, was head of the Fujian Microbiology Research Institute under the Chinese Academy of Sciences. He didn't die like his brother during the Cultural Revolution, but he was held in custody for several years before being 'liberated' in 1974. It's worth noting the officially used term 'liberated' in this context, because it implies that the Cultural Revolution authorities had the right to oppress people and then bestow liberation on them. No one dared question the term at the time or even afterwards. Rather, official newspapers continued to declare that victims should be grateful for being 'rehabilitated' and not ask who had created all this suffering in the first place.

Wang Yue was held in his work unit's 'ox pen' rather than a proper prison. One of his alleged crimes was 'illicit relations with a foreign country'; he had studied in the US in the 1940s under Selman Abraham Waksman. Born in the Ukraine, Waksman became a US citizen in 1916 and had been teaching at Rutgers University for many years. After more than a decade of research he discovered streptomycin, the first antibiotic found after penicillin and effective in treating diseases such as pulmonary tuberculosis. Waksman's discovery of other antibiotics that made a great contribution to treating human illness led to him being awarded the Nobel Prize in 1952.

Wang Yue was studying in the United States just as Waksman was making major progress with streptomycin, and after he obtained his PhD, he returned to China and served his country by engaging in the preparation of antibiotics. In the early 1960s, when China began manufacturing gentamicin, Wang wrote to his former teacher asking for help. Reportedly, he had obtained permission from the Fujian Provincial Party Committee before doing so; even before the Cultural Revolution, exchanging letters with Americans was a serious political problem, despite the Chinese Constitution ostensibly granting its people freedom of communication. Professor Waksman replied to his former student's letter, providing him with reports and information on manufacturing antibiotics. During the Cultural Revolution, Wang Yue's correspondence with Waksman was submitted as evidence of his 'illicit relations with a foreign country'.

Wang Yue was framed by his 'special investigation group' but the fact is that it was the Cultural Revolution's leaders who made 'illicit relations with a foreign country' a major target of attack. 'Certain Stipulations by the CCP Central Committee and State Council Regarding the Enhancement of Public Security Work During the Great Proletarian Cultural Revolution', promulgated on 13 January 1967,[26] and referred to during the Cultural Revolution as the 'Public Security Six Articles', included this crime in its first article. Such documents guided the Revolution and took precedence even over law. The persecution of the Wang brothers for 'illicit relations with a foreign country' occurred first and foremost because of Article 1 of this document.

Nowadays it would be impossible for anyone to follow the logic of the Cultural Revolution: How could an exchange of letters between Wang Yue and his American professor regarding the manufacturing of antibiotics constitute 'illicit relations with a foreign country'? First of all, the communication discussed science and technology, and had nothing to do with politics or state security. Second, the letters couldn't possibly involve 'selling

---

[26] Central Committee Document No. 19 [1967].

intelligence' or 'stealing state secrets' because Waksman knew much more about antibiotics than Wang did, and American medicine was far more advanced than China's, so it could only be Wang obtaining information from Waksman and not the other way round. Third, the result was that Wang developed a new antibiotic that brought enormous relief to millions of Chinese. His contribution should have been lauded and rewarded. But in fact, the very knowledge that earned Wang Yue's teacher a Nobel Prize turned Wang Yue into a victim of persecution.

The frenzied investigation and punishment for 'illicit relations with a foreign country' was meant to cut China off from the rest of the world and keep the Chinese in ignorance of how people were living in other societies, especially those with better social systems. Rather than learning from or introducing technology that had already been developed in foreign countries to improve people's lives, the Cultural Revolution attacked modern medicine, struggled doctors and forced hospitals to leave cities on the pretext of 'preventing a restoration of capitalism'. In the new society these leaders planned, ordinary people could only enjoy treatment from minimally trained 'barefoot doctors', returning medicine to the pre-scientific era. The persecution of physicians occurred against this background.

Wang Zhongfang's classmate at Beijing Xiehe Medical School, Zhang Anlang, a doctor in Xiamen, was also persecuted during the Cultural Revolution, although I've been unable to learn the details. From what I've been able to determine, every hospital had doctors who were struggled and put under 'isolation and investigation', many of them being persecuted to death. These crimes have never been clearly described or recorded.

Wang Zhongfang died, but his younger brother survived. In 1985, Wang Yue went to the United States and visited his teacher's son. Waksman had died in 1968 at the age of eighty while Wang Yue was locked up and unable to express his condolences for the former teacher whose letters had resulted in his persecution.

Wang Xiongfei, a doctor at the Shanghai Pudong Liuli Centre Public Health Clinic, was one of three people in his family who killed themselves after his son, Wang Zude, also a doctor, was imprisoned in 1968 for a remark he made about Mao's health. Wang Zude was sentenced to twelve years in prison as a 'current counter-revolutionary' because in a private conversation he had said, 'Mao Zedong had a stroke and asked a famous Shanghai doctor, Lu Shouyan, to give him acupuncture and moxibustion.' Because of this, Wang Xiongfei was also put under long-term 'isolation and investigation', and after learning in 1969 that his wife and young daughter had committed suicide, he hanged himself in his isolation cell. Wang's wife, **Zhang Qixing**, was also a doctor.

Wang's son, Wang Zude, was admitted to the Shanghai No. 1 Medical School in 1955, and the 1957 Anti-Rightist Campaign occurred while he was still a naïve eighteen-year-old student. As a result of some innocuous comments, he was designated a 'marginal Rightist'. When graduation came, his Rightist classmates were all sent to 'reform through labour'. As merely 'problematic', Wang Zude was assigned a job with the Tongji University clinic. Knowing he was on the register of disreputable people, Wang worked conscientiously to be the best doctor he could possibly be.

When the Cultural Revolution began, Wang Zude was denounced as a 'Rightist who had slipped through the net', and his home was ransacked. Prior to 1949, Wang Xiongfei and his wife had run a private clinic. Private clinics were prohibited from the 1950s onwards, so they went to work for state-owned hospitals. Wang Xiongfei was renowned as a brilliant and energetic practitioner, and he also served as a delegate to the County People's Congress and People's Political Consultative Conference. But the new Revolution required new enemies, and after the *People's Daily* published its editorial in June 1966 on 'sweeping away all ox demons and snake spirits', Wang Xiongfei's age and position resulted in his being included in the first batch of targets for attack. His son was added later.

Given that Wang Zude and both of his parents were doctors, Wang had a lot of contacts in medical circles, and through the grapevine he heard that Mao had had a stroke in the 1950s, and that he had asked a famous Shanghai doctor, Lu Shouyan, to go to Beijing to give him acupuncture treatment. He mentioned this to his younger brother, who was a mathematics student at Fudan University, and his brother told friends about it. After this matter was 'exposed', Wang Zude's brother was labelled a 'reactionary student' and Wang Zude came under investigation for a 'venomous attack on the Great Leader Chairman Mao'. Big-character posters were put up at Tongji University, and in January 1968 he was locked up on campus.

The number of people held in 'isolation' steadily increased until two floors of Wang Zude's prison-building were filled. Li Guohao, who after the Cultural Revolution became the university's president, was also held there.

At that time, Tongji University was under the control of a Revolutionary Committee made up of representatives from the military, 'revolutionary cadres' and 'revolutionary masses'. The first thing Revolutionary Committees did was to launch 'struggle against the enemy', which provided more systemisation and authority to the extrajudicial imprisonment and even killing of people that had been going on since 1966. While Wang Zude was in 'isolation' he was interrogated almost daily, accompanied by beatings and humiliation. It was mainly students who were punishing him, along with some people from the clinic. Wang calmly faced his 'problems' and admitted to saying what he'd said, hoping that once he'd clarified everything, the process could be concluded one way or another.

Instead, the people dealing with him took the opportunity to launch a 'counter-revolutionary case' to earn themselves merit in the 'struggle against the enemy'. At that time, whenever a 'class enemy' or 'counter-revolutionary clique' was nabbed, banners would go up all over the school celebrating the 'Great Victory of Mao Zedong Thought'. The special investigation groups ceaselessly made demands that were impossible to satisfy, requiring Wang Zude to produce weapons and transmitters, and going after his entire family. People from Tongji University ransacked Wang Zude's home several times without finding anything. They called his family a 'little Taiwan' and an espionage organisation. They tied up Wang Xiongfei and locked him up in a nearby room; father and son were not allowed to see or talk to each other, but they could hear each other cry out as they were beaten. This was even more agonising to Wang Zude.

By September 1968, Wang Zude had been in 'isolation' for eight months. He was constantly struggled and beaten, spending hours with a heavy placard hung around his neck as he stood in the 'aeroplane' position. In all this time, he hadn't been able to see any friends or family members, only the people interrogating or struggling him. The only voice he heard from a family member was his father's cries of pain while being beaten. Physically and psychologically devastated, he lost hope and tried to hang himself in his isolation cell, but the rope broke, and he survived.

During this time of despair and anger, Wang Zude decided he would rather die than keep living this way, so he did two particular things – in one of his 'confessions' he wrote a quote from Bai Juyi's famous poem, 'Song of Eternal Sorrow': 'Heaven and Earth shall all pass away; Only my sorrow will forever stay.' Writing these words was construed as a kind of resistance, so he was beaten even more savagely. After that, he took a portion of his spectacle frame (which had been broken while he was being beaten) and used it to scribble on the wall. Then he called in the special investigation group and said he had written 'Down with Mao Zedong', hoping to be locked up in prison and executed rather than being kept at the school. On that basis, the Tongji University authorities reported him to the Shanghai Public Security Bureau and had him arrested. After his arrest was announced at a struggle rally at the Tongji University auditorium in September 1968, Wang Zude was taken to the Shanghai No. 1 Detention Centre, arriving with a crippled leg and a body covered with wounds. He was thirty years old.

Wang Zude didn't yet know what price his family had paid for his remark about Mao's health. His younger sister, **Wang Zuhua**, a second-year student of Chinese literature at Shanghai Normal College, had been denounced as a 'reactionary student' because of him. Unable to bear the humiliation, she threw herself in front of a speeding car. She was twenty years old.

Wang's fifty-eight-year-old mother, **Zhang Qixing**, was beaten in her home by Red Guards from Tongji University. Unable to bear the torment of a son and husband in 'isolation', her second son labelled a 'reactionary student' and her daughter's suicide, Zhang Qixing poisoned herself to death. With no one else at home, her body wasn't discovered until several days later.

Meanwhile, Wang Xiongfei had been moved from Tongji University to continue his isolation at the public health clinic where he worked. He was completely cut off from the outside world and had no idea what had happened to his family. One day in 1969, a person he didn't know happened to mention that a mother and daughter living in his street had killed themselves. It was only then that Wang Xiongfei learned that the wife and daughter he'd been longing for all this time were dead, and that his eldest son had been arrested. Soon afterwards, he hanged himself.

While Wang Zude was being held on the second floor of the No. 1 Detention Centre, Fudan University professor **Wang Zaoshi** was being held on the first floor, and eventually died there. Cries rang through the prison at night as people were tortured. Wang Zude's trial proceeded rapidly because he just wanted to end it all, and he admitted to everything he was accused of, including the most heinous of all crimes, writing reactionary slogans and making a 'venomous attack against the Great Leader'. After being held in the detention centre for two months, Wang was sentenced to twelve years in prison for the crime of 'current counter-revolution'.

After being tried and sent to prison, Wang Zude was finally allowed family visits, and that's when he learned of the tragic end his family had met. His wife had said she would wait for him as long as it took, but when their children, one and seven years old, began to be victimised because of him, his wife asked for a divorce, and he immediately agreed.

Wang was sent to Shanghai's Tilanqiao Prison, where he was held on the fifth floor of Cell Block No. 3, which was set aside for counter-revolutionaries. The prison authorities allowed him to provide medical treatment to other prisoners. He registered the names and illnesses of the prisoners, more than 10,000 'counter-revolutionaries' in Cell Block No. 3 alone. Many counter-revolutionaries at Tilanqiao Prison were sent on to other places such as Qinghai, Xinjiang and Anhui, hundreds or a thousand at a time. Wang expected similar treatment, but perhaps because he'd made a good impression on the prison authorities, he was allowed to stay at Tilanqiao.

Wang Zude provided emergency treatment to many prisoners. Some had attempted suicide after being beaten by other prisoners at the instigation of prison guards. Some people went mad, but they were accused of faking it and were beaten all the same. Some people were locked in prison cells just a metre square, with rubber walls that insulated noise. Some were made to wear headgear with only eye holes, so they couldn't cry out when they were beaten. Wang Zude did his best to treat them all, even giving mouth-to-mouth resuscitation when necessary, although he was himself in utter despair.

In 1974, Wang's sentence was reduced by six years, which was extremely rare. But he still wore the 'counter-revolutionary' cap, and the instrument and meter factory where he was sent to work was a labour camp, with some of its workers being released prisoners like Wang who were given little more freedom than serving prisoners.

Mao died in 1976, and two-and-a-half years later, in January 1979, Wang Zude was rehabilitated as a 'case of injustice'. His father, mother and sister were also posthumously rehabilitated. A rehabilitation meeting was held for Wang at the Tongji University auditorium where eleven years earlier he'd been denounced and arrested. He went back to work at the university clinic, but he had no family left.

Why did Wang Xiongfei's family suffer this tragic fate? It was no secret that Mao had suffered a stroke in the 1950s – while attending the International Congress of Communist and Workers' Parties in Moscow in November 1957, Mao mentioned it to explain why he wasn't able to stand while giving his speech.

Persecution for 'venomous attack' based on the most imaginary slights was all too common. A young English teacher at Peking University, Zheng Peidi, was savagely beaten and humiliated and held in the university's makeshift jail for nearly a year merely because she'd told a roommate that Mao's wife, Jiang Qing, had once cohabitated with her cousin. An inmate at Hunan Province's Cendan labour reform farm was a peasant surnamed Fu whose first son was born when he was forty. In his joy, Fu had hugged his baby and sung the anthem 'The East Is Red', but changed the words 'China has produced a Mao Zedong' to 'My family has produced a Fu Maomao.' For that, he was imprisoned for seven years.

What harm did any of these words actually do to Mao? But for the sake of establishing someone's paramount power, Wang Zude and other ordinary people suffered such horrendous pain and calamity. The acupuncturist who had treated Mao, **Lu Shouyan**, director of the Shanghai Institute of Traditional Chinese Medicine, was also persecuted to death during the Cultural Revolution. Placed under 'isolation and investigation' in March 1969, he was tortured into giving a confession. Lu leaped to his death on 27 April 1969, aged sixty.

What I've recorded here is just a broad outline of what the Wang family suffered, and even these bare facts forced me to stop several times as I typed, too distressed to go on. The truth is that the physical and emotional torment that Wang Zude suffered far exceeded what is described here. His story calls to mind the Russian classic *Doctor Zhivago*, by Boris Pasternak. Compared with the tragedy of Dr Wang Zude, the poems and letters Dr Zhivago left behind, and the brother who preserved them for him, seem like a luxury the Chinese can never emulate. It can only be hoped that someday Dr Wang Zude will be able to write about his journey as a witness to history and humanity.

Liu Hao, a forty-two-year-old orthopaedist at the Beijing Army General Hospital, was placed under 'isolation and investigation' in 1968 on accusations of being a secret agent. He was found hanged while in custody on 31 May that year leaving behind five children ranging in age from three to fifteen years. After learning of her son's death, Liu's aged mother in Shandong killed herself.

The Beijing Army General Hospital, now known as the Military General Hospital of Beijing, was located in Dongcheng District. Liu Hao was a skilled orthopaedist who had been transferred to Beijing from Tianjin, and senior military officers would sometimes send a car to fetch him to treat their ailments at home.

When the Cleansing of the Class Ranks began in 1968, Liu was denounced, savagely beaten and then exposed as a 'secret agent' and 'plucked out' for investigation during a rally at the hospital. Liu's wife, the head nurse of the hospital's department of gynaecology and obstetrics, was forced to take part in the struggle rally.

Liu Hao was locked up in one of a row of sheds the hospital used for that purpose. One day, Liu's wife saw several robust young soldiers standing in a circle near the sheds and assaulting an elderly orthopaedist, **Shen Tianjue**, whose face and neck were already swollen from the beating. Two female cadres came over and said, 'Stop or you'll beat him to death!' Shen Tianjue killed himself soon after that.

Liu Hao's family lived in the hospital's residential quarters, but under 'isolation and investigation' he wasn't allowed to see his family. A few days before Liu died, his fifteen-year-old eldest son was walking through the hospital and suddenly saw his father, who said, 'I miss Xiaoliang. Bring him over to see me.' Xiaoliang was Liu's three-year-old youngest son. The older boy hurried home and fetched his little brother, never guessing that it was the last time he would ever see his father.

Liu Hao was found hanged in a dressing room that contained sheets and other items. A sheet had been torn into pieces to form the noose, combined with a shoe lace to make it long enough. Liu's wife insisted on seeing his body and noticed that his hands were dark blue. She suspected that someone had tied his hands and strangled him, and then made it look as if he'd hung himself. She never believed that the man who had so loved life and his children would kill himself. She sought out a senior administrator and asked 'Can someone be hanged with a shoelace?' The administrator replied 'Why not?' She said, 'You try to hang me with a shoelace.' But no one paid her any attention, and she loathed those 'political and ideological work cadres' from then on.

Liu Hao was extremely fond of his five children and had spent 400 *yuan* to buy a camera to take photos of them. He had taken his family out for Mongolian hotpot on snowy days, and to North Lake Park and the Summer Palace on Sundays. After he died, his wife was left to support the family on her single salary, sometimes foraging next to a vegetable cellar for cabbage stalks meant to feed chickens. When her youngest child was six years old, he asked her why other children had daddies but he didn't. She told him, 'Your dad went to the moon.' She spent as much time as she could with the children when she finished work, doing her best to meet their psychological and material needs. Overwork and pressure resulted in her becoming semi-paralysed and bedridden from 1977 onwards.

Liu Hao's mother, living in their native village in Zhanhua County, Shandong Province, was so distressed when she heard of her son's death that she poisoned herself with pesticide. Her family didn't dare tell other villagers why she'd killed herself, because Liu Hao had been labelled a counter-revolutionary and secret agent, and killing oneself over such a person would be considered a great crime. They could only lie and say it was because she couldn't get along with her daughter-in-law.

Liu's ashes were taken back to his home village and placed next to the family tomb, but the family didn't dare erect a gravestone for him. After the Cultural Revolution, when Liu was rehabilitated, the hospital wanted to hold a ceremony to lay his remains to rest, but when his family went to the grave to fetch his ashes, they couldn't find them, so they placed some soil in the urn and took it back to Beijing.

After Liu Hao was rehabilitated in 1978, his family was paid compensation of 4,000 *yuan*, and the children who were still too young to work were paid 20 *yuan* per month. Now his children are grown, but they've never forgotten their father. Beginning in 1995, on the anniversary of his death, his wife put up his photo and burned incense in front of it along with food and flowers. The children also came home and bowed before their father's portrait.

Han Guoyuan, a dentist at the Guiyang Aluminium Company Hospital, graduated from the West China Medical Centre of Sichuan University in 1950. During the Cultural Revolution, he was brutally struggled as a 'reactionary academic authority'. He fled Guiyang in 1967 and hid in his younger sister's home in Changsha, Hunan Province, but fearing that people would pursue him from Guiyang, he decided to leave China. His sister's daughter, a secondary school student, fled with him. They were apprehended in northeastern China, after which Han was executed, and his niece was sentenced to ten years in prison. His brother-in-law, Dr **Lou Shouping**, was accused of being an accessory to the crime and sentenced to fifteen years in prison, dying in a labour camp in 1974.

Lou Shouping, born in 1904, was an anatomy instructor at the Hunan College of Traditional Chinese Medicine. Lou graduated from the Xiangya Medical School in Changsha, Hunan Province, in 1938 as a surgeon. He was designated a Rightist in 1957 and was then seized and struggled during the Cultural Revolution.

In 1998, I talked with someone who had been persecuted during the Cultural Revolution, and he showed me material he'd written about another victim, hoping I would copy-edit it for him. His essay entitled 'Medical Professor Lou Shouping' was so well-written that it required no polishing or editing. I passed on this essay to exiled dissident Su Xiaokang, who published it in his online journal, *Minzhu Zhongguo* (No. 4, 1999). It was subsequently reposted in another online magazine.

The writer of this article had been a young student during the Cultural Revolution, and had been imprisoned for 'counter-revolutionary crime'. He came to know Lou Shouping in the labour reform camp. By then, Lou was sixty-seven years old, and given the poor nutrition and arduous labour in the camp, combined with his mental torments, he died after serving only four years of his fifteen-year sentence. One of the reasons the article was so moving was that it realistically recorded what happened, including the writer's own experience, but the writer felt compelled to use a pseudonym.

I understand the pain of the man who preferred to use the pen name 'Jiang Yan' when writing of his experience. The victims have no rights and no power, and writing their stories under their own names exposes them to powerful people who can make trouble for them whilst causing no harm to the perpetrators. Remembering and writing about the obscure death of someone encountered in a labour camp is a noble act, yet the writer feels compelled to conceal his own name.

Even so, 'Jiang Yan' only came to know Lou Shouping during the last few years of his life. Prisoners weren't allowed to talk about their 'cases', so in order to further understand Lou's story, it was necessary to find someone who knew him before he went to prison. Furthermore, both Jiang Yan and I had a deep desire to find out what happened to Lou Shouping's daughter, who might still be alive if she survived her ten years in prison. I therefore kept waiting after the posting of Jiang Yan's essay on the Internet, hoping that a reader who knew Lou or his daughter might come forward as Jiang Yan had done so that these two people wouldn't become lost to history. Finally, after two years, an email arrived.

Although websites such as *Minzhu Zhongguo* can carry information around the world in a second, the 'Great Firewall' blocks them from most readers in China. Consequently, although Lou Shouping's story was published on the Internet in 1999, it followed a very long and tortuous course and passed through many hands before reaching the appropriate individuals in China. Likewise, the email responding to it went through many twists and turns before arriving on my computer screen. I can only be thankful for each of the people who played a role in this process, which remains so slow even in the era of the Information Highway. Here is what I learned as a result of this two-year wait:

Lou Shouping grew up in poverty, and his education was a rather complicated process. The Xiangya Medical School from which he graduated in 1938 was China's first modern medical school, founded by Yale University, and it provided systematic and rigorous training for students who had to study for seven years in order to graduate. After graduation, Lou Shouping became a surgeon and director of Changsha Hospital. He then returned to the medical school as a professor of anatomy after 1949. He had no particular interest in politics and didn't belong to any political party.

When Lou Shouping was designated a Rightist in 1957, it wasn't because he believed the lies the authorities told about 'making suggestions to the Party' and 'helping the Party rectify its work style'. He was in fact a very cautious, even timid, man. When Hunan's provincial Party secretary, Zhou Xiaozhou, called on everyone to 'freely air their views' and criticise the Party, Lou Shouping told others not to do it and to be careful about what they said. He wrote a doggerel poem to a friend that contained the line: 'When in suspicious surroundings, say little; when not among your own, remain wary.' The meaning was obvious: don't speak out or 'make suggestions'. But later that doggerel was passed on to the leader of Lou's work unit and became 'evidence' for designating him as a Rightist. The leaders of the Anti-Rightist Campaign said, 'You said it yourself: you're not among "your own," so you must be a Rightist.'

After being designated a Rightist, Lou Shouping was demoted and transferred to the Hengyang Medical School. As punishments of Rightists went, this was relatively lenient, but it deprived him of the opportunity to serve the ill. Eventually Hengyang Medical School was disbanded, and Lou was transferred to the Hunan College of Traditional Chinese Medicine, where he taught anatomy.

Lou Shouping's brother-in-law, Han Guoyuan, was also a doctor, having graduated in 1950 from the Sichuan West China University of Medical

Sciences as a student of dentistry. Like Xiangya Medical School, this was a modern institution along Western lines that required eight years of study. In 1949, someone advised Han Guoyuan to go to Hong Kong, but he still had one more year of medical school before graduating and didn't want to give up his degree. He very reasonably thought, in any case, that dentistry was unrelated to politics, and that regardless of the social system, there would always be a need for dentists.

After graduating from medical school, Han Guoyuan was assigned a position at the Guiyang Central Aluminium Company. He had been an outstanding student, and after a year of work, his excellent performance put him an entire grade higher than his classmates, in spite of his 'political factors'. Han Guoyuan was unmarried, and he had only one younger sister, who was Lou Shouping's wife.

Once the Cultural Revolution began, Lou Shouping had 'reactionary academic authority' added to his 'Rightist' label, and he was denounced at the Hunan College of Traditional Chinese Medicine. Over at the Guiyang Central Aluminium Company, Han Guoyuan was likewise struggled as a reactionary academic authority.

We don't know what kind of torments Han Guoyuan suffered, because I have yet to find anyone who knew him then, but we do know there was a great deal of Cultural Revolution violence in Guiyang. One interviewee who lived in there at the time said that Red Guards from the Tsinghua University Affiliated Secondary School arrived in summer 1966 during the 'great revolutionary networking' and beat up many people at the provincial cultural bureau, including performers in its Peking Opera troupe. The director of the cultural bureau's nursery, a middle-aged mother of four who was not a primary target of the Cultural Revolution, had her head shaved and was beaten savagely with Red Guard belt buckles. With the Red August violence of Beijing imported to Guiyang, Han Guoyuan fled the province in 1967 and went to his sister's home in Changsha.

When Han Guoyuan arrived in Changsha, he found his sister's family in a similar predicament. He also knew that his personal dossier included his 'social relations' – his work unit would quickly trace him to his sister's home. If he were caught, he'd have the crime of 'taking flight' added to his offences, causing him even more suffering. For this reason, he didn't dare stay long in Changsha. His niece, Lou Shouping's daughter, wanted to leave with him. At first they thought they could just lie low, but in fact there was no way to hide, so they decided to find a way to leave China, which in fact was the only way of escaping the persecution of the Cultural Revolution.

Lou Shouping's daughter, Lou Yufang, was a lower-secondary school student at the time. She went with her uncle to Guangzhou and then to the northeast. They crossed over into North Korea, but were sent back and arrested on charges of 'betraying the country and going over to the enemy', for which Han Guoyuan was sentenced to death and Lou Yufang to ten years in prison.

Meanwhile, Lou Shouping, who had never left home, was taken into custody. After being detained for two years, he was sentenced on 27 September 1970 to fifteen years in prison as a 'current counter-revolutionary' for allegedly assisting Han Guoyuan and Lou Yufang in their crime.

1970 was the year of the One Strike and Three Antis campaign, which specifically targeted counter-revolutionaries. Following the dictates of CCP Central Committee documents and under the leadership of the newly constituted Revolutionary Committees, every locality arrested large numbers of counter-revolutionaries. The main crimes for which people were executed or handed lengthy prison terms were 'venomously attacking the Great Leader Chairman Mao' and 'betraying the country and going over to the enemy'.

Lou Shouping was tried in Changsha on 27 September 1970, in the kind of mass public trial that was emblematic of the Cultural Revolution. It did not involve evidence or defence or state the law on which the prosecution was based, and in being carried out before thousands of people, its main purpose was to intimidate the masses. After the public trial, the convicted individual was paraded through the streets in the back of a truck so that even more people could be intimidated. Lou Shouping was loaded into the truck with a placard around his neck identifying him as a 'current counter-revolutionary'. His family members weren't allowed to attend the 'public trial', but when they learned the route of the parade, they waited in the doorway of the Xinhua Bookshop in Huang Xing Road to watch him pass. It was the last Lou Shouping's family ever saw of him.

After his trial, sixty-six-year-old Lou Shouping was taken to the Cendan Labour Reform Farm on the Hunan–Hubei border. Prisoners never had a full meal at the labour camps, and they were forced to engage in extremely heavy labour. Lou managed to endure these conditions for four years before he finally died. His fellow prisoner 'Jiang Yan' saw something of Lou's life in the *laogai* camp and witnessed his death.

After Lou Shouping was imprisoned, his family lost their main source of income. Lou's wife was unemployed, and there were three young children left after the eldest daughter was imprisoned. There was no way to make money through temporary work during the Cultural Revolution without being accused of 'capitalism'. Lou Shouping's family therefore suffered not only discrimination as a 'counter-revolutionary's family' but also extreme financial distress. There was a period of three months during which the family didn't have money to buy even the cheapest vegetables.

In the labour camp, each prisoner was given 1.50 *yuan* to buy soap, cigarettes and other items, but because the quality and quantity of the prison meals were so poor and the work so arduous, prisoners more often used this pocket money to buy extra food. The lucky ones had family outside who sent them food or money to improve their living conditions, but Lou Shouping sent his own pocket money back to his wife and children.

Lou Shouping's youngest daughter was born in the early 1960s and could not even remember her father being arrested. As the daughter of a counter-revolutionary, she grew up under the worst possible conditions in terms of nutrition and mental stress, and never grew taller than 4'8". Eventually she became deranged and killed herself.

Lou Yufang was less than eighteen years old when she was sentenced. She was sent to Hunan's Chaling Labour Reform Farm and then released after serving her ten-year sentence. After the Cultural Revolution, she became a custodian at a hospital. She worked hard to educate herself and was finally admitted to a medical school. She graduated in the 1990s and became a doctor of acupuncture and moxibustion at the Changsha No. 4 Hospital.

It is my hope to some day interview Lou Yufang. Stories like hers should not be forgotten; they help us understand the world and the many unreasonable and unjust things that can happen to people. There is an evil force in the world that ran amok during the Cultural Revolution and destroyed countless lives. Lou Yufang's story can also serve as a testament to the power of life, and help us see that with enough effort in a time of relative peace a person can create a decent life for herself.

My even greater hope is that one day people can freely write the history of the Cultural Revolution. We can't change the past or bring victims back to life, but at least we can write their stories and declare that killing them was a crime. We can loudly proclaim historical truth, speak of the persecution of ourselves and others, of our physical and spiritual suffering, without concealing our names, and without fearing the threat of evildoers. Let us work towards that end.

The following are excerpts from Jiang Yan's essay, 'Professor of Medicine Lou Shouping':

> In September 1971, I was sent to Hunan's Cendan Farm to serve out my sentence for 'current counter-revolutionary crime'. This farm was situated in the Changde region, and in fact was an island encircled by rain pools and springs, which had been reclaimed and cultivated through years of labour by prisoners. It consisted of 51,000 *mu* of cultivated land and 18,000 *mu* of freshwater aquaculture surface. In 1971, about 10,000 current and former prisoners were working on the farm, with eight agricultural production brigades and subordinate aquatic farming teams, machine maintenance teams, transport teams, a processing plant, hospital, school for cadre dependents

and an educated youth farm. It was one of many labour farms under the jurisdiction of Hunan's provincial public security bureau, and the leading body was the Farming Department Military Control Commission.

I was assigned to the No. 4 unit of the No. 1 production brigade. I remember that after work on my second day at the farm, I heard someone in the prison cell speaking with a northern accent. As a northerner, I hadn't heard that sound in a long time, so I went over to introduce myself. The speaker was an old man whose hair was almost completely grey, not tall but solidly built. He wore a pair of tattered black cotton trousers, and on his clothing was stamped 'labour reform prisoner' in big yellow characters. He wore a pair of mud-caked plastic-soled shoes of the kind sold in the labour teams, and a black cotton hat that had been repeatedly mended, but the eyes behind his black-rimmed glasses looked kind and intelligent.

In the course of conversation, I learned that this old man's name was Lou Shouping, that before his arrest he'd taught at the Hunan College of Traditional Chinese Medicine, and that he was a native of northern Anhui Province, born in 1904 and therefore sixty-seven years old at the time. I asked him if he was able to tolerate the heavy labour, and he said that his team was made up of old and sickly people, making him one of the healthiest among them. I asked about his family, and he just shook his head and didn't answer. I didn't understand at the time how a university professor could become a counter-revolutionary. Constrained by the rule against 'discussing each other's cases', I didn't ask what he'd been sentenced for and only later found out from another prisoner...

Because Lou Shouping had told his daughter, 'Find a way to save yourself,' he was sentenced to fifteen years in prison for 'abetting a defection to the enemy', which is how he came to the Cenli Labour Reform Farm. His daughter was only seventeen years old, so she was sent to Hunan's Chaling County Labour Reform Tea Plantation for women and juveniles. A prisoner who had once been held there had seen the girl.

After hearing about his tragic experience, I naturally greeted him whenever I saw him, and exchanged a few words with him as we went out and came back from work, hoping to share a little of his grief. His group of old and infirm was usually sent to the work shed to dry grain and cotton, sort cotton and other tasks that didn't require much strength, but the work days were very long, and they came back later than us. When I went back to the cell, I always saw him busily drying grain or repairing tools or coiling rope. Some prisoners joked with him, 'Old Lou, why are you working so hard? Don't you want to get out of here alive?' He just smiled and kept at his work. He later told me that if he was idle, he became agitated, but if he kept busy, he stayed calmer.

Our No. 1 production brigade was located at the south end of the Cenli Farm, and the prison cells were enclosed by a tall, electrified wire fence with guard towers in the southwest and northeast corners where armed police stood sentry day and night. There were four blocks of cells in the enclosure for four units, units 1 and 4 designated for 'counter-revolutionaries' and units 2 and 3 for 'criminals', with a total of more than 1,000 prisoners.

Our No. 4 unit was also called the 'agricultural science unit', handling rice paddies and cotton and managing plant breeding for the whole farm. There were eleven production teams under it, labelled A, B, C, D and so on, divided up according to the working strength of the prisoners and the food rations, referred to by the euphemism of 'socialist distribution according to work done'. The prisoners' food was mainly a set amount of rice, cabbage and turnips, 150 grams of meat per month and 150 grams of vegetable oil, but we were forced to engage in heavy labour ten to fourteen hours a day, so we were always underfed, and our stomachs rumbled with hunger all day long.

For the autumn harvest, Lou Shouping's group of old people in their sixties and seventies was sent to the fields to cut and gather the rice. When their backs hurt, they were allowed to kneel or sit to do their work... On the first day of the harvest, the leader of the No. 4 unit, Tang Denghe, came down to the fields to inspect the work. This man was the head of the farm's rebel faction, which had taken over control of the farm, so people called him 'Commander Tang'. He was a cruel and merciless man who was always berating and beating the prisoners. When he saw Lou Shouping and the other old prisoners kneeling and sitting as they worked, he immediately yelled, 'You bunch of old geezers, you were always sloughing off while you were free and you haven't even tried to reform in the labour team, working as little as you can! When do you ever see poor and lower-middle peasants sitting so comfortably while cutting rice?' That night, Commander Tang scolded the old prisoners again. When there was an interval for discussion, I consoled Lou Shouping by saying, 'He's just saying that to scare us younger prisoners,' and told him not to take it to heart. He smiled bitterly, 'I know.' A few days later, Commander Tang saw he really couldn't get any more work out of these old prisoners, so he sent them back to drying grain.

... In April 1973, our unit's doctor was dismissed for stealing the prisoners' pocket money, and the unit decided to have Lou Shouping replace him. The prisoners didn't have a proper clinic, and all of the medical supplies were stuffed into a small chest. In fact, Lou Shouping had previously served as the prisoners' doctor and had carried that medicine chest around on his back. But one day, when there was an electrical stoppage and oil lamps were being used, and someone asked for belladonna for stomach pains, Lou Shouping's poor eyesight, combined with the poor lighting, led him to misread a label and giving the patient mercurochrome instead. For this he'd been dismissed and ridiculed, and the cadres had organised several denunciations of him as a 'reactionary academic authority'.

Now that he'd been made the prisoners' doctor again, Lou Shouping was very cautious, and he made a space in the storeroom for prisoners' belongings where he separated his medicines into categories and arranged them tidily so he wouldn't grab the wrong one. When he saw me looking sallow and asked the reason, I said I'd contracted acute jaundice while in college and it had never been fully cured before the various political campaigns had started and I'd landed in prison. Lou Shouping remembered this, and in a free moment gave me a full medical exam, saying there was tenderness and enlargement around my liver, and he pushed unsuccessfully for me to be sent to the farm's hospital for an examination. I wrote to my mother about Lou's diagnosis, and she wrote to the farm demanding improvements in my living and working conditions and also started regularly sending me nutritional supplements, which saved my life.

As mentioned before, Lou Shouping had to keep busy or else he'd become agitated and unable to sleep. Beginning in summer 1973, every night after 'political study', he'd be up writing under the light, and several times when I got up in the middle of the night to use the toilet, I saw him still there writing, unable to sleep. He never told me what he was writing, but a cadre later told me that Lou was a Christian, and part of what he was writing was religious knowledge and the perplexity of life, and another part was his worries about China's future following the 'Lin Biao Incident'. I don't know what ever happened to his writings.

One day at the beginning of 1974, the weather was very cold. Cenli Farm was surrounded by water in the winter, and the prisoners always had to use straw rope to tighten their padded jackets around them to keep out the cold. But that day after work, I saw Lou Shouping in the cell washing himself with cold water. I knew he had insisted on washing in cold water all his life, even in midwinter, but that day was especially cold and windy, and I went up to him and said I was afraid he'd catch the flu. He smiled and said, 'Don't worry, I'm used to it.'

But in fact he did catch the flu the next day. I went to see him after work, and he was lying in bed. He said he'd taken aspirin and I needn't worry. That night he suddenly took a turn for the worse and fell into a coma, and after they took him to the hospital he never came back. The production brigade's cadre doctor said he's died from a 'sudden stroke'.

A year after Lou Shouping died, the No. 1 production brigade sent over a new cadre doctor surnamed Nie who had been a student of Lou Shouping's at the Hunan College of Traditional Chinese Medicine. He said Professor Lou had been a very learned man and a vivid lecturer, modest and amiable, and one of the college's most respected and beloved professors.

Twenty-five years have passed since then, and I'm over fifty now. Sparing no effort, I went from being a young labour reform prisoner at Cenli Farm to getting my PhD in the United States. Whenever I spot a grey-haired Asian professor here on my campus across the ocean, I can't help but think of my old companion in hardship, Lou Shouping, and his northern Anhui accent seems to hover near my ear... May he rest in peace!

Han Guangdi, a dentist living in Fulin Town, Hanyuan County, Sichuan Province, was arrested in the summer of 1968 for remarks he made about a mango that Mao presented to the Capital Workers and Peasants Mao Zedong Thought Propaganda Team. After being locked up for an extended period, he was sentenced to death in 1970 for 'current counter-revolutionary crimes' and executed on the outskirts of Fulin Town.

The 7 August 1968 edition of the *People's Daily* published a headline taking up nearly half of its front page:

> The Greatest Concern, the Greatest Trust, the Greatest Support and the Greatest Encouragement
>> The Heart of Our Great Leader Chairman Mao Is Ever Linked to the Masses
>>> Chairman Mao Presents a Valuable Gift from Foreign Friends to the Capital Workers and Peasants Mao Zedong Thought Propaganda Team

A summary followed in bold print:

> The Great Leader Chairman Mao personally presented this mango to commemorate the red-letter day of the second anniversary of Chairman Mao's 'Bombard the Headquarters' big-character poster and the 'Resolution of the Central Committee of the Chinese Communist Party Regarding the Proletarian Great Cultural Revolution.' Once this happy news circulated, the masses' cries of 'Long live Chairman Mao!' echoed through the heavens for a long time.
>
> The vast revolutionary masses expressed their limitless loyalty to Chairman Mao, and their even closer unity with the proletarian

headquarters led by Chairman Mao and Vice-chairman Lin, their united will, united pace and united action, resolutely and unflinchingly implementing Chairman Mao's newest directive, resolutely criticising the reactionary 'polycentrism' and promptly seeing through and smashing the schemes and intrigues of a smattering of class enemies vainly attempting to sabotage Chairman Mao's proletarian headquarters, thereby seizing total victory for the Great Proletarian Cultural Revolution.

This is the mango that led to Han Guangdi being sentenced to death. Mangos are tropical fruit that can only be grown in few parts of China, and during the economic hardships of the 1960s, many people had never seen one. At that time, Pakistan's Minister of Foreign Affairs was visiting Beijing, and he presented a mango to Mao. Mao in turn presented the mango to the Mao Zedong Thought Propaganda Teams that had just been stationed at Tsinghua and Peking Universities as a token of his support for them. At the same time, just as Mao's every directive was immediately executed throughout the country, the news of the presentation of the mango was immediately and worshipfully disseminated even to the small Sichuan town where Han Guangdi lived.

Regarding Han's arrest and execution, someone who was a primary school student in the town back then sent me the following essay entitled 'Can't Bear to Recall':

I recall an incident that happened in my hometown during the Cultural Revolution. I can't remember exactly what year it was, but it was when Chairman Mao gave a mango to some propaganda team.

My native place produced a lot of fruit; starting in March, we'd have cherries, loquat, apricots, plums, peaches, apples, pears, jujube, persimmons, chestnuts, walnuts and melons on the market, as well as smaller amounts of longans and bananas. But we'd never produced mangoes or even heard of them.

That day, my town was buzzing with excitement. There was the beating of gongs and drums and crowds of people fighting for the first look at what a mango was – especially a mango presented by Chairman Mao!

I was twelve or thirteen at the time and less than 1.3 metres tall, so I stood on tiptoes to look through the crowd, but all I could see were several rifle-bearing soldiers standing sternly on either side of a Liberation model truck. Inside the truck was the chairman of our county Revolutionary Committee, but all I could see was his hands holding a plate that had been covered with a gold-embroidered scarlet cloth, and in the middle of the plate was an elliptical object that resembled a sweet potato – this was the mango that Chairman Mao had presented to the propaganda team!

After seeing it, I felt a bit disappointed. The mango looked pretty much like a sweet potato (but maybe its appearance had changed after being taken on a tour of the entire country).

I went home dispirited and with an inexpressible feeling of loss. Perhaps I'd exaggerated its beauty in my previous imaginings.

The next day, before I'd even gotten out of bed, I was awoken by a sudden pounding at the door.

It was my second cousin, who lived about 500 metres from us. He had never dropped in on us this early before! I pricked up my ears to listen…

'Uncle!' my second cousin said to my grandfather, 'Old Mr Han was arrested by the PSB!'

'Why?' asked my grandfather anxiously.

Old Mr Han was a good friend of my grandfather and had opened a private dental office. My grandfather's dentures had been fitted by Old Mr Han.

'They say he's a current counter-revolutionary who attacked Chairman Mao.'

'What did he say?'

'Yesterday when he looked at the mango, he said, "That mango looks like a sweet potato. It's not worth looking at – it's nothing special!" Someone reported it to the county Revolutionary Committee, and they arrested him at midnight last night.'

After saying this much, my second cousin looked at my grandfather and said, 'Uncle, be careful what you say – people can't be trusted these days.'

'I haven't seen a thing. I know how to mind myself!' My grandfather sighed and said, 'Go on now, you don't want to be late for work.'

After my second cousin left, my grandfather called us all over and told us not to ever speak carelessly outside, because we could end up being arrested. I remember I was really scared at the time – scared the PSB would arrest me because I thought the mango looked like a sweet potato.

Because of that one remark, Old Mr Han was arrested, and because he was unrepentant and told his sons he would appeal the injustice against him, he was designated someone who made no effort to reform. Eventually Old Mr Han was sentenced to death for the crime of current counter-revolution.

The day Old Mr Han was executed, my grandfather drank nearly a pint of liquor, and I saw tears in his eyes.

After Old Mr Han died, his three sons were all chased out to the countryside, and his wife, unable to bear up under the sudden attack, went to Heaven with her husband. A good family was completely destroyed.

From then on, our town no longer had a private dental office.

The author of this essay was a student at the Hanyuan No. 1 Primary School at the time, and he saw Han Guangdi being paraded through the streets in a truck before his execution. A soldier grasped Han by the hair to keep his face raised, and that face was as pale as death. The truck then drove to Gangou Lane, on the outskirts of Hanyuan Town, where Han was executed by gunfire. This student didn't go to the execution site because his grandfather wouldn't allow it.

The fact is that the mango sent to Hanyuan Town wasn't the real mango presented by the Foreign Minister of Pakistan – the real mango would have rotted long before then. What was displayed in Hanyuan was one of countless wax reproductions created at the time. This occurred right at the time of the 1968 Cleansing of the Class Ranks, the campaign in which the largest number of people were persecuted to death, and the height of Mao's cult of personality. Apart from the multitude of Mao figurines of every size, the mango also became an object of worship. Ruthless persecution and fanatical worship developed in tandem.

The people of Hanyuan Town, including many primary school students, watched Han Guangdi's execution, and the spectacle is certain to have had a deep and lasting influence on them. People watching such an event were unlikely to dare to say anything regarding Mao or offer any comment of their own. They would have become extremely circumspect. Even decades later, they would have misgivings about discussing incidents of this kind. This sort of psychic wound is profound but not readily apparent. All we can perceive is the phenomenon of many middle-aged and older people with bad teeth. Everyone knows how important healthy teeth are to a person's quality of life, not to mention their personal appearance. But good teeth require a dentist, and the lack of dentists has plagued the Chinese with bad teeth. Back during the attempt to seize 'total victory for the Great Proletarian Cultural Revolution', it was hard enough to save a life, much less teeth.

The dentist Hang Guangdi's given name meant 'glorious family status', reflecting his parents' hopes. But because of a comment about a mango, he was executed, his sons were expelled from the town, and his wife soon followed him to the grave. And the people of Hanyuan Town lost far more than dental hygiene services.

I gathered some additional information on deaths among medical personnel in various parts of China:

BEIJING

Chu Guocheng, a cadre in the personnel office of Beijing's Fuwai Hospital, killed himself while locked up in 1968 for 'historical problems'. It is said that Chu had previously taken part in the Communist Party's Dongjiang guerrilla force in Guangdong Province, but doubts had been raised about this 'revolutionary history' during the Cultural Revolution. Chu was held in a small room inside the hospital, where he was beaten and otherwise abused. He wanted to kill himself but could find nothing at hand but an iron poker used in the stove, so he placed it against the wall and then thrust his head against it. A doctor at Fuwai Hospital said that he was called to attend Chu, and found him with the poker driven into his forehead. The doctor didn't know how to help. If he pulled out the poker, Chu would die immediately, but if he didn't pull it out, Chu still couldn't be saved. Chu soon died in any event, leaving behind a wife and children. His wife was poorly educated, and the family soon fell into desperate straits. (The writer Shi Bei provided this record.)

Hu Zhengxiang, a professor at Beijing Xiehe Hospital and a prominent pathologist, had studied in the US, where his wife had grown up as an overseas Chinese. After graduating, the couple returned to China, and they lived in the hospital's residential quarters in Dongcheng District. In 1966, Hu Zhengxiang was subjected to struggle as a 'reactionary academic authority'. Hu was researching bacteria and diseases, and people at the hospital insisted that the US had used germ warfare during the Korean War, and the biological weapons the US had used contained bacteria developed by Hu Zhengxiang. In August 1966, the rebel faction at Xiehe Hospital and Red Guards from a nearby secondary school ransacked Hu's home and brutally beat him and his wife. At that time, Hu's son was working in Ningxia, and Hu's twelve-year-old grandson was staying with them. The grandson was a student at the Beijing No. 2 Experimental Primary School. After the Red Guards beat Hu Zhengxiang, they forced his grandson to hit him as well. Hu Zhengxiang killed himself with scissors, and his wife then also killed herself. Their home became a headquarters for the Red Guards.

SHANGHAI

Ye Ying, a professor of parasitology at Shanghai First Medical College, had translated for American military personnel during the War of Resistance against Japan, and in the 1940s he went to the US to study, specialising in protozoology. This 'historical problem' led to his being targeted in the Campaign to Eliminate Counter-Revolutionaries in the 1950s, and he had to repeatedly write confessions before being released. This old matter was resurrected during the Cultural Revolution, when he was subjected to repeated brutal struggle. Unable to bear the protracted physical and mental torment, he tried to kill himself by riding his bicycle into the path of a truck. Instead, he was only badly injured and crippled, but not long after that he died of pneumonia.

Many other medical personnel at the Shanghai First Medical College died around this time: **Gu Jingyan**, professor and head of the pathology research section and a prominent pathologist, and **Zhang Changshao**, head of the pharmacology teaching and research section and a famous pharmacologist, both poisoned themselves. **Wang Zhifu**, associate professor and head of the pharmaceutical chemistry teaching and research section, and **Wu Hongjian**, associate professor and head of the physics and chemistry teaching and research section of the pharmaceuticals department, both drowned themselves. **Tang Jingyi**, a doctor and deputy director of Zhongshan Hospital under the Shanghai First Medical College, leaped to his death. **Wan Dexing**, an associate professor and heart surgeon at the Zhongshan Hospital, hanged himself.

There were also deaths at other Shanghai medical schools.

Xing Deliang, a cadre in the general affairs department of the Shanghai Second Medical College, was pushed into a burlap sack and beaten to death by members of the 'rebel faction'. **Yu Hangsheng**, a lecturer in the pathology and physiology teaching and research section, and **Chen Bangxian**, professor and head of the hygiene teaching and research section, both poisoned themselves, as did **Tang Shiheng**, a professor and head of the gynaecology and obstetrics department of the Ruijin Hospital under the Shanghai Second Medical College.

Yang Zhaogui, deputy political commissar of the training department of Shanghai's Second Military Medical University, hanged himself in his office after being persecuted early in the Cultural Revolution. **Yao Jiongming**, deputy political commissar of Shanghai Hospital under the Second Military Medical University, was beaten to death by the rebel faction while under 'isolation and investigation'.

In Wuxi, near Shanghai, **Zhu Wanxing**, a doctor at the Wuxi First People's Hospital, killed himself in August 1968 after being locked up and tortured for several months. More than fifty people in the Wuxi Hospital system were driven to suicide during the Cultural Revolution.

Ji Gaicheng, director of the Wuxi Nursing School, was repeatedly beaten in June 1968. Soon after that, Ji killed his two young children, and then he and his wife committed suicide.

TIANJIN

Lei Aide, a doctor in his fifties, was once head of the teaching materials department of the Tianjin University of Medical Sciences and was highly respected in his field. His keen sense of humour resulted in his being politically persecuted, and he was designated a Rightist in 1957. After being sent to an 'ox pen' during the Cultural Revolution, Lei took an overdose of sleeping pills in 1968.

Fan Zaoshen, born in 1913, was director of the Tianjin Guangji Hospital (a psychiatric hospital). After being deeply humiliated by the 'rebel faction', he and his wife hanged themselves in 1967. Fan's wife was a doctor at the Hebei Normal School. She was pretty and amiable, and the two, although childless, were deeply attached to each other.

Bi Jinzhao, director of the Paediatrics Department at the Tianjin General Hospital since the 1950s, killed himself in 1968. He was around sixty years old. A highly skilled professional, Dr Bi was a graduate of the Qilu Medical School (now known as Shandong University of Medical Sciences) and had studied overseas. Because he had worked in a military hospital under the Nationalist government, he was accused of being a 'KMT spy' during the Cultural Revolution and ordered to hand over his (nonexistent) weapons.

Ji Zhongshi, a librarian at the Tianjin Medical Library, leaped to his death from a window in the Bureau of Public Health in 1969 after he was struggled and his home ransacked.

Wang Bingyao, a forty-five-year-old doctor at the Qikou Public Health Clinic in Huanghua County, just south of Tianjin, was denounced and locked up for being a 'historical counter-revolutionary'. On 21 August 1968, his family received a telegram informing them that Wang had 'committed suicide to escape punishment'. The family hurried to the scene but were not allowed to view the body. Wang had been brutally tortured before his death.

In the early 1940s, Wang Bingyao had accompanied his father, Wang Honghan, to Gegu Town in Tianjin and then to Qikou in Huanghua County to run a family clinic. During the movement towards 'joint state-private ownership' in 1956, the clinic was confiscated and made part of the Qikou Public Health Clinic. Wang Bingyao continued to work there until the Cultural Revolution began, while his family continued to live in Tianjin.

Wang was an art lover, and in his youth he had joined a spare-time arts organisation under the KMT's Three People's Principles Youth Corps. Because of that, he was accused of being a 'historical counter-revolutionary' and became a focal target to be seized and struggled. He was locked up at the clinic and forbidden to go home.

When Wang's family received the telegram notifying them of his suicide, Wang's eldest son, Wang Peizhi, immediately went to Qikou to identify the body. Fearing he would be attacked as a 'counter-revolutionary family member', he asked a distant relative with a good class background to accompany him. Upon arriving in Qikou, Wang Peizhi was told that the body had already been buried, but no one could say where.

Years later, Wang Bingyao's family learned from local relatives that Wang had been tortured horrendously, with rocks hung around his neck with fine cords, most of his hair torn out, and his legs crippled from beating. He had been kept alive by former patients bringing him food in custody. He had attempted suicide several times, only to be tortured even more because suicide was regarded as 'resisting the dictatorship of the proletariat'.

Wang Bingyao's family never learned exactly how he died, and although they never found his remains, they harboured no hope that he could still be alive. In May 1993, Wang's six children went to Qikou and held a heart-rending ceremony to recall his spirit, and they placed an empty urn for him at the Gugu Town funeral parlor in Tianjin's Tiannan District. Wang Peizhong told me his father's story.

CHONGQING

Yang Juyuan, director of the Chongqing Changjiang Shipping Branch Office Staff Hospital, killed himself after being struggled. An elderly staff doctor, **Tian Zunrong**, slit his wrists after being denounced.

JIANGXI PROVINCE

Chen Yaoting, a teacher at the Jiangxi Gannan Medical School, and his wife, **Xie Juzhang**, sent out more than ten anonymous articles criticising the Cultural Revolution from October 1966 to December 1967. The letters were investigated nationwide as an 'exceptionally major counter-revolutionary case' in July 1967. Chen Yaoting was arrested on 31 December 1967, and Xie Juzhang on 11 February 1968. Chen was sentenced to death on 16 March 1970, and executed four days later. Xie was handed a suspended death sentence and died at the Jiangxi Labour Reform Farm on 11 July 1971. Both were rehabilitated in 1980.

WUHAN, HUBEI PROVINCE

Gao Jingxing, the fifty-four-year-old director of Wuhan's Xiehe Hospital, was a graduate of Yenching University and Xiehe Medical School and an orthopaedist. Because of a 'historical problem', Gao was beaten by rebels in 1968, breaking his ribs and fingers. He leaped to his death from the fifth-floor balcony of a hospital operating room.

Gao's so-called 'historical problem' was that around 1940 he had worked in a military hospital under the Nationalist government. During the Cultural Revolution, he was accused of being a 'member of a Kuomintang local Party Committee' (if he had been, in fact, he should have been designated a 'historical counter-revolutionary') and a 'latent secret agent'. Xiehe Hospital was a teaching hospital of Wuhan Medical School. Students from the medical school ransacked Gao Jingxing's home in search of a letter of appointment from Chiang Kai-shek. Others who were driven to suicide in this same case included:

Fan Lecheng, deputy director of Wuhan Medical School and Gao Jingxing's former classmate; **Wang Xianglin**, a doctor at Nanchang No. 1 Hospital; and **Sun Ming**, director of the Nanchang Maternity and Child Hygiene Hospital. A famous obstetrician, Sun was a friend and former colleague of Gao Jingxin and had delivered a baby for Gao's wife.

PART SIX

The 1970 One Strike and Three Antis Campaign

GU WENXUAN AND THE 'RIGHTISTS'

Political persecution during the Cultural Revolution occurred in stages, but often also as part of a continuum. Certain stages targeted certain kinds of people, but often they had also been the victims of earlier campaigns. For example, many people were attacked during the Cultural Revolution because they had been labelled Rightists during the 1957 Anti-Rightist campaign; teachers who survived persecution at the outset of the Cultural Revolution sometimes died under further abuse during the 1968 Cleansing of the Class Ranks. And people imprisoned during the Anti-Rightist movement or at an earlier stage of the Cultural Revolution were sometimes executed as part of the crackdown during the One Strike and Three Antis Campaign in 1970, which nominally targeted corruption, profiteering and waste, but actually focused on counter-revolutionaries. Gu Wenxuan, previously mentioned in the section on university victims in 1966, falls into the category of people who were imprisoned as Rightists, targeted early on in the Cultural Revolution, and then executed as counter-revolutionaries.

Gu Wenxuan, admitted to Peking University's Western Languages Department as a student of English in 1956, was designated a Rightist the following year, after publishing an essay in a student magazine and was imprisoned for five years. During the One Strike and Three Antis Campaign he was sentenced to death as a counter-revolutionary and executed on 5 March 1970, at the age of thirty-six.

During the Cultural Revolution, people sentenced to death for counter-revolutionary crimes were summarily executed. The term 'summarily executed' means not only that the execution was carried out immediately, but also that no appeal of any kind was allowed. Even if the Chinese authorities granted public access to files from 1966 to 1976, we would not find any appeals or other forms of self-defence for people like Gu Wenxuan. During the Cultural Revolution, prison authorities didn't allow counter-revolutionaries sentenced to death to write a final letter, nor would they save their journals or letters, and they wouldn't allow those condemned to death to say anything in public, so we also have no posthumous papers of Gu Wenxuan's. After being labelled a Rightist and imprisoned in 1957, he never married, so left behind no wife or children who could provide information about his life. I interviewed other Peking University students and teachers who were designated Rightists at the same time as he was, but no one knew him.

Due to these obstacles, my account of Gu's life is based on a 1970 document listing the 'crimes' of fifty-five counter-revolutionaries, him included; a paragraph about Gu's 1957 activities in a book on the history of Peking University published in 1998; two sentences in a copy of the *People's Daily* from 1957; and 'My Experience', the essay he published in 1957 in the Peking University student magazine *Forum*.

To research the life of a victim from such fragmentary material is like an archaeologist trying to carry out research on a historical personage from ancient times based on some unearthed bamboo slips and phrases from history books. Yet the textual records I've found regarding Gu Wenxuan relate to critical stages that form a rough outline of his life. Put together, these fragments show that his fate was sealed by three political movements launched by China's highest authorities: the Campaign to Eliminate Revolutionaries, the Anti-Rightist Campaign and the Cultural Revolution.

SENTENCED TO DEATH DURING THE CULTURAL REVOLUTION

I first came across Gu Wenxuan's name in a notice regarding fifty-five 'counter-revolutionaries'. This document was discovered by a collector of old books, who passed it on to me. At the top of the first page are printed two 'Highest Directives' – the phrase applied at that time to Mao's words – related to 'suppressing counter-revolutionaries' and 'strengthening revolutionary dictatorship'. Official documents and even private correspondence always began with Mao quotes in the special literary style that was in vogue for at least five years during the Cultural Revolution era.

The second half of the first page carries the main text of the notice:

In order to strengthen dictatorship over a smattering of counter-revolutionary forces, ruthlessly attack the sabotage of current counter-revolutionaries and further improve revolutionary order in the capital, a new batch of current counter-revolutionaries has recently been sentenced in public trial. This document listing Gu Wenxuan and fifty-four other criminals is issued to all work units. All levels of Cultural Revolution Committees and Worker and PLA Mao Zedong Thought Propaganda Teams are asked to organise the revolutionary masses for serious discussion and to quickly submit opinions to the Municipal Public Security, Procuratorial and Judicial Military Control Commission regarding how to deal with this matter.
>   Chinese People's Liberation Army Beijing Municipal Public Security, Procuratorial and Judicial Military Control Commission
>   11 February 1970

The rest of this notice consists of the names and 'crimes' of these fifty-five people. Gu Wenxuan tops the list, and this is what is written about him:

> Current counter-revolutionary Gu Wenxuan, male, thirty-six, a native of Zhejiang Province, counter-revolutionary, employed at the Beijing Qinghe Labour Reform Farm, was sentenced for counter-revolutionary crimes.
> Current counter-revolutionary Zhou Hongdong, male, thirty-seven, a native of Liaoning Province, from a capitalist family, a counter-revolutionary, employed at the Beijing Qinghe Labour Reform Farm, was sentenced for counter-revolutionary crimes.
> Gu and Zhou stubbornly persisted in their reactionary standpoint, regularly disseminated reactionary speech and venomously attacked our Party and the socialist system; while employed following completion of their sentences, they repeatedly plotted to betray the country and surrender to the enemy. On 19 July 1966, they crossed the border to Vietnam to betray the country, surrender to the enemy and sell our country's important intelligence. They were then extradited back to China.

Based on these paragraphs, the Military Control Commission sentenced Gu Wenxuan and Zhou Hongdong to death.

Let's first look at their 'reactionary speech'. The document asked the masses to discuss how to 'handle' Gu Wenxuan, but didn't state what 'reactionary speech' he actually uttered, merely making a sweeping statement that he 'venomously attacked our Party and the socialist system'. During the Cultural Revolution, especially in the One Strike and Three

Antis Campaign, this became a formal crime so widely applied that the operatives of the 'organs of dictatorship' shortened it to 'venomous attack'. Although a 'venomous attack' was a major crime punishable by death, its substance was never publicly stated, so there is no way to know what Gu Wenxuan actually said. However, I was able to investigate the case of Wen Jia, who was No. 39 on the list and the youngest of the fifty-five. Wen Jia was sentenced to twenty years in prison.

When the Cultural Revolution began, Wen Jia was a third-year student at the Beijing Normal University Affiliated Girls' Secondary School. Her father was executed during the Campaign to Suppress Counter-Revolutionaries in the early 1950s (he was posthumously rehabilitated after the Cultural Revolution). Wen Jia and her elder brother were raised by her maternal uncle. Because of her 'family background' she was struggled by Red Guards who beat her and broke her glasses. In late summer 1968, her classmates were assigned work, some of them in a Beijing factory, but because of her family background, the school administrators wanted Wen Jia to be sent to the countryside. Knowing nothing about farming and certain that she would be unable to support herself, Wen climbed in the window of an unused school toilet in winter 1968 and prepared to starve herself to death there. When discovered and interrogated by the 'school defence team', she said she simply wanted to die and expressed dissatisfaction with the Cultural Revolution. It was further said that she tore up a book of *Quotations from Chairman Mao* (which people always carried with them at the time). The school's Revolutionary Committee's political work section proclaimed her a counter-revolutionary and handed her over to the Xicheng District Public Security Bureau detention centre.

Since 'venomous attacks' were designated 'anti-proliferation material', Wen Jia's 'reactionary speech' has never been made public, and only those who interrogated her know what she actually said to justify the sentence of twenty years of penal servitude that was handed down against her on 5 March 1970.

In 1979, a little more than two years after Mao's death, Deng Xiaoping's new policies resulted in the release of many people imprisoned for 'venomous attacks'. By then, Wen Jia had been in prison for more than ten years. In 1993, I interviewed a personnel cadre at her secondary school who said that Wen Jia came to the school hoping for 'policy implementation' (an expression used by victims of political persecution, referring to restitution under the Party's new policies). She seemed to be in poor health and somewhat mentally disturbed. The school authorities said that if she'd been a university student at the time of her sentencing, the university might find a job for her, but because she was a secondary school student, there was nothing the school could do for her. Eventually I learned that Wen had been diagnosed with schizophrenia after being sent to the detention centre, but was handed a lengthy prison sentence all the same. Wen Jia has never recovered and cannot support herself. Although rehabilitated, she received no compensation of any kind. Her fate highlights the stark contrast between the 'freedom of speech' guaranteed in the PRC Constitution and the reality of people being imprisoned or executed for exercising this freedom.

Gu Wenxuan's second crime was fleeing China, referred to in the materials as 'betraying the country and surrendering to the enemy'. Until the 1980s, ordinary people were almost never given a passport, and could only leave China secretly. This was very dangerous; they could be killed en route, or if they were captured, their escape attempt could be grounds for the death penalty.

From the perspective of the Cultural Revolution authorities, making 'venomous attacks' and 'betraying the country and surrendering to the enemy' into capital offences was highly advantageous to establishing their authority. Making these two crimes punishable by death minimised the likelihood of anyone criticising Mao or the Cultural Revolution, prevented people from yearning for places that had developed in a different direction from China, and deprived people of a way out of the country. These two crimes are the most common alleged against the fifty-five people on the list. Gu Wenxuan had the misfortune of being convicted of both, and he was executed on 5 March 1970.

I've been unable to find the actual judgment against Gu Wenxuan, because my inquiries show that neither the convicted person nor their family members were ever given copies of their judgments during the Cultural Revolution. We know when Gu was executed, however, because it was alongside **Yu Luoke** in a 'public trial' at the Beijing Workers' Stadium. Yu Luoke's family was very supportive of him, and they remember that he was killed on 5 March 1970.

DEATH SENTENCES WITHOUT A BASIS IN LAW

It should be noted that when the Military Control Commission convicted Gu Wenxuan, it cited no legal statute; that is, it didn't say which law he had broken.

Solzhenitsyn's *Gulag Archipelago* describes the Stalin era, when enormous numbers of Russians were arrested and executed or sent to labour camps. Interrogation methods were brutal, and judgment was swift. Many of these people were convicted and sentenced on the basis of Article 58 of the Soviet Union's criminal law, promulgated in 1926. Solzhenitsyn notes sarcastically, 'In all truth, there is no step, thought, action, or lack of action under the heavens which could not be punished by the heavy hand of Article 58.'[1] Even so, Stalin at least felt that sentencing people required a basis in law. When Gu Wenxuan was executed, the Cultural Revolution authorities never gave any legal basis for their decision. In this sense, Mao went even farther than Stalin in trampling on human rights and sabotaging the legal system.

It should be noted that when the courts imprisoned Rightists during the Anti-Rightist Campaign, the style of the sentencing was different. The 1959 judgment against Lin Xiling, a student at Renmin University of China, read thus:

> ... In summation, in accordance with the stipulations under Article 10.3 of the Regulations of the People's Republic of China to Punish Counter-Revolution, the judgment is as follows: The defendant Cheng Haiguo (Lin Xiling) is sentenced to fifteen years in prison for the crime of counter-revolution (starting on 22 July 1958 and ending on 1 July 1973) with an additional five years' deprivation of political rights.[2]

Regardless of whether or not these regulations are legitimate, at least they were cited in a judgment against a 'counter-revolutionary' in 1959. During the Cultural Revolution, the Military Control Commission convicted many 'counter-revolutionaries' but never cited any legal clause. This change was part of the substance of the Cultural Revolution.

DEATH SENTENCES PASSED BY THE 'TRIUMVIRATE' OF PUBLIC SECURITY, PROCURATORIAL AND JUDICIAL ORGANS

This notice was signed by the 'People's Liberation Army Beijing Municipal Public Security, Procuratorial and Judicial Military Control Commission'.

As early as February 1967, before the Beijing Cultural Revolution Committee was established, the Ministry of Public Security and the Beijing Garrison Command Headquarters issued a notice that on orders from the State Council and Central Military Commission, the Beijing Garrison Command Headquarters took over management of the Beijing Public Security Bureau and established a Military Control Commission.

---

[1] *The Gulag Archipelago*, Vol. 1, Part 1, Chapter 2.
[2] Quoted in *The Seventies* Monthly (Hong Kong), September 1983.

The Military Control Commission then quickly took over unified management of the procuratorate and courts as well. In democratic societies, the legislative, executive and judicial branches have separation of powers. In China prior to the Cultural Revolution, there was no 'independent' legal and judicial apparatus in theory or practice. However, the public security, procuratorial and judicial bodies were separate within that apparatus, and each had clearly delineated responsibilities. The Public Security Bureau investigated crimes, the procuratorate prosecuted and the judiciary passed judgment. During the Cultural Revolution, the three were melded into a single work unit and placed under military control.

Even now, some people still endorse the positive contribution of the Cultural Revolution in 'opposing the bureaucratic system', because Mao said he wanted 'crack troops and streamlined administration' and to 'smash the redundant administrative structure' (March 1968). Yet, what the Cultural Revolution actually did was to abolish the separation of the public security bureaus, procuratorates and courts and the legal procedures for trying and convicting people for crimes, which enhanced the efficiency of persecution to a horrific extent.

In his article 'A Critique of the "16 May Circular"', Professor Tan Zongji of the Central Party School wrote: 'In Beijing alone, 9,804 people, including cadres and the masses, died as a result of miscarriage of justice in the Cultural Revolution.'[3] I once asked Professor Tan the source of his figure. He would only say that it came from a 'central document' – obviously a 'top secret document for internal circulation' that ordinary people cannot access.

Before the Cultural Revolution, the courts would put up notices of death sentences or prison sentences, which clearly stated the name of the presiding judge. When judgment was passed on Gu Wenxuan, however, the public security, procuratorial and judicial bodies had been consolidated, and there was no individual official named, only the collective name of the 'Military Control Commission'. This kind of collective entity confronted the convicted person with an anonymous group, allowing no avenue for dialogue or appeal, while also keeping the general public from knowing who these people were, which encouraged unscrupulous conduct.

The person in charge of Beijing's merged public security, procuratorial and judicial apparatus for a full ten years was Liu Chuanxin, formerly a deputy commissar in the Nanjing Military Region. After Mao died in 1976, the Gang of Four was arrested, and the veteran cadres Liu Chuanxin had imprisoned and persecuted during the Cultural Revolution returned

---

[3] See Tan Zongji, *Evaluation Ten Years Later*, Beijing, Zhonggong dangshi ziliao chubanshe, 1987, p. 21.

to positions of power. On 27 January 1977, Liu was removed from his position as director of the Beijing Public Security Bureau and put under 'isolation and investigation' in his home in the Legation Quarter. On 18 May 1977, he was notified of a 'rally to denounce Liu Chuanxin' at the Beijing Public Security Bureau the next day. He hanged himself from a tree late that night.

Liu Chuanxin can be considered a typical case in the political persecution apparatus. He's like the cold-blooded secret police chiefs Nikolai Yezhov and Lavrentiy Beria in the Soviet Union, who were responsible for the execution and banishment of countless people. They themselves met suitably bleak ends. But people like Liu Chuanxin in China have still not been clearly written about and analysed.

DEATH BY CAMPAIGN

Gu Wenxuan was executed during the 'Campaign to Strike Against Counter-Revolutionaries' (One Strike and Three Antis Campaign). A series of campaigns comprised the Cultural Revolution, and most of its victims were killed as a result of these repeated crusades. My inquiries have found that the two movements with the largest numbers of victims were the 'Red Guard Smashing of the Four Olds' campaign in summer 1966 and the 'Cleansing of the Class Ranks' campaign in 1968 and 1969. Most of these operations were carried out via the 'dictatorship of the masses'. The 1970 campaign to 'Strike Against Counter-Revolutionaries' was built on the foundation of previous mass dictatorship, and used the organs of dictatorship – i.e. the merged public security, procuratorial and judicial apparatus – to arrest, imprison and execute so-called 'current counter-revolutionaries'.

On 31 January 1970, with Mao's memo of approval, the CCP Central Committee issued its 'Directive Regarding the Campaign to Strike Against Counter-Revolutionaries' [Central Committee document No. 4 (1970)]. A number of 'current counter-revolutionaries' had already been arrested and killed prior to this, but the new campaign greatly enhanced the scale of these arrests and executions throughout the country.

In October that year, the Beijing Revolutionary Committee submitted a report to the Central Committee entitled 'Situation Report Regarding the Earnest Execution of Policy and In-depth Development of the "One Strike and Three Antis" Campaign', which stated:

> Since the One Strike and Three Antis Campaign began, 4,823 traitors, spies, counter-revolutionaries and bad elements have been ferreted

out, three-quarters of them since June; 934 counter-revolutionaries and bad elements who had infiltrated Beijing have been ferreted out, two-thirds of them since June. At the same time, at least 3,138 cases of counter-revolution or major crime have been uncovered, along with major cases of collaboration with the enemy, treason and plotting revolt. A batch of sly and treacherous counter-revolutionaries has been arrested, leading to a drop in cases of current counter-revolution and a reduction in cases of murder, robbery, arson and other crimes injurious to public order.

It should be noted that the 4,823 local Beijing residents and 934 outsiders 'ferreted out' during the One Strike and Three Antis campaign is in addition to the more than 80,000 'class enemies' unearthed shortly before that during the Cleansing of the Class Ranks (according to the November 1968 report of the Beijing Revolutionary Committee).

Wang Nianyi's history of the Cultural Revolution, *Era of Turmoil*[4] states: 'According to statistics, more than 1.84 million "traitors" "spies" and "counter-revolutionaries" were unearthed in the ten months from February to November 1970. More than 284,800 were arrested and thousands were killed.' When I asked the author where he got his information, he said the figures came from Central Committee documents that were not accessible to the general public.

During the Campaign to Strike Against Counter-Revolutionaries, death sentences were passed by the judicial Military Control Commission. That is, people weren't beaten to death by 'mass organisations' like the Red Guards as before, but rather were killed by the organs of political power, which means there should be a written record. The figure of 'thousands' provided in Wang Nianyi's book is too vague. Clearly this is because so many people were killed in such an arbitrary manner that no one bothered to keep a record. In addition, the figure of 'thousands' is almost certainly a gross understatement, given the large number of mass executions throughout China at the time.

DESIGNATED AND IMPRISONED AS A RIGHTIST IN 1957

The 'notice' above stating Gu Wenxuan's sentencing for counter-revolutionary crimes mentions that he was designated a Rightist in 1957 and sentenced to a term of imprisonment.

---

[4] Henan renmin chubanshe, 1988, p. 333.

The two-volume *Chronicle of Peking University (1898–1997)* contains one record regarding Gu Wenxuan (p. 571):

> 25 May [1957]
> In the afternoon, some students acting in the name of the English class and Party branch of the Western Languages Department held a denunciation rally against the 'three harmfuls' in the office building assembly hall. Students Gu Wenxuan and Zhou Duo concocted many sensationalistic 'facts' to denounce 'the Party's three harmful crimes'. That night, after a film screening at the eastern sports ground, university Party secretary and vice-president Jiang Longji gave a speech to all of the school's students criticising that 'complaint rally' and warned those people not to exceed the scope of the rectification of incorrect work styles.

This is why Gu Wenxuan was designated a Rightist.

The 'three harmfuls' mentioned in this text were 'subjectivism, bureaucratism and sectarianism'. On 13 and 16 May 1957, the Party Committee of Peking University held two enlarged meetings to discuss plans for the 'rectification of incorrect work styles' in compliance with the Central Committee's directive. 'Opposing the three harmfuls' was a phrase used in this rectification campaign.

On 19 May 1957, some of the university's students put up big-character posters asking why the university Youth League Committee's representatives at the Third National Congress hadn't been elected. After that, students began putting up posters criticising other matters, and several student organisations were formed, including one called the White Flower Study Group. This period of 'freely airing views' was very short-lived. One month later, on 21 June, the *People's Daily* declared Peking University's White Flower Study Group to be a 'reactionary organisation', and students who had 'aired their views' were subjected to public criticism before the entire university, as well as being designated Rightists.

During this very short phase, certain dates and sequences of events are especially worthy of notice. In fact, as early as 15 May, Mao's essay 'The Situation is Changing' explicitly put forward the need to attack 'Rightists', who supposedly made up 10% of the population. This essay was circulated among the Party's top cadres at the time, while ordinary people and even cadres at the middle and lower levels knew nothing about it. It wasn't until twenty years later, in 1977, that this essay was made public in Volume 5 of the *Selected Works of Mao Zedong*.

It was Mao's essay that prompted Peking University students to respond to appeals from its Party Committee to 'air their views' on 19 May, and Gu Wenxuan delivered his remarks on the 'three harmfuls' six days after that.

QUOTAS FOR ATTACKING RIGHTISTS

The Chronicle of Peking University (1898–1987) records that on 31 January 1958, during the 1957 Anti-Rightist Campaign and its supplementary campaign in early 1958, Peking University designated 589 students and 110 teachers (a total of 699 people) as Rightists. That book's section on 1982 (when the 'Rightists' returned to the school for a 'correction' and to be rehabilitated) states that the university designated 716 people as Rightists (p. 890). There is a discrepancy in the numbers – either the first statistic is incomplete, or more people were added later.

At that time, the university had a total student body of 8,983, plus 1,399 teachers and administrators, so that means 7% were designated Rightists.

In a speech at the Shanghai cadre conference on 9 July 1957, Mao said: 'Rightists are only a tiny minority; as just mentioned concerning Peking University, only 1, 2 or 3%. That's for students. Professors and associate professors are somewhat different; around 10% are Rightists.'[5]

If Gu Wenxuan had not come forward with his complaints, someone else would have been labelled a Rightist in order to meet this arbitrary quota.

THE OUTCOME FOR THE PEKING UNIVERSITY PARTY SECRETARY

The Chronicle of Peking University (1898–1997) states: 'Students Gu Wenxuan and Zhou Duo concocted many sensationalist "facts."' This was obviously what Jiang Longji and the university's other authorities said at the time. Yet it's also clear that they never investigated whether what Gu said was true or not, because Jiang Longji denounced what Gu Wenxuan and Zhou Duo said that same night, and could not possibly have had the time to inquire into the veracity of their comments.

Jiang Longji was also in charge of designating hundreds of people at the university as Rightists via its Party Committee. Even at that, the higher-ups didn't think Jiang Longji went far enough; on 1 November 1957, the Beijing Municipal Party Committee gave notice that he was demoted to Second Party Secretary. Lu Ping was transferred to Peking University as First Party Secretary, where he designated even more people as Rightists. In January 1959, Jiang Longji was transferred to serve as president and Party secretary of Lanzhou University. As noted in his biography in Part

---

[5] *Selected Works of Mao Zedong*, Vol. 5, 'Beat Back the Assault by Bourgeois Rightists'.

One, Jiang soon became a key target of the Cultural Revolution and killed himself on 25 June 1966.

FEI XIAOTONG'S SYMPATHY AND FORGETFULNESS

I found an article in the 4 July 1957, edition of the *People's Daily* relating to Gu Wenxuan. The lead story by 'Min Ganghou' on the newspaper's second page, entitled 'Zhang Bojun Calls an Urgent Meeting', 'uncovered' a conversation that Zhang Bojun had with six Peking University professors on 6 June:

> After Zhang Bojun talked of how the situation in the schools was very serious and asked them all to think about what work they should do during the movement, Fei Xiaotong first said that university students had become active, their emotions were intense, and based on the many problems uncovered by the movement, the situation was very serious. He'd heard that Peking University had two students who complained that they'd been wrongfully denounced during the Campaign to Eliminate Counter-Revolutionaries, bringing some who heard it to tears, and this is intolerable for intellectuals. 'It is hard to believe that such things are still happening after Liberation – it's just too dark. Today a new feeling has risen in my heart. I sympathise with the things the students have brought to light. Now that students are doing this, the situation might easily become magnified. Right now the students are going around looking for leadership, and if teachers join in, the situation could become more serious. Of course it's easy enough to suppress them with three million troops, but their hearts are gone and so is the Party's credibility with the masses.' He said, 'The problems today have been created by the system. Non-Party members have positions but no power, and Party and Youth League members have all the power and are acting tyrannically. I don't think it's a matter of individual work styles, but of the system.'

The two students Fei referred to were Gu Wenxuan and Zhou Duo, and from his remarks we know that they complained about being 'wrongfully denounced' during the 1955 Campaign to Eliminate Counter-Revolutionaries. It is very telling that a mature, experienced person such as Fei Xiaotong was moved by Gu Wenxuan and Zhou Duo's speeches.

    Like Gu, Fei Xiaotong was labelled a Rightist. The authorities penalised prominent individuals less harshly than obscure and ordinary ones. Famous professors were typically punished through demotion and salary reductions but were retained at their schools. Most university students, however, were constantly denigrated as 'little Rightists', and the penalty for a single speech or big-character poster was to be sent to a labour farm, where they were debased to the lowest spiritual and material level. From the perspective of those in power, this was clearly effective for controlling those who were designated Rightists and for warning and intimidating society at large.

Fei Xiaotong, born in 1910, was educated at Tsinghua University and obtained a PhD in Economics from the London School of Economics. In 1957, he was a professor at the Central Institute for Nationalities (now Minzu University of China), and he remained at the institute after being designated a Rightist. During the Cultural Revolution, Fei was denounced and held in an 'ox pen' as a member of the school's 'labour reform team'. His Rightist status was subsequently 'corrected' and he began to serve in high positions, enjoying privileges similar to those of Party and national leaders. He also regularly published articles in newspapers and magazines, but he seems never to have written about his experiences during the Anti-Rightist Campaign, or to have mentioned Gu Wenxuan or Zhou Duo, of whom he'd so movingly spoken years before.

In spring 2002, I wrote two letters to Fei Xiaotong telling him I was working on an article about Gu Wenxuan and asking for information. Unfortunately, he never replied. He died in 2005.

THE SENTENCING OF GU WENXUAN

Ding Shu mentions Gu Wenxuan in his book *Open Conspiracy*, about the Anti-Rightist Campaign:[6]

> During the 'airing of views', a lecturer in Peking University's Western Languages Department, Huang Jizhong, held a complaint rally during which student Gu Wenxuan and other innocent people who had been struggled during the Campaign to Eliminate Counter-Revolutionaries mounted the podium to make their complaints. Huang had been designated an 'ultra-Rightist' and sent to the Qinghe Labour Farm.
>
> After being designated a Rightist, Gu Wenxuan had nowhere to seek redress, so he naively ran back to his home in Hangzhou to see his mother. The result was that he was arrested and sent back to Beijing and sentenced to five years in prison. After being released on completion of

---

[6] Ding Shu, *Open Conspiracy*, Hong Kong, The Nineties Publishing, 1995, p. 330.

his sentence, he was retained at the labour farm for 'employment' and was never able to rejoin society. One day, he went to visit his former Peking University professor Huang Jizhong at the Qinghe Labour Farm, and told him, 'I don't think I'll be able to visit you much from now on.'

By then, Gu Wenxuan had already given up and had decided to flee. He managed to reach the Soviet Union, but the KGB just bundled him into a gunnysack like an animal and took him to Moscow for interrogation, after which they sent him back to the Far East and extradited him to China. Gu Wenxuan was executed during the 'One Strike and Three Antis Campaign' in 1970.

Huang Jizhong went to the United States in the 1980s, teaching at Bennington College before retiring. When his American colleagues and former landlord discovered that I wished to contact Huang, they helped me find where he'd moved after leaving the school. However, he was already seriously ill by then, and died in 2001.

The Chronicle of Peking University (1898–1997) doesn't record Gu Wenxuan's arrest, but it notes: 'On 27 July 1957, a school-wide rally exposed and criticised Qian Ruping (a third-year mathematics student) for speech and actions attacking the Party and socialism, and announced that he would be sent to the public security organ to be dealt with in accordance with law.'[7] Clearly, Qian Ruping was the same kind of victim as Gu Wenxuan.

ZHOU DUO'S TRAGIC FATE

Although I was unable to find anyone who knew Gu Wenxuan, I interviewed many people who knew Zhou Duo, the student who spoke with Gu at the 25 May 1957 'complaint rally'. Zhou's story is also tragic.

Born in a southern village, Zhou Duo was admitted to Tsinghua University in 1949 as a student of English. In 1951, before he graduated, Zhou was transferred to the public security bureau to work as an interpreter. At that time, the public security organs had arrested a number of overseas Chinese and was accusing them of being foreign spies, and needed to interrogate these people through an English interpreter. Zhou was one of two students from Tsinghua's Foreign Languages Department who was sent to do this work.

Eventually Zhou Duo asked to leave the Public Security Bureau and finish his studies, but by then Tsinghua University's humanities courses had

---

[7] *Op. cit.*, p. 152.

been eradicated as part of the 1952 'restructuring' of China's universities and colleges. Zhou therefore resumed his studies at Peking University's Western Languages Department in 1954.

Zhou Duo told his schoolmates and teachers that he'd seen people beaten, berated and tortured during interrogations at the Public Security Bureau. When Professor Huan Jizhong heard of this, he felt the lawlessness of the state organs was a serious problem, and he asked the head of the Western Languages Department, Feng Zhi, to report it to the upper levels. Feng Zhi was a famous poet and translator as well as a delegate to the National People's Congress at the time. Feng reportedly asked Zhou Duo to write up a report, which he did, and also spoke publicly of his experiences at the 25 May rally. The content of Gu Wenxuan and Zhou Duo's speeches caused an uproar among the rally's large audience.

Because of his speech, Zhou Duo was labelled an 'ultra-Rightist' and punished through penal labour under surveillance. Peking University physics professor Li Shuxian was also labelled a Rightist in 1957 and was sent to a labour farm in the Mentoudou District of Beijing's suburbs. She said that she saw Zhou Duo while labouring at Malan Village. His face was swollen, he limped and he was nearly bald. That was during the Great Leap Forward, when the village was practising 'deep ploughing' under Mao's instructions. This not only covered rich soil with immature soil that was worse for growing crops, but was also backbreaking toil. Rightists who wanted to have their 'caps removed' had to put in an even greater effort in their work and political performance. For this reason, even other Rightists would have nothing to do with Zhou Duo because he was considered particularly problematic for having complained about the Communist Party.

After four years of penal labour, Zhou Duo had his student status restored in 1961 and resumed his studies, but after graduating in 1962 he wasn't assigned a job, and just worked at a factory at Peking University.

When the Cultural Revolution began, Zhou became a member of the 'ox demon and snake spirit labour reform team'. He was forced to sew the words 'Rightist Zhou Duo' on a black over-sleeve and wear it every day.

In 1968, Zhou Duo was held in the 'supervision and reform compound' of Peking University, also known as the 'reactionary compound', located where the Arthur M. Sackler Archaeological Museum now stands. This jail held more than 200 people and was a typical 'ox pen'.

One professor who was held there told me that Zhou Duo was beaten more often than others. His trousers were always stained with blood from when the Red Guard jailers beat him with bamboo strips, an especially painful form of punishment. The Red Guards particularly loved to toy with Zhou Duo by calling him and hitting his legs with a rod as he stood before them. Once a donkey cart arrived with some goods, and while the donkey was being watered, Red Guards had Zhou Duo and a Law Department professor pull the cart around the compound like donkeys.

Another professor who was held with him said that Zhou Duo may have pretended to go mad, or it may have been real. It was normal to give the 'ox demons and snake spirits' steamed corn buns to eat rather than wheat buns, but one time when wheat buns were given out, Zhou Duo still ate corn buns. When someone asked him why, he said, 'I'm a criminal, so I can only eat corn buns.' Early on cold mornings, he would get out of bed and stand outside the door for an hour holding his Little Red Book but not turning a page, just staring blankly. He would pick up persimmon peels and clay from the ground and eat them. Since inmates were not allowed to converse with each other and could not raise their heads while walking, these two professors were unable to talk with Zhou Duo to ascertain whether he had actually been driven mad by his torments. His physical infirmities were more obvious; he lost nearly all his teeth and hair and became emaciated and anemic-looking.

After being held in the 'supervision and reform compound' for eleven months, Zhou Duo and other 'ox demons and snake spirits' from the Western Languages Department were transferred to its 'ox pen' in building No. 41. Most of the people held there were older professors, the so-called 'reactionary academic authorities', but there were also two younger Rightists. Everyone slept in bunk beds, and Zhou Duo slept above the elderly professor Zhu Guangqian.

One student from the department was especially brutal while supervising the 'ox demons and snake spirits'. He always kicked open the door, and when he entered, all the inmates had to stand and he always made a point of slapping Zhou Duo hard in the face. The other inmates were outraged but could do nothing. Years later, the two Western Languages Department instructors angrily claimed that Zhou had been tortured to death, and they wondered how that brutal student, now living comfortably, could sleep at night.

When the people being struggled finally had their handling decided, Zhou Duo was released in what was called 'lenient handling'. The Worker and PLA Mao Zedong Thought Propaganda Team in control of the school held a campus-wide leniency and severity rally to reflect their execution of the Party's policy of 'giving people a way out' and of 'treating honesty with leniency and resistance with severity'. Anyone who was not handcuffed and was allowed to return home was considered to have been handled leniently, and Zhou Duo was one of them. Since being labelled a Rightist, he had suffered every kind of persecution and his life had been squeezed dry, yet he was obliged to play the part of willingly professing his guilt and thanking his oppressors for their 'leniency'.

By then, Zhou Duo's health was already extremely poor, and he died soon after leaving the university. He had never married and had no family, and today no one knows exactly where or when he died.

If Gu Wanxuan hadn't fled the labour reform farm and illegally crossed the border, he may not have been executed, but there is little doubt that he would have continued to be denounced, tortured and humiliated just like Zhou Duo.

IMPRISONED DURING THE 1955 CAMPAIGN
TO ELIMINATE COUNTER-REVOLUTIONARIES:
GU WENXUAN'S AUTOBIOGRAPHY –
'MY EXPERIENCE'

I tried to gain an idea of what exactly Gu Wenxuan said during the 'complaint rally'.

Chen Fengxiao was a student of mathematics at Peking University in 1957, and after being labelled a Rightist, he was imprisoned for fifteen years. He said Gu Wenxuan adapted his speech into an essay that appeared in *Forum*, the magazine published by the White Flower Study Group. The magazine only produced a single issue, and although Chen was one of its editors, he no longer had any copies in his possession.

Locating a copy was much harder than I expected. I contacted other Peking University students who had been labelled Rightists and also requested help from the university's two libraries, as well as writing to current professors in its History and Chinese Departments, but without success.

This magazine had served as 'evidence' for harshly punishing a group of students. When Lin Xiling, a student at Renmin University, was sentenced to fifteen years in prison, her judgment listed her support for *Forum* as one of her crimes, yet the magazine itself could not be found. The fact that so many people had suffered and even died because of a magazine that had disappeared, and whose contents were unknown, was a Kafkaesque absurdity. I finally obtained a copy from Lin Xiling, who by then was living in exile in Paris.

Lin Xiling, born Cheng Haiguo in 1935, was about to graduate with a degree in law from Renmin University when she was declared a Rightist in 1957. On 23 May 1957, she had given a speech at Peking University criticising the persecution of individuals in the Campaign to Eliminate Counter-Revolutionaries. Two days later, Gu Wenxuan gave his speech about his own persecution in this campaign, but Lin Xiling didn't know Gu and never even knew his name. She was arrested on 21 July 1958, the reason given being that she had 'beaten' a student who was supervising her, and eventually she was formally charged with 'counter-revolutionary crimes' and sentenced to fifteen years in prison. Minister of Public Security Luo Ruiqing personally went to Renmin University to arrange for her punishment. The students labelled Rightists in 1957 were in fact scattered individuals with no ties among them. It was not until twenty-one years later, when they were given the opportunity to have their reputations restored, that much was written about their common fate and history.

Gu Wenxuan's essay appeared on page 14 of *Forum* under the title 'My Experience'. The magazine had been handwritten on stencil and then mimeographed, and the surviving copy is nearly illegible but can be read with effort.

Gu Wenxuan began his speech with a poem expressing that he was motivated by opposition not to the Party, but to errors committed by the Party.

> At first, I didn't dispute my misfortune,
> I felt that time,
> That onrushing current, would wash it all away;
> At that time, as in the time before my injury,
> I enjoyed happiness and peace in my life;
> But I was incapable of shaking off those painful memories,
> Constantly awakened by nightmares in the depths of night.
> My wounded dignity could not be healed,
> The sound of shackles jangling in my brain.
> Our era is a bright spring
> Over which dark clouds have gathered;
> It is those dark things
> That have stripped so many of their precious youth;
> I can no longer be silent!
> I must cry out at this injustice.
> Let all see the face of the 'three harmfuls'
> And join in lighting the torch of truth that burns them away.

Gu wrote that he was fifteen when the People's Republic was founded in 1949, and that he 'joined the revolution' in Hangzhou as a member of the Communist Youth League and then worked at the Hangzhou Public Security Bureau. When the Campaign to Eliminate Counter-Revolutionaries began in mid-June 1955, 'I paid no attention, because I had no problems nor any relatives overseas, nor were any of my friends or relatives landlords, rich peasants or counter-revolutionaries; there was no reason for the campaign to affect me personally more than studying even more with the others. I never guessed that one afternoon, a leader in our organisation would arrange for the others to struggle me. The material he seized on was mainly that I had slanderously attacked leaders and created a clique, and that I had reactionary literary thinking.'

Gu Wenxuan felt that his tragedy was his 'excessive frankness, naivety and honesty', which had aroused the envy and hatred of the leader and some less ethical colleagues. As to his 'reactionary literary thinking', all he did was write a couple of stories, one of which depicted a village-born cadre who abandoned his wife after moving to the city.

After being denounced for several days in a row without admitting any crimes, Gu was beaten one evening by a group of colleagues. When he tried to defend himself, they accused him of hitting someone, handcuffed his wrists behind his back and tied him with rope. They then telephoned the Bureau's deputy director, after which Gu Wenxuan was taken to Hangzhou Prison. He was put in handcuffs and fetters and held for four months.

Gu Wenxuan said his arrest was unlawful because he was not issued with an arrest warrant or brought before the court within thirty-six hours. He provided full details, including the names of those who had beaten him and where and when it had happened, as well as everything he was fed in prison, and he averred that everything he said was true and could be investigated.

From the legal perspective, even if there were some inaccuracies in what Gu wrote, it didn't constitute a crime. In any case, his description has the ring of truth, and that's why Fei Xiaotong was so moved at the time.

THE TERROR OF THE CAMPAIGN TO ELIMINATE COUNTER-REVOLUTIONARIES

One of the guiding documents of the Campaign to Eliminate Counter-Revolutionaries was entitled 'The Central Group of Ten's Provisional Stipulation Regarding Policy Guidelines for Interpreting and Dealing with Counter-Revolutionaries and Other Bad Elements'; it was issued on 10 March 1956. Apart from listing the various categories that could be designated 'counter-revolutionaries', one clause stated: 'An element of extremely degenerate character. This person does not have to be included among the approximately 5% of evildoers, and is handled within the scope of cadre vetting.'

This stipulation provides indirect but clear evidence that each work unit had a 5% quota of targets for attack. Some people who took part in the Campaign to Eliminate Counter-Revolutionaries told me that each work unit established a 'group of five' to lead the campaign, and that they had to carry out whatever threats or coercion were necessary to round up enough counter-revolutionaries to meet the 5% quota. This was due to pressure from the upper-level leadership, but also to the compulsion of people within the work units to score points through active participation.

It should be noted that there had already been a Campaign to Suppress Counter-Revolutionaries before this 1955 operation. According to officially published reports, from December 1950 to mid-1952, '270,000 counter-revolutionaries of various types were imprisoned, 230,000 were put under supervision, and 710,000 received capital punishment [execution].'[8] At the 1959 Lushan Conference, Mao himself stated that one million were killed.

The Campaign to Suppress Counter-Revolutionaries was also carried out through a quota system. The Resolution of the Third National Public Security Conference held from 10 to 16 May 1951, states:

> The figures on the number of counter-revolutionaries killed in each locality must be restricted to a certain percentage: In the villages, it should not exceed 0.1% of the population, and in the cities it should not exceed 0.05%. In the Party, government and military administration, in the education and cultural, commercial and industrial and religious sectors, and in each of the democratic parties and civic organisations, the number of purged counter-revolutionaries sentenced to death should in principle be 10% to 20%.[9]

This quote was later published in *Selected Works of Mao Zedong*,[10] but with the percentages for the villages and cities edited out.

The percentage may look small, but 0.1 or 0.05% of a country's population is an enormous number. After killing and imprisoning so many counter-revolutionaries, proceeding to carry out another nationwide Campaign to Eliminate Counter-Revolutionaries required not only broadening the definition of 'counter-revolutionary' but also increasing the number of investigators and putting pressure on them in various ways. To this end, 750,000 cadres were assigned the task of eliminating counter-revolutionaries and carrying out 3.28 million investigations.[11]

Writer Zhu Zheng provides this analysis: more than 1.3 million people were purged during the Campaign to Eliminate Counter-Revolutionaries. At that time, 6.7 million people worked in China's government bodies,

---

[8] Ma Yuping, Huang Yuchong (eds), *China Yesterday and Today, 1840–1987 National Handbook*, Jiefangjun chubanshe, 1989, p. 737.
[9] *Record of Major Events in Modern China*, Beijing, Hualing chubanshe, 1993, p. 277.
[10] Vol. 5, p. 40.
[11] Ma Yuping, Huang Yuchong (eds), *China Yesterday and Today, 1840–1987 National Handbook*, op. cit., p. 740.

organisations, schools and enterprises, which means that one out of every five people became targets of the purge.[12]

Gu Wenxuan's essay 'My Experience', quoted above, says he had no 'problems' and shouldn't have been targeted as a counter-revolutionary, but he was still denounced as soon as the campaign began, clearly in order to meet the 5% quota.

There were too many people who were attacked like Gu Wenxuan during the Campaign to Eliminate Counter-Revolutionaries, as a result of which criticising the campaign was one of the most common items in what was subsequently labelled 'Rightist speech' in 1957. The 'Standards for Designating Rightists' passed by the Third Plenum of the Eighth Central Committee particularly stipulated that 'those who attack the struggle to eliminate counter-revolutionaries' should be classified as Rightists. This was the trap Gu Wenxuan fell into.

It should be pointed out that claiming to have been the victim of injustice is different from fundamentally questioning or refuting the Campaign to Eliminate Counter-Revolutionaries. Gu Wenxuan didn't condemn the campaign, but merely declared that he'd been wrongfully denounced. Even so, this was considered a serious crime, because the top authorities would not allow any criticism of it. The lack of opposition to the campaign or any in-depth negation of it meant that student Gu Wenxuan became a trailblazer who was knocked down before anyone else. Putting such a large number of people under investigation and then designating some as 'enemies' subject to perpetual punishment had become so routine that many Chinese never considered questioning or opposing it.

EXECUTION BY 'MASS DISCUSSION'

The 10 February 1970 notice by the Public Security, Procuratorial and Judicial Military Control Commission states: 'Revolutionary Committees at all levels and PLA Mao Zedong Thought Propaganda Teams are to organise serious discussion by the revolutionary masses.' If the masses were actually supposed to discuss how to deal with Gu Wenxuan, they should have been told what he had said. The real purpose of the 'discussion' was to intimidate the masses so they wouldn't dare say anything that could subject them to accusations of 'reactionary speech'.

Some of my interviewees took part in the 'discussion' that was required in order for the 'revolutionary masses' to decide how to handle the fifty-five

---

[12] *Summer of 1957: From the Hundred Flowers Movement to Contention between Two Schools of Thought*, Henan renmin chubanshe, 1998, pp. 256–261.

people listed in the document. They said the only voice that came out during the discussion was, 'Execute them! Execute them!' One interviewee said, 'Do you have any idea how evil people were in Beijing at that time? They didn't think anything of a person's life. After shouting out, "Execute them! Execute them!", they went home and ate their dinner.'

One of the fifty-five counter-revolutionaries on the list with Gu Wenxuan was Zhang Langlang, who at that time was a student at the Central Academy of Fine Arts. At first, a decision was made behind closed doors to execute him as well. He told me that he was shackled and escorted to his school to have the teachers and students there express their views on how to deal with him. His father and sixteen-year-old brother were also dragged out and stood below the stage listening to the chorus of voices calling for his execution. What Zhang never forgot was two art teachers, Huang Yongyu and Liu Xun, who refused to attend that rally. The two of them claimed to be ill and didn't go to school that day.

Zhang Langlang and his 'accomplice' Zhou Qiyue (a student at the Beijing Foreign Languages Institute), were twenty-ninth on the list, accused of the following 'crime':

> Zhang and Zhou have reactionary thinking and are extremely antagonistic to the Party and the socialist system. During the Great Proletarian Cultural Revolution, Zhang and Zhou disseminated reactionary speech, venomously slandered the proletarian headquarters and repeatedly plotted to betray the country and go over to the enemy. In February 1966, Zhang and Zhou made contact with foreign embassy personnel for the purpose of selling large quantities of our country's military, political and economic intelligence.

Zhang Langlang and Zhou Qiyue were ultimately sentenced to ten years in prison. Zhang says they were not handed death sentences as originally planned because their parents were long-time CCP members and high-level officials, so they were handled 'leniently'.

Zhang and Zhou were imprisoned for ten years merely because they had made friends with several students from France – who were in fact Leftists yearning for revolution, which is why they'd come to study in China. After the French students went home, all of the Chinese classmates they'd had contact with were arrested and harshly sentenced as 'secret agents' and 'counter-revolutionaries'.

When the 'revolutionary masses' were ordered to discuss whether to impose the death penalty on Zhang and Zhou, the people most sympathetic to them, Huang Yongyu and Liu Xun, could do nothing more than absent themselves from the rally. At that time, this was considered heroic conduct, and it was as rare as a unicorn. That alone shows what a horrific environment existed at the time. Even maintaining one's silence was extremely difficult. Demonstrating a sense of loyalty or justice and standing forward on behalf of others were concepts that simply didn't exist.

CONCLUSION

Tracing Gu Wenxuan's life chronologically, we see that he was brutally purged in 1955, and when he expressed his dissatisfaction with this in 1957, he was punished even more harshly. When he found his treatment unbearable, he decided to flee China in 1966, as a result of which he was punished even more harshly a third time in 1970. He would have no further opportunity to protest his treatment because this time it was the death penalty.

In 1949, Gu was just a fifteen-year-old boy. From then on he was persecuted in a series of political campaigns culminating in his execution. It is to my great regret that I could only pull together such a fragmentary record of his life. We know almost nothing about him as an individual – whether he was tall or short, fat or thin or what kind of temperament he had. On the other hand, this lack of information can be excused, because we can see that his personal qualities had nothing to do with his fate, which was tangled up in three 'political campaigns' that pushed him and millions of other ordinary Chinese towards suffering and death.

What was examined here was the fate of one man, Gu Wenxuan, who was ruthlessly persecuted to death. What makes his story so shocking is that there is nothing that distinguishes him from the rest of us.

Yu Luoke, born in 1942, was an apprentice at the Beijing People's Machine Factory. Yu's parents had been designated Rightists in 1957, so he wasn't allowed to go to college. In 1966 he wrote 'On Family Background' and other essays criticising the persecution of young people from 'bad family backgrounds', and he criticised the Cultural Revolution in his journal. He was arrested on 5 January 1968, and locked up in Beijing's Banbuqiao Detention Centre. On 5 March 1970, Yu Luoke was executed with a group of other 'counter-revolutionaries', including Gu Wenxuan.

Yu Luoke's younger brother, Yu Luowen, published a book[13] describing his upbringing and his experiences during the Cultural Revolution.

---

[13] Yu Luowen, *My Family*, Beijing, Zhongguo shehui kexue chubanshe, 2000.

Yu Luoke's essays are included in *Yu Luoke: Posthumous Writings and Recollections*.[14]

Yu's case led indirectly to the death of another young person. **Zheng Xiaodan**, a twenty-one-year-old student at the Beijing Institute of Geology Affiliated Secondary School, was detained on 26 April 1968 and died on 6 June, after being brutally tortured. Zheng had suffered bias and oppression after her father was designated a Rightist in 1957, and she preserved and disseminated Yu Luoke's essay opposing bias against young people from 'bad family backgrounds' while also expressing her own doubts regarding the Cultural Revolution. The parents of Zheng Xiaodan and Yu Luoke carried out a joint memorial service for the two young people in 1980.

Wang Peiying, born in 1915, a native of Kaifeng, Henan Province, was a child-care worker in the kindergarten of the Beijing Railway Design Institute. Prior to the Cultural Revolution, she had been forced to resign from the Party because she criticised Mao's general and specific policies, and in 1965 she was forcibly committed to a mental institution. During the Cultural Revolution, the mental institution sent her back to her work unit for incarceration, and she was arrested in 1968 for yelling, 'Down with Mao Zedong!' in the work unit's canteen. She was executed on 27 January 1970.

Wang Peiying was one of the many victims of the Cultural Revolution, but also one of the very few heroes of the resistance against it. The Revolution's brutality ensured that those who resisted were attacked and killed as soon as they stepped forward, before others could even know they existed.

Wang Peiying had already been arrested by a public security organ in 1968, but it was as a result of the Campaign to Attack Counter-Revolutionaries that she was put on trial on 1 January 1970, before some 100,000 spectators at what was then Beijing's largest venue, the People's Sports Stadium. There the Chinese People's Liberation Army Beijing Municipal Public Security and Judicial Military Control Commission sentenced her to death, and she was summarily executed. She and those sentenced with her were the first of several batches of 'counter-revolutionaries' tried and executed during the campaign.

An old document found in Beijing's antique book market was one of the documents released to every work unit in Beijing for 'mass discussion' before the handing down of death sentences, and this one pertained to Wang:

---

[14] Xu Xiao et al. (ed.), Zhongguo wenlian chubanshe, 1999.

> Current counter-revolutionary Wang Peiying, female, fifty-four years old, a native of Henan Province, a landlord element, engaged in odd jobs at the Railway Ministry's Railway Design Institute.
> Wang has stubbornly persisted in a reactionary standpoint. From 1964 to October 1968, she wrote more than 1,900 counter-revolutionary slogans and more than thirty reactionary rhymes, which she publicly disseminated at Tiananmen Square, the Xidan Market, work unit canteens and other public venues, and on numerous occasions shouted reactionary slogans, with extreme venom vilifying and slandering the proletarian headquarters and China's socialist system. While in custody, Wang persisted as an enemy of the people and wantonly cursed our Party, her counter-revolutionary arrogance insufferable to the extreme.

As with other judgments delivered during the Cultural Revolution, ordinary people were not told the content of Wang's 'counter-revolutionary slogans' and 'reactionary rhymes' or exactly how she 'venomously vilified and slandered the proletarian headquarters and China's socialist system'. She was executed on the same day that her judgment was delivered.

Through the father of a victim of the Cultural Revolution I was able to contact Wang's third son, Zhang Dazhong, who told me his mother's story:

> My mother, Wang Peiying, worked in the nursery of the Railway Design Institute. My father had become a refugee while a student during the War of Resistance against Japan, and he met and married my mother in Kaifeng. Mother was the only daughter of a wealthy local businessman and had graduated from Kaifeng's Jingyi Girls' Secondary School, which was run by the Catholic Church.[15] Father joined the CCP during the War of Resistance and eventually took Mother to Zhengzhou and then to Beijing, where he became a section chief in the Railway Ministry. Father died of illness in 1960, leaving Mother to raise seven children. Beginning in 1963, Mother began writing some things criticising Mao, and in 1965 she was forced to resign from the Party. Her work unit sent her to a mental institution.
> After Father died, our family received a supplementary allowance for one year, according to regulations. Mother's wages were 50 *yuan* per month. With seven children, that made life hard, and sometimes she became distraught, but for the most part she was normal. It was normal for her to discuss social problems with her family. I've also

---

[15] This school was established by American nuns, and in 1948 its founders went to Taiwan to run a school of the same name, which is known in English as Providence University.

read Mother's poems. They're what people would call doggerel. They cannot be called great poetry, but they're clear and coherent and there's nothing confused about their logic.

In 1965, I went every Sunday to the Anding Hospital's[16] Huilongguan ward to visit Mother. At that time she was still writing often. She said she was being open and aboveboard, and she mailed what she wrote to the Party Central Committee expressing her dissatisfaction. I didn't understand much at the time, but I was afraid and thought it imprudent.

One time at the hospital she told my sisters and brothers and me to have a photo taken, 'So I can look at you.' So we had a photo taken together. Another time she told me, 'Son, I've committed a serious crime and it may drag the rest of you down.' I didn't understand what she meant and just told her, 'Don't say that, just get better.' I started going to high school around that time.

During the Cultural Revolution, Kang Sheng[17] issued a special directive stating, 'Specific analysis has to be carried out on the mentally ill.' What he meant was that there were counter-revolutionaries among the mentally ill. In 1968, Anding Hospital expelled Mother, declaring that she was not mentally ill, and told her work unit to take her back. The work unit put her into its ox pen, and I was unable to see her from then on.

After the Cultural Revolution, I visited a Russian interpreter and two old cadres who had been locked up with Mother for more than three months. They told me what Mother had shouted the day she was arrested, and how she had been beaten. They also told me some details about the ox pen. They said that every day they had to do chores for the rebel faction, and my mother did her work meticulously and with full attention. When cleaning out cinders, she would set aside the coal that hadn't been burned through so it could be burned again. When she turned the cabbage, she would pile it up evenly, using a long wooden stick to keep the cabbage level, and then put the next layer of cabbage on top of that so the air would circulate around it. At that time, she was given only a small part of her wages, and she was only allowed to buy vegetables and no meat at the canteen. In order to save money, she didn't even buy fresh vegetables, but ate only steamed corn buns and salted vegetables every day. She told the women that she missed us, especially my youngest sister, who was the only girl in our family. The women said that my mother was mentally sound and a kind-hearted woman. They said that while in the ox pen, my mother wrote short notes that she would distribute when she went out to work. When the rebel faction found out about it, they burst into the ox

---

[16] Beijing's psychiatric hospital.
[17] At the height of his power, Kang Sheng was the fourth most powerful person in China.

pen and pushed her to the ground and beat and kicked her and made her 'confess her counter-revolutionary crimes', but she never made a sound. The other women urged her not to write any more, but it was no use. She said, I'm not the same as the rest of you. You'll all get out. (Meaning she would not) They said my mother would 'rather die than submit'.

On 1 October 1968, the 'ox demons and snake spirits' were escorted to the canteen, which was full of people. My mother stood before everyone and said in a loud voice, 'Down with Mao Zedong!' A group of 'revolutionary masses' charged over and beat Mother until she lost consciousness, then took her to the Public Security Bureau. There was no legal paperwork after that, but she was held for one year and four months.

In early 1970, my eldest brother's work unit was in Beijing building the subway, and the name list of counter-revolutionaries that the work unit discussed included our mother. At that time, this kind of material was sent to every work unit to 'educate' people, and whatever complaints ordinary people might have, they didn't dare say them. My mother was sentenced on 27 January, and the execution was carried out immediately. I didn't know it until 6:00 that night. Along the road, I heard a conversation between people who had attended the rally – the Workers' Stadium... public trial... death sentence. The neighbourhood committee posted the death sentence judgment in our courtyard in black and white with the names crossed out in red.

Three months later, someone came to our home saying they'd been sent by the court's military control commission. They had a paper that had to be signed. My eldest brother signed it. The man said just a few words and then left. My impression is that the man was dressed very sloppily. He let us read the document but didn't leave us a copy. Was it the judgment? No one gave judgments to family members. It was just some kind of form.

In 1977, I appealed on Mother's behalf. There was no doubt that Mother had said and written those things. Her 'attack on the proletarian headquarters' was genuine; she had really shouted those slogans and said 'Down with Mao Zedong.' But it was also true that she had once been sent to a mental hospital. My mother was eventually rehabilitated in 1980 on the grounds that 'the mentally ill cannot be held responsible for a crime.'

The life and death of Zhang Dazhong's mother took less than an hour to narrate and about 2,000 Chinese characters to write. Although I'd heard and written many tragic stories of victims of the Cultural Revolution, I still felt a suffocating sadness. Unable to think of what to say, I could only tell Zhang Dazhong, 'I have a document about your mother.'

The document found at the antique book stall described the 'nature of the offence' of twenty 'current counter-revolutionaries', and Wang Peiying was number eleven. She did in fact write poems and essays opposing the Cultural Revolution and Mao, but the document says she distributed 1,600 'reactionary' leaflets, a number that is clearly exaggerated. Even so, writing a 'reactionary' text is her only alleged criminal act. Nazi Germany's concentration camp regulations stated that anyone who in a letter or other document vilified the National Socialist Party or the head of state would be placed in custody for two weeks and whipped twenty-five times.[18] The brutality of the Cultural Revolution makes even this notorious dictatorship pale in comparison.

In terms of legal process (in law, the process is especially important), Wang Peiying was never given even a kangaroo court hearing. She was sentenced to death without being given the right to appeal, which existed even in ancient China. When she was condemned, her family members were not notified or allowed to say their goodbyes, and she was not allowed to leave last words for them.

Wang Peiying was a person with her own thinking and opinions, which everyone should have a right to. But in an era in which it was forbidden to criticise the authorities and supreme leader, a person with a different voice became 'mentally ill', and during the Cultural Revolution, with no legal system, with violence and persecution running rampant, the death penalty became the most convenient and thorough means of dealing with these alternative voices. Even after the Cultural Revolution was negated, it was only possible to rehabilitate someone on the grounds that they were 'mentally ill' rather than by explicitly declaring that freedom of expression is necessary, and no one should be convicted of a crime on the basis of their views.

Even today we have no way of knowing what she said that led to her death. Apart from the 'rehabilitation document' and court verdict, there is no file relating to her case or copies of the poem or essay for which she lost her life. The result of this Revolution is so clean and thorough that later generations don't know the names of many of the victims or what happened to them, much less what they were thinking.

I've never seen anyone as courageous as Wang Peiying, nor can I ascertain whether such a person could actually do any good. My mother once said that the number of people persecuted during the Cultural Revolution was horrific enough, but not hearing of anyone who dared to pass moral judgement upon it, even a minor criticism, made one feel even greater despair. If at that time she had heard Wang Peiying's voice, it would have made her feel less alone. The majority of people either stopped thinking

---

[18] See William L. Shirer, *The Rise and Fall of the Third Reich: A History of Nazi Germany*, English edition, p. 272. The Chinese edition was translated by Dong Leshan.

about it or surrendered to silence. But Wang Peiying was different; she surpassed ordinary people and became a hero.

After Wang was rehabilitated, the court gave her family 3,000 *yuan*, and her work unit paid another 4,000 *yuan*, which allowed 1,000 *yuan* for each of her seven children (at that time, an ordinary worker earned only 100 *yuan* per month). But the authorities were never willing to explicitly acknowledge that this was compensation for a wrongful judgment. Zhang Dazhong used his 1,000 *yuan* to open a small electrical appliance workshop, and over time he eventually became a major entrepreneur in China.

Over the telephone, Zhang Dazhong said that when he visited the US, he once saw a bronze statue commemorating a young man bound hand and foot, and he wept because it made him think of his mother. He didn't know the name of that man, but I located that bronze statue in Chicago. It commemorates Nathan Hale, a hero of the American War of Independence, who was only twenty-one years old when he lost his life. At the base of the statue are engraved his famous words: 'I only regret that I have but one life to lose for my country.'

People create statues of heroes in hopes that their name and spirit will circulate among humankind through the ages. One can only hope that someday a statue can be dedicated to Wang Peiying. But before than can happen, something else as meaningful as a bronze statue must be done, and that is to clarify the truth and insist on justice. Zhang Dazhong produced a documentary film entitled *My Mother, Wang Peiying*. Besides this, after obtaining a copy of the original rehabilitation judgment, he continued to appeal, and in 2011 he received a second rehabilitation judgment. The verdict consists of eight words: 'The defendant Wang Peiying is not guilty.'

Short and to the point, it declares a person who criticised Mao's policies and the Cultural Revolution, a person who cried out 'Down with Mao Zedong,' not guilty. As for whether Wang Peiying was mentally ill, whether she actually shouted that slogan, whether what she wrote regarding China's economic policies around 1960 and the content of her leaflets regarding the Cultural Revolution were correct, the court did not pass judgment, because none of these things have anything to do with whether she was 'guilty' or 'not guilty'.

The importance of the second rehabilitation judgment for Wang Peiying is in her 'reactionary leaflets' or 'reactionary slogans' being irrelevant to her guilt. This changed not only the verdict of a case, but also the standards for conviction. From a judicial standpoint, this is a significant difference. From a historical standpoint, this is a significant change. From a practical standpoint the power of the judicial verdict is that it is applies not only to an individual case, but also to all other cases of this kind, because in theory the law is supposed to be applied in the same way to all people. If the second rehabilitation judgment on Wang Peiying affects other cases, this is a precious gift that her sacrifice has given to the Chinese people, and we should be grateful to her.

Ren Daxiong, an assistant instructor in the Department of Mathematics and Mechanics at Peking University (from which he graduated in 1955), was labelled a Rightist in 1957. While serving time at a labour reform farm in 1960, he was sentenced to life imprisonment for 'organising a counter-revolutionary group' and 'attempting to betray China and go over to the enemy'. During the Cultural Revolution he was accused of 'actively participating in a counter-revolutionary riot' and was executed on 28 March 1970,[19] at the age of thirty-eight.

An interviewee who was an assistant instructor in Peking University's Biology Department in 1957 remembers reading Ren Daxiong's translation of Nikita Khrushchev's secret report 'On the Cult of Personality and its Consequence' in the library. Ren Daxiong posted his manuscript in the newspaper reading room and updated it every two or three days. My interviewee heard that Ren Daxiong had discovered the report in a newspaper of the Communist Party of the United Kingdom and had translated it paragraph by paragraph. Khrushchev delivered the report on 25 February 1956, to the Twentieth Congress of the Communist Party of the Soviet Union to criticise Stalin's purges, but the average Chinese reader had no access to it.

I have identified seven students among the 716 people labelled Rightists at Peking University who were eventually sentenced to death. Huang Zhongqi, a student in the Philosophy Department, was arrested on 30 January 1958, and then executed. The others were put to death during the Cultural Revolution: **Lin Zhao**, **Gu Wenxuan**, **Shen Yuan** and **Zhang Xikun** are profiled elsewhere in the book. In addition, **Wu Sihui**, a student of Physics, was executed in Luoyang, Henan Province, on 5 March 1970, at the age of thirty-seven.

Lu Lushan, a student at the Beijing Agricultural Machinery Institute, was designated a Rightist in 1957 and sent to re-education through labour. In early 1970, Lu was executed along with **Yao Zuyi**, **Wang Tongzhu** and **Sun Benqiao** in Nanjing for 'attempting to illegally cross the border and inciting educated youth to return to the city'. Lu's companions had also been designated Rightists in 1957 and sent to re-education through labour. Sun Benqiao had been a student at the Beijing University of Industry, Wang

---

[19] Criminal judgment of the People's Liberation Army Military Control Commission of the Public Security Organs of Datong City, No. 29, 1970.

Tongzhu had been a Russian translator with the CCP Central Committee's Bureau for the Compiling and Translating of the Works of Marx and Lenin, and Yao Zuyi was a graduate of Yenching University's Economics Department who had served as an English translator in the Ministry of Foreign Trade.

Lu Lanxiu, the fifty-three-year-old deputy director of the Suzhou Library, was sentenced to death as a 'counter-revolutionary' on 4 July 1970, after sending a petition to Mao requesting that the Cultural Revolution be ended. This was at the height of the campaign against counter-revolutionaries, and tens of thousands of people attended Lu's public trial in Suzhou. She was paraded through the streets before being executed.

In 1982, the Jiangsu Provincial Party Committee and Suzhou Municipal Party Committee issued a formal document retroactively recognising Lu as a 'revolutionary martyr' and restoring the Party membership that had been stripped from her after 1949.

Lu Lanxiu did something no one else had dared to do by petitioning Mao to immediately end the Cultural Revolution 'so that the revolutionary people of the world would not lose their way, so that the Marxist undertaking would not be broken off, and in order to liberate all of China's people and restore social order.'

In his preface to the book *Blood Flowing through Mountains and Passes: The life of a distinguished modern woman, Lu Lanxiu*, Li Rui wrote that Lu Lanxiu joined the Party in 1942 while a student at Wuhan University, that she was beaten during the Xiaguan Incident in Nanjing in 1946,[20] and that Zhou Enlai himself paid for dentures and a watch for her. After she was arrested, she studied *The Complete Works of Marx and Engels* in her prison cell. Lu Lanxiu attributed the Cultural Revolution to Mao's 'arrogance' and felt it deviated from the trajectory of Marxism.[21] In other words, she criticised the Cultural Revolution on the premise of Marxism and Mao Zedong Thought, or perhaps it could be said that when Lu Lanxiu was memorialised in 1996, it was on the basis of this principle, as in the case of Zhang Zhixin.

Lu Zhili, a young man in his twenties from Ningxia, joined with a dozen other young people to establish the Communist Self-Study University, which was alleged to be a 'counter-revolutionary organisation carrying the banner of studying Marxism and Mao Zedong Thought for the purpose

---

[20] TN: In June 1946, members of a delegation from Shanghai who went to Nanjing to petition the Nationalist government to end the Civil War were badly beaten.
[21] Li Rui, *People in My Heart*, Beijing, Sanlian shudian, 1996, p. 175.

of toppling our country's socialist dictatorship of the proletariat'. During the campaign against counter-revolutionaries in March 1970, Lu Zhili and his co-defendants, Ningxia natives **Wu Shuzhang** and **Wu Shusen**, were sentenced to death, while twenty-two-year-old **Xiong Manyi** committed suicide.

This case is described in Liu Xiaomeng's essay 'The Case of the Communist Self-Study University' in the *Encyclopedia of China's Educated Youth*.[22] The Communist Self-Study University was established in Yinchuan in November 1969 by thirteen university and newly graduated secondary school students, three of whom were educated youth who had been sent 'up the mountains and down into the villages'. The eldest of them was twenty-six years old, and the youngest twenty-one. In the Code of Conduct for the university they wrote:

> We wish to foster and bring up a group of revolutionary warriors who will grasp the historical development of Marxism in practice and not only in form, reliably and not superficially, courageously and not with cowardice; who have political components, who have the capacity for independent thinking and work, who are full of the spirit of sacrifice, who wish to explore and understand the patterns of modern social movements, who swear their allegiance to the interests of the absolute majority of people in the world, and who will steadfastly devote their lives to struggling for the communist cause.

Because the members didn't all live in the same place, the Code of Conduct also said that the Self-Study University 'carried out study centred on reading materials and through the combined methods of self-study, exchange and discussion'. The founders used their own money to print two issues of the university journal, which included an editorial and five other essays along with three village survey reports.

In March 1970, during the campaign against counter-revolutionaries, this organisation was labelled 'a current counter-revolutionary clique with organisation, guiding principles, plans, strategies, discussion and operations' and 'a thoroughly imperialist revisionist reactionary commando unit.' The evidence of their crime consisted of the essays they had published in their journal and the letters they'd exchanged with each other.

Among the thirteen founders, Wu Shusen, Wu Shuzhang and Lu Zhili were executed, while Chen Tongming was sentenced to life in prison, Xu Zhaoping to fifteen years, Zhang Weizhi to eight years and Zhang Shaochen

---

[22] Chengdu, Sichuan renmin chubanshe, 1995.

to three years. The remaining six were put into solitary confinement at their work units and struggled, as a result of which twenty-two-year-old Xiong Manyi killed herself.

Eight years later, in August 1978, the defendants in this case were rehabilitated, as reported in the *Ningxia Daily* on 7 August 1978, and in the 29 September 1978 edition of the *People's Daily*, which also published a commentary entitled 'The Drive of Revolutionary Youth Cannot be Stifled'. This essay commended these youths for 'engaging in strenuous physical labour in farms, commune production teams and factories while also assiduously studying the works of Marxism–Leninism and Chairman Mao with the spirit of intensively scrutinising theory and exploring truth'. It would appear from this article that if they had actually criticised Marxism–Leninism, they would not have been rehabilitated, which leads to the question of whether Communist theory can be criticised, and whether criticising it should lead to the death penalty.

In addition to the lack of a systematic and clear account of the people victimised during the Cultural Revolution, there has also been no critical examination of the theoretical and ideological sources of this persecution.

Shen Yuan, employed in the History Institute of the Chinese Academy of Sciences, was designated a Rightist while a student of history at Peking University in 1957. Targeted and persecuted during the Cultural Revolution, he smeared black shoe polish on his face and entered the embassy of an African nation, pleading for help to leave China, only to be arrested by the Chinese authorities. Shen Yuan was sentenced to death in March 1970. He was in his thirties.

Cheng Shuming, born in Beijing in 1925, was a researcher at the Shanghai Observatory. Cheng graduated with a degree in physics from Tsinghua University in 1948 and had made outstanding achievements relating to the astronomical clock. When the Cultural Revolution began, Cheng was put under 'penal labour under surveillance' for the crime of being a 'bourgeois reactionary technical authority'. In 1971, someone reported him for language 'injurious to the image of Jiang Qing' and he was once again put into isolation. He hanged himself while in custody.

Zuo Shutang, a resident of Shanghai's Urumqi Road, was beaten to death in 1970. A young worker who was under 'isolation and investigation' claimed that he'd heard Zuo listening to Voice of America and BBC broadcasts at home, which was a 'counter-revolutionary crime'. Zuo's home was searched, his son, Zuo Weimin, was put under 'isolation and investigation', and his daughter, Zuo Weizhen, was made to dig air-raid shelters. Zuo Shutang died while under investigation. When his family came for his body, they found it covered with wounds.

Zuo Weimin was accused of being a 'current counter-revolutionary' and wasn't rehabilitated until 1979. The young man who had accused Zuo Shutang was released and killed himself in a cave near Hangzhou's Lingyin Temple.

Cui Rongxing, born in 1945, was a student of mathematics in the class of 1968 at Fudan University. After graduation, Cui was assigned work on a military reclamation farm on Shanghai's Hengsha Island. In 1970, his schoolmate Fang Xiyuan (aka Fang Nong) was accused of being a member of the 'Hu Shoujun counter-revolutionary clique'.[23] Cui Rongxing had nothing to do with this 'clique', but because he had corresponded with Fang Xiyuan, he was put under 'isolation and investigation' at the farm. Added to that, his father had been an agricultural advisor to the Nationalist government before 1949, so he came under even greater pressure and was interrogated under torture. Cui Rongxing hanged himself sometime in 1970.

Tan Yuanquan, a worker at the Shanghai Steel Pipe Factory, was sentenced to death on 25 April 1970, because he used tunes from a Shanghai opera to sing a revolutionary model opera. The Shanghai Municipal Higher People's Court re-examined the case in April 1979, and the Shanghai Municipal Cultural Bureau declared Tan Yuanquan not guilty of the charge and posthumously restored his reputation.

Fang Yunfu, employed at the Chongqing branch of China People's Construction Bank, was sentenced to death by the Chongqing Municipal Public Security, Procuratorial and Judicial Military Control Commission on 6 March 1970, because he openly objected to the unjust treatment of President Liu Shaoqi. Fang was posthumously rehabilitated in 1980.

Zhu Shouzhong, sent to Ningxia as a Rightist in 1957, was executed in 1970 for 'current counter-revolutionary crimes'.

After graduating from the Politics and Economics Department of Fudan University in 1943, Zhu began teaching at Shanghai's Fuxing Secondary School, and joined the CCP in 1950. He later became vice-president of the Shanghai No. 1 Accelerated Normal School (originally located in Sichuan North Road). After being designated a Rightist in 1957, he was expelled from the Party and dismissed from his position, and was sent to Ningxia to teach at a secondary school. He appealed his punishment in 1965, but without success, and during the Socialist Education Movement he was designated a 'bad element'. In 1968, Zhu Shouzhong was sent to the Helan

---

[23] TN: Hu Shoujun was a student at Fudan University who opposed the January 1967 power seizure in Shanghai by Zhang Chunqiao and Yao Wenyuan (who later became members of the Gang of Four). Hu Shoujun and others were imprisoned as current counter-revolutionaries during the Cleansing of the Class Ranks and One Strike and Three Antis campaign.

County Laogai Farm for labour reform, and while there he expressed some personal views regarding the Cultural Revolution. He was executed on 11 February 1970, at the age of fifty.

Zeng Qinghua, a teacher at the Shiqian County Secondary School in Guizhou Province, opposed the Cultural Revolution's methods. A county-wide public trial on 3 August 1970, pronounced Zeng a current revolutionary, and he was sentenced to death and summarily executed. Zeng was rehabilitated in 1980 and his remains were moved to the Shiqian Revolutionary Martyr's Cemetery.

Cai Hanlong was a mechanic and team leader at the Kunming Steelworks thermoelectricity workshop. During the Cultural Revolution, order and discipline broke down at the factory, and in 1970 one of the workshop's medium-sized boilers burned out. The matter was reported to a higher level just as a central government leader, Xie Fuzhi, was visiting Kunming. Xie Fuzhi said, 'This has to be counter-revolutionary sabotage.' The two team leaders, Cai Hanlong and **Ma Shaoyi**, were accordingly sentenced to death and executed as counter-revolutionaries.

Xiong Yifu was a worker on the 1228 drilling crew of the Sichuan Petroleum Management Bureau. On 11 January 1971, the Chongqing City Ba County Procuratorate Military Control Commission charged Xiong with 'venomously attacking the Great Leader Chairman Mao and Vice-Chairman Lin' and sentenced him to death as a 'current counter-revolutionary'. The Ba County People's Court reviewed the case in 1980 and found that Xiong had been suffering from mental illness, and reversed the original death sentence.

Sun Fengdou, a student carrying out specialised research in electrification in the Machinery and Power-Generating Equipment Department of the Beijing Institute of Construction Materials (which had relocated to Changde, Hunan Province in 1969), was 'exposed' for 'reactionary language' in May 1970 and locked up. He attempted to escape but was caught, and while being escorted back to the school, he committed suicide by colliding with a tractor.

Sun came from an 'upper-middle peasant' family in a rural village. They didn't qualify as 'black elements' but once Sun Fengdou was designated a counter-revolutionary, his parents became 'counter-revolutionary family members'. After the People's Commune learned of Sun's death, it held a rally to denounce his parents, and they died soon afterwards.

A former classmate of Sun Fengdou said that at that time, some students had discussed things relating to the Cultural Revolution's leaders, but very few could understand enough to criticise the Revolution. No one seems to know what Sun is supposed to have said. The institute had three students who were arrested and imprisoned for seven years for 'reactionary language' during this time; several others were labelled 'reactionary students' and put under long-term 'labour under surveillance'.

The 'military representatives' in charge of the school at the time were young soldiers. Some of them went back to the military ranks after leading the Cleansing of the Class Ranks, the One Strike and Three Antis campaign and the campaign to 'Root out the May 16 Clique', and were promoted. After the death of Lin Biao, some were punished for being members of the 'small armada' of trusted followers of Lin's son, Lin Liguo, but their punishment had nothing to do with causing the deaths of Sun Fengdou and other ordinary people.

PURGE OF THE 16 MAY CONSPIRATORIAL CLIQUE

The investigation of a small group of 'radical' students at the Foreign Languages Institute in 1967 was revived with a much wider scope in March 1970 and continued into 1972, overlapping with the One Strike and Three Antis Campaign. An estimated 100,000 people died after being targeted as '16 May Elements'.

The 'logic' of the campaign against the May 16 Clique was that Qi Benyu, a member of the Central Cultural Revolution Small Group, had just been 'struck down', and Qi had publicly supported the movement to 'pluck out Liu Shaoqi' in July 1967. Back then, a small student organisation named after the 16 May Circular had been active in this movement, but it had been 'crushed' by October 1967. Nevertheless, any student leaders who had called for Liu Shaoqi's ousting at that time were accused of having taken part in a counter-revolutionary movement as members of that tiny and ephemeral group.[24] On 27 March 1970, the CCP Central Committee issued a 'Notice Regarding Thoroughly Investigating the 16 May Counter-revolutionary Conspiratorial Clique'. During the ensuing investigation, some prominent leaders of revolutionary rebel groups came under attack and investigation. Interrogated under torture by some of the same methods they had previously used against others, many gave 'frank debriefings' about completely nonexistent 'counter-revolutionary plots'.

---

[24] For more details on this surrealistic episode, see Yang Jisheng, *The World Turned Upside Down* (Stacy Mosher and Guo Jian, trans.), Farrar, Straus and Giroux, 2021, pp. 284–304.

The formal report on the incident at that time continued to refer to Liu Shaoqi as 'Thief Liu' while concluding that the students who organised the 'pluck Liu' campaign had 'used it as a cover, and their hunger strike as an artifice, to create public opinion and raise a force to stage a rebellion with the objective of opposing the Premier and with its spearhead aimed directly at the proletarian headquarters headed by Chairman Mao and Vice-chairman Lin, in a vain attempt to subvert the dictatorship of the proletariat and carry out a counter-revolutionary power seizure.'[25]

Dong Linping, a student in the Silicon Department of the Beijing Institute of Building Materials, killed herself on 4 August 1970, after coming under investigation during this purge.

At the outset of the Cultural Revolution, Dong Liping was a second-year student, and her father was a high-ranking military cadre. Someone who knew her described her as a tall, delicate and pretty young woman. When the Cultural Revolution began, Dong was 'purged' for opposing the work group sent to the institute and attempted suicide. After Mao ordered the university work groups to withdraw, Dong became leader of a 'revolutionary rebel group' called the Red Guard 1 August Combat Unit, established on that date in 1966. The Combat Unit became increasingly powerful at the institute over the next two years, and rose to fame by organising the 'pluck Liu' rally outside the government's Zhongnanhai residential compound in 1967.

After the 'pluck Liu' rally was designated a cover for rebellion against the proletarian headquarters, members of the Combat Unit confessed under torture to belonging to a 'conspiratorial clique' that required members to fill out a secret form and allowed only 'one-way contact' among members, and that one of the 'counter-revolutionary objectives' of their siege of Zhongnanhai was to prevent Premier Zhou Enlai from getting a good night's sleep. These details were later found to have been completely fabricated.

Wang Deyi, a teaching assistant in the Foreign Languages Department of Beijing Normal University, committed suicide while being interrogated about the May 16 Clique in 1970. He was survived by his wife, Qian Yuan.

Li Mingzhe, a lecturer at the Beijing Institute of Geology, was investigated as an alleged member of the May 16 Clique while attending the May 7 Cadre School of the Jiangxi Xiajiang Institute of Geology in 1971. He fled while in custody, and his decomposed corpse was later found on a barren hillside.

---

[25] 'Regarding the Seige of Zhongnanhai: A Preliminary Exposure, Debriefing and Investigation, Beijing Institute of Building Materials Investigation Group', 25 February 1971, mimeographed typescript.

Men Chunfu, a musician with the Central Philharmonic Orchestra, killed himself in the basement room where he was being held and interrogated in 1970 during investigations into the May 16 Clique.

Qian Xinmin, in his twenties, was a teacher in the Computer and Mathematics Department of Nanjing University. After being criticised, struggled and beaten during the purge of the May 16 Clique, he fled to the outskirts of Nanjing and jumped to his death from Swallow Rock.

Shi Tianxi, a technician in the Wuhan Hydrobiology Institute of the Chinese Academy of Sciences, had once served as head of a rebel faction and had been involved in struggling other people. He hanged himself after coming under investigation as a member of the May 16 Clique in 1971. Four of the Hydrobiology Institute's 400 staff killed themselves after being struggled and investigated during the Cultural Revolution.

Yan Kai, born in 1946, was a student of folk music at the Shanghai Conservatory of Music. His parents were high-level cadres in Shanghai, and at the outset of the Cultural Revolution, he was an active Red Guard. Later Yan's parents were 'struck down', and he was locked up and interrogated during the investigation of the May 16 Clique. He killed himself by slitting his wrists on 8 March 1970.

Yi Gang, a thirty-two-year-old teacher at the Nanjing Forestry Institute, threw himself in front of a train after being accused of being a member of the May 16 Clique in 1971. Yi Gang had been a counsellor for the Young Pioneers at the Shanghai Fuxing Secondary School in 1960, and had studied at the Wuhan Institute of Surveying.

Zhu Yaoxin, an astronomy teacher at Nanjing University, was sent to the Liyang Labour Reform Farm as a 'sprout of revisionism'. During the campaign against the May 16 Clique he was put under 'isolation and investigation' and harshly beaten. He attempted to escape during the night, but drowned after falling into a lake.

ZHEJIANG, QIAOSI MILITARY RECLAMATION FARM

The Cultural Revolution caused delays to the graduation and job assignments of university students, and many were first assigned to military reclamation farms to work before being given permanent jobs. One group of Shanghai University students who should have graduated in 1967 were sent in 1968 to the Qiaosi Military Reclamation Farm, which incarcerated people undergoing reform through labour. A group of students at the Qiaosi

Farm committed suicide during the One Strike and Three Antis Campaign and the investigation of the May 16 Clique in 1970, including these three, whose full names I have not been able to ascertain:

- A student of folk music at the Shanghai Conservatory of Music who had been a member of its Revolutionary Committee, surnamed Lin.
- A returned overseas Chinese who was a student of vocal music at the Shanghai Conservatory of Music hanged himself after coming under investigation as a 'major counter-revolutionary' when a packet of Mao's portraits was discovered in a toilet pit. As an overseas Chinese, he was considered politically unreliable.
- A student from the Shanghai Institute of Finance and Economics, nicknamed 'little tailor' because of his sewing skills, killed himself with scissors.

PART SEVEN

Late Cases

After the second upsurge in violence beginning in 1968, the CCP became increasingly riven with inner conflict, culminating in the death of Mao's chosen successor, Lin Biao, during an attempt to flee China in September 1971. Coupled with the general public's exhaustion with constant political compaigns, persecution deaths diminished in number. Even so, it is worth noting that people continued to be persecuted to death and executed even after the death of Mao in September 1976 as a result of earlier political 'crimes'.

Yan Shuangguang, the forty-two-year-old deputy director of metallurgy at the No. 132 Factory in Chengdu, Sichuan Province, was beaten to death in a 'Mao Zedong Thought Study Session' at the Lanzhou Air Force Headquarters on 7 September 1971.

In 1996, I interviewed Yan's younger brother, Yan Siguang. He told me that when he and another younger brother went to Chengdu three days later to arrange for Yan Shuangguang's funeral, they saw that his body had no obvious wounds but was swollen, and he had only one tooth left. They heard that their brother had been beaten with an iron chain wrapped in plastic. 'Down with Yan Shuangguang' was written in large script on the walls and floors.

The servicemen who spoke with the brothers disappeared a few days later, and were said to be connected with the Lin Biao Incident, which occurred on 13 September. Later the leader of the Mao Zedong Thought Study Session was locked up in Beijing's Qincheng Prison (which was used for incarcerating high-level cadres and special political criminals). Yan Siguang decided to go there and ask that person how his brother had died. After Yan Siguang had filled out the necessary forms and waited for several hours, a prison official came out and asked why he was there. He said, 'Because my brother was tortured to death.' The official replied, 'Just that one person?'

'I'll never forget his tone of voice and the expression on his face,' Yan Siguang said. 'What he meant was, if only one person died, it wasn't worth asking about. One person being beaten to death was a minor matter. I wasn't allowed to see the prisoner. We just said one person was tortured to death, and that person did it with his own hands, but it wasn't worth mentioning.'

When Yan Shuangguang died, his father, Yan Jici, took over raising his nine-year-old son Yan Xiaoxiong. Yan Jici, born in 1900, had studied physics in France, and was one of the key people who brought Western modern physics to China. After the Cultural Revolution, he was appointed director of the Chinese Academy of Sciences. Yan Xiaoxiong always believed his father had died as the result of an accident during a chemical experiment. It was only when Yan Shuangguang was rehabilitated after the Cultural Revolution that his son learned the truth.

Sun Boying, born in 1935, was a teacher at the Sui County Hongshan Primary School in Hubei. He was brutally denounced during the Cultural Revolution, and was deprived of his pay and food rations. Accused of 'being dissatisfied with the Cultural Revolution', he was savagely beaten again in May 1968 and sent to the county Public Security Bureau, which refused his case. He was sent to the county for investigation again on 17 March 1971, but again the local PSB refused to sentence him, and he was sent home eight months later. In order to prevent his family from becoming involved in his troubles, Sun left his home on 28 March 1972, and hid in the caves of Kuifeng Mountain, living like a wild man. He was arrested on 30 September 1972, and jailed for 'opposing the Cultural Revolution'. He refused to admit his crime, respond to questioning or wear a jail uniform. Sun died in prison on 22 June 1973 and was rehabilitated in 1980.

Li Jingwen, around forty years old, was a language teacher at Shanghai's May 7th Secondary School. He had been a teacher of Chinese at Fudan University, but in the early 1960s was transferred to Shanghai's Fuxing Secondary School as a language teacher. Targeted during the 1968 Cleansing of the Class Ranks, he was transferred to the newly established May 7th Secondary School. After the announcement of Mao's death was broadcast on 9 September 1976, Li was accused of 'celebrating Chairman Mao's death' because he drank liquor at dinner that night. He killed himself a few days before the Cultural Revolution ended.

Zhang Xikun, admitted to Peking University as a chemistry student in 1954, was designated a Rightist in 1957 and held in a 'labour reform team' in Sichuan throughout the Cultural Revolution. Zhang was executed in Yanyuan, Sichuang Province, on 26 August 1975, for 'attempting to organise a prison break.' His younger sister, Zhang Xizheng, rejected the 'rehabilitation certificate' that the government offered after the Cultural Revolution, saying, 'It's meaningless to my brother.'

Li Jiulian, born in 1946, was a student in the Ganzhou No. 3 Secondary School in 1966 and was assigned an apprenticeship in a factory in 1968. After expressing alternative views of the Cultural Revolution, she was sentenced to death on 14 December 1977. Her case was re-examined under orders from Hu Yaobang in 1980, and she was rehabilitated.

Xinhua journalist Dai Huang looked into Li Jiulian's case in 1980 and read her file, and he provided the details in his subsequent book, *Hu Yaobang and the Redress of Unjust Cases*.[1]

Before the Cultural Revolution, Li had served as propaganda head for the Ganzhou No. 3 Secondary School Communist Youth League, and during the Cultural Revolution was deputy commander of the Weidongbiao (meaning 'defend Mao Zedong and Lin Biao') Rebel Corps. While working at the factory, she was arrested in 1969 after expressing doubts about Lin Biao in a letter to her boyfriend. After Lin Biao died, her case was designated 'a contradiction between the enemy and us handled as a contradiction among the people.' Appealing repeatedly without result, in spring 1974, she wrote a big-character poster entitled 'Opposing Lin Biao is not a crime' and demanded rehabilitation. An 'Investigation Committee on the Li Jiulian Problem' was established locally, and in May 1975, the Xingguo County People's Court sentenced her to fifteen years in prison. After Mao died, Li expressed her dissatisfaction with Hua Guofeng's arrest of the Gang of Four and also criticised Deng Xiaoping. This led to her being sentenced to death for the 'counter-revolutionary crime' of 'venomously attacking the Wise Leader Chairman Hua'. She was executed on 14 December 1977.

After Dai Huang reported Li Jiulian's case in the Xinhua News Agency's *Internal Reference* in January 1981, Hu Yaobang issued a memo calling for the case to be re-examined and redressed.

The most significant aspect of this rehabilitation is that once Deng Xiaoping took over from Hua Guofeng as China's paramount leader in 1978, ordinary people who made comments about top leaders were no longer sentenced to death. This was obviously an extremely important advancement in terms of the basic rights of China's people.

More than fifty people were reportedly executed under conditions similar to Li Jiulian's during Hua Guofeng's brief rule, including **Wang Shenyou**, a student at Shanghai's East China Normal University. After writing some opinions in his journal, Wang was imprisoned for two years early in the

---

[1] Beijing, Zhongguo wenlian chuban gongsi, Xinhuan chubanshe, 1998.

Cultural Revolution and then made to 'labour under supervision' at the university. In 1976, he wrote a long letter to a female friend explaining his views of politics and life, as a result of which he was sentenced to death in April 1977 at the age of thirty-one. More than 30,000 people attended his public trial and execution.

Veteran *People's Daily* reporter Jin Feng read Wang Shenyou's file in Shanghai in 1980, and felt he was a hero in the same mould as Zhang Zhixin. But after Jin Feng finished her lengthy article, the CCP Central Committee's Propaganda Department barred it from publication.[2]

From Jin Feng's description, we learn that Wang Shenyou was a Marxist, that he criticised the Cultural Revolution, and that he commended Zhou Enlai and Deng Xiaoping, all of which are consistent with official propaganda from 1978 onwards. That suggests that Jin Feng's story on Wang Shenyou was banned not because Wang's thinking was unacceptable, but because his imprisonment and execution based on his journal, letters and 'confessions' would lead people to question the entire system.

Jin Feng's article also stated: 'The leaders of the Shanghai Municipal Revolutionary Committee authorised fifty-six death sentences in one day, taking an average of six minutes to approve one death sentence, and Wang Shenyou had the misfortune to be among them.' We don't know anything about the other fifty-five cases.

Four months after Wang Shenyou was executed, in August 1977, the CCP held its Eleventh Party Congress. At that groundbreaking meeting, Central Committee Chairman Hua Guofeng declared that by virtue of the 'Smashing of the Gang of Four', the Cultural Revolution had ended.

---

[2] See Jin Feng, 'He Fell under the Muzzles of the "Two Whatevers"' in *The Days We All Experienced*, Beijing Shiyue wenyi chubanshe, January 2001.

Alphabetical Index of Victims

An Daqiang 449
An Tiezhi 355
Aunty Guo 248
Aunty Ma 249–50
Aunty Zuo 249–50

Bai Jingwu 191
Bai Sulian 270
Bi Jinzhao 495
Bian Jiannian 449
Bian Yulin 339
Bian Zhongyuan 390
Bian Zhongyun 23–4, 118–28, 129–31, 133–40

Cai Hanlong 532
Cai Liting 101
Cai Qiyuan 450–1
Cao Shimin 456
Cao Tianxiang 232–3
Chang Xiping 32
Chen Bangjian 267
Chen Bangxian 494
Chen Baokun 159–60, 161–2
Chen Boming 438–9
Chen Buxiong 435–6

Chen Chuanbi 452
Chen Chuangang 16
Chen Fuzhong 450
Chen Haoxuan 432
Chen Jing 467
Chen Lian 46–7, 330–1
Chen Mengjia 101–4, 291
Chen Tianchi 449
Chen Tongdu 74, 375
Chen Yanrong 194–203
Chen Yaoting 496
Chen Yinglong 385–6
Chen Yonghe 372–3
Chen Youqin 445
Chen Yuanzhi 233–5
Chen Yurun 236, 238
Chen Ziqing 459
Chen Zixin 299
Chen Zudong 382–3
Cheng Guoying 384
Cheng Min 158–9
Cheng Shihu 385
Cheng Shuming 530
Cheng Xiance 78–85
Cheng Xiandao 431
Cheng Yingquan 384

Cheng Yuan 366
Cheng Zhengqing 294
Cheng Zhuoru 110, 259–60
Chu Anping 294–5
Chu Guocheng 493
Cui Rongxing 531
Cui Shumin 447
Cui Xiongkun 333, 370–1

Dai Shuwan 64, 377, 380–1
Dang Qingfan 273–7
Deng 462
Deng Tuo 324
Ding Suqin 433
Ding Xiaoyun 105
Ding Yuying 278
Dong Huaiyun 87–8
Dong Jifang 386
Dong Linping 534
Dong Silin 259
Dong Tiebao 371–2
Dong Yaocheng 232
Dong Youdao 440–2
Du Fangmei 298
Du Mengxian 309–10, 463
Duan Hongshui 339

Fan Bugong 457
Fan Changjiang 329–30
Fan Gengsu 439
Fan Jisen 110
Fan Lecheng 497
Fan Mingru 431
Fan Ximan 179
Fan Xueyin 116–17
Fan Ying 430
Fan Zaoshen 495
Fang Junjie 252–3
Fang Shicong 433
Fang Tingzhi 411, 412, 415
Fang Yingyang 295–6
Fang Yunfu 531

Fei Mingjun 106–7
Feng Shikang 280
Feng Tingzhi 174
Feng Wenzhi 443
Fu Guoxiang 387
Fu Lehuan 70
Fu Lei 297–8
Fu Manyun 109
Fu Qifang 422
Fu Weiliang 33

Gao Bin 117
Gao Jiawang 399
Gao Jingguo 416
Gao Jingshan 452
Gao Jingxing 496–7
Gao Wanchun 164–5
Gao Yangyun 33–4
Gao Yunsheng 16
Ge Panyu (wife of) 220–1
Geng Ligong 346
Gong Qiwu 116
Gong Weitai 368–70
Gu Eryi 305
Gu Jingyan 494
Gu Shengying 299–300, 301–2
Gu Wenxuan 498–503, 505–16, 518, 519, 520, 527
Gu Woqi 299–300
Gu Yuzhen 434
Guang Kaimin 100
Guo Dun 306
Guo Lanhui 145–6
Guo Shiying 355
Guo Wenyu 241–2

Hai Mo 306
Hai Tao 336
Han Guangdi 489–92
Han Guoyuan 480–1
Han Junqing 307
Han Kang 264–5

ALPHABETICAL INDEX OF VICTIMS | 543

Han Liyan 461
Han Zhen 453
Han Zhiying 270
Han Zhongxian 340, 342–4
Han Zongxin 252–3
Hao Li 428
He Dinghua 240
He Guanghan 419
He Hancheng 216, 220
He Houye 90
He Hui 294
He Ji 24, 114
He Jiefu 89, 90, 91
He Peihua 266–7
He Shenyan 231
He Sijing 356–7
He Wuqi 305
He Xiaoqiu 443–4
He Yitang 375
Hu Junru 116
Hu Maode 327
Hu Ming 105
Hu Shuhong 359–60
Hu Xiuzheng 388–98
Hu Zhengxiang 493
Hua Jin 174–8, 390
Huang Bixin 114–16, 462
Huang Guozhang 116–17
Huang Jiahui 438
Huang Mengzhang 262
Huang Ruiwu 236–9
Huang Weiban 236, 238
Huang Wenlin 446–7
Huang Xinduo 467
Huang Yaoting 428
Huang Zhongxiong 455
Huang Zhongxiu 457
Huang Zubin 265–6

Ji Gaicheng 494
Ji Xinmin 421
Ji Zhongshi 495

Jian Bozan 64, 376–81
Jiang Cheng 453
Jiang Feng 100
Jiang Longji 11–16
Jiang Nan 465–6
Jiang Peiliang 178–9
Jiang Tiyun 36
Jiang Yiping 328
Jiang Yongning 422, 423
Jiang Zhong 347
Jiao Qiyuan 431
Jiao Tingxun 419–20
Jin Danan 428
Jin Huan 235–6
Jin Zhengyu 179
Jin Zhixiong 256

Kang Zhaoming 456
Kong Haikun 203
Kong Mumin 224
Kou Huiling 248

Lao She 146, 283–91
Lei Aide 494–5
Li Bingquan 328–9
Li Changgong 297
Li Congzhen 180, 181
Li Cuizhen 110, 300
Li Da 25–7
Li Dacheng 373–4
Li Dashen 439
Li Dehui 267
Li Guangtian 34–6
Li Guoquan 298
Li Guorui 361
Li Guozhong 33
Li Jianping 240
Li Jie 404, 406–8
Li Jigu 424–5, 427–8
Li Jingpo 206–7
Li Jingwen 538
Li Jisheng 330

Li Jiulian 539
Li Keng 361
Li Liang 335
Li Mingzhe 534
Li Peiying 239
Li Piji 383
Li Pingxin 46, 70, 104–5, 300
Li Qichen 376
Li Qiuye 32–3
Li Quanhua 347
Li Shaobai 259
Li Shibai 347–8
Li Shunying 278
Li Tiemin 16
Li Wen 263
Li Wenbo 181–5, 187–91
Li Wenyuan 340
Li Xin 386
Li Xiqin 459–60
Li Xiurong 236, 238
Li Xiuying 431
Li Xueying 260
Li Yuan 367–8
Li Yushu 454
Li Yuzhen 385
Li Zaiwen 299
Li Zhongming 24, 114
Li Zonghua 354
Liang Baoshun 308
Liang Guangqi 185–6
Liang Qiuse 95
Liang Xikong 398–9
Liao Jiaxun 307–8
Liao Peizhi 453
Lin Hongxun 385
Lin Lizhen 436–7
Lin Moyin 345
Lin Qinglei 472
Lin Xiuquan 261
Lin Zhao 352–4, 527
Liu Chengxian 382
Liu Chengxiu 419

Liu Dezhong 107–8
Liu Guilan 169
Liu Hao 479–80
Liu Jihong 458
Liu Jingxia 438
Liu Junhan 472
Liu Kelin 134, 325
Liu Pansui 95–8
Liu Peishan 336
Liu Shaoqi 310, 311–16, 318–24
Liu Shiqin 356
Liu Shousong 455
Liu Shuhua 147–51, 152–7, 187
Liu Wang Liming 331–4
Liu Wenxiu 183, 191
Liu Yongji 112
Liu Zhongxuan 356
Liu Zongqi 346
Lou Hedong 348
Lou Shouping 481–9
Lou Wende 309
Lu Guyu 458
Lu Hong'en 300, 301, 302–5
Lü Jianyuan 266
Lu Jiaxun 116
Lü Jingzhen 89
Lu Jinren 88–9
Lu Lanxiu 528
Lu Lushan 527
Lü Naipu 72
Lu Shouyan 478
Lü Xianchun 330
Lu Xikun 368
Lu Xiutang 110
Lu Xueming 385
Lü Zhenxian 241–2
Lu Zhiheng 98–9
Lu Zhili 528–30
Luo Fengjiao 116
Luo Guangbin 345–6
Luo Guitian 170
Luo Juemin 33

ALPHABETICAL INDEX OF VICTIMS | 545

Luo Sen 443
Luo Zhengfu 339
Luo Zhongyu 356

Ma Guifang 446
Ma Qishuang 110–11
Ma Shaoyi 532
Ma Siwu 432–3
Ma Te 99
Ma Tieshan 231–2
Ma Yinchu 53–5
Ma Ying 451–2
Ma Youyuan 428
Mao Qingxian 109
Mao Yiming 457
Mei Fenglian 468
Men Chunfu 535
Meng Fudi 366
Meng Xiangyun 159
Meng Zhaojiang 241–2
Miao Zhichun 309
Mo Ping 170, 420–1
Mu Shuqing 452–3

Nan Hanchen 327
Nan Helong 192–4

Pan Guangdan 37–9, 42–3, 48, 50,
 51–2, 55–7, 58–61, 330
Pan Zhihong 340
Pang Chengfeng 451
Pang Hongxuan 241
Peng Kang 30–1
Peng Peng 109

Qi Huiqin 230–1
Qi Qinghua 222–4
Qi Shiqian 104, 134
Qi Xiangyun 109
Qian Pinghua 339
Qian Songqi 258
Qian Xianlun 457

Qian Xingsu 109
Qian Xinmin 535
Qin Shenyi 299
Qin Song 255
Qiu Fengxian 257
Qiu Qingyu 248
Qiu Shupei 451
Qu Fuzi 280

Rao Yutai 371
Ren Daxiong 527
Ren Fuyan 457
Rong Guotuan 422, 423–4
Ruan Jieying 420

Sa Zhaochen 265–6
Sha Ping 170–2
Shang Hongzhi 449
Shangguan Yunzhu 305–6
Shao Kai 27
Shen Baoxing 91–5
Shen Jiaben 458
Shen Jie 256
Shen Naizhang 86–7
Shen Shimin 191
Shen Xianzhe 176, 390
Shen Xin'er 106
Shen Yaolin 308
Shen Yuan 527, 530
Shen Zhibai 445
Shen Zongyan 458
Sheng Zhangqi 258
Shi Jimei 436–7
Shi Qingyun 269–70
Shi Tianxi 535
Shi Zhicong 239
Shu Sai 308–9
Song Liwu 456
Su Tingwu 211–12, 419
Su Yuxi 258
Sun (woman surnamed) 279
Sun Benqiao 527–8

Sun Bin 335
Sun Boying 538
Sun Chifu 262
Sun Di 226–9
Sun Fengchi 449
Sun Fengdu 532–3
Sun Guoying 432
Sun Huilian 309
Sun Jingxiang 257, 438
Sun Keding 348
Sun Lan 331
Sun Liangqi 246–7
Sun Lisheng 174, 411, 412–19
Sun Meisheng 98
Sun Ming 497
Sun Mingzhe 345
Sun Qikun 221
Sun Rongxian 456
Sun Ruojian 428
Sun Weidi 349
Sun Yang 27–8
Sun Yukun 221
Sun Zhaolu 449
Sun Zuoliang 250

Tan Huizhong 456
Tan Liping 442–3
Tan Runfang 252–3
Tan Yuanquan 531
Tang Guoquan 454
Tang Hai 386
Tang Jiahan 375–6
Tang Jingyi 494
Tang Lin 28–30
Tang Pinsan 420
Tang Shiheng 494
Tang Xingheng 458
Tang Zheng 267–9
Tao Qian 462
Tao Zhong 457
Tian Han 294
Tian Tao 337

Tian Xin 27
Tian Yue 205–6
Tian Zunrong 496
Tong Junting 112
Tong Mingyuan 462

Wan Dexing 494
Wang Bi 327
Wang Bingyao 495–6
Wang Bogong 272–3
Wang Dashu 385
Wang Dehong 457
Wang Deming 309
Wang Deyi 534
Wang Gengcai 111
Wang Guanghua 213–16, 434
Wang Guopang 458
Wang Hailian 457
Wang Hanying 211–12, 419
Wang Hong 101
Wang Hou 404
Wang Huichen 384
Wang Huilan 248–9
Wang Huimin 443
Wang Jia'en 445
Wang Jian 70, 74–5, 76
Wang Jimin 112
Wang Jin 263–4
Wang Leng 270–3
Wang Maorong 310, 462–3
Wang Nianqin 347
Wang Peiying 521–7
Wang Peiyuan 162, 163
Wang Qingping 243–6
Wang Renli 110
Wang Shaoyen 309
Wang Shengguan 241
Wang Shenyou 539–40
Wang Shouliang 420
Wang Shu 458
Wang Sijie 111
Wang Songlin 340

Wang Tongzhu 527–8
Wang Xianglin 497
Wang Xiongfei 474–9
Wang Yimin 261
Wang Ying 306
Wang Yonghai 138–9
Wang Yongting 116
Wang Yunqian 258
Wang Yuxiu 459
Wang Yuzhen 409–10
Wang Zaoshi 109, 477
Wang Zhanbao 251–2
Wang Zhaojun 162, 163–4
Wang Zhenguo 458
Wang Zhicheng 451
Wang Zhifu 494
Wang Zhixin 349
Wang Zhongfang 469–74
Wang Zhongyi 325
Wang Zuhua 476–7
Wei Siwen 28
Wen Duansu 269
Wen Jiaju 344
Wen Jie 298, 300
Weng Chao 431
Wu Aizhu 89
Wu Bixi 109
Wu Disheng 105
Wu Han 282, 324
Wu Hongjian 494
Wu Jingcheng 108
Wu Shuqin 456
Wu Shuqiu 111
Wu Shusen 529–30
Wu Shuzhang 529–30
Wu Sihui 527
Wu Supeng 222, 224
Wu Weiguo 109
Wu Weijun 89, 355
Wu Weineng 375
Wu Xiaofei 450
Wu Xiaoyan 282

Wu Xinghua 77–8
Wu Xinyou 258
Wu Xiyong 387
Wu Yaxiong 450

Xi Lusi 112
Xia Zhongmou 265
Xia Zhongshi 335
Xiang Chong 100
Xiang Da 75–6
Xiao Chengshen 428
Xiao Guangyan 463–4
Xiao Jing 239
Xiao Luolian 464
Xiao Shikai 251
Xiaobaiyu Shuang 187
Xie Jiarong 100–1
Xie Juzhang 496
Xin Zhiyuan 462
Xing Deliang 494
Xing Zhizheng 267
Xiong Huaqi 24, 113–14
Xiong Manyi 529–30
Xiong Yifu 532
Xu Bu 335
Xu Guangda 327–8
Xu Hui'er 100
Xu Jiqing 267
Xu Lai 306
Xu Lanfang 162, 163
Xu Peitian 176, 216–18, 219
Xu Tao 305
Xu Xingqing 279
Xu Yin 386
Xu Youfen 386–7
Xu Yueru 366–7
Xu Zhengyang 111
Xu Zhizhong 460–1
Xu Zhong 159
Xue Shimao 468–9
Xue Tinghua 101

Yan Fengying 307
Yan Huizhu 306–7
Yan Jufeng 267
Yan Kai 535
Yan Shuangguang 537–8
Yan Yuyou 445–6
Yan Zhixian 431
Yang Aimei 451
Yang Bi 430–1
Yang Dairong 111
Yang Hanqing 256
Yang Jiaren 110, 259–60
Yang Jingfu 384
Yang Jingyun 279
Yang Jiugao 259
Yang Jun 409
Yang Juyuan 496
Yang Leisheng 429
Yang Shijie 455
Yang Shunji 257
Yang Shuo 291–4
Yang Suhua 112
Yang Wen 458–9
Yang Wenheng 360–1
Yang Yaqin 361
Yang Yuzhong 345
Yang Zhaogui 494
Yang Zhenxing 269
Yao Bingyu 428
Yao Daogang 346
Yao Fude 278
Yao Jianming 240–1
Yao Jiongming 494
Yao Peihong 459
Yao Qijun 106
Yao Qin 324
Yao Shuxi 169–70
Yao Su 334
Yao Tongbin 385
Yao Xuezhi 267
Yao Zuyi 527–8
Ye Maoying 262

Ye Shaoji 109
Ye Wencui 261
Ye Ying 493–4
Ye Yiqun 298
Ye Zudong 279
Yi Gang 535
Yi Guangzhen 225
Yin Damin 428
Yin Gongzhang 384
Ying Yunwei 306
Yu Binghe 310
Yu Dayin 85–6
Yu Gongsan 403–4
Yu Gongshan 421
Yu Hangsheng 494
Yu Luoke 520–1
Yu Nanqiu 108
Yu Qiyun 114, 115–16, 462
Yu Ruifen 203–4
Yuan Guangfu 459
Yuan Lihua 453
Yuan Xuanzhao 277
Yuan Yunwen 457
Yuan Zhen 282
Yun Liangchen 453

Zeng Qinghua 532
Zeng Ruiquan 262
Zeng Zhaolun 86
Zhai Yishan 450
Zhai Yuming 111
Zhang Aizhen 256
Zhang Baihua 246
Zhang Bingjie 225
Zhang Changshao 494
Zhang Dongsun 70–2
Zhang Fang 399–403
Zhang Fengming 262
Zhang Furen 165–7, 168–9
Zhang Fuyou 448–9
Zhang Fuzhen 165, 166–7, 168–9
Zhang Guanghua 259

Zhang Guoliang 445
Zhang Huaiyi 99–100
Zhang Jian 432
Zhang Jifang 455
Zhang Jingfu 434–5
Zhang Jingren 36
Zhang Jingzhao 375
Zhang Kezhi 452
Zhang Linzhi 326
Zhang Meiyan 172, 412
Zhang Qixing 474, 477
Zhang Ruidi 99
Zhang Ruxiu 108
Zhang Shen 434
Zhang Shouying 279–80
Zhang Shuxiu 457
Zhang Wenbo 296–7
Zhang Xiaonong 62
Zhang Xikun 527, 538–9
Zhang Xutao 340
Zhang Yanqing 421
Zhang Yonggon 453
Zhang Youbai 262
Zhang Youliang 305
Zhang Yun 269
Zhang Zhendan 109
Zhang Zhixin 336–7
Zhang Zigong 454–5
Zhang Zongsui 72–4
Zhang Zongying 72, 73–4
Zhao Danruo 107–8
Zhao Fuji 461–2
Zhao Jiuzhang 385
Zhao Qianguang 247
Zhao Shouqi 398
Zhao Shuli 298
Zhao Xiangheng 247–8
Zhao Xiaodong 387–8
Zhao Xibin 355–6
Zhao Zhihua 110
Zhao Zongfu (Zhao Jinzhi) 16
Zhen Suhui 464

Zheng Enshou 335
Zheng Junli 305
Zheng Siqun 16–19
Zheng Wenquan 472
Zheng Xiaodan 521
Zheng Zhaonan 225
Zhong Xianhua 454
Zhou Fuli 254–5
Zhou Hexiang 349
Zhou Jincong 344–5
Zhou Ruipan 259
Zhou Shaoying 439
Zhou Shougen 458
Zhou Shoujuan 456
Zhou Tianzhu 24, 114
Zhou Wenzhen 112–13
Zhou Xinghua 437
Zhou Xingrong 300
Zhou Xuemin 398
Zhu Benchu 437–8
Zhu Heming 447
Zhu Huang 117
Zhu Meifu 297
Zhu Ningsheng 454
Zhu Qi 452
Zhu Qingyi 264
Zhu Qiquan 368
Zhu Shiguang 264
Zhu Shouzhong 531–2
Zhu Shunying 433
Zhu Wanxing 494
Zhu Xianji 112
Zhu Yaoxin 535
Zhu Zhenzhong 438
Zou Lianfang 431
Zou Zhiqi 384
Zuo Shutang 530–1